WORLD WAR II

WORLD WAR II

H.P. WILLMOTT • CHARLES MESSENGER • ROBIN CROSS

Introduction by RICHARD OVERY

With contributions from

MICHAEL BARRETT • MARK GRANDSTAFF
MICHAEL PAUL • DAVID WELCH

LONDON, NEW YORK, MELBOURNE,
MUNICH AND DELHI

Senior Designer Juliette Norsworthy
Designers Victoria Clark, Jerry Udall, Phil Gamble
Senior Editors Jane Edmonds, Ferdie McDonald
Editorial Consultants Haruo Tohmatsu, Winfried Heinemann
Editors Michelle Crane, Elizabeth Wyse
Picture Researcher Franziska Marking
Special Photography Gary Ombler
Digital maps created by Advanced Illustration
Project Cartographers Rob Stokes, Iowerth Watkins
DTP John Goldsmid
Production Joanna Bull

Editorial Direction Andrew Heritage
Art Director Bryn Walls
Managing Editor Debra Wolter
Managing Art Editor Louise Dick

AT BROWN REFERENCE GROUP
Art editor Stefan Morris
Designers Thor Fairchild, Alison Gardiner,
Colin Tilley-Loughrey
Editors Dennis Cove, James Murphy, Henry Russell
Picture Researcher Susy Forbes
Art Director Dave Goodman
Managing Editor Tim Cooke
Editorial Director Lindsey Lowe

First American Edition 2004
09 10 11 12 13 14 15 16 10 9 8 7 6 5 4 3 2
Published in the United States by
DK Publishing, Inc
375 Hudson Street
New York, New York 10014
This edition published in 2009
Copyright © 2004 Dorling Kindersley Limited
A Penguin Company

Library of Congress Cataloging-in-Publication Data
Willmott, H.P.
World War II / H.P. Willmott, Robin Cross, Charles
Messenger.
p. cm.
Includes index.
ISBN 978-0-7566-5142-8 (alk. Paper)
1. World War, 1939-1945. I. Title: World War Two. II. Title:
World War 2. III. Cross, Robin. IV. Messenger, Charles, 1941 –
V. Title.
D743.W525 2004
940.54'002'2--dc22

2004049351

Color reproduction by GRB, Italy
Printed and bound in Singapore by Star Standard Pte Ltd

For our complete catalog visit

www.dk.com

US artillery bombardment
US Marines of the 4th Division shell concealed Japanese
positions from the beach on Iwo Jima. The Americans
landed in strength on the tiny volcanic island in February
1945 and secured it after four weeks' fighting.

CONTENTS

INTRODUCTION

WORLD WAR II was the largest and costliest war in human history. The deaths directly and indirectly caused by the war may have reached 60 million; the war, or more properly the wars, fought between 1939 and 1945 involved literally the entire globe. At its peak more than 50 million men and women were serving in the armed services; two-thirds of the national product of the major combatants was devoted to waging war. War was the product not only of a profound disequilibrium in world affairs; it reflected deep hatreds and powerful imperial ambitions inherited from the Great War of 1914–18, where lay the seeds of the second, and larger conflict.

The attempt to produce a stable world order in 1919 was undermined from the start. In East Asia, China collapsed politically and Japan slowly expanded at Chinese expense. In the Mediterranean and Middle East, the end of Ottoman rule provoked a nationalist Italy under Mussolini to carve out a new "Roman Empire". In Europe the

Bolshevik Revolution of 1917 created a permanent sense of social crisis, while the Versailles Treaty created festering political sores which contributed to the rise of Hitler and the breakdown of the balance of power in the late 1930s.

The new war was the last fling of the wars for empire that had been the hallmark of the rise of Europe since the 17th century. Britain and France wished to preserve their world empires. Italy, Japan, and Germany all wanted empires of their own. These imperial ambitions led to the largest and most destructive conflicts of World War II: the German war against the Soviet Union and Japan's war against China.

Britain and France declared war over the German invasion of Poland in September 1939, but Anglo-French efforts on their own to stem the tide of violent imperialism were futile. They were swept aside by German forces in a matter of weeks in the summer of 1940 thanks largely to a revolution in warfare made possible by the aeroplane and the tank—weapons whose potential had been apparent at the end of the war of 1914–18.

The desolation of war
A Japanese soldier surveys the destruction of Hiroshima in an area near the centre of the atomic blast in September 1945.

In combination with radio communication, they gave armies a mobile striking power that could win sudden, annihilating victories. Slowly, ways were found to contain or limit the effectiveness of the tank, aircraft, and radio attack system, but it proved irreversible when the Germans first used it, and when German armies were in turn pushed back by reorganized and heavily-armed Soviet, British, and American forces.

By September 1940 the three new imperial powers, Germany, Italy, and Japan, signed the Tripartite Pact, which divided the world into new spheres of imperial interest. Over the next year they each embarked on vast imperial wars: Italy attacked Greece and tried to drive Britain from North Africa and the Middle East; Germany launched war against the Soviet Union in June 1941; by January 1942 Japan had seized control of most of Southeast Asia and the Western Pacific. The effect of these wars of conquest was to unite the rest of the world against the violent revision of the globe. Britain, undefeated but powerless on its own to reverse the tide of conquest, was joined by the Soviet Union and, in December 1941, by the United States. This proved an alliance just powerful enough to stem the imperial wars after four years of bitter, costly, and massively destructive warfare.

Victory was won for many reasons. The Soviet Union won the war on land by learning to organize its forces in the same way as the Germans, and by channeling its entire society and economy into the waging of "total war". Britain and the United States focussed on winning the war at sea and in the air in order to be able to fight a global war at lower cost. Bombing was central to Western strategy and hundreds of thousands of Germans and Japanese were killed by bombing attacks. Naval power gave the west exceptional flexibility in moving forces and supplies and strangling the economic lifelines to the enemy. By the time Britain and the United States assaulted Europe on land the defeat of Italy and Germany was already assured. Japan was not even invaded. The first and only use of nuclear weapons in war ended Japanese resistance in August 1945.

The final defeat of imperialism produced a reconfiguration of the world and a stabilization of the international order. Britain and France had to give up the global empires they had fought to defend. Communism came to control much of Asia and eastern Europe, while the United States used its economic and military power to preserve its interests in the non-communist world. The war had brought a precarious peace, but only at the price of misery for the hundreds of millions caught in its merciless crossfire.

Richard Overy
May 2004

THE PATH
TO WAR
1919–39

THE CAUSES OF WORLD WAR II LAY IN THE AFTERMATH
OF WORLD WAR I AND THE GLOBAL ECONOMIC CRISIS
OF THE 1930s. IN THE 1920s AND EARLY 1930s, RIGHT-WING
DICTATORS ROSE TO POWER IN A NUMBER OF EUROPEAN
COUNTRIES BY OFFERING MILITARISTIC SOLUTIONS TO
ECONOMIC AND SOCIAL PROBLEMS. IN EAST ASIA JAPAN'S
GROWING IMPERIAL AMBITIONS EVENTUALLY LED TO THE
OUTBREAK OF FULL-SCALE WAR WITH CHINA. FROM 1934
ADOLF HITLER'S GERMANY DEFIED EUROPE TO REARM
AND EXPAND EASTWARD. THIS COURSE OF ACTION LED
IN SEPTEMBER 1939 TO A WAR THAT MANY SAW AS A
CONTINUATION OF THE EARLIER CONFLICT.

Warm welcome
Joyful Austrians welcome German troops
to the city of Salzburg on March 13, 1938.
The *Anschluss*, the German annexation of
Austria, was widely popular in both countries
and encouraged German leader Adolf Hitler's
territorial ambitions.

THE RISE OF EXTREMISM

THE SEEDS OF WORLD WAR II WERE SOWN IN THE 1920S, WHEN ECONOMIC HARDSHIP AND NATIONAL HUMILIATION DROVE THE GERMAN PEOPLE TO ADOLF HITLER, WHO PROMISED TO RESTORE NATIONAL PRIDE AND PROSPERITY.

WORLD WAR I, fought between 1914 and 1918, resulted in over 10 million deaths and traumatized a generation. When peace came in November 1918 it brought few solutions and many new problems. The European economy was left in ruins and the social structure severely disrupted. The peace settlements failed to resolve the tensions that had caused the conflict and gave rise to such resentment that it soon became clear that they would not provide the framework for a lasting peace. Indeed, they contributed significantly to the outbreak of World War II in Europe in September 1939.

THE TREATY OF VERSAILLES, 1919

Although the "peacemakers" who met at Versailles, near Paris, France, in January 1919, reconstructed the map of the Middle East, Africa, and Asia, they saw these areas as being relatively unimportant. The so-called "war to end all wars" had been, despite its geographical range, a struggle for mastery of Europe. The three leading statesmen at Versailles—French prime minister Georges Clémenceau, British prime minister David Lloyd George, and US president Woodrow Wilson—had to establish immediate and lasting peace in a continent still in turmoil. The conflict was Europe's first experience of "total war," in which whole economies had been geared to the war effort, with profound effects on society. The challenge of restoring political and economic stability was correspondingly huge.

The Treaty of Versailles was by far the most important of a number of settlements at the end of the war. It saw Wilson's vision of a better world, in which rights and freedoms were guaranteed, enshrined in a swathe of new democracies across Europe—from the Baltic to the Balkans—all with new, liberal constitutions. Yet the triumph of idealism and liberalism would prove short-lived.

One problem confronting the new democracies related to territory and population. Newly independent states such as Poland, Czechoslovakia, Yugoslavia, and Hungary were created under the principle of national self-determination. However, 30 million people still found themselves as national and racial minorities. The long-term consequences of incorporating minority populations into new states would be a source of tension and discontent into the 1930s.

Versailles failed to satisfy victors and vanquished alike. In Germany, dissatisfaction stemmed from a widespread belief that, although the Germans had signed an armistice, they had not actually been defeated on the field of battle. The Germans were not invited to participate in the discussions at Versailles. When the terms of the treaty were announced, even political moderates saw them as being harsh and vindictive.

The treaty—which the Germans condemned as a *diktat*, or dictated peace—fixed the blame for the war solely on Germany and its allies, and demanded reparations. Germany, moreover, was forced to disarm and its African colonies were taken away. The fledgling Weimar Republic was thus tainted from its inception with the humiliation of having accepted the imposed terms of Versailles.

One of the noblest features of the Treaty of Versailles was the establishment of the League of Nations as an agency for maintaining international peace and for protecting the new democracies. However, the League was fatally weakened by the failure of the United States to join it or to ratify the Versailles Treaty. The League was also damaged by initially excluding Germany and the Soviet Union, and its authority was further undermined by the preference of many states to sign peace agreements independently. In Asia, Japan, which had profited economically from the war, was unhappy with attempts to impose limitations on naval and arms development. Not surprisingly, when challenges did occur, notably in the 1930s, the League of Nations was found wanting.

EUROPE IN TURMOIL

The political and economic impact of the war contributed to the fragility of democracy. It sharpened class tension which, in turn, was fueled by the triumph of Bolshevism in Russia. Moreover,

The new world order
Nazi storm troopers and Berliners gather around a bonfire at a book-burning ceremony in May 1933. More than 20,000 volumes were destroyed. Hitler came to power determined to wipe out "degenerate" culture, which included many pillars of the liberal European tradition and the works of Jewish and other writers.

the disappointment of ex-servicemen with the conduct of their politicians, and their perception that they had been betrayed at the conference table, fed widespread discontent. In Germany and Italy, government reliance on right-wing paramilitary groups to neutralize the threat of Soviet-style revolution legitimized political violence. The very real fear of revolution among Europe's middle

"Germany is not a warlike nation. It is a soldierly one, which means it does not want a war, but does not fear it. It loves peace, but also loves its honor and freedom."

ADOLF HITLER
ADDRESSING THE REICHSTAG IN 1938

classes and the inability of some of the Western democracies to defuse class warfare contributed substantially to the collapse of liberal democracy and the meteoric rise of fascism.

The Versailles Treaty's failure to support Italy's territorial claims on its northeastern borders only exacerbated the country's political and economic problems. Between 1919 and 1922 five governments failed to take decisive action that might have helped to resolve Italy's developing crisis. In an atmosphere of tension, characterized by strikes and riots, there seemed to be a real danger of a left-wing revolution. Amid the turmoil, the founder of the Italian Fascist Party, former socialist Benito Mussolini, posed as the savior of the state against communism. By 1922 he felt confident enough to seize power.

The abandonment of parliamentary democracy for right-wing fascism was repeated in Germany and later in Spain. Like Italy, both countries had comparatively little experience of operating a democratic parliamentary system. In Germany, the Weimar Republic was plagued by economic crises, which the government failed to solve permanently. Adolf Hitler's National Socialist German Workers' Party (or Nazi Party) started life as a radical group opposed to Versailles and the parliamentary system. The rise of the Nazis, fostered by economic crisis, helped bring the downfall of the republic.

Japan, like Germany, had a long tradition of militarism and weak democratic roots. World War I had seen an increase in Japanese influence in Asia, especially in China, and in industrial growth at home. However, the trading boom of the war years lasted only until 1921, when Europe was able to recover lost markets. Thereafter unemployment and industrial unrest grew. Democratically elected governments seemed unable to solve the problems, and as the fragile

prestige of parliament suffered, conservative and military groups, attracted by fascism, reasserted themselves. In 1930 a strong nationalist government controlled by the army seized power.

THE LEAGUE FAILS

By the early 1930s the idealistic hope that the League of Nations would preserve the peace by arbitration or conciliation was challenged by fascist regimes

intent on pursuing imperialistic ambitions by aggressive means. Collective security gave way to old-style bilateral diplomacy. The continued policy of isolationism in the United States encouraged the drift to extremism. In 1931 Japan seized Manchuria, an important economic region in China. In 1935 Italy invaded Abyssinia (Ethiopia), and in Germany Hitler embarked on an extensive rearmament program and also introduced conscription.

Pride of a nation
The Japanese battleship *Fuso* nears the completion of its refit in dry dock in April 1933. The Imperial Navy of Japan saw strengthening the fleet as vital to national pride after the limitations imposed by the Washington and London naval treaties were cast aside.

The failure of the League to respond to any of these violations of international treaties significantly undermined its authority and persuaded Hitler to take a calculated risk. In March 1936 he ordered his troops to reoccupy the Rhineland, which under the peace treaties had been demilitarized since 1919. Again the League and the Western powers failed to act. Emboldened, Hitler signed the Rome–Berlin Axis with Mussolini in October 1936, and the following month Germany and Japan agreed to an Anti-Comintern Pact. By 1937 Germany, Italy, and Japan had all withdrawn from the League of Nations.

In July 1936 Spanish right-wing nationalists led by General Francisco Franco rose in an attempt to overthrow the democratically elected republican government. The Spanish conflict rapidly assumed international significance when Hitler and Mussolini sent military help to Franco, while the republicans received aid from the Soviet Union. The resolutions that the League passed in response showed it to be sympathetic to the plight of the legitimate Spanish government but largely ineffectual.

By supporting the League's principle of non-intervention, Britain and France—still Europe's major powers—revealed the timidity and moral indifference of the parliamentary democracies when challenged from both the left and the right. Moreover, the ideological issues of the Spanish war polarized public opinion in Britain and France and helped shape their policy of appeasement, under which concessions were granted to Hitler and Mussolini. With Europe preoccupied with events in Spain, in July 1937 the Japanese embarked upon a full-scale invasion of northern China, precipitating a war that was to last until 1945. The United States, the only power that was capable of effectively resisting Japan, continued its policy of isolationism.

GERMAN EXPANSION

The Rome–Berlin Axis had changed the balance of power in Europe, and in March 1938 Hitler fulfilled a long-cherished ambition by annexing Austria and proclaiming *Anschluss* (union) with Germany. Britain and France continued to believe that appeasement was the only way to deal with successive crises. In Munich in September 1938 they

Peace in our time
British prime minister Neville Chamberlain brandishes Hitler's promise that Germany has no territorial ambitions in Europe after its claims on Czechoslovakia. In fact, the Munich Pact of September 30, 1938, failed to halt German rearmament or expansion.

acceded to Hitler's claims on the Sudetenland, a German-speaking region of Czechoslovakia, on the understanding that this would be Hitler's final territorial demand. The agreement, acclaimed as guaranteeing "peace in our time," was soon broken.

The German invasion of Czechoslovakia in March 1939 gave rise to a new resolve in the British and French governments to confront aggression and guarantee Poland's independence. The controversial signing of the Nazi–Soviet Non-Aggression Pact on August 23, 1939, was widely seen as a cynical reversal of ideological allegiances by Hitler and Stalin. Hitler believed that the pact would show the British and French the futility of the promises they had made to Poland in the wake of the invasion of Czechoslovakia. When, however, Germany invaded Poland on September 1, the British and French declared war two days later, and World War II began in Europe. Twenty-one years after the war to end all wars, Europe was to be torn apart again.

"Provided China perseveres in the war of resistance and in the united front, the old Japan will surely be transformed into a new Japan and the old China into a new China, and people and everything else in both China and Japan will be transformed."

MAO ZEDONG, CHINESE COMMUNIST LEADER,
LECTURE ON THE SINO-JAPANESE WAR, MAY 1938

The failure of the Treaty of Versailles and the League of Nations to resolve the social, political, and economic problems after World War I brought radical politics to center stage throughout Europe. The Wall Street Crash and the Great Depression plunged the continent into an economic crisis that allowed fascism to flourish in Germany.

1919

MARCH 23, 1919
Mussolini among those who form the Fascist Fighting Corps

JUNE 28, 1919
Germany signs Treaty of Versailles with the Allies

NOVEMBER 19, 1919
US Senate refuses to ratify Treaty of Versailles

1920

APRIL 25, 1920
Poland invades Russia

APRIL 1, 1920
German Workers' Party, with program drafted by Hitler, renamed Nazi Party

NOVEMBER 15, 1920
First session of League of Nations Assembly is held

MARCH 18, 1921
Russia and Poland sign Treaty of Riga, giving Poland most of the land seized in 1920

MAY 15, 1921
Fascists win 35 seats in elections

APRIL 16, 1922
Germany and Russia sign Treaty of Rapallo, enabling Germans to establish arms factories in Russia

OCTOBER 28, 1922
50,000 fascist Blackshirts begin their march from Milan to Rome

OCTOBER 30, 1922
Mussolini is invited by King Victor Emmanuel to form a government

JANUARY 11, 1923
French and Belgian troops begin occupation of the Ruhr following German failure to maintain reparations payments

NOVEMBER 9, 1923
As chairman of the infant National Socialist Workers' (Nazi) Party, Hitler launches an unsuccessful armed coup in Munich

1925

DECEMBER 1, 1925
Locarno Pact, signed by Germany with Britain, France, Belgium, and Italy, confirms Germany's western borders with France and Belgium as established by the Treaty of Versailles

SEPTEMBER 10, 1926
Germany joins League of Nations

AUGUST 27, 1928
Kellogg-Briand Pact is drawn up, renouncing war as a means of settling international disputes; it is eventually signed by nearly all of the world's nations

OCTOBER 29, 1929
Collapse of US stock market in the Wall Street Crash heralds the start of the Great Depression

1930

APRIL 22, 1930
US, Britain, and Japan sign London Naval Treaty, in which they agree to restrict tonnages of warships

SEPTEMBER 14, 1930
With unemployment at 3 million, Nazi Party makes first electoral breakthrough in Reichstag elections, winning 107 seats

MARCH 13, 1932
Hitler comes second after Hindenburg in presidential elections, gaining 30 percent of the vote

JULY 31, 1932
Nazis win 230 of 609 seats in national elections, but Hitler refuses to join a coalition

JANUARY 30, 1933
President Hindenburg appoints Hitler as chancellor

MARCH 5, 1933
Nazis secure 44 percent of the vote

MARCH 23, 1933
Enabling Act passed, giving Hitler dictatorial powers

AUGUST 2, 1934
Hitler merges offices of president and chancellor to become Führer and Supreme Commander

OCTOBER 14, 1933
Germany leaves League of Nations

■ Mussolini's rise to power Mar 23, 1919–Oct 30, 1922
■ Other events
■ Hitler's rise to power Apr 1, 1920–Aug 2, 1934

POSTWAR EUROPE

THE TREATY OF VERSAILLES achieved two things: it imposed peace terms on Germany—terms even some of the victors considered harsh—and established an international organization, the League of Nations, to preserve the peace and settle disputes by arbitration and conciliation. However, Versailles was fatally weakened by the failure of the United States to either ratify the treaty or join the League. Germany was not allowed to join until 1926, and the Allies were so determined to isolate the Bolshevik regime that they barred the Soviet Union until 1934. Consequently, for the first few years of its existence the League was deprived of the involvement of three of the world's most important powers.

Germany was excluded from the discussions at Versailles; it was simply presented with the terms and told to sign. German grievances were further fueled by the War Guilt Clause (Article 231), which stated that Germany took responsibility for starting the war, and the subsequent reparations. The Reparations Commission established by the treaty agreed in May 1921 on a total of $26 billion to be paid by Germany and its allies. Germany's promise to pay reparations, together with its very reluctant acceptance of an unfavorable territorial settlement, had a profound effect on postwar politics. The decision to exclude Germany from the League only reinforced the complaints of right-wing German nationalists, who condemned Versailles as a dictated peace that should not have been signed.

POLITICAL UPHEAVAL

Following the abdication of Kaiser Wilhelm II in November 1918, Germany experienced mounting instability and violence. In February 1919 the National Assembly met and set up the Weimar Republic, named after the city where it first met. The new republic was immediately beset by challenges. Communist movements, such as the Spartacists led by Karl Liebknecht and Rosa Luxemburg, attempted to overthrow the government. However, a poorly organized uprising in 1919 was crushed by the army and independent groups formed by ex-servicemen, known as the *Freikorps*. Similar uprisings in Bremen and Munich were also crushed. At the other political extreme, right-wing monarchists such as Wolfgang Kapp, together with other *Freikorps* units, engineered a successful military *putsch*, or seizure of power, in March 1920. It was eventually defeated by a general strike, but not before armed conflict between left and right had broken out in a number of German cities.

POSTWAR REVOLT

Grievances with the postwar peace settlements and fear of communism were not confined to Germany. The rise of fascism in Italy was a direct result of the strains produced by World War I and the postwar economic fluctuations that a succession of liberal governments failed to resolve. The failure of the Versailles Treaty to support Italy's territorial claims served only to exacerbate the country's political and economic problems. The subsequent rise to power of Benito Mussolini was aided by the breakdown of the existing political system and the rise of political extremism. Mussolini, who had begun his political career as a socialist, founded the Fascist Party in 1919 with a radical program and a promise of establishing strong government and restoring national pride. By focusing on the threat that communism posed, the fascists tapped into a latent fear on the

Revolution in Berlin
A group of armed communists patrol Berlin in November 1919. Many former soldiers were among the recruits to the extreme right- and left-wing groups who clashed in pitched battles in the streets of postwar Germany.

After Versailles
Germany was split in two, as East Prussia and Upper Silesia went to a restored Poland. The treaty also created new states in the Baltic region and in central and eastern Europe.

part of many sections of Italian society. Above all, fascism offered the prospect of dynamic action and leadership in contrast to the inertia of parliamentary politics. By the end of 1921 Mussolini had gained the support of property owners who saw him as a guarantor of law and order. He also gave up his republican ambitions, thus allowing the king to support him. The Italian socialists, for their part, were in disarray.

Posing as the saviors of the state from the threat of communism, Mussolini and 50,000 Blackshirts launched their famous "March on Rome" in October 1922. Although Italian prime minister Luigi Facta was prepared to resist, King Victor Emmanuel III refused to declare a state of emergency and instead addressed the crisis by summoning Mussolini to form a new government. Once in power, Mussolini moved quickly to suppress all opposition to his rule and to establish laws that removed any need for parliamentary approval of legislation. In December 1928 he replaced the parliamentary system with the

MUSSOLINI AND THE FASCISTS

School for fascists
Young blackshirts are drilled in Batilla, Italy. Modeled on Mussolini's Fascist Party Blackshirts, this organization was similar to the Hitler Youth movement in Germany, but not as successful.

Italian propaganda
In this propaganda poster in support of Mussolini, every soldier looks like the fascist dictator.

BENITO MUSSOLINI (1883–1945) was the first fascist dictator in Europe. Born the son of a blacksmith and schoolteacher, he turned to politics and joined the Socialist Party in 1910. Mussolini's rise inside the party was meteoric and following the Libyan War of 1912 he was elected editor of *Avanti!*, the party's official newspaper. However, in October 1914 he was expelled from the party for attacking its neutralist position, an experience he never forgot nor forgave. During World War I he was wounded at Isonzo and returned to Milan as editor of a new daily newspaper *Il Popolo d'Italia*. He also formed groups *(fasci)* of working men in order to agitate for revolutionary social changes. These groups, including the black-shirted Arditi, were merged into a Fascist Party *(Fascio di Combattimento)*.

Fascism varied from nation to nation—it emerged in different forms in Germany, Portugal, and Spain. In essence, it was a doctrine that sanctified the interests of the nation-state and minimized the rights of the individual. In Italy, fascism began to transform itself into a mass-movement when it took on a paramilitary edge, exemplified by Mussolini's Blackshirt supporters. Assuming dictatorial powers upon forming a government in November 1922, Mussolini established a Fascist Grand Council, carried out an extensive program of public works at home, and embarked upon a foreign policy designed to restore Italian prestige abroad.

Departing army
French soldiers garrisoned in the Ruhr in Germany march out of Essen on their way home. In 1925, when this photograph was taken, all Allied forces were ordered home and withdrawn from the Ruhr.

Fascist Grand Council. This put the finishing touches to the dictatorship and effectively gave Mussolini and the Fascist Party total political control in Italy.

DEATH OF A NATION

In Germany the period 1919–23 brought uprisings, political assassinations, and economic collapse. The fledgling Weimar Republic was experiencing a series of financial problems that caused the government to fall behind with reparations. Disagreements about whether Germany could afford the reparations caused tensions between Britain and France. Meanwhile in 1922 Russia and Germany signed a treaty of mutual respect—the Treaty of Rapallo. This canceled any reparations between the two states and demonstrated the recovery of both from isolation. The French, who needed the income from reparations in order to balance their own budget and pay their debts to the United States, decided in January 1923 to send troops into the Ruhr—the industrial heartland of Germany— to seize factories and mines. The occupation paralyzed the Ruhr and the effect on the whole

German economy was catastrophic. It led to the collapse of the German mark and hyperinflation. In December 1922 the exchange rate stood at 8,000 marks to the US dollar; by November 1923 it had reached 4,200 million marks to the dollar.

Throughout the Ruhr crisis a little-known agitator by the name of Adolf Hitler, leader of the National Socialist German Workers' Party, had kept up a barrage of criticism against the Republic. On November 8, 1923 Hitler and his right-wing supporters attempted a *putsch* in Munich, the capital of Bavaria. The intention was to take control of the state government and then lead a revolution to overthrow the national government in Berlin. The uprising was easily crushed, but the subsequent trial of Hitler for high treason gave him a nationwide platform from which to launch an attack on the Weimar Republic. The trial had the effect of turning the farce into a propaganda coup. Hitler was sentenced to five years' imprisonment in the fortress

Money to burn
A housewife uses German currency to light a stove during the period of hyperinflation in Germany, 1922–23. So low was the value of the German mark that it was worth more as fuel than as a method of payment.

of Landsberg in February 1924, but he was set free after only nine months. In prison, he dictated the first volume of his autobiographical manifesto *Mein Kampf* (*My Struggle*) to his loyal follower, Rudolf Hess.

EMERGING FROM DEFEAT

In August 1923 a new German government, led by the liberal politician Gustav Stresemann, began to take measures to stabilize the financial situation and to improve Germany's diplomatic position. Stresemann developed a close working relationship with the French foreign minister, Aristide Briand, which began in 1924 with the Dawes Plan. The plan eased reparations, allowing Germany to pay what it could afford. The relationship culminated in the signing of the Locarno Pact in December 1925. This confirmed the inviolability of the Franco-German and Belgo-German frontiers, and the demilitarized Rhineland, and repudiated the use of force to revise Germany's western border. The measures gave rise to international optimism known as the "spirit of Locarno" and cleared the way for Germany's entry into the League of Nations the following year. Two years later, in 1928, 65 nations signed the Kellogg-Briand Pact renouncing war, and in 1929 the Young Plan further reduced German reparations. Europe seemed set for a peaceful future. The fragile harmony of Locarno was destroyed, however, by the death of Stresemann in 1929 and by the Wall Street Crash that same year. In the subsequent world economic crisis, the Nazi Party began to flourish.

HITLER'S RISE TO POWER

With unemployment exceeding 6 million and the Weimar Republic entering its final death throes, the elections of 1932 were fought in a growing atmosphere of political violence and disorder. After the July Reichstag elections, the Nazis emerged as the largest party, but in the November 1932 elections the Nazi vote fell by 2 million, with their Reichstag seats reduced from 230 to 196. While the Nazi vote appeared to be in decline and the party's tactics in disarray, an increase in support for Germany's communists persuaded many industrialists and bankers to transfer their backing from the ineffectual conservatives and liberals to the Nazis. They were seen as the only bulwark against the growth of communism. In December 1932, after a series of further political intrigues, Kurt von Schleicher succeeded Franz von Papen as chancellor. However, in January 1933 Papen acted as a power-broker between business interests and landowners in political maneuvers that were intended to oust Schleicher. The ensuing negotiations eventually resulted in Hitler becoming chancellor. The fatal miscalculation made by Papen—indeed by the conservative right and the German establishment in general—was to believe that Hitler and the Nazis could be "tamed" once in power. The establishment tried to use Hitler and his party to give itself legitimacy for a new authoritarianism. In reality it served only to legitimize Nazism. Out of a labyrinth of intrigues, Hitler emerged the victor.

The Ehrhardt Brigade in Berlin
After World War I Hitler was sent by the German Army to observe right-wing groups. In this capacity he witnessed the short-lived Kapp *Putsch* of March 1920 by the Freikorps Ehrhardt Brigade in Berlin.

HITLER AND NAZISM

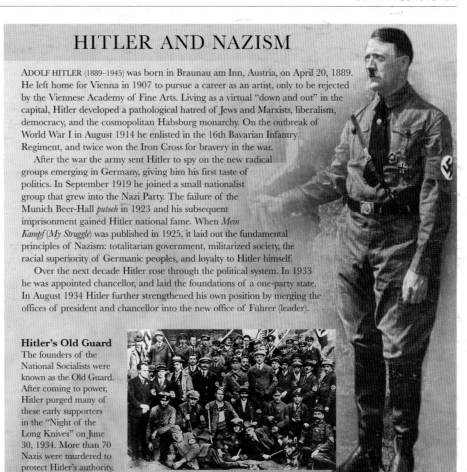

ADOLF HITLER (1889–1945) was born in Braunau am Inn, Austria, on April 20, 1889. He left home for Vienna in 1907 to pursue a career as an artist, only to be rejected by the Viennese Academy of Fine Arts. Living as a virtual "down and out" in the capital, Hitler developed a pathological hatred of Jews and Marxists, liberalism, democracy, and the cosmopolitan Habsburg monarchy. On the outbreak of World War I in August 1914 he enlisted in the 16th Bavarian Infantry Regiment, and twice won the Iron Cross for bravery in the war.

After the war the army sent Hitler to spy on the new radical groups emerging in Germany, giving him his first taste of politics. In September 1919 he joined a small nationalist group that grew into the Nazi Party. The failure of the Munich Beer-Hall *putsch* in 1923 and his subsequent imprisonment gained Hitler national fame. When *Mein Kampf (My Struggle)* was published in 1925, it laid out the fundamental principles of Nazism: totalitarian government, militarized society, the racial superiority of Germanic peoples, and loyalty to Hitler himself.

Over the next decade Hitler rose through the political system. In 1933 he was appointed chancellor, and laid the foundations of a one-party state. In August 1934 Hitler further strengthened his own position by merging the offices of president and chancellor into the new office of Führer (leader).

Hitler's Old Guard
The founders of the National Socialists were known as the Old Guard. After coming to power, Hitler purged many of these early supporters in the "Night of the Long Knives" on June 30, 1934. More than 70 Nazis were murdered to protect Hitler's authority.

ANTI-SEMITISM IN GERMANY

AS ELSEWHERE IN EUROPE, anti-Semitism grew during the 19th century in Germany, where Jews were prominent in culture and business. Conservatives and radical nationalists feared that the assimilation of Jews would only increase their influence and strengthen the left. After World War I the Jews became the scapegoats for Germany's defeat; later they were similarly blamed for the political and economic chaos of the Weimar Republic.

Anti-Semitism was a main theme of Nazi ideology. Between taking power in 1933 and 1939 the Nazis waged three main campaigns against the Jewish population. In March 1933 rank-and-file party activists went on the rampage, assaulting Jews, damaging Jewish shops, and demanding a boycott of Jewish businesses. In April 1933 Jews were banned from the civil service and the legal and medical professions. Despite continued local harassment, there were no further official moves against Jews until September 1935, when Hitler announced the Nuremberg Laws. These deprived Jews of German citizenship and political rights, and forbade marriage and sexual relations between Jews and non-Jewish Germans.

The position of Jews deteriorated further with the *Kristallnacht* ("Crystal Night") of November 1938, when Nazis burned down synagogues and placed 20,000 Jews in concentration camps. However, the unpopularity of *Kristallnacht* with the German public convinced the Nazi leadership that the solution to the so-called "Jewish Question" would be implemented outside Germany and well away from public sight. *Kristallnacht* was a crucial junction on the road to Auschwitz.

Public torment
Jews and gentiles who associated with each other were publicly humiliated by the SA and the SS.

The Eternal Jew
A poster for an anti-Semitic documentary commissioned by Josef Goebbels plays on a Jewish stereotype that had been common in Europe for many decades before the rise of the Nazis.

Covered in shame
A woman hides her face from the photographer in an anonymous German town in 1938. The sign on the bench reads "For Jews only."

Swastikas on parade
German soldiers carry swastika flags styled in the same manner as the standards of the Roman legions. The swastika symbol is over 3,000 years old, and the term is derived from two Sanskrit words; *su asti*—"well-being."

Despite the political intrigue and machinations that led to his appointment, Hitler became chancellor constitutionally; the suggestion that he somehow "seized" power is misleading. On February 27, 1933, shortly after he gained power, an arson attack destroyed the Reichstag, the German parliament. A communist sympathizer was blamed, although his guilt remains a matter of controversy. The Nazis used the fire as a pretext for suspending civil liberties and conducting an election campaign in circumstances highly favorable to themselves.

LIFE UNDER THE NAZIS

Hitler's rise to power had exploited the weaknesses of the political establishment, but the Nazis also enjoyed popular support, particularly for their promise to tackle unemployment. They introduced public works programs, such as building a system of *autobahns* (highways), and used tax concessions to encourage industrial growth. By the summer of 1934 unemployment had fallen to 2.4 million, and many Germans had renewed hope for the future, despite their loss of the right to unionize or strike. Inflation was low, wages stable, and public satisfaction high.

Economic success was not as strong as it seemed, however, and may not have been sustainable into the 1940s if war had not broken out. Government expenditure from 1933 to 1939 was 101.5 billion marks, but government revenue was only 62 billion marks. Some 60 percent of public expenditure went on rearmament. Business profited, but it was at the price of increased control by central government over what and how much it could produce.

Nazi control extended to German society. By the end of 1933 all youth organizations had been banned except the Hitler Youth and a few Catholic groups. Many boys were in the Hitler Youth, which was

> "The primitive simplicity of their minds renders them a more easy prey to a big lie than a small one, for they themselves often tell little lies but would be ashamed to tell a big one."

ADOLF HITLER ON WINNING THE SUPPORT OF THE GERMAN PEOPLE,
MEIN KAMPF, 1925

initially popular for providing opportunities for leisure activities. The *Kraft durch Freude* (Strength through Joy) movement extended the opportunity for vacations to ordinary Germans. Meanwhile, women's organizations summed up the role of the ideal mother in the Third Reich in the slogan "*Kinder, Küche, Kirche*" ("Children, Kitchen, Church").

Nazi influence spread to culture and the arts. While party rallies and parades became common, Nazi propaganda minister Josef Goebbels staged exhibitions of art designed to reinforce "German" values and young Nazis burned thousands of books condemned as being "un-German."

For many Germans the 1930s were a period of order, calm, and prosperity. For others, however, they brought terror and repression. A number of artists and intellectuals fled abroad. Anti-Semitism was enshrined in law; the first concentration camps for political prisoners opened in 1933. In June 1934 it was the turn of some of Hitler's allies to feel the

force of repression, when the SS—Hitler's elite bodyguard—executed around 150 senior members of the Brownshirts, the Nazi paramilitaries who had aided Hitler's rise to power, including their leader Erich Röhm. Now that he had control, the Führer was taking no chances of any opposition to his rule.

Nazi poster
The slogan of this Nazi poster—"Our Last Hope: Hitler"—appealed to the despair that many Germans felt.

Women Hitlerites
Enthusiastic female supporters of Adolf Hitler give the Nazi salute during a military parade through Berlin. Hitler enjoyed widespread support among German women who appreciated his oratorical skills.

JAPANESE EXPANSION IN CHINA
1930–1939

The 1930s saw Japan, suffering under the Great Depression, embark on an increasingly assertive policy in East Asia. Militant nationalism was tied to a perceived need to secure raw materials, markets, and areas of settlement. The natural focus of Japanese attention was China, particularly Manchuria.

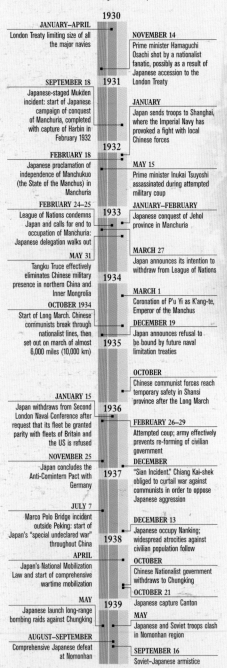

1930

JANUARY–APRIL
London Treaty limiting size of all the major navies

NOVEMBER 14
Prime minister Hamaguchi Osachi shot by a nationalist fanatic, possibly as a result of Japanese accession to the London Treaty

1931

SEPTEMBER 18
Japanese-staged Mukden incident: start of Japanese campaign of conquest of Manchuria, completed with capture of Harbin in February 1932

JANUARY
Japan sends troops to Shanghai, where the Imperial Navy has provoked a fight with local Chinese forces

1932

FEBRUARY 18
Japanese proclamation of independence of Manchukuo (the State of the Manchus) in Manchuria

MAY 15
Prime minister Inukai Tsuyoshi assassinated during attempted military coup

FEBRUARY 24–25
League of Nations condemns Japan and calls for end to occupation of Manchuria: Japanese delegation walks out

1933

JANUARY–FEBRUARY
Japanese conquest of Jehol province in Manchuria

MAY 31
Tangku Truce effectively eliminates Chinese military presence in northern China and Inner Mongolia

MARCH 27
Japan announces its intention to withdraw from League of Nations

1934

OCTOBER 1934
Start of Long March. Chinese communists break through nationalist lines, then set out on march of almost 6,000 miles (10,000 km)

MARCH 1
Coronation of P'u Yi as K'ang-te, Emperor of the Manchus

DECEMBER 19
Japan announces refusal to be bound by future naval limitation treaties

1935

OCTOBER
Chinese communist forces reach temporary safety in Shansi province after the Long March

JANUARY 15
Japan withdraws from Second London Naval Conference after request that its fleet be granted parity with fleets of Britain and the US is refused

1936

FEBRUARY 26–29
Attempted coup; army effectively prevents re-forming of civilian government

NOVEMBER 25
Japan concludes the Anti-Comintern Pact with Germany

DECEMBER
"Sian Incident." Chiang Kai-shek obliged to curtail war against communists in order to oppose Japanese aggression

1937

JULY 7
Marco Polo Bridge incident outside Peking: start of Japan's "special undeclared war" throughout China

DECEMBER 13
Japanese occupy Nanking; widespread atrocities against civilian population follow

1938

APRIL
Japan's National Mobilization Law and start of comprehensive wartime mobilization

OCTOBER
Chinese Nationalist government withdraws to Chungking

OCTOBER 21
Japanese capture Canton

MAY
Japanese launch long-range bombing raids against Chungking

1939

MAY
Japanese and Soviet troops clash in Nomonhan region

AUGUST–SEPTEMBER
Comprehensive Japanese defeat at Nomonhan

SEPTEMBER 16
Soviet–Japanese armistice

■ Events in Japan 1930–1939   ■ Events in China and Manchuria 1930–1939   ■ Other events

JAPANESE IMPERIALISM

ALTHOUGH THE TIDE of conflict barely washed its shores, East Asia was profoundly affected by the events of World War I. Decades of Western, primarily European, predominance in the area and in the Western Pacific was over. The presence of certain powers was ended, permanently in the case of Germany and Austria-Hungary, and temporarily in the case of Russia. Even the victorious powers found their status and power weakened, partly because the war had meant a withdrawal of forces from the area and partly because Japan had been immensely strengthened as a result of the conflict.

For Japan, World War I was "an opportunity that comes once in a thousand years." Prior to 1914 Japan had only limited industrial and financial resources; by the war's end the cessation of European imports had guaranteed profitability for Japanese industry. The disappearance of Western shipping left Japanese lines free to dominate the Pacific and Indian oceans. Japan also ended the war holding possession of all Germany's Pacific islands north of the equator and its trading concessions in China, such as Tsingtao. Moreover, although allied to Britain, and thus

Japanese naval power
The Japanese battleship *Yamashiro*, which was commissioned in 1917, opens fire. The *Yamashiro* and its class were among the leading battleships in the world.

associated with France and the United States, Japan was free to take as much or as little part in the war as it chose. Its contribution consisted of sending destroyer formations to the eastern Mediterranean and heavier units and formations to Australia, and consequently, its casualties were light.

JAPAN AFTER WORLD WAR I

Japan's position at the end of the war was not, however, entirely advantageous. Japan faced two significant problems. The first stemmed from the "Twenty-one Demands," its clumsy 1915 attempt to ensure itself a position of dominance in China. The Japanese sought financial, trading, and other

Chungking in flames
Chinese refugees flee through the wrecked streets of Chungking after it was bombed by the Japanese during the Sino-Japanese War that began in 1937.

economic concessions that would leave China in a position of dependence. The action aroused deep suspicion and resentment among the Chinese and, more importantly, the opposition of both Japan's wartime associates and the United States. Under pressure, Japan abandoned its claims. However, over the next three years it secured local but far-reaching gains that in effect gave it possession of Germany's prewar concessions, which legally should have been returned to China.

At the same time Japan's relations with the United States grew more difficult. The sting was temporarily drawn from the China question by the Lansing–Ishii agreement of November 1917, which included recognition of Japan's right to protect its special interests in areas of China bordering on Japanese territory. The fact remained, however, that the United States reserved for itself a special position in China and, by virtue of its possession of the Philippines, the Western Pacific. Meanwhile, Japan's wartime domination of shipping in the Pacific prompted a determination in the United

States to develop naval yards and national shipping on the west coast. This determination was made all the greater by increasingly strident nationalism that in the western states in particular took the form of opposition to Chinese and Japanese immigration.

Even in the first decade of the 20th century, Japan and the United States had begun to measure themselves against one another in terms of naval programs. With the declaration in 1916 of the American determination to acquire a navy "second to none," the two countries found themselves committed to construction programs specifically

directed against the other. Involvement in World War I temporarily curbed American ambition, but it revived at the war's end to pose diplomatic dangers. In any case, the sheer financial cost of an arms race was enough to lead the representatives of the major powers to meet in November 1921, in Washington, D.C., to hammer out a comprehensive series of treaties governing China, the Western and Central Pacific, and naval building programs.

The next four months produced seven accords, including the Naval Limitation Treaty of February 6, 1922. This treaty dealt primarily with battle

JAPANESE SOCIETY

THE TRANSFORMATION OF JAPANESE SOCIETY from feudal to modern was accelerated after victory in the Russo–Japanese War of 1904–05. Japanese liberals wanted to copy Western democracy and ways of life, while traditionalists resented Western influence. After the Allied victory in World War I, the popularity of Western sports, music, and fashion soared. The people enjoyed greater freedoms throughout the 1920s than at any time previously, and the standard of living in Japan was the highest anywhere in Asia.

The accession of Emperor Hirohito in 1926 initially seemed to signal a continuation of the liberal period, but the Great Depression hit Japan very hard and, just as in Europe, the failure of economic liberalism discredited its political counterpart. The collapse of parliamentary rule, right-wing nationalism, the increasingly aggressive attitude of the army in China, and increasing conformity were the hallmarks of Japan in the Thirties. The most famous, or infamous, part of this process involved the idea of *Kokutai*—"the Body of the Nation"—which held that Japan's divine's origins meant that modern political definitions and ideas were not merely irrelevant but deeply offensive and tantamount to blasphemy. After 1935 the worship of the emperor and imperial family became state and personal obligations.

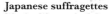

Japanese suffragettes
Wearing Western dress, Japanese women bring petitions calling for female suffrage to the Japanese parliament in the 1920s.

Emperor Hirohito
Hirohito's 1926 coronation used specially devised rituals that were falsely claimed to have been handed down over generations— a reflection of Japan's increasing obsession with historical example and values.

The rise of baseball
Members of the Waseda University Baseball Team toured the United States in 1925. The growing popularity of baseball in Japan was one of a number of signs of the Westernization of the country.

forces, and set down the 5:5:3 ratio by which Britain and the United States were afforded 500,000 tons of capital ships, while Japan was allotted 300,000 tons, and France and Italy 175,000 tons. The treaties, plus Japan's agreement to return a number of concessions to China, resolved immediate disputes among the Great Powers and avoided the dangers of a naval race. Within a decade, however, the arrangements had begun to unravel.

JAPANESE MILITARISM GROWS

As the Washington treaties unraveled and general war in East Asia seemed increasingly likely, events were largely shaped by Japanese actions. These were influenced by a number of factors, of which the widespread distress caused by the Great Depression—particularly in the countryside—was the most significant.

Just as the Depression brought in its wake the upheavals that resulted in the demise of liberal democracy in much of Europe, so it closed a decade of unprecedented prosperity within Japan. That prosperity, however, had been flawed in three long-term ways. Most notably, while the 1920s in Japan were marked by "Constitutionalism at home,

Patriotism on parade
Members of the Young Women's Patriotic Association celebrate the first birthday of Japan's crown prince in January 1935. Such groups were typical of the increasing militarization of Japanese society.

Imperialism abroad,"—the phrase did not actually imply an unbridled, aggressive form of imperialism—the Imperial Army found itself involved in the Russian Civil War and its aftermath, and then China's civil wars. These conflicts saw forces on the ground obliged to decide policy and operational priorities without reference to superior civil and military authorities. The habit, once acquired, was not lost.

This development came in parallel with an unforeseen consequence of the 1924 reduction of the Imperial Army by four divisions. Many of the officers released from service were directed into the state

education service to supervise a newly introduced program of compulsory military training for children. Retired officers and noncommissioned officers were heavily represented in the *seinengakko* (youth school) system, which provided vocational training for youths with relatively poor educational records. This system was especially strong in the countryside and played an important role in the provision of job opportunities for its students. Meanwhile, a growing population meant that more people were subject to conscription. The result of these factors was that ex-soldier associations became increasingly powerful pressure groups during the 1920s and 1930s, while the emergence of the *seinengakko* system pointed in

Winter campaign
Japanese infantry warm themselves beside a fire during the campaign for Jehol in February 1933. Once Jehol was secured, the Japanese set about encroaching on Chinese positions astride the Great Wall.

THE CHINESE CIVIL WARS

AFTER 1916 CHINA WAS WRACKED by power struggles between local warlords, but by the mid-Twenties one political party, the Kuomintang under Chiang Kai-shek, was the leading single grouping in southern and central China. A real civil war, about the nature of society, developed after 1926, when Chiang set about purging the Kuomintang's communist associates: the communists established themselves in provinces in central China, specifically Kiangsi, and sought to overthrow the Kuomintang in a largely urban-based struggle. By 1934 Kuomintang offensives forced the communists to abandon their existing base areas. Thus in October 1934 began the Long March, a journey by some 100,000 communists, soldiers, and civilians that ended a year and 6,000 miles (9,600 km) later in Shansi province. The Kuomintang sought a final effort that would have brought the communists' defeat, but the Sian Incident in December 1936 brought an end to conflict and the creation of a common front by the Kuomintang and the communists in the face of Japanese aggression.

The Long March
Chinese communists cross a mountain in 1935 on the arduous retreat to Shansi province. Of the 100,000 who began the journey, only around 10,000 reached the destination.

Nationalists on patrol
Kuomintang troops patrol through the city of Canton in late 1925 as part of a nationalist campaign to wrest power from China's numerous warlords.

Communist masterminds
Mao Zedong (left) and Zhou Enlai led the combination of rural insurgency and people's war that ultimately brought the Chinese communists to power in 1949.

the direction of the gradual imposition of military values on the countryside and the process of general low-key militarization of Japanese society.

This phenomenon developed in association with the process whereby, when universal suffrage was introduced in 1925, it was in association with the *Chian ijiho* (the National Security Act), which provided for the suppression of communist, socialist, anarchist, or any other political movement thought to pose a threat to the imperial system. In many ways such a provision amounted to a mandate for the *Tokubetsu Koto Keisatsu* (Special High Police)—or more commonly the *Tokko* (Thought Police—which had been established in Tokyo and certain prefectures in 1911. After 1928 the *Tokko*, which was already notorious for its manipulation of policial parties, intervention in legitimate party activities, and controlling the press, was established in every prefecture.

THE CAMPAIGN IN MANCHURIA

Such was the background against which the Kwantung Army, the Japanese garrison formation in southern Manchuria, a northern region of China, deliberately initiated a process in 1931 whereby it was able to overrun three of Manchuria's four provinces. The onset of the Depression and an increasingly volatile nationalism within Japan were

the basis of a Kwantung calculation that Tokyo would be unable to repudiate its action. The growing success of Chiang Kai-shek's nationalist Kuomintang suggested that China's civil wars might be drawing to a close, which could harm Japanese aspirations in China. Kwantung commanders suspected too that the great powers were indifferent to Manchuria: in 1928 a Soviet intervention provoked by local authorities there had gone unchecked. Consequently, in 1931 the Kwantung Army enjoyed maximum opportunity and minimal risk.

The campaign in Manchuria was the first of three Japanese offensive efforts north of and across the Great Wall: within Manchuria, in Inner Mongolia, and in northern China. These successive campaigns lasted until early 1937, by which time Japan had secured Manchuria and largely neutralized Chinese influence in Inner Mongolia and northern China, specifically Shansi, Hupei, and Shantung provinces.

Events north of the Great Wall had three phases. The main effort, from September 1931 to March 1932, saw the conquest of Heilungkiang, Kirin, and Fengtien, although mopping-up operations went on until November 1932. Next, between January and March 1933 the Japanese occupied Jehol, although fighting in the area of the Great Wall continued into the summer of 1932. Finally, from November

1932 to December 1935 the Japanese forces in effect established the basis of a move into Inner Mongolia. Much of this last phase was, in fact, not military but involved direct negotiations in which blandishments were combined with implied threats. Nevertheless, it resulted in Japan being the power with the greatest influence in Inner Mongolia.

SOUTH OF MANCHURIA

The Japanese constituted their gains as the puppet state of Manchukuo (the State of the Manchus) on March 1. Its president was the last emperor of the Qing (Manchu) dynasty, P'u Yi, who became the Emperor K'ang-te when Manchutikuo (the Empire of the Manchus) was proclaimed on March 1, 1934, amid what the Japanese official communiqué was to describe as "wild scenes of high nostalgia."

While the Manchurian campaign continued, the greatest single Japanese military effort had come farther south in China. In January 1932 Imperial Navy personnel in Shanghai provoked fighting that drew in the Imperial Army. Local Chinese forces resisted for a month, but a local truce was not concluded until May 5, by which time Japanese attention was directed toward Jehol province and Inner Mongolia. The completion of the conquest of Jehol in early 1933 proved to be merely the start

Noble tradition
Recruits in the Chinese Army learn to use traditional swords in this image from the late 1930s. The military in both China and Japan professed to follow ancient and honorable codes of warfare: the reality was often different.

Gas drill
Japanese troops practice putting on their gas masks during a training drill shortly before the outbreak of the Sino–Japanese War in 1937.

> "The Japanese are a disease of the skin. The Communists are a disease of the heart."

CHIANG KAI-SHEK, CHINESE NATIONALIST LEADER, DECEMBER 1941

of a continuing process of incidents, truces, and imposed agreements that resulted in successive Chinese surrenders to Japanese demands.

Kwantung Army encroachments upon Chinese positions north of the Great Wall went hand-in-hand with Japanese sponsorship of local collaborationist regimes and with what was dubbed "government-by-assassination" in Tokyo. In September 1931 the government led by Wakatsuki Reijiro, confronted by the refusal of the Army Ministry and Korean and Manchurian commands to obey its instructions, and outmaneuvered by a military with public opinion on its side, capitulated to army intransigence. The Wakatsuki cabinet remained in office, but not in power, until December 11, when it was replaced by

the government of Inukai Tsuyoshi. Inukai was prime minister until May 15, 1932, when he was killed by a group of naval officers and army cadets.

The military increasingly dominated the political process within Japan. After Inukai's assassination, an attempt to secure a government of national unity foundered because an administration could only be formed with the assent of the military—and only if it granted military demands. When a government was formed in 1936 under Hirota Koki, the new prime minister found that effectively the army minister had the power of veto over all appointments.

In these same years Japan associated itself with Germany in the Anti-Comintern Pact of November 25, 1936, but by the spring of 1937 it was isolated

and largely friendless. Japan had not helped itself by a refusal to engage in any serious discussion about naval limitation. The Imperial Navy had accepted the 1930 London Treaty—imposing new limits on shipbuilding—only because financial and economic considerations precluded opposition, but was determined that the treaty would be the last. The navy had its way between December 1934 and January 1936 and was freed from treaty limitation thereafter, but by the year's end a development within China had heralded general war in July 1937.

Within China, Kuomintang head Chiang Kai-shek had emerged as national leader. His priority was the pacification of Chinese communists rather than resistance to Japan in the north. Kuomintang forces conducted five major offensives in 1936 that brought the communists to the verge of defeat. However, a sixth offensive was conducted by Chiang's Manchurian allies, who had no interest in civil war while the Japanese occupied their homeland. When Chiang went to Sian in central China in December to enforce his orders, he was taken into custody and forced to bargain with the Manchurians and the communists. The price of release was an end to the civil wars and an undertaking to form a united front to oppose Japanese aggression.

The significance of these events was not lost on the Japanese. Their gains in Manchuria and northern China had been made possible because of Chinese

Japan's puppet
P'u Yi, the last emperor of China, was installed as first chief executive and then emperor in the Manchurian states established by the Japanese between 1932 and 1934. He was a mere figurehead; real political, economic, and military power lay in Japanese hands.

weakness and internal divisions. The Sian Incident, in which Chiang Kai-shek was held hostage, served notice that China would attempt to resolve its internal disputes in order to present Japan with a united front. Such a development was nothing short of incitement to Japanese militarists and hard-liners to move quickly before China had a chance to make something of its intent.

THE CAMPAIGN IN CHINA
On July 7, 1937 a Japanese patrol and Chinese troops skirmished at the Marco Polo Bridge in Wanping, just outside Peking. Such events had often been used by the Japanese as a pretext to browbeat Chinese authorities into local concessions. The Marco Polo Bridge incident, however, proved the first step to full-scale war. In late July 1937 there was a massacre of Japanese soldiers, police, and civilians in Tungchow. Then, as a result of provocation by the Imperial Navy, fighting broke out in Shanghai on August 13. As in 1932, the Japanese Navy was unable to win the fight it had started; the army had to send reinforcements to help, which made mobilization necessary. Once ordered, on August 17, 1937, mobilization ensured full-scale war in China.

Thus began the Sino–Japanese War, which lasted until August 1945. Its first phase, between summer 1937 and October 1938, saw the Japanese gain the upper hand. Two initial advances, in northern and central China, came together on May 19, 1938,

THE RAPE OF NANKING

ALSO KNOWN AS THE NANKING MASSACRE, the Rape of Nanking ranks as one of the most infamous episodes in the history of modern warfare. The city in Kiangsu province had been the capital of the Nationalist Chinese from 1928 to 1937. Chiang Kai-shek's troops had already left the city when it was captured by the Japanese Central China Front Army on December 13, 1937. The destruction of Nanking was ordered by the Japanese commanding officer, General Matsui Iwane, and in the weeks that followed, some 50,000 Japanese troops went on a spree of mass killing and violence. Brutality was not uncommon from either side in the Sino–Japanese War, but even by these standards the events in Nanking were breathtaking. The soldiers bayoneted, shot, burned, buried alive, and decapitated their victims, and, according to eyewitness accounts, mutilated corpses lined the streets of the city.

The total number of Chinese killed in the Nanking massacre has been the subject of much debate, with most estimates ranging from around 100,000 to more than 300,000. It is almost certain that the accurate figure will never be known. In addition, it is thought that a total of 20,000 Chinese women and girls were raped before being murdered. As well as the mass human slaughter, the Japanese army looted and burned

the city and surrounding towns, destroying more than one-third of the buildings in the process. In 1940 the Japanese made Nanking the capital of a Chinese client regime headed, until 1944, by Wang Ching-wei, the most senior member of the Kuomintang to have defected. Japan officially surrendered to China in Nanking on September 9, 1945. At the end of World War II Matsui and Tani Hisao, a lieutenant who had participated in murder and rape in Nanking, were tried for war crimes. They were found guilty and executed.

The conqueror's spoils
A Japanese soldier holding the national flag looks over the ruins of Nanking after the city's occupation in December 1937.

Buried alive
Japanese troops herd Chinese prisoners into a pit where they will be buried alive. The Japanese also committed other atrocities, including using live prisoners for bayonet practice.

with the capture of Suchow, which gave the Japanese possession of overland communications between Peking and the port of Shanghai. The Japanese effort then divided against the cites that lay in central China between the Yellow River in the north and the Yangtze River to the south. The first phase of the war ended when the Japanese drove along the Yangtze to capture the Wuhan cities—Wuchang, Hanyang, and Hangkou. The campaign was notable for a number of reasons: the deliberate Japanese bombing of British and American warships at Shanghai, the Japanese atrocities at Nanking, and the breaching by the Chinese of dikes along the Yellow River in order to slow the Japanese advance. The Japanese incurred some defeats, mainly in the early weeks of the air war, when it became all too apparent that their bombers, without adequate fighter cover, were vulnerable to Soviet-supplied Chinese fighters.

Such defeats were, however, minor. The Japanese met with no real, sustained resistance as they conquered large areas of northern and central China.

Onward to victory

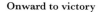

Japanese troops speed past a railroad sign during the March 1939 occupation of the strategically vital city of Nanchang, the capital of Kiangsi province in southeast China. By the time the Japanese arrived, retreating Chinese forces had destroyed most of the city's infrastructure.

Children of war

A famous—and possibly staged—photograph of the China conflict: Shanghai station after a bombing raid in August 1937. The Sino-Japanese conflict saw the first sustained employment of air power against civilian targets.

JAPAN'S FURTHER PLANS

The Japanese faced an age-old military truism: conquering territory was one thing, but holding on to it was quite another. They might be able to defeat Kuomintang forces, but they could not defeat the Kuomintang. What was more, there was no political option. On December 26, 1937 Chiang Kai-shek announced a policy of protracted resistance that precluded negotiations. Likewise, the Japanese would not deal with Chiang. They thus faced a dilemma. They had not conquered vast territories in order to set up client regimes that possessed real power, which might then be used against themselves. Yet without establishing popularly-based government in occupied China, they had no chance of securing support from the Chinese population.

Members of the Japanese military who were prepared to acknowledge the dilemma proposed genuine cooperation with a properly constituted alternative to Chiang and the Kuomintang. Some figures, such as Ishihara Kanji (the main architect of the Manchurian Incident in 1931), helped found the *Toa Remmei* (East Asian League) in October 1938. The league promoted war in East Asia as the means of creating a united continent in which Japan would be the equal partner of other Asian nations. Such a goal was opposed by Lieutenant-General Tojo Hideki, the Kwantung Army's chief of staff and the founder of the governmental *Koa Domei* (Agency for Developing Asia). The agency argued for the military conquest of Asia, and absolute Japanese domination of conquered areas in preparation for a "final war" with the Western races. Tojo and like-minded officers increasingly came to dominate political and military life.

While the war in China could not be won by political or military means, the effort of conquest worsened the international trading position on which the overpopulated, under-resourced Home Islands depended. Exploitation of the natural resources of Manchuria and northern and central China demanded capital investment that could only be secured at the expense of domestic programs. Similarly, the massive rise in state spending and concentration on military production imposed cuts on domestic consumption that were severe even by 1940. Moreover, with the outbreak of war in Europe in 1939, Western commercial shipping in the Pacific and international credits all but disappeared, with obvious implications for a Japan that lacked sufficient

The start of battle
Soviet tankmen prepare to attack Japanese forces and their local allies at Nomonhan, in Manchuria, in July 1939. The clash was the most significant Soviet military action before the outbreak of the war itself.

Japanese gains
Japanese gains in China during the occupation of Manchuria and the Sino-Japanese War in the 1930s were substantial.

shipping to meet its import requirements. Japan thus found itself facing a disastrous war in China that reached indecisively into the future at the very time when in Manchuria, around Nomonhan, its forces were being defeated in battle with Soviet forces. With its German ally signing a non-aggression treaty with the Soviet Union even as this defeat took shape, Japan chose caution and waited upon events to unfold before deciding its next course of action.

JAPANESE EXPANSION
1930–1939

- Japanese empire 1930
- Japanese sphere of influence 1930
- Japanese conquests 1931–33
- Japanese conquests 1937–39

BUILD-UP TO WAR IN EUROPE

OCTOBER 1, 1934–SEPTEMBER 1, 1939

On attaining power in 1933, Adolf Hitler set about rearming Germany in preparation for military conquests abroad. His expansion of the Reich met with little initial resistance from Britain and France, and Hitler acquired Austria and Czechoslovakia with little difficulty. However, when he sent German troops into Poland in 1939, the course for war was set.

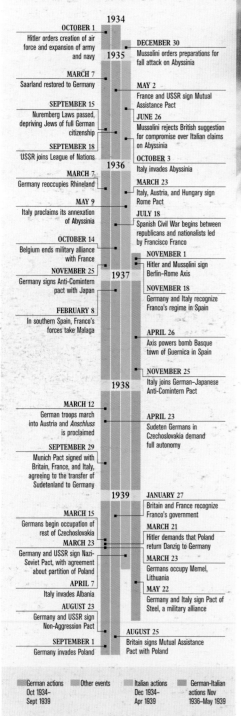

1934

OCTOBER 1
Hitler orders creation of air force and expansion of army and navy

DECEMBER 30
Mussolini orders preparations for fall attack on Abyssinia

1935

MARCH 7
Saarland restored to Germany

MAY 2
France and USSR sign Mutual Assistance Pact

SEPTEMBER 15
Nuremberg Laws passed, depriving Jews of full German citizenship

JUNE 26
Mussolini rejects British suggestion for compromise over Italian claims on Abyssinia

SEPTEMBER 18
USSR joins League of Nations

OCTOBER 3
Italy invades Abyssinia

1936

MARCH 7
Germany reoccupies Rhineland

MARCH 23
Italy, Austria, and Hungary sign Rome Pact

MAY 9
Italy proclaims its annexation of Abyssinia

JULY 18
Spanish Civil War begins between republicans and nationalists led by Francisco Franco

OCTOBER 14
Belgium ends military alliance with France

NOVEMBER 1
Hitler and Mussolini sign Berlin–Rome Axis

NOVEMBER 25
Germany signs Anti-Comintern pact with Japan

NOVEMBER 18
Germany and Italy recognize Franco's regime in Spain

1937

FEBRUARY 8
In southern Spain, Franco's forces take Malaga

APRIL 26
Axis powers bomb Basque town of Guernica in Spain

NOVEMBER 25
Italy joins German–Japanese Anti-Comintern Pact

1938

MARCH 12
German troops march into Austria and *Anschluss* is proclaimed

APRIL 23
Sudeten Germans in Czechoslovakia demand full autonomy

SEPTEMBER 29
Munich Pact signed with Britain, France, and Italy, agreeing to the transfer of Sudetenland to Germany

1939

JANUARY 27
Britain and France recognize Franco's government

MARCH 15
Germans begin occupation of rest of Czechoslovakia

MARCH 21
Hitler demands that Poland return Danzig to Germany

MARCH 23
Germany and USSR sign Nazi-Soviet Pact, with agreement about partition of Poland

MARCH 23
Germans occupy Memel, Lithuania

APRIL 7
Italy invades Albania

MAY 22
Germany and Italy sign Pact of Steel, a military alliance

AUGUST 23
Germany and USSR sign Non-Aggression Pact

AUGUST 25
Britain signs Mutual Assistance Pact with Poland

SEPTEMBER 1
Germany invades Poland

German actions Oct 1934–Sept 1939	Other events	Italian actions Dec 1934–Apr 1939	German-Italian actions Nov 1936–May 1939

REARMAMENT AND EXPANSION

WITHIN 18 MONTHS of becoming chancellor of Germany on January 30, 1933, Adolf Hitler turned his attention to three foreign policy goals that were central to his avowed goal of restoring national prestige. First, the military restrictions imposed by the Versailles Treaty of 1919 should be lifted. Second, Germany should be restored to its rightful place as the strongest European power, and a "Greater Germany" should be created, to include German-speaking Austria, the Czech Sudetenland, and regions lost after World War I. Third, the German empire should be expanded to encompass Poland and European Russia.

Hitler had no concrete plan for attaining his ambitions. Instead, he would take what opportunities presented themselves. As his success grew, however, so did his appetite for conquest and his recklessness.

Defending the homeland
Mussolini's invasion of Abyssinia on October 3, 1935, was designed to acquire a glorious Italian empire. It was fiercely resisted by Abyssinian soldiers.

Hitler's rhetoric during the 1920s had made it clear that, should he come to power, Germany would set about rearming. For Europe, sapped by the effects of the Depression, the timing could not have been worse. Both Britain and France lacked the military means to oppose Hitler with force, and the economic resources to fund military programs.

In March 1933 Hitler argued that only Germany had disarmed in accordance with the Versailles Treaty, and that either other nations should disarm or Germany should be allowed to raise its own level of armaments. Later that year he threatened to quit the League of Nations if Germany was not granted parity. On October 19, he duly ordered his delegation to walk out of the League. The move shocked Europeans, but many Germans saw it as a sign that their national honor was at last being restored.

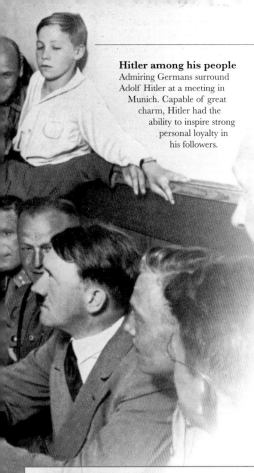

Hitler among his people
Admiring Germans surround Adolf Hitler at a meeting in Munich. Capable of great charm, Hitler had the ability to inspire strong personal loyalty in his followers.

DEVELOPMENTS IN AUSTRIA

A natural prize in the quest for a Greater Germany was Hitler's homeland, Austria, where in May 1932 Engelbert Dollfuss became chancellor. He began economic reforms and sought allies, especially Mussolini's Italy, to help him oppose a union with Germany. In May 1933 he dissolved parliament and banned the major political parties. Putting down an armed uprising in May 1934, Dollfuss proclaimed a new constitution modeled on that of fascist Italy, to the anger of German and Austrian Nazis. In July 1934 Austrian Nazis killed Dollfuss in a failed coup.

In response Mussolini, who saw Austria as a useful buffer between Italy and Hitler's Germany, sent three divisions of troops toward the Brenner Pass. The gesture made it clear that, if Germany came to the aid of the Nazi conspirators, war would ensue. Not yet in a position to fight such a war, Hitler could only watch as the new government banned the Austrian Nazi Party and executed the conspirators. Hitler's foreign policy was at its nadir.

GERMAN REARMAMENT

In early 1935 Hitler announced that Germany would build what military forces it chose. He also staged a lavish ceremony to reveal the existence of a new German Air Force, the 2,500-plane Luftwaffe, which he had been secretly building for two years. The Germans celebrated wildly, but Germany's neighbors were not so enthusiastic. Italy, France, and Britain forged the "Stresa Front" to resist German violations of the Versailles Treaty. Hitler saw the gesture for what it was: an empty show of strength, disguising the Allies' true weakness.

Versailles had also limited Germany's navy, but Hitler now sensed that he could increase it without reprisal. He forced Britain to allow him a surface navy equivalent to one-third of the tonnage of the British surface fleet and an equal tonnage of submarines. The British accepted that Germany would expand its navy with or without a treaty, and reluctantly signed an agreement to Hitler's naval expansion on June 18, 1935. Similar German agreements with France and the Soviet Union followed. The Versailles Treaty was dead.

ITALY'S INVASION OF ABYSSINIA

Mussolini, meanwhile, decided that if Hitler could flout treaties, so could he. He needed an overseas adventure to distract from the domestic troubles caused by the Depression. His target was Abyssinia (now Ethiopia) in East Africa, where on a previous colonial adventure in 1898 Italy had suffered a humiliating defeat at the hands of African troops.

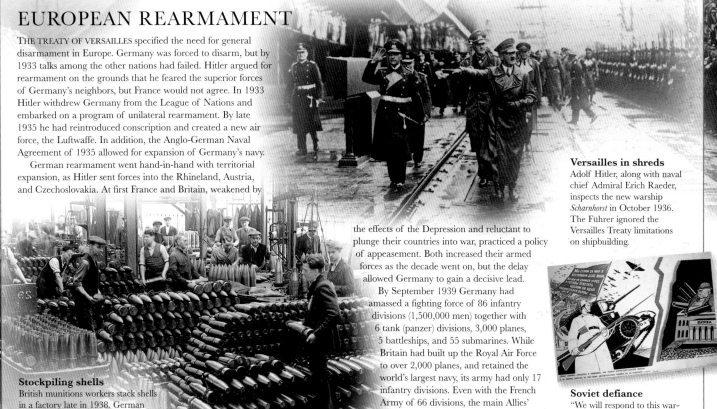

EUROPEAN REARMAMENT

THE TREATY OF VERSAILLES specified the need for general disarmament in Europe. Germany was forced to disarm, but by 1933 talks among the other nations had failed. Hitler argued for rearmament on the grounds that he feared the superior forces of Germany's neighbors, but France would not agree. In 1933 Hitler withdrew Germany from the League of Nations and embarked on a program of unilateral rearmament. By late 1935 he had reintroduced conscription and created a new air force, the Luftwaffe. In addition, the Anglo-German Naval Agreement of 1935 allowed for expansion of Germany's navy.

German rearmament went hand-in-hand with territorial expansion, as Hitler sent forces into the Rhineland, Austria, and Czechoslovakia. At first France and Britain, weakened by the effects of the Depression and reluctant to plunge their countries into war, practiced a policy of appeasement. Both increased their armed forces as the decade went on, but the delay allowed Germany to gain a decisive lead.

By September 1939 Germany had amassed a fighting force of 86 infantry divisions (1,500,000 men) together with 6 tank (panzer) divisions, 3,000 planes, 5 battleships, and 55 submarines. While Britain had built up the Royal Air Force to over 2,000 planes, and retained the world's largest navy, its army had only 17 infantry divisions. Even with the French Army of 66 divisions, the main Allies' combined military might was still smaller than that of Nazi Germany.

Versailles in shreds
Adolf Hitler, along with naval chief Admiral Erich Raeder, inspects the new warship *Scharnhorst* in October 1936. The Führer ignored the Versailles Treaty limitations on shipbuilding.

Stockpiling shells
British munitions workers stack shells in a factory late in 1938. German rearmament triggered a reciprocal arms build-up in Britain and France.

Soviet defiance
"We will respond to this war-mongering" declares a 1934 Soviet propaganda poster.

SPANISH CIVIL WAR

THE SPANISH CIVIL WAR (1936–39) was a full-scale military revolt by conservative nationalists against the leftist republican government. Under the leadership of General Francisco Franco, the rebel forces coalesced around the policies of the fascist Falange Party. Adolf Hitler despatched Luftwaffe transports and fighters to assist Franco, and allowed his own forces to go to Spain as "volunteers" in the Condor Legion. Hitler used the conflict as a test-bed for equipment and new military doctrines—the introduction of area or carpet-bombing techniques in the attack on Guernica in 1937 was an innovation that reemerged in World War II—but the Führer's motives were more generally concerned with spreading fascism and sowing the seeds of disunity among the Western powers. Likewise, Mussolini also sent men and equipment, seeing the nationalist cause as an opportunity to bolster Italy's international standing and to gain respect for its armed forces.

The republicans asked for help from the Western democracies and the Soviet Union. In France and Britain, divided public opinion prevented official involvement, while Stalin offered limited support. However, Western neutrality could not stop volunteers from joining the war. Thousands of young men flocked to Spain to fight fascism. Most served in the republican International Brigade, but some

Women snipers
Female republican fighters take cover in the early stages of the Spanish Civil War. Control of Spain's cities, where much of the fighting took place, was vital to the eventual victory of Franco's nationalists in March 1939.

formed their own national units. From the United States, for example, came the Abraham Lincoln and George Washington Brigades; refugees from Germany formed the Ernst Thälmann Brigade. Nonetheless, by 1938 the fighting had clearly tilted in Franco's favor. In March 1939 the Spanish fascists achieved final victory. In May the German troops returned home to a heroes' welcome, and the "volunteers" rejoined their units.

In addition to dividing the Western powers, the Spanish Civil War cemented Benito Mussolini's relationship with Adolf Hitler, culminating in the Rome–Berlin Axis Agreement of September 1937, a fascist alliance that would have profound effects on the course of World War II.

Spanish propaganda
The cover of this right-wing magazine reflects the influence of Spanish artist Salvador Dalí. Both sides were quick to exploit graphic art such as posters to drum up support.

Symbolic city
A lone dog stands in a ruined street in the city of Guernica, in northern Spain, destroyed by a German bombing raid on April 26, 1937.

Fleeing for their lives
Uncertainty marks the faces of women and children fleeing Spain's capital, Madrid, in December 1936. Thousands of civilians were caught up in the fighting.

Isolated and poor, Abyssinia lay within easy reach of Italy's colonies in Eritrea and Somaliland. Starting a campaign, however, would leave Italy vulnerable to any punitive sanctions imposed by the League of Nations. Mussolini gambled that he could eliminate Abyssinia before the League of Nations had time to react and thus present it with a *fait accompli*.

Accordingly, Italian troops invaded Abyssinia on October 3, 1935. Abyssinian emperor Haile Selassie pleaded with the League to react. The League realized, however, that any form of military intervention would come too late to affect events and that any economic sanctions might drive Mussolini into alliances with non-League members such as the Soviet Union or Germany. The League made a hopeless compromise: it imposed minimal sanctions that caused no harm but succeeded in angering the Italians. On the ground, the Italians routed the Abyssinians. By the time the "dispute" came to the top of the League's agenda, Abyssinia had ceased to exist as an independent nation.

HITLER AND THE RHINELAND

Hitler, in turn, reasoned that if Italy could get away with such naked aggression, so could Germany. In March 1936 the major European powers watched helplessly as he ordered troops into the German Rhineland, in defiance of the Versailles Treaty.

An effective reaction to the remilitarization of the Rhineland was partly prevented by political paralysis within France, where a Popular Front—an alliance of socialists and communists—expected to win a parliamentary majority in elections in April 1936. By May 1936, when the Popular Front finally came to power, the German Army had been stationed in the Rhineland for more than two months.

Among those who were most alarmed by the German move into the Rhineland were Hitler's own generals, who knew that their forces' training

Nazism on display
Hitler Youth parade in the form of a stylized swastika during the Berlin Olympic games in 1936. Hitler tried to turn the event into a publicity coup for Aryan ideals, but German athletes failed to achieve the success he craved.

and equipment were inadequate. German troops had no modern artillery or tanks. The infantry had no transport. The generals wrung a concession from Hitler: if the French mobilized their troops, Hitler would order the German forces back.

However, Hitler had read the French well. The Maginot Line along the German border revealed a mentality more suited to defense than attack. Hitler was also right that the French would not fight alone, and that Britain, the most important ally of France, would not go to war over the Rhineland. His gamble succeeded, and his popularity at home rose to unprecedented levels.

On November 5, 1937 Hitler told his defense staff that his focus lay on creating a Greater Germany, involving the amalgamation into the Reich of German-speaking Austrians, the Germans of the Czech Sudetenland, the areas lost in post-World War I plebiscites, and the coastal city of Danzig at the head of the Polish Corridor. He also indicated that he would turn east in a bid to establish *Lebensraum*, or "living space," for the expanded German populace.

The implications were clear: unless Poland and the Soviet Union agreed to surrender territory, only war could bring about Hitler's goals. The Führer told his audience to be ready for war by late 1942 or early 1943. But he also warned them to prepare to take advantage of any earlier opportunities that might arise.

After firing those ministers and generals who were clearly less than enthusiastic about his plans, Hitler took his first step toward creating an expanded Germany—the *Anschluss*, or annexation of Austria. Using as a pretext the refusal of Chancellor Kurt von

Schuschnigg to lift the ban on the Austrian Nazi Party, illegal since the attempted coup in 1934, Hitler presented the Austrian leader with a document that essentially imposed Nazi control on the country. Browbeaten and shattered, Schuschnigg signed. On March 12, 1938, German troops marched into Austria, which was rapidly and fully incorporated into Germany as the Ostmark province.

DEMANDS FOR THE SUDETENLAND

Hitler now looked to the region of Czechoslovakia bordering Germany. Known as the Sudetenland, it was home to some 3 million ethnic Germans. Hitler instructed the local Nazi leader, Konrad Henlein, to begin a campaign for greater autonomy for Sudeten Germans. Throughout the summer of 1938, no sooner did the Czech government offer a concession than Henlein would make new demands.

Dictators in tandem
Hitler and Mussolini take the salute during Il Duce's state visit to Berlin in September 1937. The visit cemented the military alliance between Germany and Italy, which would have long-term consequences for the fate of Europe.

> "…the lost land will never be won back by solemn appeals to God, nor by hopes in any League of Nations, but only by the force of arms."
>
> ADOLF HITLER, SPEAKING OUTSIDE THE REICHSTAG IN 1936

EXPANSION OF NAZI
GERMANY
MAR 1935–MAR 1939

Germany 1933

Area of German expansion
Mar 1935–Mar 1939

German defensive lines

The quest for "living space"
German expansion from
1936 to 1939 concentrated
on territories with large
German minorities—but
further eastern expansion
seemed inevitable.

The Czech president, Edouard Benes, foresaw the
eventual outcome and began to prepare for war. He
appealed to France, with whom Czechoslovakia had
a defensive alliance, and France called for assistance
from Britain. Prime Minister Neville Chamberlain
made several trips to Germany to try to defuse the
crisis, but eventually gave up. Hitler ordered his
army to prepare an attack for October 1.

Faced with certain defeat in the event of a
German mobilization, in September 1938 Benes
agreed to cede the Sudetenland in six months'
time. Hitler increased the stakes. The Czechs
must hand over the Sudetenland immediately,
he said. Chamberlain mobilized British forces in
anticipation of a military conflict that appeared
to be inevitable. The French took similar measures,
and Europe prepared for war.

Some of Hitler's generals were as unhappy
as Europe's leaders. Led by Army chief of staff
General Ludwig Beck, they regarded Hitler's
ultimatums with horror. Beck wanted to expose
Hitler's recklessness so that the army might be able
to act against him. Risking the death penalty for
treason, he approached the British political maverick
Winston Churchill, urging him to tell the British
government to stand up to Hitler. Chamberlain
ignored Churchill's pleas for action.

Meanwhile, German military units moved to the
Czech border in readiness for the invasion. Hitler
had counted on popular support, but the Germans
looked on sullenly. As he rethought the situation,
intervention came from an unexpected source:
Mussolini, fearing a European-wide conflagration,
urged Hitler to give peace one more chance.

Accordingly, Germany invited France and Britain
to a meeting to discuss the crisis. The Czechs were
not asked to attend. In Munich in September 1938
Hitler offered France and Britain a pledge that the
Sudetenland marked the end of his quest to create
a Greater Germany. To Chamberlain and French
premier Edouard Daladier this offered the chance
of an honorable exit. Daladier told the Czechs that
Hitler's forces would occupy their country within 48
hours, and no opposition would be voiced by Britain
or France. Appeasement had reached its zenith. On
October 1, 1938, Czech border guards stood aside
as German troops occupied the Sudetenland.

THE FALL OF CZECHOSLOVAKIA

Hitler, however, remained unsatisfied. He was no
closer to his goal of "living space" for the German
people than before the Czech crisis had arisen, a
situation he was determined to rectify by invading
the remainder of Czechoslovakia. With winter
approaching, the earliest feasible date for such an
action was March 1939. As the moment neared,
the new Czech president Emil Hacha visited Berlin.
Aged 67, and a diabetic in poor health, Hacha was
harangued until at 4:00 am on March 15, 1939,
he agreed to invite the Germans to enter.

Bohemia and Moravia and establish a "protectorate." Unopposed, German troops crossed the border later that day, to remain there for the next six years.

Chamberlain and Daladier had been duped. Knowing what Hitler's next target would be, they extended promises to Poland to protect its territorial integrity if Germany invaded. Hitler's response was to set his sights on the Polish Corridor.

INVASION OF POLAND

The Polish Corridor, which separated East Prussia from Germany, was a daily reminder for Germans of the humiliation of the Versailles Treaty. The Poles had expelled most Germans from the area, but at the top of the corridor was Danzig, whose German inhabitants made growing demands for autonomy. In a familiar pattern, any concessions by the Poles were met only with more demands. France and Britain now sought assistance from the Soviet Union in the belief that if Stalin would give support to Poland, Hitler could not attack.

Hitler sent his foreign minister, Joachim von Ribbentrop, to Moscow to broker a deal with Stalin. Ribbentrop offered what the Allies

THE FREE CITY OF DANZIG

UNDER THE TERMS of the Treaty of Versailles, the port of Danzig, on the Vistula River at the top of the corridor through Germany that gave Poland access to the Baltic Sea, became a "free city." The former capital of the German province of West Prussia, Danzig was under the protection of the League of Nations, but had special administrative ties

Staking a claim
"Danzig is German": this propaganda postcard printed by the Nazis in 1938 shows the imperial eagle above a stylized view of the free city.

with Poland. Poland could use the harbor without paying duty, and was in charge of foreign policy. The arrangement irked both the city's 96 percent German majority and Germans everywhere. Economic and political developments in Danzig mirrored those in Germany. In late 1930 the Nazis emerged as the second-largest political party in the city. After taking power in elections in 1933, they outlawed opposing parties and introduced racial laws that led to an exodus of Jewish inhabitants.

Throughout the 1930s Danzig's Germans lobbied for increased autonomy, and in March 1939 Hitler demanded the cession of Danzig to Germany and the restoration of a land link with East Prussia. Poland rejected these demands and obtained French and British guarantees against German aggression.

On the march
Hitler Youth march past Danzig harbor in June 1930. That same year the Nazi Party emerged from nowhere to become one of the major powers in the city.

could not: the eastern half of Poland and non-intervention should Stalin try to repossess Finland and states on the Baltic which had broken away from the Soviet Union. Not yet ready for war, Stalin accepted. On August 23, 1939, Europe learned that Hitler and Stalin had signed a Non-Aggression Pact.

The Poles mobilized their armed forces. Hitler still expected Britain and France to back off from any military action, as they had done previously over Czechoslovakia. To give them a means of doing so without losing face, he staged a "border outrage" in order to make it appear that the Poles were the aggressors. Responding to this "provocation," German troops crossed the border into Poland at 4:30 am on September 1. Britain and France presented an ultimatum. When Hitler failed to halt the German invasion, to his surprise the allies honored their guarantees to Poland by quickly declaring war on Germany. On September 3, 1939, World War II in Europe began.

Military on the move
German-speaking inhabitants of the Czech village of Waldheusel welcome Nazi troops during Hitler's occupation of the Sudetenland in October 1938.

Politics as spectacle
Thousands of Nazi supporters crowd an
arena at Buckeberge to mark Thanksgiving
Day, January 1, 1937. The Nazis used mass
rallies, particularly at Nuremberg, to reinforce
the impression of power and discipline.

WAR BEGINS IN EUROPE
1939–40

DURING THE FIRST PHASE OF THE WAR IN EUROPE

THERE WAS ACTION AT SEA AND FOUR CAMPAIGNS

ON LAND: THE GERMAN AND SOVIET INVASION OF

POLAND, A WINTER WAR BETWEEN THE SOVIET UNION

AND FINLAND, THE GERMAN INVASION OF DENMARK AND

NORWAY, AND FINALLY, AFTER MANY MONTHS IN WHICH

LITTLE HAPPENED IN WESTERN EUROPE, THE GERMAN

ASSAULT ON FRANCE AND THE LOW COUNTRIES.

THIS ATTACK WAS A DEVASTATING DEMONSTRATION

OF THE NEW GERMAN HIGH-SPEED WARFARE AND,

AT THE END OF IT, BRITAIN STOOD ALONE.

Germans marching in Warsaw
The Germans unleashed their attack on
Poland on September 1, 1939. The Polish
army, with its largely obsolescent weapons,
was no match for them, and Warsaw was
forced to surrender on September 27.

BLITZKRIEG AND TOTAL WAR

EUROPE WENT TO WAR IN SEPTEMBER 1939 IN A MOOD OF GRIM ACCEPTANCE THAT THE EFFORTS OF THE PEACEMAKERS IN 1919 TO CREATE A EUROPE AT PEACE WITH ITSELF HAD FAILED. THE TECHNOLOGICAL ADVANCES OF THE PREVIOUS 25 YEARS WOULD RESULT IN A CONFLICT VERY MUCH MORE TOTAL THAN WORLD WAR I, WITH CIVILIANS IN THE FIRING LINE AS NEVER BEFORE.

A WIDELY HELD BELIEF had grown up between the two world wars that any future war would open with mass attacks by bombers, armed with gas bombs, on cities. It had been argued that air power was now the decisive weapon of war since it had the ability to strike at the heart of a nation and destroy its will to fight, thus making armies and navies virtually superfluous. Incidents such as the bombing of Guernica during the Spanish Civil War and Japanese air attacks in China appeared to confirm that the aircraft was now the dominant weapon, although in no instance was poison gas actually used. Consequently, in the months leading up to the outbreak of war, the belligerent nations had begun to prepare their citizens for such an event, even to the extent of issuing them with gasmasks and arranging for the evacuation of children from cities.

USE OF AIR POWER

The fact that massed air attacks on cities did not immediately take place was largely through fear of instant retaliation in kind. The air forces of both sides were under strict instructions to confine themselves to military targets. By the same token, while some nations held stocks of poison gas, governments laid down that it would only be employed if the other side used gas warfare first. Consequently, air power was employed primarily in support of ground forces, both on the battlefield itself and to the rear in attacks on communications. There was a need to gain air superiority over the battlefield, which for the German Luftwaffe meant that the first priority in any campaign was to destroy the opposing air force, ideally by attacking its aircraft on its airfields. The Luftwaffe did, in fact, stray beyond military targets when it attacked Warsaw in September 1939, Rotterdam in May 1940, and refugees in the Low Countries and

France. Its defense was that the two cities refused demands to surrender, hence making themselves military targets. As for attacks on refugees, the justification was that creating panic would hamper the movement of enemy military forces.

An adjunct to air power was the employment by the Germans of a new form of warfare in the campaigns in both Norway and the west. They used paratroops and airlanded forces to secure key points, enabling the troops on the ground to advance quickly. The success enjoyed by the German airborne forces prompted both the British and the Americans to establish their own.

BLITZKRIEG TACTICS

On land the fighting would be dominated by the new German style of warfare—blitzkrieg ("lightning war")—that made great use of tanks and aircraft. The Poles were the first victims in September 1939, when they paid the penalty for their lack of modern equipment. The French and British might have hoped to cope better in May 1940, especially since they had had nine months in which to prepare for the German attack. Their armies, however, were suffering from prewar parsimony. In France much of the defense budget had gone into constructing the Maginot Line, while in Britain greater priority had been given to rearming the navy and air force. Cooperation between both the British and French air force and army was not nearly as close as that between the German Army and the Luftwaffe. Furthermore, it was only late in the day that the French began to concentrate their tanks into armored divisions, while the one British armored formation was only ready to be deployed in late May. Finally, Allied communications, especially at the higer levels of command, were too cumbersome to enable commanders to react sufficiently quickly to rapidly changing situations.

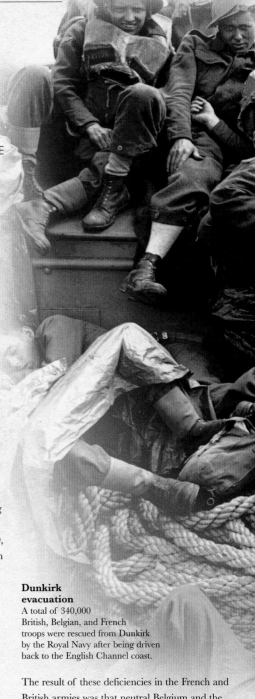

Dunkirk evacuation
A total of 340,000 British, Belgian, and French troops were rescued from Dunkirk by the Royal Navy after being driven back to the English Channel coast.

The result of these deficiencies in the French and British armies was that neutral Belgium and the Netherlands were quickly overrun and France was forced to sign a humiliating armistice. Much of the British Army in France did manage to escape, largely thanks to the Royal Navy, which rescued it from the beaches of Dunkirk. It was not the first time, since the navy had also had to carry out evacuations of Allied forces from Norway. This was in parallel with a grim campaign that it had been waging from the outbreak of war—the defense of Britain's maritime communications.

"We must be very careful not to assign to this deliverance the attributes of a victory. Wars are not won by evacuations."

WINSTON CHURCHILL ADDRESSING THE HOUSE OF COMMONS ON JUNE 4, 1940
AFTER THE END OF THE DUNKIRK EVACUATION

WAR AT SEA

At sea the main focus was on the Atlantic, as it had been during World War I. Indeed, the second Battle of the Atlantic would be the longest running campaign of World War II, the first victim being on September 3, 1939 (the liner *Athenia*), and the last in May 1945 during the dying days of the war in Europe. The French and British had agreed that the Royal Navy, still the most powerful in the world, would be responsible for the Atlantic and North Sea, while the French took care of the Mediterranean, which did not become a theater of war until June 1940, when Italy finally entered the conflict. The British imposed a maritime blockade on Germany, as they had during World War I. Otherwise, the Royal Navy's main task was keeping Britain's sea communications open.

Hitler, with his fleet in the midst of an expansion plan when war broke out, recognized that, although modern, it lacked the strength to meet the Royal Navy head on. Instead, the German Navy would concentrate on throttling Britain's maritime communications, something it had very nearly succeeded in doing in 1917. In September 1939, the German U-boat arm was still comparatively small, and from the outset the British limited the amount of damage it could inflict on merchant vessels by instituting a convoy system. This was despite a grave shortage of escort ships. Consequently, most of the U-boat victims were ships sailing on their own. On the other hand, few

French refugees
Possibly as many as 5 million French civilians took part in a vast southward exodus ahead of the advancing Germans, sometimes greatly hampering the movements of Allied troops. Here, refugees arrive by train in an area of France not yet occupied by the Germans.

U-boats were sunk and they did cause two major embarrassments. One sunk the aircraft carrier *Courageous* in the North Sea in September 1939 and another managed to penetrate the British Home Fleet anchorage in Scapa Flow in the Orkneys and sink the battleship *Royal Oak*. More serious were the German surface-raiders, the fast and heavily armed

pocket battleships. Most notable of these was the *Graf Spee*, which had sailed from Germany before the outbreak of war and caused havoc in the Indian Ocean and South Atlantic. At one point as many as five Allied naval task forces were attempting to hunt her down. Eventually she was brought to bay and trapped by three British cruisers off the South American coast in December 1939. Her captain scuttled her rather than face the disgrace of surrender. It was one of the few bright spots for the Allies during the lengthy period of waiting and relative inactivity in the west, between September 1939 and May 1940, known as the "Phoney War."

"The final German victory over England is now only a question of time. Enemy offensive operations on a large scale are no longer possible."

GENERAL ALFRED JODL, CHIEF OF STAFF GERMAN ARMED FORCES HQ,
DIARY ENTRY, JUNE 30, 1940

Fleeing civilians
As the Germans advanced rapidly through the Netherlands, Belgium, and France in May–June 1940, literally millions of civilians took to the roads to flee from the fighting. Often in columns, they were an easy target for German machine-gun fire from the air.

One other aspect of the war at sea that grew in significance was maritime air power. The British had aircraft carriers, while the Germans did not, but initially they saw little action, aside from off Norway in April 1940, when they provided some air support to the forces ashore. Norway, however, also revealed the threat of land-based aircraft to ships. This would become even more apparent in the Mediterranean, as would the carrier's ability to strike at the enemy from long range, something that would be employed to great effect in the Pacific war.

Another type of warfare that would come to dominate much of the conflict—but was used only tentatively in the first phase of the war—was amphibious warfare. The events at Gallipoli during World War I had made many believe that landings on a hostile coast were no longer viable. As a result, little specialized shipping, such as landing craft, was available to either side when they executed landings in Norway. Faced with the prospect of a cross-Channel invasion of Britain, the Germans did realize that air superiority over the landing area was essential, but when they failed to achieve this during the Battle of Britain, Hitler postponed the invasion indefinitely. By then he had turned on Britain's cities, hoping to bomb the country into submission.

TOTAL WAR

"City busting," as it came to be known, helped to make World War II a total war, in which civilian populations were not only in the firing line, but were also mobilized as never before to support the war effort. In particular, and notably in Britain, women

A factory in occupied France
The Germans expected the civilians in the countries they occupied to contribute to the German war effort. Some factory workers were forced to leave their homes and go to work in Germany where, by 1943, foreigners made up 20 percent of the workforce.

were conscripted. They not only worked in the factories to produce the weapons, but also helped to operate them. Strict food rationing, too, was a fact of life in the belligerent nations and those under Axis occupation. An even grimmer aspect of total war was what is today termed "ethnic cleansing." Hitler's persecution of Jews had, of course, begun almost as soon as he gained power in Germany. After the outbreak of war the policy was expanded to include the entire Jewish population of Europe. By the fall of 1940 all Jews in German-occupied Europe were under threat. In Poland they were already being confined to ghettoes, but it was to be another year before the Nazis adopted a policy of wholesale extermination.

In the meantime, Britain was being nightly hammered by the Luftwaffe. Yet while Churchill was certain that the British people would remain steadfast and that the danger of a German invasion was receding, he accepted that his country lacked the resources to defeat the fascist powers on its own, even with the British Empire taken into account. Only the entry of the United States into the war could achieve victory. Thus, from the summer of 1940, he began to woo President Franklin Roosevelt. But while Roosevelt had every sympathy for Britain's plight and admired the way in which the British were fighting on, he knew that the vast majority of Americans were still isolationist and had no wish to become involved in what they saw as yet another European squabble. In the months to come the US president would give Britain what help he could, as well as preparing his own country for what he believed was ultimately inevitable. The United States' actual entry into the war was, however, still a long way off.

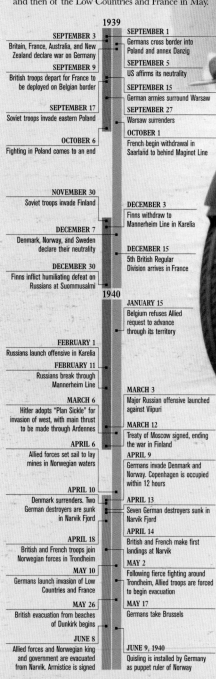

INVASION OF POLAND AND SCANDINAVIA

SEPTEMBER 1, 1939–JUNE 9, 1940

While Germany and the Soviet Union dismembered Poland, little happened in the west. The British and French only became actively involved on the ground with the German invasion of Norway in April 1940 and then of the Low Countries and France in May.

1939

SEPTEMBER 3
Britain, France, Australia, and New Zealand declare war on Germany

SEPTEMBER 9
British troops depart for France to be deployed on Belgian border

SEPTEMBER 17
Soviet troops invade eastern Poland

OCTOBER 6
Fighting in Poland comes to an end

NOVEMBER 30
Soviet troops invade Finland

DECEMBER 7
Denmark, Norway, and Sweden declare their neutrality

DECEMBER 30
Finns inflict humiliating defeat on Russians at Suommusalmi

1940

FEBRUARY 1
Russians launch offensive in Karelia

FEBRUARY 11
Russians break through Mannerheim Line

MARCH 6
Hitler adopts "Plan Sickle" for invasion of west, with main thrust to be made through Ardennes

APRIL 6
Allied forces set sail to lay mines in Norwegian waters

APRIL 10
Denmark surrenders. Two German destroyers are sunk in Narvik Fjord

APRIL 18
British and French troops join Norwegian forces in Trondheim

MAY 10
Germans launch invasion of Low Countries and France

MAY 26
British evacuation from beaches of Dunkirk begins

JUNE 8
Allied forces and Norwegian king and government are evacuated from Narvik. Armistice is signed

---

SEPTEMBER 1
Germans cross border into Poland and annex Danzig

SEPTEMBER 5
US affirms its neutrality

SEPTEMBER 15
German armies surround Warsaw

SEPTEMBER 27
Warsaw surrenders

OCTOBER 1
French begin withdrawal in Saarland to behind Maginot Line

DECEMBER 3
Finns withdraw to Mannerheim Line in Karelia

DECEMBER 15
5th British Regular Division arrives in France

JANUARY 15
Belgium refuses Allied request to advance through its territory

MARCH 3
Major Russian offensive launched against Viipuri

MARCH 12
Treaty of Moscow signed, ending the war in Finland

APRIL 9
Germans invade Denmark and Norway. Copenhagen is occupied within 12 hours

APRIL 13
Seven German destroyers sunk in Narvik Fjord

APRIL 14
British and French make first landings at Narvik

MAY 2
Following fierce fighting around Trondheim, Allied troops are forced to begin evacuation

MAY 17
Germans take Brussels

JUNE 9, 1940
Quisling is installed by Germany as puppet ruler of Norway

▨ Campaign in Poland
Sept 1–Oct 6, 1939

▨ Campaign in Finland Nov 30, 1940–Mar 12, 1940

▨ Campaign in Denmark and Norway
Apr 9–June 8, 1940

▨ Other events

FIRST CONQUESTS

THE GERMAN PLAN for the assault on Poland had been drawn up by a small team headed by the Prussian Gerd von Rundstedt, who was nominally in retirement. In essence, General Fedor von Bock's Army Group North was to seal the base of the hated Polish Corridor and drive south from East Prussia to cut off the withdrawal of the Polish forces defending the German frontier. Rundstedt himself was to take command of Army Group South and advance rapidly on the Polish capital Warsaw.

The Poles, who had not begun serious planning until spring 1939, faced a dilemma. They had a number of well placed river lines, notably the Warthe and the Vistula, on which to anchor their defenses. However, to do so would mean abandoning the most

Polish cavalry
The Poles considered the cavalry to be the cream of their army. It was, however, ill-equipped to combat blitzkrieg, and claims that it charged German tanks were baseless.

heavily populated and economically developed part of the country in the west. In addition, with Slovakia now under Nazi thrall, they had to worry about their southern border. There was also the threat from the German Third Army in East Prussia. Consequently, they felt forced to adopt a linear defense along their borders. This left them with just one army in reserve

German motorcyclists in Warsaw
German troops poured into Warsaw after its surrender on September 27. For the Poles this day was to mark the end of 20 years as an independent state and the beginning of nearly six years of intense suffering.

and placed to guard the approaches to Warsaw from the west. The Poles hoped, however, that a German attack would immediately precipitate an assault by the French and the British on Germany.

THE INVASION OF POLAND

Hitler's original intention was to launch his invasion on August 26, but the Anglo-Polish Alliance signed the previous day, together with Mussolini's declaration that he was not yet ready for war, caused him to delay at the last moment. He finally ordered that the attack should begin in the early hours of September 1. The invasion opened at 4:45 am with the guns of the elderly battleship *Schleswig-Holstein*, which was on a goodwill visit to the Polish port of Danzig (Gdansk), pounding the Polish garrison at nearby Westerplatte. Minutes later, the skies thundered to the sound of German aircraft, their main target Polish airfields. The Poles, however, had taken the precaution of dispersing many of their aircraft to satellite airfields, so frustrating the German goal of destroying the air force on the ground in one blow. Then, as dawn broke, the ground forces, spearheaded by the panzer divisions and supported by artillery, crossed the border. The Poles fought bravely, with the Westerplatte garrison not surrendering for a week, but they lacked the mobility to counter the new form of blitzkrieg warfare. Even so, the Germans

were not without their problems. Most had never been under fire before and maneuvers that had worked like clockwork on the training ground were now marked by a hesitancy, but it was not enough to halt the advance. By the end of two days' fighting the Polish Corridor was sealed and on September 5 Army Group South had broken through the Poznan and Lodz Armies in the center (see map page 47). Having destroyed the infrastructure of the main Polish airfields, the Luftwaffe now turned its attention to communications and this soon began to affect the Polish supply lines.

The British and French declarations of war on September 3 may have boosted Polish morale, but they did nothing to impede the German advance. The Pomorze Army, now trapped in the Corridor was totally destroyed, while the Modlin Army was forced to withdraw. The Polish Air Force was being shot out of the skies and was running out of fuel due to the disruption to its logistics. Indeed, by September 9 it was virtually grounded. With the German Third Army now advancing south from East Prussia, and the Eighth and Tenth Armies from the west, the threat to Warsaw was growing by the day. To restore the situation, on the 9th the Poznan Army counterattacked from Kutno into the flank of the Eighth Army. In the three-day battle that followed, the Poles decimated one German infantry division.

The Poles were courageous, but they could not halt the remorseless advance of the German panzer divisions. Polish communications were breaking down and it proved impossible to establish a coherent defense on the Vistula and San Rivers. The Poznan Army was trapped and destroyed, and by September 15 Warsaw was surrounded.

WARSAW BESIEGED

Demands that the Poles surrender their capital were met with defiance. Not wishing to become embroiled in costly street fighting, the Germans subjected Warsaw to a prolonged artillery and air bombardment. To outside observers it seemed that

STALIN AND THE SOVIET UNION

JOSEF VISSARIONOVICH DZHUGASHVILI (1879–1953) was born in Tiflis, the son of a cobbler, and in his youth was a candidate for the priesthood in the Russian Orthodox Church. He changed his name to Stalin, meaning "Man of Steel," on becoming involved in revolutionary politics in 1903. Stalin became a close associate of Lenin during the Bolshevik Revolution of 1917 and later a member of the Revolutionary Military Council. By 1928 he had emerged from a bitter leadership struggle as the dictator of the Soviet Union, and he then launched a Five-Year Plan to develop heavy industry and collectivize agriculture. The plan was ruthlessly implemented, transforming the economy at the cost of millions of lives.

In the 1930s Stalin responded to opposition to his reforms by instituting a wholesale purge of the ruling hierarchy in which most of his former Bolshevik comrades were sentenced to death. The purges spread downward into every stratum of society and hundreds of thousands were shot or sent to the rapidly expanding network of

labor camps in the far north. Subsequent purges of the Soviet armed forces cut a swathe through the officer corps, destroying morale and throwing into reverse the reforms introduced by Marshal Tukhachevsky, a proponent of armored warfare.

In the weeks leading up to Germany's invasion of Poland, Stalin was only too aware that his country was not ready for war. He signed a nonaggression pact with his archenemy, Hitler, in the belief that being allowed half of Poland and a free rein in the Baltic States would provide him with a land buffer against a possible future German invasion.

State propaganda
Throughout the 1930s Stalin was portrayed in state propaganda as a benign leader committed to the good of the Soviet people.

Stalin
A ruthless dictator, Stalin's driving ambition was to turn the Soviet Union into a modern industrial state in just 10 years.

MILITARY STRENGTH OF THE COMBATANTS IN 1939

IN THE WEHRMACHT (German Armed Forces), a new philosophy of high-speed warfare had been adopted. However, the instruments of this new style of warfare were not perfected by 1939. The navy's expansion plan was not due for completion until 1942, and much of the army was still reliant on its feet and horsedrawn transportation. Only the Luftwaffe, with its imposing fleet of modern aircraft, was ready for war.

The French had strong armed forces on paper, but they had developed a wholly defensive mentality. The British placed their faith, as always, in the Royal Navy, still the strongest navy in the world. The Royal Air Force had modernized, but was still small when compared to the Luftwaffe, while the army had serious equipment deficiencies. On the sidelines, for the moment, stood Italy and the Soviet Union. Mussolini had created a

modern navy, which rivaled the British in the Mediterranean. His air force, too, appeared capable, but the army had much still to do to prepare itself. In terms of numbers, the forces of the Soviet Union, especially the Red Army, dwarfed those of other countries, but morale had suffered as a result of the purges, which had also snuffed out any vestige of individual initiative.

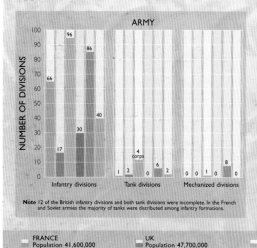

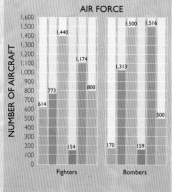

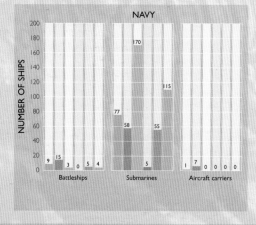

Note 12 of the British infantry divisions and both tank divisions were incomplete. In the French and Soviet armies the majority of tanks were distributed among infantry formations.

| FRANCE Population 41,600,000 | UK Population 47,700,000 | USSR Population 170,000,000 | POLAND Population 34,600,000 | GERMANY Population 68,400,000 | ITALY Population 43,800,000 |

the Luftwaffe was repeating what had happened at Guernica in the Spanish Civil War, but Hitler had ordered that indiscriminate attacks were not to be made on urban areas and in this instance it was mainly the public utilities that were bombed.

Throughout the siege of Warsaw the Poles lived in hope that the Western Allies would attack Germany. True, the French did make a limited advance into the Saarland, but they halted before getting beyond the range of the guns in the Maginot Line. The British, still deploying troops to France and under the overall control of the French, were in no position to do anything. The Poles, however, would continue to fight as long as they still possessed territory. Their

determination to do so was shaken on September 17, when the Soviet Union suddenly attacked from the east. Stalin, surprised by the rapid German advance, decided that he should act before the Germans occupied the whole of Poland and placed themselves on the Soviet border. With the bulk of their forces engaged with the Germans, the Poles were in no position to counter the Red Army, despite its huge deficiencies. Thus, after just two days the Soviet troops met German troops at Brest-Litovsk on the Bug River.

The ultimate outcome was now in no doubt. Polish troops began to fight their way into neutral Romania and Hungary in the hopes of evading capture by either of their two most bitter enemies. Yet, in spite of the battering it was receiving, Warsaw continued

Soviet and German troops near Brest-Litovsk
There was much mutual suspicion when German and Soviet troops met in Poland, a reflection of the hatred their countries had recently borne for each other.

to hold out, as did the fortress of Modlin to its north, where 10 divisions had been trapped since September 10. The suffering of the citizens in the capital increased by the day and, with the city's utilities almost destroyed, the military commander decided, on the 27th, that it was time to surrender. Modlin fell the next day. Isolated pockets of Polish troops remained, but by October 6 all resistance had ended.

This first demonstration of the German blitzkrieg, with its rapidly moving armored formations, closely supported by air power, making pincerlike moves to trap opposing forces in pockets that were then reduced by the follow-up infantry, deeply impressed the world at large. It was in stark contrast to the trench-bound warfare of World War I. The casualties suffered by both sides demonstrated its effectiveness. The German losses were some 40,000 killed, wounded, and missing, while the Poles had some 200,000 killed and wounded, with very many more being made prisoner. Soviet losses were just

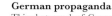

over 3,000, an indication of the paucity of Polish forces in the east. Poland itself was now split in two. The Soviet Union took possession of the eastern part of the country up to the line of the Bug River, which had been Russian territory until the war with Poland in 1919–20. The remainder fell under German rule. The agendas of the two occupying powers differed, however. The Soviet government was determined that Poland should never regain its independence

German propaganda
This photograph of German troops feeding Polish children disguised the fact that the Germans treated the Poles very much as a subject people.

and, to this end, it incarcerated all the members of the intelligentsia it could find. Many officers were placed in camps in Russia, while others, together with their men, were transported to Siberia. In 1940 up to 4,500 officers were massacred at Katyn near Smolensk. The Nazis, on the other hand, targeted the Polish Jews, who represented a sizeable minority of the population. Initially, they were forced into ghettos and virtually starved, but ultimately a grimmer fate awaited most of them—the extermination camps.

Hitler at the Warsaw victory parade
Many of the triumphant troops in Poland would soon be sent across Germany to prepare for the planned invasion of the Low Countries and France.

Despite the dismemberment of their country, the Polish spirit of resistance had not been extinguished. In Poland itself an underground organization, the Home Army, was set up. Abroad, General Wladyslaw Sikorski formed a government-in-exile, the first of many, in Paris, and some 90,000 of his countrymen, including many who managed to escape from Poland itself, flocked to his banner, placing themselves under French command so as to continue the fight. As for Hitler, he was now looking westward and was determined to strike at the French and British as soon as possible. Circumstances would conspire against him and it would be many months before this could be done.

FINLAND INVADED

In the immediate aftermath of the Polish campaign, attention switched to Finland, a country that had broken away from the Russian Empire during the revolution of 1917. Finland was, however, strategically significant in Soviet eyes. Its border was only 20 miles (32 km) from Leningrad (St. Petersburg) and the northern coast of the Gulf of Finland—the sea approach to the city—was Finnish. The entrance to the vital Soviet northern port of Murmansk was also guarded by Finnish territory. Stalin, fearful that Finland would come under German influence, proposed an exchange of territory. If the Finns would cede territory on the shores of Lake Ladoga and the Gulf of Finland, as well as leasing ports, notably Viipuri in the south and Petsamo in the extreme north, they would gain some desolate terrain in southern Karelia. Negotiations dragged on through much of October and November 1939, but the Finns refused to agree. Stalin decided that force was the only answer. He attacked on November 30.

On paper, the Finns stood little chance. They could call only 150,000 men to arms and their one set of fixed defenses covering their long border with the Soviet Union was the Mannerheim Line, which ran between the Gulf of Finland and Lake Ladoga. In contrast, the Leningrad Military District of the Red Army, which was to conduct the campaign, had some 700,000 men. In the far north the Soviet 14th Army quickly seized Petsamo and cut off Finnish access to the Barents Sea, while the Eighth and Ninth Armies attacking from Karelia also made rapid progress. In the extreme south it was a different matter. The Finns conducted a fighting withdrawal back to the Mannerheim Line and when the Soviet troops attempted to storm it they were bloodily repulsed. By mid-December there was stalemate. The condition of the postpurge Red Army was starkly revealed. Incompetent officers and a poor supply system, with many men still wearing summer uniform, resulted in numerous unnecessary casualties, a significant proportion from frostbite.

The reactions of other nations to this David versus Goliath contest were mixed. Denmark, Sweden, and Norway had no wish to see the fighting spill over into their territory and reaffirmed their neutrality. The League of Nations expelled the Soviet Union and called on member states to give

Captured Soviet soldier
Ill-equipped and poorly led, Soviet prisoners had little idea why they were fighting the Finns and were often just pleased to be out of the fighting.

Finnish ski troops moving up for an attack
The ability of the Finnish ski troops to infiltrate the Soviet positions noiselessly and strike unsuspecting units to the rear did much to enable the Finns to hold out for so long against numerically superior forces.

Finland all possible support. The United States, although not a League member, launched strong protests to Moscow. The British and the French went even further and began to draw up plans to send munitions and troops to Finland.

FINNISH COUNTERATTACKS

In late December the Finns launched a series of counterattacks on the Karelian front. Their highly skilled ski troops came into their own, penetrating deep into the Soviet lines. At Suomussalmi they destroyed two Soviet divisions and captured much equipment. Stalin had already realized that all was not well with his high command, and at the beginning of January he appointed one of the few competent generals to have survived the purges, Semyon Timoshenko, to take over command. Timoshenko began to build up his forces for a major assault, but his first attempt, across the ice-bound Viipuri Bay, failed at the beginning of February, when the few remaining Finnish bombers attacked his troops as they were crossing the ice. By now, Anglo-French plans for sending troops to help the Finns had been finalized. They necessitated ignoring Norwegian neutrality by sending troops through the north of the country. At this juncture

Antitank rifle
All the belligerent nations used antitank rifles, such as this Finnish model, early in the war. But they were only effective up to 330 yd (300 m) and soon gave way to more powerful antitank guns.

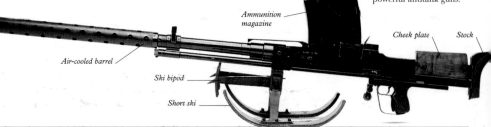

Ammunition magazine

Air-cooled barrel

Ski bipod

Short ski

Cheek plate

Stock

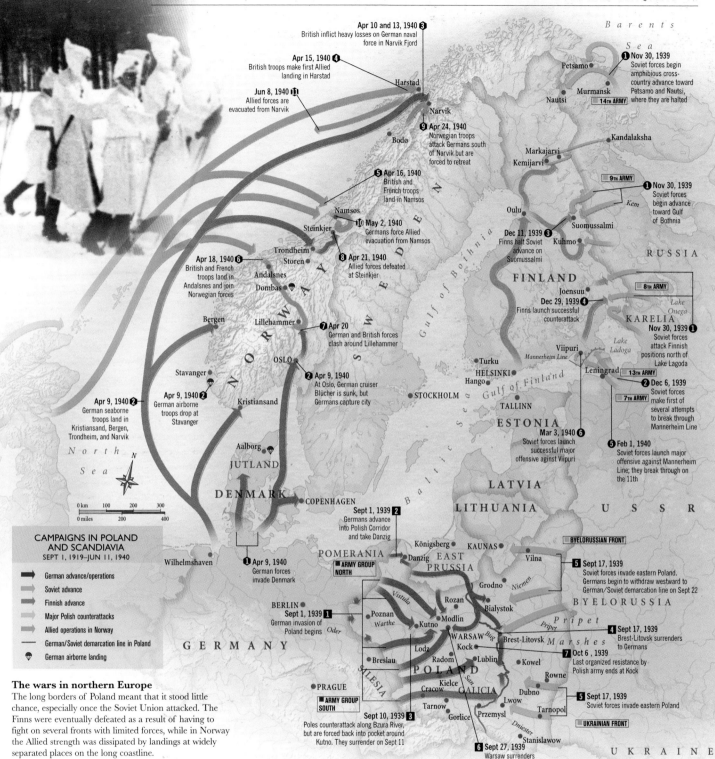

Apr 10 and 13, 1940 ❸
British inflict heavy losses on German naval force in Narvik Fjord

Apr 15, 1940 ❹
British troops make first Allied landing in Harstad

Jun 8, 1940 ⓫
Allied forces are evacuated from Narvik

Apr 24, 1940 ❾
Norwegian troops attack Germans south of Narvik but are forced to retreat

Apr 16, 1940 ❺
British and French troops land in Namsos

May 2, 1940 ❿
Germans force Allied evacuation from Namsos

Apr 21, 1940 ❽
Allied forces defeated at Steinkjer

Apr 18, 1940 ❻
British and French troops land in Andalsnes and join Norwegian forces

Apr 20 ❼
German and British forces clash around Lillehammer

Apr 9, 1940 ❷
At Oslo, German cruiser Blücher is sunk, but Germans capture city

Apr 9, 1940 ❷
German seaborne troops land in Kristiansand, Bergen, Trondheim, and Narvik

Apr 9, 1940 ❷
German airborne troops drop at Stavanger

Apr 9, 1940 ❶
German forces invade Denmark

Sept 1, 1939 ❶
German invasion of Poland begins

Sept 1, 1939 ❷
Germans advance into Polish Corridor and take Danzig

Sept 10, 1939 ❸
Poles counterattack along Bzura River, but are forced back into pocket around Kutno. They surrender on Sept 11

Nov 30, 1939 ❶
Soviet forces begin amphibious cross-country advance toward Petsamo and Nautsi, where they are halted
14TH ARMY

Nov 30, 1939 ❶
Soviet forces begin advance toward Gulf of Bothnia
9TH ARMY

Dec 11, 1939 ❸
Finns halt Soviet advance on Suomussalmi

Dec 29, 1939 ❹
Finns launch successful counterattack
8TH ARMY

Nov 30, 1939 ❶
Soviet forces attack Finnish positions north of Lake Lagoda
13TH ARMY

Dec 6, 1939 ❷
Soviet forces make first of several attempts to break through Mannerheim Line
7TH ARMY

Feb 1, 1940 ❺
Soviet forces launch major offensive against Mannerheim Line; they break through on the 11th

Mar 3, 1940 ❻
Soviet forces launch successful major offensive against Viipuri

Sept 17, 1939 ❺
Soviet forces invade eastern Poland. Germans begin to withdraw westward to German/Soviet demarcation line on Sept 22
BYELORUSSIAN FRONT

Sept 17, 1939 ❹
Brest-Litovsk surrenders to Germans

Oct 6, 1939 ❼
Last organized resistance by Polish army ends at Kock

Sept 17, 1939 ❺
Soviet forces invade eastern Poland
UKRAINIAN FRONT

Sept 27, 1939 ❻
Warsaw surrenders

CAMPAIGNS IN POLAND AND SCANDIAVIA
SEPT 1, 1919–JUN 11, 1940

- German advance/operations
- Soviet advance
- Finnish advance
- Major Polish counterattacks
- Allied operations in Norway
- German/Soviet demarcation line in Poland
- German airborne landing

0 km 100 200 300
0 miles 200 400

Place names on map: Barents Sea, Petsamo, Murmansk, Nautsi, Kandalaksha, Markajarvi, Kemijarvi, Oulu, Suomussalmi, Kuhmo, RUSSIA, FINLAND, Joensuu, Lake Onega, KARELIA, Lake Ladoga, Viipuri, Mannerheim Line, Leningrad, Turku, HELSINKI, Hango, Gulf of Finland, STOCKHOLM, TALLINN, ESTONIA, LATVIA, LITHUANIA, U S S R, Königsberg, KAUNAS, Vilna, Grodno, Niemen, BYELORUSSIA, Pripet, Pripet Marshes, Brest-Litovsk, Kowel, Rowne, Dubno, Lwow, Tarnopol, Stanislawow, Dniester, UKRAINE, Harstad, Narvik, Bodø, Namsos, Steinkjer, Trondheim, Storen, Andalsnes, Dombas, Bergen, Lillehammer, OSLO, Stavanger, Kristiansand, Aalborg, JUTLAND, DENMARK, COPENHAGEN, Wilhelmshaven, North Sea, Gulf of Bothnia, Baltic Sea, POMERANIA, Danzig, EAST PRUSSIA, ARMY GROUP NORTH, BERLIN, Poznan, Warthe, Oder, Vistula, GERMANY, SILESIA, Breslau, PRAGUE, ARMY GROUP SOUTH, Rozan, Modlin, Kutno, WARSAW, Kock, Lodz, Radom, Lublin, Bialystok, Bug, San, POLAND, GALICIA, Cracow, Kielce, Tarnow, Gorlice, Przemysl, NORWAY, SWEDEN

The wars in northern Europe
The long borders of Poland meant that it stood little chance, especially once the Soviet Union attacked. The Finns were eventually defeated as a result of having to fight on several fronts with limited forces, while in Norway the Allied strength was dissipated by landings at widely separated places on the long coastline.

Timoshenko attacked again and finally breached the Mannerheim Line, forcing the Finns to retire to a second line of defenses. Moscow now broadcast its final conditions for peace. Finland was to cede territory in the south, while the Soviet Union would hand back Petsamo. Again, the Finns refused and, at the end of February, Soviet forces broke through the second defense line on the Karelian isthmus. Viipuri then came under direct attack and the Finns, realizing that they could not resist much longer, sent a peace delegation to Moscow. On March 12 a peace treaty was signed. The terms were harsh, requiring the Finns to hand over the whole of the Karelian isthmus, including Viipuri, other parts of Karelia, including Lake Ladoga, and Petsamo. The Soviet Union also extracted a 30-year lease on the Hango peninsula at the entrance to the Gulf of Finland. Stalin had thus gotten everything he wanted, but at the cost of 85,000 Soviet troops killed or missing, and 186,000 wounded.

In constrast, the Finnish casualties were 25,000 killed and 45,000 wounded. Clearly the Soviet armed forces were in particularly urgent need of reorganization. The campaign left Finland embittered, but it would have the chance for revenge. As for the Western Allies, they had for a second time been powerless to provide timely help to a distant ally. The conflict, though, would continue to focus on Scandanavia.

THE PHONEY WAR

Prior to the outbreak of war, the British and French, seemingly secure behing the Maginot Line, had agreed to adopt a strictly defensive strategy and to wait. The only positive action on the ground was the advance by the French into the Saarland, but they quickly withdrew. In the air, fear that inflicting civilian casualties might bring about German retaliation in the form of aerial bombardments of Allied cities resulted in attacks being restricted to warships in port. Allied bombers were also used to drop propaganda leaflets over Germany. The only real activity took place at sea, with the beginning of the Battle of the Atlantic (see pages 80–83).

Parisians with gas masks
The French practiced protecting themselves against the gas bombs that they feared would be used against them by the Germans.

Child's gas mask
In Britain colorful "Mickey Mouse" gas masks were issued to young children, who were taught to carry their masks with them at all times.

Hitler wanted to attack west as soon as possible after the Polish campaign, and he issued orders to this effect on October 9, 1939. The intention was to avoid the Maginot Line and attack through the neutral Low Countries, thus destroying the northern Allied armies and securing the North Sea and English Channel coasts. Bases from which to wage an air and sea campaign against Britain could then be established. Hitler wanted to attack in November, but his commanders argued that they needed time to put into effect the lessons from Poland. They were also well aware of the apparent strength of the French Army, which, on paper at least, was equal to that of the German Army. The onset of a particularly severe winter caused further postponement.

ALLIED PREPARATIONS

The Allies, too, had been planning. They anticipated a German attack through the Low Countries, but there were few natural obstacles close to the Belgian border on which to base a defense. Consequently, they decided that they would have to advance into Belgium once the Germans had invaded, and take up positions based on the Meuse and Dyle rivers and the Albert Canal. This "Plan D," as it was called, would be executed by the northern Allied armies under General Pierre Billotte's First Army Group, comprising the best of the French and the British Expeditionary Force (BEF). But the Allied chain of command was cumbersome. Immediately above Billotte was General Alphonse Georges, commanding the northeast of France, while in overall charge was General Maurice Gamelin, who envisaged Georges controlling the whole battle, but according to Gamelin's plan. The problem was that there was mutual antipathy between Georges and Gamelin. Furthermore, there was a plethora of headquarters with inadequate communications, which relied on an imperfect telephone system and despatch riders. It was hardly the infrastructure with which to combat high-speed warfare. Meanwhile, the troops on the ground spent some time training and the remainder in attempting to improve the Belgian border defenses.

On January 10 Hitler commanded that the invasion take place in a week's time. However, that same day a German light aircraft carrying a Luftwaffe liaison officer made a forced landing inside Belgium. He was carrying details of the German plan and although he and the pilot set the plane on fire, they could not be sure that the Belgians remained in ignorance. Furthermore, there had been rumblings among the German high command over the plan itself. Rundstedt and, more especially, his chief of staff, Erich von Manstein, argued that the emphasis should be on completely cutting off the Allied forces in the north and then turning on the remainder of France. In the circumstances, Hitler decided that the invasion should be postponed until the spring. He then approved the Manstein plan under which Army Group B in the north

Digging a British air-raid shelter
During the Phoney War British civilians continued to make preparations for a German attack. With the encouragement of the government, many constructed air raid shelters in their backyards.

would advance into the Netherlands and Belgium to draw the British and French forward, while Army Group A, with the bulk of the panzer divisions, would thrust through the Ardennes and make for the English Channel. Army Group C would remain opposite the Maginot Line to tie down the forces manning it. Meanwhile, Hitler received reassurance from Mussolini that Italy would join in the invasion.

In the Allied camp the long months of inactivity had done little for morale. True, the BEF had been able to double its strength during the early months of 1940, but many of the British divisions now arriving in France lacked essential equipment and were poorly trained. The French had begun to concentrate some of their tanks into armored divisions in the German style, but they had not yet developed cohesion among these formations. Many were beginning to hope and, indeed, believe that Hitler might have had second thoughts. Both sides, however, now became distracted by Norway.

PLANS FOR NORWAY

Allied attention had been drawn to Norway as a means of sending troops and supplies to the Finns. Indeed, just before the Finnish surrender the British and French finalized their plans for landing at Narvik and Trondheim—the former a port that handled the Swedish exports of iron-ore that were vital to the German war industry.

Patrolling the line
Thirteen divisions were committed to manning the line in 1939.

Location of the line
The main Maginot Line covered the Franco-German border. There was, however, another belt of defenses protecting the border with Italy.

THE MAGINOT LINE

PLANS TO PROTECT France's eastern frontier were drawn up following the huge losses suffered in World War I. Serious construction began in 1929 under war minister André Maginot with the goal of providing an impenetrable wall.

A complication was added in 1936, when Belgium renounced its military alliance with France in favor of neutrality. An extension of the main Maginot Line began to be established, but this was by no means continuous, especially since the general view was that the hilly and wooded Ardennes region of southern Belgium and Luxembourg was impassable to invading troops. With their

subterranean forts topped by armored cupolas mounting a wide range of guns, the fortifications were sufficiently impressive to deter invaders. However, they lulled the French into a false sense of security, and the money spent on them, which was twice the original estimate, meant that modernization of the armed forces was held back.

Section through the line
The gun cupolas above the ground concealed a web of passages, living quarters, and command bunkers.

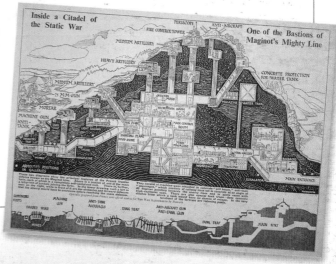

British destroyer HMS _Bittern_ in Namsos Fjord
Even though the Royal Navy enjoyed domination of the North Sea, it was unable to prevent the Germans from making several landings in Norway. While it sank several warships during the campaign, it also suffered losses.

German troops in northern Jutland
Denmark's armed forces were too small to offer anything other than a very token resistance to the forces that invaded on April 9, and by the end of the day the country was in German hands.

There was, too, in February 1940 the affair of the *Altmark*, a German vessel carrying crews of British merchant vessels sunk by the *Graf Spee* battleship during her rampage in the Indian Ocean and South Atlantic. The Norwegians gave sanctuary to the *Altmark* in their waters and, when she was boarded by the crew of a British destroyer, they complained that their neutrality had been violated. The British countered that Norway had allowed its neutrality to be abused by the Germans.

The Germans had been considering establishing bases in Norway for waging the maritime war against Britain since October 1939. Hitler was so attracted to the idea that at the end of January 1940 he took over personal control of Weser Exercise, as the invasion of Norway was codenamed. This would also embrace the occupation of Denmark. On February 20 General Niklaus von Falkenhorst was appointed to command the invasion force and the final plan took shape. A number of simultaneous landings would be made, from Narvik in the north to Oslo Fjord, and airborne forces would be used for the first time to secure airfields at Oslo and Stavanger.

ACTION IN NORWEGIAN WATERS

The Allies did not believe that the Germans could invade Norway because of the dominance of the North Sea by Britain's navy. At the end of March they agreed to mine Norwegian territorial waters so as to force the iron-ore ships leaving Narvik into the open sea, where the Royal Navy could deal with them. Anticipating German attempts to interfere with the mining, they also began to reconstitute the forces that had been earlier assembled for securing the routes through Norway to Finland.

German paratroopers landing at Narvik
The use of paratroops in support of land forces had not been tried by either side before the German campaign in Denmark and Norway.

On April 2 Hitler gave orders that the landings were to take place in seven days' time, and German merchant vessels carrying troops set sail for Narvik, Trondheim, and Bergen. On April 6, British minelayers, with a powerful escort, set sail, and the following day the landing forces boarded their vessels. Simultaneously, an RAF aircraft spotted German warships. Bombers were sent to attack them but did no damage. That evening, the British Home Fleet set sail to intercept the invasion force. On April 8 the British laid mines at the entrance of Vertsj Fjord, north of Bodo. Bad weather prevented the Home Fleet from locating the Germans, except for one straggling British destroyer, which rammed a German cruiser and was sunk.

DENMARK AND NORWAY INVADED

The following day the invasion began. Both the Danish mainland (Jutland) and islands were overrun within 24 hours, with the Danes offering little or no resistance. By this time, the Norwegian government had ordered a partial mobilization and it enjoyed an early success when coastal batteries sank the German cruiser *Blücher* in Oslo Fjord and seriously

French Chasseurs Alpins near Narvik
Unlike the British troops who landed at Narvik and elsewhere in Norway, the Chasseurs Alpins were well trained in mountain and winter warfare.

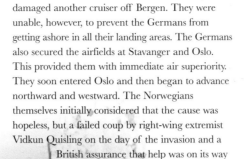

damaged another cruiser off Bergen. They were unable, however, to prevent the Germans from getting ashore in all their landing areas. The Germans also secured the airfields at Stavanger and Oslo. This provided them with immediate air superiority. They soon entered Oslo and then began to advance northward and westward. The Norwegians themselves initially considered that the cause was hopeless, but a failed coup by right-wing extremist Vidkun Quisling on the day of the invasion and a British assurance that help was on its way gave them the resolve to fight on.

The first positive Allied response came on April 10, when British destroyers entered Narvik Fjord and sank two German destroyers and some transport ships. They returned three days later to sink the remainder of the German naval force, thus leaving the troops on shore isolated. In the meantime, an Allied landing force set sail for Narvik, while during April 13–18 other troops landed in the Namsos area and in Andalsnes with the intention of isolating the German force in Trondheim. They also began to land in Harstad close to Narvik.

British prisoners in Norway
The losses of the Allies, including Norwegians, during the campaign in Norway were 4,000 dead, missing, or taken prisoner. The Germans lost 5,300 men and subsequently required up to 350,000 troops to occupy the country.

The Allied forces labored under a number of major disadvantages. Rapid changes of plan and a cumbersome command structure caused confusion. In the haste to mount the expedition, the ships had been loaded in a totally haphazard fashion and on landing in Norway the troops often found there was a lack of essential items such as radios and mortar ammunition, and sometimes even artillery and antiaircraft guns. This put them at a serious disadvantage from which they never recovered.

The Norwegians also had their problems. Because there had been no general mobilization before the invasion, the Norwegian Army had to try to organize its forces and fight the Germans at the same time. The scattered Norwegian units did their best, but could not slow the German advance northward. The decisive factor was German airpower, to which the Allies had no answer aside from some RAF Gloster Gladiator biplanes that were unable to make much of an impression.

The remorseless German advance from the south and successful link-up with their troops in Trondheim necessitated the evacuation of the Allied forces in Namsos and Andalsnes in early May. The focus then switched to Narvik. The Allies landed further forces, including French and Poles, and on May 28 they drove the isolated German garrison out of Narvik. It was a short-lived triumph. By this time King Haakon and his government had been taken by the Royal Navy to Britain. Worse, far to the south in France, the Allied situation was becoming desperate. In consequence, the Allies had no option but to evacuate Narvik. The whole of Norway was now in German hands, with a puppet government established under Quisling. The Germans had totally outwitted the Allies.

FIGHTING IN THE SNOW

THE IMPORTANCE OF TROOPS well equipped for winter warfare was demonstrated during the Soviet-Finnish War. In particular, it was the skill of the Finnish ski troops that was a significant fact in enabling Finland to hold out for so long. The German mountain troops were also well trained for winter warfare, as were the French Chasseurs Alpins. The "lowland" countries, like Britain, had paid little or no attention to this art before the war, although one British battalion was hastily trained as ski troops for possible use in Finland.

In Norway, with the advent of spring, expertise in fighting in the snow was not really a factor, even though snow was still on the ground in the northern part of the country. Indeed, after Finland, the ability to operate in the extremes of winter would not be fully tested until late 1941 in the Soviet Union. The Red Army was used to these conditions, but the Germans were initially taken by surprise over the effect of a plummeting thermometer on weapons and equipment, and many of their soliders were to suffer from the lack of adequate winter clothing.

Finnish ski soldier
Many Finns were brought up on skis and were at home in the snow. The white smocks and trousers worn by the ski troops provided ideal camouflage.

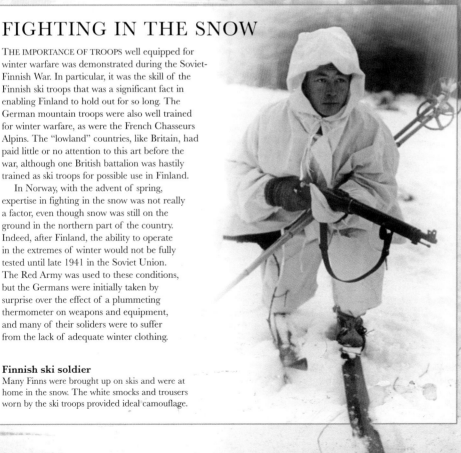

The campaign in the west consisted of two phases. In the first the Germans overran the Netherlands, Belgium, and northern France, forcing the Allied evacuation from Dunkirk on the English Channel coast. In the second the Germans turned south and conquered a lot more of France, forcing the French to seek an armistice.

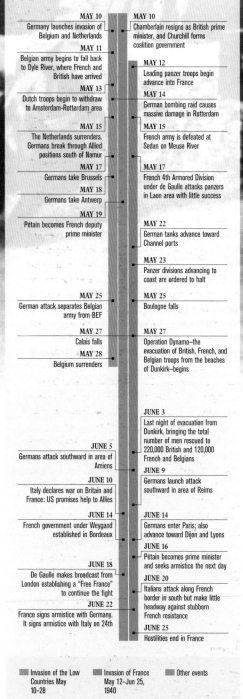

MAY 10
Germany launches invasion of Belgium and Netherlands

MAY 10
Chamberlain resigns as British prime minister, and Churchill forms coalition government

MAY 11
Belgian army begins to fall back to Dyle River, where French and British have arrived

MAY 12
Leading panzer troops begin advance into France

MAY 13
Dutch troops begin to withdraw to Amsterdam-Rotterdam area

MAY 14
German bombing raid causes massive damage in Rotterdam

MAY 15
The Netherlands surrenders. Germans break through Allied positions south of Namur

MAY 15
French army is defeated at Sedan on Meuse River

MAY 17
Germans take Brussels

MAY 17
French 4th Armored Division under de Gaulle attacks panzers in Laon area with little success

MAY 18
Germans take Antwerp

MAY 19
Pétain becomes French deputy prime minister

MAY 22
German tanks advance toward Channel ports

MAY 23
Panzer divisions advancing to coast are ordered to halt

MAY 25
German attack separates Belgian army from BEF

MAY 25
Boulogne falls

MAY 27
Calais falls

MAY 27
Operation Dynamo–the evacuation of British, French, and Belgian troops from the beaches of Dunkirk–begins

MAY 28
Belgium surrenders

JUNE 3
Last night of evacuation from Dunkirk, bringing the total number of men rescued to 220,000 British and 120,000 French and Belgians

JUNE 5
Germans attack southward in area of Amiens

JUNE 9
Germans launch attack southward in area of Reims

JUNE 10
Italy declares war on Britain and France; US promises help to Allies

JUNE 14
French government under Weygand established in Bordeaux

JUNE 14
Germans enter Paris; also advance toward Dijon and Lyons

JUNE 16
Pétain becomes prime minister and seeks armistice the next day

JUNE 18
De Gaulle makes broadcast from London establishing a "Free France" to continue the fight

JUNE 20
Italians attack along French border in south but make little headway against stubborn French resistance

JUNE 22
France signs armistice with Germany. It signs armistice with Italy on 24th

JUNE 25
Hostilities end in France

■ Invasion of the Low Countries May 10–28 ■ Invasion of France May 12–Jun 25, 1940 ■ Other events

GERMAN INVASION OF THE WEST

AT DAWN ON MAY 10, 1940, the Luftwaffe attacked airfields in the Netherlands, Belgium, and France, aiming, as they had done in Poland, to establish immediate air superiority. A second wave then took off to attack known headquarters, communications centers, railroads, and military camps. Paratroops were dropped over the Netherlands, their objectives an airfield in Rotterdam, three in The Hague, and crossings over major river defense lines. Not all went according to plan, especially since the Dutch had learned lessons from Norway and were prepared for airborne operations. In Belgium further airborne troops seized crossings over the Meuse River in the Maastricht area, while a small glider-borne force was used to deal with the key fortress of Eben Emael, near the junction of the Meuse with the Albert Canal (see map page 54).

ADVANCE IN THE LOW COUNTRIES

As Rundstedt's Army Group A and Bock's Army Group B crossed the Belgian and Dutch borders, the northern Allied armies—three French and the British Expeditionary Force (BEF)—began to move into Belgium to establish themselves on the defense line along the Dyle River. The Dutch made life difficult for the German airborne troops. But after many years of strict neutrality they were no match for the Germans, who within 48 hours had penetrated deep into the country. The Dutch withdrew to the protection of some fortifications in the south, and German attention now focused on Rotterdam. Its capture would signal the end for the Dutch, and they fought fiercely to protect it. The city had, however, already surrendered when the Germans launched a wave of bombers against it. Radio orders for the bombers to abort the mission did not get through, and over 1,000 civilians lost their lives as Rotterdam was devastated. It was too much for the Dutch, who had already begun to run low on ammunition. On May 15 they surrendered.

In Belgium the Germans thrust toward Brussels, while panzer spearheads forced their way through the Ardennes, brushing the Belgian forces aside. Luftwaffe attacks against airfields and other targets continued. There were fierce battles in which the Germans gradually wore down the Allied fighter

WINSTON CHURCHILL

WINSTON SPENCER CHURCHILL (1874–1965) was one of the greatest war leaders of all time. He spent his early career as a soldier and war correspondent before entering politics. In 1911 he was appointed First Lord of the Admiralty, with ministerial responsibility for the Royal Navy. His support for the ultimately disastrous 1915 Dardanelles campaign caused his fall from office and he then spent time on the Western Front. In 1917 he became minister of munitions and subsequently served as minister of war and air, and chancellor of the exchequer. He fell from grace in 1929 and spent the next 10 years in the political wilderness. His dire warnings on German rearmament did not accord with the general policy of appeasing Hitler. On the outbreak of war in 1939, he was reappointed First Lord of the Admiralty and then became prime minister on the day the German invasion of the west opened. While Churchill's hands-on approach to the conduct of the war often put severe pressure on military staff, his inspirational speeches fired all in the Allied camp, and he was single-minded in his determination to secure ultimate victory.

German troops in action
The speed of the German advance into the Low Countries and France took the Allies by surprise. They had no answer to the Germans' blitzkrieg tactics.

strength. In desperation, the French called on Britain to send more fighters across the Channel. Against the advice of Sir Hugh Dowding, in charge of RAF Fighter Command, Churchill ordered the despatch of further Hurricanes, but to no avail. RAF and Belgian fighter-bombers also tried to destroy the Maastricht bridges, across which

German forces continued to pour. Most were shot down and the bridges remained intact.

On May 12 the German tanks reached the east bank of the Meuse to the consternation of the French. The following day the tanks crossed, broke through the defenses on the other bank, and began to sweep westward toward the English Channel. To their north, elements of Army Group B closed up to the Dyle Line, which initially held them. As the panzers rampaged westward, the Allies realized that their armies in Belgium were under increasing threat of being cut off. Accordingly, on May 16 they began to withdraw from Belgium. On the following day Brussels fell. Simultaneously, a French armored division, commanded by General Charles de Gaulle, attacked the southern flank of the German panzers, but made little impression. Hitler, however, was concerned that the panzer divisions were becoming overextended and ordered a temporary halt to allow the infantry to catch up.

For the Allied armies in the north it was a bewildering period. Aside from the French Seventh Army, which had been unable to extend the Dyle Line to the North Sea coast because of the rapid Dutch collapse, the Allied troops felt that they had given a good account of themselves in keeping Bock's Army Group B at bay and were perplexed by the orders to withdraw. Nevertheless, they pulled back in an orderly fashion. One major problem they did face was that of refugees. They had come across them on the move up to the Dyle, but now life was made much more difficult by the fact that civilians were fleeing in the same direction and clogging up the roads that the troops wanted to use. The situation was made even worse when the Luftwaffe instilled panic among the refugees by machine-gunning them from the air. It was just as well for the Allies that the troops of Army Group B were advancing with a degree of caution. This was out of recognition that the decisive blow was being struck by Rundstedt's Army Group A to their south.

On May 19 Gamelin was replaced as the French commander-in-chief by Maxime Weygand. At the same time, Marshal Henri Pétain, the great French hero of 1914–18, was appointed deputy prime minister. The changes came too late. Rundstedt's tanks were on the move once more and on May 20 they reached the mouth of the Somme. The Allied armies were now totally split. The following day it was the British turn to counterattack, but all

French defenders
This light machine-gun team was among the French troops who struggled to withstand the German onslaught. Many were demoralized from the outset.

that was available were two battalions of slow-moving infantry tanks and some infantry. At Arras they struck at the 7th Panzer Division, under Erwin Rommel, and briefly knocked it off balance, causing Hitler further concern over the vulnerability of the flanks of his panzer formations. The British force was, however, too weak to cause any lasting damage and the German thrusts continued.

ALLIED RETREAT TO THE COAST

The northern Allied forces, now comprising the remnants of the Belgian Army, the French First Army, and the BEF, were being squeezed into an ever tighter pocket by Army Group B pressing from the north and Army Group A from the south and west. The Allied troops were also becoming increasingly

Attack in the west
German Army Group A thrust through the Ardennes and cut off the Allied forces in northern France, while Army Group B dealt with the Netherlands and the remainder of Belgium. Both army groups then turned south and cut swathes through the rest of France.

exhausted by the seemingly endless cycle of withdrawal, followed by preparing fresh defensive positions and then receiving orders to abandon them. The skies above appeared dominated by the Luftwaffe and movement on the roads during daylight hours became ever more dangerous. Yet, they still largely maintained their cohesion. The German troops, too, especially those in Army Group A, were beginning to suffer from the rapidity of their advance. In particular, Rundstedt was conscious of the increasing wear and tear on Army Group A's armor after almost two weeks of constant action. Indeed, some panzer divisions had only a third of their tanks still running. Knowing that the remainder of France still had to be conquered, on May 23 he ordered the bulk of them to halt,

believing that Army Group B and his own infantry could deal with the Allied pocket. The following day, Hitler approved his halt order. Rundstedt's forces were now seeking to overrun the Channel ports so as to cut off the BEF, especially, from its homeland. In spite of last-minute reinforcement, Boulogne fell on May 25 and Calais, after a brave defense, two days later. Meanwhile, worse had befallen the Allies.

INVASION OF THE LOW COUNTRIES AND FRANCE
MAY 10–JUN 22, 1940

— Allied front line May 16
--- Allied front line May 21
— Allied defensive line May 28
--- Allied front line Jun 4
··· Allied front line Jun 21
— Approximate line reached by German advance Jun 25

→ German advance
→ Allied movement
→ Italian attack
↓ Airborne assault
⌄ Maginot Line

May 14 ❸ Bombing raid on Rotterdam causes widespread destruction. Dutch surrender next day

May 10 ❶ Germans launch invasion of the Netherlands and Belgium with both ground attacks and airborne assaults

May 12 ❷ French fail to halt German advance at Breda and withdraw to Antwerp

May 17 ❹ Germans take Brussels

May 27–Jun 4 ❾ 340,000 Allied troops are evacuated from Dunkirk in Operation Dynamo

May 27 ❽ Germans capture Calais

May 25 ❼ Germans capture Boulogne

May 21 ❻ British counterattack at Arras but are forced back the next day

Jun 5 ❿ Germans launch attack over Somme and Aisne Rivers

May 17–19 ❺ French attack southern flank of German forces but fail to halt German advance

Jun 14 ❶ Germans enter Paris

Jun 14 ❷ Germans begin advance toward Dijon and Lyons

Jun 22 ❺ French troops around Épinal surrender

Jun 19 ❸ Evacuation of 190,000 French and Polish troops from Bayonne to Britain begins

Jun 20 ❹ Italians launch attack but fail to advance beyond border

Belgian refugees
As the Germans advanced, civilians took to the roads, sometimes fleeing without any possessions in order to get away from the fighting.

To the northeast the withdrawal of the now cut-off northern Allied armies continued. For the remains of the Belgian Army on the coast, it was a repeat of August 1914, when the Belgians had found themselves left holding just one strip of their country. Hopes of achieving even this were now fading. The BEF and the French First Army still maintained their cohesion, but the endless retreats were sapping morale and their exhaustion was growing. Matters were not helped by growing rumors of fifth columnists and disguised German paratroops, some apparently dressed as nuns, operating in their rear. These added to the increasing sense of confusion and the stark truth was that the northern Allied forces were being progressively squeezed into a pocket from which there appeared to be no escape.

Weygand, who had taken over command from Gamelin on May 20, had proposed an ambitious plan to extricate the forces in northern France from the trap in which they now found themselves. The BEF and French First Army would attack out of the pocket, while the French Seventh and 10th Armies did so from the south, with the goal of cutting off the German armor. Given the German pressure and poor communications, this proved impossible to accomplish. Then, on May 25 the Belgian high command warned the French and British that its remaining forces, which were on the left flank of those troops facing Army Group B, could not hold on for much longer. Lord Gort, commanding the BEF, now decided that his duty lay in saving as much as he could of his force rather than continuing to fight on and lose it all. Without telling his allies, he ordered the BEF to withdraw to Dunkirk, on the English Channel coast, and asked the British government to evacuate it by sea. This proved fortuitous since the Belgians decided to surrender on May 28. That night the evacuation of the BEF from Dunkirk began. The Germans, rather than using their ground forces to destroy the shrinking pocket, decided to rely on airpower after Reichsmarschall Hermann Göring had boasted that his Luftwaffe could do the task on its own.

SOUTHWARD ADVANCE

On May 29, with the Dunkirk evacuation gathering momentum, Hitler ordered his forces to turn south to deal with the remainder of France. The new offensive was launched on June 5, the day after German troops finally entered Dunkirk. On the same day, de Gaulle was appointed the French deputy war minister, but like the earlier changes, it was too late to make any difference. The Germans quickly secured crossings over the Somme River and once again the panzer divisions were on

BLITZKRIEG TACTICS

THE CONCEPT OF BLITZKRIEG or "lightning war" was born out of the infiltration tactics practiced by the German storm troops in 1917–18 and the development of mechanized warfare, especially the tank. Rather than the bludgeonlike tactics that had dominated much of World War I, blitzkrieg was more like the thrust of a rapier and was designed not to destroy the opposing forces *per se*, but to fatally degrade the ability to command and control them through sheer pace of operations. A key to the secret of the success of blitzkrieg during the early part of the war was radio. This enabled the quick passing of orders, and the immediate response of aircraft providing close support—especially the Junkers Ju 87 dive-bombers—to calls for assistance from the ground. Commanders were encouraged to position themselves well forward and to identify the *Schwerpunkt*, or critical point on the battlefield. The Germans did, however, have a major problem in that in any advance the great majority of their infantry relied on their feet and horsedrawn forms of transportation. Furthermore, there was always the danger that the tip of the blade, represented by the fast-moving panzer and panzergrenadier formations, would advance too far in front of the main body and thus put itself in danger of being cut off.

Stuka dive-bomber
The Ju 87 was a key element of blitzkrieg, with its ability to attack pinpoint targets. Its siren had a terrifying effect.

Sidecar with panniers and spare wheel

Pannier for gear or ammunition

Panzer Mark II
Armed with a 20-mm gun and a 7.92-mm machine-gun, this tank had a crew of three and was generally used for reconnaissance.

Zündapp KS750
A light machine-gun was often mounted in the sidecar of this motorcycle combination that was largely used by reconnaissance troops.

Gas tank

Unit symbol

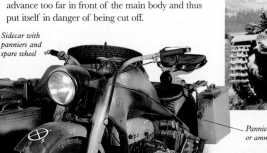

Half-track vehicle
The Sd Kfz 251 became the main vehicle of the Panzer Grenadiers, many of whom were still truck-borne in May 1940. The tracks enabled it to accompany tanks when moving cross-country.

Allied troops line up for evacuation
The Allied troops awaiting rescue on the beaches were very vulnerable to attack by the Luftwaffe, which also wrought havoc among the rescue ships.

EVACUATION FROM DUNKIRK

AS EARLY AS MAY 20 preparations had begun for a possible evacuation of at least part of the BEF in France. Thus when the order came, on May 26, to mount Operation Dynamo, as it was codenamed, there were ships available. No one believed, however, that more than a small proportion of the BEF could be rescued before Dunkirk fell. During May 27–28 some 25,000 troops were evacuated from the port, but there were problems. Because Calais was in German hands, ships had to use an indirect route that first ran parallel to the Belgian coast, and because the Luftwaffe

Some who got away
Exhaustion, relief, and bewilderment are etched on the faces of these British troops waiting to be picked up from a pontoon.

had put Dunkirk's port facilities out of action, the troops had to be rescued from the beaches. The privately-owned craft from the navy's "small vessels pool" were pressed into service to take the troops to the ships waiting offshore, and they were joined by other volunteer private vessels. Collectively, they became known as the Little Ships.

For the men waiting in Dunkirk it was a terrible experience to huddle on the sandy beach as the Luftwaffe's bombs exploded all around them. Many were required to march into the sea up to their necks again and again before finally getting into a boat. During most of the evacuation, French troops held much of the perimeter and bought valuable time. However, only British troops were allowed to leave, causing French bitterness. RAF Fighter Command was increasingly unable to provide the ships with full protection from the Luftwaffe, making it necessary on June 1 to restrict the evacuation to the hours of darkness. By now the alternative route along the Belgian coast had become too vulnerable to German torpedo-boats, and another route had

The aftermath
When the Germans finally entered Dunkirk on June 4, 1940, they found many corpses. Among those who had died in the fighting in and around the town were the largely French rearguard.

to be opened. It was only at this point that French and Belgian troops were taken off. With the Germans on the outskirts of Dunkirk, the night of June 3 was to be the last of the evacuation. In all, 220,000 British and 120,000 French and Belgian troops were taken to England, though almost all the French quickly returned to France to continue the fight. Some 200 ships and 177 Allied aircraft were lost. Yet the fact that so many men were brought home did much to stiffen British resolve to fight on.

The smallest ship
Tamzine—14 ft (4.4 m) long—was the smallest of more than 900 "Little Ships" that ferried men from the beaches to deep-water vessels.

the rampage, spreading panic among French civilians who began to flee from their homes in huge numbers. Perhaps over 5 million took to the roads that went southward; about 2 million fled from the Paris region alone. Even the government joined the exodus, leaving Paris for Tours on June 10.

Fearing that their capital might suffer the same fate as Warsaw and Rotterdam, the French declared Paris an open city and the Germans entered it in triumph on June 14. Pleas were sent for the British to send more RAF fighters to France, but this time Churchill heeded the advice of Dowding, who was now certain that the fighters would be needed to defend Britain, and refused. Even so, two British divisions were still fighting with the French. One had been gaining combat experience on the Maginot Line when the Germans invaded and the other was the only British armored division, which had not crossed to France until late May. Churchill now decided to send a second BEF to Cherbourg to help the French form a redoubt in Brittany. But in view of the rapidly deteriorating situation, the force was recalled just as it was about to land. The 51st Highland Division and four French divisions were trapped by Rommel's tanks, but the British 1st Armoured Division did get back to England.

FRENCH-GERMAN ARMISTICE

On June 16 the French prime minister, Paul Reynaud, whose government had fled to Bordeaux, resigned. He was replaced by Marshal Pétain, who decided to seek an armistice.

Slowly they came, bewildered and shocked, yet the faces of hundreds showed the great joy of once again being on dry land, above all their homeland. Even the troops of other nations accepted thankfully the greeting and helping hand from those waiting on the quayside... Sodden and bloodstained uniforms were gratefully exchanged for trousers, jackets, shirts and dressing gowns.

W. E. WILLIAMSON, RAILWAY CLERK, ON THE ARRIVAL IN WEYMOUTH OF TROOPS RESCUED FROM DUNKIRK

De Gaulle got himself flown to Britain and, once there, broadcast to the French people. He told them that he would continue the struggle and called for volunteers to join him. While an armistice meeting was being set up, there was a development in southeastern France. On June 10 Mussolini had declared that his country would be at war with Britain and France from

the following day. Ten days later, his troops invaded France. While the main Maginot Line had now been enveloped from the rear and penetrated by the Germans, the Alpine extension kept the Italians out. But it made no difference. The French signed an armistice with the Germans on June 22 in the same railroad car that had been used to bring World War I to an end in November 1918. Two days later, they also signed with the Italians. The campaign in the west officially came to an end on June 25. Allied losses were 100,000 killed and—as a result of the surrender of the Dutch, Belgians, and French—the huge figure of 2,200,000 taken prisoner. German losses were 45,000 killed and missing.

In just six weeks Hitler had achieved what Imperial Germany had failed to do during the whole of 1914–18. France and the Low Countries were now under Nazi occupation, although the southern half of France was given a degree of limited autonomy under Pétain's Vichy government, which was prepared to bow to Germany's every command. Just a few rallied to de Gaulle, now seen as a traitor in his own land. Dutch and Belgians also joined the various "free" forces being formed in Britain to one day liberate their countries. Yet, for Britain itself, shorn as it was of European allies and with only its far-flung empire still on its side, the future looked bleak. Few outside observers gave the country any chance of holding out against a now triumphant and seemingly invincible Hitler.

Germans occupy Paris
The Germans' triumphant march down the Champs Elysées marked a high point in their conquest of France.

THE BATTLE OF BRITAIN AND THE BLITZ

MARCH 1940–JULY 1941

In the summer of 1940, while Germany prepared to invade Britain, the Luftwaffe was ordered to gain control of the skies. In the ensuing Battle of Britain it failed to do this, but by a very narrow margin. German strategy then switched to a bombing campaign aimed at London and other major industrial cities—the Blitz.

1940

MARCH 16
German bombers attack British Grand Fleet at Scapa Flow in Orkney Islands

MARCH 19
British air raid on German seaplane base on island of Sylt in retaliation for raid on Scapa Flow

APRIL 15
British raid on German port of Wilhelmshaven

MAY 22
British break Luftwaffe's Enigma code

JUNE 3
Germans launch 300-bomber raid on Paris

JULY 10
Germans attack Channel convoys and launch raid on Swansea docks and arms factory in Wales

AUGUST 11
Numerous air battles over English Channel and south coast of England. Attacks directed at ports, airfields, and radar stations

AUGUST 13
Adlertag (Eagle Day). Official start of Göring's offensive to gain control of the skies over Britain prior to invasion (Operation Sea Lion)

AUGUST 15
Greatest German effort to date with more than 1,000 German planes in action

AUGUST 25
Night raid on Berlin—in retaliation for accidental bombing of London the night before

SEPTEMBER 7
Start of London Blitz. Luftwaffe directs bombing offensive at London and other major cities

SEPTEMBER 17
Hitler calls off invasion of Britain (planned for September 21)

SEPTEMBER 30
Last large daylight raid on Britain. Total civilian air-raid casualties for September are 6,954 killed and 10,615 injured

OCTOBER 3
Over 170,000 people spend night in London Underground stations

NOVEMBER 14
Night raid by 449 bombers virtually destroys city of Coventry

DECEMBER 16
Largest air raid on Germany to date. 134 bombers attack Mannheim

DECEMBER 29
Massive incendiary raid on City of London, but winter weather now restricts number and size of raids until March

1941

JANUARY 20
Compulsory fire-watching introduced in Britain

FEBRUARY 10
RAF raid on oil-storage tanks in Rotterdam

MARCH 2
RAF raid on Cologne

MARCH 13
Raid on Clydebank near Glasgow leaves 35,000 homeless

MARCH 31
After let-up in bombing over winter, German raids intensify. Civilian casualties for March total 4,259 killed and 5,557 injured

MAY 1
First of seven consecutive raids on Liverpool

MAY 10
1,436 killed in largest ever raid on London

MAY 16
Heavy raid on Birmingham. Blitz now comes to an end as Luftwaffe transfers bombers from France and Low Countries for invasion of USSR

JUNE 8
RAF sends 360 aircraft on largest raid yet on Germany

JULY 27
German raid on London is first for 10 weeks. July casualty figures: 501 civilians killed in raids on Britain

■ Battle of Britain
Jul 10–Sept 6, 1940

■ The Blitz
Sept 7, 1940–May 16, 1941

■ Other events

BRITAIN IN PERIL

VICTORY IN FRANCE had brought the German army to the Channel coast. While German officers viewed the white cliffs of Dover through the warm summer haze, Hitler pondered his options, weighing the advantages of a cross-Channel operation against his evolving plan for an invasion of the Soviet Union. On July 16, 1940, he issued Führer Directive No 16, stating, "I have decided to prepare a landing operation against England, and, if necessary, to carry it out." Preparations for the invasion of Britain, codenamed *Seelöwe* (Sea Lion), were to be completed by the middle of August.

THE OPPOSING FORCES

An essential precondition of Sea Lion was the securing of air control over the English Channel. The commander of the Luftwaffe, Hermann Göring, was brimming with confidence. He estimated that a mere four days would be sufficient to eliminate the RAF from southern England. At the Luftwaffe's disposal were three *Luftflotten* (air fleets). The largest, Luftflotte 2, was based in Belgium and northern France, facing England from the east. Luftflotte 3 was stationed in Normandy and poised to strike at the southwest and south coasts. The smaller Luftflotte 5, based in Denmark and Norway, was tasked with attacking targets in the north of England and Scotland.

RAF Fighter Command, led by Sir Hugh Dowding, faced the German threat with its squadrons organized into four Groups. In the critical southeastern sector, 11 Group was commanded by Air Vice-Marshal Keith Park; in the Midlands and East Anglia, 12 Group was led by Air Vice-Marshal Trafford Leigh-Mallory. In mid-July, 10 Group became operational in the west of England; the rest of the UK—the

Heinkel He 111 over London
Photographed on the first day of the Blitz, September 7, 1940, a Heinkel bomber flies over the Thames River in the East End of London, where the capital's docks and factories were concentrated.

north of England, Scotland, and Northern Ireland was covered by 13 Group. Group areas were divided into sectors, each consisting of a main airfield (sector station) and several satellite stations.

HEAVY LOSSES

On the eve of battle, both sides were licking the wounds sustained in the Battle of France. Between May 10 and June 20, the British had lost 944 aircraft, including 386 Hurricanes and 67 Spitfires. Not counting losses over Dunkirk, they had also lost 350 fighter pilots killed, missing, wounded, or taken prisoner. Nor had the Luftwaffe escaped lightly. In the fighting of May–June 1940, it had lost some 1,100 aircraft on operations, plus 200 more in accidents and 145 damaged. By July 20, RAF Fighter Command could field just 531 operational aircraft compared with the 725 operational fighters and 1,280 combat-ready bombers of Luftflotten 2, 3, and 5. The British, however, enjoyed a significant advantage in the "Chain Home" system of 30 radar stations established on the coastline from Land's End in the southwest to Newcastle in the northeast.

With hindsight the Battle of Britain can be seen as the prelude to a battle that was never fought—the invasion of England. It passed through a number of phases, each triggered by the Luftwaffe's decisions to switch targets. The first phase opened in early July as the Luftwaffe launched a series of attacks on coastal targets and convoys, seeking to draw Fighter Command out over the Channel.

EAGLE DAY

At the end of July Hitler ordered Göring to prepare "immediately and with the greatest haste … the great battle of the German air force against England." On August 2 Göring issued the final order for *Adlertag* (Eagle Day) on which the destruction of Fighter

RADAR

AN ACRONYM FOR "Radio Direction and Ranging," radar was originally known as "RDF" (Radio Direction Finding) by the British. Its principle is that of sending out a pulse of radio energy to strike a target and then detecting the energy reflected back. As the speed of the pulse is known, measuring the time between transmission and reception enables radar operators to calculate the target range. In the 1930s the concept was developed independently in Britain, France, Germany, and the United States.

In Britain, radar was first developed for defensive purposes, and by 1939 a chain of 30 radar stations had been established around the southwest, southern, and eastern British coastlines. Reports from radar stations were fed back to Fighter Command headquarters along with information

Operations room
Members of the Women's Auxiliary Air Force (WAAF) track incoming German aircraft. One of the Luftwaffe's greatest blunders in 1940 was its failure to appreciate the effectiveness of Britain's radar.

Cierva C-30 autogiro
In the years immediately preceding the war Cierva autogiros were used by the RAF to test and calibrate Britain's chain of coastal radar stations.

from observation posts. The cross-checked results were then transmitted to the relevant Fighter Command Group and sector stations, where controllers would scramble interceptor aircraft to meet the incoming enemy bombers. Radar avoided the wasteful system of flying standing patrols and was a vital element in the narrow margin of victory secured by Fighter Command in the Battle of Britain.

Command was to be accomplished. This was set for August 10, but bad weather caused its postponement for three days while the air fighting intensified. On August 12 Luftflotte 2 struck at England's central south coast. Targets included the docks and war industries in Portsmouth and Southampton, and the radar station in Ventnor on the Isle of Wight. This last target, with its tall, latticed masts, was assigned to 15 Ju 88s, operating in their dive-bomber role. The station was put out of action but within three days was replaced by a mobile station. The Luftwaffe then decided, fatally, not to press home its attack on the radar stations.

Scramble
RAF pilots always raced to their fighters when they were "scrambled." Time was precious and a few extra seconds allowed them to gain height before engaging the enemy.

Luftwaffe operations on August 13—the rescheduled Eagle Day—were disrupted by bad weather and it was on August 15 that the most intensive phase of the Battle of Britain began. For the first and last time, all three Luftflotten took part in the attack, throwing five successive waves of aircraft against Britain—over 2,000 sorties, some two-thirds of them by fighters. The Luftwaffe was unable to coordinate operations against southern England with those in the north, and Luftflotte 5 was withdrawn from the battle after suffering heavy losses. It also failed to coordinate the operations of Luftflotten 2 and 3. At no point were attacks timed to catch the British fighters on the ground refueling and rearming. Thus, when Luftflotte 3 launched its main attack in the west with some 200 aircraft, 10 and 11 Groups were able to concentrate 170 fighters against them, a move that would have been impossible an hour earlier. In the evening, Luftflotte 2 had the opportunity to launch a series of raids at full strength, but sent barely 100 aircraft over southeast England.

Loading a Heinkel 111 with bombs
In the short-range missions of the Battle of Britain the He 111 operated reasonably efficiently as a bomber, but for the longer-range missions of the Blitz, its bombload had to be reduced by half to 2,200 lb (1,000 kg).

At the end of the day's fighting, both sides claimed success, but the Luftwaffe had lost 69 aircraft and 190 aircrew while Fighter Command had lost only 34 aircraft and 13 pilots. On what the Germans called "Black Thursday," the Luftwaffe had sustained its worst losses in a single day of the Battle of Britain. The vulnerable Ju 87 (Stuka) dive-bomber was pulled out of the battle on August 18.

CHANGES IN STRATEGY

The Luftwaffe now narrowed its goal to the destruction of 11 Group's seven sector stations—Biggin Hill, Debden, Hornchurch, Kenley, Northolt, North Weald, and Tangmere. On August 30 Biggin Hill suffered the first of six major attacks. Littered with wreckage, with most its buildings destroyed and much of its vital equipment being worked in the open, the airfield nevertheless remained operational.

Both sides were now feeling the strain. In the first six days of September, the Luftwaffe lost 125 aircraft. The twin-engined Me 110s had proved no match for Spitfires and Hurricanes. In the same period Fighter Command lost 119 aircraft, and its reserve of experienced aircrew was running low. The rate of fighter production was impressive—476 were delivered in August—but the aircraft were of no use without trained pilots to fly them.

The weight of the Luftwaffe's attacks had fallen most heavily on 11 Group—12 Group lay beyond the range of Me 109 escorts—and Park's tactics were aimed at engaging the enemy as early as possible,

often despatching single unsupported squadrons against formations of 100 or more enemy aircraft. Park's tactics attracted criticism, not least from Leigh-Mallory, commander of 12 Group, who argued for the use of wings of up to five squadrons. But these so-called "Big Wings" took time to assemble, and Park believed that the short time available for interception, and the need to protect vital airfields and factories, should be the key determinants in this desperate phase of the battle.

My nerves were in ribbons and I was scared stiff that one day I would pull out and avoid combat. That frightened me more than the Germans and I pleaded with my CO for a rest. He was sympathetic but quite adamant that until he got replacements I would have to carry on. I am glad now that he was unable to let me go. If I had been allowed to leave the squadron, feeling as I did, I am sure that I would never have flown again.

PILOT OFFICER J.H. "GINGER" LACEY, 501 SQUADRON

Ju 88 bombsight
German bombsights were more sophisticated than British ones and allowed for ground speed, wind speed and direction, and drift.

Turn and drift knob

The Luftwaffe's main problem was fighter escort. From mid-August the fighters had been pulled in to fly above, ahead, and on the flank of bomber formations, reducing both their combat efficiency and endurance. The short range of the Me 109 became an increasing handicap.

At this point the Luftwaffe's strategy took a new turn. Late in the afternoon of September 7, it launched its first daylight raid on London, ordered by Hitler in retaliation for an RAF raid on Berlin on the night of August 25/26. A total of 348 bombers, escorted by 617 fighters bombed the oil tanks at Thameshaven and the London docks. Throughout the night a steady procession of 318 Heinkels and Dorniers added 300 tons of high-explosive and 13,000 incendiary bombs to the flames below. The city's antiaircraft defenses downed just one bomber.

On the basis of German intelligence estimates that Fighter Command could now muster only 100 aircraft, a new pattern of bombing was adopted. The Luftwaffe would continue to bomb London by night, while smaller daylight raids—escorted in overwhelming strength—would clear the sky of the remnants of Fighter Command. The pressure was taken off the battered sector stations, allowing them to attack in larger formations—the moment of vindication for Leigh-Mallory's Big Wing tactics.

THE OPPOSING AIR FORCES

THE LUFTWAFFE went into the Battle of Britain with a significant numerical advantage over the RAF. Britain's aircraft, however, were probably better equipped for the roles they had to play in the battle—in particular the two single-seater fighters, the Hurricane and the Spitfire. Even so, these had to land frequently to rearm. On the German side, the Ju 87 Stuka dive-bomber, proved far too vulnerable, while the Ju 88, He 111, and Do 17 medium bombers were limited in their range and had to reduce their bombloads in order to carry sufficient fuel. The principal German fighter, the Messerschmitt Bf 109 was the equal of the Spitfire, but was crucially hampered by its limited range.

Junkers Ju 88A-1

Over 15,000 Ju 88s, of which 9,000 were bombers, were produced in 1939–45. Arguably the most versatile aircraft of the war, the Ju 88 was heavily armored against stern and quarter attacks, but unprotected against head-on attack. Pilots used the dive as an evasive maneuver—the plane had been designed to perform as a dive bomber.

Engines 2 × 1,200 hp Junkers Jumo 211B-1	
Wingspan 65 ft 8 in (19.8 m)	Length 51 ft (15.6 m)
Max Speed 286 mph (460 kph)	Crew 4
Armament 6 × 7.92-mm machine-guns; maximum bombload 5,510 lb (2,500 kg)	

Dornier 17Z-2

Nicknamed the "Flying Pencil" because of its long, thin fuselage, the Dornier medium bomber, like the Heinkel 111, started life as a commercial airplane in the 1930s. Production ceased in 1940 as it became clear that the Junkers 88 was a much better aircraft, but large numbers of Dorniers were used during the the Battle of Britain and as night bombers during the Blitz.

Engines 2 × 1,000 hp Bramo 323P Fafnir	
Wingspan 59 ft (18 m)	Length 52 ft 6 in (15.95 m)
Max Speed 265 mph (426 kph)	Crew 4 or 5
Armament 6 × 7.92-mm machine-guns; bombload 2,200 lb (1,000 kg)	

Heinkel He 111H-3

Designed ostensibly as a civil airliner, the He 111 made its combat debut in the Spanish Civil War. It proved vulnerable in daylight raids without heavy fighter escort and was switched to night bombing, mine-laying, and torpedo-bombing. The ventral gondola, dubbed "the Death Bed," was a favorite target for RAF fighter pilots.

Engines 2 × 1,340 hp Junkers Jumo 211F-1	
Wingspan 74 ft 2 in (22.6 m)	Length 54 ft 6in (16.6 m)
Max Speed 258 mph (415 kph)	Crew 5
Armament 7 × 7.92-mm machine guns; maximum bombload 4,400 lb (2,000 kg)	

Light metal alloy monocoque (weight-bearing) fuselage

Liquid-cooled V-12 Rolls Royce Merlin engine

Elliptical-section wing, housing machine-guns and the retracted undercarriage

Messerschmitt Bf 109E-3

As a weapon of blitzkrieg, operating at the forward point of contact with the enemy, the Me 109 (seen here in desert markings) was a formidable aircraft. But range was less important in France than it was in the skies over southern England. The Me 109 had wooden drop tanks to extend its range, but these had degraded in northern France and were not used in the Battle of Britain.

Engine 1,350 hp Daimler Benz DB 601 E	
Wingspan 32 ft 4 in (9.87 m)	Length 28 ft 2 in (8.64 m)
Max Speed 348 mph (560 kph)	Crew 1
Armament 2 × 20-mm cannon, 2 × 7.9-mm machine-guns	

Boulton Paul Defiant

The Defiant had no fixed forward firing armament but featured instead a power-operated revolving turret immediately behind the pilot. Designed as a bomber destroyer, which could fly alongside enemy aircraft, pouring fire into their unprotected flanks, the Defiant was no match for enemy fighters, but had some success against bombers as a night fighter during the Blitz.

Engine 1,030 hp Rolls Royce Merlin III	
Wingspan 39 ft 4 in (10.77 m)	Length 35 ft 4 in (11.99 m)
Max Speed 304 mph (489 kph)	Crew 2
Armament 4 × .303-in Browning machine-guns	

Supermarine Spitfire I

The Spitfire became synonymous with the success of the British fighters in the Battle of Britain, although Hurricanes were more numerous and shot down more enemy planes. But the Spitfire had a certain mystique and won the affection of all the pilots that flew it. In combat the Spitfire had the edge on the Messerschmitt Bf 109 in speed and climb and in turning circle. The Me 109, however, outperformed the Spitfire over 20,000 ft (6,000 m), a height at which the prewar RAF had not expected dogfighting. When flown to its limits a Spitfire could shake off a pursuer by means of a flick and half roll and a quick pull out of the subsequent dive. However, at the start of the Battle of Britain the Me 109 had the advantage in a steep dive because its direct-injection engine kept running under negative gravity while the Spitfire's Merlin cut out as the Spitfire tried to follow.

Engine 1,030 hp Rolls Royce Merlin III	
Wingspan 36 ft 10 in (11.23 m)	Length 29 ft 11 in (9.12 m)
Max speed 357 mph (575 kph)	Crew 1
Armament 8 × .303-in Browning machine-guns	

Hawker Hurricane I

The Hurricane was the RAF's first monoplane fighter, entering service in 1937. The principal fighter in the Battle of Britain, it was a rock-solid gun platform, immensely maneuverable, and capable of absorbing a huge amount of battle damage. Its roomy cockpit, excellent all-around visibility, responsive handling, and reliable engine made it a true pilot's aircraft.

Engine 1,030 hp Rolls Royce Merlin II or III	
Wingspan 40 ft (12.1 m)	Length 32 ft 2 in (9.8 m)
Max Speed 329 mph (529 kph)	Crew 1
Armament 8 × .303-in Browning machine-guns	

On the morning of September 15, 100 Do 17s crossed the English coastline, battling into a strong headwind. Their slow approach forced their escorts to turn back as their fuel ran low and also gave Fighter Command time to deploy. The Dorniers were harried all the way to the outskirts of London, where they were met by five squadrons of the Duxford Big Wing—60 fighters attacking in close formation—which shot down six Dorniers as the raiders jettisoned their bombs and turned for home.

In the afternoon, British radar operators picked up the slow assembly, over their airfields in France, of another large formation. The raiders flew in over Kent to be met by over 160 fighters of 11 Group. By the end of the day nearly 300 British fighters were operating over London. The Luftwaffe lost 55 aircraft and at least 25 percent of the remainder suffered severe damage. Hitler ordered the indefinite postponement of Sealion and the He 111s and Do 17s were switched to night operations.

THE BLITZ

Between September 7 and November 12 London was spared bombing on a mere 10 nights. Some 13,000 tons of high explosive and almost one million incendiaries fell on the city, killing 13,000 people and injuring 20,000 more. At this stage in the war, the RAF's night defenses were little more than a collection of hasty improvisations. Only a handful of fighters were equipped with a primitive form of airborne radar. Nor had the Luftwaffe's bombers much to fear from antiaircraft guns. In September 1940 an expenditure of some 20,000 shells was needed to down one plane.

The Germans, moreover, had a secret weapon, described by Churchill as "a radio beam which, like an invisible searchlight, would guide bombers… to their target." Dubbed *Knickebein* (crooked leg), it consisted of two radio beams directed from stations in Europe. Aircraft would fly along one beam and release their bombs when the first beam was intersected by the second. The Luftwaffe had foolishly tested the system over Britain in March 1940, at a time when it was not contemplating large-scale night-bombing operations. The examination of an He 111 shot down by a night fighter enabled scientists to work out how to jam the beams. A more sophisticated version of this system—X-Verfahren—used four beams and a clockwork timer linked to the beams and bomb release. A crack unit, Kampfgruppe (KGr) 100, was formed early in 1940 to test this system. By mid-October a regular pattern of night raids had emerged: KGr 100 acted as a pathfinding force, marking targets for the main force flying in behind.

The bombing of Coventry
In an 11-hour attack, 554 people were killed and over 1,200 injured. Some 60,000 buildings were destroyed or damaged, including the city's medieval cathedral, which was completely gutted.

Map labels

Orkney Islands

Scapa Flow

1 Mar 16, 1940
Luftwaffe attacks Scapa Flow naval base. First British civilian casualty of the war

SCOTLAND

Aberdeen

6 Mar 13/14, 1941
Luftwaffe attacks Clydebank in attempt to destroy its shipyards. Homes, factories, and a munitions plant are obliterated

Dundee

Apr 1941 **8**
Belfast, an important ship-building center, suffers two heavy raids

Clydebank Glasgow EDINBURGH

11 May 15, 1941
111 German bombers carry out a massive assault against Birmingham

Newcastle-upon-Tyne Tyne

NORTHERN IRELAND

Workington Middlesbrough

BELFAST 13 GROUP Catterick

Isle of Man

IRELAND

Irish Sea

North Sea

5 Nov 14/15, 1940
449 German bombers devastate Coventry, leaving one-third of its inhabitants homeless

Church Fenton Hull
Manchester Humber
Liverpool

May 31, 1941 **12** DUBLIN
Bomb falls on Dublin. Neutral Ireland occasionally bombed in error

Sheffield Kirton in Lindsey
Stoke-on-Trent Digby
Nottingham
Wittering

3 Sept 7, 1940 –
Nov 12, 1941
Raids kill over 15,000 in London and make more than 250,000 homeless

Birmingham Norwich

May 1–7, 1941 **9**
Luftwaffe targets Liverpool for second time, subjecting it to seven successive nights of bombing

Coventry 12 GROUP
WALES ENGLAND Duxford

NETH.

AMSTERDAM
Soesterberg
Nijmegen

Pembrey Swansea
Filton North Weald Debden
Severn Oxford Northolt Hornchurch
Thames Chatham

Gilze-Rijen Eindhoven

CARDIFF Bristol LONDON
Kenley
10 GROUP

Antwerp

Jul 10, 1940 **2**
In first major attack, Luftwaffe bombs Swansea docks and Royal Ordnance factory in Pembrey

Yeovil 11 GROUP
Middle Wallop Dover
Exeter Lympne Calais BRUSSELS St Trond
Weymouth Hastings Lille
Portland Brighton Biggin Hill BELGIUM

Apr 1941 **7**
Five relentless bombing raids virtually reduce Plymouth to rubble

Plymouth Southampton Isle of Wight

LUFTFLOTTE 2

10 May 10, 1941
London suffers largest raid so far. Thousands left without electricity, gas, or water

Tangmere Portsmouth

Sept 30, 1940 **4**
Luftwaffe pounds Westland aircraft factory

English Channel

Cherbourg

Laon

Rouen/Rennes Beauvais

Caen Evreux Seine PARIS
St André-de-l'Eure
Dreux Orly
Brest Dinard Chartres Melun
LUFTFLOTTE 3 Etampes

Châteaudun

Vannes

FRANCE

N

0 km 50 100 150
0 miles 50 100 150

Legend

GERMAN BOMBING OF BRITISH CITIES
MAR 1940–MAY 1941

- Major air raids or towns suffering repeated bombing
- Other important air raids
- Main British industrial areas
- British fighter base
- German air base

The war in the air over Britain
When Hitler called off his planned invasion of Britain from northern France, he ordered the Luftwaffe to bomb the country into submission instead. The most intense period of bombing (the Blitz) lasted from September 1940 to May 1941.

Late in the afternoon of November 14 an X-beam was detected crossing the Midlands, an area as yet largely unscathed by heavy night raids. This confirmed reports that the Germans were planning a major night offensive, code-named *Mondscheinserenade* (Moonlight Serenade), timed to take advantage of the full moon.

Less than two hours later the first of 13 He 11s of KGr 100 arrived over Coventry. The aiming point was to the east of the city center and when the last of the Heinkels flew away, numerous fires had been started. These lit the way for 449 bombers which dropped 1,500 high-explosive bombs, 50 huge parachute and land mines, and some 30,000 incendiaries. The city was

London firefighters
On the first night of the Blitz 25,000 auxiliary firefighters rushed to assist the London Fire Brigade. On many nights there were over 2,000 major fires in the city, as well as countless minor spot fires.

devastated and 21 factories—12 of them connected with the aircraft industry— severely damaged. Yet Coventry quickly recovered. Just over a month of industrial output was lost but most of the factories were back in production within days. Nor had civilian morale collapsed. After the initial shock there was no mass panic.

Throughout January and February, in the face of winter weather, the Luftwaffe fought to maintain the pressure on London, the industrial centers of

the Midlands, and Britain's western ports, the last links in the Atlantic supply chain. However, air defenses were now making life more difficult for the German bombers. By March, improved radar equipment was reaching the night fighter squadrons. In March, night fighters shot down 22 bombers and AA guns claimed another 17. In April, the figures rose to 48 and 39 respectively and reached a peak in May, with 96 fighter victories and 32 claimed by the guns.

The final phase of the Blitz began in mid-April 1941 and concluded with a heavy raid on London on the night of May 10/11 in which some 1,436 civilians were killed and 16 aircraft were brought down by the air defenses, the highest total in a single night. These losses were not sufficient in themselves to bring a halt to the Blitz. Rather it was the transfer to the East of units earmarked for the invasion of the Soviet Union, which Hitler launched on June 22, 1941. By the end of June two-thirds of the Luftwaffe had been removed from the bombing operations against Britain.

"The whole sky to the east was blazing red… it seemed as though half of London must be burning… In Shaftesbury Avenue, five miles from the blaze, it was possible to read an evening paper."

AIR RAID WARDEN BARBARA NIXON
ON SEPTEMBER 7, 1940

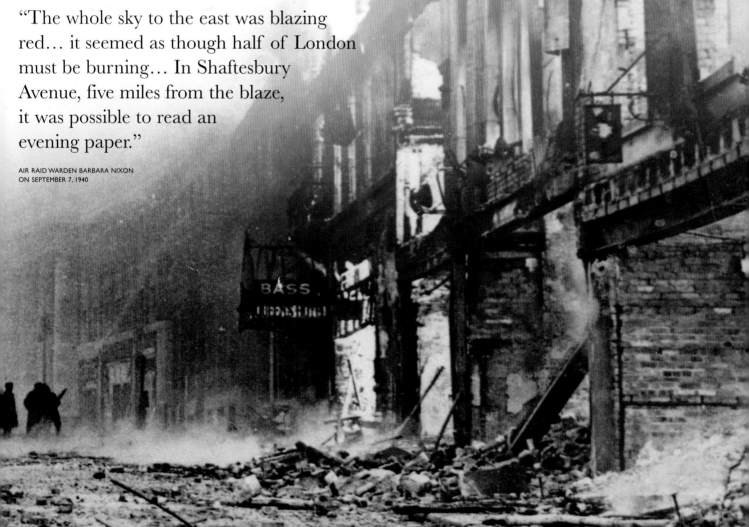

Rescuing a victim of the Blitz
A Heavy Rescue Squad pulls a survivor from the remains of a bombed building. Some 40,000 civilians were killed in the Blitz, in which London and other British cities were bombed over a nine-month period. The Blitz failed, however, to affect British morale.

THE BRITISH, FRENCH, AND GERMAN HOME FRONTS

SEPTEMBER 1939–JUNE 1943

World War II was a "total war" in which civilians were mobilized to contribute to their countries' war effort more fully than ever before. This was particularly the case in Britain and Germany, where rationing was introduced almost immediately and the government took control of the economy. Women played a major part in military hardware production, to which resources were increasingly diverted.

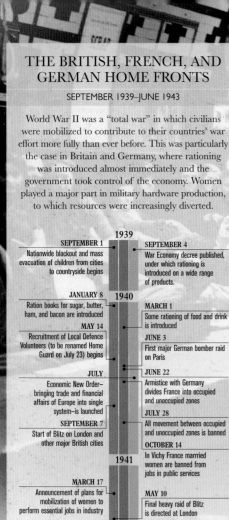

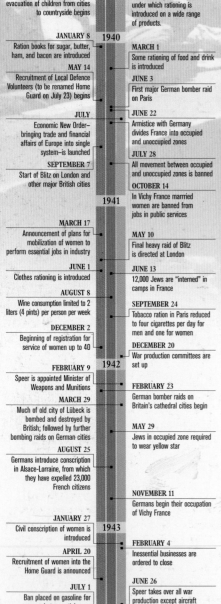

1939

SEPTEMBER 1
Nationwide blackout and mass evacuation of children from cities to countryside begins

SEPTEMBER 4
War Economy decree published, under which rationing is introduced on a wide range of products.

1940

JANUARY 8
Ration books for sugar, butter, ham, and bacon are introduced

MARCH 1
Some rationing of food and drink is introduced

MAY 14
Recruitment of Local Defence Volunteers (to be renamed Home Guard on July 23) begins

JUNE 3
First major German bomber raid on Paris

JULY
Economic New Order–bringing trade and financial affairs of Europe into single system–is launched

JUNE 22
Armistice with Germany divides France into occupied and unoccupied zones

JULY 28
All movement between occupied and unoccupied zones is banned

SEPTEMBER 7
Start of Blitz on London and other major British cities

OCTOBER 14
In Vichy France married women are banned from jobs in public services

1941

MARCH 17
Announcement of plans for mobilization of women to perform essential jobs in industry

MAY 10
Final heavy raid of Blitz is directed at London

JUNE 1
Clothes rationing is introduced

JUNE 13
12,000 Jews are "interned" in camps in France

AUGUST 8
Wine consumption limited to 2 liters (4 pints) per person per week

SEPTEMBER 24
Tobacco ration in Paris reduced to four cigarettes per day for men and one for women

DECEMBER 2
Beginning of registration for service of women up to 40

DECEMBER 20
War production committees are set up

1942

FEBRUARY 9
Speer is appointed Minister of Weapons and Munitions

FEBRUARY 23
German bomber raids on Britain's cathedral cities begin

MARCH 29
Much of old city of Lübeck is bombed and destroyed by British; followed by further bombing raids on German cities

MAY 29
Jews in occupied zone required to wear yellow star

AUGUST 25
Germans introduce conscription in Alsace-Lorraine, from which they have expelled 23,000 French citizens

NOVEMBER 11
Germans begin their occupation of Vichy France

1943

JANUARY 27
Civil conscription of women is introduced

FEBRUARY 4
Inessential businesses are ordered to close

APRIL 20
Recruitment of women into the Home Guard is announced

JULY 1
Ban placed on gasoline for anyone but essential users

JUNE 26
Speer takes over all war production except aircraft

■ Events in Britain   ■ Events in France   ■ Events in Germany

THE HOME FRONT IN WESTERN EUROPE

Wᴏʀʟᴅ ᴡᴀʀ ɪɪ involved civilians on a scale never experienced before, both as contributors to the war effort and as victims. The number of civilian casualties in western Europe did not approach the number reached in eastern Europe. Even so, as many as 2 million were killed in Germany, 170,000 in France, and 65,000 in Britain.

The single greatest cause of civilian casualties in western Europe—apart from the Nazi death camps—was aerial bombardment. An early warning of the massive destruction that could be inflicted on cities by bomber planes came during the German invasion of Poland in September 1939, when Warsaw was bombed into submission. The following May

the bombing of Rotterdam, which resulted in the death of over 1,000 civilians and 78,000 being made homeless, was followed by the Blitz on British cities between September 1940 and May 1941, in which some 40,000 people lost their lives.

Training for the British Home Guard
In 1940, when volunteers to the Home Guard were first recruited, the training was patchy and equipment either nonexistent or outdated. Both improved greatly in 1941.

CIVILIAN EVACUATIONS

IN 1932 THE WARNING of the British politician, Stanley Baldwin, that "the bomber will always get through" made a deep impression in Britain, the only state to make serious plans to evacuate civilians from large towns before the war started. The Germans did not expect to be bombed, but when they were, the *Kinder Land Verschickung* was set up to evacuate children from the north and west to the south. Child casualties of the bombing in cities in the south were possibly one-third of those in the north and west. In France, between the outbreak of war and defeat in June 1940, many parents in the cities sent children to stay with relatives in the country. Others were taken in by Catholic schools and orphanages.

Encouraging evacuation
Only a minority of children were evacuated from London and other cities, despite the authorities' efforts.

In Britain, plans to evacuate 4 million children, mothers, and expectant mothers were put into effect as soon as the war began. About 1.5 million actually went, plus another 2 million privately. But the bombers did not come, and about half the evacuees returned home within four months. Air raids during the Blitz of 1940 prompted a new evacuation, although patchy and unplanned. In the summer of 1944, the arrival of the V-1 and V-2 was to prompt the evacuation of another 1.5 million Londoners.

Children went first to "reception areas," where they were allotted to households judged able to take them. Billeting was compulsory if sufficient volunteers were not forthcoming. Such close contact between city slums and rural prosperity caused problems. Evacuees, especially poor Roman Catholics from the Liverpool and Glasgow slums, were often resented. Some mothers never returned to reclaim their children, and there were cases of physical and sexual abuse. There were also benefits—greater social awareness on both sides and, more tangibly, good country food for poor city children.

Sheltering in a subway station
London's underground stations were not always as safe as people supposed them to be. In October 1940 a bomb falling on Balham station killed or injured 600 people.

Evacuees
For many city children, evacuation to the countryside was a frightening experience. Sometimes it involved having to live with a family that clearly did not want them.

The German bombs were a combination of high-explosive, ranging from several pounds to 2.5 tons, and incendiaries of various types. The incendiaries were far more effective. A high-explosive bomb might destroy a building but an incendiary could set fire to a huge area. Although it only caused a small explosion, it ignited chemicals that burned for a few minutes at very high temperature, long enough to set fire to the surroundings.

Scenes of destruction were horrific. In some cases whole families were wiped out, and from a high vantage point most of east London on a bad night in the Blitz seemed to be on fire. London Transport lost so many buses it had to borrow 500 from other cities. In the notorious raids on Coventry in November 1940 and April 1941, when most of the city center was destroyed, 50,000 houses were rendered uninhabitable. Rehousing the homeless caused severe difficulties here and elsewhere: prefabricated houses were not built until 1944. Yet paradoxically the "Blitz," which was expressly designed to break British morale, actually raised it. Large-scale bombardment of civilian targets in Germany did not begin until 1943, when Hamburg was the chief victim, with 40,000 of its citizens dying in one night. Even this huge figure was to be far exceeded by the casualties in German cities during the massive Allied raids of 1944–45.

CIVIL DEFENSE

In Britain plans had been laid for rationing, evacuation, and aspects of civil defense before the war began. The Anderson air-raid shelter, which could be dug into any backyard, was widely distributed from February 1939. It was followed by the indoors Morrison shelter, a reinforced iron cage that doubled as a table. Both required scarce steel and provided inadequate protection against direct hits. Public shelters, usually brick, also proved inadequate. People preferred their own barricaded homes or, against the initial resistance of the authorities, impregnable underground railroad stations. Better, deeper shelters were then built, too late for the Blitz but useful when the V-1s and V-2s arrived toward the end of the war.

LEAVE THIS TO US
SONNY—**YOU OUGHT**
TO BE OUT OF LONDON

MINISTRY OF HEALTH EVACUATION SCHEME

Gas masks were issued to all citizens, who were urged to carry them at all times, though they proved an unnecessary precaution. Considerable chaos was caused by a nationwide blackout: the road accident rate doubled in the first month of its operation but later fell with less stringent lighting restrictions and the rationing of gasoline (later withdrawn entirely for private use). In Germany the blackout began the day before war started, and flashlights soon joined the growing number of articles unobtainable in stores. Buses crawled along darkened Berlin streets bearing a single, ghostly, blue light. Pedestrians wore a phosphorescent button on their coats.

Windows had to be blacked out, too, and were usually also crisscrossed with gummed newspaper strips as protection against splinters. Blackout discipline was maintained in Britain by ARP (Air Raid Protection) wardens, volunteers who had generally done a day's work first. The cry "Put out that light!" became another wartime watchword.

The call in Britain for ARP wardens—made in 1937—had met with a big response. This was repeated in May 1940 with the Local Defence Volunteers, soon to be renamed the Home Guard. Within one month of the government's appeal, 1.5 million men had volunteered. They included men of every age and class, though perhaps the core was made up of World War I veterans, now too old for the army. Their main task was to guard factories, airfields, and other sensitive places, and to man coastal defenses. In such a role they were immensely valuable, but few people put much faith in their ability to resist a German invasion.

The fear of imminent invasion led to a plethora of security measures—such as barricades, camouflage, and obstacles against enemy tanks—of which some were of doubtful utility. The removal of signposts from road junctions, for example, overlooked the fact that the Germans had maps. Encouraged by official urging to avoid careless talk ("you never know who is listening"), fantasies about German agents, even German paratroopers, being everywhere, proliferated during the Phoney War. They largely subsided when the situation became more serious.

Women in war work
In Britain women were recruited to the industrial workforce on a huge scale. By 1943 all those under 40 were in war work unless they had particularly heavy domestic responsibilities. They were employed in all forms of industry and acquired a wide range of skills, including welding.

LIFE UNDER GERMAN OCCUPATION

The wartime experience of civilians naturally varied greatly from one country to another, even in those under German occupation. Moreover, conditions changed, invariably for the worse, as time went on.

Reactions to occupation varied widely, while the German attitude toward conquered peoples depended on Nazi racial prejudices. In the Netherlands the German regime was, to begin with, comparatively mild, since the Dutch were regarded as racially akin to Germans and potential members of a future Greater Reich. Scandinavians were also acceptable. The Nazi hope of enlisting Norwegians, Danes, and Dutch in support of the war against

INTERNMENT OF CIVILIANS

AT THE OUTBREAK OF WAR most combatant nations arrested and held without trial "enemy aliens"—residents who were citizens of enemy states, had been born there, or in some cases were merely descended from people born there. Initially, Britain and Germany allowed some aliens to return home, whereas in France all German males were interned. When the Germans invaded, many more were arrested in Belgium and the Netherlands as well as France, where they were sent to camps in the far south. In Britain only those people considered "high-risk" were held in camps in 1939, but during the spy scare of May 1940 more were interned, including refugees from Naziism. The sinking of a ship carrying 600 internees to Canada provoked popular protest, leading to the majority being freed by mid-1941.

Camp in Huyton, near Liverpool
In the summer of 1940 around 27,000 men, women, and children were interned in camps in Britain, often in very poor conditions.

communism, to which, after the attack on the Soviet Union in June 1941, a hefty propaganda effort was directed, induced Hitler initially to avoid putting native Nazi sympathizers in power. However, apart from a small minority of collaborationists on the one hand and resistance members on the other, the great majority of civilians in the occupied countries opted for a policy of pragmatism, cooperating nenthusiastically with the German authorities and only so far as necessary to avoid trouble. After all, until 1943, German dominance looked likely to be long-lasting, if not permanent.

The extent to which the Germans took direct control of civil administration reflected their racial attitude, with the Netherlands, and still more Denmark, retaining a large measure of authority for the first two years. But the economies of all occupied countries rapidly became wholly subservient to the German war effort. Foreign workers were encouraged, and later compelled, to take work in Germany, where by 1943 they made up nearly 20 percent of the workforce. Sometimes factories were dismantled and their machinery transported to the Fatherland.

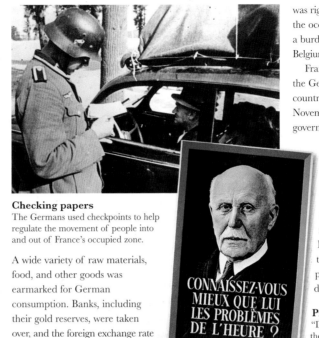

Checking papers
The Germans used checkpoints to help regulate the movement of people into and out of France's occupied zone.

A wide variety of raw materials, food, and other goods was earmarked for German consumption. Banks, including their gold reserves, were taken over, and the foreign exchange rate was rigged to favor the mark. The costs of the occupation were borne by its victims, a burden exacerbated, particularly in Belgium and France, by runaway inflation.

France was an unusual case because the Germans did not occupy the whole country between May 1940 and November 1942, and left the Vichy government headed by Pétain in sole charge of the center and south. The veneer of French national unity at the outbreak of war soon cracked as old animosities resurfaced. The Vichy regime represented the reactionary, anti-republican Right, as much anti-British as anti-German, and hostile to the liberal Left, reflecting a profound division in French society dating from the 1789 Revolution.

Promotion of a personality cult
"Do you know more than he does about the problems of the moment?," asked this poster featuring Marshal Pétain.

" I collaborate: therefore I have the right to contribute my own thought and individual effort to the common cause."

THE BISHOP OF ARRAS, MGR. HENRI-ÉDOUARD DUTOÎT, ATTEMPTING TO JUSTIFY THE DECISION OF PÉTAIN AND HIS FOLLOWERS TO COLLABORATE WITH THE GERMANS

Germans in Paris
From June 1940 Paris was the seat of the German Military Administration that governed the occupied section of France.

The old watchwords, Liberté, Egalité, Fraternité, were replaced by Travail, Famille, Patrie (Work, Family, Fatherland), and the government was increasingly dominated by fascist collaborators.

In both zones of France, as elsewhere, most people settled for minimal cooperation if not tacit collaboration. However, despite the extra difficulties imposed by the division of the country, viable resistance —to both Germans and the Vichy government— was active in the north within weeks of the armistice and developed later with equal strength in the south.

THE ROLE OF WOMEN

Women were recruited to the labor force throughout Europe. In Britain, for example, about 80 percent of the workers added to the British labor force in 1939–43 were women who had not formerly figured in the labor market, the majority having been housewives. Later, certain categories of women were

Vichy propaganda poster
The Vichy government was both authoritarian and patriarchal, and it cooperated with the Germans on a major scale. Its people were exhorted to work in support of the German war effort.

conscripted for work in war industries, learning hitherto masculine trades such as carpentry or welding. By 1943, when workers in the munitions industry had expanded from 1.25 million (1939) to 8.5 million even grandmothers were being recruited. Women workers were not always popular, sometimes because the admission of women to a factory freed men for military service, and there was considerable discrimination. In a team assembling Lancasters, men and women did the same work side by side, but the women's pay was half that of the men.

Women were also required to take the place of absent farmworkers. In Britain the Women's Land Army, popularly known as Land Girls, eventually numbered over 80,000. It attracted office girls yearning for an outdoor life, though working long hours in all weather for £1.40 ($5.60) a week plus room and board dented some illusions. It was perfectly possible to join the Land Girls to get away

from the Blitz, only to find oneself on a farm near an airfield that was a regular target of German air raids.

At the beginning of the war, Germany made less use of women workers. Hitler believed that to remove women from family life was bad for morale, and the Nazi concept of the woman as a Nordic domestic goddess devoted exclusively to husband and children continued to prevail. Women were theoretically subject to civil conscription under prewar legislation, but in June 1940 only 250,000 had been recruited and they did not affect the workforce total because all had previously been employed. Generous family allowances, nearly three times their equivalent in Britain, discouraged soldiers' wives from taking jobs.

Ministers who, as time went on, urged greater employment of women, came up against Hitler's prejudices. When the Soviet Union was cited as an example, Hitler replied that "slim, long-legged German women" could not be compared with "dumpy, primitive . . . Russian women." He even disliked mobilizing domestic servants, who decreased in numbers in 1939–45 by only 15 percent, while in Britain they virtually disappeared. However, in a

RADIO PROPAGANDA

PROPAGANDA IN ALL FORMS was a vital force in raising public morale, and all governments established a ministry of propaganda. Paper shortages notwithstanding, posters and leaflets urged people to contribute to their country's war effort. Slogans, such as the British "Dig for Victory" and "Mend and Make-do," assaulted both eye and ear. While sometimes being criticized for putting too much emphasis on exhortation and not supplying enough facts, radio was particularly effective. In Germany it was largely responsible for continued confidence in the government after defeat had become inevitable. Churchill and Hitler, in rather different styles, exploited radio with skill.

Broadcasts to occupied Europe by the British Broadcasting Corporation (BBC), which was independent though supportive of the British government, reached eager listeners who risked death if caught. In general it broadcast what it believed to be the truth, though not necessarily the whole truth. The BBC's German service had perhaps 1 million listeners in Germany in 1943. Josef Goebbels, appointed the German minister of propaganda in 1933, recognized the advantages of truthfulness in propaganda, though he was often overruled. Radio Suisse could also be relied on for relative accuracy.

Listening to Churchill
Through speeches broadcast on the radio, Churchill did much to raise public morale in Britain.

"Black" propaganda aimed at the enemy or, by the Germans, at the people of occupied countries, was less successful, though under the guidance of Goebbels it played a part in damaging French morale before June 1940. The broadcasts of "Lord Haw-Haw," from Germany to Britain, by a British traitor, William Joyce, who had a very upper-class accent, met with general derision. Similarly, British broadcasts pretending to emanate from Germany and aiming to undermine morale in the German army and U-boat crews apparently had little effect.

Earpiece

Secret radio
Owning a radio was forbidden in many countries. This radio hidden in a tin was used by a Dutch family to listen to BBC broadcasts.

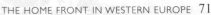

German aircraft factory, 1940
Resources were diverted from the civilian to the military economy on an even greater scale in Germany than elsewhere. However, there was not a corresponding increase in the production of weapons and aircraft until 1942.

country where 6.6 million men were recruited to the armed services during the first two years of the war, it was inevitable that women should be required to join the workforce, whether on a paid or voluntary basis. In the countryside, from which many of the army recruits were drawn, women had to take on a greater share of the work on often unmechanized farms, while in the towns they took over from men in transportation, commerce, and administration. They also worked in the armaments industry, though not on as great a scale as would have been necessary if Germany had not begun to use foreign workers.

Hitler refused to contemplate equal pay for women, and sexist discrimination was common everywhere. For example, the huge contribution of women to the Resistance in France, as well as to French society generally under the occupation, is now well known, yet the attitude toward women of the male-dominated Resistance, even the Communist Party, was not much different from the paternalistic attitude of the Vichy regime, which banned married women from jobs in public services. Women were highly praised, but as defenders of their families and supporters of those "actively engaged" in the fight against the Nazis.

RATIONING AND FOOD

Rationing was introduced everywhere at the beginning of the war, or as soon as a program could be set up. Such programs were so extensive that they amounted to near-total government control of food. In Britain the only basic food items not rationed were bread and potatoes, while other, nonessential foods were "rationed" by simple nonavailability. When a supply of something scarce appeared in a local store, large lines quickly formed. In prosperous western Europe, there was scope for reducing consumption without severe hardship. Although some people had to make sacrifices, the overall effect of rationing in Britain, assisted by subsidies, price controls, and higher wages, was,

ironically, an overall improvement in the national diet. Child mortality rates and developmental diseases such as rickets registered a marked fall, whereas in France and other occupied countries, health and diet deteriorated. Even in Britain, the wartime diet was far from ideal, however, being short on protein and Vitamins A and D.

The rationing system adopted in Britain was to allocate a minimum quantity—for example, 2 oz (60 grams) of butter per week—to each individual, obtainable only with coupons from a ration book. Although rigid, this ensured that no one was undernourished. A more flexible system, which gave some choice, operated for clothes and consumer goods. In Germany citizens needed seven ration books, each color-coded for a specific type of food.

Britain imported nearly two-thirds of its food in 1939, hence the importance of the Battle of the Atlantic. More needed to be produced at home.

THE TREATMENT OF JEWS IN EUROPE 1939–41

BEFORE 1939 GERMANY had passed a series of measures against the Jews that included their effective exclusion from all economic life. The next step was to push them out of Germany. Various plans for expulsion were considered, Madagascar being one favored destination. Some Jews in eastern Germany were deported across the border to Poland as early as 1938. The question became more pressing for the German authorities with the conquest of Poland and, in 1941, the invasion of the Soviet Union, which resulted in a huge increase in the number of Jews under German rule. Some massacres of Jews and other "undesirables" were carried out by mass shootings. Elsewhere the Jews were rounded up and forced into ghettos with the intention of starving them to death. The numbers were, however, too large for this generally to be a practicable course of action. Consequently, in the fall of 1941 preparations began for the extermination of Jews in eastern Europe by gassing.

In the occupied countries of western Europe, measures against the Jews were not introduced as quickly as in the east and initially were less extreme. This was partly due to the decision not to permit the SS carte blanche, but also because the Jews were proportionately fewer and more integrated. Jews were expelled from public life, not allowed

Anti-Semitic poster
Jews were often portrayed as being in an alliance with the communist Soviet Union against Europe.

Determining Jewishness
German officials could go to extreme lengths—such as measuring the length and width of a person's nose—to establish whether he or she was a true "Aryan" or had Jewish blood.

to use public transportation and were encouraged to emigrate. Their property was frequently confiscated.

Nazi racial policy often contradicted other goals of German policy. For instance, the Germans were hopeful of gaining the cooperation of the Dutch people, but an attack on the Jewish district in Amsterdam provoked a 48-hour strike by Dutch workers. By contrast, the Vichy regime in France cooperated fully with the Nazis. It introduced anti-Semitic laws of its own. As early as July 1940 it deprived naturalized Jews of French citizenship and one year later interned 12,000 in camps.

The country most successful in thwarting Nazi destruction of its Jews was Denmark, where a large majority of the 8,000 Danish Jews were safely smuggled to Sweden and the king boldly wore a star of David.

The yellow star
Jews in the occupied countries were ordered to wear a yellow star of David as a way of making them feel like outcasts and to facilitate rounding them up into ghettos and camps.

"I saw German soldiers dragging Jewish men from their houses, and kicking and beating them in the street…"

AREK HERSH, AGED 11, AT THE OUTBREAK OF WAR IN SIERADZ, POLAND

Jews in Warsaw
The Jews in Poland were treated with great brutality as soon as the Germans took over. In 1940 they were rounded up in the cities and herded into sealed-off ghettos.

Everywhere in Britain, unproductive land was cultivated. Even elegant Greenwich Park in London was dug up for gardens, and the government urged people to "Dig for Victory" while bombarding them with "economy" recipes. Some schools and other groups raised a communal pig on kitchen scraps. (In France, Parisians took to keeping rabbits on their balconies.) Along with the National Wheatmeal Loaf, the Woolton Pie (named after the minister of food) appeared, its ingredients infinitely variable, but excluding meat.

Circumstances varied from country to country and district to district, but in general, and unsurprisingly, people everywhere ate better if they lived in the country rather than an urban environment—especially in occupied countries where townspeople were more closely watched—and if they had the means to take advantage of the black market. This was ubiquitous though illegal, and also expensive. In France the official price of butter in 1942 was 66 francs per kilo (30 francs per lb);

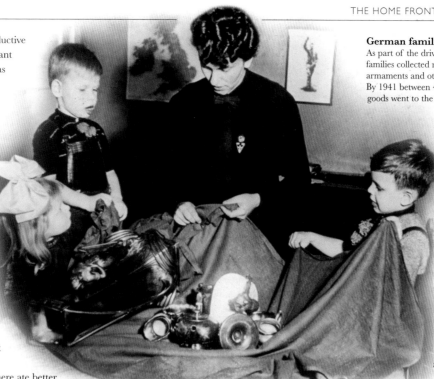

German family collecting metal
As part of the drive to help the German war effort, families collected metal for use in the production of armaments and other goods for the armed forces. By 1941 between 40 and 50 percent of consumer goods went to the military, leaving little for civilians.

France was only one-third that of his or her German equivalent, while the bread ration was one-half. There were shortages in virtually all kinds of consumer goods throughout Europe, including—though to a lesser degree—neutral countries such as Sweden. Some industries disappeared altogether, or were diverted to different purposes, for the course of the war. Children's toys were just one example of goods that soon became almost unobtainable.

on the black market it was 175 francs. In some occupied countries, such as Belgium, the turnover of the black market was possibly greater than that of the official food outlets.

In Germany, where rationing was introduced for a wide range of foodstuffs following the publication of the War Economy Decree in September 1939, civilians were probably worse off than in Britain even in the early years of the war. With the exception of workers in heavy industry who received extra rations, they were certainly less well fed—and this despite the additional food resources drawn from the conquered countries. Supplies of meat and fresh foods were reserved for the armed forces, with the result that most people's diet consisted of potatoes, black bread, and *ersatz* (substitute) foods of the type produced during World War I, such as "meat" made of vegetable flour, barley, and mushrooms. Real meat and eggs were occasional luxuries. The supply of manufactured clothing was little better, with over 40 percent being diverted to the armed forces. In 1939–40 a man's clothing allowance was 100 coupons, but he needed 80 coupons for a suit (*ersatz* cloth at that). In the occupied countries, official rations were even lower. The meat ration of an industrial worker in

THE WAR ECONOMY

The governments of the combatant nations adopted extensive powers that enabled them to impose tight controls on virtually all aspects of the economy and society and divert resources to where they were needed. In Germany they were transferred from the civilian to the military economy on a greater scale than elsewhere. This did not mean, however, that Germany's requirements for armaments were met from the outset. The armed forces established a system of inspectorates to oversee armaments production, but attempting to do the same job were the Economics and Labor Ministries. The resulting lack of centralization meant that the war economy was extemely inefficient, a situation that Hitler sought to rectify by appointing Albert Speer as minister for armaments and munitions in February 1942. By rationalizing the whole system, Speer succeeded in trebling armaments production. Only in 1944, when the Allied bombing of German cities and industrial installations caused major devastation, did Speer begin to struggle to maintain the output of the war economy.

German air-raid poster
Germans were warned to observe the blackout during bombing raids with the words "The Enemy Sees Your Light."

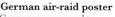

Der Feind sieht Dein Licht!

Verdunkeln!

GERMANY TRIUMPHANT
1940–41

THE EVACUATION OF THE BRITISH EXPEDITIONARY FORCE (BEF) FROM DUNKIRK AND THE FALL OF FRANCE IN JUNE 1940 OPENED NEW STRATEGIC HORIZONS FOR HITLER. WHILE THE BRITISH REFUSED TO BEND TO HIS WILL, HE WAS NOW IN A POSITION TO MULTIPLY THE FRONTS ON WHICH THEY WOULD BE FORCED TO FIGHT—IN THE ATLANTIC, THE MEDITERRANEAN, AND NORTH AFRICA. ABOVE ALL, HE COULD NOW GIVE HIS ATTENTION TO A LONG-CHERISHED CAMPAIGN—THE INVASION AND CONQUEST OF THE SOVIET UNION.

Military pride
Hitler gives the Nazi salute to the Wehrmacht guard of honor at a march past in Unter den Linden, Berlin, on March 16, 1941. In Nazi Germany the day commemorated national heroes.

THE FÜHRER IN COMMAND

HITLER HAD SECURED A STUNNING VICTORY IN THE BATTLE OF FRANCE, WHICH NOW ALLOWED HIM TO DOMINATE GERMAN DECISION MAKING ON THE STRATEGIC COURSE OF THE WAR. WHILE BEING CONVINCED OF HIS OWN MILITARY GENIUS, HITLER WAS IN FACT A POOR STRATEGIST, AND HE COMMITTED GERMANY TO FIGHTING ON AN EVER-WIDENING NUMBER OF FRONTS. THIS WAS TO LEAD TO A FATEFUL DECISION.

ON JULY 19, 1940, in the first flush of the victory won in France, and in a conscious echo of Napoleon, Hitler created 12 new field marshals and elevated Hermann Göring, chief of the Luftwaffe, to the rank of Reichsmarschall. He also made an hour-long speech in which, as "the victor speaking in the name of reason," he appealed to the British to come to terms. He "could see no reason why this war should go on." Almost a month later he told his new field marshals that Germany "was not striving to smash Britain" because the ultimate beneficiaries of its destruction would not be Germany, but rather Japan in the east, Russia in India, Italy in the Mediterranean, and the United States in world trade. He still hoped for peace with Britain—indeed, he considered it inevitable that Britain would have no alternative but to capitulate.

THE FIRST "HAPPY TIME"

The capture of naval bases on the Norwegian and French Atlantic coasts gave Germany the chance to starve the British into submission by deploying its U-boat fleet, commerce raiders, heavy units of its surface fleet, and long-range patrol aircraft. The British had adopted the convoy system in 1939, but they were hamstrung by a shortage of escorts, many of which were retained in home waters until the fear of invasion passed. This left the field free for Admiral Karl Dönitz's U-boats to operate in "wolf packs," attacking the U-boats at night. The U-boat crews were to remember this period as the "Happy Time," and between July and October 1940 they sank 217 ships for the loss of only two U-boats.

The commander-in-chief of the German Navy, Grand Admiral Erich Raeder, urged Hitler to strike at Britain in the Mediterranean Sea by capturing Gibraltar at the western end, in the so-called Felix Plan, and to apply pressure at the eastern end in the Balkans. He also advocated the seizure of French North Africa—as a means of supporting Italy in Libya and threatening the British in Egypt— and the capture of the Spanish and Portuguese possessions of the Azores, Canaries, and Cape Verde islands, so severing Britain's supply lines in the western and mid-Atlantic. This prospect appealed to Hitler, but would also further exacerbate Germany's relations with the United States. At this stage, Hitler did not rate the United States as a military power. Nevertheless, he was an unqualified admirer of its industrial might and was reluctant to add it to his growing list of enemies.

CAMPAIGNS IN THE BALKANS

On October 4, 1940, Hitler met Mussolini at the Brenner Pass, on the border between Germany and Italy. Here it was decided to enlist the support of a third dictator, the Spanish General Franco, in the Felix Plan by offering him part of French North Africa. Vichy France would be compensated with a chunk of British West Africa. However, neither Franco nor Marshal Pétain, the leader of Vichy France who impressed Hitler with his hostility to Britain, would entertain the plan. Hitler's calculations were thrown into further disarray when, on October 28, Mussolini—piqued at not being consulted about the movement of German troops into Romania earlier in the month—launched an invasion of Greece from Albania. There was, perhaps, a sound strategic reason for Mussolini to deprive the British of naval and air bases in the Adriatic, but the principal driving force for his Greek adventure was an overweening desire to emulate Hitler, a former admirer whose power now far outstripped his own.

The immediate effect of the Italian invasion of Greece was to torpedo Hitler's attempts to secure the Balkans as a compliant satellite zone by peaceful diplomacy. Hard on its heels came the British decision to occupy the islands of Crete and Lemnos, placing the Romanian oilfields—the principal source of German oil—within the range of British bombers. The invasion foundered as soon as it ran into determined Greek resistance, which steadily pushed the Italians back beyond the Albanian border. Hitler watched with growing

"We've already reached our first objective, which we weren't supposed to get to until the end of May. The British are falling over each other to get away. Our casualties small. Booty can't be estimated."

GENERAL ERWIN ROMMEL IN A LETTER TO HIS WIFE, DESCRIBING
THE GERMAN OFFENSIVE IN NORTH AFRICA IN APRIL 1941

Tank battle in Libya
Panzer Mark IIs of Rommel's Afrika Korps
block the progress of the British offensive,
Operation Crusader, in November 1941.
A grim two-week tank battle was fought
around the airfield at Sidi Rezegh as the
British tried to break through to Tobruk.

"The fight will be very different from the fight in the west; in the east harshness is kindness toward the future. The leaders must force themselves to sacrifice their scruples."

FROM THE DIARY OF FRANZ HALDER, GERMAN ARMY CHIEF OF STAFF, AFTER A SPEECH BY HITLER TO SENIOR OFFICERS, MARCH 30, 1941

concern before deciding to intervene. In March 1941 he successfully pressured Bulgaria into joining Germany and Italy in the Axis and then did the same to a reluctant Yugoslavia, which subsequently agreed to permit the transit of German troops.

OPERATIONS IN AFRICA

Mussolini, who was fast becoming a strategic embarrassment, also needed propping up. Luftwaffe formations were despatched to Sicily and, in February 1941, General Rommel was appointed commander of the German force sent to support the Italian troops in Libya, where in the previous three months a large Italian army under Marshal Rodolfo Graziani had been forced to retreat by the much smaller British Western Desert Force under General Sir Richard O'Connor. A month later, O'Connor was taken prisoner during Rommel's first offensive in North Africa. Between March and June 1941 Rommel was to recapture all of the territory taken by the British since December 1940.

On March 27, 1941 the government of Yugoslavia was overthrown (just two days after the country had joined the Axis), and the regent, Prince Paul, was forced into exile. The new government immediately

made friendly overtures to the Soviet Union and Britain. Hitler's response was to go on the offensive in the Balkans in Operation Marita, which was launched on April 6, 1941. Yugoslavia was overrun in ten days, and the conquest of Greece took just over two weeks. The British evacuated some 18,000 troops from Greece to Crete, which was captured by the Germans at the end of May after an airborne invasion. Nine British warships were sunk and a total of 17 badly damaged in a second evacuation.

The German victory in Crete was gained at a cost of nearly 10,000 casualties. Alarmed by the scale of these losses, Hitler canceled a proposed airborne seizure of the strategically crucial British colony of Malta, in the central Mediterranean, which was supplied by regular naval convoys from Gibraltar. Both the convoys and the island continued to suffer constant attacks from the Luftwaffe and the Italian air force, but the island remained an Allied stronghold, serving as the vital link in the supply line between Gibraltar and Alexandria.

RELATIONS WITH THE SOVIET UNION

In early November 1940 Hitler had conferred with the Soviet foreign minister, Molotov, in Berlin, but their talks had been unproductive. Molotov was unimpressed by an offer to share with Germany the spoils of a dismembered British Empire and insisted on the full implementation of the terms of the Nazi-Soviet Pact. He also demanded that the Soviet Union should be free to annex Finland and should have freedom of access to the North Sea via the Baltic—a matter of extreme sensitivity to Germany. In addition, he wanted Bulgaria's borders to be guaranteed. When he finally departed, an enraged Hitler was convinced that the final confrontation with Bolshevism could be delayed no longer.

Since October 1940, when Hitler had canceled Operation Sea Lion—the projected invasion of England—his overriding strategic preoccupation had been the invasion of the Soviet Union. He was

German troops at the Parthenon
The Germans entered Athens almost unopposed on April 27, 1941, while Greek troops helped cover the evacuation of the British expeditionary force. The Germans had conquered Yugoslavia and Greece in less than three weeks.

driven by the conviction that German hegemony in Europe could be secured only by the seizing of *Lebensraum* (living space) in the east and, with it, the industry and agricultural land that would ensure Germany's survival as a world power. A new German empire would reach a line stretching south from Archangel to Astrakhan, the so-called "A-A line," some 2,000 miles (3,200 km) east of Berlin.

In July 1940 Hitler informed Field Marshal Walther von Brauchitsch, commander-in-chief of the German Army, and General Franz Halder, his chief of staff, that the transfer of divisions from western Europe to the east was to be accelerated. By the spring of 1941, 120 German divisions would be massed on the border of the Soviet Union, ostensibly as a response to the Soviet occupation of the Baltic states of Latvia, Lithuania, and Estonia in June 1940, and the annexation of Bessarabia and Bukovina from Romania in the same month.

PLANNING THE INVASION

From the summer of 1940 both OKW (the German armed forces high command) and OKH (the German Army high command) were preoccupied

with drafting plans for the invasion of the Soviet Union. The evolution of the operation went through three distinct phases. In August 1940 the initial plans placed the principal thrusts in the north, through Byelorussia and toward Moscow, and in the south toward Kiev. In December, Halder proposed a variant, adding a third thrust in the direction of Leningrad and strengthening the drive on Moscow, where Soviet political authority was concentrated, at the expense of the advance on Kiev. To this Hitler added his own variant, in which the emphasis shifted north, with Leningrad as the main objective, while the operation in the south was reduced to the occupation of the western Ukraine.

At joint staff discussions held in Berlin on December 5, the specter of Napoleon's retreat from Moscow in 1812 was a nagging reminder of the perils inherent in an invasion of the Soviet Union. The sheer scale of the country's interior threatened to swallow the armies of the Third Reich just as it

had devoured Napoleon's Grande Armée in 1812. However, Hitler believed that the Red Army could be destroyed close to the frontier in a series of "cauldron battles" in which fast-moving German armor would encircle the Red Army's major elements in huge pockets before they were ground to bits by the follow-up infantry.

The joint staff deliberations of early December 1940 were embodied in Führer Directive 21, which was issued on December 18. At Hitler's insistence the directive emphasized the destruction of the Red Army in the Baltic region and the capture of Leningrad at the expense of the drive on Moscow in the central sector. The directive also gave the operation a codename, Barbarossa, after the medieval Holy Roman Emperor, and laid down that planning was to be completed by mid-May 1941.

German treatment of Soviet partisans
Members of a German army execution squad force Soviet partisans to dig their own graves. The German troops who invaded the Soviet Union in June 1941 often treated civilians in the conquered territories with great cruelty.

Hitler's intervention in the Balkans in the spring of 1941 was to delay the launch of Operation Barbarossa by approximately a month, to June 22, 1941. The extent to which this affected the operation's outcome is debatable. What is certain is that the delay had less of an impact than the confusion about the operation's precise goals, which had been introduced by Hitler at the planning stage in December 1940. Combined with the unforgiving Soviet climate, this confusion was fatally to undermine Hitler's greatest strategic gamble.

NAVAL WAR IN EUROPEAN AND ATLANTIC WATERS

SEPTEMBER 1939–SEPTEMBER 1941

Despite losses to U-boats, bombers, and mines and the failure of the Allied expedition to Norway, up until June 1940 Britain was able to contain the German threat at sea. The fall of France in June 1940 altered everything. From their new bases in western France U-boats began to wreak havoc on British convoys.

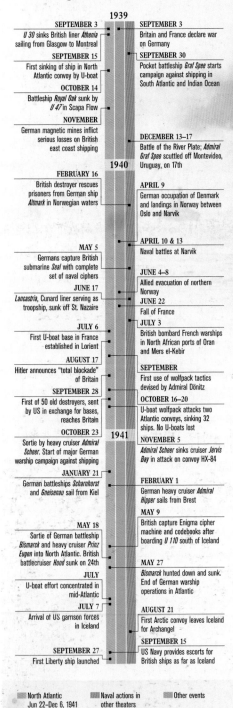

1939

SEPTEMBER 3
U 30 sinks British liner *Athenia* sailing from Glasgow to Montreal

SEPTEMBER 3
Britain and France declare war on Germany

SEPTEMBER 15
First sinking of ship in North Atlantic convoy by U-boat

SEPTEMBER 30
Pocket battleship *Graf Spee* starts campaign against shipping in South Atlantic and Indian Ocean

OCTOBER 14
Battleship *Royal Oak* sunk by *U 47* in Scapa Flow

NOVEMBER
German magnetic mines inflict serious losses on British east coast shipping

DECEMBER 13–17
Battle of the River Plate; *Admiral Graf Spee* scuttled off Montevideo, Uruguay, on 17th

1940

FEBRUARY 16
British destroyer rescues prisoners from German ship *Altmark* in Norwegian waters

APRIL 9
German occupation of Denmark and landings in Norway between Oslo and Narvik

APRIL 10 & 13
Naval battles at Narvik

MAY 5
Germans capture British submarine *Seal* with complete set of naval ciphers

JUNE 4–8
Allied evacuation of northern Norway

JUNE 17
Lancastria, Cunard liner serving as troopship, sunk off St. Nazaire

JUNE 22
Fall of France

JULY 6
First U-boat base in France established in Lorient

JULY 3
British bombard French warships in North African ports of Oran and Mers el-Kebir

AUGUST 17
Hitler announces "total blockade" of Britain

SEPTEMBER
First use of wolfpack tactics devised by Admiral Dönitz

SEPTEMBER 28
First of 50 old destroyers, sent by US in exchange for bases, reaches Britain

OCTOBER 16–20
U-boat wolfpack attacks two Atlantic convoys, sinking 32 ships. No U-boats lost

OCTOBER 23
Sortie by heavy cruiser *Admiral Scheer*. Start of major German warship campaign against shipping

NOVEMBER 5
Admiral Scheer sinks cruiser *Jervis Bay* in attack on convoy HX-84

1941

JANUARY 21
German battleships *Scharnhorst* and *Gneisenau* sail from Kiel

FEBRUARY 1
German heavy cruiser *Admiral Hipper* sails from Brest

MAY 9
British capture Enigma cipher machine and codebooks after boarding *U 110* south of Iceland

MAY 18
Sortie of German battleship *Bismarck* and heavy cruiser *Prinz Eugen* into North Atlantic. British battlecruiser *Hood* sunk on 24th

MAY 27
Bismarck hunted down and sunk. End of German warship operations in Atlantic

JULY
U-boat effort concentrated in mid-Atlantic

JULY 7
Arrival of US garrison forces in Iceland

AUGUST 21
First Arctic convoy leaves Iceland for Archangel

SEPTEMBER 27
First Liberty ship launched

SEPTEMBER 15
US Navy provides escorts for British ships as far as Iceland

■ North Atlantic
Jun 22–Dec 6, 1941

■ Naval actions in other theaters
Jun 22–Dec 6, 1941

■ Other events

THE WAR AT SEA

AT THE OUTBREAK OF WAR in September 1939, Britain and France enjoyed a major strategic advantage over Germany at sea. Their geographical position allowed them to cut off German lines of communication with the world beyond Europe, and their command of ports, coaling stations, and narrows throughout the world meant that German oceanic trade all but ended with the start of war. A total of 76 ships returned to Germany, evading Allied patrols, but the greater part of German shipping outside Europe sought the safety of neutral ports.

Britain and France also had a huge advantage in terms of numbers. For most of the interwar period the size of the Kriegsmarine (the German Navy) and of individual warships was limited by treaty, and the coming of war in 1939 found Germany

massively outnumbered in every type of warship. In September 1939 it had just four battleships, three armoured, one heavy, and three light cruisers, 34 destroyers, and 57 submarines. It also had no air arm of its own, and in the early part of the war the Luftwaffe proved uncooperative. Jealous of its independence and primarily committed to air support of the army, the Luftwaffe had little interest in naval operations. At any rate, it had very few long-range aircraft suitable for operations over the sea.

Coastal U-boat
In 1939 Germany had more Class II coastal U-boats than any other kind. These were only suitable for operations in the Baltic or North Sea, not for long-range missions.

British minesweepers in the North Sea
At the start of the war the greatest danger to British shipping was not the U-boat, but mines. The danger was contained, but only at the expense of a heavy defensive commitment. In May 1945 the British had over 700 minesweepers and auxiliaries.

In the interwar period the German Navy, despite the failure of its submarine campaign against shipping in World War I, convinced itself that the war at sea was an economic, not a military struggle. The seeking of battle at sea was a distraction to be avoided. German naval staff argued that if they could sink 750,000 tons of shipping every month for a year Britain would be defeated. This was exactly the same "tonnage war" argument that it had used in 1916, the necessary tonnage having increased slightly in the intervening years.

BRITISH ASSUMPTIONS

Throughout the interwar period Britain had paid little attention to the defense of shipping. There was a general confidence that use of convoys—along with ASDIC, the sonar system for locating submerged submarines—would be enough to defeat the U-boat menace. With the outbreak of war the British intention was to close the Dover Strait by defensive mining and to mine and patrol northern waters, while RAF Coastal Command covered the North Sea. Any threat outside these waters, it was believed, would be small and short-lived.

FIRST U-BOAT CAMPAIGN

The first seven months of war more or less bore out these British calculations. Without a balanced fleet and supporting air arm, German naval effectiveness was limited. At the outbreak of war Germany had only 27 ocean-going U-boats, of which 17 were at sea. There were striking successes by individual U-boats against warships, such as the sinking of the aircraft carrier *Courageous* while on antisubmarine duty in the Western Approaches and of the battleship *Royal Oak* at Scapa Flow. The U-boat campaign against merchant shipping, however, did not give Britain cause for serious alarm. In 1939 German submarines sank 114 merchantmen, but only 12 of these were sailing in convoy. The cycle of operations, with U-boats returning to port for refitting, meant that the rate of monthly sinkings actually declined in November–December 1939.

SURFACE RAIDERS AND MINES

For the first six months of the war most German surface warships remained in port. The armored cruiser (or "pocket battleship") *Admiral Graf Spee* made a menacing sortie and succeeded in sinking nine merchantmen in the South Atlantic and the Indian Ocean. She was eventually intercepted by three cruisers in December at the Battle of the Plate River. The captain scuttled the ship after seeking refuge in Montevideo. The first German auxiliary cruisers sailed in March 1940. In all, six of these raiders—converted merchantmen with concealed guns and torpedo tubes, equipped for long voyages—sailed in the spring of 1940. It was not until July, however, that these raiders managed to sink 10 merchantmen in a single month.

In many ways the most effective German weapon in the early months of the war was the mine. Between September 1939 and April 1940 a total of 128 merchantmen of 429,899 tons were sunk by mines

Torpedo room
The standard German torpedo was electrically driven. Armed with a warhead of 617 lb (280 kg), it was 21 in (53.3 cm) in diameter.

This latter part of the action has attracted many spectators and, unfortunately, their cars. Headlights along the shore with other illuminations possibly allow Graf Spee to detect our stealthy approach, and at 20:48 when we race past, guns in her huge turrets wave like a robot's arms elevating whilst training on to our blurred outline. And then she lurches under her own heavy recoil, thunder rolls across a grey sky to quicken the heartbeats of excited Uruguayans watching her vivid gunflashes through enveloping bursts of cordite smoke.

FROM *HMNZS ACHILLES* BY JACK HARKER, WIRELESS TELEGRAPHIST ON THE *ACHILLES* AT THE BATTLE OF THE PLATE RIVER

laid by German U-boats, destroyers, and aircraft. This was about a third of all Allied and neutral losses to mines in the course of the whole war. The reason for this success was the use of a magnetic firing mechanism that detonated as a ship passed over the mine. Fortunately for the British merchant fleet, metal hulls could be demagnetized and new methods of minesweeping were soon developed to counter the threat. Even so, mines continued to cause serious delays and disruption to shipping.

ENIGMA AND ULTRA

ENIGMA, THE GERMAN ENCODING MACHINE developed in the 1920s and 1930s, was a portable electromechanical device resembling a typewriter. Each keystroke set in motion a series of rotors and electrical circuits. The Germans believed that the system was totally secure. Even with a captured machine, the enemy needed to know the current code and settings for the day. The German services each had different codes: the Luftwaffe's were relatively simple, those of the navy the most complex. The Poles had managed to read some Enigma messages during the 1930s and their assistance was of great value to the British decryption unit set up in Bletchley Park in 1939.

Intelligence gathered from Enigma intercepts was highly sensitive. The Allies could not let the Germans know that they were able to read coded radio signals. Intelligence gathered in this way was code-named Ultra and was used with extreme caution. The Germans never realized that their Enigma codes had been cracked.

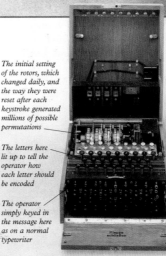

The initial setting of the rotors, which changed daily, and the way they were reset after each keystroke generated millions of possible permutations

The letters here lit up to tell the operator how each letter should be encoded

The operator simply keyed in the message here as on a normal typewriter

Enigma machine
As the machine spelled out the coded message, this was copied down letter by letter, then transmitted in Morse code.

U-boat surfacing
Enigma gave a fairly constant picture of U-boat positions, often allowing convoys to be rerouted.

The war at sea was completely transformed in spring 1940 with the German occupation of Norway and northern and western France. At a stroke German warships, submarines, and bombers could reach far out into the North Atlantic to strike directly at Allied shipping. At the same time the threat of invasion meant that the British navy had to keep large numbers of warships in home waters even at the expense of the shipping and trade on which Britain depended. In addition, Italy's entry into the war meant a greater naval commitment in the Mediterranean and also forced shipping to make the lengthy diversion around the Cape of Good Hope. Such were the circumstances that made for what the Germans came to call their first *Glückliche Zeit* (Happy Time), when their submarines began to inflict serious losses on Allied and neutral shipping.

A TRIPLE ASSAULT ON SHIPPING
Between September 1939 and July 1941 German U-boats sank 848 British, Allied, and neutral merchantmen of 4,058,909 tons, for the loss of just 43 of their number. U-boats, however, were not the only threat to Britain's vital trade. In the first five months of 1941, when Allied shipping losses averaged 490,456 tons a month, the Luftwaffe accounted for about 30 percent of the total. The Luftwaffe did not begin operations in the Atlantic under the control of the U-boat arm until February 1941. Many of its successes in this period, however, were obtained not in the Atlantic, but in the eastern Mediterranean by short-range bombers during the German conquest of Greece in April 1941.

These results were complemented by four sorties into the Atlantic by warships between October 1940 and May 1941,

The apparatus was powered by rechargeable battery

The telephone was used principally by the captain for issuing orders and receiving status reports

Portable telephone from *U 219*
Telephones were used for communication between the various parts of a U-boat, for example the boiler room, the torpedo rooms, and even the conning tower.

which accounted for 47 merchantmen of 254,759 tons and caused massive disruption in convoy sailings. The most successful cruise was that of the pocket battleship *Admiral Scheer*, which sailed on October 27, 1940, sank 16 ships, including three in the Indian Ocean, evaded all her pursuers, and returned to Bergen on March 30, 1941. The battleships *Scharnhorst* and *Gneisenau* enjoyed similar success, together sinking or capturing 22 ships between January and March 1941.

Perhaps the main weakness of the German war against shipping was the fact that for most of the war it was pursued primarily by the U-boat service with very little support from the Luftwaffe or from the rest of the navy. In this period, however, with major contributions from the Luftwaffe and from warships, the combined effort achieved a level of success that seemed to augur very badly for Britain.

REVERSING THE TREND
By spring 1941, however, various factors were combining to bring this period of easy German success to an end. The brief, ill-fated sortie of the battleship *Bismarck* in May spelled the end of raiding operations by major warships. After her sinking on May 27, 1941, the German naval staff concluded that, with Britain's air search and carrier strike capabilities in the North Atlantic, such operations were now too risky. This was followed by the German attack on the Soviet Union in June 1941, which led to a long-term commitment of air power to the Eastern Front. The Luftwaffe's contribution to the German effort at sea declined sharply after

Dining aboard a U-boat
Living conditions on a U-boat, with its cramped berths and limited sanitary arrangements, were not good. The men, however, were well fed. When fresh food ran out, there were hams and sausages, and canned vegetables and fruit.

May 1941. In 1941 the Luftwaffe accounted for 23.5 percent of Allied losses, but this was reduced to a mere 9 percent in 1942.

STRENGTHENING THE CONVOYS

The most important British countermeasure was the introduction in July 1941 of continuous two-way escort across the North Atlantic. Despite the loss of 55 destroyers and eight escorts, Britain now had 395 escorts with another 306 under construction. It was slowly acquiring sufficient numbers to establish a comprehensive convoy system throughout and beyond the North Atlantic. Since January 1941 escorts had been equipped with radar, the first step in stripping U-boats of their invisibility when conducting attacks on the surface under cover of darkness. This was backed up by new, more powerful depth charges and more effective firing patterns.

Convoys could now count on reconnaissance and support provided by increasing numbers of aircraft, equipped with effective airborne radar and improved weapons, including airborne depth charges. Aircraft were deployed to Iceland in April 1941 and the first escort carrier accompanied a convoy in September.

For the first 18 months of the war the German Navy had held a clear intelligence advantage over the British. B-Dienst (Beobachtungs-Dienst, the

U-boats in dry dock
German U-boats *U 106* and *U 124* undergo repairs in the French port of Brest. Only a small fraction of total U-boat strength was operational at any one time.

German intelligence service) had broken British naval codes and could quickly decipher radio traffic. In the course of 1941, however, the British managed to crack the German Navy's Enigma code. Messages took time to decipher, but the two sides were now competing on more equal terms. The British had also developed better means of locating and tracking broadcasting U-boats.

In April 1941 the United States claimed that its defense zone extended as far as 26° West, almost to Iceland. After July all US shipping was escorted to and from Iceland and after September US ships also escorted British shipping in the Western Atlantic. Hitler, seeking to avoid a clash with the United States, scaled back German operations in the North Atlantic. U-boats now operated chiefly in waters where British escorts were at their most numerous. Construction programs, meanwhile, lagged behind the German Navy's requirements. In February 1941 just 21 U-boats were operational. There were simply not enough to take advantage of British vulnerability. Between June and December 1941 monthly Allied shipping losses fell to an average of 268,039 tons, a decrease of 5.4 percent from the average over the previous five months.

THE SINKING OF THE BISMARCK

AT 42,000 TONS AND ARMED with eight 15-in (38-cm) guns, the *Bismarck* and her sister ship the *Tirpitz* were Germany's two most powerful battleships. The British had been awaiting their completion with some trepidation. First to be commisssioned was the *Bismarck* in August 1940. After trials in the Baltic she sailed from Gotenhafen in the Gulf of Danzig in May 1941. Then, accompanied by the heavy cruiser *Prinz Eugen*, she left the Baltic for the North Sea.

The British knew the ships were heading for the Atlantic and despatched patrols to hunt for them. On May 23 the two ships were spotted in the Denmark Strait between Iceland and Greenland and the following day the battleship *Prince of Wales* and the battlecruiser *Hood* intercepted them. Both the *Bismarck* and the *Prinz Eugen* concentrated their fire on the *Hood*. A shell struck the British ship's magazine, causing a massive explosion, and she split in two. Only three of her crew of 1,421 survived.

The *Bismarck* had been damaged in the encounter and received minor damage that night when hit by a Swordfish torpedo-bomber from the carrier *Victorious*. Her admiral then decided to make for Brest, but on May 26 she was spotted by a Catalina flying boat, then crippled in an attack by Swordfish from the carrier *Ark Royal*. The next day, as British warships from across the Atalantic closed in for the kill, she was sunk by the battleships *King George V* and *Rodney*.

The fortunate few
Survivors from the *Bismarck* struggle to climb aboard the cruiser *Dorsetshire*. Only 115 of the 2,222 officers and men in the *Bismarck* were rescued.

The *Bismarck* in action
This picture of the *Bismarck* firing on the *Prince of Wales*, after the sinking of the *Hood*, was taken from the *Prinz Eugen* on the morning of May 24.

AFRICA, THE MIDDLE EAST, AND THE MEDITERRANEAN
JUNE 1940–FEBRUARY 1942

Italy aimed to challenge Britain for control of the Mediterranean and to move on Egypt and the Suez Canal, and the British colonies in East Africa. In addition to these threats, the British had to fight to counter German influence in the Middle East. Early in 1941, as Italian offensives collapsed, Germany was forced to come to the aid of its weaker ally.

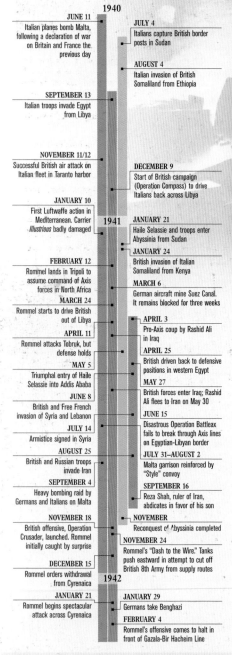

1940

JUNE 11
Italian planes bomb Malta, following a declaration of war on Britain and France the previous day

JULY 4
Italians capture British border posts in Sudan

AUGUST 4
Italian invasion of British Somaliland from Ethiopia

SEPTEMBER 13
Italian troops invade Egypt from Libya

NOVEMBER 11/12
Successful British air attack on Italian fleet in Taranto harbor

DECEMBER 9
Start of British campaign (Operation Compass) to drive Italians back across Libya

JANUARY 10
First Luftwaffe action in Mediterranean. Carrier *Illustrious* badly damaged

1941

JANUARY 21
Haile Selassie and troops enter Abyssinia from Sudan

JANUARY 24
British invasion of Italian Somaliland from Kenya

FEBRUARY 12
Rommel lands in Tripoli to assume command of Axis forces in North Africa

MARCH 6
German aircraft mine Suez Canal. It remains blocked for three weeks

MARCH 24
Rommel starts to drive British out of Libya

APRIL 3
Pro-Axis coup by Rashid Ali in Iraq

APRIL 11
Rommel attacks Tobruk, but defense holds

APRIL 25
British driven back to defensive positions in western Egypt

MAY 5
Triumphal entry of Haile Selassie into Addis Ababa

MAY 27
British forces enter Iraq; Rashid Ali flees to Iran on May 30

JUNE 8
British and Free French invasion of Syria and Lebanon

JUNE 15
Disastrous Operation Battleax fails to break through Axis lines on Egyptian-Libyan border

JULY 14
Armistice signed in Syria

JULY 31–AUGUST 2
Malta garrison reinforced by "Style" convoy

AUGUST 25
British and Russian troops invade Iran

SEPTEMBER 16
Reza Shah, ruler of Iran, abdicates in favor of his son

SEPTEMBER 4
Heavy bombing raid by Germans and Italians on Malta

NOVEMBER
Reconquest of Abyssinia completed

NOVEMBER 18
British offensive, Operation Crusader, launched. Rommel initially caught by surprise

NOVEMBER 24
Rommel's "Dash to the Wire." Tanks push eastward in attempt to cut off British 8th Army from supply routes

DECEMBER 15
Rommel orders withdrawal from Cyrenaica

1942

JANUARY 21
Rommel begins spectacular attack across Cyrenaica

JANUARY 29
Germans take Benghazi

FEBRUARY 4
Rommel's offensive comes to halt in front of Gazala-Bir Hacheim Line

■ Mediterranean Jun 1940–Feb 1942   ■ East Africa Jul 1940–Nov 1941
■ North Africa Sept 1940–Feb 1942   ■ Middle East Jun–Sept 1941

CAMPAIGNS IN AFRICA AND THE MIDDLE EAST

MUSSOLINI'S DECISION to bring Italy into the war immediately opened another theater—the Mediterranean and North Africa. With France rapidly collapsing, the initial phase would be fought just between an Italy determined to make the Mediterranean its own and expand its African empire and a Britain desperate to maintain its lines of communication through the Mediterranean and the Suez Canal. While the British Mediterranean Fleet and Force H based in Gibraltar could match the Italian Navy, on land and in the air British forces faced overwhelmingly superior numbers. Including those based on the mainland, the Italians had some 1,700 aircraft; the British had a mere 205 serviceable planes in Egypt and a further 163 in East Africa. Most were obsolete or obsolescent and, with the Battle of Britain about to begin, there was little prospect of any reinforcement. On the ground the situation appeared even more desperate. To protect Egypt and police Palestine and Iraq, the British had just 63,000 troops. The main threat came from Libya, which had 250,000 Italian and indigenous troops, while to the south 300,000 more Italian and native troops in Abyssinia and Eritrea faced a mere 10,000 British troops in Sudan, British Somaliland, and Kenya. At sea the British were determined to bring the Italians into battle, but elsewhere they naturally opted for the defensive.

FIRST CLASHES
There were minor bombing raids by both sides during the first few weeks. A naval clash took place off the Calabrian coast on July 9, 1940. The Italian fleet withdrew to port after its flagship was damaged. On the ground, the British were expecting the Italians to invade Egypt from Libya. To keep them off balance, they adopted a policy of aggressive patrolling on the Libyan side of the border. The first Italian move, however, came on July 4, when they seized a number of frontier posts on Sudan's borders with Abyssinia and Eritrea. This was followed in early August by an invasion of British Somaliland from Abyssinia. After two weeks' fighting, the small British garrison was withdrawn to Aden. Churchill now took the brave step, in view of Britain's parlous position, of sending further ships to reinforce the

German reinforcements, April 1941
Airplanes and tanks made operations in Libya extremely mobile, as the two sides took turns pursuing the other across the desert. Here, German light tanks, recently arrived in Tripoli, are marshaled in preparation for Rommel's first offensive in March 1941.

Mediterranean Fleet and a troop convoy, which included 150 tanks. This, however, had to be routed around the Cape of Good Hope and did not reach Egypt until late September. By this time, the Italians had entered Egypt from Libya. After advancing a mere 60 miles (100 km), they halted and established a network of fortified camps. The arrival of the additional British tanks deterred them from pressing toward the Suez Canal.

BRITISH SUCCESS
General Sir Archibald Wavell, the British commander in the Middle East, now set in motion preparations for a counteroffensive in Egypt and for the conquest of Italian East Africa. At sea, the British adopted the policy of using supply convoys to Malta to tempt the Italian fleet out of the port. This was unsuccessful and so Admiral Sir Andrew Cunningham conceived a daring plan. On the night of November 11–12, 1940, carrier-borne torpedo-armed Swordfish aircraft attacked the naval base at

Taranto, severely damaging three of Italy's six battleships, and forcing its fleet to withdraw to more distant bases on Italy's west coast.

Wavell's attack on the Italians in Egypt was launched in the early hours of December 9. The troops

The Swordfish had a top speed of 138 mph (222 kph) and just one rear machine-gun for protection

Fixed undercarriage

The normal bombload was a single 1,610-lb (730-kg) torpedo carried under the fuselage

Aircraft carriers
British aircraft carriers, such as the *Ark Royal* (above), played a vital role in the protection of Mediterranean convoys. The main offensive carrier aircraft was the obsolete torpedo-bomber, the Fairey Swordfish (left).

taking part thought that it was merely an exercise until shortly before H-hour. This tight security worked, since the Italians were taken totally by surprise. Within two days their camps had been overrun and after a further 24 hours they were left with just three small toeholds in Egypt. At this juncture, Wavell replaced the 4th Indian Division, which was sent to Sudan in preparation for the offensive against East Africa, with the newly arrived

6th Australian Division. The Australians took the port of Bardia on January 5 and advanced along the coast, reaching Tobruk two days later. The port was besieged, but the British needed to pause since their rapid advance was overstretching their supply lines, a problem that was to characterize the Desert War. However, the fall of Tobruk on January 22 did much to ease the supply situation. Wavell now gave orders to push on to Benghazi.

THE ISLAND OF MALTA UNDER SIEGE

MALTA'S KEY STRATEGIC POSITION made it the traditional base of the British Mediterranean Fleet. When Italy declared war in June 1940, one of its first acts was an air attack on the island, which lies just 60 miles (100 km) from Sicily. The Italians knew that if they could seize it, they would deny the British the central Mediterranean and remove a major threat to their supply lines to North Africa. The air offensive against Malta intensified when Luftwaffe units were deployed to Sicily at the beginning of 1941. Even though they had moved their main fleet base to Alexandria, the British were determined to hang on to Malta, but the cost would be high. Every supply convoy had to have a heavy naval escort and during the two years beginning August 1940 over one-third of the merchant vessels sent out never reached the island. Food became desperately short and the Maltese had to endure starvation rations, as well as the destruction of much of the island's infrastructure.

Valletta under bombardment
During March and April 1942 alone, Axis aircraft dropped twice the bomb tonnage on Malta that London had endured in the Blitz.

The bombing did ease in June 1941, when many Luftwaffe units were redeployed for the invasion of the Soviet Union, but at the end of the year it resumed in intensity. Even so, Malta-based aircraft and submarines continued to disrupt the Axis supply lines. The German commander-in-chief in the Mediterranean, Field Marshal Albert Kesselring, was determined to break Malta's resistance. The Axis had laid so many minefields in the waters around Malta that it was almost impossible for a ship to get in or out and by early May Kesselring was convinced that Malta had been neutralized. He therefore diverted many of his Luftwaffe units to other missions. The arrival, however, of some much needed replacement fighters restored morale on the island, as did the clearance of lanes in some of the minefields. But the crisis was not yet over.

In June a crucial convoy failed to get through and rations on the island were cut to 1,500 calories per day. Kesselring then launched a further air assault in October, but Montgomery's victory at El Alamein and the subsequent capture of the Axis airfields in Libya eased the situation once more. The siege was not yet over, but food and other essentials now got through on a regular basis.

George Cross
In recognition of the steadfast resistance of the islanders, King George VI awarded Malta the George Cross, Britain's highest decoration for civilian bravery.

While the Australians pursued the Italian 10th Army along the coast road, the 7th Armoured Division was sent inland to the base of the Cyrenaican "bulge," which is dominated by the semimountainous Jebel el Akhdar. The Australians were temporarily stalled by a strong Italian position just to the west of Derna. Simultaneously, RAF reconnaissance reported that the Italians were evacuating the port of Benghazi. General Dick O'Connor, the operational commander, decided to send the 7th Armoured Division to cut the coast road south of Benghazi. The tanks drove 150 miles (240 km) in 33 hours over rock-strewn terrain and arrived at the road, 70 miles (110 km) south of Benghazi, late on February 5. They were just in time to establish a blocking position.

During the next two days, as the Australians secured Benghazi, the 7th Armoured Division fended off repeated Italian attempts to break through. Eventually, the Italians decided that they had had enough and 20,000 surrendered, adding to the total of 100,000 prisoners already netted during the campaign. The Battle of Beda Fomm marked the final destruction of the Italian 10th Army and the capture of the whole of the eastern Libyan province of Cyrenaica. It was also the British Army's first significant victory of the war. The triumph would, however, be short-lived.

ERITREA AND ABYSSINIA

Meanwhile, Wavell had launched another offensive, this time into Italian East Africa. His plan was for General William Platt, with two Indian divisions, to attack into Eritrea from Sudan. At much the same time, three divisions under General Alan Cunningham, brother of the Admiral, were to advance into Abyssinia from the south. Emperor Haile Selassie and his small force would enter from the west. Sensing what was about to happen and demoralized because of the increasingly grim news from Libya, the Italians withdrew from the outposts they had captured in Sudan just before the offensive opened. Platt crossed into Eritrea on January 19, 1941. The subsequent campaign was to be no walk-over, however. After a fierce battle for Agordat, the Italians withdrew to the mountain fortress of Keren, which guarded the only approach to Asmara, the Eritrean capital. Platt closed up to this position on

The battle for Keren
Indian troops survey the debris of a skirmish near the fortified town of Keren. An Italian truck lies beside the road. Keren proved the critical battle in the British campaign in the Italian colony of Eritrea.

February 3, but, with the Italians holding all the high ground, it proved impossible to force. He therefore decided to pause in order to strengthen his forces and improve his logistics.

In contrast, Cunningham made good progress in the more open country of southern Abyssinia. On February 25, he captured the port of Mogadishu and his forces then turned northward in two separate prongs, one aimed at the western part of the country and the other the center. A further element was added on March 16, when troops from Aden landed at Berbera and, within a week, had liberated British Somaliland. By now, Platt had resumed his attacks on Keren and, after two weeks' tough fighting, the fortress finally fell on March 27. This broke the back of the Italian resistance and within two weeks both Asmara and the port of Massawa were in British hands. Simultaneously, 11th African

THE RETURN OF THE EMPEROR

IN SPITE OF THEIR CONQUEST of Abyssinia in 1935, the Italians were unable to subdue the more remote mountainous areas. But, while the British gave Emperor Haile Selassie sanctuary, they were not prepared to provide open support for any resistance.

The situation changed once Italy entered the war. In June 1940 the emperor was flown out to Sudan and settled near Khartoum under the alias of Mr. Smith. Word soon got around that he had come to reclaim his throne. British plans included an offensive from the west, which the emperor would accompany. The principal element of this offensive was Gideon Force, under the command of Orde Wingate, a British officer who had established a reputation for irregular warfare in Palestine. Haile Selassie raised his standard inside Abyssinian territory on January 21, 1941. Gideon Force then began its advance. Wingate relied on bluff and daring. All forage and

food was paid for in Maria Theresa silver thalers dated 1764, which had been specially minted in Britain and was the one currency the locals respected.

Wingate's first major action came at the end of February, when, with 450 men, he surprised and routed a force of 7,000. Gideon Force then drove the Italians out of Debra Markos. Abyssinians had flocked to join their emperor and the Italians thought a whole British division was advancing against them. General Cunningham's troops had already taken Addis Ababa, but Haile Selassie, accompanied by Gideon Force, did enter his capital in triumph at the beginning of May.

Haile Selassie reviews his troops
Gideon Force, the irregular force that accompanied Haile Selassie, was made up of a Sudanese battalion and one of Abyssinian refugees known as the Patriots.

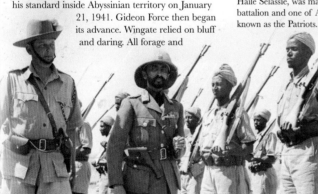

German and Italian cooperation
This propaganda photograph from the German *Signal* magazine shows German troops helping Italians manhandle a gun into position in the Libyan desert.

Division entered Addis Ababa on April 6. Yet, even with the Abyssinian capital in British hands, the campaign was not over. The Italian commander-in-chief, the Duke d'Aosta, had decided to make a stand in the fortress of Amba Alagi. It took 18 days to reduce the defenses in the hills surrounding the fortress, which finally surrendered on May 18, with the duke the last to leave it. Four days later, the fall of Soddu marked the end of the campaign in the south. The Italians continued to hold out in the mountains around Lake Tana in the northwest of Abyssinia and it would not be until the end of November 1941 that the last stronghold, Gondar, finally surrendered.

GERMAN SUPPORT FOR ITALY

Mussolini may have lost his East African empire, but in Egypt and Libya the situation changed dramatically during spring 1941. Hitler decided to give his ally some material support. He had, at the beginning of 1941, deployed elements of the Luftwaffe to Sicily to help in the air assault on Malta and an early victim was the carrier *Illustrious*, which was attacked by Stukas on January 10 and badly damaged. He also decided to send two mechanized divisions, as well as further aircraft, to Libya. Their commander, Erwin Rommel, arrived in Tripoli on February 12

and two days later his Deutsches Afrika Korps (DAK) began to unload its vehicles at the quayside. On the British side, the victors of the overrunning of Cyrenaica, 7th Armoured and 6th Australian Divisions, were sent back to the Nile Delta to reequip. Their places were taken by the newly arrived 2nd Armoured and 9th Australian Divisions, but part of the former was then diverted to Greece, where Churchill had ordered Wavell to send troops. Because there were insufficient fit British tanks available, part of the new division had to be equipped with inferior captured Italian models. At the time, though, it was not believed that the Axis would make an early attempt to regain Cyrenaica.

As early as February 24, DAK reconnaissance elements clashed with their British opposite numbers between Sirte and El Agheila. It was an indication that Rommel was impatient for action. By March 11, the first of his two divisions, the 5th Light, had deployed close to the border with Cyrenaica, but he himself was then ordered by his German superiors to await the arrival of the other division, which

Bersaglieri offroading
The Bersaglieri were a crack Italian corps of sharpshooters, who traditionally rode to the front on bicycles. In North Africa the more fortunate were issued with motorcycles.

was not due until the end of May, before attacking. Rommel was not, however, prepared to sit on his hands. On March 24 he drove the British out of El Agheila with comparative ease and was encouraged by this success to press on further. A week later he seized Mersa Brega and decided to clear the whole of Cyrenaica. The British were so taken by surprise that they decided on a voluntary withdrawal, but it was almost too late. Sending an Italian division up the coast road to Benghazi, Rommel took his own 5th Light Division and the Ariete Armored Division south of the Jebel el Akhdar, thus mirroring in reverse the British clearance of Cyrenaica at the beginning of the year.

By April 7, Rommel had cleared the Cyrenaican bulge and such was the British confusion that the new commander in Libya, General Philip Neame, and General O'Connor, who had been asked by Wavell to give him advice, were both captured. Some of their men were evacuated by sea from Tobruk, which was now to be held by 9th Australian Division with an additional brigade sent by sea from Egypt. The remainder withdrew back into Egypt. Given the disintegration of his opponent, Rommel would have liked to continue as far as the Suez Canal, but was ordered to halt on the Egyptian border and concentrate on capturing Tobruk, which had already resisted his initial attacks.

WAVELL UNDER PRESSURE

April 1941 was indeed a time of trouble for Wavell. The forces he had sent to Greece had to be withdrawn after another German blitzkrieg campaign. Then there was a revolt in Iraq led by Rashid Ali, who was in the pay of the Germans. An Indian brigade en route for Malaya had to be

*The tank's main armament was
a 2-pounder (40-mm), most
effective as an antitank weapon*

*The Matilda's strength was its
armor. At the front of the hull,
it was 3 in (78 mm) thick*

*This form of camouflage—sand,
blue, and gray—was widely used
in the desert campaign*

Matilda II
The British Matilda tank performed well in the opening exchanges in North Africa against antitank guns, but its armor was no match for the mighty German 88-mm gun.

The overrunning of Crete was another disaster, but no sooner had this occurred than Wavell was further distracted. Concern had been growing that the Vichy French in Syria were preparing to allow the Germans use of their airfields. This would have presented a grave threat to the British position in the Middle East. Therefore, on June 8, 1941, on Churchill's orders, Wavell invaded Syria. He had hoped that the Vichy French would offer only token resistance, but this was not to be. Not until mid-July did hostilities come to an end. By this time, Wavell had been relieved of his command.

Churchill had been determined that he strike once more at Rommel and lift the siege of Tobruk and had agreed to sending a reinforcement of tanks through the Mediterranean. This duly arrived and Wavell mounted another attack, code-named Battleaxe, on June 15. It was a disaster. Capuzzo was regained for a short time, but within 48 hours Rommel had driven the British back to their start line, with the loss of over 90 tanks. It was the last straw, as far as Churchill was concerned. Wavell was replaced by General Sir Claude Auchinleck.

THE GERMAN THREAT IN IRAN

Despite pressure from Churchill to resume the offensive against Rommel, Auchinleck wanted to wait until he had rebuilt his forces. He remained confident, however, that Tobruk would hold out. But before he could start preparing for a fresh attack, he was faced with another problem. The spectacular success the Germans were enjoying

Australian troops in Syria
The Syrian campaign was fought by Australian, Indian, British, and Free French forces. The Australians, advancing from Palestine, had nearly reached Beirut when the Vichy French requested an armistice on July 10, 1941.

in the Soviet Union created the possibility that they might launch an assault on the Middle East from the Caucasus. The Shah of Iran had adopted an anti-British stance and there were fears that he might allow the Germans free passage through his country. The Russians were equally concerned and both they and the British demanded access to Iran. When the Shah refused, they had no option but to invade, which they did on August 25. After two days, the Iranians asked for a ceasefire and installed a government more sympathetic to the Allies. Later, the Allies demanded that the Shah expel all Axis nationals and, when he was slow to do so, their troops occupied Tehran. The Shah promptly abdicated in favor of his son. Allied troops remained in Iran for the rest of the war and it became one of the routes used to keep the Soviet Union supplied with munitions from the West.

German supply planes in Libya
German and Italian forces often had to rely on aircraft for supplies. Most of planes here are Junkers Ju 52s, the three-engined transport plane that was the workhorse of the Luftwaffe throughout the war. In the right foreground is a Messerschmitt Bf 110 fighter.

hastily diverted and landed at Basra to protect the RAF airfield in Shaibah, but this did not deter Rashid Ali from laying siege to the other British air base in the country, Habbaniyah. Two more Indian brigades were landed during May, but Habbaniyah could only be relieved from the west and so Wavell had to organize a force in Palestine for this purpose. Not until the end of May was the revolt crushed.

FURTHER SUCCESS FOR ROMMEL

In the meantime, Wavell had suffered further reverses. On May 15 he launched Operation Brevity against the Axis positions on the frontier with Libya. His troops succeeded in regaining Capuzzo, Sollum, and the Halfaya Pass. But Rommel counterattacked the following day and recaptured the first two. Before the end of the month, and now finally joined by 15th Panzer Division, he also drove the British out of the Halfaya Pass. These battles brought the British up against the German 88-mm gun for the first time. Although essentially an antiaircraft weapon, it proved highly effective against armor, completely outranging the guns of the British tanks.

ERWIN ROMMEL

ERWIN ROMMEL (1891–1944) made his mark as a young officer during World War 1. He came to Hitler's attention after he had written a book on infantry tactics and commanded the Führer's security detachment during the Polish campaign. Hitler rewarded him with command of a panzer division for the campaign in the West, then in 1941 with command of the Afrika Korps. Rommel soon became a national hero, also gaining the respect of the British. He always liked to lead from the front and had an ability to sense the critical point on the battlefield. In summer 1942 he became the youngest German Field Marshal, but, after being stalled at El Alamein, was forced onto the defensive, conducting a skillful withdrawal into Tunisia. By March 1943 he was a sick man and left North Africa, but was then appointed to command Army Group B, responsible for the defense of northern Italy. He later conducted the battle for Normandy before being badly wounded. His name was linked with the July 1944 Bomb Plot and he was forced to commit suicide to save his wife and son from the Gestapo.

The siege of Tobruk
The first siege of the port lasted from April to December
1941. The Italians had built strong defenses around the
town, to which the Australian and British troops added
trenches, foxholes, and gun emplacements.

Auchinleck now turned his attention to his
forthcoming offensive. Given the reinforcements
that he was receiving, which included a sizeable
quantity of American tanks, he decided that not
only would he relieve Tobruk, but once more seize
the whole of Cyrenaica. This would also deny the
Axis airfields from which to attack Malta and supply
convoys sailing to it. At the end of September, the
British and Dominion troops in the Western Desert
were formed into the Eighth Army under Sir Alan
Cunningham, one of the victors of the Abyssinian
campaign. A week later Cunningham presented his
final plan for Operation Crusader. In essence, his
XXX Corps, which contained the bulk of his tanks,
was to tie down Rommel's armor, while XIII Corps
advanced on Tobruk, whose garrison would break
out and link up with it. Rommel himself was to be
the target of a raid by Commandos, who would
be landed by submarine and attack his suspected
headquarters in the Jebel el Akhdar. Another
Special Forces operation would involve the newly
created L Detachment of the Special Air Service
(SAS), which was to be dropped behind enemy
lines to destroy aircraft on the ground.

OPERATION CRUSADER

Crusader got off to a bad start, with the failure of
both special operations, which were launched the
night before the main attack. The Commandos'
target turned out to be merely a logistics HQ and
almost all of them were killed or captured. At any
rate, Rommel was in Rome at the time. The aircraft
carrying the SAS were blown off course in a

Antiaircraft gun defending Tobruk
Not only did the defenders of Tobruk have to
withstand attacks on three sides on land, but they
also had to fight off night raids by Axis bombers.

Opening advances

The campaign began as it would continue, with the opposing armies taking turns pursuing each other across the desert until forced to halt by fuel and supply shortages. All the territory lost by the Italians was recaptured by Rommel by May 1941.

Operation Crusader and Rommel's response

In the face of Operation Crusader (November 1941), Rommel withdrew from Cyrenaica, but counterattacked in January 1942 and drove the British back to Gazala.

---

sandstorm and their drop was widely scattered, with many of them also being lost. Crusader itself was launched at 6:00 am on November 18. It initially caught the Axis by surprise and the tanks of XXX Corps reached the airfield at Sidi Rezegh, just 10 miles (16 km) southeast of Tobruk. XIII Corps also made good progress, capturing Sidi Omar and Capuzzo. Rommel, now returned from Rome, sent the DAK against XXX Corps. After two days of bitter struggle in Sidi Rezegh, the British armor was brought to a grinding halt and the Tobruk garrison break-out had to be postponed. XIII Corps, however, continued its advance.

THE DASH TO THE WIRE

Rommel now seized the initiative. He took his tanks on a dash across the frontier into Egypt with the goal of cutting off the Eighth Army from its supply lines. This caused such confusion that Cunningham wanted to withdraw. Auchinleck refused to countenance this. He immediately replaced Cunningham, with his own deputy chief of staff, Neil Ritchie, telling him

that Crusader must continue. What encouraged him was the fact that the New Zealand Division in XIII Corps had managed to link up with the Tobruk garrison in El Duda. Rommel had hoped to capture a British fuel dump, but failed to find one and was running short of fuel. The DAK was also being harried by the Desert Air Force. Aware, too, of the situation in El Duda, Rommel was forced to turn back. On December 5 he gave orders for the eastern part of the perimeter around Tobruk to be evacuated and mounted another attack on XXX Corps. When this failed, Rommel withdrew from Tobruk, which was relieved on December 7.

Eight days later, Ritchie attacked Rommel in Gazala. The Axis position here had an exposed desert flank that could be easily turned. Rommel therefore decided on a further withdrawal across Cyrenaica and by early January 1942 he was back in El Agheila in Tripolitania. The Eighth Army, exhausted after six weeks of continuous fighting, was in no position to advance farther westward.

The final act of Crusader was the capture of Bardia, the port close to the Egyptian border, which had been bypassed at the beginning of the offensive.

The situation in Libya was now more or less what it had been 11 months earlier. Not believing that the Axis forces were in a fit state to launch another offensive, Ritchie withdrew some of his divisions to reequip in preparation for continuing the advance. Rommel, however, encouraged by the arrival of two ships' worth of replacement tanks and learning through lax radio security that the British had few serviceable tanks, decided not to allow his adversary time to draw breath.

Without informing his more cautious Italian masters or Kesselring, his immediate German superior, Rommel launched his attack on January 21, 1942. He caught the novice 1st Armoured Division, a recent arrival, with its tanks widely dispersed, and scattered it, trapping and destroying 70 of its tanks in the Antelat area. He then almost succeeded in cutting off Fourth Indian Division in the Benghazi area and it looked as though he was about to repeat his success of the previous spring. Ritchie, however, decided to hold him and hastily constructed defenses between Gazala and Bir Hacheim. The remainder of the Eighth Army withdrew to this line. Rommel followed up, but was now too short of fuel to be able to push the British back any farther.

The port of Benghazi
Axis shipping, damaged by bombing raids, lies in the harbor. Benghazi fell to the British in December 1941, but was retaken by Rommel the following month.

THE WAR IN THE BALKANS AND CRETE

SEPTEMBER 27, 1940–JUNE 1, 1941

War in the Balkans began with Italy's unsuccessful invasion of Greece. Hitler then turned his attention to the region in preparation for his attack on the Soviet Union. The two countries that refused to submit to Hitler's will, Yugoslavia and Greece, were swiftly overrun despite support from Britain.

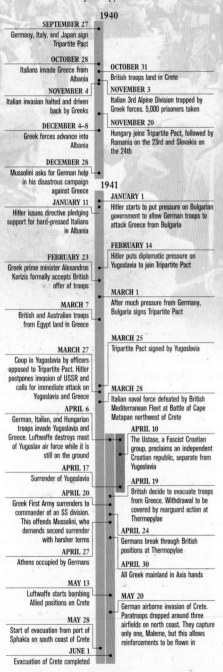

1940

SEPTEMBER 27
Germany, Italy, and Japan sign Tripartite Pact

OCTOBER 28
Italians invade Greece from Albania

OCTOBER 31
British troops land in Crete

NOVEMBER 4
Italian invasion halted and driven back by Greeks

NOVEMBER 3
Italian 3rd Alpine Division trapped by Greek forces. 5,000 prisoners taken

DECEMBER 4–8
Greek forces advance into Albania

NOVEMBER 20
Hungary joins Tripartite Pact, followed by Romania on the 23rd and Slovakia on the 24th

DECEMBER 28
Mussolini asks for German help in his disastrous campaign against Greece

1941

JANUARY 11
Hitler issues directive pledging support for hard-pressed Italians in Albania

JANUARY 1
Hitler starts to put pressure on Bulgarian government to allow German troops to attack Greece from Bulgaria

FEBRUARY 23
Greek prime minister Alexandros Korizis formally accepts British offer of troops

FEBRUARY 14
Hitler puts diplomatic pressure on Yugoslavia to join Tripartite Pact

MARCH 1
After much pressure from Germany, Bulgaria signs Tripartite Pact

MARCH 7
British and Australian troops from Egypt land in Greece

MARCH 25
Tripartite Pact signed by Yugoslavia

MARCH 27
Coup in Yugoslavia by officers opposed to Tripartite Pact. Hitler postpones invasion of USSR and calls for immediate attack on Yugoslavia and Greece

MARCH 28
Italian naval force defeated by British Mediterranean Fleet at Battle of Cape Matapan northwest of Crete

APRIL 6
German, Italian, and Hungarian troops invade Yugoslavia and Greece. Luftwaffe destroys most of Yugoslav air force while it is still on the ground

APRIL 10
The Ustase, a Fascist Croatian group, proclaims an independent Croatian republic, separate from Yugoslavia

APRIL 17
Surrender of Yugoslavia

APRIL 19
British decide to evacuate troops from Greece. Withdrawal to be covered by rearguard action at Thermopylae

APRIL 20
Greek First Army surrenders to commander of an SS division. This offends Mussolini, who demands second surrender with harsher terms

APRIL 24
Germans break through British positions at Thermopylae

APRIL 27
Athens occupied by Germans

APRIL 30
All Greek mainland in Axis hands

MAY 13
Luftwaffe starts bombing Allied positions on Crete

MAY 20
German airborne invasion of Crete. Paratroops dropped around three airfields on north coast. They capture only one, Maleme, but this allows reinforcements to be flown in

MAY 28
Start of evacuation from port of Sphakia on south coast of Crete

JUNE 1
Evacuation of Crete completed

▨ Axis conquest of Greece and Crete Apr 6–Jun 1, 1941

▨ Axis conquest of Yugoslavia Apr 6–17, 1941

▨ Other events

THE BALKAN CAMPAIGN

Mussolini, jealous of Hitler's territorial acquisitions in Central Europe, had long harbored ambitions of carving out a similar empire in southeast Europe. His first victim was Albania. The country had been under Italian influence for some years, when in March 1939 Mussolini demanded that Albania allow in Italian troops. When King Zog refused, he invaded and, after brief resistance, the monarch fled to neighboring Greece, leaving his country in Italian hands. Greece itself appeared to be Mussolini's next target, but he declared that he had no designs on the country. Unconvinced, Britain and France pledged themselves to uphold Greek and Romanian independence.

On Italy's declaration of war in June 1940, Mussolini again stated that he had no interest in Greece, which declared its neutrality. Even so, that fall he began to make threatening noises, accusing Greece of helping Britain. Mussolini now decided to attack, convinced that it would be an easy victory, even though his generals warned him that it was too late in the year. On October 27, 1940, he informed Hitler of his intention, but rejected his offer of participation by German troops. The following day, two Italian armies invaded from Albania. They advanced a short way into the country, but the Greeks then drove the Italians back across the border and advanced deep into Albania, with only the wintry weather slowing their progress.

DIPLOMATIC MOVES

Churchill, eager to uphold Britain's prewar guarantee, offered the Greeks troops and aircraft, but all they would accept was five RAF squadrons. They did, however, allow a British brigade to garrison Crete so as to release Greek troops to fight on the mainland. The Greek government did not want to antagonize the Germans and they were right to be cautious. Hitler was now turning his eyes toward southeast Europe. His

Ready to invade

German airborne troops prepare to embark in Junkers Ju 52 transport planes prior to the invasion of Yugoslavia. With help from Hungary and Italy, Germany overran Yugoslavia in just 11 days.

mind was firmly set on invading the Soviet Union, but first he needed to secure his southern flank. He therefore launched a diplomatic offensive. Before the end of November Hungary, Romania, and Slovakia—all countries with Fascist-style governments—had agreed to join the Tripartite Pact, the alliance formed by Germany, Italy, and Japan that September.

Hitler, meanwhile, ordered plans to be drawn up for a possible invasion of Greece, but he needed the compliance of Bulgaria so that it could be used as a launching pad. At the beginning of January 1941 Hitler opened negotiations with the Bulgarians, but they decided to play for time. The Italians had managed to halt the Greek advance in Albania, but Mussolini refused a further offer of German troops because he feared that Hitler would take over Albania.

The British now decided to counter Hitler's diplomatic offensive. In February Foreign Secretary Anthony Eden toured the Balkans in an effort to create an anti-Axis pact. Yugoslavia refused to see him, as did Turkey. Aware of their growing isolation, only the Greeks showed any interest. This was largely because General Ioannis Metaxas, the dictator who had resisted a formal alliance with the British, had died at the end of January. The new pro-British government agreed that British troops should be sent to Greece.

On March 1 Bulgaria signed up to the Tripartite Pact and German troops began to move into the country on the following day. German attention now concentrated on Yugoslavia. Hitler demanded rights of passage, offering the port of Salonika and part of Macedonia in recompense. Eventually, on March 25, Yugoslavia succumbed and joined the Pact, although many in the country were unhappy.

British and Commonwealth troops began to land on the Greek mainland on March 7. W Force would eventually consist of the New Zealand Division, two Australian divisions, and a British armored brigade

under the command of General Maitland Wilson. Two days later, the Italians launched an offensive against the Greeks in Albania, but failed to break through. At sea, the Italian Navy attempted to intercept the troop convoys going to Greece. On March 28 it clashed with the Mediterranean Fleet off Cape Matapan, west of the Peloponnese. The battleship *Vittorio Veneto* was badly damaged by a torpedo, while three Italian cruisers and two destroyers fell to the guns of the British ships.

THE INVASION OF YUGOSLAVIA

There was also dramatic news from Yugoslavia. On March 27 a group of air force officers overthrew the regency of Prince Paul in a bloodless coup. They established a government of national unity and made his 17-year-old nephew, Prince Peter, monarch in his place.

The new government then signed a non-aggression pact with the Soviet Union and expressed interest in a pact with Britain.

Operation Punishment

On the first day of the invasion of Yugoslavia, German dive-bombers attacked the airfields of the Yugoslav air force, destroying most of its planes before they could take off.

The invasion of the Balkans

Germany's conquest of Yugoslavia and Greece in spring 1941 was a well-planned, swiftly executed campaign. The Yugoslavs were totally unprepared, while the British and Greek forces in their defensive positions were easily outflanked by the mobile German forces. The airborne invasion of Crete also succeeded, but cost many more lives.

Hitler, furious over what he saw as Yugoslavia's treachery, ordered an immediate invasion of the country—Operation Punishment—with Greece to be attacked at the same time.

Yugoslavia was ill-equipped to face an Axis assault. While its army could call upon over one million men, they were poorly armed and badly trained. The country's long frontiers also did not help. On April 6 the Axis invaded, with Germans and Italians attacking from the north, Germans and Hungarians from the east, and Italians from Albania in the south. Much of the Yugoslav air force was destroyed on the ground at the start of hostilities and within a week Belgrade, the capital, had been occupied. Yugoslav resistance was minimal and a mere 150 German soldiers were killed during the brief campaign, which ended on April 17.

THE CONQUEST OF YUGOSLAVIA AND GREECE
APR 6–JUN 1, 1941

➡ Axis advance
🪂 Parachute/glider landing
⌐⌐⌐ Allied defensive position April 6, 1941

❻ Apr 11–12, 1941 Hungarian army overruns area of northern Yugoslavia, which is then annexed by Hungary

❶ Apr 6, 1941 Heavy bombing of Belgrade. Yugoslav high command paralyzed

❷ Apr 6, 1941 First Panzer Corps under General Paul von Kleist invades from Bulgaria and reaches Belgrade on the 12th

❼ Apr 16, 1941 Fall of Sarajevo

❹ Apr 9, 1941 German motorized corps reaches Monastir

❺ Apr 10, 1941 British troops start to fall back from Aliakmon Line

❽ Apr 20, 1941 Greek First Army surrenders

❸ Apr 9, 1941 Germans take Salonika, trapping Greek troops defending Metaxas Line

❾ Apr 24, 1941 Germans break through British positions at Thermopylae

❿ Apr 24–30, 1941 British evacuation from Piraeus and ports in the Peloponnese

⓫ Apr 25, 1941 German paratroops take Corinth

⓬ May 20, 1941 German airborne invasion of Crete

⓭ May 28–Jun 1, 1941 British and Commonwealth troops evacuated from Sphakia to Alexandria

THE INVASION OF GREECE

The rapid collapse of Yugoslavia was fatal for Greece. The Greek army's defensive plan was based on two sets of fortifications: the Metaxas Line in eastern Macedonia facing the border with Bulgaria and the Aliakmon Line along the southern boundary of Macedonia. It had been the British understanding that the Greeks would give up Macedonia and concentrate on defending the Aliakmon Line. This was where W Force was deployed, thus leaving their forces considerably less extended. The Greeks, however, planned to do this only if the Yugoslavs offered no resistance to the passage of German troops through their territory. That the Yugoslavs had opposed the Axis, albeit ineffectually, meant that the Greek Second Army remained in the Metaxas Line and was immediately outflanked by a German thrust from southeastern Yugoslavia to

the port of Salonika. It was quickly forced to surrender. A thrust through Monastir threatened to do the same to W Force in the Aliakmon Line and the British troops began to withdraw on April 10, although the line itself held for another eight days.

REARGUARD ACTIONS

By now it was clear that little could be done to halt the German blitzkrieg and the Greeks agreed that Wilson could withdraw his troops. Further disaster occurred on April 20, when the Greek First Army was trapped in the west of the country and

surrendered. W Force began its evacuation, covered by a rearguard which managed to hold off the Germans at Thermopylae for five days. On April 25 German paratroops seized the port of Corinth and two days later the Germans entered Athens. The British evacuation was completed the following day.

Operation Marita, as the overrunning of the Balkans was code-named, was another devastating demonstration of blitzkrieg and left Churchill's Balkans strategy in tatters, especially since it convinced Turkey to remain neutral. W Force had to leave all its heavy equipment behind along with 900 men killed and some 10,000 taken prisoner. The Greek king and his government fled—first to Crete and from there to Egypt. While some from W Force were taken back to Egypt, the bulk were landed in Crete. The British hoped to use the

Advance through Greece
An infantry column of the German 12th Army marches past Mount Olympus, having broken British and Greek resistance on the Aliakmon Line.

Germans rounding up prisoners
Over 11,000 British and Commonwealth troops were taken prisoner by the Germans on Crete. A few men escaped to the mountains, where they continued to fight alongside the Cretan resistance.

On May 19 the surviving aircraft were withdrawn, leaving Crete with no air cover whatsoever. On the following day the invasion began. Initially it did not go well. Some 2,000 paratroops were killed and none of their objectives captured. All the German commanders, aside from Student, wanted to abort the operation, but he was determined to continue. That night the battalion defending Maleme abandoned the airfield because of misunderstood orders. The Germans captured it the following day and began to land reinforcements. The British mounted a

counterattack, but it failed and the fate of Crete was sealed. Even though the Royal Navy was able to scatter the German seaborne reinforcements, Freyberg decided that it was impossible to hold the island. He had too many problems of command and control, while the Luftwaffe had complete domination of the skies. On May 28 he was given permission to withdraw to the south coast, where the Royal Navy would evacuate his men.

By June 1 Crete was in German hands. The navy managed to rescue some 12,000 men, but at the cost of three cruisers and six destroyers sunk, all victims of the Luftwaffe. Germany's victory in the Balkans and the success of its airborne troops, along with Rommel's victories in North Africa, reinforced the Wehrmacht's growing aura of invincibility. It boded well for Hitler's most momentous undertaking—the invasion of the Soviet Union.

island as a base from which to attack the Romanian oilfields at Ploesti, which were vital to the German war effort. The Royal Navy had also been using Suda Bay in the north of the island as a forward anchorage, although it was now within range of the Luftwaffe in Greece and there were few British aircraft on the island to defend ships using the bay.

AIRBORNE ASSAULT ON CRETE

The Germans also recognized the importance of Crete. On April 21, as the battle for Greece raged, General Karl Student, commander of Germany's paratroops, presented Hitler with a plan for an airborne invasion of the island. Hitler needed some persuasion, but eventually gave his approval and four days later issued a directive for Operation Mercury. German intelligence did not believe that there were more than 5,000 troops on the island, so only two divisions were to be used for the attack. In fact there were some 42,000, although they were poorly equipped after being evacuated from Greece. The 7th Parachute Division, which was deployed from Germany, was to make a series of drops, seize the airfields at Maleme, Rethymno, and Heraklion and also secure the harbor of Suda Bay. The bulk of the other division, 5th Mountain, would be flown in to the airfields once they had been secured, and reinforce the paratroops. Suda Bay was to be used by reinforcements arriving by sea, which would bring in heavy weapons, including tanks.

In command of the British defense of Crete was General Bernard Freyberg, commander of the New Zealand Division in the Middle East and a Victoria Cross winner from World War I. He knew of German intentions from Ultra, but was convinced that the main assault would come from the sea and did not pay sufficient attention to defense of the airfields.

On May 13 the Luftwaffe began to attack Crete. Because of Germany's overwhelming air superiority the RAF refused to reinforce the 25 fighters, most of them obsolete, that they had on the island.

AIRBORNE FORCES

AIRBORNE FORCES USUALLY COMPRISED three elements: paratroops, glider-borne troops, and airlanded troops—those landed by plane on an airfield that had already been secured. Most airborne operations combined at least two of these elements—in the case of Crete all three. Prior to the war only the Soviets and the Germans had created airborne forces, although during 1939–45 the former used theirs only in small-scale operations, the concept falling out of favor during Stalin's purges. The German successes in Norway and the 1940 campaign in the West prompted the British and Americans to create airborne forces of their own. These were first used on a significant scale during the Allied landings in French northwest Africa in November 1942.

Airborne operations are always fraught with risk. On Crete, many German paratroops were shot as they descended to the ground. Operation Mercury also demonstrated the vulnerability of their transport aircraft, which had to fly on a steady course as they approached and flew over the dropping zone. Indeed, so heavy was the loss of Junkers Ju 52 transport planes during the Crete campaign that the Germans never again mounted an airborne operation on this scale. Gliders were likewise prone to being shot down or wrecked on landing. Poor navigation and high winds resulted in a very scattered drop, which created problems once the paratroops had landed. The Allies experienced

German parachute drop over Crete
When they landed in a well-defended area, casualties among paratroops were high. Those who were not shot in the air were likely to be bayoneted as they struggled to get free of their harnesses.

this during the assault on Sicily in July 1943 and again, to some extent, on D-Day, June 6, 1944. Airborne forces were also lightly equipped and could not hold out for long on their own before ground forces linked up with them. The Allies learned this the hard way at Arnhem in September 1944, when much of the British 1st Airborne Division was lost because the ground advance could not reach them in time. The lesson was learned by the time it came to the Rhine crossings in March 1945, where Allied airborne forces played a key role in securing a bridgehead on the east bank.

German column under attack in Serbia
When Axis troops invaded Yugoslavia in April 1941, they met with little opposition. Most resistance came from the Serbs, who, after the conquest, quickly organized guerrilla resistance to the occupying forces.

GERMAN–SOVIET CONFLICT

JUNE 22–DECEMBER 6, 1941

In launching Operation Barbarossa the Germans planned to destroy the Soviet army before it could retreat into the vast Russian interior and extend the campaign into the winter. Initially the German forces achieved considerable success as they advanced toward Leningrad in the north, Moscow in the centre, and into the Ukraine in the south. They failed, however, to secure a quick and total victory, and by December they had come to a halt before Moscow.

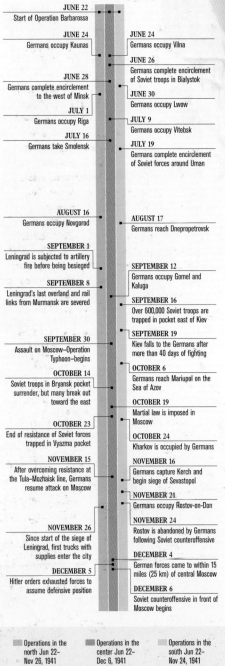

JUNE 22
Start of Operation Barbarossa

JUNE 24
Germans occupy Kaunas

JUNE 24
Germans occupy Vilna

JUNE 26
Germans complete encirclement of Soviet troops in Bialystok

JUNE 28
Germans complete encirclement to the west of Minsk

JUNE 30
Germans occupy Lwow

JULY 1
Germans occupy Riga

JULY 9
Germans occupy Vitebsk

JULY 16
Germans take Smolensk

JULY 19
Germans complete encirclement of Soviet forces around Uman

AUGUST 16
Germans occupy Novgorod

AUGUST 17
Germans reach Dnepropetrovsk

SEPTEMBER 1
Leningrad is subjected to artillery fire before being besieged

SEPTEMBER 12
Germans occupy Gomel and Kaluga

SEPTEMBER 8
Leningrad's last overland and rail links from Murmansk are severed

SEPTEMBER 16
Over 600,000 Soviet troops are trapped in pocket east of Kiev

SEPTEMBER 19
Kiev falls to the Germans after more than 40 days of fighting

SEPTEMBER 30
Assault on Moscow–Operation Typhoon–begins

OCTOBER 6
Germans reach Mariupol on the Sea of Azov

OCTOBER 14
Soviet troops in Bryansk pocket surrender, but many break out toward the east

OCTOBER 19
Martial law is imposed in Moscow

OCTOBER 23
End of resistance of Soviet forces trapped in Vyazma pocket

OCTOBER 24
Kharkov is occupied by Germans

NOVEMBER 15
After overcoming resistance at the Tula–Mozhaisk line, Germans resume attack on Moscow

NOVEMBER 16
Germans capture Kerch and begin siege of Sevastopol

NOVEMBER 21
Germans occupy Rostov-on-Don

NOVEMBER 24
Rostov is abandoned by Germans following Soviet counteroffensive

NOVEMBER 26
Since start of the siege of Leningrad, first trucks with supplies enter the city

DECEMBER 4
German forces come to within 15 miles (25 km) of central Moscow

DECEMBER 5
Hitler orders exhausted forces to assume defensive position

DECEMBER 6
Soviet counteroffensive in front of Moscow begins

Operations in the north Jun 22–Nov 26, 1941

Operations in the center Jun 22–Dec 6, 1941

Operations in the south Jun 22–Nov 24, 1941

OPERATION BARBAROSSA

A T 3:30 AM ON JUNE 22, 1941, a total of seven German infantry armies, their advance led by four panzer groups, invaded the Soviet Union. They had opened the greatest land war in the history of military operations. Some 3 million German soldiers, supported by 3,580 tanks, 7,184 guns, and nearly 2,000 aircraft were on the move along a 1,000-mile (1,600-km) front, stretching from Memel on the Baltic to Odessa on the Black Sea.

The operation, which was code-named Barbarossa, had a long period of gestation. A plan for the invasion of the Soviet Union had first been drawn up in August 1940, but it did not emerge in its final form until the spring of 1941.

A call to arms
Following the launch of Operation Barbarossa men from all parts of the Soviet Union were exhorted to defend their "motherland" and avenge the deaths of their wives and children.

Army Group North, commanded by Field Marshal Ritter von Leeb, was to attack from East Pusssia toward Leningrad, aided by the Finns advancing into the Karelian isthmus. The strongest formation, Army Group Center under Bock, was to drive north of the natural barrier of the freshwater Pripet marshes to Smolensk, the route followed by Napoleon in 1812. To the south of the Pripet marshes, Rundstedt's Army Group South was to advance to the black-earth country of the Ukraine—the Soviet Unions's breadbasket—and the oil-rich industrial areas of the Donetz, the Volga, and the Caucasus. The cream of the German Army was poised to advance into a vast area—about 1,000,000 sq miles (2,600,000 sq km)—of steppe, forest, and swamp.

The invasion of the Soviet Union was the culmination of the twin obsessions that had driven Hitler throughout his career: the seizing of *Lebensraum* ("living space") in the east and, with it, the industry and

Soviet prisoners of war
Soviet troops were totally unprepared for the attack that was unleashed against them on June 22. Many on the frontier were taken prisoner before they had any idea that their country was now at war with Germany.

hunted look in the eyes of the generals showed all too plainly the constant fear in which they lived. It was nauseating to see brave men reduced to such servility." Furthermore, in the spring of 1941 Stalin's complex psychological makeup had resulted in him deeming as "unreliable" the numerous strong intelligence indications he had received of German intentions: from his own networks, from British diplomatic channels, and from Ultra information, which had been laundered to mask its source (see page 82). He had insisted on maintaining compliance with the terms of the Nazi-Soviet Pact of 1939, to the extent that trainloads of minerals and raw materials bound for Germany's war industries continued to rumble across the Soviet frontier until the small hours of June 22, 1941.

Stalin had also insisted on cramming the bulk of the Red Army fronts (army groups) into the incomplete line of fortifications, known as the "Stalin Line," on the Soviet frontier. The shallowest of German penetrations would place these formations at the risk of rapid envelopment.

THE STORM BREAKS

The Luftwaffe prepared the way for Army Group Center's attack. On the morning of June 22 it destroyed 528 Soviet aircraft on the ground and 210 in the air. When darkness fell across the German front on June 22, the Red Air Force had lost approximately 25 percent of its strength, some 1,600 machines. By June 26 Army Group Center was completing encirclements in Brest-Litovsk on the Soviet frontier, and in Bialystok, thus entombing tens of thousands of Soviet troops in what the Germans called "cauldron battles" (see map page 101). By then Army Group Center's two panzer groups had raced 200 miles (300 km) east to launch an encirclement of hard-fighting Soviet troops west of Minsk.

At this stage in the campaign the Soviet Union's primitive roads, and a rail network of a different gauge to that in Germany, posed few problems, although both factors had been underestimated by German military intelligence during the planning of Barbarossa. Racing through flat,

> The bombs were falling with a shriek. The army headquarters building we had just left was shrouded in smoke and dust. The powerful blasts rent the air and made our ears ring. The German bombers dived confidently at the defenseless military settlement. When the raid was over, thick black pillars of smoke billowed up from many places. Part of the headquarters building was in ruins. Somewhere a high-pitched, hysterical female voice was crying out.
>
> AN ENGINEER OFFICER AT SOVIET 4TH ARMY HEADQUARTERS DESCRIBING THE ATTACK BY THE LUFTWAFFE ON JUNE 22

open terrain, whose earth had been baked hard by the scorching sun, the panzer spearheads covered around 50 miles (80 km) a day, halting only to snuff out resistance or take in supplies. Behind them labored the infantry, marching an average of 20 miles (30 km) a day under a pitiless sun while carrying 50 lb (23 kg) of equipment, ammunition, and rations. The landscape through which they passed bore testimony to the savagery of the fighting. One infantryman recalled that "burning villages, staring bodies of fallen Russian soldiers, swollen carcasses of dead horses, rusting, blackened and burnt-out tanks were the signs of the march."

By the end of June the German encirclement west of Minsk had resulted in the capture of 324,00 Red Army soldiers. Army Group

German 240-mm howitzer in action
Soviet defenses came under attack from over 7,000 artillery pieces in the opening phase of Barbarossa. In the seven largest encirclement battles the Germans seized or destroyed over 9,300 tanks and 16,170 guns, as well as taking over 2,250,000 prisoners.

agricultural land that would ensure Germany's survival as a great power, and his contempt for the "Jewish-Bolshevist" government of the Soviet Union, whose Slav and Asiatic population would be enslaved or expelled into a wasteland beyond the "A-A line" stretching from Archangel to Astrakhan.

THE STATE OF SOVIET DEFENSES

The Soviet Union's Red Army was in no state to resist the German onslaught. Under Marshal Georgi Zhukov, chief of staff since January, a wholesale reorganization had begun, with tank formations that had been disbanded during Stalin's purges of the 1930s being reestablished. It would, however, be some time before the damage inflicted on the army by the purges was fully overcome. The fear engendered by both them and the ever-present NKVD (the Soviet secret service, whose many responsibilities included ensuring the political reliability of the armed forces) had sapped the morale of the army at all levels. Visiting Moscow in October 1941, the British General Ismay noted that when Stalin entered a room, "every Russian froze into silence and the

HEINZ GUDERIAN

AFTER SERVICE AS A STAFF OFFICER in World War I, Heinz Guderian (1888–1954) became a specialist in armored warfare. In 1937 he published *Achtung Panzer!*, a book that made him the leading advocate of blitzkrieg warfare, and in 1938 he was appointed Chief of Mobile Forces. In September 1939, at the head of XIX Panzer Corps, he put theory into practice in Poland and eight months later led the same formation in France. His breakthrough at Sedan provided persuasive proof of his prophetic prewar thinking on the employment of armored formations. In Operation Barbarossa, Guderian commanded 2 Panzer Group in a breakneck drive into the heart of the European Soviet Union. On being brought to a halt by the onset of winter and stiffening Soviet resistance, he ordered a tactical withdrawal, and so was dismissed by Hitler in December 1941. He became chief of the army general staff after the bomb plot to kill Hitler in July 1944 failed. Plagued by ill-health, he was a sardonic observer of the collapse of the Third Reich, of which he gave an informative account in his autobiography, *Panzer Leader* (1952).

Center's panzer groups pressed on, crossed the Dnieper on July 10 and closed on Smolensk, beating off determined Red Army counterattacks on both flanks. At Smolensk another 300,000 men of the Red Army surrendered and were marched into captivity. A total of 3,205 tanks and 3,120 guns were also captured. Denied any organized means of transportation to the rear, tens of thousands of Soviet prisoners were to die while marching vast distances or packed like cattle in railroad wagons.

THE SLOWING OF THE ADVANCE
Army Group Center had now penetrated over 400 miles (650 km) into the Soviet Union, but the breakneck pace of the advance was slowing. Although Moscow was only 200 miles (325 km) away, the conditions were beginning to take their toll on the Ostheer (the German Army in the east). An hour or two of heavy rain brought tanks,

wheeled vehicles, and horses to a halt in seas of glutinous mud. They remained stuck fast in columns stretching tens of miles until the sun came out. (The Germans' dependence on horses can be gauged from the fact that more than 750,000 were used in the opening phase of Barbarossa, with an average loss of 1,000 animals a day.) Victory also exacted its own price. By the middle of August there were 500,000 German casualties.

After the fall of Smolensk on July 16, Army Group Center halted for several weeks to bring up supplies. Ammunition was running low and tank strength had fallen by nearly half. Meanwhile, there were growing divisions within the German high command that needed to be settled. Field Marshal von Bock wanted to drive on to Moscow

behind a renewed panzer thrust, but on July 19 Hitler intervened. He issued a new directive: one of Bock's two panzer groups was to wheel south to aid Army Group South in another huge encirclement in northern Ukraine. The other was to swing north to reinforce the advance of Army Group North on Leningrad and cut Soviet communications with Moscow. This meant that Bock now had only infantry with which to push toward Moscow.

The ensuing argument over the priorities of the Ostheer lasted a month before Hitler settled matters with an order, issued on August 21, in which he shifted the emphasis to the south and the envelopment of four Soviet armies east of Kiev by Rundstedt's Army Group South. With firm orders from Stalin not to withdraw, the Soviet troops in and around Kiev fought on grimly until September 19, when 665,000 were taken prisoner. After the shock of the German invasion and advance in June and July, Stalin was regaining his grip on the levers of command. He was now supreme commander of the armed forces, and commissar for defense, and sat at the head of the Soviet Supreme High Command, or Stavka as it was known.

ADVANCE TO LENINGRAD
Torn between the competing options of the drive on Moscow, the advance to Leningrad at the head of the Baltic, and the huge maneuver in Kiev, Hitler had opted for the third. However, in the final

Street battle
German infantry fight behind a Panzer Mark III. There were nearly 1,500 in service in 1941, forming the backbone of the panzer divisions in the opening stages of Barbarossa. But they were no match for the Red Army's T-34s.

Advance through the Soviet Union

The Germans launched Operation Barbarossa along a 1,000-mile (1,600-km) front on June 22. They advanced to Leningrad in the north, to Moscow in the center, and beyond Kiev in the south. By December they were just 15 miles (25 km) from Moscow.

planning stages of Barbarossa he had given priority to the capture of Leningrad as the preliminary to a drive on Moscow from the north. By shuttling his forces up and down a vast front, Hitler was fatally dissipating the early stunning successes of Operation Barbarossa.

By July 20 Leeb's Army Group North had been poised to take Leningrad, but the growing exhaustion of his troops, hardening Soviet resistance, and Hitler's intervention had destroyed the chance of its early capture. At the end of August, as Leeb's armor nosed into the outskirts of the city, the Führer had ordered a halt, possibly fearing heavy losses in a street-by-street battle for the city. Moreover, the Finns had been showing a reluctance to extend their operations beyond the Karelian isthmus once they had succeeded in regaining their 1939 border.

Hitler had ordered Leningrad to be besieged. By September 8 all land communications with the city had been severed, and the only way in which food supplies could be delivered was by using air and river links. These were constantly harassed by the Germans, while Leningrad itself was pounded by German artillery and bombers. In October starvation

Crossing the steppe

Many German soldiers were oppressed by the sheer size and emptiness of the Soviet steppe.

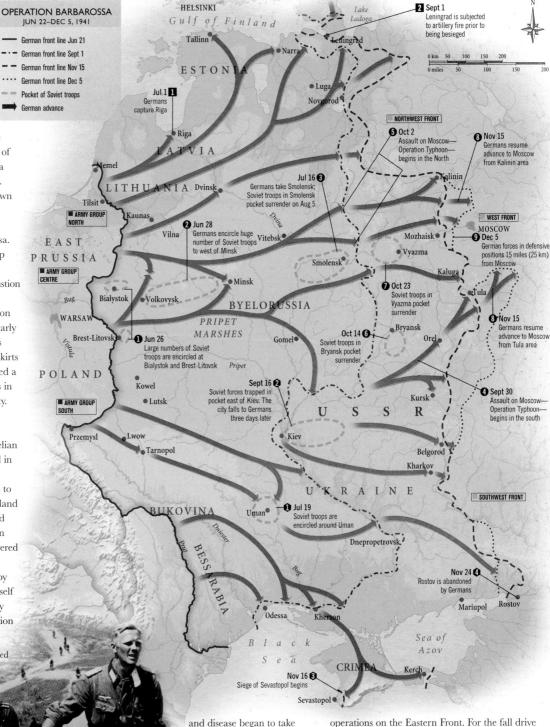

OPERATION BARBAROSSA
JUN 22–DEC 5, 1941

— German front line Jun 21
-·- German front line Sept 1
--- German front line Nov 15
··· German front line Dec 5
▨ Pocket of Soviet troops
➜ German advance

2 Sept 1 Leningrad is subjected to artillery fire prior to being besieged

Jul 1 1 Germans capture Riga

5 Oct 2 Assault on Moscow— Operation Typhoon— begins in the North

8 Nov 15 Germans resume advance to Moscow from Kalinin area

Jul 16 3 Germans take Smolensk; Soviet troops in Smolensk pocket surrender on Aug 5

2 Jun 28 Germans encircle huge number of Soviet troops to west of Minsk

9 Dec 5 German forces in defensive positions 15 miles (25 km) from Moscow

7 Oct 23 Soviet troops in Vyazma pocket surrender

8 Nov 15 Germans resume advance to Moscow from Tula area

Oct 14 6 Soviet troops in Bryansk pocket surrender

1 Jun 26 Large numbers of Soviet troops are encircled at Bialystok and Brest-Litovsk

Sept 16 2 Soviet forces trapped in pocket east of Kiev. The city falls to Germans three days later

4 Sept 30 Assault on Moscow— Operation Typhoon— begins in the south

1 Jul 19 Soviet troops are encircled around Uman

4 Nov 24 Rostov is abandoned by Germans

Nov 16 3 Siege of Sevastopol begins

NORTHWEST FRONT
WEST FRONT
SOUTHWEST FRONT
ARMY GROUP NORTH
ARMY GROUP CENTRE
ARMY GROUP SOUTH

and disease began to take a grip, and it was not long before 300 of Leningrad's civilians were dying every day.

By then Hitler's attention had belatedly swung back to Moscow. Buoyed by the encirclement of Kiev, he resisted Rundstedt's cautious advice to call a temporary halt to operations on the Eastern Front. For the fall drive on the Soviet capital, Army Group North's panzer spearhead was transferred from the Leningrad sector and joined Army Group Center's Fourth Army. To the north of the Fourth Army was the Ninth Army and Panzer Group 3; to the south was the Second Army and Panzer Group 2, commanded by General Heinz Guderian, Germany's leading exponent of armored warfare.

EINSATZGRUPPEN ATROCITIES

DURING THE INVASION OF POLAND in 1939 the German armies were accompanied by special units—*Einsatzgruppen*—charged with the liquidation of priests and members of the Polish intelligentsia.

Their successor units, initially comprising 3,000 men and directly responsible to Heinrich Himmler and his deputy Reinhard Heydrich, were tasked with the mass murder of Jews, communists, Romanies, and other non-Aryans in the territories occupied during Barbarossa. Gruppe A was attached to Army Group North and cleared the Baltic states and northeast Russia, Gruppe B followed Army Group Center through Minsk and Smolensk, Gruppe C followed Army Group South through the Ukraine, and Gruppe D tracked the 11th Army to the Crimea. In June 1941 their orders were to eliminate Jewish males aged 17 to 45, but by mid-summer Jewish women and children were also being rounded up, many of them betrayed by anti-Semitic inhabitants of the Baltic states and the Ukraine.

The principal method of the *Einsatzgruppen* was mass shooting, although small numbers of gas trucks were also employed in which the victims were killed by exhaust from the motors. Almost all the victims of these gas experiments were women and

Execution by shooting
Throughout the *Einsatzgruppen's* reign of terror the great majority of their victims were Jewish, often killed by shooting in the back of the head.

Soviet partisan victims
In a trench they have been forced to dig themselves, Soviet partisans await execution. The Germans did not believe they should apply the laws of war to partisans.

children. The *Einsatzgruppen* were occasionally aided by the Wehrmacht and, more frequently, by local militia groups willing to participate in the massacres. For example, on October 28–29, 1941, in Kaunas in Lithuania, local militia joined *Einsatzgruppe* A in the murder of some 9,200 Jews. The dead were then looted for money, watches, jewelry, and clothing. In Lithuania between July 4 and November 25, 1941, some 130,000 people were killed by *Einsatzgruppe* A. In the Soviet Union between 1941 and 1944 the *Einsatzgruppen* executed between 1.5 million and 2 million people, the great majority of them Jewish.

THE DRIVE ON MOSCOW

On September 30, in Operation Typhoon, Guderian opened the drive on Moscow, thrusting toward Orel. To the north, the German attacks went in two days later, and within a week nine Soviet armies had been cut off in pockets west of Vyazma and Bryansk, consigning another 600,000 Red Army soldiers to captivity. Neither Stalin nor the Stavka had anticipated that the Germans would launch an offensive so late in the year. However, the weather came to their aid. At the end of the first week in October, the heavy fall rains—the Russian *rasputitsa*—set in, slowing the German advance in a vast sea of mud.

General Günther von Blumentritt, the German Fourth Army's chief of staff, recalled: "After the Russian forces had been rounded up, we pushed on toward Moscow. There was little opposition for the moment, but the advance was slow—for the mud was awful, and the troops were tired. Moreover, they met a well-prepared defensive position on the Nara River, where they were held up by the arrival of fresh Russian forces. Most of the commanders were now asking, 'where are we going to stop?'"

Snow had fallen as early as the first week in October. By now most of the German front-line units had been in action, without relief, since June 22. Few had warm winter clothing, making it all but impossible for most troops to remain out in the open during the increasingly severe night frosts. Exhaustion exacerbated minor wounds and increased the misery of depleted units with punishing workloads. Hot food seldom arrived in the front line as it froze solid on its short journey forward. Lice thrived and leather boots disintegrated in the musty air of earth dugouts. As the thermometer dropped, the sentries' duty was limited to a maximum of one hour and their goggles froze to the flesh of their faces. Men survived by stripping the clothing from the bodies of the Soviet dead.

A rallying cry
The Russians were rallied to the defense of their country with the slogan: "We will destroy the murderers of our children."

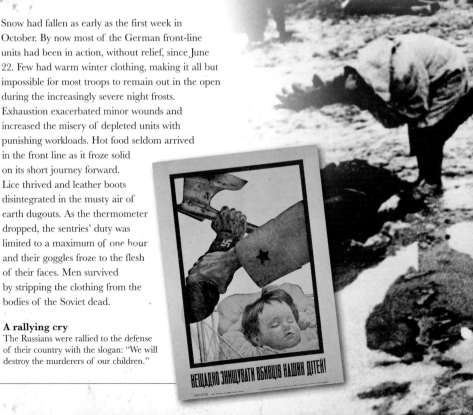

By the end of October, forward German units were 40 miles (65 km) from the outskirts of Moscow. At night they could see the flash of antiaircraft guns over the Soviet capital. Roads that had been hardened by frost offered a fleeting chance for a final offensive on November 15. However, Zhukov was now in command of the Soviet forces barring the route to Moscow, and these had been reinforced by fresh divisions transferred from Siberia and fully equipped for fighting in winter.

By November 27 the leading panzer units had reached the Volga Canal, within 20 miles (32 km) of Moscow's northern suburbs. Patrols could see the sun glinting on the domes of the Kremlin. But the Germans were unable to advance any farther, and the forward units were pulled back on December 5. The next day, as the Germans considered a tactical withdrawal to a defensive line, Zhukov delivered a crushing counterblow. Hitler's gamble on victory in the Soviet Union by September had failed, and the German people were warned, for the first time, that they should expect a long war. Priority was now to be given to the air raid defense of the Reich.

Trenches outside Moscow
Following the launch on September 30 of the German drive against Moscow, over 500,000 Muscovites responded to the call for help in constructing fortifications outside the city.

Identifying the dead
Soviet civilians search for their loved ones after a massacre by the Germans. Nazi ideology ensured that the war in the east was fought with unparalleled savagery.

The human and material costs of Barbarossa had been on a colossal scale. By the beginning of December the Ostheer had sustained total losses of 743,000 men (not counting the sick) and was short of 340,000 men, approximately 50 percent of the fighting strength of the infantry. In Germany only 33,000 replacements were available. Of the 500,000 trucks that had started the campaign, 150,000 had been written off and nearly 300,000 were in need of repair. It was estimated that it would take at least six months to bring each battered armored division up to full strength again.

These losses paled beside those suffered in the same period by the Red Army. Between June and early December it had lost nearly 3 million killed in action and 3.5 million taken prisoner. The German high command comforted itself with the conviction that this massive bloodletting had exhausted Soviet manpower—but this was by no means the case.

THE WAR BECOMES GLOBAL
1941–42

THE JAPANESE ATTACK ON PEARL HARBOR ON DECEMBER 7, 1941, WAS ONE OF THE DEFINING MOMENTS OF 20TH-CENTURY HISTORY. FROM THIS POINT TWO ALLIED POWERS, THE UNITED STATES AND BRITAIN, WOULD FIGHT THE WAR IN BOTH THE EUROPEAN AND THE ASIAN AND PACIFIC THEATERS, UNITING WHAT HAD BEEN TWO SEPARATE CONFLICTS. WHILE THE ALLIES MADE COMMON CAUSE TO DEFEAT THEIR ENEMIES, ON THE AXIS SIDE GERMANY AND JAPAN HAD SEPARATE WAR GOALS. GERMANY SOUGHT THE DESTRUCTION OF THE SOVIET UNION AND MASTERY OF EUROPE, JAPAN POLITICAL AND ECONOMIC PRIMACY IN ASIA.

Spheres of influence
High-ranking German officers and a Japanese military attaché in Berlin discuss the progress of the war in March 1941. Although the two powers regularly shared intelligence, Hitler did not inform Japan of his intended invasion of the Soviet Union.

NEW THEATERS OF WAR

IN THE LATE 1930S THE UNITED STATES HAD STOOD ASIDE AS JAPAN'S ARMY SECURED LARGE TRACTS OF NORTHERN AND COASTAL CHINA. WHEN WAR BROKE OUT IN EUROPE IN 1939, THE AMERICAN REACTION WAS AGAIN NOT TO GET INVOLVED. JAPAN, PREOCCUPIED BY THE ONGOING WAR IN CHINA AND SMARTING FROM ITS DEFEAT BY THE SOVIET UNION IN 1938–39, WAS SIMILARLY CAUTIOUS IN ITS RESPONSE TO THE EUROPEAN WAR. ALL THIS CHANGED IN SPRING 1940 WITH GERMANY'S RAPID CONQUEST OF NORTHWEST EUROPE.

THE CHANGED SITUATION in Europe had far-reaching implications, both for the United States and Japan. The defeat of France and the likely defeat of Britain forced the Americans to look to their own defenses. In July 1940 Congress passed the Two-Ocean Naval Expansion Act, which authorized a huge increase over the next few years in the strength of the US fleets in the North Atlantic and the Pacific.

In January 1941 President Roosevelt appealed to Congress to support the nations fighting in defense of what he called the "Four Freedoms": freedom of speech, freedom of religion, freedom from want, and freedom from fear. These were noble sentiments, but what Britain needed was a supply of arms on easier terms than the "cash and carry" basis on which they had been supplied since the outbreak of war.

Roosevelt's answer was the Lend-Lease Act, passed by Congress in March 1941. This allowed Britain to borrow war supplies from the United States against a promise of later repayment. By the end of March, Congress had voted $7 billion to Lend-Lease, the first installment in a program that would eventually total over $50 billion.

In taking "all steps short of war" to sustain the British, Roosevelt was maneuvering indirectly toward war itself. At the end of March 1941 Axis ships in American ports were seized. On May 28, following the torpedoing of the US freighter *Robin Moor* by a U-boat, Roosevelt declared a state of unlimited national emergency. Axis credit in the United States was frozen and Axis consulates closed in June.

On August 9, 1941, Roosevelt and Churchill met in Placentia Bay in Newfoundland to discuss their war goals. They agreed that the defeat of Nazi Germany was the priority and issued the Atlantic Charter, which embodied Roosevelt's Four Freedoms and provided the seed from which the United Nations grew. However, it was also agreed that joint American and British military action could not be undertaken until the United States was at war with Germany. By the end of the year the United States would be at war with Germany, not as a result of a direct confrontation, but through the actions of Japan.

JAPANESE INTENTIONS

For Japan, the defeat of France and the Netherlands in spring 1940 and the apparently impending defeat of Britain presented a golden opportunity. The possessions of the three imperial powers in Southeast Asia had long been coveted by Japan as sources of valuable raw materials, such as rubber and oil. But there remained one important obstacle to a policy of military conquest in Southeast Asia. The Japanese had to decide whether they should risk provoking a war with the United States.

On August 29, 1940, Vichy France bowed to pressure from the Japanese and allowed them to establish bases in northern Indochina. In response, Roosevelt placed an embargo on the export of various raw marterials to Japan. When, in July 1941, the Japanese secured base facilities in southern Indochina, this was a more serious development, posing a threat to the American possession of the Philippines, the British possessions of Malaya and Burma, and the Dutch East Indies. Roosevelt, acting in concert with Britain, froze all Japan's assets in the United States and imposed an oil embargo.

At a stroke Japan was deprived of 90 percent of its oil supplies and 75 percent of its foreign trade. If the Japanese could not secure new supplies of raw materials, they would be forced to accede to American demands that they relinquish all the territory they had gained in China and suffer a humiliating loss of face. In the words of Admiral Osami Nagano, Chief of the Japanese General Staff, Japan was like "a fish in a pond from which the water is gradually being drained away."

Japanese plans for war, begun in earnest in mid-summer 1941, involved two widely separated areas of operation. The seizure of the so-called Southern Resources Area would start with an offensive against the Philippines, accompanied by a simultaneous attack on Malaya. Japan's southern drive was to be coordinated with a preemptive carrier strike on the US Pacific Fleet at its base, Pearl Harbor on the Hawaiian island of Oahu. This part of the plan was the brainchild of Admiral Yamamoto Isoroku, commander-in-chief of the Japanese Combined Fleet since 1939. Yamamoto had suggested this operation as early as January 1941, but it was not until October 1941 that it was given the go-ahead.

The bombing of Pearl Harbor
US servicemen survey Ford Island airbase after the Japanese raid on Pearl Harbor. Contrary to Japanese hopes, the surprise attack did not weaken American fighting spirit, but inflamed the desire for revenge.

"You will not only be unable to make up your losses but will grow weaker as time goes on…we will not only make up our losses but will grow stronger as time goes on. It is inevitable that we shall crush you before we are through with you."

ADMIRAL HAROLD N STARK, CHIEF OF NAVAL OPERATIONS,
TO ADMIRAL NOMURA KICHISABURO, JAPANESE
AMBASSADOR TO THE UNITED STATES

In September 1940 Japan had signed the Tripartite Pact with Germany and Italy. This bound the three nations to mutual support in the event of any one of them being attacked by a country not yet at war. In April 1941 Japan also negotiated a nonaggression pact with the Soviet Union. This would allow the planned Japanese operations in Southeast Asia to go ahead without any fear of a Soviet attack in Mongolia and Manchuria. The harmony of the Tripartite Pact was temporarily disturbed by Hitler's invasion of the Soviet Union in June 1941, of which Japan received no advance warning.

One man who had played a prominent role in negotiating the Tripartite Pact was General Tojo Hideki, the Japanese minister of war. Tojo's view, endorsed by the Japanese Army, was that provoking war with the United States was a risk worth taking. The seizure of Southeast Asia and the resources denied Japan by the Western powers would present them with a *fait accompli*. This would place Japan in a position of great strength in any subsequent peace negotiations. The Americans would surely flinch from the task of fighting across the territories and vast tracts of ocean that would be contained behind Japan's perimeter defense and would come to terms.

The battle for Stalingrad
Red Army soldiers duck and crouch as they advance cautiously across the rubble of Stalingrad. So constant was fighting in the ruined city, troops rarely exposed themselves to enemy fire in this way. They moved around by means of rat runs through the ruins.

On October 17 Tojo succeeded Konoye as prime minister. On November 2 he told Emperor Hirohito that Japan must seize its advantage or become a "third-class nation in two or three years." The war plans were approved by Admiral Nagano on November 3, and Yamamoto's carrier strike force assembled in the Kurile Islands north of Japan. In the meantime diplomatic talks in Washington, ostensibly aimed at averting hostilities, continued on their futile course. By now, the Americans were aware of Japanese intentions since they had been decoding Japanese radio traffic for months, but they remained ignorant of the precise Japanese plans.

REACTIONS TO PEARL HARBOR

The Japanese attack on the US Pacific Fleet at Pearl Harbor on December 7, 1941 transformed the war into a global conflict. The United States immediately declared war on Japan and, on December 11,

Germany declared war on the United States. Hitler addressed the Reichstag, declaring jubilantly that the Japanese had followed the German precept of always striking first. He was now convinced that Germany could not possibly lose the war. The Japanese, after all, were a nation that had not been vanquished in three thousand years. Churchill's reaction was more measured. On being given the news of the attack on Pearl Harbor he reached the same conclusion as Hitler, but from the British perspective, observing, "So we have won after all."

On December 22, 1941, Churchill, Roosevelt, and their respective staffs met in Washington, D.C., at the conference code-named "Arcadia." In formulating a general policy for prosecuting the war, Roosevelt came under intense pressure from his admirals to make the Pacific theater the major priority. However, Roosevelt confirmed the "Germany first" policy agreed in Placentia Bay in August 1941.

"Each position, each yard of Soviet territory must be stubbornly defended to the last drop of blood. We must cling to every inch of Soviet soil and defend it to the end."

JOSEF STALIN IN HIS ORDER TO THE RED ARMY ON JULY 28, 1942

Driven from their homes
Hundreds of families camp in fields on the outskirts of Stalingrad in September 1942 to escape the furious German shelling of the city.

To achieve this, both sides agreed that the continent of Europe would have to be invaded and that Britain would be the springboard for this operation. Furthermore, the Soviet Union was to be kept in the war at all costs, and this could best be achieved by extending to Stalin the terms of Lend-Lease.

HITLER'S GRAND DESIGNS

Hitler, meanwhile, was in the grip of his ambitious strategic plans for 1942, encompassing the seizure of the oil fields of the Middle East, which would destroy the basis of British power in the region and provide the fuel to sustain his panzer armies

in perpetuity. This ambitious long-term objective was the background to the German summer campaign of 1942, code-named Operation *Blau* (Blue) and outlined by Hitler in Führer Directive No 41. One of the principal goals of the campaign was to destroy "the entire defense potential remaining to the Soviets and to cut them off, as far as possible, from their most important centers of war industry."

One of the centers of war industry that the invading Germans would attempt to destroy was the city of Stalingrad on the Volga River. From midsummer 1942 Stalingrad was to exercise a morbid hold over Hitler. It would eventually assume an even more terrible significance, when the soldiers of the Red Army demonstrated that they were prepared to sacrifice themselves in their hundreds of thousands to deny the city to the Germans.

A TRULY GLOBAL WAR

The scale on which the war was being fought in the Soviet Union, along a front of more than 1,500 miles (2,400 km), already dwarfed that of any previous conflict. To this was now added a vast new theater of war in Asia and the Pacific.

In order to wage war, Britain and the United States, until 1945 the only great powers involved in both the German and Japanese wars, needed to move manpower, war material, and food around the globe. In addition to the constant flow of Allied shipping across the Atlantic, American ships now sailed across the Pacific to Australia, and through the Indian Ocean to the Persian Gulf in order to get supplies overland to their Soviet ally.

For the moment it was hard to predict how the war in the Pacific would develop. By provoking American wrath, the Japanese had awakened a sleeping giant. Through their own choices, both Japan and Germany had brought the United States into the ranks of their enemies. American military and air power in 1941 may have been modest, but in terms of financial, industrial, and demographic resources, the United States was incomparably the greatest power in the world.

EVENTS LEADING TO THE ATTACK ON PEARL HARBOR

MARCH 1940–DECEMBER 1941

US policy in this period was governed by opposition to Japan's war in China and Japanese designs on Southeast Asia, with its rich oil reserves and other natural resources. Japan knew that sooner or later war with the US was inevitable and decided to strike first before the Americans had time to build a larger navy.

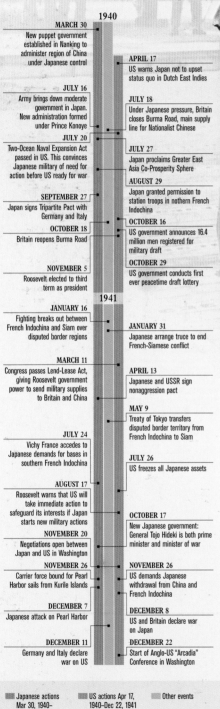

1940

MARCH 30
New puppet government established in Nanking to administer region of China under Japanese control

APRIL 17
US warns Japan not to upset status quo in Dutch East Indies

JULY 16
Army brings down moderate government in Japan. New administration formed under Prince Konoye

JULY 18
Under Japanese pressure, Britain closes Burma Road, main supply line for Nationalist Chinese

JULY 20
Two-Ocean Naval Expansion Act passed in US. This convinces Japanese military of need for action before US ready for war

JULY 27
Japan proclaims Greater East Asia Co-Prosperity Sphere

AUGUST 29
Japan granted permission to station troops in nothern French Indochina

SEPTEMBER 27
Japan signs Tripartite Pact with Germany and Italy

OCTOBER 16
US government announces 16.4 million men registered for military draft

OCTOBER 18
Britain reopens Burma Road

OCTOBER 29
US government conducts first ever peacetime draft lottery

NOVEMBER 5
Roosevelt elected to third term as president

1941

JANUARY 16
Fighting breaks out between French Indochina and Siam over disputed border regions

JANUARY 31
Japanese arrange truce to end French-Siamese conflict

MARCH 11
Congress passes Lend-Lease Act, giving Roosevelt government power to send military supplies to Britain and China

APRIL 13
Japanese and USSR sign nonaggression pact

MAY 9
Treaty of Tokyo transfers disputed border territory from French Indochina to Siam

JULY 24
Vichy France accedes to Japanese demands for bases in southern French Indochina

JULY 26
US freezes all Japanese assets

AUGUST 17
Roosevelt warns that US will take immediate action to safeguard its interests if Japan starts new military actions

OCTOBER 17
New Japanese government: General Tojo Hideki is both prime minister and minister of war

NOVEMBER 20
Negotiations open between Japan and US in Washington

NOVEMBER 26
Carrier force bound for Pearl Harbor sails from Kurile Islands

NOVEMBER 26
US demands Japanese withdrawal from China and French Indochina

DECEMBER 7
Japanese attack on Pearl Harbor

DECEMBER 8
US and Britain declare war on Japan

DECEMBER 11
Germany and Italy declare war on US

DECEMBER 22
Start of Anglo-US "Arcadia" Conference in Washington

| ▓ Japanese actions Mar 30, 1940– Dec 22, 1941 | ▓ US actions Apr 17, 1940–Dec 22, 1941 | ▓ Other events |

THE US JOINS THE WAR

WHEN WAR BROKE OUT in Europe in 1939, Japan's high command was understandably cautious. Germany had secretly and treacherously signed a nonaggression pact with the Soviets, whose army had recently inflicted a resounding defeat on Japanese forces in Nomonhan. After agreeing to a cease-fire with the USSR, Japan chose to remain neutral and see how events unfolded.

EFFECTS OF THE FALL OF FRANCE

The German victory in northwest Europe in the spring of 1940 altered Japanese thinking. After the fall of France, the defeat of Britain seemed to be only a matter of time. The European colonies in Southeast Asia—the Dutch East Indies, French Indochina, Burma, and Malaya, the region Japan saw as its Southern Resources Area—lay virtually defenseless. Taking advantage of this situation, the Japanese sought to close supply routes to the Chinese

Nationalists via Indochina and Burma. The French were forced to close the Hanoi-Nanning railroad, and on July 24, 1940, the British closed the Burma Road between Lashio and Chungking (see map page 118).

In July 1940 a new government was formed, headed by Prince Konoye Fumimaro, a former prime minister, who was closely associated with the military. The preconditions of the army and navy for allowing him to form a government were prior acceptance of their demands for a treaty with Germany and Italy, a nonaggression treaty with the USSR, and an expansionist strategy in Southeast Asia.

What seemed an impending German victory in Europe also produced far-reaching policy changes in the United States. Throughout its history, the security of the United States had largely depended on a divided Europe. Faced now with a German victory in Europe and the Japanese threat in the Far East, the United States sought to ensure its security

Aboard an aircraft carrier of the Pacific Fleet
The US response to the Japanese threat in the Pacific was slow, but in May 1940 Roosevelt decided that the Pacific Fleet, which had been conducting exercises off Hawaii, should remain at Pearl Harbor and not return to California.

in both the North Atlantic and the Pacific with the Two-Ocean Naval Expansion Act of July 1940. The act authorized the construction of 11 battleships, 6 battlecruisers, 18 fleet carriers, 27 cruisers, 115 destroyers, and 43 submarines, in addition to the 130 warships already under construction.

Over the next few months the Japanese high command gradually realized the implications of the act. Its provisions would be completed around 1948, but, after 1944, the United States would enjoy an overwhelming advantage in naval strength over Japan. In a way the act presented Japan with a "now or never" dilemma, a window of opportunity around the end of 1941 when Japanese building and mobilization would be complete, but before American construction came on line.

SOUTHEAST ASIA

On September 22, 1940, the French authorities in Saigon were forced to accept Japanese demands for occupation rights in northern Indochina and in the same month Japan concluded the Tripartite Pact with Germany and Italy. From its renewed association with Germany, Japan came into possession of intelligence material obtained from the British steamer *Automedon* by the German raider *Atlantis* off the Nicobar Islands in November 1940. The *Automedon* was carrying mail for Singapore that included the minutes of the British cabinet meeting of August 12, 1940. These revealed that Britain could not oppose any Japanese move against either Indochina or Siam, and would be unable to send a fleet to the Far East in the event of war with Japan. The contents of the papers were sent by signal to Berlin (and were read by British intelligence, though Singapore was not informed) and were then presented by the Germans to the Japanese attachés in Berlin and to representatives of the army and navy staffs in Tokyo.

The revelation of British defenselessness in Southeast Asia was like scales falling from the eyes. The Japanese army now began serious

Battle-hardened troops
Japan's well-trained army had been at war since 1937. Here Japanese infantry and artillery pursue remnants of the Chinese Nationalist army in Honan province north of the Yangtze River in November 1941.

FRANKLIN DELANO ROOSEVELT

FRANKLIN D. ROOSEVELT (1882–1945), the 32nd president of the United States, led his country from 1933 to 1945. The Democratic candidate for vice president in 1920, he was struck down by poliomyelitis in 1921, but refused to give up politics. He is remembered for two great achievements: first for the hope he gave the American people with his "New Deal" policies during the Depression of the 1930s, then for his leadership in World War II. The American economic recovery was completed by the full employment of the war years, allowing the United States to emerge as the dominant political and economic force of the postwar world.

Before his country was drawn into the war by the attack on Pearl Harbor, Roosevelt had faced an isolationist public, although his own feelings on the war in Europe were made clear in his policy of acting as the "arsenal of democracy." In 1944 he was elected to a historic fourth term, but his health declined and on April 12, 1945, he died, less than a month before the German surrender.

training for operations in the south. The troops that were to lead the campaign in Malaya practiced landings on Hainan and training in jungle warfare began on Formosa in February 1941. At the same time Japanese naval staff began to take seriously a suggestion made in October 1940 for a preemptive attack on the US Pacific Fleet at Pearl Harbor.

ECONOMIC WARFARE

Relations between the United States and Japan had been steadily worsening. In January 1940 Washington had refused to agree to a new commercial treaty with Japan. After July 1940 a series of US measures

deprived Japan of aviation fuel, high-grade scrap and, after January 1941, virtually every raw material and metal of any real importance. In March 1941 the Japanese forced the French to accept Japanese occupation of Saigon airport and to turn over the whole of Indochina's rice surplus. Having proclaimed their intention to create a new international order throughout Southeast Asia in February 1941, the Japanese announced what amounted to a claim upon exclusive interest in the resources of the area. Then, in April 1941, came the Japanese conclusion of a nonaggression treaty with the USSR, the essential prerequisite for a move into Southeast Asia.

When Germany attacked the Soviet Union in June 1941, it appeared at first that the Germans were certain to win. On June 25 the two Japanese services met to discuss this new development. They decided to concentrate on the intended takeover of Southeast Asia before dealing with whatever situation existed in the wake of Germany's victory over the Soviet Union. When the imperial conference of July 2 had confirmed this decision, the army called up a million reservists. These were to be deployed in the Home Islands, Manchuria, and China, thus freeing existing divisions for service in Southeast Asia. On July 21 the navy formally declared itself in favor of the occupation of parts of the Southern Resources Area even at the risk of war with the United States and, on July 25, Japanese forces occupied southern

YAMAMOTO ISOROKU

COMMANDER-IN-CHIEF of the Japanese Combined Fleet in 1941, Yamamoto Isoroku (1884–1943), was the originator of the plan for the attack on Pearl Harbor. As a young ensign he fought against the Russians at Tsushima (1905), where he lost two fingers on his left hand. After World War I he spent time in United States, first as a student at Harvard, then as a naval attaché in Washington. He foresaw the importance of airpower in naval warfare and in 1933 was given command of the First Carrier Division. The apparent success of the Pearl Harbor operation made him a national hero, but his Central Pacific offensive in June 1942 resulted in disaster at Midway. Yamamoto retained command of the Combined Fleet, moving his headquarters to Truk. He was killed when the aircraft he was flying in was shot down over Bougainville on April 18, 1943. Yamamoto remains a figure of controversy. He is usually portrayed as one of the more moderate Japanese officers, fearful of American power, but, whatever misgivings he had about war with the United States, these did not prevent him from attaining the highest ranks.

The *West Virginia* sinking in flames
In the attack on Pearl Harbor, the battleship *West Virginia* was hit by six torpedoes and two bombs. After the ship had sunk to the bottom, she continued to burn until the following afternoon.

French Indochina under the terms of a joint Franco-Japanese condominium. Roosevelt immediately froze all Japanese assets and halted US trade with Japan. Britain and the Netherlands followed suit, ending the trade with Southeast Asia on which Japan depended. Japanese attempts to get the American embargo lifted failed because of US insistence that Japan give up all its gains on the Asian mainland. The Japanese therefore decided that the only escape from this deadlock was war.

THE ATTACK ON PEARL HARBOR

In attacking the American fleet at its Hawaiian base at the outset of war the Japanese sought to neutralize the only force that could oppose their planned seizure of Southeast Asia and various island groups in the Pacific. The Japanese plan was to secure these areas and establish a vast perimeter defense around them. The Americans, after fighting to exhaustion against this

This is no drill
This message was sent to all ships in the Hawaii area announcing the air raid on Pearl Harbor minutes after the first bombs and torpedoes had struck.

defensive barrier, would be forced to come to a negotiated settlement. The specific goal of the attack on the fleet at Pearl Harbor was to forestall American countermoves by destroying four battleships. The Japanese calculated that this would limit American offensive capability sufficiently to provide a six-month period in which Japan could complete its planned conquests and prepare for the next phase of war.

The scale of the Japanese raid on the US Pacific Fleet on the morning of Sunday, December 7, 1941, was unprecedented. It was a massed attack involving two waves of aircraft (350 in total) from six fleet carriers. The British air attack on the Italian fleet at Taranto in November 1940 had involved just one carrier and 21 elderly Swordfish biplanes. The thoroughness of the Japanese planning and the successful timing needed to achieve complete surprise were equally impressive. An attack over such a large distance was possible only because of refueling under way, something the units of the carrier force had practiced for the first time in the three weeks before sailing.

THE ATTACK IS LAUNCHED
At 6:05 am on the day of the attack the fleet was 220 miles (350 km) north of Oahu. The Japanese aircraft had to take off in strong winds and heavy seas, the worst conditions the fleet had encountered in its 13-day voyage from the Kurile Islands. In spite of this, the first wave, which consisted of 49 Kate bombers, 40 Kate torpedo-bombers, 51 Val dive-bombers, and 43 Zero fighters, was airborne within 15 minutes, with just two planes lost in the process. The second wave—54 Kate bombers, 78 Vals, and 35 Zeros—was ready for takeoff at 7:15 am.

The air attacks were backed up by five midget submarines launched from their parent submarine close to the entrance to Pearl Harbor during the night. One of the submarines was actually spotted at 3:42 am; another (or the same one) was spotted and sunk shortly before 7:00 am. The second incident was reported but the craft's identity was unknown and no further action was taken. A radar sighting of a large number of aircraft approaching from the north was made at about the same time, but it was assumed these were US planes flying in from the mainland. At any rate, by now, there was hardly any time to take effective action against attack.

THE EXTENT OF THE DAMAGE
The first wave of planes inflicted considerable damage, especially the Kates' attack on "Battleship Row," where seven battleships were moored. The Val dive-bombers and Zero fighters were also extremely effective in neutralizing American air power on Oahu. The second wave, which struck an

JAPANESE AND US CARRIER PLANES

OF ALL THE MAJOR POWERS, Japan was best prepared for a new era in naval warfare dominated by aircraft. In 1941 the Japanese navy had 10 front-line aircraft carriers; the American navy had only three in the Pacific. Both navies agreed on the types of aircraft needed—fighters to gain control of the air, along with dive-bombers and torpedo-bombers to attack enemy ships—but the US planes were markedly inferior to their Japanese counterparts. The Japanese also had better-trained, more experienced crews. Although the Japanese realized the importance of the aircraft carrier, they still believed that battleships—their principal targets at Pearl Harbor—were the key to any major naval action. Both sides soon discovered that this was not the case. Entire naval battles would be fought without any ships coming within range of the other side's guns. Carriers also became launching pads for bombing raids on airfields and other military installations on shore.

Nakajima B5N2 ("Kate")
The B5N2 was Japan's torpedo-bomber. Armed with the advanced Type 95 torpedo, this formidable aircraft enjoyed great success for the first two years of the war. An earlier model, the B5N1, was used as a level-altitude bomber, deployed chiefly in China. Late in the war Kates were used as Kamikaze planes.

Engine 1,115 hp Nakajima Sakae 21 air-cooled 14-cylinder radial	
Wingspan 50 ft 11 in (15.5 m)	Length 33 ft 9 in (10.3 m)
Top speed 235 mph (378 kph)	Crew 3
Armament 2 × 7.7-mm machine-guns, 1 × 7.7-mm machine-gun in rear; 1 × 1,765-lb (800-kg) torpedo	

Radio mast. The Zero was one of the first Japanese carrier aircraft to be equipped with radio

Mitsubishi A6M Reisen ("Zero" or "Zeke")
At the outbreak of war the Japanese Zero was superior to any other carrier fighter and a match for existing shore-based fighters. "Zero" is the translation of the Japanese "Reisen." The lightweight aircraft had unparalleled range for the period. The A6M2 (the model in use at the time of Pearl Harbor) had a mission range of over 1,600 miles (2,500 km). New models of the highly maneuverable Zero continued to be developed—shown here is the A6M5—and by the end of the war a total of almost 11,000 had been built.

Wing-mounted cannon. In earlier models these were concealed within the wing

On some models the wingtips folded up so the plane could fit into standard carrier elevators

Three-bladed propellor

Engine 1,300 hp Nakajima NK1C Sakae 21 14-cylinder radial	
Wingspan 36 ft 1 in (11 m)	Length 29 ft 11 in (9.1 m)
Top speed 346 mph (557 kph)	Crew 1
Armament 2 × 20-mm cannon in wings, 2 × 7.7-mm machine-guns on fuselage; wing racks carry 2 × 132-lb (60-kg) bombs	

Douglas SBD-3 Dauntless
The US Navy's main dive-bomber at the start of the war, the Dauntless carried a greater bombload than the Japanese Val. Though slow and vulnerable to fighters, it could absorb considerable damage. Dauntlesses were involved in the destruction of six Japanese carriers in 1942. Nearly 6,000 were built.

Engine 1,000 hp Wright R-1820-52 Cyclone 9-cylinder radial	
Wingspan 41 ft 6 in (13.9 m)	Length 33 ft 1 in (10.1 m)
Top speed 250 mph (402 kph)	Crew 2
Armament 2 × 0.5-in machine-guns in nose, 2 × 0.3-in machine-guns in rear cockpit; 1,200-lb (545-kg) bombload	

Aichi D3A ("Val")
A dive-bomber used by the Japanese navy at Pearl Harbor, the Val was feared for its impressive accuracy in the first two years of the war, but after 1943 its lack of armor made it an easy target for US fighters. Its fixed undercarriage made its silhouette easily recognizable.

Engine 1,080 hp Mitsubishi Kinsei 44 air-cooled 14-cylinder radial	
Wingspan 47 ft 1 in (14.4 m)	Length 33 ft 5 in (10.2 m)
Top speed 272 mph (460 kph)	Crew 2
Armament 2 × 7.7-mm machine-guns (1 in nose, 1 in rear); 1 × 550-lb (250-kg), 2 × 66-lb (30-kg) bombs under wings	

MAGIC: CRACKING THE JAPANESE CODES

"MAGIC" WAS THE CODE NAME the Americans gave to deciphered Japanese radio messages, particularly those in the code known as "Purple," used for diplomatic communications. This code was introduced in early 1939, replacing one code-named "Red" that the Americans had already deciphered. The cipher machine that generated the Purple code consisted of two typewriter keyboards connected by a bewildering array of circuits and switches, based on the technology of a telephone switchboard. Not all Japanese embassies were issued with these new machines and they continued to use the "Red" code. This helped

Deciphering Japanese messages
Intelligence analysts work with Purple code machines at the headquarters of the US Army cryptanalysis service in Arlington, Virginia.

Purple machine
The Americans never managed to capture a Japanese Purple encoding machine. Once they had understood how it worked, they simply built their own.

the decryption team at the US Army Signals Intelligence Service, as the same message was sometimes sent out in the two codes. The team of cryptanalysts, headed by William F. Friedman, worked tirelessly for 18 months to crack the code. A vital contribution was made by Harry L. Clark, a naval cryptanalyst, who guessed that the Japanese were not using rotors as on the German Enigma machine, but standard telephone equipment. Success came on September 25, 1940, when the first complete message was deciphered. The team then set about constructing Purple analogue machines.

After the failure of the US intelligence services to foresee the attack on Pearl Harbor, vast resources were devoted to breaking other Japanese codes. The Japanese naval code, JN-25, was never cracked completely, but was understood sufficiently to warn the US Navy of the Japanese attack on Midway in June 1942. Top secret information derived from Japanese coded radio traffic was given the same "Ultra" designation as information gathered from German Enigma communications (see page 82).

through an unrestricted submarine campaign. Moreover, the losses inflicted on the Americans were really of little account. In the course of the war the US Navy brought into service 104 fleet, light fleet, and escort carriers, eight battleships, 46 cruisers, 349 destroyers, 493 destroyer escorts and frigates, and 203 submarines; the aircraft losses incurred at Pearl Harbor represented less than two days' production by March 1944.

WHAT MIGHT HAVE BEEN

Some commentators maintain that Japan's mistake was to leave Pearl Harbor's docks, workshops, power plants, and oil depots virtually intact. Despite the heavy loss of warships, the Americans were left with a more or less functional naval base. Given America's industrial output over the next three years, however, whatever damage might have been inflicted on these facilities would have been repaired very quickly. Others suggest that the Japanese should have conducted not an air strike, but an assault landing with the intention of securing Oahu, yet even this would probably have done little to alter the course of the war.

From the American point of view, commentators have pointed out that by the fall of 1941 signals intelligence had cracked a number of Japanese ciphers and was reading a large amount of radio traffic. But the Japanese Navy in its preparation and training for the attack on Pearl Harbor did not need to use radio and nothing in the signals read by the Americans gave any inkling of a war beginning with an attack on the fleet at its Hawaiian base.

In the build-up to the attack the Japanese Navy had employed a number of deceptive measures. A large number of its sailors had been granted leave in Tokyo over the weekend and wide publicity was given to the sailing of the *Tatsuta Maru* in order to collect Japanese nationals being repatriated from the United States.

hour later, was less successful, largely because smoke from the burning oil spewing from the stricken battleships obscured the attackers' view. In all, the attack accounted for 18 warships either sunk, destroyed, or damaged to some degree, and 198 aircraft destroyed and 174 damaged. A total of 3,748 US service personnel were killed or wounded. American civilian casualties numbered 103.

Of the ships, only three, the battleships *Arizona* and *Oklahoma*, and the target ship *Utah*, were total losses, though the *Oklahoma* was raised in order to clear the anchorage. The *Arizona* was struck by a bomb that penetrated the ship's forward magazine, causing a tremendous explosion and a huge fireball. Nearly 1,000 of its crew were killed and the vessel sank within nine minutes. The battleships *California* and *West Virginia*, and the headquarters ship *Oglala*, were sunk, and the battleship *Nevada*, after suffering extensive damage, was run aground. All four ships, however, were raised, then underwent massive reconstruction and were returned to service. The light cruisers *Helena* and *Raleigh*, and the destroyer *Shaw* were moderately damaged, and were returned to service in 1942; the destroyers *Cassin* and *Downes* were very badly damaged, but were rebuilt and

reentered service in 1944. The damage inflicted on the battleships *Maryland*, *Tennessee*, and *Pennnsyvania*, the light cruiser *Honolulu*, and the auxiliaries *Curtiss* and *Vestal* was minor. Japanese losses numbered 29 aircraft, with at least another 111 damaged.

For all the success registered against the US fleet, the attack was disastrous for Japan. It brought into the war a United States roused in righteous anger and determined to wage war either to total victory or to defeat. The attack forced the US navy to reconstitute its tactical formations around the aircraft carrier rather than the battleship and to carry the war immediately to Japanese shipping

Pearl Harbor
This Japanese aerial photograph of the attack shows Ford Island in the middle of the harbor with the row of US battleships lined up on the far side of the island.

As well as these measures, intended to demonstrate "business as usual," a signals unit in Japan's Inland Sea simulated radio signals from aircraft carrier units, and these, it seems, had the desired effect.

In the aftermath of the attack, the Americans naturally wanted to know what had gone wrong and to find scapegoats on whom to pin the blame. There was little appreciation of the tight security measures taken by the Japanese. Perhaps no more than 100

Assessing the damage

American sailors walk over the wreckage of the destroyers *Downes* (left) and *Cassin* after the Japanese attack on Pearl Harbor. The battleship *Pennsylvania*, flagship of the Pacific fleet, is visible behind the two destroyers.

officers in the Imperial Navy outside the task force earmarked for the operation were aware of the plan. Nor were critics prepared to accept the fact that the United States had no God-given ability to predict the future. The Americans and British had both realized that the Japanese were about to go to war, but in the days immediately before the attack, their attention had been focused on the impending offensives throughout Southeast Asia. This had clouded their appreciation of the strategic picture to the east, in the Central Pacific. The Japanese opening move, spread across nine time zones and over 7,000 miles (11,000 km), was something so utterly without precedent that it could never have been foreseen.

Behind me, a marine lay dead on the deck, his body split in two. I began to realize there were dead men all around me. Some men were burning, wandering aimlessly. The sound of someone shouting "put out the fire" cut through the sound of the battle, but it was obvious the ship was doomed. I made my way to the side of the ship, which by this time was sinking fast, and jumped off the fantail. The shoreline of Ford Island was only a short distance. There was burning oil all around the ship, but the aft was clear. After swimming to shore, I was taken to the naval air station. Every table in the mess hall had a man on it.

GEORGE D. PHRANER, AVIATION MACHINIST'S MATE 1ST CLASS, SURVIVOR OF THE USS *ARIZONA*

BINOCULARS FROM THE BRIDGE OF THE USS ARIZONA

THE PACIFIC AND SOUTHEAST ASIA

DECEMBER 1941–JUNE 1942

The attack on Pearl Harbor was synchronized with the start of Japanese invasions of the American, British, and Dutch colonies in Southeast Asia. For six months the Japanese enjoyed an uninterrupted run of victories, but in June 1942 suffered a serious setback in the carrier battle with the US fleet at Midway.

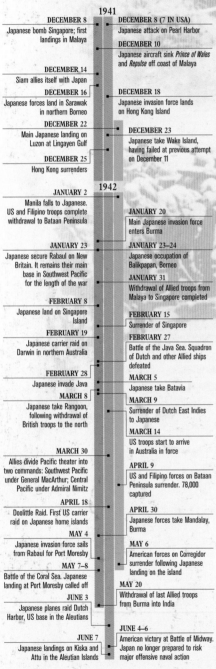

1941

DECEMBER 8
Japanese bomb Singapore; first landings in Malaya

DECEMBER 8 (7 IN USA)
Japanese attack on Pearl Harbor

DECEMBER 10
Japanese aircraft sink *Prince of Wales* and *Repulse* off coast of Malaya

DECEMBER 14
Siam allies itself with Japan

DECEMBER 16
Japanese forces land in Sarawak in northern Borneo

DECEMBER 18
Japanese invasion force lands on Hong Kong Island

DECEMBER 22
Main Japanese landing on Luzon at Lingayen Gulf

DECEMBER 23
Japanese take Wake Island, having failed at previous attempt on December 11

DECEMBER 25
Hong Kong surrenders

1942

JANUARY 2
Manila falls to Japanese. US and Filipino troops complete withdrawal to Bataan Peninsula

JANUARY 20
Main Japanese invasion force enters Burma

JANUARY 23
Japanese secure Rabaul on New Britain. It remains their main base in Southwest Pacific for the length of the war

JANUARY 23–24
Japanese occupation of Balikpapan, Borneo

JANUARY 31
Withdrawal of Allied troops from Malaya to Singapore completed

FEBRUARY 8
Japanese land on Singapore Island

FEBRUARY 15
Surrender of Singapore

FEBRUARY 19
Japanese carrier raid on Darwin in northern Australia

FEBRUARY 27
Battle of the Java Sea. Squadron of Dutch and other Allied ships defeated

FEBRUARY 28
Japanese invade Java

MARCH 5
Japanese take Batavia

MARCH 8
Japanese take Rangoon, following withdrawal of British troops to the north

MARCH 9
Surrender of Dutch East Indies to Japanese

MARCH 14
US troops start to arrive in Australia in force

MARCH 30
Allies divide Pacific theater into two commands: Southwest Pacific under General MacArthur; Central Pacific under Admiral Nimitz

APRIL 9
US and Filipino forces on Bataan Peninsula surrender. 78,000 captured

APRIL 18
Doolittle Raid. First US carrier raid on Japanese home islands

APRIL 30
Japanese forces take Mandalay, Burma

MAY 4
Japanese invasion force sails from Rabaul for Port Moresby

MAY 6
American forces on Corregidor surrender following Japanese landing on the island

MAY 7–8
Battle of the Coral Sea. Japanese landing at Port Moresby called off

MAY 20
Withdrawal of last Allied troops from Burma into India

JUNE 3
Japanese planes raid Dutch Harbor, US base in the Aleutians

JUNE 4–6
American victory at Battle of Midway. Japan no longer prepared to risk major offensive naval action

JUNE 7
Japanese landings on Kiska and Attu in the Aleutian Islands

■ Japanese conquest of Southeast Asia and Dutch East Indies Dec 1942–Jun 1943

■ Japanese conquest of the Philippines Dec 1942–May 1943

■ Other events

JAPANESE ONSLAUGHT

O N THE SAME DAY as their strike against the US Pacific Fleet—December 7 in the United States and at Pearl Harbor, December 8 in Japan and the Western Pacific—the Japanese unleashed a series of other carefully prepared attacks. In the Pacific, these included a bombardment of the island of Midway and attacks on Wake Island and Guam. Bombers from Formosa launched an air strike against American airfields on the island of Luzon in the Philippines, destroying 103 aircraft, most of them while they were still on the ground. The Japanese then went ahead with preliminary landings on the islands to the north of Luzon. Meanwhile, troops from the Chinese mainland entered the New Territories in order to seize the British colony of Hong Kong. In Southeast Asia, some Japanese troops moved overland into neutral Siam from southern Indochina, while others carried out a series of landings in southern Siam and northern Malaya.

Only at Wake did Japanese plans miscarry. On December 11 the garrison of American Marines managed to repel the invasion force, but the Japanese, with the assistance of two of the carriers returning from the Pearl Harbor operation, were able to secure the island on December 23.

By that date the Japanese had overrun the New Territories, and the garrison on Hong Kong Island surrendered on December 25. In Malaya, the British hoped to put up more substantial resistance. On December 8 they despatched a naval force—the battleship *Prince of Wales*, the battlecruiser *Repulse*, and four destroyers—from Singapore to counter the Japanese landings on the east coast of Malaya and Siam. The ships were spotted and, on the morning of December 10, attacked by land-based torpedo-bombers. In less than three hours both the *Prince of Wales* and the *Repulse* had been sunk.

RAPID ADVANCE

The British fared little better on land. As the Indian, British, and Australian troops retreated south along the Malayan peninsula, they were caught between trying to fight a delaying action and preparing defensive positions. The Japanese, well trained in

Advance into Burma

A column of Japanese troops crosses an improvised bridge in northern Burma. Beside it lie the remains of a metal bridge destroyed by the retreating British forces as they withdrew to the safety of northern India.

jungle fighting, employed light armor on the roads and infantry infiltration through the jungle to get around British defenses. The British abandoned Penang on December 19 and the Japanese were able to bring the nearby airfield in Butterworth into service on the following day to provide air support for their continued advance.

AMERICAN WITHDRAWAL

In the Philippines, the Japanese staged a series of landings by small forces at various points on Luzon and at Davao on southern Mindanao. The main landings took place on December 22 in Lingayen Gulf north of Manila. These were followed by the withdrawal of the main American forces into the Bataan Peninsula, allowing the Japanese to advance to Manila and enter the city on January 2, 1942. In this first phase of the invasion the Americans managed to avoid defeat, but the refuge they had chosen in the Bataan Peninsula would turn out to be a trap. Despite having planned for such an eventuality, they had not prepared or prestocked their defenses. With the Japanese in control of the sea and the air, supplies could only reach the beleaguered forces by submarine. The defensive positions across the mountainous peninsula might prolong resistance, but there was no doubting the outcome of the campaign. For the time being, however, the Japanese command chose to ignore the American sidestep to Bataan. Its main concern at this stage was to free forces from the Philippines for moves against the Indies, and it was not until after the fall of Manila that Japanese attention turned to Bataan, but by then they did not have sufficient forces to overrun the peninsula.

TOJO HIDEKI

PRIME MINISTER OF JAPAN at the outbreak of war, General Tojo (1884–1948) was prominent among the hard-line militarists who came to dominate Japanese politics in the 1930s. He was a founder of the Asian Development Union, which embraced a policy of Japanese conquest and control throughout Asia. Respected both as a staff officer and as a field commander, he became chief of staff of the Kwantung army in Manchuria in 1937 and in the following year vice minister of war in the government of Prince Konoye. When Konoye formed another government in 1941, Tojo was his minister for war. As negotiations with the United States stalled, Tojo ousted Konoye and, in October 1941, established an administration that committed Japan to war. As the tide of war turned against Japan, Tojo took on ever more positions: by February 1944 he was minister of war and army chief of staff as well as prime minister. Tojo and his whole cabinet resigned in July 1944. After the Japanese surrender he made an unsuccessful attempt to kill himself, but was arrested and stood trial as a war criminal. He was hanged in December 1948.

SOUTHEAST ASIA

By this time the Japanese had won resounding victories throughout Southeast Asia. On the Malayan peninsula they continued their drive south to Singapore, advancing sometimes through the jungle, at other times by means of amphibious operations. On the western side of the peninsula they used light craft captured during their advance to outflank British positions with a series of small landings along the coast.

The sinking of the *Prince of Wales*

On December 10, 1942 the *Prince of Wales* was sunk by torpedoes in the South China Sea along with the *Repulse*. About 1,000 men were lost, but 2,081 were picked up by British destroyers.

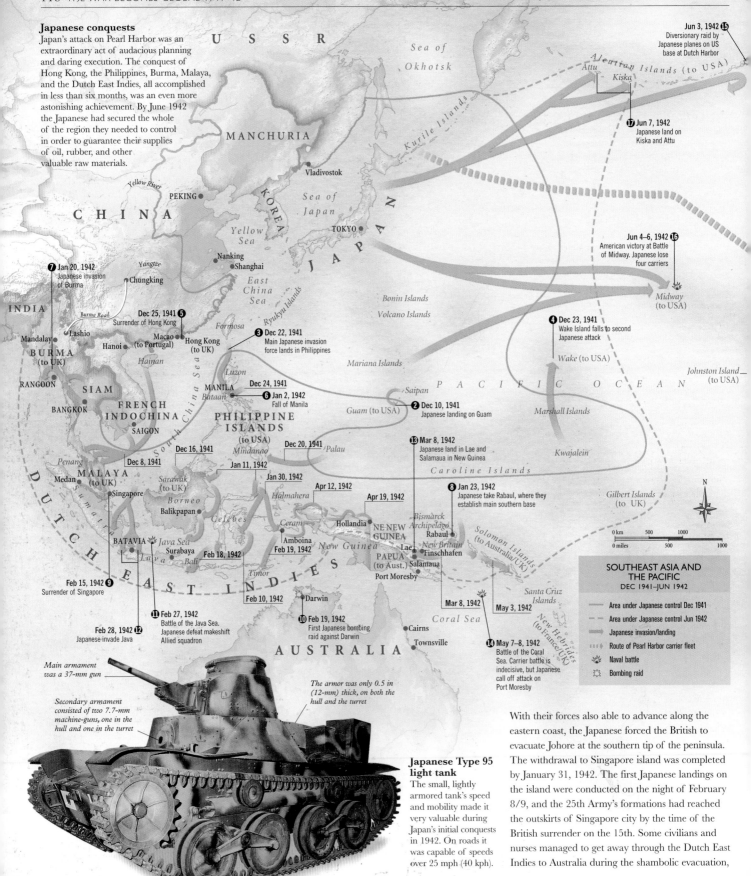

Japanese conquests

Japan's attack on Pearl Harbor was an extraordinary act of audacious planning and daring execution. The conquest of Hong Kong, the Philippines, Burma, Malaya, and the Dutch East Indies, all accomplished in less than six months, was an even more astonishing achievement. By June 1942 the Japanese had secured the whole of the region they needed to control in order to guarantee their supplies of oil, rubber, and other valuable raw materials.

Jun 3, 1942 ⑮
Diversionary raid by Japanese planes on US base at Dutch Harbor

⑰ Jun 7, 1942
Japanese land on Kiska and Attu

Jun 4–6, 1942 ⑯
American victory at Battle of Midway. Japanese lose four carriers

❼ Jan 20, 1942
Japanese invasion of Burma

Dec 25, 1941 ❺
Surrender of Hong Kong

❸ Dec 22, 1941
Main Japanese invasion force lands in Philippines

❹ Dec 23, 1941
Wake Island falls to second Japanese attack

Dec 24, 1941

❻ Jan 2, 1942
Fall of Manila

❷ Dec 10, 1941
Japanese landing on Guam

Dec 16, 1941

Dec 20, 1941

❽ Mar 8, 1942
Japanese land in Lae and Salamaua in New Guinea

Dec 8, 1941

Jan 11, 1942

❽ Jan 23, 1942
Japanese take Rabaul, where they establish main southern base

Jan 30, 1942

Apr 12, 1942

Apr 19, 1942

Feb 18, 1942

Feb 19, 1942

Feb 15, 1942 ❾
Surrender of Singapore

Feb 10, 1942

❶❶ Feb 27, 1942
Battle of the Java Sea. Japanese defeat makeshift Allied squadron

Feb 28, 1942 ❶❷
Japanese invade Java

❶⓿ Feb 19, 1942
First Japanese bombing raid against Darwin

Mar 8, 1942

May 3, 1942

❶❹ May 7–8, 1942
Battle of the Coral Sea. Carrier battle is indecisive, but Japanese call off attack on Port Moresby

Japanese Type 95 light tank

Main armament was a 37-mm gun

Secondary armament consisted of two 7.7-mm machine-guns, one in the hull and one in the turret

The armor was only 0.5 in (12-mm) thick, on both the hull and the turret

The small, lightly armored tank's speed and mobility made it very valuable during Japan's initial conquests in 1942. On roads it was capable of speeds over 25 mph (40 kph).

SOUTHEAST ASIA AND THE PACIFIC
DEC 1941–JUN 1942

- Area under Japanese control Dec 1941
- Area under Japanese control Jun 1942
- Japanese invasion/landing
- Route of Pearl Harbor carrier fleet
- Naval battle
- Bombing raid

0 km   500   1000
0 miles   500   1000

With their forces also able to advance along the eastern coast, the Japanese forced the British to evacuate Johore at the southern tip of the peninsula. The withdrawal to Singapore island was completed by January 31, 1942. The first Japanese landings on the island were conducted on the night of February 8/9, and the 25th Army's formations had reached the outskirts of Singapore city by the time of the British surrender on the 15th. Some civilians and nurses managed to get away through the Dutch East Indies to Australia during the shambolic evacuation,

Surrender in Singapore
Japanese troops with fixed bayonets round up a demoralized British unit after the fall of Singapore on February 15, 1942. The humiliating defeat by a despised and underrated enemy was a severe blow to British imperial prestige.

❶ Dec 7, 1941
Japanese attack on Pearl Harbor

Hawaiian Islands (to USA)
Pearl Harbor

but a large number of troops, including 32,000 Indians, 16,000 Britons, and 14,000 Australians, were made prisoners of war. The Japanese treated the Chinese civilian population of Singapore very differently from the prisoners of war. According to some accounts, the Japanese army killed about 120,000 Chinese in the three months after the surrender.

THE DUTCH EAST INDIES

The security of the Dutch empire in the East Indies had rested upon successive lines of defense—French Indochina, the American Philippines, and British Malaya. Once these had fallen the Dutch empire lay open to defeat and dismemberment. In fact, even before the defeats of the Americans and British were completed, the Japanese made their first moves against the islands, conducting a series of landings along two main axes of advance—one through the Macassar Strait between Borneo and Celebes, the other through the Molucca Sea, which separates Celebes from Halmahera and western New Guinea. The Japanese moves were synchronized and mounted behind a front secured by land-based air power.

As the Japanese moved southward through the Dutch East Indies, their only real losses occurred outside Balikpapan, the main port serving the valuable oil fields of eastern Borneo. On January 24–25, 1942 a group of American destroyers caught four of the transports carrying the Japanese landing force. The night action was fought against a background of flaming oil wells, which had been set alight by the Dutch. Even this reverse, however, did not delay the Japanese. The port was captured and the airfield in Balikpapan was returned to service on January 28.

With the British on the verge of defeat in Singapore, the Japanese mounted a further offensive to the west. Landings were made in southern Sumatra, even as Japanese forces came ashore on Timor and Bali. At the same time Japanese carrier planes raided Darwin in northern Australia. The defense of Java resulted in a vain Allied attempt to meet the Japanese at sea before their forces could come ashore, but this resulted in defeat at the Battle of the Java Sea on February 27–28. The Japanese landings on Java were followed by a naval action in the Sunda Strait and further losses as Allied naval forces abandoned the Indies. The Japanese occupied Batavia (Jakarta) on March 5 and four days later the Dutch East Indies surrendered. Japanese forces had already been operating south of Java, in the Indian Ocean, trying to destroy shipping escaping to Australia. In mid-March Japanese forces from Malaya occupied Medan in northern Sumatra and in early April other forces occupied various small ports on the Vogelkop Peninsula in western New Guinea. From there they advanced along the north coast of the island to Hollandia.

At first we thought these planes were ours, and then we noticed some silver-looking objects dropping from them. It was not long before we knew what they were as they exploded in smoke and dust on the town and waterfront. More Japanese planes came in from another direction. These were dive-bombers, and they attacked the ships in the harbor... They began strafing us from almost mast height. As the only armament we had against aircraft was a Lewis machine gun, and this had been disabled by a Japanese bullet hitting the magazine pan, the skipper was firing at them with his .45 revolver... Our casualties were nine wounded out of a crew of thirty-six, and one of these died on the hospital ship Manunda on the following day.

CHARLIE UNMACK, STOKER ABOARD THE MINESWEEPER HMAS *GUNBAR*, IN DARWIN HARBOR ON FEBRUARY 19, 1942

NIMITZ AND MACARTHUR

IN 1942 THE UNITED STATES found itself fighting a war along a front stretching from New Guinea to the Aleutians. It also had the problem of supporting and supplying the Nationalist forces in China. A new kind of command structure was needed to implement American strategic goals. The logical solution would have been to put the US Navy in overall command, but the US Army would not agree to this, nor would the navy agree to put the Pacific Fleet under the command of the army. They eventually appointed two commanders, one from the navy, the other from the army, each responsible for one particular theater. Admiral Chester W. Nimitz, commander-in-chief of the US Pacific Fleet since Pearl Harbor, was also made commander-in-chief of the Pacific Ocean Areas. General Douglas A. MacArthur, despite his poor handling of the defense of the Philippines, was made Supreme Allied Commander South West Pacific Command, with his headquarters in Australia. The two were very contrasting characters. Nimitz was a modest man, who deliberately chose able subordinate commanders, while MacArthur was an individualist, obsessed with his own importance and the creation of his own legend.

Joint commanders
MacArthur (with his trademark corncob pipe) and Nimitz study a map. Rivalry between the army and the navy was a constant source of tension between the two, but somehow the job got done.

US troops in Australia
The first American soldiers reached Australia on December 22, 1941. General MacArthur arrived in March 1942, setting up his headquarters in Melbourne.

BURMA

The Japanese victories in Malaya, the Indies, and the Philippines were not the only victories recorded in this period. The Japanese move into Siam at the outbreak of hostilities was the prelude to an invasion of the British colony of Burma. Siam, with very little choice in the matter, allied itself to Japan, allowing its territory to serve as a base for operations against Malaya and Burma.

The Burmese campaign proved a remarkable Japanese success. By the end of April 1942, and at a cost of just over 4,000 dead, the Japanese had captured Lashio and were on the point of occupying

While Aussies shed their precious blood, Ole man Roosevelt finds his selfish aims going according to schedule.

Japanese advance in the Philippines
Once the main American force on the Bataan peninsula had surrendered in April 1942, the Japanese gradually mopped up the other scattered pockets of resistance. Here troops are crossing a river on Type 89 medium tanks.

Japanese propaganda
The Japanese tried to alienate Australians from the Allied cause. This cartoon shows Australians fighting vainly to hold back the Japanese advance, while Roosevelt helps himself to their homeland.

Mandalay. By the end of May the Japanese had secured virtually the whole of Burma. The few British forces that had been in Burma and the Chinese Kuomintang troops that had entered the country in January 1942 were unable to put up any resistance to the Japanese at any point during their advance. The victory was comprehensive, but brought a defensive commitment at the end of a long, vulnerable line of communication. In time, Japan's enemies were certain to launch a counteroffensive.

THE END IN THE PHILIPPINES

The humiliation of the United States was completed by the surrender of its remaining forces in the Philippines. The Americans and Filipinos

on the Bataan Peninsula had resisted Japanese attacks in January and February, but many were struck down by malaria and by February supplies of quinine were running short. Food was an even greater problem , since Japanese air superiority meant that hardly any supplies were reaching the beleaguered troops. There was no fodder at all for the horses and mules, which all had to be killed.

In Washington, Roosevelt accepted that the defense of the Philippines was doomed and on February 23 ordered General MacArthur to leave for Australia to take command of the Allied effort in the Southwest Pacific. On March 11 MacArthur and his family were taken by torpedo boat to Mindanao and from there by Flying Fortress to Australia. Reinforced with fresh troops, the Japanese renewed their attacks on the exhausted defenders of the Bataan Peninsula. On April 9 the American and Filipino forces surrendered. The American forces on Corregidor, off the tip of the peninsula, resisted until the night of May 5, when the Japanese managed to land a battalion on the island. The following day Lieutenant-General Jonathan M. Wainwright, the US commander since

THE BATAAN DEATH MARCH

WHEN THE AMERICAN AND FILIPINO forces on the Bataan Peninsula surrendered on April 9, 1942, the Japanese had a plan for the transportation of the prisoners from Mariveles near the tip of the peninsula to Camp O'Donnell, a trip of about 90 miles (145 km). For some of the way the prisoners would be expected to walk, for other parts of the journey, transportation—either by rail or by truck—would be provided. But Homma Masaharu, the Japanese commander, had imagined there would be no more than 25,000 prisoners. As it turned out, there were 76,000, many already weakened by malaria and months of living on starvation rations. The great majority were Filipinos; about 12,000

were American. For the first day of the march no food was given to the prisoners, who were expected to have their own rations with them, and there was no medical care for the sick and wounded. Random acts of violence were committed against the prisoners: beatings and bayonetings administered by guards and taunts and assaults delivered by Japanese soldiers traveling in the opposite direction. Some prisoners were given water, others were denied it.

The number of prisoners marching grew as they were joined by others who had surrendered at various points along the route. Conditions grew worse as, in baking heat, white dust covered the

marchers as they made their way northward. When the prisoners reached the railroad station, some were packed into freight cars and many died as they stood upright for the journey of 25 miles (40 km). Others were forced to walk the whole way.

Nobody knows how many died on the march, but perhaps 15,000 of those who set out did not reach their destination. A number of these, however, were Filipinos who managed to escape. In 1946 Homma was tried for the actions of his men during the "Death March." He maintained he had been unaware of the conditions endured by the prisoners, but he was convicted and sentenced to death.

Prisoners on the march
American and Filipino soldiers are herded into captivity on the Bataan Peninsula after surrendering to the Japanese on April 9, 1942.

the departure of MacArthur, negotiated terms of surrender for all the forces on the Philippines. It was not until June 9, however, that the process of surrender throughout the islands was completed.

The Japanese victory in Southeast Asia was a triumph. With no overall margin of superiority in terms of military forces available, Japan had totally outfought its three enemies. The American, British, and Dutch troops had all been deployed defensively, but had failed to make any use of this advantage.

The Japanese success was the result of detailed planning and preparation. The United States and Britain had totally underestimated the effectiveness of Japanese air and naval power. Their comprehensive defeat was totally deserved.

AMERICAN FLAME-THROWER

Pressure to propel the flame was provided by compressed nitrogen

Flame-throwers were fuelled with petrol thickened with napalm

Attack on Corregidor
Japanese troops use a flame-thrower to drive American defenders out of a bunker. The island of Corregidor was heavily fortified with an intricate system of underground tunnels.

EXTENDING THE PERIMETER

As the campaign in the Philippines drew to a close, the Japanese were undertaking further landings in the Southwest Pacific. In January they had taken Rabaul in New Britain and from there they set about a series of offensives aimed at giving depth to their position. Their immediate objective was to secure eastern New Guinea and the Solomon Islands in order to develop the airfields needed to fight a defensive battle in this theater. This was to be part of the perimeter along which the Americans would be fought to exhaustion.

Following the outbreak of war the Americans found themselves with defensive commitments throughout the Central and Southwest Pacific. These precluded any serious attempt to interfere with Japanese moves, but in February 1942 they were able to mount a few small-scale carrier raids on Kwajalein, Rabaul, and Wake. The following month, however, on the basis of signals intelligence, the Americans were in a position to counter the Japanese landings at Lae and Salamaua in eastern New Guinea on March 8. Two days later, when Japanese forces came ashore at Finschhafen, American carrier aircraft attacked Japanese shipping off Lae and Salamaua. While losses were modest in terms of numbers, they were serious enough to jeopardize the next moves the Japanese had planned.

Initial Japanese success bred a belief that Japan could not go over to the defensive but should continue with offensive operations, a confidence that came to be known as "Victory Disease." At this stage the Imperial Navy was committed to a carrier operation in the Indian Ocean against British warships and merchantmen, but the main focus of its attention was upon the question of where in the Pacific its next moves should be made.

On April 18, 1942, the Americans carried out a raid on Tokyo and other targets in the Japanese home islands by B-25 medium bombers launched from the aircraft carrier *Hornet*. Led by Lieutenant Colonel James H. Doolittle, the "Doolittle Raid" gave a boost to US morale, but was derisively dismissed by the Japanese as the "Do Nothing Raid." The raid, however, silenced any misgivings about what the next Japanese moves should be. The fleet already had plans in place to extend Japan's defensive perimeter: first by a landing at Port Moresby in New Guinea, then by the occupation of Nauru and Ocean islands by forces from the Solomons. The main effort, however, involved an initial attack on the Aleutian Islands before an assault on Midway.

The Japanese fleet's plan envisaged the Americans having to commit their carrier force in response to the Japanese landings

A telling advantage
Douglas Dauntless dive-bombers stand on the deck of an Essex-class carrier. At the Battle of Midway in June 1942 the Japanese navy lost four of its carriers to American aircraft.

on Midway, but the Japanese carrier force supporting the landings would only be able to stay on station for perhaps ten days. Meanwhile, the aircraft that would subsequently operate from Midway were embarked in the carrier bound for the Aleutians, so it is not exactly clear how the various parts of the operation were to hang together. The Japanese plans envisaged a withdrawal of the fleet—after winning "the decisive battle"—to Truk. Subsequent offensives were already planned against New Caledonia, Fiji, and Samoa in July and against Johnston Island in August, as a prelude to an invasion of the Hawaiian Islands.

BATTLE OF THE CORAL SEA

Japanese plans miscarried from the outset. The operation against Port Moresby required a series of preliminary landings in the lower Solomons and in the islands off the eastern tip of New Guinea.

This dispersal of effort allowed the American carrier force to conduct a series of damaging strikes. These succeeded in neutralizing intended air bases and sinking the light carrier *Shoho* on May 7.

Aircraft from the Japanese and US carrier forces now sought each other out and on the following day fought what was the first naval battle in which the warships of the two opposing fleets never sighted one another. The Americans lost the carrier *Lexington* and the *Yorktown* suffered considerable damage, as

The Battle of Midway
The US carrier *Yorktown* burns after being hit by Japanese dive-bombers. She was the only US warship to be attacked from the air during the battle.

did the *Shokaku* on the Japanese side. Japanese aircraft losses, however, were so serious that they could not continue the battle and, as a result, the planned landing in Port Moresby was abandoned.

The Battle of the Coral Sea was the first real check to Japanese intentions. The basis of the setback was the staging of an operation with no margin of superiority over enemy forces known to be in the area. But the damage to the *Shokaku* and the aircraft losses added another dimension to the Japanese reverse. The *Shokaku* and another carrier, the *Zuikaku*, which had lost virtually all its planes, were unable to take part in the operation against Midway. Had these two carriers been present at the Battle of Midway they would have given the Japanese a significant margin of superiority over US forces. The Americans, meanwhile, had broken Japanese signals security and were forewarned of Japanese intentions when

the attack was unleashed on June 4. As a result they were able to put two carrier groups on station, northeast of Midway.

THE BATTLE OF MIDWAY
After an initial Japanese air strike on the island, the American carriers launched a series of attacks. These caught three of the four Japanese carriers some 30 or so minutes from being able to relaunch their own aircraft. The *Kaga* and *Soryu* sank that evening. The remaining

Japanese carrier was able to inflict heavy damage on the *Yorktown*, but in the last attacks of the day the American carriers caught the *Hiryu* and inflicted such damage that she, along with the *Akagi*, sank the following day. The *Yorktown*, having been abandoned but then reboarded, was under tow when hit by a spread of torpedoes from a submarine, which also accounted for a destroyer alongside. This cumulative damage put an end to attempts to salvage the ship, and the *Yorktown* sank on the morning of June 7.

Victory at the Battle of Midway was seen by the American public as revenge for the attack on the US Pacific Fleet at Pearl Harbor. It was not, as is often claimed, the decisive battle of the Pacific War, but the Coral Sea and Midway were the first in a series of battles over a six-month period, at the end of which the initiative lay clearly in American hands.

> "Pearl Harbor has now been partially avenged. Vengeance will not be complete until Japanese sea power is reduced to impotence."
>
> ADMIRAL NIMITZ, IN A COMMUNIQUÉ
> AFTER THE BATTLE OF MIDWAY, JUNE 6, 1942

THE HOME FRONT IN THE UNITED STATES AND JAPAN

NOVEMBER 1941– OCTOBER 1944

The contrast between the American and Japanese home fronts could not have been greater. At the time of Pearl Harbor, Japan's industry was already on a war footing. American industry had just begun to emerge from recession through the supply of war material and food to Britain, but its huge potential lay virtually untapped. By the end of the war the Americans had gained a new prosperity, while the defeated Japanese faced poverty and starvation.

US home front	Japanese home front
1941	
DECEMBER 8 Following attack on Pearl Harbor, US declares war on Japan	**NOVEMBER** Coupon system for rice, salt, and sugar rations already in use in major cities is extended to whole of Japan
1942	
JANUARY 7 Roosevelt announces first war budget. $13,250 million to be spent on defense	**JANUARY 31** Private car production suspended to maximize war effort
FEBRUARY 19 Over 100,000 Japanese living on Pacific coast moved to detention camps	**FEBRUARY 23** Japanese submarine shells coast of California
APRIL 18 Blackout enforced along eastern seaboard to counter shipping losses to U-boats	**APRIL 18** Doolittle Raid launched from carrier *Hornet* on Tokyo and other Japanese cities
APRIL Japanese junior schools reorganized along militarist, nationalistic principles	**MAY 15** Petrol rationing imposed in 17 US Eastern states
AUGUST 28 Japanese seaplane, launched from submarine, bombs forests in Oregon	
DECEMBER Gasoline rationing nationwide	**DECEMBER 1** Coffee rationing introduced. Ended in July 1943
1943	
JANUARY 11 In budget for second year of war, $100 billion is earmarked for war effort	
MARCH 29 Meat ration in the United States set at 28 oz (about 800 g) per week	**APRIL 1** Prices and wages frozen in order to put a brake on inflation
MAY 29 First appearance of Norman Rockwell's heroic figure "Rosie the Riveter" on cover of *Saturday Evening Post*	**MAY 27** Roosevelt issues executive order forbidding racial discrimination by government contractors
JULY 1 Pay-as-you-go income tax introduced in the United States	**JUNE 22** Race riots in Detroit; 34 killed
	NOVEMBER Air Defense Headquarters set up. Makes preparations for air raids, such as public tunnel shelters
1944	
	FEBRUARY Mobilization of teenaged students. 1.5 million new recruits conscripted into Japanese armed forces during 1944
MAY 3 Meat rationing ends in the United States, except for certain special cuts	
JUNE 22 Roosevelt signs GI Bill of Rights, entitling all veterans to subsidized education and other benefits after the war	**JUNE 15** First American B-29 raid on Japanese Home Islands from China. Parents start evacuating hundreds of thousands of children from cities to rural areas
OCTOBER 12 Endo case. Detention of Japanese-Americans whose loyalty is not in doubt found unconstitutional	**JULY 18** Tojo Hideki resigns as prime minister following US capture of Saipan

THE HOME FRONT IN THE US AND JAPAN

PARTICIPATION IN WORLD WAR II had far-reaching political, economic, and social effects on the United States, despite the fact that no enemy ever invaded its shores. Politically, the president and his advisers gained more power to run the country than ever before. Moreover, the Supreme Court helped endorse this new authority by refusing to hear cases that challenged it. During the war the number of federal civilian employees escalated from 1 million in 1940 to nearly 4 million. Many of these new government workers naturally felt a loyalty to President Roosevelt and the Democratic Party. Consequently, the majority party remained the Democrats, the voting constituency staying much the same as that of the 1930s, and Roosevelt won decisive victories in 1940 and 1944.

The Republicans, however, were able to reduce the Democrats' control of Congress and join with conservative Democrats in order to dismantle the social programs of the "New Deal." Military spending caused the administration to slash funding for the Civilian Conservation Corps, the Work Progress Administration, and the National Youth Administration. Because the programs were designed to help the poor and those who faced job discrimination, its demise especially affected blacks, women, and the elderly. There were also changes in the federal bureaucracies, as businessmen who disliked social welfare programs replaced the New Deal's social and economic "brains trust."

THE US ECONOMY

Wartime mobilization affected many aspects of the US economy and effectively ended the Great Depression. The government began to play an increasing role in keeping the economy healthy by "priming the pump" with orders for military goods. Companies with government contracts hired more

Quality control
A young woman checks the cartridge cases of 40-mm artillery shells at an American munitions factory.

Mass production
Production line methods developed in the automobile industry were adopted by aircraft factories. Here fuselages of B-17 Flying Fortress bombers await the next stage of production at the Boeing plant in Seattle, Washington.

people, set longer working hours, and increased production capacity. In 1940 there were 8 million unemployed Americans. By 1943 unemployment was virtually unheard of and there were actually labor shortages in some industries. The average working week in manufacturing durable goods increased from 38 hours in 1939 to 47 hours in 1943. In 1940 steel mills operated at 82 percent capacity, producing 67 million tons; by 1944, they were working at 100 percent capacity producing 89 million tons, half the world's output. From 1940 to 1945, American workers turned out 80,000 landing craft, 100,000 tanks and armored cars, 300,000 aircraft, 15 million guns, and 41 billion rounds of ammunition. The gross national product grew at an unprecedented rate from $91 billion in 1939 to $214 billion in 1945, a 235 percent increase. The national income doubled and consumer spending and savings increased significantly.

WOMEN ON THE US HOME FRONT

THE WAR BROUGHT MAJOR CHANGES to the lives of American women. Before the war, there had been a huge pool of female labor, consisting largely of young, single women. Many jobs were closed to them and they were effectively restricted to working in domestic service and retail businesses. Wartime production requirements, however, combined with the loss of the men who entered the military, provided women with the opportunity to move into a far wider range of jobs.

The response to the US government's request for more women workers was overwhelming and the changes remarkable. In 1941 there were 14.6 million women workers; by 1944 the number had grown to over 19.4 million. At one point during those years, more than 50 percent of American women worked and by 1945 half of all women workers were over 35 years old.

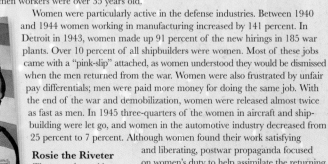

Equipping a bomber
A group of women workers installs interior fixtures in the tail fuselage section of a B-17 Flying Fortress at the Douglas plant, Long Beach, California, in October 1942.

Women were particularly active in the defense industries. Between 1940 and 1944 women working in manufacturing increased by 141 percent. In Detroit in 1943, women made up 91 percent of the new hirings in 185 war plants. Over 10 percent of all shipbuilders were women. Most of these jobs came with a "pink-slip" attached, as women understood they would be dismissed when the men returned from the war. Women were also frustrated by unfair pay differentials; men were paid more money for doing the same job. With the end of the war and demobilization, women were released almost twice as fast as men. In 1945 three-quarters of the women in aircraft and ship-building were let go, and women in the automotive industry decreased from 25 percent to 7 percent. Although women found their work satisfying and liberating, postwar propaganda focused on women's duty to help assimilate the returning veteran into society by "making him the man of the house again." When the war ended, many women left work to take up the duties of homemaking and child rearing.

Rosie the Riveter
The muscular emblem of American women's war work was created by the artist Norman Rockwell in 1943.

Wartime demand also brought new prosperity to farmers as the government kept prices high, provided low interest loans, and helped farmers apply the latest technological advances to increase crop production. Farmers produced all that they could for high prices, with the result that net income soared from $5.3 billion in 1939 to $13.6 billion in 1944. Because the government only provided aid to farmers with large acreages, the number of tenant and small farmers declined drastically. New technologies such as the enhanced grain combine also displaced many farm workers, who moved to urban areas looking for jobs in industry. The rise of the large-acreage farmer supported by government programs and price subsidies ushered in the era of "Big Agriculture."

Rita Hayworth
The Hollywood film star shows she is doing her bit for the war effort by sacrificing her car bumpers for use as scrap metal.

PATRIOTIC DUTY

It was personal sacrifice that lay at the heart of war mobilization and helped to forge a unified society. One of the major goals of the Roosevelt administration was to prepare people for a long, hard effort against Germany and Japan. In addition to military service, which eventually involved some 15 million men and women, those on the home front, through advertisements, magazine stories, films, and radio programs, were encouraged to "do their part." The Office of War Information commissioned a series of movies produced by Major Frank Capra entitled *Why We Fight* to help Americans (especially soldiers) understand why the war began, what was at stake, and why sacrifice was necessary. Stars such as Ronald Reagan, Robert Taylor, and Clark Gable were drafted into the army and then worked in Hollywood on such projects. Public service advertisements attempted to shame Americans into supporting the war effort. One government poster, for instance, showed a dead GI accompanied by the words, "He died today. What did you do?" Others demonstrated how both servicemen and home-front workers were soldiers in the fight for freedom—each making sacrifices for the cause. In all cases, the American GI was shown as a heroic figure, concerned about his family back home, yet dedicated to fighting for freedom and the American Way.

The government encouraged Americans to support their heroes by conserving and recycling materials. They were told that a donated shovel could make four hand grenades or help build a tank; lipstick tubes could be converted into bullet casings, while aluminum foil from gum wrappers would build fast, deadly aircraft. Furthermore, the government rationed certain goods, such as gas, coffee, sugar, and meat, and encouraged citizens to plant "Victory Gardens" to help save on foods needed for the front. Celebrities such as Bob Hope, Frank Sinatra, and Bing Crosby appeared at Savings Bond drives to convince Americans to donate

Recycling metals
This huge site in Brooklyn, New York, was set up for the public to donate cooking pots and pans, and other household objects made of aluminum. The metal was used principally in the manufacture of aircraft.

Standing in line
Members of the public line up at the local rationing board in New Orleans in 1943. There they would be issued with ration books, like that of the famous poet Robert Frost (right).

the migration of more than 700,000 blacks to the North and West during the war led to increased racial conflict. Between 1940 and 1946, the black population in urban areas increased significantly. In San Francisco, it grew by some 560 percent compared with a 28 percent increase in the white population. In Los Angeles, the figure was 105 percent compared with 18 percent for whites, in Detroit 47 percent compared to 5.2 percent for whites. Industrial employers discriminated because they paid black workers only a fraction of what they paid whites

doing the same job. Frustration came to a head in the summer of 1943 when race riots broke out in Detroit, Michigan, and Harlem, New York. In the Detroit riot 34 people were killed and 700 injured.

Yet it was during the war years that the Civil Rights movement gained some impetus. Black leaders such as A. Phillip Randolph, head of the Sleeping Car Porters' Union, demanded change. Randolph went as far as threatening President Roosevelt with a million-man march on Washington should he not do something about workplace discrimination. Concerned that the Nazis would humiliate him by making a comparison between discrimination against blacks in the United States and anti-Semitism in Germany, Roosevelt issued Presidential Order 8802, which set up the Fair Employment Practices Committee for federal government hiring procedures.

money to the war effort and be repaid with interest later. The government also became involved in the fashion business as it dictated styles that would conserve metal and cloth for the war. Out went three-piece suits and cuffs on pants. Women's skirts became shorter and narrower and the scandalous two-piece swimsuit was introduced to save on cloth and rubber. The new styles were dubbed "Patriotic Chic."

SOCIAL CHANGES

A more unified citizenry and the wartime economy had significant effects on American society. Although people were already moving to the North and West, and to suburban areas of major industrial centers, this trend would accelerate during the war as one in five Americans made a significant move. This helped strengthen the feelings of unity toward the war effort as citizens came into contact with others from different parts of the country, but it also contributed to racial and class conflict.

African-Americans faced continued discrimination and prejudice in the military and in industry. They served in separate units during the war. Some, such as the Tuskegee Airmen, distinguished themselves, but most were restricted to menial jobs such as steward or cook. Many whites refused to salute or take orders from black officers. The secretary of war, Henry Stimson, believed that African-Americans did not have leadership ability. On the home front,

Building a cargo ship
American shipyards competed to see which could build a new ship in the least time. The Kaiser shipyard in Richmond, California, completed the *Robert E Peary* in just four days, 15 hours, and 29 minutes.

JAPANESE INTERNMENT

AMONG THE INDIRECT VICTIMS of the war were the Japanese who lived in the United States. The majority of these lived in the US territory of Hawaii, which had been bombed by Japan, but they met with much less hostility there than did the Japanese living on the mainland. At the beginning of the war, approximately 120,000 Japanese lived on the West Coast, the majority in California. Despite a lack of credible evidence, Roosevelt succumbed to insistence that the Japanese-Americans should be classified as "enemy aliens." On February 19, 1942, he signed Executive Order No. 9066, which gave the US Army the authority to designate areas from which "any or all persons may be excluded." The military decreed that all people of Japanese descent be removed from the West Coast states of California, Oregon, and Washington, which were declared strategic areas. They were to sell their property, often at ridiculously low prices, abandon their homes, and settle in one of 10 relocation centers.

A number of Japanese-Americans brought cases protesting at this severe violation of their civil liberties, but the courts initially upheld the evacuation and detention orders. However, in the 1944 case Endo v. United States, the Supreme Court found that it was inappropriate in time of war to detain persons whose loyalty was not in question. In late 1944, the authorities began to close some of the camps and families were allowed to return to the West Coast. By this time there were Japanese-American units fighting in Italy and France. In spite of this, discrimination against Americans of Japanese descent continued long after the war.

Forced to sell
A Japanese-owned toy shop in Los Angeles announces it is closing down in 1942.

Evacuation
A young Japanese-American girl sits with her family's belongings, waiting to be transported to an assembly center.

Since the 1970s the record of Japanese-American soldiers and the conscience of a new generation of Americans has reduced levels of prejudice and helped in the assimilation of Japanese immigrants into the American mainstream. Japanese-Americans were not the only Americans placed in detention centers during the war. Conscientious objectors shared a similar fate. They were objects of hatred and ridicule, many calling them cowards, communists, or Nazi sympathizers. The government, unsure of how to deal with an irate public which had lost many sons during the war, built detention centers for them as well. While they were there, conscientious objectors were expected to help the war effort by growing crops or doing light factory work. Those who refused were sent to jail.

Farming at Manzanar
Japanese-American internees farm a field at the Manzanar relocation center in California. In many cases, communities flourished despite the harsh, remote regions they were sent to.

Relocation center
New arrivals survey the bleak interior of their accommodation block at the Manzanar relocation center in eastern California on March 24, 1942.

The committee did very little to stop unfair and discriminatory labor practices, but the very fact that a black leader had succeeded in forcing the president's hand set a precedent for the leaders of the Civil Rights Movement after the war.

Italians, Jews, Japanese, and Mexican-Americans also faced discrimination and prejudice during the war. In 1943 whites targeted Mexican-Americans in the Los Angeles "zoot suit" riots. Japanese-Americans were the most harshly treated when they were forced to give up their homes and relocate into internment camps. Nevertheless, for many other immigrants, especially those from southern and eastern Europe, the war gained them greater social

and economic opportunities as they became more integrated into the fabric of American life. Women also made gains because of wartime demand for industrial workers (see page 125). By 1945, women made up 36 percent of the workforce as they worked in jobs once reserved for men.

With much of the nation on the move, the increasing rates of marriages and births made housing a critical issue. Typically, the housing provided for migrating workers was of inferior quality. A great many of the young women who married in wartime, however, stayed with their parents until their soldier husbands returned from the war. The severe housing shortages inspired a postwar boom,

that would satisify many people's needs with a plentiful supply of new single-family dwellings. The increasing marriage rate helped to set off a corresponding baby boom that did not abate until the 1960s. Between 1940 and 1943 the rate of first births jumped from 293 to 375 per 10,000 women. The rate of subsequent births also went up—from 506 to 540. With more children, women working, and little housing available, the government was forced to pass legislation establishing daycare centers and providing some social housing. As the war progressed, an increase in juvenile delinquency caused some to blame working mothers and these daycare centers as a major part of the problem.

THE JAPANESE HOME FRONT

When the war started between Japan and China in July 1937, the Japanese government began a propaganda campaign meant to revitalize Japanese culture and instil an attitude of racial superiority. In October 1937, the Japanese prime minister, Konoye Fumimaro, promoted a three-year "National Spiritual Mobilization Movement" to rally the people in support of the war against the Chinese "mongrels." Ceremonies, parades, and a campaign to simplify dress, hairstyles, and diet were all aimed at promoting national pride and spiritual renewal.

By 1940 the state had completed its propaganda efforts by forming the people into local "patriotic" units. Each member worked in a job supporting some aspect of the war, such as national defense, street sweeping, fire watching, or public health. Many of them were run by community leaders, who ensured that people were doing their "duty."

In October 1941, to underline the seriousness of the conflict with China and the bitter diplomatic arguments between Japan and the United States, Konoye initiated a "New Order Movement." This centralized many of the local civil patriotic units. Although it never worked quite as envisioned, the movement did increase the number of units, which began to impose local food and clothing rationing.

THE JAPANESE WAR ECONOMY

With regard to economic planning prior to 1941, most Japanese, including members of the government, believed the war with China would be short. Hence, they saw no need for full-scale mobilization of the country's population. Traditional gender roles prohibited women from working outside the home and this further militated against reorganizing society in order to drive the war economy. Japanese civilians celebrated their country's military victories, but few took a sustained war effort seriously.

In December 1941, when Japan went to war with the United States, the government began a focused effort to gear up the economy for war and the people began to understand the seriousness of their situation. Many people took up jobs in farming or work in arms factories. By 1944 the workforce consisted of more than 33.5 million out of a population of 74 million.

Heroic airman
Japanese propaganda tended simply to extol the might of the army, navy, and air force.

> After six months in a barracks at the Santa Anita Racetrack, we were sent to Heart Mountain, Wyoming. We arrived in the middle of a blinding snowstorm, five of us children in our California clothes. When we got to our tar-paper barracks, we found sand coming in through the walls, around the windows, up through the floor. The camp was surrounded by barbed wire... But throughout our ordeal, we cooperated with the government because we felt that in the long run, we could prove our citizenship.

NORMAN MINETA QUOTED BY OTTO FREDERICK IN "A TIME OF AGONY FOR JAPANESE AMERICANS", *TIME* (DEC 2, 1991)

At first women were not required to work because there were enough teenaged boys and older men who volunteered to work. This changed in 1944 when many unmarried women under the age of 25 were conscripted into the workforce.

Food shortages forced many families to enter the black market to find day-to-day living necessities. Obtaining black-market goods was especially difficult for farm workers, who earned about two-thirds the wages of their urban factory counterparts. Rationing became a way of life and had long-term repercussions. By early 1942, every citizen received a daily rice allotment of just 12 oz (330 g). Clothes also were rationed through a points system, with farm workers receiving fewer points than the factory workers. As the war progressed, food became increasingly scarce. Japan normally imported much of its food and by the fall of 1944 its heavy merchant shipping losses were becoming critical.

The "economy of scarcity" caused by the war had an important social-cultural impact on the Japanese people. It was probably as a result of an insufficient diet that younger Japanese men and women were shorter and lighter in 1946 than those a decade earlier. Overcrowded urban areas spawned an outbreak of tuberculosis. Children also received only a modicum of education. Officially, during the war Japanese children went to school for six years. The reality was that, in the latter part of the war, school was shortened to one hour per day in order for older children to work. There was little respite from work and the business of finding food. The government banned most foreign films and music, and closed down bars and amusement parks.

From late November 1944 until the end of the war, American bombers dropped over 160,000 tons of explosives and incendiaries on 66 Japanese cities, destroying about a quarter of all Japanese homes, 42 percent of the industrial areas and killing over half a million civilians. Thus, by mid-1945, the Japanese people knew only the necessity of back-breaking work, little food, mourning for dead relatives, and death from the skies.

A send-off for heroes
Japanese women line the streets of Tokyo in December 1941 as troops leave the country to reinforce the formations that have begun the invasion of Malaya and Singapore.

WARTIME CINEMA

IN WORLD WAR II, films—both features and documentaries—became powerful instruments of national propaganda, while continuing to provide escapist entertainment and a relief from the privations of war. At the start of the war in Europe, US neutrality made most of the major Hollywood studios reluctant to adopt a strong anti-Nazi stance. However, after the release of Warners' *Confessions of a Nazi Spy* (1939) other studios took up the theme. Among the influential anti-Nazi films made in America before the attack on Pearl Harbor were Charles Chaplin's *The Great Dictator* (1940), Alfred Hitchcock's *Foreign Correspondent*, and the émigré German director Fritz Lang's *Man Hunt* (1941).

After America's entry into the war in December 1941, some 40,000 of Hollywood's 250,000 technicians, actors, producers, and directors went into uniform. A number of distinguished directors, among them John Huston and William Wyler, put their energies into hard-hitting documentary depictions of war. In 1942, Wyler's fantasy version of the British home front, *Mrs. Miniver*, won seven Oscars. After joining the USAF, Wyler forsook the studio for the skies over Germany, in *Memphis Belle* (1945) and *Thunderbolt* (1945). Another Hollywood stalwart, John Ford, filmed *The Battle of Midway* (1942) and later became head of the Field Photographic Branch of the OSS. Many Hollywood stars joined the armed forces, including Clark Gable, Robert Montgomery, Robert Taylor, and Douglas Fairbanks, Jr. James Stewart enlisted in the USAAF, rising to the rank of colonel and flying 20 bombing missions over Europe.

In the midwar years, some 90 million Americans went to the movies every week. The Hollywood production line adapted all the stock film genres—crime thrillers, musicals, cartoons, even the B Western—to accommodate wartime themes. Nazis rode the range and stalked the streets of Sherlock

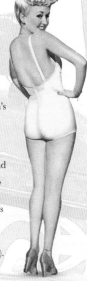

Betty Grable
The actress was the most popular pin-up with US servicemen.

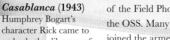

The Great Dictator
Charlie Chaplin's 1940 film lampooned Hitler (Adenoid Hynkel)—and in this scene, Mussolini (Napaloni)—and sent a message of hope to the world's oppressed.

Casablanca **(1943)**
Humphrey Bogart's character Rick came to embody the dilemma of American neutrality.

Henry V **(1944)**
This appeal to British patriotism was filmed in neutral Ireland. Lawrence Olivier directed and played the king in the most heroic of Shakespeare's history plays.

James Stewart
Still in USAAF uniform after his return home in September 1945, James Stewart talks on the telephone at his father's hardware store.

Holmes' London. Combat films tended to reinforce the romantic stereotypes of war, and it was not until the end of the conflict that Hollywood came to terms with the reality in feature films such as William Wellman's *The Story of GI Joe*, and John Ford's *They Were Expendable*, both released in 1945.

In Britain the realist school of filmmaking found an outlet in a stream of superb documentaries, among them Harry Watt's *Target for Tonight* (1941) and Humphrey Jennings' *Listen to Britain* (1942) and *Fires Were Started* (1943). These documentaries, and compilations like *Desert Victory* (1942), placed the emphasis firmly on the waging of a "People's War." This had a significant impact on feature films such as *The Foreman Went to France* (1942), *Millions Like Us* (1943), *Waterloo Road* (1944), and *The Way Ahead* (1945), all of which focused on the lives of ordinary soldiers and civilians.

In Germany, the first year of war produced a spate of anti-Semitic films orchestrated by the Nazi minister for propaganda, Josef Goebbels. Three major films of 1940 stigmatized the Jews as racial enemies: the documentary *The Eternal Jew* and two feature films, *The Rothschilds* and *Jew Süss*.

From 1942 Goebbels presided over a nationalized film industry that combined historical epics celebrating the lives of German heroes such as Bismarck and Frederick the Great, with romantic froth and lavish entertainments such as *Münchhausen*, the most expensive film of the Nazi era. Even when facing inevitable defeat, Goebbels devoted huge resources—and the services of much-needed troops as extras—on films such as *Kolberg*, which was premiered in January 1945 and told the tale of the siege of an East Pomeranian town during the Napoleonic Wars. Ironically, by the time *Kolberg* was finished, Nazi Germany was itself under siege.

Wartime line for a movie theater
In September 1939 fear of air raids prompted the British government to shut the nation's movie theaters, but they opened again after two weeks and proved the most popular form of entertainment during the war.

Münchhausen
This spectacular color film was made to show that the German film industry in Babelsberg could compete with Hollywood.

Special prisms divided the light from the lens into its red, blue, and green components

The Eternal Jew
The film was shot in Poland in 1939–40. Its message was one of pure hate, juxtaposing images of Jews with rats to justify their extermination.

A propaganda coup
A German newsreel crew films British war material abandoned in the hasty evacuation from Dunkirk in June 1940.

Technicolor camera
The camera used a complex triple film, so color remained expensive and a relative rarity.

Ohm Kruger
This 1941 German film portrayed the British as villains of the Boer War.

OHM KRÜGER
Emil Jannings

YY 7894

GERMAN–SOVIET CONFLICT

DECEMBER 6, 1941–NOVEMBER 12, 1942

In December 1941 the Germans reached a low point in their campaign on the Eastern Front as they were driven back from Moscow. Their fortunes changed from May onward as they went onto the counter-offensive and launched Operation Blue, which took them to the outskirts of Stalingrad.

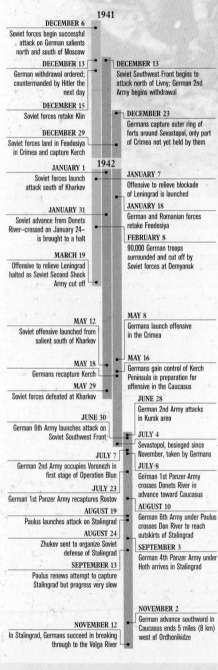

1941

DECEMBER 6
Soviet forces begin successful attack on German salients north and south of Moscow

DECEMBER 13
German withdrawal ordered; countermanded by Hitler the next day

DECEMBER 13
Soviet Southwest Front begins to attack north of Livny; German 2nd Army begins withdrawal

DECEMBER 15
Soviet forces retake Klin

DECEMBER 23
Germans capture outer ring of forts around Sevastopol, only part of Crimea not yet held by them

DECEMBER 29
Soviet forces land in Feodosiya in Crimea and capture Kerch

1942

JANUARY 1
Soviet forces launch attack south of Kharkov

JANUARY 7
Offensive to relieve blockade of Leningrad is launched

JANUARY 18
German and Romanian forces retake Feodosiya

JANUARY 31
Soviet advance from Donets River–crossed on January 24– is brought to a halt

FEBRUARY 8
90,000 German troops surrounded and cut off by Soviet forces at Demyansk

MARCH 19
Offensive to relieve Leningrad halted as Soviet Second Shock Army cut off

MAY 12
Soviet offensive launched from salient south of Kharkov

MAY 8
Germans launch offensive in the Crimea

MAY 18
Germans recapture Kerch

MAY 16
Germans gain control of Kerch Peninsula in preparation for offensive in the Caucasus

MAY 29
Soviet forces defeated at Kharkov

JUNE 28
German 2nd Army attacks in Kursk area

JUNE 30
German 6th Army launches attack on Soviet Southwest Front

JULY 4
Sevastopol, besieged since November, taken by Germans

JULY 7
German 2nd Army occupies Voronezh in first stage of Operation Blue

JULY 8
German 1st Panzer Army crosses Donets River in advance toward Caucasus

JULY 23
German 1st Panzer Army recaptures Rostov

AUGUST 10
German 6th Army under Paulus crosses Don River to reach outskirts of Stalingrad

AUGUST 19
Paulus launches attack on Stalingrad

AUGUST 24
Zhukov sent to organize Soviet defense of Stalingrad

SEPTEMBER 3
German 4th Panzer Army under Hoth arrives in Stalingrad

SEPTEMBER 13
Paulus renews attempt to capture Stalingrad but progress very slow

NOVEMBER 2
German advance southward in Caucasus ends 5 miles (8 km) west of Ordhonikidze

NOVEMBER 12
In Stalingrad, Germans succeed in breaking through to the Volga River

▮ Soviet attacks in the north and center Dec 6, 1941–Mar 19,1942

▮ Action in the Crimea Dec 23, 1941–Jul 4, 1942

▮ Action in the Ukraine Dec 13, 1941–May 29, 1942

▮ German action in the south Jun 28–Nov 11, 1942

FROM MOSCOW TO STALINGRAD

THE GERMANS HAD BEEN brought to a halt before Moscow in late November 1941. It was only after much heated debate that Hitler had then given permission for a general withdrawal to a secure winter line along the Ugra River, some 200 miles (300 km) to the west of the city. Despite reports from German reconnaissance aircraft of the assembly of large numbers of Soviet troops in the Moscow sector, the German high command was confident that the Red Army had utterly exhausted its reserves of manpower. In fact, when it had become clear that the Japanese would not attack in Siberia, Soviet divisions had been rapidly transferred from the east to reinforce the 59 divisions deliberately withheld from the battle for Moscow. Unlike the Germans, these formations were fully equipped for winter warfare. By early December nearly 720,000 men, 8,000 guns and mortars, and 720 tanks, many of them T-34s, were assembled on the Soviet central front.

COUNTEROFFENSIVE AT MOSCOW

On November 30 Stalin had given Zhukov orders to launch a counteroffensive. The troops moved off, in a violent snowstorm, at 3:00 am on the morning of December 5. Zhukov, who initially had expressed reluctance to go on the attack but had been overruled by Stalin, had devised a characteristically simple plan. Massed artillery was to lead the counterblow before Moscow by delivering an earth-shattering barrage. The two armored German pincers, which were to the north and south of Moscow and threatened to encircle it, would then be driven back to their November start lines.

Zhukov's offensive caught the Ostheer —the German Army on the Eastern Front—at the start of its painfully won withdrawal and immediately prompted a fresh order from the Führer: "The Fourth Army is not to retire a single step." Order and counterorder left the Fourth Army dangerously exposed. Guderian's battered Panzer Group lay beyond the Fourth Army's right wing, around Tula, and was pushed back over the Oka River by the force of the Red Army counteroffensive. On the Fourth Army's left wing, General Erich Höpner's Fourth Panzer Group came under increasing pressure in its forward position and was in danger of being outflanked as a preliminary to the encirclement of the Fourth Army. Soviet cavalry formations, supported by sled-borne infantry, advanced across the frozen rivers to harry

Soviet infantry advance in winter
In the depths of the Soviet winter, temperatures plummet to well below zero. In 1941 Soviet forces were generally better equipped than the Germans to cope with such conditions.

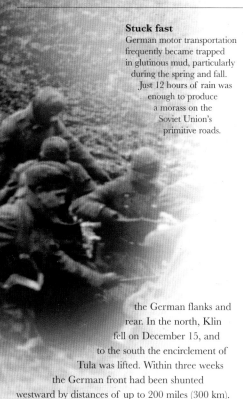

Stuck fast
German motor transportation frequently became trapped in glutinous mud, particularly during the spring and fall. Just 12 hours of rain was enough to produce a morass on the Soviet Union's primitive roads.

GEORGI ZHUKOV

Marshal Zhukov (1896–1974)—one of the very few men with the courage to stand up to Stalin—was indispensable to Soviet victory. He was conscripted into the Russian Army in World War I and later became a specialist in armored warfare. In August 1939 he masterminded the defeat of the Japanese at Khalkin Ghol. In January 1941 he became chief of staff, and later in the year he directed the defense of Leningrad and then of Moscow, before planning the Soviet counterattack at Moscow. In August 1942 he became deputy commissar for defense, effectively Stalin's second-in-command, and directed the defence of Stalingrad. In 1943 he oversaw the defense of the Kursk salient and coordinated the massive Soviet counter-offensive in the Ukraine. Having planned Operation Bagration in 1944, he led the First Byelorussian Front in its advance to Berlin. By Western, though not Soviet, standards, he brought great ruthlessness to the battlefield. In 1945–46 he commanded the Soviet occupation forces in Germany.

the German flanks and rear. In the north, Klin fell on December 15, and to the south the encirclement of Tula was lifted. Within three weeks the German front had been shunted westward by distances of up to 200 miles (300 km).

"HEDGEHOG" TACTICS

The German withdrawal was made in the worst of the winter weather—with night temperatures falling to far below freezing and horses struggling through snow up to their bellies. As the Red Army infiltrated the German lines, local penetrations became breaches. But the piecemeal withdrawal did not

degenerate into a total rout. Commanders learned to move back from one hastily prepared defensive position, known as a "hedgehog," to the next. In mid-December a sudden thaw gripped the Red Army in a sea of mud, allowing the hedgehogs to be strengthened before freezing temperatures returned. These strengthened positions gave the German troops the chance to stand fast while reserves were assembled in the rear to plug the gaps in the line.

The rapid development of hedgehog tactics led to the introduction of another feature of the war on the Eastern Front, in which German formations allowed themselves to be encircled. While Red Army cavalry, armor, ski-troops, and great masses of infantry swept around and past them, the

hedgehogs' defenders were able to inflict heavy casualties and deny the enemy the road and rail junctions it needed to sustain the momentum of its advance. The German pockets had to be supplied by air, often stretching the resources of the Luftwaffe to the limit. While, for example, sustaining the 90,000 men of II Corps isolated in the large Demyansk pocket south of Lake Ilmen between January and May 1942, the Luftwaffe lost some 250 aircraft.

These tactical developments were taking place against a backdrop of structural upheaval within the German Army's high command. On December 1 Rundstedt had been removed from command of Army Group South, having protested at Hitler's "no withdrawal" order. No fewer than 35 army corps and divisional generals were dismissed, among them Guderian, for

Retreat from Moscow
In December 1941 there was a breakdown in the
Ostheer's military cohesion, and morale dropped
considerably. It was not until 1942 that steps were
taken to equip the troops for winter warfare.

making unauthorized withdrawals. On December
17 the commander-in-chief of the German Army,
Field Marshal von Brauchitsch, was relieved of his
command, to be succeeded by Hitler himself. From
now on, operations in the Soviet Union, down to
battalion level, were to be executed according to
directives and orders issued by the Führer.

STALIN SEIZES THE INITIATIVE
It seems that in June 1941, during the first days of
Operation Barbarossa, Stalin had come close to a
mental breakdown and had even briefly considered
abandoning Moscow. Once he had recovered, his
characteristic reaction had been to consolidate
control of the war in his own hands. Thus in June
1941 he had created the State Defense Committee,
or GKO, which oversaw all political, military, and
economic aspects of the war and whose original
members were Stalin, Foreign Minister Molotov,
Marshal Voroshilov and Lavrenti Beria, head of the
NKVD. The GKO administered military matters
through the Stavka, which drew up battle plans and,
through the general staff, organized the preparation
and execution of strategic operations. In all cases
the final decision lay with Stalin, who had appointed
himself in the position of supreme commander on
August 8. The two dictators and military amateurs,
Hitler and Stalin, were now locked in a head-to-
head battle for survival on the Eastern Front.

With the entry of the United States into the war
in December, Stalin aquired an ally with almost
unlimited potential economic power. Emboldened
by this change in his fortunes, on January 5, 1942,
he ordered a general offensive to drive the Germans
back along the entire Eastern Front before the
spring rains signaled the onset of the *rasputitsa*:
Leningrad was to be relieved, Army Group Center
rolled up, and the Ukraine liberated. Only Zhukov
dissented, arguing that such an offensive would
weaken the critical central counteroffensive and
place an intolerable strain on Soviet resources.

A temporary respite for German troops
In the winter of 1941–42 many German commanders
forbade the lighting of fires by day to prevent wisps of
smoke from betraying positions to the enemy.

THE SOVIET GENERAL OFFENSIVE
One of the principal objectives of Stalin's all-out
offensive was to pinch out the distended center of
the German line. The Fourth Shock Army attacked
from north of Moscow toward Vitebsk and Smolensk
with the goal of severing German supply lines, while
the Bryansk Front drove west to isolate the German
Fourth Army. The fighting along the German salient
between these two Red Army drives was exceptionally
savage as Soviet forces strove to break through, but
were then encircled and cut off.

In February and March, Stalin harried his high
command to press home the faltering offensive. But
the resistance of the Germans was hardening, and
their commanders' more flexible battlefield reflexes
were exacting a rising toll on Soviet forces. By the
end of March the Red Army had lost some 450,000
dead and the offensive had lost all momentum.
German losses were also mounting. In the Ninth
Army one regiment that had begun Barbarossa
with over 2,000 men now had a strength of just 35.

By early April both sides were in the glutinous
grip of the *rasputitsa* and the Red Army offensive
slithered to a halt. Since December 1941 the
German Army Group Center had lost 265,000
men, while approximately 350,000 had become ill,
often suffering from frostbite. Even when they were
evacuated by ambulance train, the wounded and
frostbitten were not safe: the unheated trains often
arrived at their destination carrying a cargo of
corpses. Material losses included 1,800 tanks,
55,000 motor vehicles, and 180,000 horses. If the
Red Army had displayed a higher degree of tactical
competence, the losses would have been far greater.

RED ARMY INFANTRY WEAPONS

BY THE END OF 1942 THE RED ARMY infantryman's standard submachine-gun was the 7.62-mm PPSh-41. By the end of the war some 5 million had been made. In common with all items of Red Army kit, it was simple to manufacture, easy to maintain, and immensely robust and reliable, with a 71-round drum, or 35-round box-type, magazine. It was also one of the few Soviet weapons to be adopted by the Germans in large numbers, and many were adapted to fire German 9-mm ammunition. Up to the summer of 1943, Red Army infantry formations were expected to manage on their initial ammunition allocation, which lasted about 10 days.

Tokarev pistol
Closely modeled on the Colt M1911, and introduced in 1930, the 7.62-mm Tokarev was the standard Red Army sidearm of the war. It had an 8-round magazine.

Hooded foresight

PPS-43 submachine-gun
This variant of the PPSh-41 was manufactured during the siege of Leningrad. The PPSh-41 had a wooden stock.

Ammunition magazine/hand grip

Pistol grip

Metal stock

Grenades
A Soviet infantry-man usually carried three grenades in his pocket or in a linen haversack.

FIGHTING IN THE SOUTH

While the fighting fell away on the central front, it flared again in the south. By early March the Red Army had been thwarted in its attempt to retake Kharkov, but Stalin, champing at the bit, ordered a second offensive to be delivered, in a right hook from Volchanksk, in May. Simultaneously, the Germans were preparing to eliminate the Soviet salient around Barvenkovo, which had bitten into the German front 100 miles (160 km) south of Kharkov. On May 12 the Red Army launched offensives from north and south of the city, aiming to take it in a pincer movement, but the Germans contained the thrusts and on May 17 launched their own counterblow. Within a week they had eliminated the threatening salient to the south of Kharkov and driven back the right hook to the north of the city.

At the southern tip of the battle line, 20,000 men of the Soviet 44th and 51st Armies had landed on the Kerch peninsula to relieve Sevastopol, which had been besieged by Manstein's 11th Army. The Red Army force was expanded and redesignated the Crimean Front but was effectively checked by Manstein, who left five divisions at Sevastopol while he launched a counteroffensive with heavy Luftwaffe support. The Soviet forces were routed, losing nearly 200,000 men and all their heavy equipment before the 90,000 survivors were evacuated to the Taman peninsula. Manstein turned back to Sevastopol, sealed it off from the sea, and subjected it to an intense air and artillery bombardment. The battle for the city raged until the end of June, with the German and Soviet forces fighting over ground that had been very hotly contested nearly 100 years before in the Crimean War. Finally, their supplies of ammunition exhausted, the remaining Red Army defenders were evacuated.

Germans advancing in May 1942
From December 1941 to April 1942 the Red Army appeared to be gaining the initiative. However, by May the Germans were again on the offensive, in both Ukraine and the Crimea.

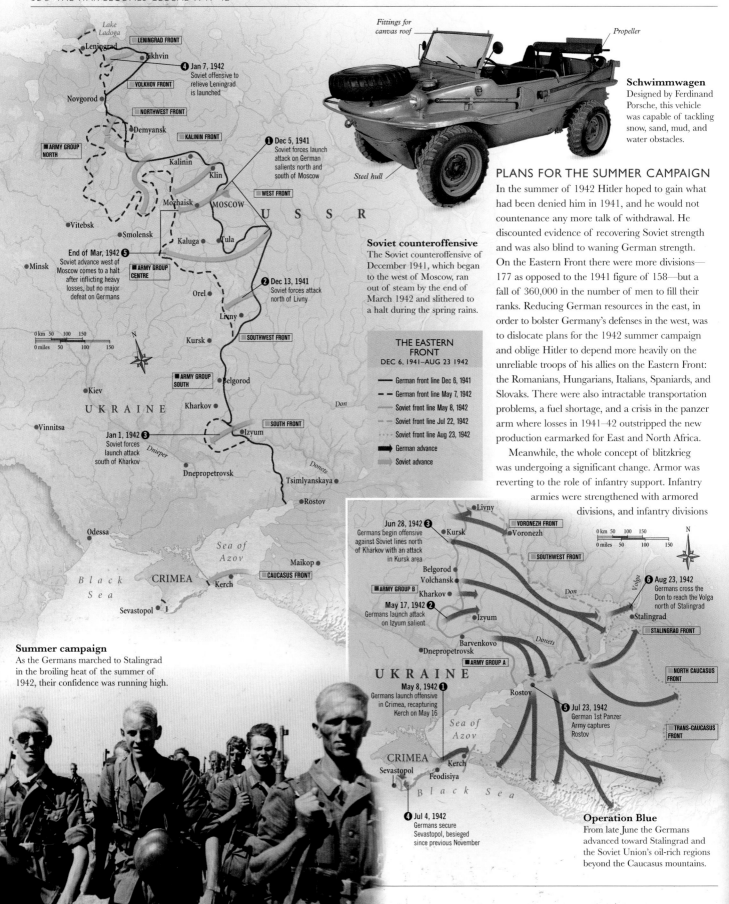

Schwimmwagen
Designed by Ferdinand Porsche, this vehicle was capable of tackling snow, sand, mud, and water obstacles.

Fittings for canvas roof

Propeller

Steel hull

PLANS FOR THE SUMMER CAMPAIGN

In the summer of 1942 Hitler hoped to gain what had been denied him in 1941, and he would not countenance any more talk of withdrawal. He discounted evidence of recovering Soviet strength and was also blind to waning German strength. On the Eastern Front there were more divisions— 177 as opposed to the 1941 figure of 158—but a fall of 360,000 in the number of men to fill their ranks. Reducing German resources in the east, in order to bolster Germany's defenses in the west, was to dislocate plans for the 1942 summer campaign and oblige Hitler to depend more heavily on the unreliable troops of his allies on the Eastern Front: the Romanians, Hungarians, Italians, Spaniards, and Slovaks. There were also intractable transportation problems, a fuel shortage, and a crisis in the panzer arm where losses in 1941–42 outstripped the new production earmarked for East and North Africa.

Meanwhile, the whole concept of blitzkrieg was undergoing a significant change. Armor was reverting to the role of infantry support. Infantry armies were strengthened with armored divisions, and infantry divisions

Leningrad / Moscow map labels

Lake Ladoga

LENINGRAD FRONT
Leningrad
Tikhvin

④ Jan 7, 1942
Soviet offensive to relieve Leningrad is launched

VOLKHOV FRONT

Novgorod

NORTHWEST FRONT

Demyansk

KALININ FRONT

■ ARMY GROUP NORTH

Kalinin
Klin

① Dec 5, 1941
Soviet forces launch attack on German salients north and south of Moscow

WEST FRONT

Mozhaisk
MOSCOW

U S S R

Vitebsk
Smolensk
Kaluga   Tula

End of Mar, 1942 ⑤
Soviet advance west of Moscow comes to a halt after inflicting heavy losses, but no major defeat on Germans

■ ARMY GROUP CENTRE

Minsk

② Dec 13, 1941
Soviet forces attack north of Livny

Orel

Soviet counteroffensive
The Soviet counteroffensive of December 1941, which began to the west of Moscow, ran out of steam by the end of March 1942 and slithered to a halt during the spring rains.

Livny

Kursk

SOUTHWEST FRONT

0 km 50 100 150
0 miles 50 100 150

N

■ ARMY GROUP SOUTH

Kiev
Belgorod

U K R A I N E

Kharkov

Don

Jan 1, 1942 ③
Soviet forces launch attack south of Kharkov

Vinnitsa

Dnieper

Izyum

SOUTH FRONT

Donets

Dnepropetrovsk

Tsimlyanskaya

Rostov

Odessa

Sea of Azov

Maikop

Black Sea

CRIMEA   Kerch

CAUCASUS FRONT

Sevastopol

THE EASTERN FRONT
DEC 6, 1941–AUG 23 1942

— German front line Dec 6, 1941
- - German front line May 7, 1942
— Soviet front line May 8, 1942
- - Soviet front line Jul 22, 1942
···· Soviet front line Aug 23, 1942
➤ German advance
➤ Soviet advance

Summer campaign
As the Germans marched to Stalingrad in the broiling heat of the summer of 1942, their confidence was running high.

Operation Blue map labels

Jun 28, 1942 ③
Germans begin offensive against Soviet lines north of Kharkov with an attack in Kursk area

Livny
Kursk

VORONEZH FRONT

Voronezh

SOUTHWEST FRONT

Belgorod
Volchansk

■ ARMY GROUP B

Kharkov

0 km 50 100 150
0 miles 50 100 150

N

Don

Volga

⑥ Aug 23, 1942
Germans cross the Don to reach the Volga north of Stalingrad

May 17, 1942 ②
Germans launch attack on Izyum salient

Izyum

Stalingrad

STALINGRAD FRONT

Barvenkovo

Donets

Dnepropetrovsk

■ ARMY GROUP A

NORTH CAUCASUS FRONT

U K R A I N E

May 8, 1942 ①
Germans launch offensive in Crimea, recapturing Kerch on May 16

Rostov

Jul 23, 1942 ⑤
German 1st Panzer Army captures Rostov

Sea of Azov

TRANS-CAUCASUS FRONT

CRIMEA

Sevastopol
Feodisiya
Kerch

Black Sea

④ Jul 4, 1942
Germans secure Sevastopol, besieged since previous November

Operation Blue
From late June the Germans advanced toward Stalingrad and the Soviet Union's oil-rich regions beyond the Caucasus mountains.

assumed a more important role in panzer armies. The production of self-propelled assault guns was stepped up so that by July 1942 they represented almost one-quarter of the Ostheer's armored strength.

Hitler had a grand strategic plan for 1942 which entailed sweeping southward from the Caucasus and northeast from Egypt, in a colossal pincer movement, to seize the oil resources of the Middle East. In fact, the only part of Hitler's plan that was to see the light of day was Operation *Blau* (Blue), a drive aimed east to the city of Stalingrad and south to the mountain passes of the Causcasus and then on to the oilfields on the western shore of the Caspian Sea. British code breakers had gotten wind of the operation and had passed the information to Stalin, who dismissed it as disinformation. He also ignored the hard evidence, retrieved by Soviet troops from a crashed German aircraft on June 19, of the planned order of battle for Operation Blue.

OPERATION BLUE

The German summer offensive began on June 28, 1942. Field Marshal von Bock's Army Group B (the Second, Sixth, and Fourth Panzer Armies) was to advance toward Voronezh and down the grasslands of the Don-Donets corridor toward Stalingrad, while Field Marshal Wilhelm List's Army Group A (the First Panzer and 17th Armies) drove for the Don crossings east of Rostov. As the panzer formations, arrayed in massive squares, advanced, Soviet resistance melted away. By July 6 Army Group B had reached the Don River opposite Voronezh.

Crossing the Don
Tanks of Army Group A ford the Don River east of Rostov in July 1942. In the initial stages of their summer offensive, the German forces appeared to be repeating their success of 1941.

It seemed like a rerun of the summer of 1941, with the front of the Red Army falling apart at the first armored impact. Bock, however, was concerned that Red Army reinforcements might attack Army Group B's left flank from the Voronezh area, and he gained Hitler's permission to secure Voronezh with armor detached from the Sixth Army, commanded by General Friedrich Paulus. Bock was now drawn into a slugging match at Voronezh, which threatened to dislocate Operation Blue's timetable. On July 13 Hitler intervened, replacing Bock with Field Marshal Maximilian von Weichs. Paulus was to wheel east toward Stalingrad, providing further protection for the extended German left flank.

In the Don-Donets corridor the Red Army was now threatened by a series of encirclements on the scale of those executed by the Germans in

Operation Barbarossa. With great difficulty, the recently appointed chief of the Soviet general staff, Marshal Aleksandr Vasilevsky, persuaded Stalin that orders to "stand fast" regardless of the strategic situation invited further catastrophe, and that it was vital for the Soviet forces in the corridor to withdraw. On July 23 Rostov, which the Red Army had lost and then retaken in the winter fighting, fell to Army Group A almost without a fight. Hitler now ordered Army Group A and General Ewald von Kleist's First Panzer Army to drive for the Caucasus oilfields while Army Group B advanced to Stalingrad.

On August 9, just six weeks after the start of Operation Blue, Kleist's forces had reached Maikop, 200 miles (300 km) southeast of Rostov, and captured the Soviet Union's most westerly oilfields. The installations had, however, been wrecked by the retreating Red Army, and the Germans were never to reach the principal sources of oil beyond the Caucasus. Ironically, they had insufficient fuel to maintain the momentum of their advance, and they faced stiffening Soviet resistance from both Red Air Force bombers and locally raised formations.

Red Army logistics
Soviet infantrymen relied heavily on horses and the carts they pulled (*panjes*), which could keep going in a wide range of conditions. *Panjes* were also used extensively by the Germans, despite their vaunted panzer spearheads.

> "It was easily the most desolate and mournful region of the east that came before my eyes. A barren, naked, lifeless steppe without a bush, without a tree, for miles without a village."
>
> A GERMAN SOLDIER DESCRIBING THE LANDSCAPE IN THE DON-DONETS CORRIDOR

ADVANCE TO STALINGRAD

While the First Panzer Army was racing to Maikop, the German Sixth Army—much of whose transportation had been temporarily transferred to Army Group A —was moving slowly down the Don–Donets corridor toward Stalingrad across a wide, treeless, and desolate steppe. By August 19 it was poised to begin its assault on Stalingrad, while the Fourth Panzer Army moved up along a northeast axis. On August 23 a total of 600 aircraft of the Luftwaffe's VIII Air Corps attacked the city, which straggled for some 20 miles (30 km) along the west bank of the Volga, and reduced its center to an inferno. Thousands of Soviet civilians—ordered to remain in Stalingrad so as not to hamper Red

Army movements—were killed in the raid. On the same day German troops entered the outskirts of Stalingrad and also carved out a salient to the north of the city along the western bank of the Volga. At Hitler's forward headquarters in Vinnitsa in the Ukraine, the mood was jubilant. The seizure of Stalingrad was expected within days as the Sixth Army plunged into country cut with gullies and ravines leading to the industrial heart of the city.

On September 5 a Red Army counterattack designed to prise the German grip off the Volga north of Stalingrad was driven off with heavy losses. Stalin was determined that Stalingrad must be held, whatever the cost, and it was only after some argument that he agreed on September 13

German mortar squad
German infantry prepare to move forward in the ruins of Stalingrad. The soldier in the center carries a mortar base plate, and the man to his right, leaning on a grenade, carries a rack of bombs.

> Stalingrad is no longer a town. By day it is an enormous cloud of burning, blinding smoke; it is a vast furnace lit by the reflection of the flames. And when night arrives, one of those scorching, howling, bleeding nights, the dogs plunge into the Volga and swim desperately to gain the other bank. The nights in Stalingrad are a terror for them. Animals flee this hell… only men endure.
>
> A GERMAN OFFICER OF 24TH PANZER DIVISION, OCTOBER 1942

to a plan presented to him by Zhukov—now in overall command of the Stalingrad sector—for a wide encirclement of the Axis forces on the Lower Volga and the destruction of Paulus's Sixth Army at Stalingrad. On the same day General Vasili Chuikov was appointed as the new commander of the Soviet 62nd Army in Stalingrad. A no-nonsense fighting officer of peasant stock, Chuikov would prove to be a streetfighter of genius. He set up his headquarters in a bunker on the banks of the Volga, across which a fleet of small boats went back and forth, carrying reinforcements, ammunition, and food to the west bank, and wounded men back to the east bank. From the outset, Chuikov urged his men to fight "as if there is no land across the Volga." At the same time the Stalingrad sector, which had now been redesignated the Stalingrad Front, came under the command of another determined and pugnacious officer of peasant stock, General Andrei Yeremenko.

Stalingrad seen from the east bank
During the battle for the city, some 35,000 wounded Soviet troops were ferried to the east bank, while 65,000 reinforcements crossed to the west.

It was a sniper's paradise, in which all freedom of maneuver and flexibility in the battlefield was lost, and blitzkrieg was replaced by attrition.

The men of the German Sixth Army edged ever closer to the steep banks of the Volga. The giant Univermag department store in Red Square, just under a mile from the ferries, was captured by the Germans after a ferocious fight and became the headquarters of the army's commander, General Paulus. Some 3 miles (5 km) to the south, on the edge of Stalingrad, a massive grain silo became the scene of a grim two-month siege as the city's defenders were slowly pushed back to the water's edge. By November 1 the Germans had chopped Chuikov's command on the western bank into four groups, forcing

Stranded civilian
The civilians stranded in Stalingrad had to endure German bombardment, starvation, and threatened execution by the NKVD if they failed to assist the city's Red Army defenders.

communication between them to be carried out on the east bank. On the 12th the Germans reached the Volga itself on the southern edge of the city, but the battle had now become for them one of the grimmest kind—one whose cost far exceeded its value. It was remorselessly sucking in units essential to sustain the dwindling hopes of a breakthrough being achieved in the Caucasus. This was all too evident to the German high command, but not to Hitler. Stalingrad had become an obsession, its occupation overriding all military sense—and, inevitably, it was the Führer's will that would prevail.

FIGHTING AMONG THE RUINS

In three days of savage fighting from September 13, the Germans inched their way through the shattered city to Stalingrad's main railroad station and Mamayev Kurgan, a vantage point some 5 miles (8 km) to the northwest, which until a few days before had housed the headquarters of the 62nd Army. Both strongholds changed hands repeatedly as Chuikov's men attacked by night and the Germans counterattacked by day, their armor nosing through a nightmare cityscape pitted with shell craters and piled high with the rubble of shattered buildings. As Chuikov's men fell back on the bank of the Volga, reinforcements from 13th Guards Division were rushed up from the interior and fed across the river. They clung to the vital jetties on the western bank but at the cost of almost 100 percent casualties.

Beneath the hulks of burning and collapsed buildings the German attackers and Soviet defenders sheltered and lived in the cellars. They fought from the cover of masonry, scrambling and slithering over dunes of bricks from one position to the next. The front lines were fluid, often no more than a grenade throw apart. Swarms of rats scurried through the carnage, feasting on the dead and dying.

Red Army assault squad
In Stalingrad, fighting raged for days over the possession of the few buildings left standing, which gave the precious advantage of height over the battlefield.

3.5x telescopic sight   MOSIN-NAGANT M91/30 SNIPER RIFLE

Rear sights

5-round fixed box magazine

Soviet sniper's rifle
Adapted with a powerful telescopic sight, the 7.62-mm M91/30 was used by the most famous Soviet sniper at Stalingrad, Vasily Zaitsev. He killed 149 German soldiers.

German tanks near Moscow
The German advance to Moscow halted in November
1941. During the subsequent Soviet counteroffensive,
the German formations were pushed back by Soviet
troops far better equipped for the winter conditions.

THE INITIATIVE CHANGES HANDS
1942–43

IN NOVEMBER 1942, AS THE GERMAN SIXTH ARMY FOUGHT

FOR THE CITY OF STALINGRAD AND HITLER ORDERED

THE OCCUPATION OF VICHY FRANCE, THE BOUNDARIES

OF THE THIRD REICH REACHED THEIR GREATEST EXTENT.

HOWEVER, THE HIGH TIDE OF NAZI EXPANSIONISM BEGAN

TO RECEDE AS THE INITIATIVE PASSED OVER TO THE ALLIES

ON THREE FRONTS: IN THE SOVIET UNION, NORTH AFRICA,

AND THE ATLANTIC. IN THE PACIFIC THE JAPANESE WERE

ALSO CHECKED, AND THEN DECISIVELY DEFEATED, AT

GUADALCANAL IN THE SOLOMON ISLANDS.

Americans welcomed in Tunis
In November 1942 Vichy French troops at first
resisted the US landings in Algeria and Morocco.
By May 1943, with the Germans and Italians
defeated in Tunisia, the French in North Africa
were firmly on the Allied side.

5

THE TIDE BEGINS TO TURN

BETWEEN THE FALL OF 1942 AND THE SPRING OF 1943 THE EXTRAVAGANT AMBITIONS THAT HAD FUELED HITLER'S PLANS FOR THE INVASION OF THE SOVIET UNION BEGAN TO DIM. AS THE TIDE OF WAR BEGAN TO TURN AGAINST GERMANY, DEBATE OVER GRAND STRATEGY GAVE WAY TO DEBATE OVER HOW THE THIRD REICH MIGHT RETAIN THE TERRITORY IT HAD WON SINCE SEPTEMBER 1939.

ON THE EASTERN FRONT the German Sixth Army had opened its assault on Stalingrad on August 19. Three months later it was still locked in a ferocious street-by-street battle with the defenders of the city. Hitler was obsessed with securing Stalingrad, while Stalin was equally determined that it should be denied him. Stalin's resolve had been hardened at a meeting with Churchill in August 1942, when he had been informed that there would be no immediate Anglo-American invasion of continental Europe to ease the pressure on the Red Army. He had then agreed to an operation proposed by Zhukov, deputy commissar for defense, in which a holding battle fought in Stalingrad would be followed by an encirclement of the Axis forces on the lower Volga and the destruction of the Sixth Army.

OPERATION URANUS

Code-named Uranus, the operation was launched on November 19, 1942 and by the end of January had secured the surrender of the Sixth Army under Field Marshal Paulus. The Red Army then drove on, threatening Kharkov and the German forces withdrawing from the Caucasus. However, there was to be a major setback for the Soviet Union in February and March 1943, when Field Marshal Manstein's Army Group Don delivered a brilliantly weighted counterblow against the overextended Red Army. When the fighting died down in the spring thaw, there was a huge Soviet salient, centered around the city of Kursk in the heartland of the Ukraine, jutting westward into the German line.

On the surface, it seemed that the rhythms of the Eastern Front would be resumed in the late spring of 1943, when the ground became firm enough to sustain armored operations. But the debacle at

Stalingrad had dealt a heavy blow to the Ostheer, while the Red Army was shrugging off the specter of defeat that had haunted it from June 1941 to the late summer of 1942. One of the reasons for this lay in the stolid figure of Stalin. Unlike Hitler, who grew to despise and mistrust the Prussian military caste that dominated the German high command, Stalin was able to develop a constructive engagement with his high command, the Stavka.

Stalin's gaining of wisdom had, of course, been acquired at the cost of millions of Soviet dead, a price that no other combatant nation could have paid and still remain in the field. Also making it possible for the Soviet Union to continue fighting was the maintenance of supplies of war materiel. In the summer of 1941 the Soviet Union had preserved a crucial part of its industrial infrastructure by shifting much of its war-making plant east, beyond the Urals and out of the reach of the Ostheer and Luftwaffe bombers. The ravages of Operation Barbarossa meant that initially output fell. Even by 1945 coal and steel production had not

"…at the bottom of the trenches there still lay frozen green Germans and frozen gray Russians and frozen fragments of human shape, and there were tin helmets, German and Russian, lying among the brick debris, and the helmets were half-filled with snow."

BRITISH CORRESPONDENT ALEXANDER WERTH DESCRIBING THE SCENE IN STALINGRAD IN EARLY FEBRUARY 1943 AFTER THE SURRENDER OF THE GERMAN SIXTH ARMY

Marching into captivity
By the end of January 1943 the Red Army
had entombed General Paulus's Sixth Army
in Stalingrad. When Paulus surrendered on the
31st, over 100,000 Axis troops were marched
into a terrible captivity that few would survive.

Meeting in Casablanca
Roosevelt and Churchill
met in January 1943 to plan
the next Allied offensive.
Attempts were also made
to bring together General
Giraud (far left), the French
commander in North Africa,
and the Free French leader
General de Gaulle.

NORTH AFRICA

By the spring of 1943
defeat was also looming
in North Africa. The
German high tide in this
theater had been reached
in August 1942 before
Montgomery checked
Rommel's Afrika Korps
at Alam Halfa. Defeat

These harsh truths bore down heavily on Germany's
allies. Europe contained a combination of cowed
occupied peoples and increasingly sullen allies. The
latter became markedly reluctant to make sacrifices
on the Eastern Front, where entire Italian, Hungarian,
and Romanian armies had been swept away in
Operation Uranus. Finland, Hungary, and Romania
began to extend secret peace feelers to the Soviet
Union, while between December 1942 and April
1943 Mussolini attempted to persuade Hitler to
make a separate political settlement with Stalin in
order to free the Axis for the fight against the British
and Americans. Hitler, however, had no illusions
about the likelihood of dividing the Grand Alliance
ranged against him. By the end of March 1943 he
was immersed in plans for the summer campaigning
season, and his gaze was increasingly fixed on the
Soviet-held Kursk salient, swelling menacingly into
the German line to the north of Kharkov.

returned to prewar levels, and at first the Soviet war
industry survived on prewar stockpiles. When these
ran down, the gap was filled by Lend-Lease materiel,
supplied by the United States under terms agreed to
by Roosevelt and Churchill at the Arcadia Conference
of December 1941. By 1945 the Soviet Union had
received some 16.4 million tons of Lend-Lease
supplies, ranging from 2,000 locomotives to a total
of 13 million boots for the Red Army. This crucial
aid enabled the Soviet war industry to focus on the
output of weaponry for the Eastern Front.

followed at El Alamein in October–November, and
on November 8 an Anglo-American army made a
number of landings in North Africa in Operation
Torch. The response of the Axis was to send
reinforcements from Germany. They joined hands
with Rommel's retreating army and fierce fighting
ensued in the mountains of Tunisia.

By March 1943 the Axis supply situation
in Tunisia had become critical. Rommel was
brought back to Germany, to be decorated
by Hitler but not to return to North Africa.
Army Group Africa was less fortunate. By
May 12 Axis resistance in North Africa was
at an end and, with the fall of Tunis, some
240,000 Axis prisoners, nearly half of them
German, passed into Allied captivity. Hitler
had gloomily anticipated this defeat but, once
again, had been unable to liquidate a front. As
a result, he had presided over another debacle.

THE WAR AT SEA

Away from the Eastern Front, the tide was to turn
abruptly in the Battle of the Atlantic after a period
of sustained German success. In March 1943 the
struggle for the sea-lanes had reached crisis point
for the Western Allies as Grand Admiral Dönitz's
U-boat "wolf packs" scored one of their greatest
successes, plundering two Allied convoys. That month
the number of ships accounted for by U-boats in the
North Atlantic was 108, a total that caused almost
fatal disruption to the seaborne lifeline between
Britain and the United States.

The moment passed. The mid-Atlantic "air
gap"—the stretch of ocean in which the U-boats
had operated free of interference from Allied long-
range patrol aircraft—was closed, and a host of
technical developments was introduced, ranging
from centimetric radar to the breaking at Bletchley
Park of the U-boats' "Shark" code. This was a
battle for technological superiority that the German
Navy was losing hands down. The "wolf packs"
would soon be withdrawn from the Atlantic to go in
search of hunting grounds that were less dangerous.

CASABLANCA CONFERENCE

Allied success made it all the more important to
agree on a common strategy. At the Casablanca
Conference, held between January 13 and 24, 1943,
Roosevelt and Churchill reached several important
decisions: to invade Sicily in the Mediterranean; to
mount a joint strategic bombing offensive against
Germany; to accelerate the build-up of US troops in
Britain for an invasion of northwest Europe; and to
demand, on Roosevelt's insistence, the unconditional
surrender of Germany, Italy, and Japan.

American troops in Operation Torch
On November 8, 1942 Allied troops made landings in
northwest Africa as part of a plan to drive out the Axis
forces. This was finally achieved in May 1943.

FIGHT-BACK IN THE PACIFIC

In two crucial naval encounters that had taken place in the Pacific—the battles of the Coral Sea (May 1942) and Midway (June 1942)—the Japanese had been decisively defeated. This had left them with the need to defend a vast ocean empire that might be attacked at any point by the Americans. The target chosen by the Americans was the Solomons chain. On August 7, 1942 a force of US Marines stormed ashore on the island of Guadalcanal, where the Japanese were building an airfield. This was quickly secured by the Marines and on August 20 it received its first delivery of aircraft. The Japanese poured reinforcements into the island to retake the airstrip, and launched naval and air offensives against the American beachhead. The fighting continued until early February 1943, when the Japanese evacuated some 10,000 troops. The campaign had provided the Allies with their first large-scale victory over the Japanese.

In driving southward, one of the chief objectives of the Japanese had been Port Moresby, the capital of New Guinea, which was situated on the south coast. Control of the town would have enabled Japan to isolate Australia. However, the check received by the Japanese at the Battle of the Coral Sea had destroyed their hopes of seizing it through a direct landing. Their next move, on June 21–22, 1942, had been to land a force on the northern coast of New Guinea to advance on Port Moresby along the Kokoda Trail, a track leading over the mountains separating the north and south coasts. The Japanese advanced to within 30 miles (50 km) of Port Mores by before being forced back by Australian troops to Buna on New Guinea's north coast. This marked the beginning of one of the most bitter campaigns of the war, fought in possibly the most unforgiving terrain and climate experienced in any theater. It was not until May 1945 that the Allies put an end to active Japanese resistance in New Guinea.

> "We have a new experience. We have victory—
> a remarkable and definite victory."
>
> WINSTON CHURCHILL ANNOUNCING THE ALLIED VICTORY AT EL ALAMEIN IN NORTH AFRICA, NOVEMBER 1942

FROM STALINGRAD TO KHARKOV

NOVEMBER 19, 1942–MARCH 18, 1943

A major Soviet counteroffensive to drive the Germans back from Stalingrad initially met with great success, leading to the surrender of the Sixth Army. However, in February 1943 it began to falter and the Germans struck an effective counterblow.

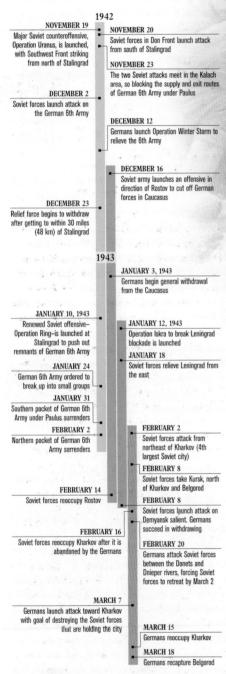

1942

NOVEMBER 19
Major Soviet counteroffensive, Operation Uranus, is launched, with Southwest Front striking from north of Stalingrad

NOVEMBER 20
Soviet forces in Don Front launch attack from south of Stalingrad

NOVEMBER 23
The two Soviet attacks meet in the Kalach area, so blocking the supply and exit routes of German 6th Army under Paulus

DECEMBER 2
Soviet forces launch attack on the German 6th Army

DECEMBER 12
Germans launch Operation Winter Storm to relieve the 6th Army

DECEMBER 16
Soviet army launches an offensive in direction of Rostov to cut off German forces in Caucasus

DECEMBER 23
Relief force begins to withdraw after getting to within 30 miles (48 km) of Stalingrad

1943

JANUARY 3, 1943
Germans begin general withdrawal from the Caucasus

JANUARY 10, 1943
Renewed Soviet offensive–Operation Ring–is launched at Stalingrad to push out remnants of German 6th Army

JANUARY 12, 1943
Operation Iskra to break Leningrad blockade is launched

JANUARY 18
Soviet forces relieve Leningrad from the east

JANUARY 24
German 6th Army ordered to break up into small groups

JANUARY 31
Southern pocket of German 6th Army under Paulus surrenders

FEBRUARY 2
Northern pocket of German 6th Army surrenders

FEBRUARY 2
Soviet forces attack from northeast of Kharkov (4th largest Soviet city)

FEBRUARY 8
Soviet forces take Kursk, north of Kharkov and Belgorod

FEBRUARY 14
Soviet forces reoccupy Rostov

FEBRUARY 16
Soviet forces reoccupy Kharkov after it is abandoned by the Germans

FEBRUARY 14
Soviet forces launch attack on Demyansk salient. Germans succeed in withdrawing

FEBRUARY 20
Germans attack Soviet forces between the Donets and Dnieper rivers, forcing Soviet forces to retreat by March 2

MARCH 7
Germans launch attack toward Kharkov with goal of destroying the Soviet forces that are holding the city

MARCH 15
Germans reoccupy Kharkov

MARCH 18
Germans recapture Belgorod

- Soviet counterattack at Stalingrad Nov 19, 1942–Feb 2, 1943
- Action in southern Russia and the Ukraine Feb 2–Mar 18, 1943
- Action in the Caucasus Dec 16, 1942–Feb 14, 1943
- Action in the north Jan 12–Feb 15, 1943

CHANGING FORTUNES ON THE EASTERN FRONT

BY NOVEMBER 12, 1942 THE SIXTH ARMY had exhausted its strength in a final desperate three-day drive to take Stalingrad. Counterattacks by the Red Army began to nibble away at the ground so painfully won by the Germans in weeks of fighting. At the same time, German military intelligence was becoming increasingly aware of a Red Army build-up on the northern and southern flanks of the Stalingrad salient. These flanks were screened by the Third Romanian Army in the north and the Fourth Romanian Army in the south. Both Romanian armies were not at full strength: under pressure from Hitler, their ranks had been bolstered by freed civilian convicts, but desertion was soon thinning their numbers. Belatedly, elements of the German reserve were sent north to bolster the Third Romanian Army. They were spared Stalingrad, but their relief was to be short-lived.

PLANS FOR A COUNTERATTACK

The Soviet build-up to the Stalingrad counterblow, code-named Operation Uranus, was typical of Zhukov's method. He read the enemy's intentions and juggled scant resources in the front line while methodically amassing a powerful reserve in the rear until the time was right to release it against an enemy at the end of its tether. By the beginning of November, Zhukov had assembled a force of over 1 million men, 14,000 heavy guns, nearly 1,000 tanks, and 1,400 aircraft. Throughout the operation the planning had been measured and methodical, in marked contrast with the 1941–42 improvisations. The lives of the defenders of Stalingrad

RED BANNER

RED STAR

Awards for Red Army soldiers
The Orders of the Red Banner and the Red Star were among the major medals. Stalin also introduced decorations named after 19th-century field marshals.

Fit for battle
Red Army troops in Stalingrad generally had better winter clothing than the Axis troops. Felt boots (*valenki*) and hats made of lamb's wool were often worn by infantrymen.

A Junkers Ju 52 takes to the air
The Germans lost nearly 500 transport aircraft, including many Ju 52s, in their failed attempt to resupply the Sixth Army.

had been traded for time while the Stavka waited for the arrival of a frost that made the ground hard enough for armor to race across country, and for the Allied landings in North Africa that would tie down German reserves in western Europe.

Stalin raised no objections when presented, on November 13, with the detailed plan for Uranus, and he allowed Zhukov to decide when to launch the attack. The date for the blow on the northern front was November 19, followed within 24 hours by an attack in the south. Chuikov, in command of the forces in Stalingrad, was not informed of this decision until the 18th, to ensure that there was no slackening in the defense of the city.

LAUNCH OF OPERATION URANUS

On the northern flank of the Stalingrad salient were the three Soviet armies of the Southwest Front, while due north of Stalingrad itself was the Don Front's two armies. To the south was the Stalingrad Front, comprising three armies. On November 19 the offensive in the north began with a pulverizing artillery barrage, which was followed by infantry advancing in human waves. Within hours the front of the Third Romanian Army had disintegrated, and Red Army tanks were moving across open country

Romanian and German prisoners
Many of the Romanians at Stalingrad lacked basic winter clothing and suffered very badly from frostbite.

in rapid pursuit of fleeing Romanian and German units. Some 30,000 Axis troops were taken prisoner. In the south, where there was no defensible front, the Fourth Romanian Army was shredded with equal speed. On November 23 the Red Army's northern and southern pincers met south of Kalach, 60 miles (95 km) west of Stalingrad (see map page 150). Paulus's Sixth Army and part of the Fourth Panzer Army—330,000 men —were trapped, separated from the rest of the German front by a corridor 100 miles (160 km) wide that was littered with cairns of frozen corpses and smashed artillery and armor. Inside the Stalingrad pocket, the Sixth Army had rations for only six days and ammunition for just two days.

On November 19 Hitler had been 1,300 miles (2,100 km) from Stalingrad in his mountain retreat at the Berghof in southern Bavaria. His immediate response was to dismiss a proposal that the Sixth Army should break out of Stalingrad. The next day the Führer ordered Paulus to hold firm at all costs.

He then ordered a command reshuffle, appointing Manstein commander of Army Group Don, with orders to break through to the Sixth Army.

On November 24 Göring promised Hitler that the Luftwaffe would supply the trapped army from the air. This air support was doomed from the outset. Paulus's minimum daily requirement was 550 tons of rations, clothing, equipment, and munitions. But the largest delivery—made on December 7—was only 290 tons. By mid-January the daily average had dipped to 60 tons and the temperature was as low as −22° F (−30° C). Soldiers survived on scant rations of bread, fat or margarine, and horsemeat. The Red Air Force dominated the skies over Stalingrad, and the cost of Göring's airlift to the Luftwaffe was nearly 500 transports, many of them Junkers Ju 52s, the workhorses of the German air force.

On the ground, Manstein's task of breaking through to Paulus was equally compromised. He estimated that he would need a minimum of four armored, four infantry and mountain, and three Luftwaffe field divisions just to make contact with the Sixth Army and restore its freedom of movement. This was the most he could hope to achieve. The strength of the Red Army forces in the corridor around Stalingrad—some 60 divisions and 1,000 tanks—was too great for him to inflict a defeat that would enable the Ostheer to resume the position it had held in early November. Manstein, however, was not granted even this modest capability, the parlous state of the Soviet railroads combining with a thaw in the Caucasus to deny him the formations he needed. His problems were compounded as units were shuffled back and forth on the Don front to plug the cracks radiating from the debacle at Stalingrad.

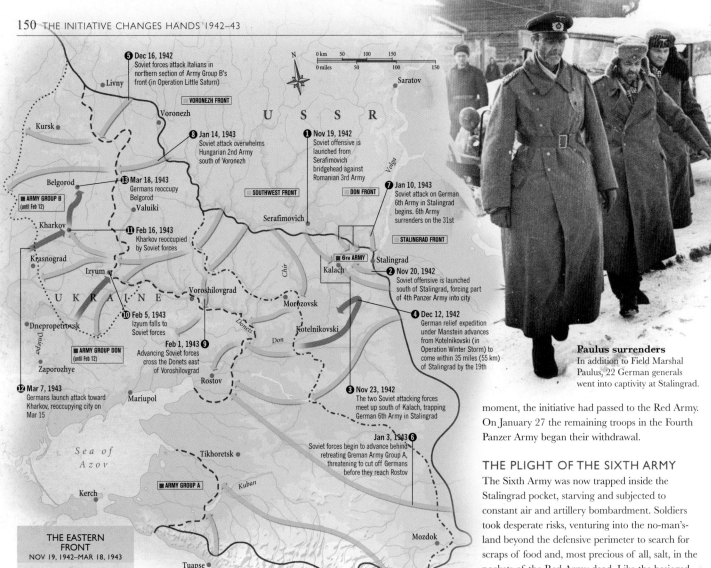

5 Dec 16, 1942
Soviet forces attack Italians in northern section of Army Group B's front (in Operation Little Saturn)

VORONEZH FRONT

8 Jan 14, 1943
Soviet attack overwhelms Hungarian 2nd Army south of Voronezh

1 Nov 19, 1942
Soviet offensive is launched from Serafimovich bridgehead against Romanian 3rd Army

SOUTHWEST FRONT

DON FRONT

7 Jan 10, 1943
Soviet attack on German 6th Army in Stalingrad begins. 6th Army surrenders on the 31st

13 Mar 18, 1943
Germans reoccupy Belgorod

ARMY GROUP B (until Feb 12)

11 Feb 16, 1943
Kharkov reoccupied by Soviet forces

STALINGRAD FRONT

6TH ARMY

2 Nov 20, 1942
Soviet offensive is launched south of Stalingrad, forcing part of 4th Panzer Army into city

10 Feb 5, 1943
Izyum falls to Soviet forces

4 Dec 12, 1942
German relief expedition under Manstein advances from Kotelnikovski (in Operation Winter Storm) to come within 35 miles (55 km) of Stalingrad by the 19th

9 Feb 1, 1943
Advancing Soviet forces cross the Donets east of Voroshilovgrad

ARMY GROUP DON (until Feb 12)

12 Mar 7, 1943
Germans launch attack toward Kharkov, reoccupying city on Mar 15

3 Nov 23, 1942
The two Soviet attacking forces meet up south of Kalach, trapping German 6th Army in Stalingrad

6 Jan 3, 1943
Soviet forces begin to advance behind retreating Greman Army Group A, threatening to cut off Germans before they reach Rostov

ARMY GROUP A

THE EASTERN FRONT
NOV 19, 1942–MAR 18, 1943

— German front line Nov 19, 1942
–·– German front line Jan 2, 1943
–– German front line Feb 2, 1943
···· German front line Feb 20, 1943
▬ Soviet advance
➤ German advance

TRANS-CAUCASUS FRONT

Advance in Ukraine
Following the German failure to relieve the Sixth Army in Stalingrad, the Red Army advanced to beyond Kharkov.

Paulus surrenders
In addition to Field Marshal Paulus, 22 German generals went into captivity at Stalingrad.

moment, the initiative had passed to the Red Army. On January 27 the remaining troops in the Fourth Panzer Army began their withdrawal.

THE PLIGHT OF THE SIXTH ARMY

The Sixth Army was now trapped inside the Stalingrad pocket, starving and subjected to constant air and artillery bombardment. Soldiers took desperate risks, venturing into the no-man's-land beyond the defensive perimeter to search for scraps of food and, most precious of all, salt, in the pockets of the Red Army dead. Like the besieged population of Leningrad, they were reduced to eating rats. Transport aircraft were still flying in and out of Stalingrad's airstrips, taking the wounded with them on the return flights, during which they came under constant attack from enemy antiaircraft guns and the Red Air Force fighters that crowded the air space over the city. The most grievously wounded men stood no chance of escape, since stretchers took up too much space.

OPERATION WINTER STORM

Manstein finally launched his counterattack, which was code-named Winter Storm, on December 12. At first it made steady progress as the Red Army forces surrounding Stalingrad had turned inward against the city. By December 17 a single corps (LVII) of the Fourth Panzer Army had fought its way to within 35 miles (55 km) of Stalingrad. Manstein requested that the Sixth Army should be allowed to break out of the city. Hitler, however, refused: the Sixth Army was to stay put. Manstein then sent one of his officers to the Stalingrad headquarters of Paulus to make one last plea that the Sixth Army should withdraw. Paulus, a polished and immaculately attired staff officer who was a

skilled planner rather than a fighting soldier, and whose willpower had been drained by the battle for Stalingrad, declared that a breakout was impossible. What was more, a surrender had been expressly forbidden by Hitler, his commander-in-chief.

By December 24 Manstein's relief force was fighting for its own life. It lost an armored division, despatched northeast to reinforce hard-pressed units on the Lower Chir, taking with it all hope of relieving the Sixth Army. For the

Wartime propaganda
The portrayal of events by the magazine *Die Wehrmacht* was in stark contrast with the fate of the Sixth Army survivors, who went into a horrifying captivity.

On January 8 the Red Army offered Paulus the chance to capitulate. He declined, and on the 12th reported to the German high command that there were no reserves and that all his heavy weapons were immobilized. He anticipated that the Sixth Army could hold out only for a few more days. On January 22 he made a personal appeal to Hitler to be allowed to open negotiations with the enemy. The Führer turned a deaf ear, and on the 30th he made Paulus a field marshal. No German field marshal had ever surrendered, and in effect Hitler was pressing a suicide pistol into Paulus's hand. Characteristically, however, Paulus did not pull the trigger. Instead, on the 31st he and 22 German generals stepped into captivity. Two days later the last defenders of Stalingrad laid down their arms.

In the Stalingrad pocket the Ostheer had lost 20 divisions and over 200,000 men. Of the 108,000 who marched into captivity, only 5,000 survived the war. Six German divisions had been destroyed outside the encirclement. Germany's allies on the Eastern Front, the Romanians, Hungarians, and Italians, had lost four armies, upward of 450,000 men, and any lingering desire they might have nursed to play an active part in Hitler's dreams of an empire in the east. For three days, German radio broadcast a continuous program of solemn music.

SOVIET INTELLIGENCE

SOVIET INTELLIGENCE NETWORKS had been active in Europe, the United Sates, and the Far East from the 1920s. In the months leading up to Operation Barbarossa in June 1941, and thereafter, they provided a stream of information which would often have proved vital had not Stalin been repeatedly determined to believe the opposite of what he was told. Among the most important of these sources was Richard Sorge, a German journalist based in Japan who had the ear of the German ambassador and a number of high-ranking Japanese officials. In March 1941 Sorge had sent microfilmed German documents to Moscow indicating a German attack in June and, ubsequently, precise details of the German order of battle. They were not believed, but his revelation in

Stalin's spy
A Soviet stamp commemorates spy Richard Sorge, executed by the Japanese in 1944.

November 1941 that Japan was preparing to move south against Britain and the United States was taken at face value, enabling the transfer of divisions from Siberia for the Soviet counteroffensive before Moscow.

High-level Soviet sources in the German high command and civil service in Berlin—the latter part of the network dubbed the "Red Orchestra" by the Germans—also provided valuable information, such as Hitler's plans in the fall of 1941 to besiege Leningrad rather than take it by storm. Elements of the Red Orchestra were based in neutral Switzerland, where the spy Rudolf Rössler was based. A German bookseller, he had sources at a high level within OKW and from 1942 was the lynchpin of the Soviet network known as "Lucy." Rössler provided Moscow with the Ostheer's order of battle for Operation Citadel at Kursk in 1943. John Cairncross, a British army officer, tranferred to Bletchley Park, the home of the British Ultra decoding service, supplied the Luftwaffe's order of battle for Citadel. By the fall of 1943 Stalin would be waging an intelligence war against his allies as well as the Germans.

Harro Shulze-Boysen
A German Air Ministry official and member of the "Red Orchestra" in Berlin, Shulze-Boysen was exposed and executed in 1942.

"The heroism of so many tens of thousands of men, officers and generals is cancelled out by a man like this... He could have freed himself and ascended into eternity and national immortality, but he preferred to go to Moscow."

HITLER ON HEARING THE NEWS OF PAULUS'S SURRENDER

THE SIEGE OF LENINGRAD

ON HITLER'S ORDERS, in September 1941 the German Army Group North and its Finnish allies had pulled back from the outskirts of Leningrad rather than become involved in a costly city battle. On the 25th the Axis forces had begun to besiege the city, subjecting it to constant air and artillery bombardment. The population had already made preparations to defend their city street by street, forming a civilian militia and erecting 17 miles (27 km) of barricades and antitank ditches. Under Marshal Zhukov's direction, mines were laid and guns were taken from ships to strengthen the defenses. Over 600,000 people had been evacuated by the end of August, but by early October the population of some 3.5 million had only enough food to last 20 days. Savage food rationing left up to 500,000 people with no entitlement, and people were driven to eating domestic animals and birds, and making soup from glue and leather.

Starvation and cold weakened even the strongest, and by January 1942 the daily death toll had risen to 5,000. There were incidents of cannibalism. When the city's arms factories ground to a halt, key workers were flown out.

There was one loophole in the blockade. When the large freshwater Lake Ladoga, northwest of Leningrad, froze in November, a road was created over the ice that provided the last link in a 240-mile (380-km) supply route from beyond the German line at Tikhvin. It became known as "The Road of Life." In December the Red Army's capture of Tikhvin, with its railhead, shortened the journey by one-third and enabled the evacuation of over 500,000 civilians. By the spring of 1942 a semblance of normality had returned: industrial production had resumed, and vegetables grown in plots and parks were being supplemented by food aid from the United States, Australia, and New Zealand. In January 1943 Soviet forces succeeded in opening a land corridor south of the lake, enabling trains to reach the city. The siege was to continue until January 27, 1944, when the Germans were driven beyond the distance from which their artillery could fire at the city. It has been estimated that during the 900 days of the siege, about 1 million of Leningrad's citizens died from starvation and other privations, or German bombardment.

A call to patriots
A stern Mother Russia promises death to the German invaders in this propaganda poster.

Digging for water
During the winter of 1941–42 the citizens of Leningrad had to endure not only starvation but a shortage of drinking water when the extreme cold and German shelling combined to interrupt the supply of water to their homes.

Ice road
A Soviet truck creeps forward over a frozen Lake Ladoga. To support the truck's weight, the ice had to be at least 8 in (200 mm) thick.

Garden plot in the cathedral square
By 1943 vegetables were being grown on over 200,000 garden plots. The threat of starvation was lifted by the spring of 1942, but not the German siege, which was to continue until 1944.

The effects of a shell explosion
For month after month, the Germans subjected Leningrad to bombardment by both artillery and aircraft every day between 8:00 am and 10:00 pm.

THE SOVIET ADVANCE CONTINUES

Hitler drew grim satisfaction from the fact that, by condemning the Sixth Army to self-immolation on the Volga, he had prevented an even more disastrous collapse on the Eastern Front. One hundred Soviet divisions had been tied down for a month, so preventing them from rolling up the entire southern wing of the Ostheer between Orel and Rostov.

By the end of the first week in February, the Soviet Southwest Front, under General Nikolai Vatutin, was over the Donets and advancing southeast of Kharkov, while to the north, Colonel General Fillipp Golikov's Voronezh Front was moving on Kharkov itself. On the German side, Manstein's Army Group Don had fallen back on Rostov at the mouth of the Don River. To Manstein's south, Kleist's Army Group A had been forced to withdraw from the Caucasus into the Taman peninsula, on the north coast of the Black Sea, separated from the Crimea by the Kerch Strait and from Army Group Don by 300 miles (500 km).

Manstein, arguably the finest operational commander of the war, had devised a plan to evacuate Rostov and take up a shorter line along the Mius River, which flows into the Sea of Azov 60 miles (90 km) west of Rostov. From here a powerful armored force could strike against the Red Army's counteroffensive. On February 6 Hitler, temporarily unnerved by the disaster at Stalingrad, agreed to the withdrawal. Manstein moved his headquarters west to Zaporozhye, on the Dnieper, and reshuffled Army Group Don in preparation for the planned strike.

SOVIET CAPTURE OF KHARKOV

The situation remained critical for the Germans. On February 8 the Soviet 60th Army had taken the city of Kursk, 120 miles (190 km) north of Kharkov. On February 14 the Germans abandoned Rostov,

Panzer Mark III
By 1942 this German tank was obsolescent and, armed with a 75-mm L/24 howitzer, served in a fire support role in panzergrenadier and heavy tank formations.

A resurgent Red Army
Soviet infantry rush a German outpost, in February 1943, during an attack which saw the retaking of both Kursk and Kharkov before Manstein's brilliant counterblow rocked the Red Army back on its heels.

and on the same day the encirclement of Kharkov itself threatened to bottle up three panzergrenadier divisions. The German high command reacted with another reshuffle. Army Group Don became Army Group South and Army Group B was broken up, with I SS Panzer Corps being absorbed into the forces defending Kharkov. General Paul Hausser, the commander of I SS Panzer Corps, was ordered to defend Kharkov to the last man and last bullet. He did not, however, emulate Paulus. On the 15th he broke out to the southeast, through the one remaining gap in the Soviet ring. Twenty-four hours later, the last of Hausser's rear parties fought their way out of the blazing city to safety. Most of Kharkov's civilian population had fled during the fighting of 1942. Of those who remained, some 250,000 had died during the German occupation, been deported as slave labor, or killed by cold and hunger. When the Red Army took over Kharkov, the Soviet Union's fourth biggest city, they found it almost deserted.

Like Hitler, Stalin wanted everything to happen at once. Both he and the Stavka were convinced that the Ostheer was in full retreat. The race was now on to beat the arrival of the spring *rasputitsa*.

Vatutin was ordered to broaden his offensive, which bulged like a huge sack toward Dnepropetrovsk and threatened to swallow Manstein's headquarters at Zaporozhye. Manstein watched these developments calmly, aware that the Red Army's supply lines were now stretched to breaking point. He proceeded to order his forces to slice into the increasingly exposed northern and southern flanks of the Soviet Sixth Army (part of Vatutin's Southwest Front).

Manstein also had to handle Hitler, who was now eager to overturn the agreement to a withdrawal that he had made on February 6. On February 16 the Führer flew to Zaporozhye to recite a familiar litany —no more withdrawals. Manstein's plan was to be set aside until Kharkov had been retaken by I SS Panzer Corps. Manstein, however, stood firm. The Southwest Front was becoming increasingly exposed to German blows from north and south. Behind it stretched supply lines running across a wasteland left by the withdrawing Germans, who had blown bridges and broken up the few passable roads. Now, before the onset of the *rasputitsa*, was the time to strike at the Sixth Army in the open as the essential preliminary to the retaking of Kharkov. Hitler wavered while the leading elements of the Sixth Army probed to within 40 miles (60 km) of Zaporozhye and the rumble of Red Army guns became audible in the distance. Hitler then flew out, leaving Manstein with a free hand.

MANSTEIN'S COUNTERBLOW

The westward movement of German armored and motorized formations had been noted by Soviet military intelligence but had been interpreted by the Stavka as confirmation of a retreat to the Dnieper. It chose to believe that the significant concentrations of armor it had detected—the First and Fourth

Panzer Armies—were covering a general withdrawal. It came as an unpleasant shock when, on February 20, Manstein's armored shears began chopping away at the right and left flanks of the Sixth Army. Within 24 hours the two Red Army commanders caught by the storm were requesting permission to pull back. They were ordered to press on to cut off the westward German escape routes.

A division of the Sixth Army's XV Tank Corps fought its way to within 10 miles (16 km) of Zaporozhye and then stuck fast, its tanks starved of fuel. Behind it the rest of XV Corps, also short of fuel, was proving to be an easy target for the German tanks on the open, rolling steppe.

Rumbling over the frozen ground at 25 mph (40 kph), the tanks drew alongside trucks packed with infantry and poured machine-gun fire into them at point-blank range. Soviet tank columns, stranded with empty fuel tanks, were shot to pieces. To the south, panzergrenadiers fanned out across the steppe to mop up in a graveyard of burned armor.

At the headquarters of Southwest Front, Vatutin was torn between apprehension of impending disaster and a reluctance to disobey the urgent orders from Stalin to "get that left wing of yours moving." By February 25, however, the greater part

Germans reach Kharkov
The Germans recaptured Kharkov on March 15 after days of savage fighting in which the Soviet defenders used dug-in T-34s and a network of strongpoints in the huge apartment blocks.

of the Soviet Sixth Army was facing encirclement, and Vatutin was obliged to suspend all offensive operations. The Third Tank Army wheeled south from Kharkov to break through to the Sixth Army. Assembling for attack, it was surprised by German armor and dive-bombers and, after four days of heavy fighting, was itself facing encirclement.

The Red Army was saved by the intense cold, which made movement at night all but impossible. The Germans could not seal off the pockets of the badly mauled Soviet forces, who withdrew across the frozen Donets River, leaving behind all their heavy equipment. Manstein now mounted the second phase of his operation, the retaking of Kharkov.

GERMAN RECAPTURE OF KHARKOV
By March 9 the Germans had sealed off Kharkov to the west and north, and after days of savage street fighting the city fell on the 15th. Belgorod, 50 miles (80 km) to the north, was then retaken on the 18th. This brought not only Kursk under threat but also the rear of the Red Army's Central Front, which formed a huge westward bulge in the Soviet line. If Manstein could now coordinate his northward drive with a southward thrust by Field Marshal Günther Hans von Kluge's Army Group Center, the Soviet armies west of Kursk would be trapped and then destroyed. Kluge, however, was of the opinion that his forces were in no shape to launch an offensive. As the Stavka frantically shored up the front around Kursk, and the *rasputitsa* set in, Manstein's chance slipped away. By the end of March the front line had stabilized from the Mius River to Belgorod.

In the course of Manstein's operation against the Southwest Front, the Red Army had lost just over 600 tanks and had left some 23,000 dead on

the battlefield. But significantly, only 9,000 Soviet troops had been taken prisoner. This was not the army that had suffered the huge defeats of 1941 in which hundreds of thousands had been taken prisoner. In 1942 the Red Army had been reshaped from top to bottom. Its officer corps had been invested with new authority—saluting, for example, had been made obligatory—and new decorations invoking the pre-Revolutionary past had been introduced. The granting of privileges had been balanced by a tightening of a military code that was already the most savage of any of the combatants in the western hemisphere. During the battle for Stalingrad, penal battalions, the *strafblats*, had been introduced for both officers and men. The influence of the Communist Party had also been much reduced with the abolition of the "dual command" system in which a formation's political officer, the commissar, shared authority with the commanding officer. With Zhukov at the helm, the Red Army was set to become a far more effective fighting force.

On the German side, Manstein had demonstrated generalship of the highest order in fighting an enemy that outnumbered his own forces by as many as 8 to 1 in vital sectors. The Ostheer had shown that it still had remarkable powers of recovery and tactical superiority in mobile operations over Red Army formations. Contrary to Hitler's unwavering conviction, giving ground was by no means an invitation to certain disaster, but a precondition for German success on the Eastern Front. Manstein's counterblow had restored the nerve of the Ostheer after the shock of Stalingrad and the initial inroads made by the Red Army counteroffensive. Germany could now plan for the renewal of offensive operations in the summer of 1943.

THE SOVIET HOME FRONT

MORE THAN ANY OTHER COMBATANT in World War II, the Soviet Union was mobilized to fight a "total war." The sacrifices and suffering endured by the Soviet people between 1941 and 1945 were both heroic and horrifying. The brunt of the civilian effort was borne by women. The armed services devoured the male population of the Soviet Union, leaving women to make up 80 percent of the rural workforce by 1944 and over 50 percent of factory workers, much of the balance being met by boys waiting for their call-up. From June 1941 many workers were forced to move eastward, and endure immense hardship, as a program for the relocation of heavy industry was implemented. The program included the transfer of the huge tank plant at Kharkov to the tractor factory at Chelyabinsk, which also housed part of the Kirov plant evacuated from Leningrad. Popularly known as "Tankograd," it was producing T-34s just 10 weeks after the last engineers left the Kharkov works.

In both factories and fields, life was lived at subsistence level and rationing of food was severe: from 1941 children and elderly dependents received just 700 calories a day, factory workers 1,300, and coalminers 4,000. Peasants did not qualify for ration cards but were able to sell food on the flourishing black market. City dwellers sustained themselves with produce from their garden plots, which by 1944 supplied 25 percent of the Soviet potato harvest.

Completely outside this system were the millions of Soviet citizens in labor camps— some 4.6 million in 1942—who were integrated into the Soviet war industry with characteristic ruthlessness. In 1943–44, as the Red Army steadily regained Soviet territory from the Ostheer, it also swept into Stalin's net millions of Soviet citizens—mere contact with the occupiers brought with it the taint of collaboration. Entire populations—the Volga Germans, Chechens, Crimean Tatars, Kalmyks—were uprooted and deported to Soviet Central Asia and Siberia in cattle trucks supervised by the ever-present NKVD or secret police. It has been estimated that at least 1.5 million people were involved in this forced migration, half of whom did not survive the war.

Field workers
This idealized picture of Russian women bringing in the grain harvest belies the fact that, for most women during the war, life was a constant struggle to survive.

Making shells
By November 1941 the Soviet male work force had fallen by 21 million. Their places in factories and on farms were taken by women.

An exhortation to workers
In the names of Lenin and Stalin, civilians were exhorted to work to support the war effort.

СОРЕВНУЙТЕСЬ НА ЛУЧШУЮ ПОМОЩЬ ФРОНТУ!

Byelorussian refugees
Soviet peasants in the war zones were helpless against German "scorched earth" tactics and anti-partisan operations. Vast numbers of refugees was created as homes were destroyed.

Tank production
Tank factories were among the heavy industries that were moved eastward with as many as 25 million workers and their families in the second half of 1941.

THE HOLOCAUST

THE GERMAN ARMY'S SUCCESSES in the first two years of the war delivered into Hitler's hands the Jewish populations of much of Europe. In the early stages of the conflict the Germans had created numerous ghettos in Poland, the largest in Warsaw, where at least 40,000 Jews died of starvation in 1941. The gains made by Germany in the summer of 1941 in the Soviet Union produced the so-called "Final Solution," a euphemism for the extermination of European Jews.

In January 1942, at a secret conference in Wannsee chaired by Reinhard Heydrich, deputy head of the SS, the Final Solution was systematized. In the east the killing had initially been undertaken by *Einsatzgruppe* units (see page 102) with the help of local auxiliaries and allies. At Odessa in the fall of 1941 up to 80,000 Jews were killed by *Einsatzgruppen* and troops from Romania, into which Odessa had been incorporated. Heydrich industrialized the killing, establishing extermination camps based on the existing concentration camp system. Clusters of camps were built in Poland—among them Treblinka, Belzec, Majdanek, Sobibor, and Auschwitz-Birkenau. Adolf Eichmann and his subordinates organized the transportation to these and other camps of Jews, Slavs, Red Army prisoners-of-war, gypsies, political prisoners, and homosexuals. They came from every part of occupied Europe, and meticulously logged railroad movements later provided much detail for historians of the Final Solution. The camps were sometimes linked to industrial complexes run by the SS, and those deemed capable of work on arrival were given a stay of execution. The rest—the old and the infirm, the children—were gassed. Auschwitz attained a rate of 12,000 victims a day. In April 1943 there was a revolt and mass escape at Treblinka, the destination for many Polish Jews. That same month, the German troops despatched to clear the ghetto in Warsaw met with armed resistance. The fighting, in which some 13,000 Jews died, ended in mid-May 1943, and the survivors were sent to extermination camps.

The Western Allies had learned about the existence of the extermination camps from intelligence sources and refuges by the summer of 1944, when the Red Army reached the abandoned camp in Majdanek in Poland. It overran many more camps in the following months, including Auschwitz, to which 450,000 Hungarian Jews—about 60 percent of the largest surviving Jewish population in Europe—had been delivered from March 1944. The Final Solution caused the death of approximately 5.7 million Jews, some 40 percent of the world's Jewish population, and at least another million more people who were either non-Aryan or deemed undesirable by the Nazis.

Arriving at Auschwitz
Many of the people sent to Auschwitz only learnt on their arrival that it was a death camp.

Distribution of camps

The system of concentration and death camps was extended with each German conquest in Europe.

CENTERS OF PERSECUTION
DURING THE WAR

- ◉ Main concentration camp
- ● Extermination camp
- ◻ Site of major mass killing
- ⊛ Ghetto
- (8,000) Estimated number of Jews killed
- — Borders Nov 1942
- Greater Germany Nov 1942
- Italy and Axis satellites Nov 1942
- Under German occupation Nov 1942
- Under German and Italian occupation Nov 1942
- Allied territory
- Neutral territory

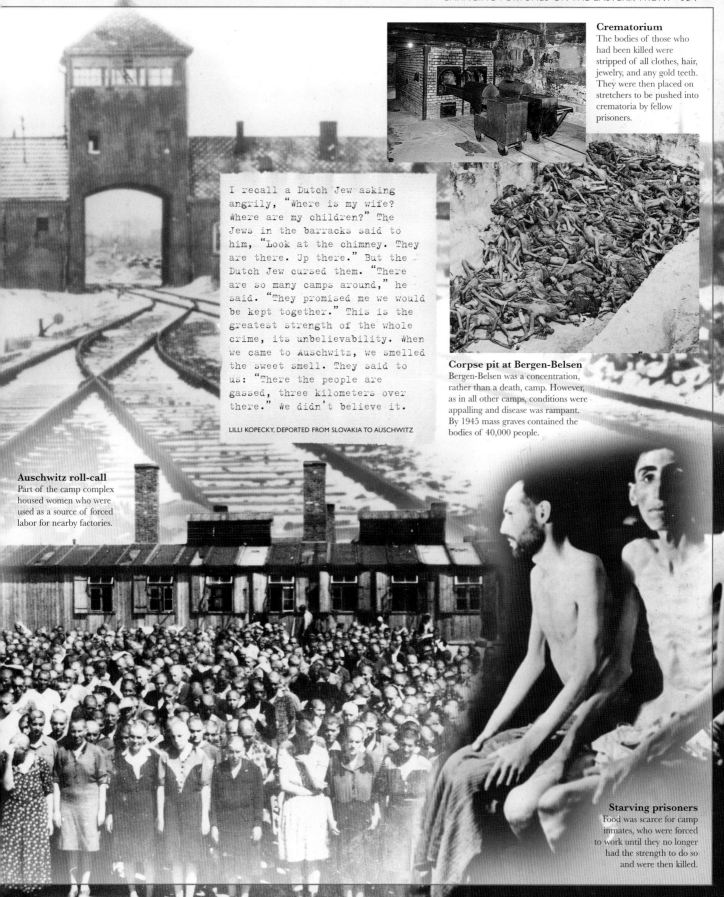

Crematorium
The bodies of those who had been killed were stripped of all clothes, hair, jewelry, and any gold teeth. They were then placed on stretchers to be pushed into crematoria by fellow prisoners.

I recall a Dutch Jew asking angrily, "Where is my wife? Where are my children?" The Jews in the barracks said to him, "Look at the chimney. They are there. Up there." But the Dutch Jew cursed them. "There are so many camps around," he said. "They promised me we would be kept together." This is the greatest strength of the whole crime, its unbelievability. When we came to Auschwitz, we smelled the sweet smell. They said to us: "There the people are gassed, three kilometers over there." We didn't believe it.

LILLI KOPECKY, DEPORTED FROM SLOVAKIA TO AUSCHWITZ

Corpse pit at Bergen-Belsen
Bergen-Belsen was a concentration, rather than a death, camp. However, as in all other camps, conditions were appalling and disease was rampant. By 1945 mass graves contained the bodies of 40,000 people.

Auschwitz roll-call
Part of the camp complex housed women who were used as a source of forced labor for nearby factories.

Starving prisoners
Food was scarce for camp inmates, who were forced to work until they no longer had the strength to do so and were then killed.

One million pairs of shoes at Lublin camp
As the Red Army advanced into Poland in 1944, it discovered many extermination camps. Among the horrifying evidence of the Holocaust in these camps were piles of the former possessions of murdered Jews.

NORTH AFRICA AND THE MEDITERRANEAN

MARCH 1942–MAY 1943

After two years of inconclusive offensives and retreats across Libya, in November 1942 the British finally won a significant victory over Rommel at El Alamein. In the same month the odds tilted dramatically with the arrival of US forces—the Torch landings—in French northwest Africa. Even so, it took the Allies another six months to drive the Axis from North Africa.

1942

MARCH 20–26
British convoy from Alexandria to Malta fights off Italian ships in Sirte Gulf, but suffers heavy losses as it nears Malta

APRIL 7
2,000-plane raid on Malta

JUNE 11
Two convoys sail for Malta: "Harpoon" from Gibraltar, "Vigorous" from Alexandria. Both suffer heavy losses. "Vigorous" turns back to Alexandria

MAY 26
German offensive begins with march to south of British Gazala Line

JUNE 21
Tobruk falls to Germans

JUNE 30
After Rommel's advance, 8th Army back on El Alamein line. In Cairo British HQ prepares for evacuation to Palestine

JULY 1
Rommel attacks at El Alamein

JULY 7
Rommel halted at El Alamein, but Auchinleck unable to launch effective counteroffensive

AUGUST 11–15
British convoy "Pedestal" sailing for Malta attacked by aircraft, submarines, and torpedo boats

AUGUST 13
Montgomery assumes command of British 8th Army from Auchinleck

AUGUST 30
Rommel launches attack on British 8th Army south of El Alamein

SEPTEMBER 2
Rommel falls back to start line–end of attempt to capture Suez Canal

OCTOBER 18
Germans and Italians halt daylight bombing raids on Malta

OCTOBER 23–24
Start of Second Battle of El Alamein

OCTOBER 27
Axis counterattacks

NOVEMBER 4
Rommel, hopelessly outnumbered in men, tanks, and aircraft, retreats

NOVEMBER 8
Operation Torch. US landings around Casablanca, Oran, and Algiers meet with resistance from Vichy French

NOVEMBER 9
German landings near Tunis

NOVEMBER 10
French end resistance to Allies

NOVEMBER 11
French in Algeria and Morocco sign armistice with Allies

NOVEMBER 13
Tobruk recaptured

DECEMBER 28
Allied advance to Tunis halted

1943

JANUARY 14–25
Casablanca Conference. Churchill and Roosevelt meet to discuss future plans for war

JANUARY 23
British 8th Army enters Tripoli

JANUARY 23
Rommel crosses into Tunisia

FEBRUARY 14–22
Battle of Kasserine Pass. Dual offensive by von Arnim's 5th Army and Rommel's Afrika Korps forces Allied withdrawal

FEBRUARY 22
Axis advance halted; Rommel turns to face British 8th Army advancing from south

MARCH 9
Rommel leaves North Africa on sick leave; replaced by von Arnim

MARCH 20
Montgomery attacks Mareth Line, Axis defensive position in southern Tunisia

MARCH 26–27
Axis troops evacuate Mareth Line after being outflanked by New Zealand Corps

MAY 6
Final Allied offensive opens

MAY 7
Bizerta and Tunis fall

MAY 13
Italian 1st Army surrenders. In all Allies take 240,000 German and Italian prisoners

 Operations in the Mediterranean Mar 1942–May 1943

Egypt and Libya May 6, 1942–Jan 23, 1943

Operation Torch and Tunisia Nov 8, 1942–May 13, 1943

THE AXIS DEFEATED IN NORTH AFRICA

AFTER ROMMEL HAD DRIVEN the British back to the Gazala Line in early 1942, a temporary stalemate existed in Libya, with both sides making preparations for renewing the offensive. Malta was still under siege and the Royal Navy was desperately struggling, in the face of Axis air superiority, to keep the island supplied. While the United States had finally joined the war, it would clearly be some time before sufficient US forces were deployed to the European theatre to have any influence on events.

Concerned over Malta, Churchill pressured Auchinleck, the Middle East commander-in-chief, to attack as soon as possible. Auchinleck was not prepared to do so until he was ready and he also wanted to strengthen the Gazala Line so that he could launch his offensive from a secure base. Churchill remained dissatisfied and threatened to remove part of the Desert Air Force to India. This galvanized Auchinleck into agreeing to make an attack on May 1, although he soon postponed this to the middle of June.

British Commonwealth Forces Quad Gun Tractor. Many of these reliable four-wheel drive vehicles were made by Ford, Canada

Exhausted German troops
Rommel's German and Italian forces crossed into Egypt and reached the El Alamein line at the end of June 1942, but their fatigue was now such that they were unable to break through the British defensive positions.

AXIS INTENTIONS

There was also disagreement in the Axis camp. While Rommel wanted to push on to the Suez Canal before the British could strengthen their defenses, his superiors remained cautious. By the end of March 1942 they decided that the seizure of Malta must be the priority because of the threat it posed to Axis supply lines across the Mediterranean. After an intensification of the air offensive against the island, a combined airborne and amphibious operation would be launched to capture it.

As far as Libya was concerned, Rommel could expect no more German reinforcements because of the planned offensive on the Eastern Front. His hands were thus tied. Eventually, though, at the beginning of May he was given leave to conduct a limited offensive to recapture Tobruk. Should he achieve this speedily, he would be allowed to advance to the Egyptian frontier, but then his air support would be removed for the assault on Malta. Only once this had taken place and been successful would Rommel be allowed to continue to the Nile Delta.

As far as Rommel was concerned, he had been given the green light and he immediately began his preparations. The Gazala Line had two major weaknesses. Although it stretched some 40 miles (65 km) south to Bir Hacheim, there was open desert beyond this point, which meant that the line could be outflanked. In addition, the defenses consisted of a number of fortified brigade-sized positions, known as "boxes," but some were too far apart to provide mutual supporting fire. Rommel decided to take his armor around the south of the line, while his Italian infantry tied down the defenders. They would then punch a hole through the defenses and establish

Camouflaged artillery
The crew prepares to fire a 25-pounder from a gun emplacement in the desert. The British field gun was manned by a crew of six.

a direct resupply route for his tanks. The Gazala Line dispositions had a further weakness, not recognized by Rommel. Although Auchinleck wanted to keep his tanks concentrated so that they could deal with any Axis outflanking move, Ritchie, still commanding Eighth Army, was worried about his supply dumps, which were situated far forward as part of his own attack preparations, and dispersed his armor to protect them.

ROMMEL'S OFFENSIVE

On the evening of May 26, 1942, Rommel began his approach march. Ritchie was convinced that it was a diversion and that the main attack would be against the Gazala Line itself. Next morning, the Axis armor swung around Bir Hacheim and began to advance north to the rear of the British defenses. Caught by surprise, the British tanks became increasing scattered. But Rommel's tanks were now beginning to run out of fuel. It was time to attack the Gazala Line itself, which the Italians did from the west and the Afrika Korps from the east. The particular box selected was soon isolated and Ritchie was unable to concentrate his armor to launch an effective counterattack. By the end of June 2 the Cauldron, as the British called it, had been overrun and an

In the first second we must have received at least four direct hits from armor-piercing shells. The engine was knocked out, a track was broken and one shell hit the barrel of the 75-mm gun and broke it. Then quite a heavy high-explosive shell dropped on the mantlet of my 37-mm gun and pushed it back against the recoil springs... I suffered nothing more than a singing in my ears. But a splinter hit the subaltern in the head and he fell to the floor of the turret dead.

REA LEAKEY, BRITISH TANK OFFICER, ON BEING HIT BY GERMAN 88-MM SHELLS

armored counterattack launched three days later was a disastrous failure, resulting in a heavy loss of tanks. The southern part of the line was now entirely in Axis hands, apart from Bir Hacheim, where the Free French garrison continued to hold out in the face of repeated attacks.

On June 11 the French were ordered to break out, which they successfully did. Rommel, meanwhile, set about destroying the remainder of the British armor to the west of El Adem. In two days' fighting, he largely succeeded and threatened Ritchie's main supply line to the northern part of the Gazala Line.

Accordingly, Ritchie withdrew his forces to prevent them from being totally cut off. The Eighth Army was now withdrawing to the Egyptian frontier, but Churchill was insistent that Tobruk be held. Unfortunately, the port's perimeter defenses had deteriorated since the long siege of the previous year. The largely South African garrison had little chance to prepare before Rommel's troops had isolated Tobruk and attacked. It fell on June 21.

British 25-pounder
This gun was the workhorse of the British artillery. It was a multipurpose gun that served primarily as a field gun, but could also be fired at a high elevation like a howitzer. In the desert it was often used in an antitank role.

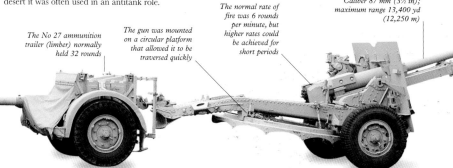

The No 27 ammunition trailer (limber) normally held 32 rounds

The gun was mounted on a circular platform that allowed it to be traversed quickly

The normal rate of fire was 6 rounds per minute, but higher rates could be achieved for short periods

Caliber 87 mm (3½ in); maximum range 13,400 yd (12,250 m)

BERNARD LAW MONTGOMERY

BADLY WOUNDED as a young infantry officer in 1914, Montgomery (1887–1976) served for the remainder of the war as a staff officer on the Western Front. He took Third Infantry Division to France in 1939 and was then made responsible for the defense of the southeast coast of England. It was when he was selected to take over the Eighth Army in Egypt in August 1942 that Monty, as he was generally known, demonstrated his best qualities. His self-confidence, clarity of thought, and insistence on showing himself to his troops and making them believe that each had a key role to play, restored the morale of the army.

Monty's victory at El Alamein made him a household name in Britain. He led his victorious army across Libya into Tunisia, then to Sicily and Italy. His brashness and lack of tact did not go down well with some of his American fellow commanders, but he was appointed to command 21st Army Group for the invasion of Europe. He conducted the Normandy campaign, but was disappointed when Eisenhower subsequently insisted on taking over command.

Two days later, Rommel continued his pursuit of the increasingly disorganized Eighth Army. He signaled Kesselring, his superior in Rome, for permission to keep going into Egypt, pointing out that he had captured large stocks of supplies in Tobruk.

DESPERATE MEASURES

In the British camp, Ritchie wanted to stand and fight at Mersa Matruh, but Auchinleck feared that this would result in the destruction of the Eighth Army. He was starting to construct a new defense line at El Alamein, which had the advantage that its southern end was anchored on the virtually impassable Qattara Depression and hence could not be outflanked. Auchinleck decided to remove Ritchie and take command of the army himself. If the Axis succeeded in penetrating the El Alamein line, he intended to hold them on the Suez Canal or, if need be, in Palestine.

Rommel had already closed up to Mersa Matruh, when he obtained grudging permission to continue his advance. Kesselring had decided that the need to capture Malta was less pressing. He now felt that air assaults and the mining of the waters around the island had effectively neutralized it as a threat to Axis supply lines. Two simultaneous British supply convoys, Harpoon from Gibraltar and Vigorous from Alexandria, had been subjected to ferocious air and sea attacks. Only two supply vessels from Harpoon reached the island, while Vigorous was forced to turn back. It was possible that the island could be starved into submission.

Back in Egypt, Rommel quickly outflanked the defenses at Mersa Matruh, as Auchinleck expected him to do, and by June 30 the Eighth Army was back on the El Alamein Line. On that same day, the Mediterranean Fleet left Alexandria for anchorages farther east, while British headquarters began to burn secret files and prepared to evacuate to Palestine. Rommel was conscious that his troops were now close to exhaustion after five weeks of very intensive combat and that he had to attack immediately to deny the British any opportunity to draw breath. Accordingly, he launched his assault on July 1. Partially thanks to a sandstorm and the

Infantry advance
At El Alamein and other battles in the Desert War Montgomery used his infantry, after an initial artillery bombardment, for what he termed the "crumbling" of Axis defenses.

efforts of the Desert Air Force, it was repulsed. Rommel made further attacks during the next two days, but although these did gain ground he could not achieve the now elusive breakthrough.

Rommel therefore decided to go over to the defensive for the time being. The British tried to dislodge him, but without success. Rommel then launched two further attacks, on July 10 and 12, but again could not break through and finally accepted that he had done all he could. Auchinleck now made further attempts to drive his adversary back, but his troops were also drained and before the end of the month he halted his attacks and a stalemate ensued.

CHANGES IN COMMAND

Disappointed that Auchinleck had failed to drive the Axis back, Churchill flew to Cairo. He decided to replace Auchinleck, appointing Harold Alexander, who had recently overseen the British withdrawal from Burma, in his place. Hardened desert veteran William "Strafer" Gott was selected to take over the Eighth Army, but he was shot down and killed while flying to Cairo to assume command and Bernard Montgomery had to be hastily sent for from Britain. He found an army that was "brave but baffled" and the first action he and Alexander took was to make it clear that there would be no retreat from El Alamein. The Eighth Army's task would be to repulse Rommel's next attack, then go onto the offensive.

Rommel himself had become ill and asked to be relieved of his command, but his request was denied. He knew he had to attack again, but was very short of fuel. Six tankers and ammunition ships were scheduled to cross the Mediterranean during August. Ultra gave the British due warning of their sailing and four were sunk, while the other two did not arrive in time. As a result, Rommel did not have the

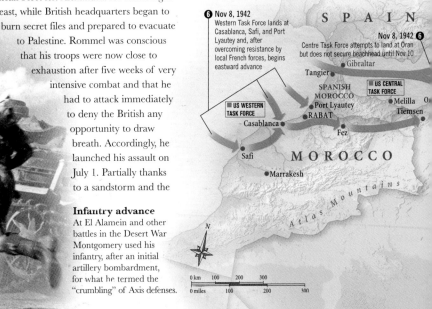

6 Nov 8, 1942
Western Task Force lands at Casablanca, Safi, and Port Lyautey and, after overcoming resistance by local French forces, begins eastward advance

Nov 8, 1942 **6**
Centre Task Force attempts to land at Oran but does not secure beachhead until Nov 10

SPAIN

Tangier • Gibraltar

SPANISH
MOROCCO
Port Lyautey
RABAT
Casablanca

US CENTRAL
TASK FORCE

US WESTERN
TASK FORCE

Melilla
Tiemsen

Fez

Safi

MOROCCO

• Marrakesh

Atlas Mountains

0 km 100 200 300
0 miles 100 200 300

fuel to reach the Suez Canal and would have to rely on capturing British dumps. Meanwhile a key convoy to Malta, Pedestal, got through from Gibraltar to reinforce and resupply the island.

Rommel began his attack late on August 30. His plan was to feint in the north, while his tanks broke through in the south and then swung north to cut the Eighth Army's supply lines. Montgomery, partly thanks to Ultra intelligence, had foreseen this and knew that his opponent had to secure the dominant Alam Halfa Ridge, southeast of El Alamein. He was therefore determined to deny Rommel the ridge and, indeed, to use it as bait in order to defeat him. The British had only light screening forces in the extreme south and Rommel hoped to be able to

The Allied victory in North Africa

After US forces landed in Morocco and Algeria in November 1942, the German and Italian forces in this theatre were heavily ounumbered. The Axis sent fresh troops to Tunisia, but they were unable to break out as the Allies closed in from east and west to trap them.

reach the ridge by dawn. Unfortunately, his armor was slowed by two belts of minefields and it was well after daylight when it began to advance toward the Alam Halfa Ridge. While the Desert Air Force attacked from the air, Montgomery's tanks engaged from the ridge itself. After two days of repeated attempts to capture it, Rommel, now desperately short of fuel, was forced to withdraw to his start line.

It was now Montgomery's turn to attack. Churchill wanted him to strike before the end of September, but both Alexander and Montgomery insisted that they would not be ready, especially since the army needed some intensive training. By mid-October the Eighth Army outnumbered the Axis forces by two to one in men and tanks and by almost the same margin in antitank guns, artillery, and aircraft. In addition, Rommel was still beset by fuel problems. Air attacks on the ports along the Egyptian and Libyan coasts had rendered them almost unusable and many of his supplies had to come by road all the way from Tripoli. He himself

German and Italian prisoners

In the aftermath of El Alamein, the Eighth Army took some 30,000 prisoners, about a third of them Germans. Here a large number of Axis troops have been rounded up after the battle by New Zealanders in armored cars.

was ill again and left for Germany for treatment on September 23. Realizing that his forces could no longer fight a maneuver battle, he left instructions for efforts to be concentrated on strengthening the minefields covering his positions.

Montgomery appreciated that there was no means of outflanking the Axis defenses and that he would have to make a frontal assault, opting to do this against the northern part of Rommel's line. Once lanes in the minefields had been cleared, he looked to his infantry to carry out the break-in operation. His armor would then draw the Axis tanks onto it and destroy them prior to the actual breakthrough taking place.

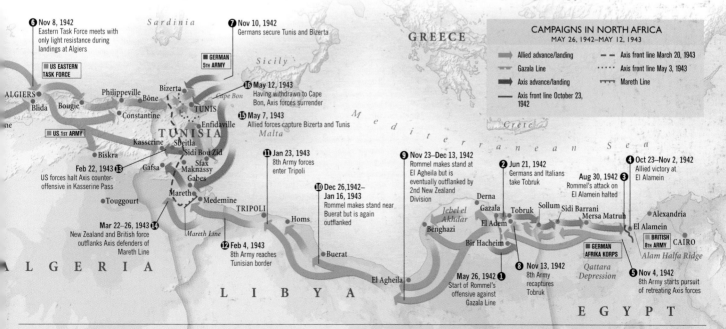

6 Nov 8, 1942
Eastern Task Force meets with only light resistance during landings at Algiers

US EASTERN TASK FORCE

7 Nov 10, 1942
Germans secure Tunis and Bizerta

GERMAN 5TH ARMY

16 May 12, 1943
Having withdrawn to Cape Bon, Axis forces surrender

15 May 7, 1943
Allied forces capture Bizerta and Tunis

11 Jan 23, 1943
8th Army forces enter Tripoli

9 Nov 23–Dec 13, 1942
Rommel makes stand at El Agheila but is eventually outflanked by 2nd New Zealand Division

2 Jun 21, 1942
Germans and Italians take Tobruk

3 Aug 30, 1942
Rommel's attack on El Alamein halted

4 Oct 23–Nov 2, 1942
Allied victory at El Alamein

US 1ST ARMY

13 Feb 22, 1943
US forces halt Axis counter-offensive in Kasserine Pass

10 Dec 26,1942– Jan 16, 1943
Rommel makes stand near Buerat but is again outflanked

14 Mar 22–26, 1943
New Zealand and British force outflanks Axis defenders of Mareth Line

12 Feb 4, 1943
8th Army reaches Tunisian border

GERMAN AFRIKA KORPS

8 Nov 13, 1942
8th Army recaptures Tobruk

1 May 26, 1942
Start of Rommel's offensive against Gazala Line

5 Nov 4, 1942
8th Army starts pursuit of retreating Axis forces

BRITISH 8TH ARMY

CAMPAIGNS IN NORTH AFRICA
MAY 26, 1942–MAY 12, 1943

Allied advance/landing	Axis front line March 20, 1943
Gazala Line	Axis front line May 3, 1943
Axis advance/landing	Mareth Line
Axis front line October 23, 1942	

Sardinia · GREECE · Sicily · Cape Bon · TUNIS · Bizerta · Philippeville · Bône · Constantine · ALGIERS · Blida · Bougie · TUNISIA · Enfidaville · Malta · Kasserine · Sbeitla · Sidi Bou Zid · Biskra · Sfax · Maknassy · Gabes · Gafsa · Mareth · Medenine · TRIPOLI · Touggourt · Mareth Line · Homs · Buerat · El Agheila · Jebel el Akhdar · Derna · Gazala · Benghazi · El Adem · Tobruk · Sollum · Bir Hacheim · Sidi Barrani · Mersa Matruh · Alexandria · El Alamein · CAIRO · Alam Halfa Ridge · Qattara Depression · Mediterranean Sea · Crete

A L G E R I A · L I B Y A · E G Y P T

On the night of October 23/24 the attack began. Nearly 900 British guns fired a preliminary barrage and the mine clearance parties, covered by infantry, began to move forward. The Axis forces were initially taken by surprise and lanes were soon created, but problems of command and control in the darkness, which slowed the passage of the tanks through the lanes, and the sheer depth of the defenses meant that progress was not as quick as was hoped. Rommel's deputy was killed during the day, and Rommel himself returned on October 25. He immediately launched a series of counterattacks against the British lodgements, but these were beaten off. Even so, Montgomery accepted that there was a growing danger that a stalemate might ensue and recast his plans. This meant a pause to reorganize, which agitated Churchill. The new attack was launched on the night of November 1/2. Given his now desperate lack of fuel, Rommel realized that if

The American disembarkation
US troops manhandle a gun up a beach on November 9, the day after the initial Torch landings. Most of the men had no experience of war when they arrived in North Africa, but learned quickly during the Tunisian campaign.

he continued to stand and fight, his army was in danger of being destroyed. He therefore began to withdraw his mobile forces. Hitler ordered him to stay put, but it was too late. By midday on November 4 the Axis forces were in full retreat.

At first Montgomery's armor was slow to take advantage of Rommel's retreat and the arrival of rain on November 6 did not help matters. Even so, El Alamein was a significant victory and a major turning point of the war in the West. It was also the last significant success by British arms alone in the theater. Some 1,800 miles (2,900 km) to the west US forces were about to enter the fray.

THE TORCH LANDINGS

On November 8, 1942 Anglo–US forces landed at points in French northwest Africa. Operation Torch was the upshot of several months of strategic debate between the United States and Britain as to where US forces in Europe could be best employed before the end of 1942. The idea was to secure Morocco, Algeria, and Tunisia quickly so as to threaten the Axis forces facing the British in Egypt and Libya in the rear and help bring about their destruction. The key to the success of the Torch landings was that the Vichy French forces would offer minimum resistance. To this end, Torch's deputy commander, General Mark Clark was taken secretly by submarine for a meeting on the Algerian coast with one of the Vichy French generals, who assured him that they would follow the

Algeria bound
US forces assemble on the deck of a troopship before the landings in Algeria. In all, 39,000 men were landed near Oran, 33,000 around Algiers, and 35,000 in Morocco.

orders of General Henri Giraud, who had been selected as the French figurehead after the Vichy French government in the region had been dissolved.

Three task forces took part in Torch. The Western Task Force under General George S. Patton sailed directly from the United States and landed at points on the Moroccan coast. The other two forces sailed from Scotland. General Lloyd Fredenhall's Center Task Force landed in Oran and General Charles Ryder's Eastern Task Force in Algiers. The latter was the only one to include British forces. These, however, had to be initially disguised as Americans because of Vichy French enmity toward the British since the bombardment of their fleet in July 1940 to prevent it from falling into German hands. There were fears that this would stiffen resistance to the landing. As it happened, the Vichy French did offer some resistance to all three landings. However, Marshal Pétain gave Admiral François Darlan, the Resident-General in North Africa, freedom to negotiate with the Allies and on November 11 an armistice came into force.

GERMAN REACTIONS

The Axis had initially been taken by surprise, especially by the landings in Algeria. Nevertheless, they reacted quickly. On November 9 the Vichy prime minister Pierre Laval gave permission for Axis troops to be deployed to Tunisia and the first of these, German paratroops, landed at an airfield outside Tunis that same day. In revenge for the signing of the armistice with the Allies, the Germans proceeded to occupy Vichy France. The French response was to scuttle their fleet based at Toulon.

The Allies now had to advance into Tunisia as fast as possible to secure it before the Axis forces built up. The forces available, under the command of General Kenneth Anderson's First British Army, were initially slim—two British infantry brigades, an Anglo–US armored task force, together with some Commandos, US Rangers, and paratroops.

ARMOR AND ANTITANK WEAPONS USED IN THE DESERT WAR

ARMOR DOMINATED THE WAR in Egypt and Libya, the desert being ideal terrain for tanks. It was also the scene of intense rivalry between the tank and the antitank gun. Dominant in this respect was the German 88-mm, which totally outranged all the tanks used by the British. The earlier models the British used in the desert were also disadvantaged because they did not have high-explosive shells, a much more effective way of neutralizing antitank guns than solid shot.

Italian CV3/35 flamethrower tankette
The basic CV3, with two machine-guns, entered service in 1933, but was too lightly armed and armored to have any effect in North Africa. The flamethrower version enjoyed virtually no success.

Crew 2	Top speed 26 mph (42 kph)
Range with full fuel tank 100 miles (160 km)	
Maximum armor thickness ½ in (14 mm)	

75-mm gun mounted in side sponson

37-mm secondary armament

British 6-pounder (57-mm) antitank gun
Designed in 1938, the gun did not enter production until 1941 and only began to replace the less effective 2-pounder (40-mm) in the Eighth Army in early 1942.

Weight of gun carriage 2,698 lb (1,224 kg)	Weight of shot 6 lb (2.72 kg)
Armour penetration at 1,000 yd (915 m) 2½ in (65 mm)	
Crew 5	

Side hatch

Muzzle break to reduce smoke visible to enemy on firing

Shield

Trail

US M3 Grant
Used by the British from summer 1942, the Grant was automotively more reliable than British tank types, but its high silhouette was a disadvantage.

Crew 6	Top speed 26 mph (42 kph)
Range with full fuel tank 120 miles (192 km)	
Maximum armor thickness 2¼ in (55 mm)	

90-mm smoke generators

88-mm high-velocity gun

British Humber armored car
Both sides made extensive use of armored cars for reconnaissance and covering their open desert flanks. The Humber was in North Africa from late 1941.

Crew 3	Top speed 45 mph (72 kph)
Range with full fuel tank 250 miles (400 km)	
Maximum armor thickness : ⅗ in (15 mm)	

7.92-mm MG 34 machine-gun

15-mm Besa gun

German PzKpfw VI Tiger heavy tank
The most formidable of all the German tanks, the Tiger made its combat debut in Tunisia. It proved particularly effective in defense, especially in northwest Europe, where its potential as an attacking weapon was limited by the terrain.

Crew 5	Top speed 23 mph (37 kph)
Range with full fuel tank 62 miles (100 km)	
Maximum armor thickness 4 in (100 mm)	

720-mm battle tracks

German 88-mm FLAK
Designed as an antiaircraft weapon, it was first used in an antitank role during the Spanish Civil War. It was in North Africa that it really came into its own.

Crew 5	Weight of shot 23 lb (10.4 kg)
Armor penetration at 1,000 yd (915 m) 4 in (103 mm)	
Weight of gun carriage 8,140 lb (3,700 kg)	

German PzKpfw III
There were a number of variants of this tank, with both 37-mm and 50-mm guns. This version is equipped with a 75-mm low velocity gun for firing high explosive.

Crew 5	Top speed 25 mph (40 kph)
Range with full fuel tank 93 miles (150 km)	
Maximum armor thickness 2¼ in (70 mm)	

Recoil chamber

Sectional interchangeable barrel

Trailer

Breech

Pivoted cruciform carriage

Anderson began by conducting a series of amphibious landings along the Algerian coast and using his paratroops to secure airfields. The two infantry brigades and Blade Force (the armor) then began to advance into Tunisia on separate axes. The first clash with Axis forces came on November 17, when a German battle group turned back the British advance in the north. The following day, however, the Axis suffered a serious blow when French forces in Tunisia declared for the Allies.

THE ALLIED ADVANCE HALTED

Anderson was now facing difficulties. His main supply line from Algiers was a single-track and rather antiquated railroad line and the passage of supplies and reinforcements was slow. Matters were not helped by heavy rain. The Allies were operating largely off grass airfields, which quickly became choked in mud, while the Axis forces had good all-weather airfields in Tunisia itself. As a consequence, they enjoyed air superiority. These problems caused Anderson to order a temporary halt to the advance, which was resumed in the last week of November. Initially it made good progress and the leading elements of his forces reached a point just 20 miles (32 km) from Tunis before the Germans launched a counterattack and drove them back. By the end of the year, both sides had taken up defensive positions and a winter campaign was now inevitable.

There was a political development in Algeria on December 24, when a monarchist French student assassinated Admiral Darlan, Resident-General of French North and West Africa. Eisenhower, as

"Ike's position just now is something like that of a hen sitting on a batch of eggs. He is waiting for the eggs to hatch, and is in the mental state of wondering if they will ever break the shell."

CAPTAIN HARRY C. BUTCHER, NAVAL AIDE TO GENERAL EISENHOWER (IKE), DIARY ENTRY APRIL 25, 1943, REFERRING TO PREPARATIONS FOR THE FINAL ALLIED OFFENSIVE IN TUNISIA

supreme Allied commander, had retained Darlan in his post as the best way of bringing the French in Algeria and Tunisia firmly on the Allied side. He now appointed Giraud, who had been acting as commander-in-chief of the French forces, in his place. The appointment, however, was not a success. De Gaulle and the Free French did not like Giraud and he also angered Eisenhower by arresting many who had collaborated with the Allies during the Torch landings. These political problems diverted Eisenhower from overseeing the campaign in Tunisia as closely as he would have liked.

GATHERING OF THE FORCES

By January 1943 the Allies in Tunisia were organized in three corps under Anderson's First Army. The British held the north, the French, who were poorly equipped, the center, and the Americans the south. The Axis forces were grouped under Jürgen von Arnim's Fifth Panzer Army. This was now joined by Rommel's Panzer Army Africa, which had been pursued the length of Libya by Montgomery. The two Axis armies now came under the command of

the Italian General Vittorio Ambrosio. Montgomery, meanwhile, paused at Tripoli to reopen the port. He needed to improve the Eighth Army's logistics before starting his advance into Tunisia.

AXIS COUNTERATTACKS

During January von Arnim had managed to seize passes in the French sector. With Rommel now on the scene, they discussed a more ambitious operation to destroy the First Army, but could not agree. Eventually, in mid-February, they launched two separate attacks, both in the US sector. Von Arnim, attacking from the east, took Sidi Bou Zid and Sbeitla, while Rommel, coming from the south, passed through Gafsa. Much to his displeasure, Rommel was now ordered north to cooperate with von Arnim, whereas he wanted to advance farther westward so as to get into the rear of the Allied

American infantry advancing through Tunisia
US troops were deployed mainly in mountainous central Tunisia. They were driven back by fierce counter-offensives led by Rommel and von Arnim, but the terrain prevented the German armor from breaking through.

The battle for the Mareth Line
Exhausted British troops sleep in their trench facing the Mareth Line in March 1943. The fortified line held up Montgomery's advance along the Tunisian coast to link up with the other Allied forces advancing from the west.

defenses. Although between them they dealt the combat-inexperienced Americans a severe blow, notably at the Kasserine Pass, they were now foiled by British reinforcements coming down from the north. Rommel was also aware that Montgomery and the British Eighth Army had finally entered Tunisia and threatened his rear. While he turned to meet his old desert adversary, von Arnim carried out a number of spoiling attacks in the north.

Montgomery had been forewarned by Ultra intelligence that Rommel intended to attack and prepared accordingly. On March 6 the Afrika Korps attacked at Medenine and was repulsed with heavy losses in tanks. Three days later, Rommel left North Africa for good for a spell of sick leave at home.

CLOSING IN

Montgomery now began to advance up eastern Tunisia's narrow coastal plain. As he did so, Patton, who had taken over US II Corps in western Tunisia, regained the territory that had been lost in February and by the end of March had secured the key pass at Maknassy. Montgomery's first obstacle was the Mareth Line, which had originally been built by the French as a defense against an Italian invasion from Libya. A frontal assault, launched on March 20, failed and so he carried out a deep westward outflanking move, which turned the Axis defenses, although it did not prevent them from withdrawing to the next defensive line at Wadi Akarit. He overturned this on April 6 and advanced north to Enfidaville, but was stalemated there by a resolute defense. Meanwhile, in western Tunisia the First Army also began to close in and was undeterred by further spoiling attacks by von Arnim in mid-April. Axis resistance

was, however, nearing its end. German and Italian supply lines to Tunisia across the Mediterranean were being throttled by Allied sea and air action.

AXIS RESISTANCE CRUMBLES

With Montgomery held up at Enfidaville, General Alexander, who had been appointed to command 18th Army Group, which embraced the First and Eighth Armies, decided that the final assault should come from the west. He ordered Montgomery to pass some of his divisions to the First Army, which began its offensive on April 22. Both Tunis and Bizerta fell, to the British and Americans respectively, on May 7 and the remaining Axis forces were trapped in the Cape Bon peninsula. Their resistance finally ended five days later. Two hundred and forty thousand men surrendered to the Allies, a disaster for the Axis comparable to that at Stalingrad. After almost three years the North African campaign was at an end and the Allies could now look northward to Europe.

THE FREE FRENCH

THOSE FEW FRENCHMEN WHO RALLIED to Charles de Gaulle's banner in London in summer 1940 did so realizing that they were regarded as traitors in their own land. De Gaulle decided to concentrate on bringing the French African colonies onto his side, but his first attempt, a landing, with British support, at Dakar in Senegal in September 1940, was a disaster. He did, however, win over other territories in Africa, most importantly Chad. From here Free French elements began to cooperate with the British Long Range Desert Group, whose patrols covered the southern Libyan Desert. Under Philippe de Hautecloque, who took on the pseudonym of Leclerc to protect his familiy in France, a small force began to advance northward from Chad in March 1941.

Meanwhile Free French pilots fought in the Battle of Britain and a French brigade was sent to the Middle East and fought in Eritrea. It was joined in Egypt by further troops. In the hope that they might persuade their fellow Frenchmen to lay down their arms, the Free French took part in the invasion of Vichy French Syria in 1941. In the end, Vichy and Free French fought one another and de Gaulle was furious that he was

not consulted over the armistice. Even so, his men continued to fight loyally for the British and their epic stand at Bir Hacheim during the Gazala battle in June 1942 cemented their reputation.

The Allied landings in French northwest Africa in November 1942 brought the French forces in Algeria, Morocco, and Tunisia onto the Allied side. Leclerc's L Force also linked up with the British Eighth Army at the beginning of 1943 and fought with it during the Tunisian campaign. De Gaulle's relations with the US, however, were not good, especially since Washington had maintained diplomatic relations with Vichy France. Roosevelt chose General Henri Giraud, who had escaped from German captivity, to head the new regime in northwest Africa. De Gaulle could not be sidelined completely and was persuaded to join Giraud in a Committee of National Liberation, where he soon became the dominant figure.

Patrol in the Western Desert
A group of French Foreign Legionnaires prepares to set off on a reconnaissance mission in the desert. They are armed with tommy guns and knives.

An invincible alliance
This poster produced in Algeria in 1943 to celebrate victory over the Axis in North Africa shows the united strength of the American, British, and Free French forces.

LA VICTOIRE DES NATIONS UNIES EST MAINTENANT CERTAINE

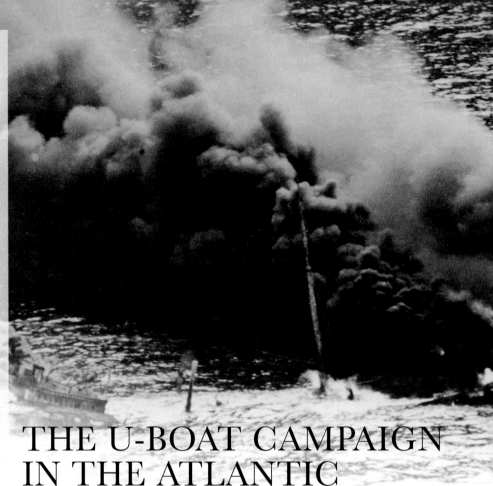

In the first half of 1942 U-boats sank unprecedented amounts of shipping in the western North Atlantic. When the Americans started regular convoys off the eastern seaboard, the U-boats switched to the central Atlantic. With improved methods of detection, however, the Allies slowly gained the upper hand.

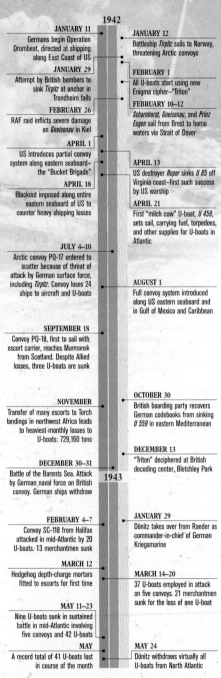

1942

JANUARY 11
Germans begin Operation Drumbeat, directed at shipping along East Coast of US

JANUARY 12
Battleship *Tirpitz* sails to Norway, threatening Arctic convoys

JANUARY 29
Attempt by British bombers to sink *Tirpitz* at anchor in Trondheim fails

FEBRUARY 1
All U-boats start using new Enigma cipher–"Triton"

FEBRUARY 26
RAF raid inflicts severe damage on *Gneisenau* in Kiel

FEBRUARY 10–12
Scharnhorst, *Gneisenau*, and *Prinz Eugen* sail from Brest to home waters via Strait of Dover

APRIL 1
US introduces partial convoy system along eastern seaboard– the "Bucket Brigade"

APRIL 13
US destroyer *Roper* sinks *U 85* off Virginia coast–first such success by US warship

APRIL 18
Blackout imposed along entire eastern seaboard of US to counter heavy shipping losses

APRIL 21
First "milch cow" U-boat, *U 459*, sets sail, carrying fuel, torpedoes, and other supplies for U-boats in Atlantic

JULY 4–10
Arctic convoy PQ-17 ordered to scatter because of threat of attack by German surface force, including *Tirpitz*. Convoy loses 24 ships to aircraft and U-boats

AUGUST 1
Full convoy system introduced along US eastern seaboard and in Gulf of Mexico and Caribbean

SEPTEMBER 18
Convoy PQ-18, first to sail with escort carrier, reaches Murmansk from Scotland. Despite Allied losses, three U-boats are sunk

OCTOBER 30
British boarding party recovers German codebooks from sinking *U 559* in eastern Mediterranean

NOVEMBER
Transfer of many escorts to Torch landings in northwest Africa leads to heaviest monthly losses to U-boats: 729,160 tons

DECEMBER 13
"Triton" deciphered at British decoding center, Bletchley Park

DECEMBER 30–31
Battle of the Barents Sea. Attack by German naval force on British convoy. German ships withdraw

1943

FEBRUARY 4–7
Convoy SC-118 from Halifax attacked in mid-Atlantic by 20 U-boats. 13 merchantmen sunk

JANUARY 29
Dönitz takes over from Raeder as commander-in-chief of German Kriegsmarine

MARCH 12
Hedgehog depth-charge mortars fitted to escorts for first time

MARCH 14–20
37 U-boats employed in attack on five convoys. 21 merchantmen sunk for the loss of one U-boat

MAY 11–23
Nine U-boats sunk in sustained battle in mid-Atlantic involving five convoys and 42 U-boats

MAY
A record total of 41 U-boats lost in course of the month

MAY 24
Dönitz withdraws virtually all U-boats from North Atlantic

■ Atlantic convoys   ■ Arctic convoys   Other events

THE U-BOAT CAMPAIGN IN THE ATLANTIC

THE SECOND HALF of 1941 saw a major improvement in the British position at sea. Sinkings in the North Atlantic fell from 345 ships, totalling 1,800,190 tons in the first half of the year to 151 ships, totalling 621,510 tons, while losses in British waters, the Mediterranean, the South Atlantic, and Indian Ocean fell from 1,082,830 tons to 364,897 tons. These reductions were largely due to the westward extension of the American neutrality zone and greater use of the convoy system. With fewer merchantmen sailing independently, U-boats were increasingly forced to attack convoys. As a result the average number of merchantmen sunk per U-boat lost fell from 21.9 in the first half of the year to 7.3 in the second half.

NEW TARGETS
The German and Italian declaration of war on the United States in December 1941 signaled the start of a new phase in the Battle of the Atlantic. The whole of the western

North Atlantic now became a theater for U-boat operations. The first Type IX long-range U-boats sailed for the coastal waters of the eastern United States as early as mid-December. They carried only 16 torpedoes each, but were under orders to conserve these for large, worthwhile targets, especially tankers. At the start of hostilities the United States was faced with a serious lack of escorts. Lack of organization meant that East Coast shipping was not protected and no blackout was imposed in coastal areas. As a result, in the first six months of 1942 the German submarines enjoyed their second "Happy Time," comparable to their period of success in the second half of 1940.

In the first half of 1942 Allied monthly shipping losses exceeded 650,000 tons on five occasions. U-boats extended their operations into the Caribbean and Gulf of Mexico and in June sank a total of 121 merchantmen in the western North Atlantic. In fact this month, June 1942, saw German operations account for 173 merchantmen of 834,196 tons with U-boats sinking 144 merchantmen of 700,235 tons. The American introduction of

FAITES VITE... FAITES BIEN

LEUR *Victoire* **SERA LA VÔTRE**

Canadian recruiting poster
Canada's navy played an important role in the war against the U-boats. By the end of the war it had grown to become the third largest navy in the world.

U-boat victim
Burning oil engulfs the sinking American tanker *Dixie Arrow*. After being torpedoed by *U 71* off the coast of North Carolina on March 26, 1942, the ship's hull broke in two.

THE U-BOAT WAR

THE CRITICAL PERIOD in the U-boat war in the Atlantic was 1942–43. Sinkings by U-boats reached their monthly peak in November 1942, but thereafter Allied merchant shipping losses, despite the occasional blip, went steadily down. This was in spite of the fact that by 1943 the Germans had four times as many U-boats as at the outbreak of war. It was also the year in which the Allies finally marshaled the aircraft, the escorts, the organization, and the new technology to wage an effective antisubmarine war.

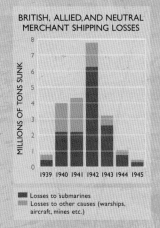

BRITISH, ALLIED, AND NEUTRAL MERCHANT SHIPPING LOSSES

MILLIONS OF TONS SUNK

1939 1940 1941 1942 1943 1944 1945

■ Losses to submarines
■ Losses to other causes (warships, aircraft, mines etc.)

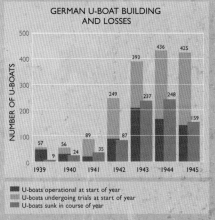

GERMAN U-BOAT BUILDING AND LOSSES

NUMBER OF U-BOATS

57 9 | 56 24 | 89 35 | 249 87 | 393 237 | 436 248 | 425 159
1939 1940 1941 1942 1943 1944 1945

■ U-boats operational at start of year
■ U-boats undergoing trials at start of year
■ U-boats sunk in course of year

convoys along the eastern seaboard spelled the end of this period of German success. There was no point in U-boats crossing the North Atlantic if shipping off the eastern seaboard was under escort. The focus of German effort after July 1942 was therefore in the central North Atlantic—in the so-called "air gap." This was the area where Allied shipping was beyond the range of Allied aircraft based in Newfoundland, Iceland, and Britain.

U-BOAT NUMBERS

The rising number of U-boats in service—from a total of 91 in January 1942 to 212 in January 1943—meant that they could be deployed in long patrol lines across the North Atlantic convoy routes. As a result, Allied shipping losses between July and November 1942 were not far short of those recorded in the first half of 1942. At the same time, however, U-boat losses rose steeply—from 22 in the first half of the year to 66 in the second.

Various factors combined to blunt the U-boat offensive. The most important was the increasing number and quality of the warships and aircraft committed to the defense of shipping. This had

been a continuing process since 1940, but in the first two years of the war escort formations had amounted to little more than collections of individual ships. Now formations were being raised on a permanent basis and trained together. Fast new frigates specifically designed for submarine hunting were entering service, and escorts were being equipped with TBS (Talk Between Ships) radio, improved sonar, and hedgehog mortars for throwing salvoes of new more powerful depth charges.

Despite these innovations, Allied shipping continued to suffer losses. These reached their peak when convoys were stripped of their

escorts to provide protection for Operation Torch—the US and British landings in French North Africa in November 1942. This month saw the highest number of sinkings by U-boats in the entire war with 729,160 tons of merchantmen sunk.

March 1943 was another bad month for Allied shipping with losses to submarines reaching 627,377 tons. In early March the German change of ciphers meant that the Admiralty temporarily lost its ability to read German naval signals and divert shipping accordingly. Even so, the month's figures were an anomaly and reversed the now established trend.

By this point in the war virtually all the factors that were to contribute to the defeat of the German war against shipping were in place.

US Coast Guard cutter *Duane*
On April 17, 1943, along with USCGC *Spencer*, the *Duane* was part of the escort group that located the *U 175*, forcing it to the surface with depth charges, and then firing on it until the crew abandoned the U-boat.

Sunderlands on patrol
The British Short Sunderland flying boat was
a very successful reconnaissance aircraft and
submarine destroyer. The Mark III, introduced
in 1942, had a range of about 2,700 miles
(4,340 km). It could carry bombs, torpedoes,
depth charges, and rockets.

RECALL OF THE U-BOATS

In May 1943 Germany's U-boats suffered their worst
monthly losses of the war with 41 sunk or destroyed.
On May 24 the Kriegsmarine recalled its U-boats
from the North Atlantic in what was tantamount to
acknowledgment of defeat. But the German

intention was to refit their boats and return to the
offensive. However, when battle was resumed in
July the losses incurred by the U-boats were still
disastrously heavy. July 1943 saw the destruction
of 37 U-boats and the following month another 25.

The period May–November 1943 effectively
decided the outcome of the campaign against
shipping. The Allied victory was the result of a
number of contributory factors: superior numbers
of escorts and aircraft, improved organization, better
weapons and radar, and more effective intelligence.
In January 1943 the British Navy had realized that
its signals were being read by the Germans. The
situation took months to rectify, but over the course
of the year the Allies acquired a distinct intelligence
advantage over the Germans.

The two most important factors were the
improvement in the quality of escorts and the massive
impact of increased air power, with many more long-
range aircraft available for antisubmarine duties.
Between the start of the war and the end of 1942,
aircraft accounted for just 46 U-boats. In May 1943

U-boat on North Alantic patrol
This propaganda photograph from 1943 shows German
sailors braving bad weather to wage war on enemy shipping.
Despite the diminishing returns of U-boat warfare, captains
and crews remained heroes in the eyes of the public.

they sank 20 and had a hand in the destruction
of five more. This increase in losses was in part the
result of the Kriegsmarine's failure to realize that
the British had developed a form of airborne radar
that U-boat search equipment could not detect.

THE OPPOSING FORCES

The Canadian Navy had grown rapidly and gained
enormous experience over the first three years of the
war. By 1943 escort duties were shared more
or less equally by the British and
Canadians, while US warships in
ordinary convoys to Britain had
all but disappeared. In contrast
to the experience gained by
Allied crews, German U-boat
officers and men were not of the
same overall quality as those of
1940–41. The growing numbers of
U-boats, combined with increased losses,
meant that boats were going to sea with
officers with no more than two operational
missions to their credit.

In addition to accelerating their U-boat
construction program, the Germans had also
developed new weaponry and tactics. They had
high hopes of a new type of acoustic torpedo,

The Allied victory in the Battle of the Atlantic was achieved by limiting shipping losses and maintaining an adequate level of imports into Britain, even though U-boat numbers continued to increase almost to the end of the war. Another factor in this victory was the simple fact that by the third quarter of 1943 American shipyards had replaced all losses incurred to date in the war. The peak of American construction was reached in March 1943 when 130 merchantmen were launched. By the end of the war US yards had built more than 34 million tons of new ships—a total that no campaign against merchant shipping was ever going to overcome.

The Battle of the Atlantic was clearly the most important part of the Allied naval effort. It ensured Britain's survival and role as the base for the liberation of northwest Europe. But the war at sea was not just an economic contest over the defense of trade. Navies were also used to carry the war to enemy territory, and to prevent raids and landings. Over a 16-month period the Allies conducted seven major landings in Europe, starting with the landings on Sicily in July 1943. In every case the German Navy proved ineffective, neither preventing invasion nor inflicting serious losses on enemy naval and amphibious forces.

ARCTIC CONVOYS

The German Navy's most powerful surviving warships, the battleships *Scharnhorst* and *Tirpitz*, were held in Norwegian waters to tie down British naval forces and menace Allied convoys sailing to Soviet ports. In July 1942 the mere threat of an attack by

Aboard an escort on an Arctic convoy
Despite the danger and hardship endured by the crews that sailed to Murmansk and Archangel, this convoy route was not crucial to the Soviet war effort.

the *Tirpitz* led to the near annihilation of a convoy. Acting on intelligence that the *Tirpitz* was about to sail, the Admiralty ordered the commander of convoy PQ-17 to withdraw his escorts and disperse the merchantmen. German aircraft and U-boats then attacked the scattered merchantmen, sinking 24 out of a total of 36. Arctic convoys were always vulnerable, but of the 17,499,861 tons of materiel sent to the Soviet Union during the war, only 3,964,000 tons was sent by this route. The German battleships did not survive to inflict much damage themselves. The *Scharnhorst* was sunk off North Cape on December 26, 1943, during a failed attack on a convoy. The *Tirpitz*, after surviving numerous attacks, was sunk by British bombers off Tromso on November 12, 1944.

which came into service in the fall of 1943, but its success was short-lived. The Allies adopted a simple countermeasure in the form of a noise-making device towed by the escorts to divert the torpedo from its real target. February 1944 saw the appearance of U-boats equipped with the *Schnorchel*, an air tube that would enable the submarine to run at periscope depth using its diesel motors, thus reducing the chances of its being discovered by radar. However, conditions inside the U-boat when the *Schnorchel* was in use were appalling—the limited supply of air was consumed almost entirely by the engines.

German U-boat crew awaiting rescue
Survivors of *U 877* cling to rubber life rafts in freezing Atlantic waters. Their U-boat was sunk northwest of the Azores in December 1944 by the Canadian escort *St. Thomas*.

"There is ground for confident estimate that the enemy's peak effort is passed. Morale and efficiency are delicate and may wither rapidly if no longer nourished by rich success."

FROM A BRITISH ADMIRALTY REPORT ON THE U-BOAT WAR, MAY 1943

Depth charge attack
This attack on *U 175* on April 17, 1943,
ended in complete success for USCGC *Spencer*.
Having located the submerged U-boat by
means of sonar, the escort ship then used
depth charges to force it to the surface.

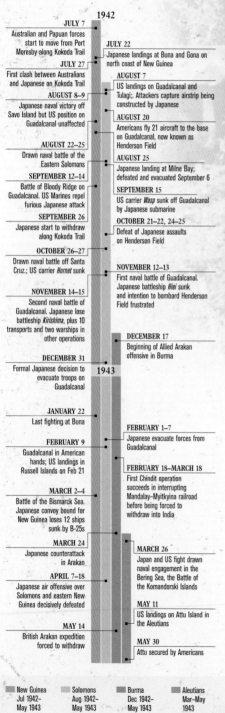

ASIA AND THE PACIFIC

JULY 1942–MAY 1943

The second half of 1942 saw the Allies assume a defensive commitment in eastern New Guinea and a limited offensive in the lower Solomons. The Japanese were defeated in both theaters by the turn of the year and the initiative passed clearly to the Americans and their allies.

1942

JULY 7
Australian and Papuan forces start to move from Port Moresby along Kokoda Trail

JULY 22
Japanese landings at Buna and Gona on north coast of New Guinea

JULY 27
First clash between Australians and Japanese on Kokoda Trail

AUGUST 7
US landings on Guadalcanal and Tulagi;. Attackers capture airstrip being constructed by Japanese

AUGUST 8–9
Japanese naval victory off Savo Island but US position on Guadalcanal unaffected

AUGUST 20
Americans fly 21 aircraft to the base on Guadalcanal, now known as Henderson Field

AUGUST 22–25
Drawn naval battle of the Eastern Solomons

AUGUST 25
Japanese landing at Milne Bay; defeated and evacuated September 6

SEPTEMBER 12–14
Battle of Bloody Ridge on Guadalcanal. US Marines repel furious Japanese attack

SEPTEMBER 15
US carrier *Wasp* sunk off Guadalcanal by Japanese submarine

SEPTEMBER 26
Japanese start to withdraw along Kokoda Trail

OCTOBER 21–22, 24–25
Defeat of Japanese assaults on Henderson Field

OCTOBER 26–27
Drawn naval battle off Santa Cruz.; US carrier *Hornet* sunk

NOVEMBER 12–13
First naval battle of Guadalcanal. Japanese battleship *Hiei* sunk and intention to bombard Henderson Field frustrated

NOVEMBER 14–15
Second naval battle of Guadalcanal. Japanese lose battleship *Kirishima*, plus 10 transports and two warships in other operations

DECEMBER 17
Beginning of Allied Arakan offensive in Burma

DECEMBER 31
Formal Japanese decision to evacuate troops on Guadalcanal

1943

JANUARY 22
Last fighting at Buna

FEBRUARY 1–7
Japanese evacuate forces from Guadalcanal

FEBRUARY 9
Guadalcanal in American hands; US landings in Russell Islands on Feb 21

FEBRUARY 18–MARCH 18
First Chindit operation succeeds in interrupting Mandalay–Myitkyina railroad before being forced to withdraw into India

MARCH 2–4
Battle of the Bismarck Sea. Japanese convoy bound for New Guinea loses 12 ships sunk by B-25s

MARCH 24
Japanese counterattack in Arakan

MARCH 26
Japan and US fight drawn naval engagement in the Bering Sea, the Battle of the Komandorski Islands

APRIL 7–18
Japanese air offensive over Solomons and eastern New Guinea decisively defeated

MAY 11
US landings on Attu Island in the Aleutians

MAY 14
British Arakan expedition forced to withdraw

MAY 30
Attu secured by Americans

New Guinea Jul 1942– May 1943	Solomons Aug 1942– May 1943	Burma Dec 1942– May 1943	Aleutians Mar–May 1943

THE PACIFIC WAR IN THE BALANCE

A FTER CORAL SEA and Midway, summer 1942 brought a pause in the Pacific as both sides readied themselves for the next phase of operations. The Japanese reorganized their carrier formations, prepared bases in the lower Solomons, and secured positions in eastern New Guinea. For the United States, the priority given to the European war and the requirements of a North African landing meant that it was possible to undertake only a limited offensive in the lower Solomons. The campaign against the island of Guadalcanal would be the first step in a general offensive in the Southwest Pacific.

STRUGGLE FOR GUADALCANAL

On Guadalcanal the initial American landing was directed against a Japanese airstrip then nearing completion. The US landings on the island and nearby Tulagi were conducted on August 7 with overwhelming force. They were promptly countered by a foray by a Japanese cruiser formation, which at Savo Island (August 8–9) inflicted a comprehensive defeat on Allied naval forces off Guadalcanal. On land, however, the Japanese were not in a position to move immediately and with adequate numbers of troops against the Marines, whose numbers and quality they drastically underestimated. The result was that, while the Americans took the defensive around the captured airfield, which they renamed Henderson Field, the battle for the lower Solomons took place on, off, and above Guadalcanal. During the struggle the Americans developed one highly significant advantage. On August 20 the first US aircraft were ferried into the completed Henderson Field. From that point on American air power was able to control the waters immediately around Guadalcanal throughout the hours of daylight.

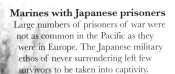

Marines with Japanese prisoners
Large numbers of prisoners of war were
not as common in the Pacific as they
were in Europe. The Japanese military
ethos of never surrendering left few
survivors to be taken into captivity.

Over the next four months this would
be a crucial advantage that the Japanese
were simply not able to overcome. In the
wake of their victory off Savo Island, however, the
Japanese did make two further efforts on Guadalcanal:
to put ashore a military force that could overrun
Henderson Field, and to conduct naval operations to
facilitate and support that offensive. But Savo Island
proved to be the first and last clear Japanese victory
of the campaign. Two further carrier actions were
fought—the battles of the Eastern Solomons
(August 22–25) and Santa Cruz (October 26–27)—
and a Japanese submarine sank the aircraft carrier
Wasp off Guadalcanal on September 15. Although
the balance of losses in these exchanges slightly
favored the Japanese, they derived no real advantage.
On the island itself, the Americans fought off the
first major Japanese assault on the defensive perimeter
around Henderson Field, the action for Bloody Ridge
in mid-September. They also launched a number of
spoiling attacks that disrupted Japanese preparations
for a second major effort.

THE CRISIS OF THE CAMPAIGN

As the Japanese commitment in the Solomons
deepened, so their plans began to unravel. On
October 11–12 the Japanese fought and lost the naval
battle of Cape Esperance. On the next night their
battleships bombarded Henderson Field, but a
further night's bombardment by heavy cruisers was
followed by transport losses that the Japanese could
not afford. The army's assaults on Henderson Field
were defeated on October 21–22 and October 24–25,

Rearming on board an aircraft carrier
Deck crew on a US carrier rearm a Douglas SBD
Dauntless dive-bomber. Air superiority was key to
victory in the land and naval battles of Guadalcanal.

and the deployment of a carrier force brought such
aircraft losses in the Battle of Santa Cruz that the
Japanese could not take advantage of their sinking
of the US carrier *Hornet*. The
Japanese made plans for
another assault on
Henderson Field and
a renewal of naval

bombardments of the airfield, but in the middle
of November they suffered two crushing defeats. On
the night of November 12/13, in an action fought
at such close range that the guns of the battleships
could not depress far enough to fire at enemy vessels,
and torpedoes did not have enough range to arm

Marines at Hell's Corner
Marines shelter on Guadalcanal as a US
plane flies above. The area was named Hell's
Corner after concentrated Japanese assaults.

Henderson Field rebuilt
Solomon Islanders work with US engineers to finish
the landing strip at Henderson Field. Interlocking
ready-made metal plates were spread out over cleared
ground to give a firm surface for takeoff and landing.

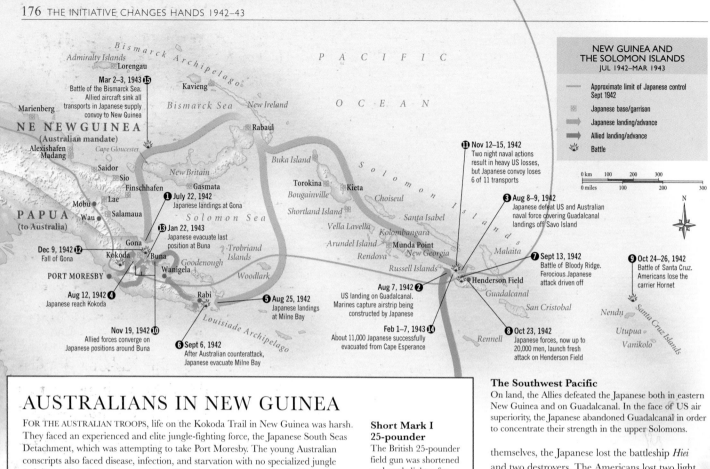

NEW GUINEA AND THE SOLOMON ISLANDS
JUL 1942–MAR 1943

— Approximate limit of Japanese control Sept 1942

⊠ Japanese base/garrison

⟹ Japanese landing/advance

⟹ Allied landing/advance

✺ Battle

Mar 2–3, 1943 ⑮ Battle of the Bismarck Sea. Allied aircraft sink all transports in Japanese supply convoy to New Guinea

Nov 12–15, 1942 ⑪ Two night naval actions result in heavy US losses, but Japanese convoy loses 6 of 11 transports

Aug 8–9, 1942 ③ Japanese defeat US and Australian naval force covering Guadalcanal landings off Savo Island

July 22, 1942 ① Japanese landings at Gona

Jan 22, 1943 ⑬ Japanese evacuate last position at Buna

Sept 13, 1942 ⑦ Battle of Bloody Ridge. Ferocious Japanese attack driven off

Oct 24–26, 1942 ⑨ Battle of Santa Cruz. Americans lose the carrier Hornet

Dec 9, 1942 ⑫ Fall of Gona

Aug 12, 1942 ④ Japanese reach Kokoda

Aug 7, 1942 ② US landing on Guadalcanal. Marines capture airstrip being constructed by Japanese

Aug 25, 1942 ⑤ Japanese landings at Milne Bay

Nov 19, 1942 ⑩ Allied forces converge on Japanese positions around Buna

Feb 1–7, 1943 ⑭ About 11,000 Japanese successfully evacuated from Cape Esperance

Oct 23, 1942 ⑧ Japanese forces, now up to 20,000 men, launch fresh attack on Henderson Field

Sept 6, 1942 ⑥ After Australian counterattack, Japanese evacuate Milne Bay

AUSTRALIANS IN NEW GUINEA

FOR THE AUSTRALIAN TROOPS, life on the Kokoda Trail in New Guinea was harsh. They faced an experienced and elite jungle-fighting force, the Japanese South Seas Detachment, which was attempting to take Port Moresby. The young Australian conscripts also faced disease, infection, and starvation with no specialized jungle training and no proper support. The stifling humidity rotted their clothing and made the physical effort needed to move in the Owen Stanley mountains extremely hard. Poor visibility in the dense vegetation often meant that the first sign of the enemy would be an eruption of gunfire. Despite the difficulties, the Australians fought surprisingly well against a force that, at times, outnumbered them by 15 to one.

Owen submachine-gun
The rugged and reliable Australian-made Owen was a favorite weapon among troops facing the exacting conditions of the jungles of the Pacific.

33-round magazine

Detachable barrel

Short Mark I 25-pounder
The British 25-pounder field gun was shortened and made lighter for use in New Guinea. Nicknamed the "Baby," it could be broken down into 14 mule-loads.

Conical flash shroud

Dial for indirect fire

Pneumatic tires

Jungle warfare
Australian soldiers force their way along a difficult jungle track during operations on New Guinea.

The Southwest Pacific
On land, the Allies defeated the Japanese both in eastern New Guinea and on Guadalcanal. In the face of US air superiority, the Japanese abandoned Guadalcanal in order to concentrate their strength in the upper Solomons.

themselves, the Japanese lost the battleship *Hiei* and two destroyers. The Americans lost two light cruisers and four destroyers, with two heavy cruisers and another two destroyers badly damaged. On the night of November 14/15 the Japanese lost the battleship *Kirishima* and a destroyer.

These defeats were accompanied by a failed Japanese attempt to put more formations ashore, in which all but one of 11 transports were lost or ran aground. The Japanese high command now faced crisis on two counts. The fleet losses could not be afforded, but with the services called upon to return shipping to the trade vital to support Japan's Home Islands, neither could the transport losses. About 750,000 tons of shipping had been committed to the operations in the Southwest Pacific. After their losses, the services required another 620,000 tons of shipping in order to continue the campaign. The result was that in December the Japanese high command decided to abandon Guadalcanal in favor of a defensive strategy based on the central and upper Solomons. By February 8, 1943 the orderly withdrawal of 11,706 men from the Cape Esperance area was completed. The Guadalcanal campaign was over. The Japanese now had to face an enemy with a choice of when and where to undertake its next offensive.

NEW GUINEA

The campaign on Guadalcanal was initially separate from, but later influential on, a simultaneous campaign being fought in eastern New Guinea. It had been the Japanese intention after Midway to move by sea and in strength against Port Moresby, the Allied base on the southern coast of eastern New Guinea. With the defeat off Midway, however, the plans were changed. On July 22, 1942 Japanese troops came ashore and secured Buna and Gona on the northern coast, intending to advance on Port Moresby along the Kokoda Trail. Japanese planners believed that this trail was a metaled road. In reality it was a 100-mile (160-km) jungle track across the forbidding Owen Stanley mountain range. For most of its length, it was too narrow for troops to walk two abreast.

The initial Japanese advance swept aside feeble opposition on the part of inexperienced Australian troops, but as Australian units that had recently been withdrawn from the Middle East were fed into the battle, the Japanese encountered mounting

Indigenous allies
A Papuan soldier takes aim with his Bren machine-gun. The local Papuan infantry co-operated with the Australians and Americans against the Japanese in eastern New Guinea, and their knowledge of the island terrain proved a great bonus to the Allies.

resistance. Australian troops lost, retook, and for a second time lost Kokoda. Then Japanese forces, with no supplies and relying on captured enemy stores to sustain themselves, bypassed Australian positions and carried the battle as far as Ioribaiwa, some 30 miles (48 km) from Port Moresby, on September 16. By this time, however, the campaign on Guadalcanal had begun to go badly for the Japanese. Forced to decide between the two efforts, and having seen a secondary landing on New Guinea checked at Milne Bay (August 25–September 7), the Japanese chose to focus their attention on the campaign in Guadalcanal and the lower Solomons.

On September 26, in an attempt to consolidate their position in eastern New Guinea, Japanese troops began a slow withdrawal along the Kokoda Trail.

The Japanese withdrawal from Ioribaiwa was followed by an Australian advance along the Kokoda Trail. Meanwhile American forces were able to

Storming New Guinea
American troops wade ashore on the New Guinea coast. The shallow beaches meant that disembarking troops often had to wade through the surf for some distance.

> "I have an idea that the name of the Kokoda Trail is going to live on in the minds of Australians, just as Gallipoli lives on. Every hour is a nightmare."
>
> GEORGE H. JOHNSTON, WAR CORRESPONDENT
> SEPTEMBER 1942

undertake an exhausting advance around the Japanese open left flank. Meanwhile, transport aircraft moved forces to occupy Wanigela on the northeast coast and Allied troops were also transported around the coast by sea. This gave the Americans and Australians an overwhelming advantage of numbers and position that enabled them to take the initiative. Japanese forces, who had been wracked by malaria, beri-beri, and dysentery caused by food stores purposely contaminated by the retreating Australian troops, resorted to cannibalism to stay alive. By the end of November they had been penned back into the Gona–Sanananda–Buna beachhead area.

The final Allied offensive against the beachhead stalled several times amid bitter recriminations, and the first Australian move against Gona was beaten back. The Japanese put ashore an extra 1,300 troops during December 1942, and the tough fighting went on in swamps that reached up to armpit level and against fieldworks that could not be seen from more than a few yards away. Still, the Australians took Gona on December 9, American troops, supported by armor, took Buna village five days later, the government building on January 2, 1943, and then Sanananda on the 14th, the day after the Japanese high command made the decision to abandon the struggle. The Allied capture of Giruwa, between Buna and Gona, on January 21 was the last action in a campaign that had cost the Australians 5,698 and the Americans some 2,400 killed and wounded; an additional 38,000 troops were evacuated at various times because of illness. The Japanese ultimately committed about 17,000 troops in eastern New Guinea, and it seems that the survivors of the campaign numbered fewer than 3,000.

JAPANESE WITHDRAWALS

The Japanese evacuation of their surviving troops from Guadalcanal in early February 1943 was soon followed by American landings in the neighboring Russell Islands in the third week of the month. In the first week of March American aicraft secured an overwhelming victory, sinking eight transport vessels and four destroyers in the Battle of the Bismarck Sea (March 2–4). Japanese losses in the course of the week were so heavy that their position south of Finschhafen was severely compromised.

It was not until September 1943, however, that Allied forces moved to secure targets in central New Guinea, including Lae, Salamaua, and Finschhafen. At the end of October, after a series of Japanese attempts to recapture Finschhafen were beaten back, local Japanese forces admitted defeat and began to evacuate the area.

By that time, too, Allied forces were moving into the upper Solomons, but for the most part the

Casualties of Buna
Dead US soldiers lie near a beached landing craft at Buna following the American assault on the Japanese stronghold. Compared with the losses suffered by the beleaguered Japanese defenders, American and Australian casualties in the operation were relatively low.

As the Japs advanced we could
hear the bushes rustle. Suddenly
all hell broke loose. Grenades
exploded everywhere on the ridge
nose, followed by shrieks and
yells. Then I gave the word to
fire. Machine-guns and rifles
let go and the whole line seemed
to light up. I knocked off two
Japs with a rifle. After a few
minutes, I couldn't swear how
long it was, the blitz became a
hand-to-hand battle. All my men
were casualties and I was on my
own. It was lonely up there.

US SERGEANT MITCHELL PAIGE DESCRIBING THE DEFENSE OF
HENDERSON FIELD, GUADALCANAL, OCTOBER 24, 1942

period between February and November 1943 saw
very few islands change hands anywhere in the Pacific
and very few naval actions. February saw a local
Japanese defeat in front of Wau in eastern New
Guinea, and April saw a much vaunted—but wholly
ineffective—Japanese air offensive in the Southwest
Pacific. One damning comment on its failure was
the ease with which American fighters shot down
a Japanese aircraft carrying the commander of the
Combined Fleet, Admiral Yamamoto Isoroku, over
Bougainville. June brought a major air battle over
the Russells and the annihilation of a Japanese air
offensive over Guadalcanal. The same month saw
US landings on southern New Georgia and Rendova
in the central Solomons, and on Woodlark and the
Trobriand Islands off eastern New Guinea. On New
Guinea itself, an American force landed in Nassau
Bay just to the southeast of Salamaua.

THE ALEUTIANS

In March an indecisive action known as the Battle
of the Komandorski Islands was fought in the
Northwestern Pacific. On the Aleutian Islands off
Alaska, which the Japanese had occupied in June
1942, May brought American landings on Attu,
where organized resistance collapsed on the 30th;
the island was secured by the following day. Little
over a week later the Japanese high command
decided to cut its losses and ordered that nearby

Japanese in the Aleutians
Japanese soldiers on Kiska in the Aleutian Islands scour
the skies for US aircraft. The Aleutians were a sideshow to
the main Pacific conflict, but they witnessed the only time
Japan occupied US territory during the war.

Kiska be abandoned. The Japanese evacuation was
complete on July 28. With no inkling that the Japanese
had already departed, the Americans subjected the
island to a full-scale assault in the middle of August.
Thereafter the Aleutians were of importance to the
wider conflict only as a base for American air and
submarine operations against Japan's Home Islands.
The first American air raid on the Kurile Islands
was an attack by eight B-25 medium bombers
staging through Attu on July 10, 1943.

THE BALANCE TILTS
Most of the operations in this period were on a very
small scale. Individually they were of little importance,
but together they represented notable, if local, gains.
More significantly, they were also actions conducted
by American forces that were now clearly possessed
of the initiative. The Americans had also acquired,
by this stage of the war, a clear superiority of
numbers and technique.

The extent of that superiority was to be revealed
after July 1943. In that month, in the wake of the
American landings in the central Solomons, and
the simultaneous American and Japanese landings
in Kula Gulf at the northern end of New Georgia,
two naval actions were fought that were effectively
the last battles in the Pacific to pitch two evenly
matched sides against one another. The battles of
Kula Gulf (July 5–6) and Kolombangara (July 12–13)
saw honors more or less shared. By the end of the
month, however, the Americans were in a position

to take the tide of war into the upper Solomons in
a strength that left the Japanese defenders without
an effective response. In around a year and a half
of war the Imperial Japanese Navy had in effect
fought both the US Navy and itself to a standstill.
By the time it had done so, however, it found itself
having to face a second US Navy. The new enemy
was not a prewar navy but a modern navy that
had been built primarily since the attack on Pearl
Harbor in December 1941 and was now being
gathered in readiness for the next phase of the war.

Captured Japanese flag
American troops proudly display a captured Japanese flag
on Guadalcanal. Such items, as well as enemy swords and
weapons, were considered prize souvenirs.

THE AXIS ON THE DEFENSIVE
1943–44

DURING THE COURSE OF 1943, THE TABLES WERE

TURNED ON GERMANY AND JAPAN. BOTH NATIONS

HAD MADE SWEEPING TERRITORIAL GAINS

IN THE OPENING PHASES OF THE WAR, IN THE WEST

AND IN SOUTHEAST ASIA AND THE PACIFIC. THESE,

HOWEVER, WERE NOW STARTING TO BE EATEN AWAY

AS THE MANPOWER RESOURCES OF THE SOVIET

UNION AND THE ALMOST LIMITLESS ECONOMIC AND

INDUSTRIAL POTENTIAL OF THE UNITED STATES

WERE BROUGHT FULLY TO BEAR ON THE AXIS.

American landing on Saipan
US troops crouch on a beach under the shelter
of their landing craft. The capture of Saipan,
Tinian, and Guam in the Marianas in June and
July 1944 gave the Americans airbases within
bomber range of the Japanese Home Islands.

THE BEGINNING OF THE END

FROM THE SUMMER OF 1943 THE THIRD REICH FACED A GRIM HOLDING OPERATION ON THE EASTERN FRONT IN THE FACE OF THE INEXORABLE SOVIET ADVANCE. IN ITALY, HOWEVER, THE BRITISH AND AMERICANS MADE SLOWER PROGRESS. IN THE PACIFIC THE AMERICANS BEGAN A DRIVE TOWARD THE JAPANESE HOME ISLANDS, BYPASSING A NUMBER OF JAPANESE BASES AND GARRISONS IN A STRATEGY KNOWN AS "ISLAND HOPPING".

FOLLOWING THE RECAPTURE of Kharkov by the Germans in mid-March 1943, fighting on the Eastern Front subsided as both sides made preparations for further offensives. Hitler calculated that the Red Army was marking time before launching another offensive in the winter of 1943. The aim of the first German offensive would be to eliminate the huge Soviet salient north of Kharkov around the town of Kursk in the Ukraine. This had been created by the success of Manstein's counterblow after Stalingrad.

Opinions differed within the German high command over how to deal with the Kursk salient. Manstein favored what became known as the "backhand solution", waiting for the Red Army to burst out of the salient and then rolling up its advancing columns as the Soviet lines of supply grew ever longer. Hitler and General Kurt Zeitzler, Chief of the Army General Staff, favored a more aggressive strategy. Having rejected a proposal for a frontal attack on the salient, the German high command settled for a pincer attack, delivered on the northern and southern shoulders of the salient with the aim of pinching out the Kursk bulge and trapping the Soviet armies holding it. The operation was codenamed *Zitadelle* (Citadel).

Operation Citadel was based on the dangerous assumption that the Red Army, well dug-in, would crumble at the first impact of German armor. It was also a measure of changing fortunes on the Eastern Front that, for all the massive preparations that preceded it, Citadel's principal objective was limited to a mere straightening of the front line. However, such was the scale of the coming offensive that it was clear to all involved in its preparation that failure would mean the complete collapse of the German strategy on the Eastern Front. Hitler confessed that every time he thought about the operation, his stomach turned over.

Launched on July 4, 1943, Citadel was abandoned within days, after the Red Army had halted both the German northern and southern drives. The advance from the south ended on July 12 at Prokhorovka, scene of the largest tank battle of the war. On the same date the Red Army launched Operation Kutuzov against the Orel salient, a mirror image of the Kursk salient, lying immediately to its north. A series of Soviet counteroffensives to the south of Kursk drove the Ostheer back to the line of the Dnieper River.

Citadel was the last major German offensive on the Eastern Front. The psychological advantage had begun to pass to the Red Army after its victory at Stalingrad. It is clear that, after Kursk, the Red Army not only seized the initiative, but also established an inexorably growing material advantage over the Ostheer that the German mobile forces were no longer able to counter with tactical initiative.

ALLIED PRIORITIES

In the spring of 1941 Hitler had increased the number of fronts on which the British were obliged to fight. Now the roles were about to be reversed. On January 14, 1943 Churchill, Roosevelt, and their chiefs of staff met at Casablanca in Morocco for a conference, codenamed Symbol, to decide their priorities for the war in the West and in the Pacific.

One of the principal fruits of Symbol was an agreement to relieve the pressure on the Soviet Union by opening a "second front" in Europe in the form of a strategic bombing offensive against Germany to be conducted by RAF Bomber Command and the US Eighth Air Force. The objectives of this offensive were twofold: the progressive destruction of the German military, industrial, and economic infrastructures; and the undermining of the will of the German people to a point where "their capacity for armed resistance is fatally weakened". The operational details of the offensive were embodied in a plan codenamed Pointblank, drawn up

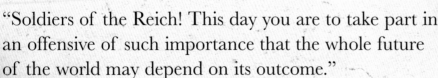

"Soldiers of the Reich! This day you are to take part in an offensive of such importance that the whole future of the world may depend on its outcome."

ADOLF HITLER JULY 4, 1943, AT THE BEGINNING OF THE BATTLE OF KURSK by General Ira C Eaker, commander of the Eighth Air Force, and issued on June 10, 1943. While Bomber Command concentrated on the area bombing of German cities by night, the USAAF flew daylight missions aimed against precise industrial targets. However, with no long-range escort fighters, the USAAF was to suffer heavy losses.

At Casablanca the Americans and British also decided that, once the US and British forces had driven the Germans and Italians out of North Africa, the first Allied objective in the Mediterranean would be the island of Sicily. The Americans argued that it was more important to

concentrate on preparations for the planned invasion of northwest Europe, but were persuaded by Churchill that, in the meantime, Sicily was a valuable prize. The Western Allies were also keenly aware of the titanic battles being fought on the Eastern Front and realized that Stalin would resent any reluctance to commit Allied forces in the one theatre of war in which they could now come to grips with the Axis. A cross-Channel assault on Hitler's "Fortress Europe" would have to wait until 1944.

DEFENDING THE MEDITERRANEAN

Hitler was keenly aware of the threat of Italian defection. He observed wryly, "The Italians never lose a war; no matter what happens, they always end up

on the winning side." Hitler therefore despatched German troops to mainland Italy and Sicily. Rommel was brought back from North Africa to command a shadow army group in the Alps, to be activated in the event of an Allied landing. Hitler also deemed it necessary to cover Italy by reinforcing German garrisons in Corsica and Sardinia.

To secure Greece and the Balkans against Allied attack, strong garrisons were also needed in Crete and Rhodes and dozens of smaller islands in the eastern Mediterranean. These would deny the British access to the Dardanelles and thus prevent the establishment of a direct seaborne supply route to the Soviet Union, while also deterring Turkey from casting its lot with the Allies.

The Battle of Kursk
German Tiger I tanks move up to their start line at the the launch of Operation Citadel on July 4, 1943. The German offensive rapidly ground to a halt at the Battle of Kursk, where the German armour was outnumbered and outfought by Soviet T-34 tanks.

Occupying forces
British troops patrol the town of Pachino, captured swiftly on the first day of the landings in Sicily, July 10, 1943.

In the Mediterranean, as on the Eastern Front, Hitler's instinct was to defend everything on the perimeters of the Nazi empire. Although he liked to compare himself with Frederick the Great, and carried a portrait of the Prussian king with him to each of his headquarters, the Führer had forgotten one of Frederick's most famous dicta—"He who defends everything defends nothing".

THE ITALIAN ARMISTICE

On July 10, 1943 the British Eighth Army and the US Seventh Army landed in Sicily, which was secured by August 17. The Italians' reaction to the invasion was to rid themselves of Mussolini. This proved easier than they had anticipated. The dictator was

deposed on July 24 by the Fascist Grand Council and imprisoned in a mountain hotel on the Gran Sasso in the Apennines. His successor, Marshal Badoglio, opened secret negotiations with the Allies and on September 3 Italy was granted an armistice, to become effective within five days.

When the terms of the armistice were published on September 8, the German troops in Italy, under Field Marshal Albert Kesselring, disarmed their former allies. Four days later, Mussolini was rescued from his mountain-top jail in a daring German airborne raid and brought back behind German lines to set up a puppet government, the Salò Republic, in northern Italy. The main Allied landings on the Italian mainland were made by the US Fifth Army

on September 9 in the Gulf of Salerno, some 40 miles (64 km) southeast of Naples. After ten days of resistance, the German defenders withdrew.

Churchill had called Italy the "soft underbelly" of the Third Reich, but its terrain was well suited to a determined defense. The Germans settled down behind the successive rivers that flow eastward and westward out of the Apennines to the sea. Whenever their line was breached they would fall back to the next carefully prepared position. In November 1943 the Allied advance was halted by the Gustav Line, running across the Italian peninsula, north of Naples, but still south of Rome.

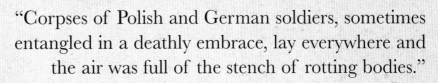

"Corpses of Polish and German soldiers, sometimes entangled in a deathly embrace, lay everywhere and the air was full of the stench of rotting bodies."

GENERAL WLADYSLAW ANDERS DESCRIBING MONTE CASSINO AFTER ITS FINAL CAPTURE IN MAY 1944

US STRATEGY IN THE PACIFIC

At Casablanca it was decided to extend operations to include the recapture of the Aleutians in Admiral Nimitz's North Pacific command area. In June 1942 the Japanese had occupied two islands, Attu and Kiska, as a diversionary maneuver in the Midway campaign.

In February 1943 the securing of Guadalcanal, in General MacArthur's Southwest Pacific command area, paved the way for the Allied drive across the Central and South Pacific command areas, the latter commanded by Admiral Halsey. In the Southwest Pacific command area, General MacArthur was to outflank the Japanese base at Rabaul, on the northeast tip of the island of New Britain, and approach the Philippines from the south. In the South Pacific Area, Halsey was to cooperate with MacArthur in isolating Rabaul and also push northwest from Guadalcanal along the Solomons. In the Central Pacific Area, Admiral Nimitz was to ensure adequate supplies to MacArthur and Halsey, while simultaneously mounting a drive through the Gilbert, Marshall, Caroline, and Mariana Islands.

The campaign in the central Solomons opened on June 21, 1943 with the assault on New Georgia and the capture of Munda airfield on August 5. At the beginning of November the US 3rd Marine Division went ashore at Empress Augusta Bay on Bougainville. By the end of the year the Americans had secured a defensive perimeter and established a naval base and

operational airstrips on the island. Much of Bougainville still remained in Japanese hands, but the eastern arm of Halsey's advance was now fully extended toward Rabaul. Landings on New Britain and the capture of the Admiralty and St Matthias Islands northwest of New Britain tightened the ring around Rabaul, which was successfully cut off by the end of March 1944. It would remain isolated and impotent until the end of the war.

In the summer and autumn of 1943, Nimitz concentrated an armada of ships, aircraft, and men for his drive in the Central Pacific. The stiffest resistance was encountered on Tarawa Atoll, in the Gilbert Islands. It was secured on November 23 after three days of heavy fighting in which all but 146 of the Japanese garrison of 4,800 were killed. This phase of operations ended on February 21, 1944, with the capture of Eniwetok in the Marshalls.

On June 15, 1944, 69 B-29 bombers flew from eastern India via China to bomb the Imperial Iron and Steel works at Yawata on the Japanese island of Kyushu. It was the first B-29 Superfortress raid on a target in the Japanese Home Islands. The date also marked the start of operations to take the islands of Saipan, Tinian, and Guam in the Marianas. These would serve as bases for a campaign against Japan itself. The capture of Saipan gave the Americans a new airbase for the B-29 1,500 miles (2,400 km) southeast of Tokyo, just within the bomber's range.

The stubborn defense of the Gustav Line throughout December and January forced the Allies to attempt to outflank it with a landing on January 22, 1944 at Anzio, 30 miles (48 km) south of Rome. Through a combination of indecisive Allied generalship and determined German resistance, the plan failed. Heavy fighting continued until May 1944, when Monte Cassino, the lynchpin of the Gustav Line defenses, was finally taken. The way now lay open to Rome, which was liberated on June 5.

The capture of Rome accelerated work on yet another German defense system, the Gothic Line. The German 10th and 14th Armies retired behind this line and awaited the Allied attempts to breach their defenses, which began on August 30, 1944.

The taking of Tarawa
A US Marine prepares to throw a hand grenade at Japanese soldiers entrenched in the ruins of their airbase during the fierce fighting to capture Tarawa in the Gilberts in November 1943.

GERMAN RETREAT ON THE EASTERN FRONT

JULY 5, 1943–MAY 12, 1944

The launch in July, near Kursk, of a major offensive called Operation Citadel was intended to signal the beginning of a German recovery. Instead, the offensive was quickly halted, and by the fall of 1943 Germany had lost the war on the Eastern Front.

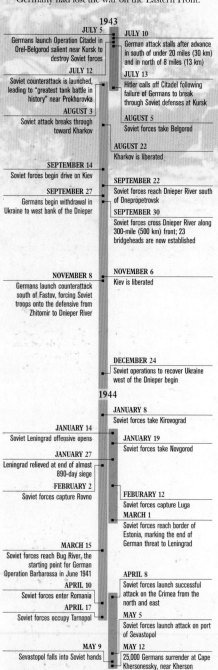

1943

JULY 5
Germans launch Operation Citadel in Orel-Belgorod salient near Kursk to destroy Soviet forces

JULY 10
German attack stalls after advance in south of under 20 miles (30 km) and in north of 8 miles (13 km)

JULY 12
Soviet counterattack is launched, leading to "greatest tank battle in history" near Prokhorovka

JULY 13
Hitler calls off Citadel following failure of Germans to break through Soviet defenses at Kursk

AUGUST 3
Soviet attack breaks through toward Kharkov

AUGUST 5
Soviet forces take Belgorod

AUGUST 22
Kharkov is liberated

SEPTEMBER 14
Soviet forces begin drive on Kiev

SEPTEMBER 22
Soviet forces reach Dnieper River south of Dnepropetrovsk

SEPTEMBER 27
Germans begin withdrawal in Ukraine to west bank of the Dnieper

SEPTEMBER 30
Soviet forces cross Dnieper River along 300-mile (500 km) front; 23 bridgeheads are now established

NOVEMBER 8
Germans launch counterattack south of Fastov, forcing Soviet troops onto the defensive from Zhitomir to Dnieper River

NOVEMBER 6
Kiev is liberated

DECEMBER 24
Soviet operations to recover Ukraine west of the Dnieper begin

1944

JANUARY 8
Soviet forces take Kirovograd

JANUARY 14
Soviet Leningrad offensive opens

JANUARY 19
Soviet forces take Novgorod

JANUARY 27
Leningrad relieved at end of almost 890-day siege

FEBRUARY 2
Soviet forces capture Rovno

FEBURARY 12
Soviet forces capture Luga

MARCH 1
Soviet forces reach border of Estonia, marking the end of German threat to Leningrad

MARCH 15
Soviet forces reach Bug River, the starting point for German Operation Barbarossa in June 1941

APRIL 8
Soviet forces launch successful attack on the Crimea from the north and east

APRIL 10
Soviet forces enter Romania

APRIL 17
Soviet forces occupy Tarnopol

MAY 5
Soviet forces launch attack on port of Sevastopol

MAY 9
Sevastopol falls into Soviet hands

MAY 12
25,000 Germans surrender at Cape Khersonessky, near Kherson

■ Campaigns in Orel-Belgorod salient
Jul 5–Aug 5, 1943

■ Relief of Leningrad
Jan 14–Mar 1, 1944

■ Advance through the Ukraine
Aug 3, 1943–Apr 17, 1944

■ The Crimea
Apr 8, 1943–May 12, 1944

RECAPTURE OF THE WESTERN SOVIET UNION

SINCE MARCH 1943 HITLER and his high command had been planning a major offensive—to be launched after the spring thaw—with the goal of excising the heavily defended salient around Kursk. A concentric attack of the type that had been so effective in the summer of 1941 would trap the Red Army forces inside a large pocket, where they could be destroyed piecemeal and provide a rich haul of prisoners. Moreover, taking Kursk would enable the Ostheer to establish a shorter front line. The operation, code-named *Zitadelle* (Citadel), was to involve two army groups, Center and South. Some 900,000 men, 2,380 tanks and assault guns, 10,000 artillery pieces, and 2,500 aircraft, many of them ruthlessly stripped from other sectors of the Eastern Front, would be sent into action.

Well informed of German intentions by the "Lucy" spy network in Switzerland and a mole inside British intelligence, the Stavka had plenty of time to strengthen the Kursk salient, which was held by the Central Front in the north and the Voronezh Front in the south. By the end of June 1943 it had packed the bulge with 1.3 million men—including 75 infantry divisions, some 40 percent of the Red Army's rifle formations—and had positioned as many as 100 guns nearly a mile along the likely German axes of advance. It had also concentrated some 3,500 tanks and self-propelled guns, of which 2,000 were deployed in the Kursk salient and the bulk of the remainder held in reserve in the Steppe Front's Fifth Guards Tank Army. In the north and south of the salient, a deeply echeloned eight-line defensive network, comprising dense minefields and trench systems linking antitank strongpoints, had been constructed. Some 330,000 civilians had been employed as auxiliaries in the preparation of these killing grounds and in the repair and maintenance of rail links from the Soviet interior.

Semiautomatic vertical sliding wedge breech mechanism

Muzzle break

Shield to protect crew

German 50-mm Pak 38
The standard German antitank gun until late 1942, the Pak 38 could penetrate 3.5 in (90 mm) of armor at a range of 1,000 yd (915 m).

Red Army tank on the move

A T-34, the mainstay of the Red Army, rolls forward with infantry aboard. On July 12, 1943 some 800 T-34s were to confront more than 600 German tanks at Prokhorovka, in the Kursk salient, in the largest tank battle of the war.

The Soviet army commanders went to considerable lengths to conceal from the Germans the depth and scale of the defense they were preparing. Measures included the creation of false troop concentrations and the construction of dummy tanks and air armies. At least 40 false airfields were built, complete with dummy aircraft, runways, and control towers. They were repeatedly bombed by the Luftwaffe in the run-up to the battle. German military intelligence anticipated that Zhukov, now deputy commander-in-chief and in overall command of the Kursk salient, was preparing to fight a grim defensive battle. They were unaware that he was planning to absorb the Ostheer's blows and then launch his own counteroffensive.

OPERATION CITADEL

The German launched a probing attack in driving rain on July 4. After a bombardment on the southern shoulder of the Kursk salient, the Fourth Panzer Army, under General Hermann Hoth, slithered forward through a quagmire to seize the low hills overlooking the German assembly areas. It took some time for Stalin to be convinced that the long-awaited offensive had begun, but eventually,

Despairing German soldier

An artilleryman contemplates captivity after the Soviet counteroffensive that followed the Battle of Kursk. The battle ended any prospect of German victory in the east.

at 10:30 pm, the Soviet artillery opened up with a colossal counterbombardment of the entire area. The following day there was more torrential rain, and massive air battles took place overhead as the Fourth Panzer Army launched its attack on the line held by the Soviet Sixth Guards Army. By nightfall on July 5 the Fourth Panzer Army had made only three small penetrations of the Red Army's line, none of them more than 7 miles (11 km) deep.

The battle on the southern shoulder of the salient was now drawing in significant elements of Zhukov's strategic reserve. On July 7 Hoth's two panzer corps, together with a third on their right flank, began to advance more quickly. For a fleeting moment it seemed as if they might burst through the Red Army's defense zone into open country. However, the armored, artillery, and antitank reinforcements were fed in from flanking sectors on the south face of the salient to meet the threat. By July 9 Hoth was still 55 miles (90 km) from Kursk.

To the north, Army Group Centre under Field Marshal Günther von Kluge had made good progress on July 5 against the Central Front. Its Ninth Army had advanced 6 miles (9 km) on a frontage of 20 miles (30 km). However, on the 7th, Red Army resistance stiffened and in the next two days the Ninth Army sustained some 10,000 casualties as it cleared the villages and wooded country on its front. By July 10 its advance had come to a standstill.

...we found ourselves taking on a seemingly inexhaustible mass of enemy armor—never have I received such an overwhelming impression of Russian strength and numbers as on that day. The clouds of dust made it difficult to get help from the Luftwaffe, and soon many of the T-34s had broken past our screen and were streaming like rats all over the battlefield...

GERMAN SOLDIER DESCRIBING THE BATTLEFIELD AT PROKHOROVKA ON JULY 12

Action in Kursk salient

The German plan at Kursk was to eliminate the massive salient—about half the size of England—with an attack at its northern and southern shoulders. It would then straighten the German line on the Eastern Front.

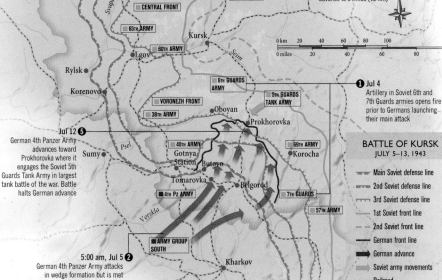

5:30 am, Jul 5 ③
German 9th Army attacks and meets with fierce resistance from Soviet 13th Army

④ Jul 7–8
In fierce fighting, German advance is halted at Ponyri, limiting German advance to 8 miles (13 km)

① Jul 4
Artillery in Soviet 6th and 7th Guards armies opens fire prior to Germans launching their main attack

Jul 12 ⑤
German 4th Panzer Army advances toward Prokhorovka where it engages the Soviet 5th Guards Tank Army in largest tank battle of the war. Battle halts German advance

5:00 am, Jul 5 ②
German 4th Panzer Army attacks in wedge formation but is met with heavy artillery fire

BATTLE OF KURSK
JULY 5–13, 1943

- Main Soviet defense line
- 2nd Soviet defense line
- 3rd Soviet defense line
- 1st Soviet front line
- 2nd Soviet front line
- German front line
- German advance
- Soviet army movements
- Railroad

Map labels: Oka, Orel, 2ND PZ ARMY, 9TH ARMY, 48TH ARMY, Malorakhangelsk, ARMY GROUP CENTRE, Pervyye Ponyri, Ponyri Station, Olkhovatka, 2ND TANK ARMY, 13TH ARMY, CENTRAL FRONT, Svapa, 65TH ARMY, 60TH ARMY, Kursk, Lgov, Seim, Rylsk, Korenovo, 6TH GUARDS ARMY, 5TH GUARDS TANK ARMY, VORONEZH FRONT, 38TH ARMY, Oboyan, Prokhorovka, 69TH ARMY, Korocha, Psel, Sumy, 40TH ARMY, Gotnya Station, Butovo, Tomarovka, Belgorod, 7TH GUARDS, 4TH PZ ARMY, Vorskla, 57TH ARMY, ARMY GROUP SOUTH, Kharkov, Donets, N

It was fast becoming apparent to Hitler and his high command that there would be no quick victory. As Anglo-American forces began disembarking in Sicily on July 10, it became clear that Germany would now have to fight in Europe on two fronts.

TANK BATTLE AT PROKHOROVKA

On July 12, at the northernmost point of the Fourth Panzer Army's advance, the German II SS Panzer Corps slammed headlong into the Soviet Fifth Guards Tank Army, which was hastening up from the Steppe Front strategic reserve. In the ensuing armored *mêlée* at Prokhorovka, the largest tank battle of the war in which armoured vehicles clashed at point-blank range, the II SS Panzer Corps was stopped dead in its tracks. It had inflicted heavy losses on the Fifth Guards Tank Army, knocking out or badly damaging at least 400 of a total of 850 vehicles at relatively small cost to itself. However, for

IL2 Sturmovich
This rugged Ilyushin ground-attack aircraft was dubbed the "cement bomber" by the Germans. Some 35,000 were built during the war.

the Fourth Panzer Army's elite units, Prokhorovka must have seemed the last straw. The terrible slog through the Red Army's defenses in which, before the clash at Prokhorovka, it had lost 330 tanks and assault guns, had already sapped morale to the point where the will to press home attacks against continuing strong Soviet resistance was beginning to ebb away.

OPERATION KUTUZOV

The Allied invasion of Sicily had taken the German high command completely by surprise. So, too, did Zhukov's counteroffensive, code-named Kutuzov, which was launched on July 12 against the northern and eastern faces of the Orel salient held by the Second Panzer Army. Kutuzov was conceived as a relieving

Soviet 76-mm antitank gun
Introduced in 1942, this robust antitank weapon had a 14,200-yd (13,000-m) range. Its three-man crew carried personal weapons to engage mechanized infantry.

Double baffle muzzle break

Shield to protect crew

Split carriage trail

attack prior to a major offensive along the entire Eastern Front, but by the evening of July 14 it had achieved an advance of over 10 miles (16 km).

On July 13 Kluge, the commander of Army Group Center, and Manstein, the commander of Army Group South, were summoned to a meeting with Hitler, in which Manstein uncharacteristically urged the Führer to continue the battle of attrition in the Kursk salient. Failure to do so, he argued, would bring powerful Soviet forces crashing down on Army Group South's long salient to the Donets Basin and Black Sea in a rerun of the crisis that had followed Stalingrad. In contrast, Kluge reported that he was making no headway and was being forced to transfer mobile forces northward to check the Red Army's eruption into the Orel salient. Operation Citadel should be abandoned.

Kluge won the day. By July 23 the Fourth Panzer Army was back on the starting line of Operation Citadel and the Red Army counteroffensive was under way.

On July 17 Soviet forces

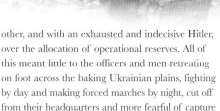

Retreating from Kharkov
After the failure of Citadel, the Germans fell back from Kharkov, which the Red Army liberated on August 22, 1943.

launched a powerful attack on the German defenses in the south both along the Mius line and across the Donets below Izyum (see map page 192). Meanwhile, north of the Kursk bulge, the Ninth Army was beginning a withdrawal from the Orel salient to escape the expanding Kutuzov drive, which was threatening to surround it. By August 18 it had regained the temporary safety of the Hagen Line, a system of fortifications across the neck of the Orel salient. The commander of the Ninth Army, General Walther Model, was soon to become one of Hitler's most trusted commanders.

FURTHER SOVIET OFFENSIVES

Operation Kutuzov was the first in a series of offensives planned to unroll along the Eastern Front in the wake of Kursk. Initially the success of all other Red Army offensives was subordinated to the objective of taking Belgorod, just below the shoulder of the Kursk salient. Once this had been achieved, on August 5, it was the turn of Kharkov, which was liberated on August 22.

Stalin now began to urge his earlier strategy of striking hammer blows along the entire front, while Hitler, who appeared to be almost completely preoccupied with the situation in the Mediterranean and the Balkans, refused to accept the need for an organized withdrawal. As a result, army group commanders such as Manstein and Kluge were reduced to squabbling with each

other, and with an exhausted and indecisive Hitler, over the allocation of operational reserves. All of this meant little to the officers and men retreating on foot across the baking Ukrainian plains, fighting by day and making forced marches by night, cut off from their headquarters and more fearful of capture by the Red Army than of death itself.

Following the capture of Kharkov, the Red Army advanced into eastern Ukraine with the goal of liberating Kiev and crossing the Dnieper River. Its forces might be under strength after the terrible losses incurred at Kursk, but the Voronezh and

Steppe Fronts now enjoyed an overall superiority over Army Group South of 3:1 in manpower, 4:1 in artillery and tanks, and 3:2 in aircraft. Greatly outnumbered, the German troops defending the Mius Line began to give way. At the end of August, Hitler reluctantly agreed to the strengthening of Army Group South and directed Kluge to assemble a strong force in front of Kiev.

Manstein—previously denied any freedom to maneuver by Hitler—now ordered a retreat to the Dnieper. However, he faced an almost impossible task, for the delays imposed by the Führer meant

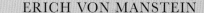

Roks-2 flamethrower in action
In the first days of the Battle of Kursk, Soviet forces attacked German tanks at close range, using grenades, gasoline bombs, and flame-throwers, as well as guns.

ERICH VON MANSTEIN

ACKNOWLEDGED BY MANY AS THE FINEST OPERATIONAL commander of World War II, Manstein (1887–1973) fought on the Western Front in World War I. In 1939 he served as Rundstedt's chief of staff in Poland and subsequently developed the Sickle Cut plan, the most significant element of Hitler's 1940 campaign in France. In September 1941 he became commander of the 11th Army and with it conquered the Crimea. Promoted to the rank of field marshal after the fall of Sevastopol, he was given command of Army Group Don in the abortive attempt to relieve the Sixth Army at Stalingrad in late 1942. In the subsequent retreat he prevented the Red Army from crossing the Dnieper and then retook Kharkov in a brilliant counterstroke. In the spring of 1943 Manstein, now in command of Army Group South, was closely involved in the planning of Operation Citadel, about which he entertained the gravest misgivings. After its failure, Manstein again demonstrated generalship of the highest skill in conducting a step-by-step retreat to the Polish frontier. His arguments for taking a long step back were, however, not heeded by Hitler, who replaced him with Model in March 1944. It was the end of Manstein's military career.

SOVIET AND GERMAN ARMOR

BY 1943 THE ARMORED BATTLES of the Eastern Front had assumed a new shape. The Red Army now fielded dedicated tank armies, whose mainstay, the T-34, accounted for almost 70 percent of Soviet tank production. In contrast, German tank development focused on the production of a new generation of massively armored vehicles—in particular, so-called "tank destroyers"—which were needed for defensive warfare. Crucially, the tank was no longer the autonomous war-winning weapon it had been in 1940. Rather, it was one, albeit vital, element in the tactics of battlefield attrition. For this new kind of warfare, Soviet armored formations used two standard vehicles— T-34 tanks and US-supplied Dodge trucks.

85-mm primary armament

PzKpfw V Panther main battle tank

The Panther entered production in 1943 as Germany's response to the T-34. It incorporated features of the T-34, including sloped frontal armor and wide tracks.

Crew 5		Max speed 29 mph (47 kph)
Range 110 miles (177 km)		Max armour thickness 4¾ in (120 mm)
Armament 1 × 75-mm gun, 2 × 7.92-mm machine-guns		

T-34/85

The T-34 was the best all-around tank of the war. It fought through the conflict without major modifications, except that in spring 1944 its main armament was upgraded from a 76-mm gun to an 85-mm gun.

Crew 5	Max speed 31mph (50 kph)
Range 186 miles (300 km)	
Max armor thickness 2⅜ in (60 mm)	
Armament 1 × 85-mm D-5T gun, 2 × 7.62-mm machine-guns	

22-in (55-cm) tracks, reducing ground pressure for running cross country

2¼-in (60-mm) thick sloping front armor

7.62-mm machine-gun

7.92-mm MG34 machine-gun

Long-barrelled 88-mm gun

Jagdpanther heavy tank destroyer

Based on the Panther chassis and armed with an 88-mm gun, which could penetrate the armor of any Allied tank, the Jagdpanther entered service in 1944 but only 382 were produced.

Crew 5	Max speed 45 mph (72 kph)
Frontal armor thickness 3¼ in (80 mm)	
Armament 1 × 88-mm L/71 Pak 43/3 gun, 1 × 7.92-mm machine-gun	

4-in (100-mm) thick Saukopf (pig's head) mantlet

KV-1B heavy tank

The KV-1 entered Red Army service in 1940 and the B version was heavily armored. About 10,500 KVs were built between 1940 and 1943.

Crew 5	Max speed 22 mph (35 kph)
Max armor thickness 3¼ in (82 mm)	
Armament 1 × 76-mm gun, 3 × 7.62-mm machine-guns	

that there was no time to prepare roads, river crossings, demolition charges, or minefields. Manstein's task was to get four armies over five major river crossings and then turn to defend a front of 450 miles (720 km).

The retreating Germans attempted to "sterilize" the rich farmlands and coalfields of the Donets Basin but were thwarted by the haste of the withdrawal. Army Group South had to abandon much of its heavy equipment and nearly 3 million horses and cattle. The Red Army tide rolled on. By the end of September, 23 bridgeheads had been established on the west bank of the Dnieper. For a while Red Army troops struggled to reinforce these bridgeheads, but by October 20 they had successfully built up the position around Lyutezh, and were ferrying tanks over the Dnieper in barges. On November 4 tanks of the Third Guards Army burst out of the bridgehead, headlights blazing and sirens howling. Two days later they were in Kiev.

COUNTING THE COST

By the fall of 1943 Germany had lost the war on the Eastern Front. The premonition of defeat that had stirred at Stalingrad had now become a daily reality for the men of the Ostheer. Hitler had intended Citadel to be a "beacon to the world" and a reaffirmation of German power to his increasingly apprehensive allies. Instead it had led to a series of convulsions which, in two and a half months, had thrown back the Ostheer around 150 miles (240 km) on a front of 650 miles (1,040 km). German manpower losses during the Battle of Kursk and the Red Army counteroffensive had exceeded those at Stalingrad, where some 209,000 "irreplaceable"

German infantryman in Kiev
Lines of exhaustion are etched on the face of a German infantryman during fighting in Kiev in the winter of 1943. The city was liberated by the Red Army on November 6.

Streetfighting in Kiev
Red Army infantrymen, armed with PPSh-41 submachine-guns, engage in house-to-house fighting in the battle to gain control of the city.

losses (dead, missing, and one-third of the wounded) had been sustained. Between July and October 1943, the number of irreplaceable losses in the east, the greater part inflicted at Kursk and during the retreat to the Dnieper, had reached 365,000. The Ostheer could not hope to match the numbers available to the Red Army. Kursk involved 1.3 million Soviet troops compared with 900,000 Germans, while on the Dnieper in October, the Red Army had 2.6 million troops against 1.2 million Germans, and a 4:1 superiority in tanks and guns.

RELIEF OF LENINGRAD

In January 1943 the Red Army's Volkhov and Leningrad Fronts had joined hands to carve out a corridor 7 miles (11 km) wide south of Lake Ladoga

through which trains could pass to the besieged city of Leningrad. By the fall a semblance of normality had returned, though regular German artillery fire, and equally regular Soviet counter-bombardments, had continued to serve as permanent reminders that the battle for the city was not over.

Relief finally came in January 1944, when the Volkhov and Leningrad Fronts fell on the German 18th Army. The army's commander, General Lindemann, was forced to give ground, in spite of the customary orders to the contrary, leaving the garrison of Novgorod, 90 miles (145 km) to the south, cut off. Its troops had to abandon the seriously wounded and fight their way out under

A call to rebuild Leningrad
In 1941 the desperate defense of Russia's old capital had been vital to save Moscow, the Soviet Union's new capital. Pounded by German artillery throughout an 890-day siege, its reconstruction from 1944 was to be an immense undertaking.

cover of darkness. By January 27 the railroad between Moscow and Leningrad had been cleared and the German Army Group North had been pushed back to the eastern shore of Lake Chuskoye, 160 miles (255 km) to the southwest. The Germans now established themselves along a line where Leningrad lay beyond the range of their artillery. As the 890-day siege of the city ended, the skies were streaked with red, white, and blue rockets of celebration. Leningrad was free, but at a terrible cost.

Red Army storms Sevastopol
The Soviet assault on Sevastopol opened on May 5, 1944. The Germans were evacuated on the 9th.

SOVIET ADVANCE IN THE UKRAINE

As the Soviet Leningrad and Volkhov Fronts were preparing to liberate Leningrad, pressure on the German Army Group South was mounting. The Red Army now enjoyed the freedom to attack where it chose and always in superior numbers. It also possessed far greater mobility than the Ostheer, the result of the Lend-Lease conveyor belt that had provided Stalin with huge quantities of American four-wheel drive and six-wheel drive trucks that could operate across country in all but the very worst weather. In contrast, German motorized formations were tied to the primitive Soviet road system. Transportation shortages were now so bad in German armored formations that they increasingly relied on Soviet *panjes* (horse-drawn carts).

Systematically, Manstein's front was picked apart, while in Germany Hitler fought the war from the map, shuttling formations back and forth and designating so-called "strongholds" that must be held at all costs. By January 28 the First and Second Ukranian Fronts—the former General Vatutin's renamed Voronezh Front—were threatening to totally encircle two German corps, about 60,000 men, in the area of Cherkassy in the center of Manstein's front. With great difficulty, and with Hitler interfering at every turn, about 30,000 men were extracted from the Cherkassy pocket, but with none of their

THE EASTERN FRONT
JUL 5, 1943–MAY 9, 1944

— German front line Jul 5, 1943
–·– German front line Sept 1, 1943
– – German front line Nov 30, 1943
····· German front line Mar 2, 1944
····· German front line Apr 8 and 17, 1944
➡ Soviet advance
➡ German attack
🛇 Major tank battle
● Campaign in Russia and Ukraine
■ Campaign in the Baltic region
⬟ Campaign in the Crimea

1 Jan 4, 1944 Soviet forces launch Leningrad offensive

2 Jan 27, 1944 Leningrad is relieved by Leningrad and Volkhov Fronts

Mar 1, 1944 3 Soviet forces reach Estonian border

3 Aug 4, 1943 Soviet forces take Orel

2 Jul 12, 1943 Soviet forces defeat Germans in major tank battle at Prokhorovka

6 Nov 6, 1943 Soviet forces take Kiev

1 Jul 5, 1943 Germans launch Operation Citadel

8 Jan 28, 1944 Soviet offensive threaten to encircle Germans at Cherkassy

4 Aug 22, 1943 Germans evacuate Kharkov

Nov 8, 1943 7 Germans counterattack south of Fastov

Apr 17, 1944 10 Soviet forces occupy Tarnopol

April 17, 1944

5 Sept 30, 1943 Soviet forces begin to cross Dnieper River along 500-mile (800-km) front

Mar 15, 1944 9 Soviet forces reach Bug River

1 Apr 8, 1944 Soviet forces launch offensive on the Crimea

April 8, 1944

2 May 9, 1944 Sevastopol's German garrison surrenders

Soviet advance
Following the failure of the German Operation Citadel in July 1943, the Red Army began a relentless advance along a front that stretched from the Baltic region to the Crimea.

0 km 50   100   150   200
0 miles   50   100   150   200

heavy equipment. By early March the same fate had befallen the First Panzer Army as it was overhauled by the First Ukrainian Front (now commanded by Zhukov after Vatutin's death at the hands of anti-Soviet partisans) and the Second Ukrainian Front, driving southeast toward the Carpathians.

Manstein was now locked in an argument with Hitler about how best the First Panzer Army might be extracted from imminent encirclement. This time Manstein prevailed and the First Panzer Army was ordered to march northwest 150 miles (240 km)— in effect a moving pocket—living off the land and supplied with ammunition, fuel, and spare parts by air drops flown by night. On April 9 the First

Panzer Army joined hands with the Fourth Panzer Army near Tarnopol, having lost all of its equipment and most of its heavy weapons. By then Manstein had been relieved of his command. His replacement was Model, who had commanded the Ninth Army at Kursk and had become commander of Army Group North in January 1944. He was a favorite of the Führer and was to become his troubleshooter on both the Eastern and Western Fronts.

ACTION IN THE CRIMEA

At this point another lull descended on the Eastern Front, except in the Crimea, where the German 17th Army was now isolated. As the crisis in the

south had deepened, Manstein had shifted north, attempting to close the dangerous gap between Army Groups South and Center. Something had to give, and it was the German 17th Army's front in the Crimea, on the Perekop isthmus, which was breached early in April by the Fourth Ukrainian Front. The Independent Coastal Army then landed on the Kerch peninsula, forcing the Germans to fall back on Sevastopol, which was taken on May 9 after two days of intense fighting.

The victory at Kursk, and its aftermath, had demonstrated the growing confidence of the Red Army. From midsummer 1943 the war in the east would be one of relentless Soviet advance.

SOVIET PARTISANS

IN A RADIO BROADCAST ON JULY 3, 1941, Stalin called for a vast partisan movement to spring up behind the advancing Ostheer. However, it was some time before the partisans became a thorn in the German side. Early resistance by scattered bands of partisans was met with savage German reprisals against the native population: in a single month in Byelorussia, the 707th Division shot nearly 10,500 "partisans" in retaliation for the death of two soldiers. This did more to promote recruitment to the partisan movement than exhortation from Moscow.

A centralized structure was imposed on the partisan movement by Stalin in the spring of 1942, after the Soviet winter offensive, and a semblance of military discipline was imposed by Red Army officers, party officials, and the NKVD. Recalcitrant partisans were summarily shot. Those who toed the line were now well supplied with food, medical supplies, and arms, including tanks and artillery. "Partisan regions" were carved out of areas where there was a limited German presence and where the terrain—dense woods and marshland—lent itself to guerrilla activity. It has been estimated that in the winter of 1942–43 up to 60 percent of Byelorussia was controlled by the partisans. Other partisan regions included the Porkhov region south of Leningrad

Poster urging partisan activity
Soviet civilians living in territory that had been occupied by German troops were exhorted to join a partisan group and "Beat the enemy mercilessly."

Women fighters
Women fought alongside men in Soviet partisan bands. Many became partisans after fleeing from the threat of forced labor.

and the forests around Bryansk, southwest of Moscow. In the Orel region some 18,000 partisans controlled an area containing nearly 500 villages and airstrips used for evacuating the wounded and flying in supplies. The partisans kept this and other occupied areas in touch with Moscow and under a form of communist control.

From the beginning of 1943, partisans waged an effective "rail war" behind German lines. In June 1943 Army Group Center logged 1,092 attacks, with 298 locomotives damaged and 44 bridges blown up. The psychological effect of these attacks on German troops was considerable. Countermeasures included the felling of trees and clearing of undergrowth for distances up to 250 yds (230 m) on either side of the track. Patrols and blockhouses kept the line clear by day, but at night the partisans laid more mines and destroyed ever longer sections of track. The partisan movement was wound up in 1944 as the Red Army liberated the last occupied regions of the European Soviet Union. Many of the partisans were then absorbed into the Red Army.

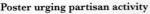

Partisan ambush
In a staged photograph, partisans lie in wait for a German patrol. The best topography for partisan activity was swampland or forest rather than open steppe.

THE SICILIAN AND ITALIAN CAMPAIGNS

JULY 1943–DECEMBER 1944

After the successful campaign in Tunisia, the Allies decided to strike at Italy by invading Sicily. This led the Italians to seek an armistice, but the Germans rushed troops into Italy and held up Allied progress with a resolute defensive campaign. By the winter of 1944 the Allies had reached northern Italy, but their advance ground to a halt south of Bologna.

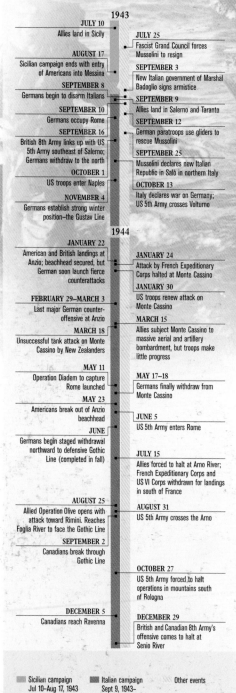

1943

JULY 10
Allies land in Sicily

JULY 25
Fascist Grand Council forces Mussolini to resign

AUGUST 17
Sicilian campaign ends with entry of Americans into Messina

SEPTEMBER 3
New Italian government of Marshal Badoglio signs armistice

SEPTEMBER 8
Germans begin to disarm Italians

SEPTEMBER 9
Allies land in Salerno and Taranto

SEPTEMBER 10
Germans occupy Rome

SEPTEMBER 12
German paratroops use gliders to rescue Mussolini

SEPTEMBER 16
British 8th Army links up with US 5th Army southeast of Salerno; Germans withdraw to the north

SEPTEMBER 25
Mussolini declares new Italian Republic in Salò in northern Italy

OCTOBER 1
US troops enter Naples

OCTOBER 13
Italy declares war on Germany; US 5th Army crosses Volturno

NOVEMBER 4
Germans establish strong winter position—the Gustav Line

1944

JANUARY 22
American and British landings at Anzio; beachhead secured, but German soon launch fierce counterattacks

JANUARY 24
Attack by French Expeditionary Corps halted at Monte Cassino

JANUARY 30
US troops renew attack on Monte Cassino

FEBRUARY 29–MARCH 3
Last major German counter-offensive at Anzio

MARCH 15
Allies subject Monte Cassino to massive aerial and artillery bombardment, but troops make little progress

MARCH 18
Unsuccessful tank attack on Monte Cassino by New Zealanders

MAY 11
Operation Diadem to capture Rome launched

MAY 17–18
Germans finally withdraw from Monte Cassino

MAY 23
Americans break out of Anzio beachhead

JUNE 5
US 5th Army enters Rome

JUNE
Germans begin staged withdrawal northward to defensive Gothic Line (completed in fall)

JULY 15
Allies forced to halt at Arno River; French Expeditionary Corps and US VI Corps withdrawn for landings in south of France

AUGUST 25
Allied Operation Olive opens with attack toward Rimini. Reaches Foglia River to face the Gothic Line

AUGUST 31
US 5th Army crosses the Arno

SEPTEMBER 2
Canadians break through Gothic Line

OCTOBER 27
US 5th Army forced to halt operations in mountains south of Bologna

DECEMBER 5
Canadians reach Ravenna

DECEMBER 29
British and Canadian 8th Army's offensive comes to halt at Senio River

▪ Sicilian campaign
Jul 10–Aug 17, 1943

▪ Italian campaign
Sept 9, 1943–
Dec 1944

Other events

THE INVASION OF ITALY

Planning for the landings on Sicily had begun in March 1943, well before the end of the Tunisian campaign. A deception plan to make the Axis believe that Sardinia was the real target was put into effect. It included the planting of a corpse dressed as a British officer, with a briefcase containing misleading documents, on the Spanish coast. As a result, Hitler ordered that Sardinia be reinforced.

Between Tunisia and Sicily lay two small islands—Lampedusa and Pantelleria. If these were not neutralized, aircraft based on them could interfere with the landings. From early May both were subjected to heavy air bombardment. British troops landed on

Wounded in Sicily
An American medical officer administers blood plasma to a wounded US soldier, watched by local Sicilians.

Pantelleria on June 11 and the Italian garrison surrendered without firing a shot. Lampedusa succumbed in the same way the following day.

THE LANDINGS ON SICILY

The landings on Sicily itself were to be on the south and southeast coasts, with Patton's newly formed US Seventh Army being responsible for the former and Montgomery's British Eighth Army the latter. The plan was that Montgomery would advance up the east coast and cut off the Axis escape route across the Strait of Messina, while Patton protected his left flank. The coastal defenses were manned by low-grade Italian divisions, but there were two well-equipped German mobile divisions on the island. The Allied assault

American troops landing in Sicily
The US Seventh Army was opposed by German aircraft and tanks when it landed on the south coast, but supporting fire from warships enabled the troops to get ashore without serious losses.

Maximum elevation of the howitzer was 45°

The hydraulic "horns" absorbed recoil

Gunsight

British 5.5-in howitzer
During the long campaign to conquer Italy, the Allies often found themselves tied down by Germans dug in behind strong defensive lines. To break through the enemy positions required the use of mortars and heavy artillery. The British 5.5-in medium howitzer was introduced in 1942 and remained in service until the 1970s.

Clinometer, for setting elevation of gun

The gun had a 60° traverse

began on July 10. It was preceded by air-drops to secure airfields and key bridges, but these were badly scattered because of high winds and poor navigation. The landings themselves generally went well and by the end of the day the beachheads had been secured.

Montgomery began to advance up the coast, but soon found his troops held up by stiff German resistance in rugged terrain that favored the defense. Patton took advantage of the fact that the western half of Sicily was held by Italian troops and sent part of his force on a drive to Palermo, the capital. Alexander, whose 15th Army Group was in overall control, wanted him to continue to concentrate on guarding the British left flank, but, after Patton protested, relented. The Seventh Army overran western Sicily and entered Palermo on July 23. Patton then turned east toward Messina, carrying out a number of amphibious landings to outflank Axis defenses. On August 3 Italian troops began to evacuate the island, leaving the Germans to provide the rearguard. By the time the Allies entered Messina on August 17, the Germans had already withdrawn to mainland Italy.

With defeat staring Italy in the face, on July 25 the Fascist Grand Council arrested Mussolini. A new

government was formed under Marshal Pietro Badoglio and this began to make secret overtures to the Allies. Fearing this might be happening, Hitler rushed forces from other theaters to northern Italy, where they came under the command of Rommel's Army Group B. The disgraced Mussolini would be rescued from imprisonment on September 12 by German paratroops.

LANDINGS ON THE MAINLAND

Eisenhower decided that the main landing in Italy should be at Salerno, south of Naples. This was the farthest north that a landing could be supported by Sicily-based fighters. To divert German forces, a preliminary landing would be made across the Strait of Messina by the British Eighth Army. The Salerno landing was to be undertaken by a new formation, the US Fifth Army under General Mark Clark, which contained both US and British troops. Overall operational control would be in the hands of Alexander's 15th Army Group. As for the Seventh Army, Patton was in temporary disgrace for slapping a shell-shocked soldier and he and his HQ were left to administer Sicily.

On September 1, the Italian government agreed to the Allied demand that the country lay down it arms and an envoy went to Sicily to sign an armistice agreement. In the event of a surrender, the Germans intended to disarm the Italians themselves and take control of the country. They now had eight divisions in northern Italy under Rommel and 10 in the south under Kesselring. Rommel's strategy was to make the Alpine region impassable to the Allies, whereas Kesselring wanted to fight a delaying action throughout the length of Italy. For the moment Hitler accepted both strategies.

A free man
Mussolini is escorted by his German rescuers to a waiting aircraft. He was flown to Rome, then to Germany for a meeting with Hitler.

A spectacular rescue
German gliders crash-landed high in the Apennines to rescue Mussolini from his Italian guards. This part of the operation was conducted by German Special Forces officer, Otto Skorzeny, who had tracked the imprisoned dictator to a mountain hotel.

1-8

On September 3 the British landed in the toe of Italy. They met minimal resistance, but their advance was initially slowed by demolitions. On the same day the Italian armistice was signed. It was due to come into effect on September 8 as the Salerno landings were being mounted. Eisenhower intended to fly the US 82nd Airborne Division into Rome to secure the city, but the Italian authorities said that they could not remove the German threat to its landing grounds and so the operation was cancelled. He also ordered Montgomery to make a landing in Taranto to prevent Italian warships based there from falling into German hands.

Eisenhower broadcast the Italian armistice on the evening of September 8, but the landings at Salerno did not take place until 3:30 am the following morning. This gave the Germans valuable warning and they immediately set about disarming the Italian Army. Kesselring had deduced where the landing would be, and the assault was met by bitter resistance from both troops on the ground and the Luftwaffe. Even so, the attackers did get ashore. The British landing at Taranto was unopposed, on the other hand, and the Italian naval squadron, as well as those based in La Spezia and Genoa, set sail for Malta, where they would formally surrender. The latter two squadrons were, however, attacked by the Luftwaffe, which sank the battleship *Roma*.

At Salerno a fierce counterattack on September 14 was beaten back only with difficulty. Two days later, the Eighth Army linked up with the Fifth Army in the beachhead and Kesselring began to pull his troops back northward. The Allies now began to

> Monday, September 13, 1943
> Guess I slept until almost 8:00. Dead tired. Slept through a hot battle. Sgts. Engstrom and Swanson were killed. Sgt. Murphy was badly wounded; his leg was shot off. Our gun position was not far away. Had a good breakfast of C ration hash mixed with genuine Italian onions, tomatoes and peppers. Boiled some potatoes; made coffee that I got from Division. A German soldier gave himself up. He got through our infantry and got to us.

FROM THE DIARY OF CORPORAL BUD WAGNER, US 151ST ARTILLERY BATTALION AT SALERNO

advance, with the Fifth Army in the west and the Eighth Army in the east. Initially, progress was good, with Clark entering Naples on October 1, while Montgomery secured Foggia on the same day.

On October 4 Hitler ordered Rommel to transfer two of his divisions to Kesselring, who was to delay the US Fifth Army for as long as possible north of the Volturno River. Simultaneously, Kesselring was preparing a formidable defensive position, the Gustav Line, which ran the breadth of Italy and took maximum advantage of the river lines and mountainous terrain. All this was an indication that Hitler now favored Kesselring's forward defense strategy and was not prepared to grant the Allies

Bombing German positions on the Volturno
A US B-25 Mitchell bomber drops its bombs on the German artillery positions defending the Volturno River. In the Italian campaign the Allies made use of superior air power to soften up the strong German defenses and to disrupt communications.

easy access to Rome. In addition, the fall rains had now arrived and provided a further brake on progress. During October the Fifth Army managed to get across the Volturno, but was then held in the mountainous country to the north. In the Eighth Army sector, Montgomery had been forcing his way over even more river lines and by early November was closing up to the Sangro River. At this time, Hitler finally came off the fence and approved Kesselring's strategy by appointing him commander-in-chief in Italy.

Eisenhower was still eager to capture Rome and obtained the agreement of the Combined Chiefs of Staff to mount an amphibious operation, codenamed Shingle, designed to outflank the Gustav Line. This would mean retaining shipping that should have been sent back to Britain in preparation for the cross-Channel invasion. Simultaneously, and accepting the Fifth Army's problems in breaking through in the south, Alexander ordered Clark to halt his attacks and for Montgomery to break through the Gustav Line in his sector and threaten Rome. The Eighth Army crossed the Sangro on November 20 during a spell of better weather and then managed to penetrate the Gustav Line. Casualties, however, were mounting and the bad weather returned. On December 27 the Canadians managed to seize Ortona. In view

Anzio harbour
American and British forces remained trapped in the beachhead around the small port of Anzio for four months between January and May 1944. Allied control of the sea and air allowed the troops to be resupplied regularly.

THE ANZIO BEACHHEAD

The Allies now resumed their efforts to break through the Gustav Line. On January 17 Clark made some territorial gains north of the Garigliano River. Three days later there was a further assault across the Rapido. This was partially successful, but was halted by the German defenses on and around the towering hill of Monte Cassino, a feature that was to dominate the fighting during the next few months. Then, on January 22, came the landings at Anzio. They were conducted by General John P. Lucas's US VI Corps, which contained both American and British troops. They initially caught the Germans by surprise and the attackers got ashore with few problems. Because of lack of clarity in his orders, Lucas did not take advantage of this to advance immediately inland, but contented himself with building up his forces in the beachhead. This gave Kesselring time to deploy forces to Anzio.

The Allies now entered what was to be the grimmest period of the whole Italian campaign. On January 24 the French crossed the Rapido to the north of Monte Cassino, but were halted in their tracks by fierce German counterattacks. Five days later, Lucas began to advance out of the Anzio beachhead. Simultaneously, the Fifth Army made another attack on Monte Cassino, which was again repulsed. On February 3 the Germans launched a counterattack at Anzio and drove the Allies back into the beachhead.

of the growing exhaustion of his troops and the fact that they were now faced with mountainous terrain, Montgomery then halted his attacks.

At the beginning of January 1944 there were major changes in the Allied higher command. Both Eisenhower and Montgomery were summoned back to Britain to prepare for Overlord, the landings in Normandy, and were replaced respectively by Generals Sir Maitland Wilson and Sir Oliver Leese. A number of veteran US and British divisions also left the theater for the same reason. They were replaced by fresh US divisions from the States, Alphonse Juin's French Expeditionary Corps from Northwest Africa and Wladislaw Anders' II Polish Corps, which had been formed in the Middle East from Poles that the Soviets had sent to Siberia and had then released.

German paratroopers

The Germans reacted swiftly to the Allied landings on the Italian mainland, first at Salerno, then at Anzio. Here, motorized units speed south to contain the Allied beachhead at Anzio.

The invasion of Italy

Despite the fact that the Italians soon surrendered and came over to the Allied side, the Italian campaign was a long and bitter struggle. The Germans took over the country and fought a defensive battle, making skilful use of the country's mountains and river valleys to hold up the Allied advance.

THE ALLIED INVASION OF ITALY
JUL 10, 1943–DEC 31, 1944

- German front line Sept 25, 1943
- German front line Mar 31, 1944
- German front line Jun 5, 1944
- German front line Dec 31, 1944
- Gothic line
- Allied landing/advance

16 Oct 27, 1944
Allied advance comes to a halt south of Bologna

17 Dec 5, 1944
8th Army enters Ravenna, as Germans withdraw to Senio River

15 Aug 25, 1944
8th Army storms Gothic line, the German defensive position

14 Aug 3–4, 1944
Retreating Germans blow up all bridges across the Arno in Florence (except the Ponte Vecchio)

8 Sept 12, 1943
German paratroopers use gliders to rescue Mussolini from hotel in the Appenines where he is being held

13 Jun 5, 1944
General Clark enjoys triumphal entry into Rome

11 Jan 22, 1944
Allied landings at Anzio. Troops pinned down in narrow beachhead until May

12 May 17, 1944
Germans finally abandon Monte Cassino after four months of fighting

10 Oct 6, 1943
Germans withdraw to line of Volturno

9 Sept 20, 1943
British 8th Army links up with Salerno forces

6 Sept 9, 1943
US and British landings at Salerno meet with strong resistance

7 Sept 9, 1943
Diversionary landing at Italian port of Taranto

2 Jul 23, 1943
US troops enter Palermo

5 Sept 3, 1943
Two divisions of British 8th Army cross to Italian mainland

3 Aug 11–17, 1943
Germans successfully evacuate troops across Strait of Messina

4 Sept 3, 1943
New Italian government of Marshal Badoglio secretly signs armistice with Allies

1 Jul 10, 1943
Operation Husky: US 7th Army and British 8th Army land in southern Sicily

ARMY GROUP SOUTHWEST
10TH ARMY
14TH ARMY
BRITISH 8TH ARMY
US 5TH ARMY
15TH ARMY GROUP
US VI CORPS
US 5TH ARMY
US 7TH ARMY
BRITISH 8TH ARMY
15TH ARMY GROUP

Genoa, Bologna, Ravenna, La Spezia, Forlì, Rimini, Pistoia, Pesaro, Pisa, Florence, Livorno, Arezzo, Ancona, Siena, Perugia, Grosseto, Pescara, Ortona, Viterbo, Civitavecchia, ROME, Anzio, Cassino, Foggia, Naples, Salerno, Potenza, Bari, Brindisi, Taranto, Reggio, Messina, Palermo, Caltanissetta, Catania, Licata, Gela, Cassibile, Syracuse, Pantelleria, Malta (to UK), Lampedusa

Elba, Sicily, Tyrrhenian Sea, APPENNINE, Mt Etna

0 km 50 100 150
0 miles 50 100 150

Alexander was still determined to seize Cassino. He transferred British, Indian, and New Zealand formations from the Eighth Army for another attack. On the very top of the mountain stood a monastery, which the Allies were convinced the Germans were using as an observation post, although in practice they were not. On February 15, Allied bombers attacked the monastery and virtually destroyed it. German paratroops occupied the ruins and turned them into a formidable bastion. On the following day the Indians and New Zealanders attacked, but could make little headway. At the same time, the Germans mounted another assault at Anzio. Only massive Allied air and artillery support prevented them from splitting the beachhead in two.

ATTACKS ON CASSINO

Realizing that he was getting nowhere, Alexander drew up a fresh plan. He now intended to deploy the bulk of the Eighth Army to the Cassino sector for an all-out assault. Simultaneously, while the Fifth Army created a diversion to tie down German

British gun emplacement at Cassino
The barrel of a Bofors antiaircraft gun projects from the ruins of Cassino. The versatile Bofors was often used for shelling defensive positions. On the hilltop above stand the bombed-out remains of the monastery of Monte Cassino.

Rome in Allied hands
American troops walk past the Colosseum. The Fifth Army's triumphal entry into Rome on June 5, 1944, was somewhat overshadowed by the news of the D-Day landings in Normandy on the following day.

troops, the Anzio force would break out and sever the German supply lines from Rome to the Gustav Line. To prepare the way, Alexander intended to mount an air campaign against German communications throughout Italy. He would not be ready to put his plan into effect until late April and wanted to retain the troops earmarked for Operation Anvil, the landings in southern France, which were scheduled to take place at the same time as those in Normandy. The Combined Chiefs of Staff eventually consented to this and Anvil was postponed until July.

On March 15 the Indians and New Zealanders also assaulted Cassino once more. They managed to enter what remained of Cassino town at the base of the mountain, but the German defenses otherwise remained impregnable and Alexander halted the attack after six days' fighting. There was now a comparative lull, while the Allied air forces launched their campaign against German communications, which was largely aimed at road and railroad bridges.

Not until the night of May 11/12 did Alexander mount his all-out offensive. This time it was the turn of

the Poles to attack at Cassino, but again they were unable to make much progress. There was, however, a development in the Fifth Army sector. Juin's French troops managed to break through in the mountains to the south and by May 14 were in a position to outflank Cassino. Realizing this, Kesselring ordered the withdrawal from the Gustav Line to begin. On May 17 the Poles attacked Monte Cassino once more and hoisted their flag on top of the monastery.

On May 23 the breakout from Anzio began, while the Germans started to fall back to a fresh defensive line, which ran through the Alban hills, south of Rome. Two days later the Fifth Army linked up with the Anzio force. The goal now was to cut off the German 10th Army's withdrawal from the Gustav Line by cutting Highway 7, the main route to Rome. Clark, however, now became mesmerized by the prize of Rome itself and directed the majority of his forces in the direction of the capital. Not only did this mean a stiff fight to break through the German defenses in the Alban hills, but it enabled the bulk of the 10th Army to escape the planned trap. Even so, Kesselring accepted that Rome could not be held. By June 4 the last of his troops had withdrawn north of the city, enabling Clark to enter it in triumph the following day.

THE GOTHIC LINE

The Allied advance came to a halt in mid-July along the line of the Arno River. To the north, Kesselring was once more taking advantage of mountainous terrain to construct another defensive barrier across the width of Italy—the Gothic Line. Alexander was determined to resume the offensive, but had to pause while the French Expeditionary

The end of the battle
Allied troops search the ruins of Cassino in May 1944 following the German withdrawal from the monastery above the town.

Corps and US VI Corps, which were required for Anvil, were replaced by the untried Brazilian Expeditionary Corps and a new US division. The new plan called for the Eighth Army to advance east of the Apennines, draw the Germans toward the Adriatic coast, and then for the Fifth Army to punch through the center of the Gothic Line and advance toward Bologna.

The new offensive opened on August 25 and by the end of the month the Eighth Army was across the Foglia River and hammering at the Gothic Line. As expected, Kesselring began to switch his forces to the east to counter this threat, which grew as the Allies broke through the German defenses and reached the Conca River before heavy rain caused a temporary halt. Then, on September 12, the Fifth Army crossed the Arno and aimed for the boundary between the German 10th and 14th Armies. Simultaneously, the Eighth Army resumed its advance. It now faced a succession of river lines, much as it had the previous fall. The American attack

Hilltop defense
A German paratrooper armed with an MP40 submachine-gun takes aim from an almost impregnable position among the ruins of Monte Cassino.

initially made good progress. Breaking through the Gothic Line, Clark headed for Bologna. If he could seize the city, the 10th Army, facing Leese in the east, would be cut off. But the fall rains, combined with the mountains, slowed his momentum and Kesselring was able to fill the gaps in his defenses. The Eighth Army continued to push forward, Leese

being replaced by General Sir Richard McCreery at the beginning of October. On the 27th of the month Clark, still in the mountains south of Bologna, was forced to halt, his casualty rate becoming unsupportable. The increasingly tired Eighth Army continued its endless river crossings, but the chances of achieving a decisive breakthrough were receding.

On November 24, Alexander succeeded Wilson as supreme theater commander, with Clark taking over 15th Army Group. The Eighth Army was still advancing, with the Canadians capturing Ravenna at the beginning of December. By the middle of the month it had reached the Senio River. More river lines lay between this and Bologna and the troops were exhausted. Alexander therefore closed down the offensive. He would wait until the spring before resuming the offensive.

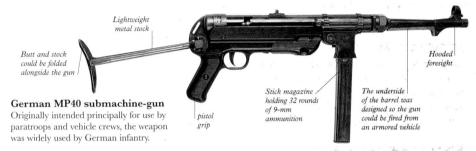

Lightweight metal stock

Butt and stock could be folded alongside the gun

Hooded foresight

German MP40 submachine-gun
Originally intended principally for use by paratroops and vehicle crews, the weapon was widely used by German infantry.

pistol grip

Stick magazine holding 32 rounds of 9-mm ammunition

The underside of the barrel was designed so the gun could be fired from an armored vehicle

ENTERTAINING THE TROOPS

USO (UNITED SERVICES ORGANIZATIONS) was founded in February 1941. By 1944, USO was run by nearly 750,000 volunteers who operated over 3,000 clubs across the United States and overseas, providing rest, recreation, and entertainment for the troops. Many Hollywood stars served in theaters of war. Bob Hope began the first of his five decades of USO service in 1942. Marlene Dietrich, a USO stalwart, was entertaining near the front line in Belgium in December 1944 when the Germans launched the Ardennes offensive. The most famous USO casualty of the war was bandleader Glenn Miller, who disappeared on December 14, 1944 on a cross-Channel flight to Paris to join his orchestra, a mystery which has never been satisfactorily solved. Between 1941 and 1947 over 7,000 "soldiers in greasepaint" put on nearly 430,000 shows for the troops, and USO continues to this day as USO Celebrity Entertainments.

Marlene Dietrich
Marlene poses on top of a piano with a group of admiring GIs at an evacuation hospital in Italy in May 1944.

The British equivalent was the Entertainments National Service Association, or ENSA. Initially, the quality of ENSA shows was extremely variable and the organization earned the nickname "Every Night Something Awful." Nevertheless, by the end of November 1939 ENSA had some 700 artistes on its books and had given nearly 1,500 shows which had been seen by some 600,000 people. ENSA crossed the Channel to entertain British troops in France, where in the winter of 1939–40 comedian George

The Forces' Sweetheart
Vera Lynn sings to a group of British servicemen, raising morale during the Blitz.

Formby kept the troops laughing and Gracie Fields sang to huge audiences. ENSA was gradually expanded to include more highbrow entertainment, and its Good Music section staged concerts by Yehudi Menuhin, Sir Adrian Boult and the BBC Symphony Orchestra. ENSA performed wonders overseas, often in the most grueling and hazardous conditions, entertaining troops from North Africa to Burma. In the spring of 1944, Vera Lynn, the "Forces' Sweetheart," toured Burma, entertaining troops in the jungle. ENSA followed the Allies into Normandy and there was even an ENSA concert party on Lüneburg Heath when on May 5, 1945, the German forces in the West surrendered to Field Marshal Montgomery. The show was lit by the headlights of six jeeps. ENSA was disbanded in 1947; at its wartime peak it was mounting 500 shows a week at home and abroad, showcasing some 4,000 artists.

Bob Hope on stage in New Georgia
Hope was one of USO's most indefatigable entertainers. Here he is playing to a vast audience on the island of New Georgia in the Solomons.

Bombing raid on Cassino
A formation of US Mitchell B-25s flies toward
Cassino. Despite persistent bombardment by artillery
and from the air, the German defenses in Cassino
held up the Allied advance in Italy for six months.

THE ALLIED BOMBING OF GERMANY

FEBRUARY 1942– DECEMBER 1943

In spring 1942 RAF Bomber Command decided to concentrate on night raids over German cities. When the US Air Force joined the campaign later in the year, it used its heavily armed bombers for daylight raids on specific targets. Without long-range fighter escorts, both air forces suffered heavy losses.

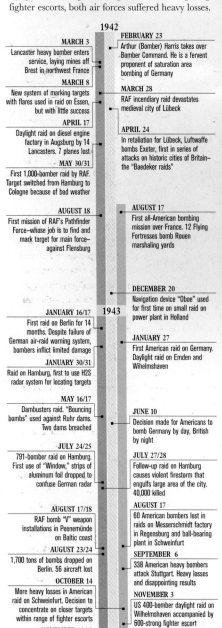

1942

MARCH 3
Lancaster heavy bomber enters service, laying mines off Brest in northwest France

MARCH 8
New system of marking targets with flares used in raid on Essen, but with little success

APRIL 17
Daylight raid on diesel engine factory in Augsburg by 14 Lancasters. 7 planes lost

MAY 30/31
First 1,000-bomber raid by RAF. Target switched from Hamburg to Cologne because of bad weather

AUGUST 18
First mission of RAF's Pathfinder Force–whose job is to find and mark target for main force– against Flensburg

FEBRUARY 23
Arthur (Bomber) Harris takes over Bomber Command. He is a fervent proponent of saturation area bombing of Germany

MARCH 28
RAF incendiary raid devastates medieval city of Lübeck

APRIL 24
In retaliation for Lübeck, Luftwaffe bombs Exeter, first in series of attacks on historic cities of Britain– the "Baedeker raids"

AUGUST 17
First all-American bombing mission over France. 12 Flying Fortresses bomb Rouen marshaling yards

DECEMBER 20
Navigation device "Oboe" used for first time on small raid on power plant in Holland

1943

JANUARY 16/17
First raid on Berlin for 14 months. Despite failure of German air-raid warning system, bombers inflict limited damage

JANUARY 30/31
Raid on Hamburg, first to use H2S radar system for locating targets

MAY 16/17
Dambusters raid. "Bouncing bombs" used against Ruhr dams. Two dams breached

JULY 24/25
791-bomber raid on Hamburg. First use of "Window," strips of aluminum foil dropped to confuse German radar

AUGUST 17/18
RAF bomb "V" weapon installations in Peenemünde on Baltic coast

AUGUST 23/24
1,700 tons of bombs dropped on Berlin. 56 aircraft lost

OCTOBER 14
More heavy losses in American raid on Schweinfurt. Decision to concentrate on closer targets within range of fighter escorts

NOVEMBER 18/19
Start of a sustained bombing campaign against Berlin

JANUARY 27
First American raid on Germany. Daylight raid on Emden and Wilhelmshaven

JUNE 10
Decision made for Americans to bomb Germany by day, British by night

JULY 27/28
Follow-up raid on Hamburg causes violent firestorm that engulfs large area of the city. 40,000 killed

AUGUST 17
60 American bombers lost in raids on Messerschmidt factory in Regensburg and ball-bearing plant in Schweinfurt

SEPTEMBER 6
338 American heavy bombers attack Stuttgart. Heavy losses and disappointing results

NOVEMBER 3
US 400-bomber daylight raid on Wilhelmshaven accompanied by 600-strong fighter escort

DECEMBER
First P-51 Mustangs delivered to Europe. With external fuel tanks, Mustangs can escort US bombers deep into Germany

■ British bombing raids Feb 1942– Dec 1943 ■ US bombing raids Aug 1942–Dec 1943 Other events

WAR IN THE AIR

THE BUTT REPORT, published in August 1941, examined the performance over three months of British bombers against targets in France and Germany. Butt, a member of the War Cabinet Secretariat, had examined hundreds of photographs taken at the moment of bomb release and concluded that, in the summer of 1941, only a third of Bomber Command aircraft had succeeded in placing their bombs within 5 miles (8 km) of the aiming point.

AREA BOMBING

In February 1942, Bomber Command received a new directive. The main weight of its operations was to be thrown into "area" attacks on German cities. The aiming points were to be built-up areas rather than specific industrial plants and facilities. Precision raids continued, but from this point to May 1945, 75 percent of the total tonnage of bombs dropped fell on area targets.

In the spring of 1942, Bomber Command was better placed to execute the new policy. Its twin-engined Wellington, Whitley, Blenheim, and Hampden bombers were gradually giving way to a generation of four-engined bombers capable of delivering bigger payloads—the Short Stirling, Handley Page Halifax, and Avro Lancaster.

Simultaneously, the Butt report was bearing fruit. Late in 1941, the first of a series of navigational aids, "Gee," was introduced. By February 1942, 200 aircraft had been equipped with Gee, a modification that led to the introduction of specialized bomb aimers. The job had previously been handled by the navigator. As Gee was going into service, a new commander arrived at Bomber Command's headquarters in High Wycombe, outside London.

The appointment of Air Chief Marshal Sir Arthur Harris was the single most important factor in the systematic organization of the bombing offensive.

Harris never abandoned the belief that the progressive destruction of the urban areas of Germany would, by itself, bring the war to

Mission accomplished
The crew of a Lancaster bomber walks away from the aircraft after a flight in April 1943, while the ground crew checks it over.

Avro Lancaster bombers

The Lancaster was the principal aircraft used on British night raids over Germany. A total of 3,345 out of 7,373 were lost on operations.

an end. His intention was to mount increasingly heavy raids compressed into progressively shorter periods of time, thus overwhelming German civil defenses on the ground.

On the night of March 3/4, 235 aircraft attacked the Renault factory in Billancourt in occupied France. The concentration achieved on this raid was about 120 aircraft an hour, a first step toward the saturation raids of the later war years. Production at the Billancourt factory was not resumed for three months.

Harris now turned his attention to the Baltic cities of Lübeck and Rostock. The latter was the site of the Heinkel aircraft factory, but the main reason for their choice as targets was their vulnerability to incendiary attack. The densely packed streets of the medieval cities were like tinderboxes. Lübeck was bombed on March 28/29, 1942, and a month later Rostock was subjected to four raids in quick succession.

THE 1,000-BOMBER RAID

Harris had a flair for publicity, which he exploited to the fullest in the 1,000-bomber raid flown against Cologne on May, 30/31, 1942. In Operation Millennium, Harris planned to throw the whole of his front-line strength, and his entire reserve, into a massive raid on a major German city. It was a

tremendous gamble, but the prize was the survival of the strategic bombing offensive. Of the 1,047 aircraft that took off that night, 367 were from training units. During the attack, which lasted just under two and a half hours, some 870 bombers dropped 1,445 tons of bombs. The fires the bombers left behind burned for several days. Some 50,000 people were "dehoused." Harris launched two more "1,000" raids, against Essen (June 1) and Bremen (June 25). Neither matched the success of the Cologne raid and both operations suffered mounting losses to the Luftwaffe's night fighters.

The man responsible for the improving German night fighter defenses was General Josef Kammhuber, who established the so-called "Kammhuber Line," a system of closely controlled fighter-defended areas covering every approach to Germany from Denmark to France. The Kammhuber Line consisted of "boxes," each of which was controlled by a small radar station deploying both long-range early-warning radar and narrow-beam systems. The latter

The bombing of Cologne

Cologne suffered many raids during the war, but none was as terrifying as the first 1,000-bomber raid. Aircrews reported seeing the framework of white-hot building joists glowing in the immense fire raging below.

could pick up and hold a bomber at a range of 30 miles (48 km) and then direct a night fighter onto the target. The major drawback of this system was that only one fighter could operate in a box at any given time. By concentrating its bombers in a "stream," Bomber Command could pass through as few as four boxes on an inward flight, although there was a tendency to spread out on the way home, bringing more night fighters into play.

COMBINED BOMBING OFFENSIVE

Even before the United States entered the war, Anglo-American strategic discussions had resulted in the decision to direct the main weight of the Allied effort against Germany. To defeat Germany, the United States pledged complete land, sea, and air participation in the Anglo-American effort. The United States Army Air Force (USAAF) was confident that, given a sufficient number of aircraft, it could conduct a strategic bombing offensive that would bring Germany to its knees. At the core of the USAAF's philosophy were two firmly held beliefs: first, that high-level daylight precision bombing could be employed to break down the key elements in the German war economy; and second, that, in the absence of a satisfactory long-range escort fighter, the heavily armed USAAF Flying Fortress and Liberator bombers could fight their way to and from their targets without suffering unacceptable losses.

> ## "There are a lot of people who say that bombing cannot win the war. My reply is that it has never been tried yet. We shall see…"
>
> AIR CHIEF MARSHAL SIR ARTHUR HARRIS, AOC-IN-C, BOMBER COMMAND, FEBRUARY 1942

Assessing the damage

Air Chief Marshal Harris and his staff study aerial photographs and reports of the latest air raids over Germany at Bomber Command headquarters in High Wycombe.

The bombers of the US Eighth Air Force began to arrive in England in July 1942 and, on August 17, twelve B-17s raided the rail yards in Rouen. The Americans spent the next five months acclimatizing and training. While the Eighth Air Force grappled with the huge logistical task of establishing bases in Britain, only 30 raids were flown—against targets in the Netherlands, Belgium, and northern France.

THE US BOMBING CAMPAIGN

The bedrock of USAAF tactics was formation flying, the success of which depended on the concentration of defensive firepower. By spring 1943, the so-called "tucked-in" wing had been introduced, which comprised three 18-aircraft squadrons stacked closely together with one squadron flying lead, one high, and one low. It could take up to three hours to assemble 300 or more bombers in combat wings of this kind before they flew on to their target. This enabled German radar and listening stations in northwest Europe, the latter counting radio sets as they were switched on, to estimate with some accuracy the strength of the force flying against them.

B-24 Liberator
Although more vulnerable than the Flying Fortress, the Liberator proved its worth as a bomber both in Europe and in the Pacific.

B-17 bombers over Germany
A squadron of B-17 Flying Fortresses maintains its tight formation on its way to bomb Stuttgart on September 6, 1943.

Early in 1943, following the Casablanca conference, the British and Americans outlined their plan for the air offensive in Europe. Its goal was "the progressive destruction and dislocation of the German military, industrial, and economic system." This strategy was embodied in the Pointblank Directive of June 1943. The USAAF's confidence ran high, but it was to be tested almost to the point of destruction in the skies over Germany.

The USAAF had begun to make shallow penetrations into Germany in January 1943, and from February losses began to mount steadily. The Luftwaffe's day fighters were as well armed as the American bombers and by fall 1943 they were equipped with 30-mm heavy cannon and 210-mm rockets. The latter were not particularly accurate but were effective in loosening up the bomber formations.

By spring 1943, heavy losses were the norm over Germany. On June 22 the Eighth Air Force mounted its first large-scale raid on the Ruhr, attacking the synthetic rubber plants in Hüls.

Only 16 bombers were lost out of 235, but of those that returned no fewer than 170 had been damaged. Operations were often handicapped by poor weather conditions. Crew who had trained for high-altitude bombing with the excellent Norden bombsight could achieve pinpoint accuracy in the clear blue skies of the Nevada desert in the United States. Bombing targets in Germany through dense cloud, smoke screens, or industrial haze was another matter, particularly with the Luftwaffe in close attendance.

The bombing of Germany
In 1942–43 raids by RAF Bomber Command and the US Eighth Air Force targeted cities and industrial complexes farther and farther from Britain. The Americans as yet possessed no long-range escort fighters, and losses in daylight raids rose steadily. Matters improved at the end of 1943 with the arrival of the Mustang P-51B and then, in spring 1944, of the P-51D, both of which were equipped with drop tanks to increase their range.

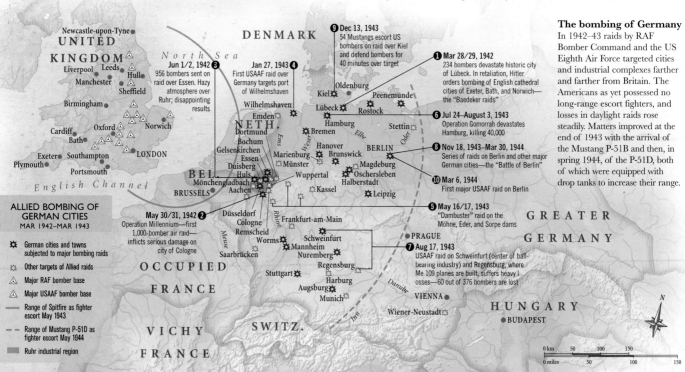

ALLIED BOMBING OF GERMAN CITIES
MAR 1942–MAR 1943

✷ German cities and towns subjected to major bombing raids
✸ Other targets of Allied raids
△ Major RAF bomber base
▲ Major USAAF bomber base
— Range of Spitfire as fighter escort May 1943
-- Range of Mustang P-51D as fighter escort May 1944
▓ Ruhr industrial region

❶ Mar 28/29, 1942
234 bombers devastate historic city of Lübeck. In retaliation, Hitler orders bombing of English cathedral cities of Exeter, Bath, and Norwich—the "Baedeker raids"

❸ Jun 1/2, 1942
956 bombers sent on raid over Essen. Hazy atmosphere over Ruhr; disappointing results

❷ May 30/31, 1942
Operation Millennium—first 1,000-bomber air raid—inflicts serious damage on city of Cologne

❹ Jan 27, 1943
First USAAF raid over Germany targets port of Wilhelmshaven

❻ Jul 24–August 3, 1943
Operation Gomorrah devastates Hamburg, killing 40,000

❽ Nov 18, 1943–Mar 30, 1944
Series of raids on Berlin and other major German cities—the "Battle of Berlin"

❿ Mar 6, 1944
First major USAAF raid on Berlin

❺ May 16/17, 1943
"Dambuster" raid on the Möhne, Eder, and Sorpe dams

❾ Dec 13, 1943
54 Mustangs escort US bombers on raid over Kiel and defend bombers for 40 minutes over target

❼ Aug 17, 1943
USAAF raid on Schweinfurt (center of ball-bearing industry) and Regensburg, where Me 109 planes are built, suffers heavy losses—60 out of 376 bombers are lost

FINDING THE TARGET

FROM THE BLITZ ONWARD, the war in the air became an electronic battle of measures and countermeasures between Allied and German scientists, technicians, and aircrews. "Gee," a British target-finding system introduced in late 1941, consisted of a master and two "slave" transmitter stations positioned on a base line some 200 miles (320 km) long. A receiver in the aircraft picked up a complex sequence of pulses sent in a predetermined order across Europe. Much depended on the skill of the navigator, who applied the time differences between pulses to a special grid chart and thus calculated the aircraft's position. The Germans, however, began to jam Gee successfully in the fall of 1942.

"Oboe," introduced in December 1942 was a blind-bombing system that depended on an aircraft flying on an arc at a constant range from a radio beam transmitted from a station in England to pass over the target. A signal conveyed by a second intersecting beam cut the arc at the correct point for bomb release. Because it could only handle one aircraft at a time, Oboe was restricted to Pathfinder Mosquitos. H2S, which went into service early in 1943, was a downward-looking radar, housed in a blister in the bomber's belly. The returning echoes, displayed on a cathode ray tube known as the Plan Position Indicator (PPI), gave a continuous picture of the terrain over which the aircraft was flying. From 1944, German night fighters equipped with Naxos radars could home in on H2S radiations, forcing bombers to switch on their H2S equipment only for very short periods.

In November 1943, Bomber Command formed 100 Group whose sole purpose was to use radar and radio countermeasures. Toward the end of the war, in a big operation, it could put up as many as 90 jamming aircraft.

Bombs away
Bombs from a USAAF bomber fall toward their target during an air raid on the docks of Bremen in December 1943.

H2S radar
First used in January 1943, H2S radar scanned the ground beneath the aircraft. The echoes were strongest from built-up areas and weaker from open country and water. The navigator compared the image created by the returning echoes with a map.

PPI SCREEN

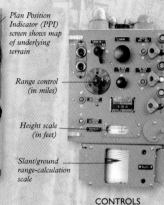

Plan Position Indicator (PPI) screen shows map of underlying terrain

Range control (in miles)

Height scale (in feet)

Slant/ground range-calculation scale

CONTROLS

At the end of July 1943, predominantly cloudless skies over Europe enabled the Eighth Air Force to mount a series of raids, during which 100 aircraft were either destroyed or written off. The attrition reached its peak on August 17 when the Eighth Air Force made its deepest penetration into the Reich, attacking the Me 109 assembly plant at Regensburg and the ball-bearing factories in Schweinfurt. Of the 376 aircraft despatched on the Schweinfurt and Regensburg raids, 60 were lost and many more written off. A second raid on Schweinfurt in October cost the Americans 77 aircraft lost and another 133 damaged out of 291 despatched. Average losses were now running at an unacceptable 10 percent and by the fall of 1943 morale had fallen. After the second Schweinfurt raid, bombing operations were temporarily suspended. Schweinfurt was hit again on February 24, 1944. Some 266 USAAF bombers attacked by day and 734 Bomber Command aircraft by night. This raid was part of Operation Argument ("Big Week"), a concerted attempt to cripple the German aircraft industry. The USAAF flew 3,300 sorties in Big Week, losing 224 bombers and 41 fighters. Help, however, was at hand. The spring of 1944 saw the introduction of the P-51D Mustang. Equipped with drop tanks, the Mustang had a range of 1,500 miles (2,400 km), enabling it to fly escort to any target in Germany, including Berlin. Thanks

principally to the P-51D, the Luftwaffe lost over 1,000 day fighter pilots between January and April 1944, a rate of attrition it could not sustain.

PATHFINDERS
By the spring of 1943, RAF Bomber Command had the weapons and navigational aids to proceed with the Pointblank directive. Gee now had only limited usefulness, as the Germans had learned how to jam it, but two new radar devices, H2S and "Oboe," were now operational. The first aircraft to receive Oboe were six Mosquitos of

Nose gun
The nose blister of a B-17 bomber housed one of a total of 13 machine-guns defending the Flying Fortress.

109 Squadron, which took it on a calibration raid against a power plant in the Netherlands on December 20/21, 1942. In the twin-engined Mosquito, Bomber Command possessed a fighter-bomber that was fast enough to outrun all the Luftwaffe's prejet fighters. 109 Squadron was part of 8 Group, known as the Pathfinder Force (PFF), which was formed in August 1942 to exploit the new radar devices in locating and marking targets.

By the end of February 1943, the Pathfinders had progressed from being a target-finding force to being a target-marking force, introducing and constantly refining systems of groundmarking and skymarking. On March 5, 1943 Bomber Command delivered the first blow in the so-called Battle of the Ruhr when a Main Force of 442 aircraft led by 36 PFF crews flew to Essen. Summer 1943 saw the introduction of a Master Bomber who remained over the target throughout the raid, instructing the Main Force where to aim its bombs.

THE AIR WAR OVER GERMANY

FROM 1942, BRITAIN AND THE UNITED STATES fielded powerful strategic bombing forces in the European theater. By the end of 1944, RAF Bomber Command's heavy bomber force was dominated by the Avro Lancaster. The duties of the US Eighth Air Force's strategic day-bombing campaign were shared by the Consolidated B-24 Liberator and the Boeing B-17 Flying Fortress. The Allied bomber chiefs' belief that strategic bombing could win the war was sorely tested in 1943–44 when both the Eighth Air Force and Bomber Command suffered heavy losses over Germany at the hands of the Luftwaffe's day and night fighters. During this period only about 35 percent of the Eighth Air Force's bomber crews could expect to complete a tour of 25 operational missions.

De Havilland Mosquito

Designed as an all-wooden unarmed day bomber, capable of outrunning any fighter, the versatile Mosquito also appeared in reconnaissance, ground-attack, night-fighter, and precision night-bomber versions. Some 6,700 were built during the war.

Engines	2 × 1,290 hp Rolls Royce Merlin	
Wingspan 54 ft (16.45 m)		Length 40 ft 6 in (12.34 m)
Top speed 408 mph (656 kph)		Crew 2
Armament 4 × 500-lb (225-kg) bombs internally plus 2 × 500-lb (225-kg) bombs underwing; or 1 × 4,000-lb (1,800-kg) bomb		

P-51D Mustang

With its ability to escort US bombers all the way to any target in continental Europe, the bubble-canopied Mustang, fitted with extra fuel tanks, changed the face of the air war in the spring of 1944. It was not only used for close escort duty, but also flew fighting patrols to seek out and destroy enemy day fighters.

Engine	1 × 1,490 hp Rolls Royce/Packard Merlin	
Wingspan 37 ft (11.27m)		Length 32 ft 3 in (9.83 m)
Top Speed 437 mph (437 mph)		Crew 1
Armament 6 × .50-in machine-guns plus 2 × 1,000-lb (450-kg) bombs or 6 × 5-in rockets on underwing racks		

Waist gunner position. In the G model (introduced autumn 1943) this was often glazed

Rear turret

Ball turret

Chin turret

Boeing B-17G Flying Fortress

The bomber's heavy defensive armament not only compromised its bombload but also, without long-range fighter escort, was not enough to ward off enemy fighters. By the end of the war some 13,000 B-17s had been built.

Engines	4 × 1,200 hp Wright Cyclone radials	
Wingspan 103 ft 9in (31. 6 m)		Length 74 ft 9 in (22.8 m)
Top speed 302 mph (486 kph)		Crew 10
Armament 13 × .50-in machine-guns; maximum bombload 12,800 lb (5, 800kg)		

Captain, navigator, 1st wireless operator, flight engineer

Mid-upper gun turret

Rear gun turret

Consolidated B-24J Liberator

Ease of manufacture led to the production of some 18,500 Liberators during the war, many of which served in the Pacific theater. Its cruising range was the highest of any land aircraft of World War II, but it was a poor formation keeper and, when damaged, it tended to catch fire or blow up very quickly.

Engines	4 × 1,200 hp Pratt and Whitney Twin Wasp radial	
Wingspan 110 ft (33.5 m)		Length 67 ft 2 in (20.5 m)
Top speed 300 mph (483 kph)		Crew 10
Armament 10 × .50-in machine-guns; maximum bombload 12,800 lb (5,800 kg)		

2nd wireless operator/air gunner

H2S downward-looking radar blister below fuselage

Avro Lancaster

Introduced to operations in March 1942, Lancasters of RAF Bomber Command flew some 156,000 sorties in World War II, dropping 609,000 tons of bombs. Originally designed to carry 4,000 lb (1,800 kg) of bombs, the Lancaster was adapted to carry much larger loads, culminating in the 22,000-lb (9,980-kg) Grand Slam bomb. Primarily a night bomber, the Lancaster flew some daring daylight operations, including a raid on Augsburg in which two Victoria Crosses were won. By 1945, Lancasters were routinely flying by day in loose formations, or "gaggles".

Engines	4 × 1,460 hp Rolls Royce Merlin	
Wingspan 102 ft (31.09 m)		Length 69 ft 6 in (21.18 m)
Top speed 275 mph (442 kph)		Crew 7
Armament 10 × .303-in machine-guns; maximum normal bombload 14,000 lb (6,350 kg)		

Messerschmitt Bf 110C-4

The Me 110 failed as an escort fighter in the Battle of Britain but proved successful as a night fighter over the Reich, particularly when equipped with radar and twin upward-firing "Schräge Musik" (Jazz Music) cannon mounted behind the cockpit. Some 6,000 Me 110s were produced by 1945.

Engines	2 × 1,475 hp Daimler Benz	
Wingspan 53 ft 4 in (16.25 m)		Length 39 ft 7 in (12.07 m)
Top speed 349 mph (560 kph)		Crew 3
Armament 2 × 30-mm cannon, 2 × 20-mm cannon 2 × 7.92-mm machine-guns		

Focke Wulf 190A-8

One of the great fighters of the war, the radial-engined FW 190 made its combat debut in the late summer of 1941, easily outclassing the Spitfire V. It was successfully adapted as a fighter-bomber and as a heavily armoured ground attack aircraft and in this role could carry up to 1,100 lb (500 kg) of bombs.

Engine	1 × 1,700 hp BMW radial	
Wingspan 34 ft 6 in (10.5 m)		Length 29 ft 5in (9 m)
Top speed 408 mph (656 kph)		Crew 1
Armament 2 × 13-mm machine-guns, 4 × 20-mm cannon		

"The sight approaching Hamburg was fantastic. It was as if a black swathe had been cut through a sea of light and flashes."

FLIGHT LIEUTENANT V WOOD, 12 SQUADRON, ON THE HAMBURG RAID OF JULY 24/25, 1943

The area bombing campaign reached its climax at the end of July 1943. The target was Hamburg, Germany's second city. For this operation, Bomber Command deployed a new weapon, codenamed "Window". More than a million metallized strips (the USAAF called the strips "Chaff") were dropped to jam German radar. On the night of July 24/25, Window achieved complete tactical surprise, disabling the Kammhuber Line and Hamburg's defenses. The raid overwhelmed the city's firefighting forces, dislocating communications and blocking streets.

Bomber Command struck Hamburg in force again on July 27/28. Over 700 aircraft set off a fire storm in eastern Hamburg. It reached its height in the small hours of the morning amid scenes of horror which were to be repeated in Dresden and Tokyo in 1945. A million of Hamburg's citizens fled into the countryside. Some 215,000 homes were destroyed, along with 600 factories and countless smaller workshops. There were two more raids on Hamburg, the last flown by 730 aircraft on August 2/3. The raids caused two months' lost industrial production, but many of Hamburg's aircraft plants,

Aftermath of the Hamburg air raids
In the four big raids of July and August 1943, 8,334 tons of bombs were dropped on Hamburg. Despite the unprecedented devastation, the city recovered with remarkable speed.

which lay at the heart of the Pointblank Directive, were quickly dispersed across the Reich by armaments minister, Albert Speer. Nor was the city's production of U-boats seriously hampered.

THE BATTLE OF BERLIN

Although Harris was happy to pay lipservice to Pointblank, he remained a fierce advocate of the area bombing of Germany's cities. On November 3, 1943 he told Churchill, "We can wreck Berlin from end to end if the US Army Air Force come in on it. It will cost us between 400 and 500 aircraft. It will cost Germany the war." The Battle of Berlin began on November 18 with a raid by 440 Lancasters. It was the first of 16 major raids on Berlin, combined with 19 attacks on other German cities. It was the last great drive to win the war by area bombing.

Berlin was too distant a target, perpetually cloud-covered and too big and well-defended. After the raids of August, the Germans had adopted new night-fighter tactics, in which twin-engined fighters were directed into the bomber streams by ground controllers. These tactics proved highly effective, particularly when the fighters were fitted with SN-2 radar, which was not affected by Window.

I set off in the direction of Hammerbrook because everything was still burning in the direction of the school where our post was. The air was hardly breathable and my injuries hurt hellishly. Dead lay everywhere. Most were naked because their clothes had been burnt away. All had become shrunken, really small, because of the heat.

HERBERT BRECHT, A TEENAGED FIREFIGHTER, ON THE HAMBURG FIRESTORM OF 27/28 JULY, 1943

On the night of March 30/31, 1944 Bomber Command mounted a raid on Nuremberg in which 95 out of 795 aircraft failed to return. This was the end of the Battle of Berlin, in which overall losses had now reached nearly 600 aircraft. Even Harris had to accept that such losses could not be sustained. In April 1944 he considered providing his bombers with escort fighters. Even under cover of darkness, Bomber Command was discovering what the USAAF had learned by day: before it could strike at the heart of the Third Reich, it had first to defeat the Luftwaffe.

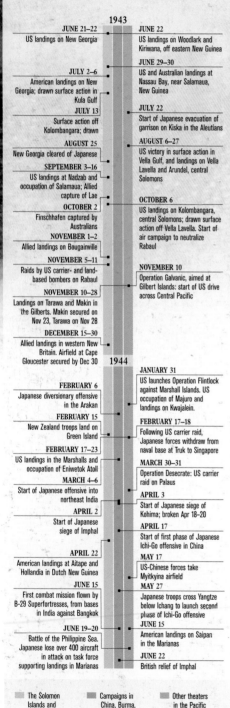

OPERATIONS IN ASIA AND THE PACIFIC

JUNE 1943–JUNE 1944

From June to October 1943 the Allies recorded minimal gains in the Pacific. In November, however, the American offensive on the Gilberts heralded the start of a drive across the Central and Southwest Pacific. It produced in June 1944 an overwhelming victory in the greatest carrier battle in history.

1943

JUNE 21–22
US landings on New Georgia

JUNE 22
US landings on Woodlark and Kiriwana, off eastern New Guinea

JUNE 29–30
US and Australian landings at Nassau Bay, near Salamaua, New Guinea

JULY 2–6
American landings on New Georgia; drawn surface action in Kula Gulf

JULY 13
Surface action off Kolombangara; drawn

JULY 22
Start of Japanese evacuation of garrison on Kiska in the Aleutians

AUGUST 25
New Georgia cleared of Japanese

AUGUST 6–27
US victory in surface action in Vella Gulf, and landings on Vella Lavella and Arundel, central Solomons

SEPTEMBER 3–16
US landings at Nadzab and occupation of Salamaua; Allied capture of Lae

OCTOBER 2
Finschhafen captured by Australians

OCTOBER 6
US landings on Kolombangara, central Solomons; drawn surface action off Vella Lavella. Start of air campaign to neutralize Rabaul

NOVEMBER 1–2
Allied landings on Bougainville

NOVEMBER 5–11
Raids by US carrier- and land-based bombers on Rabaul

NOVEMBER 10
Operation Galvanic, aimed at Gilbert Islands: start of US drive across Central Pacific

NOVEMBER 10–28
Landings on Tarawa and Makin in the Gilberts. Makin secured on Nov 23, Tarawa on Nov 28

DECEMBER 15–30
Allied landings in western New Britain. Airfield at Cape Gloucester secured by Dec 30

1944

JANUARY 31
US launches Operation Flintlock against Marshall Islands. US occupation of Majuro and landings on Kwajalein.

FEBRUARY 6
Japanese diversionary offensive in the Arakan

FEBRUARY 17–18
Following US carrier raid, Japanese forces withdraw from naval base at Truk to Singapore

FEBRUARY 15
New Zealand troops land on Green Island

FEBRUARY 17–23
US landings in the Marshalls and occupation of Eniwetok Atoll

MARCH 30–31
Operation Desecrate: US carrier raid on Palaus

MARCH 4–6
Start of Japanese offensive into northeast India

APRIL 3
Start of Japanese siege of Kohima; broken Apr 18–20

APRIL 2
Start of Japanese siege of Imphal

APRIL 17
Start of first phase of Japanese Ichi-Go offensive in China

APRIL 22
American landings at Aitape and Hollandia in Dutch New Guinea

MAY 17
US-Chinese forces take Myitkyina airfield

MAY 27
Japanese troops cross Yangtze below Ichang to launch second phase of Ichi-Go offensive

JUNE 15
First combat mission flown by B-29 Superfortresses, from bases in India against Bangkok

JUNE 15
American landings on Saipan in the Marianas

JUNE 19–20
Battle of the Philippine Sea. Japanese lose over 400 aircraft in attack on task force supporting landings in Marianas

JUNE 22
British relief of Imphal

- The Solomon Islands and New Guinea
- Campaigns in China, Burma, and India
- Other theaters in the Pacific War

AMERICAN OFFENSIVES IN THE PACIFIC

IN THE FIFTEEN MONTHS after the defeats in the Coral Sea in May and off Midway in June 1942, the Japanese suffered a series of reverses in eastern New Guinea, in the lower and central Solomons, and on Attu Island in the Aleutians. Still, the Japanese high command could take comfort from the fact that these defeats were local and in distant, remote theaters. None of the islands or places that had been lost possessed any real strategic significance. In addition, the Americans' very slow advances in the central Solomons and their lack of any real

progress in front of Lae and Salamaua in eastern New Guinea after February 1943 seemed to augur well for continuing Japanese resistance (see map page 176). After nearly two years of conflict they still held the Americans at arm's length from areas of political, economic, or military importance.

In reality, however, in the last quarter of 1943 the situation in the Pacific was transformed in two ways. First, in the Southwest Pacific the Americans adopted the island-hopping technique for the first time when they landed on Vella Lavella and

Taking the airfield at Tarawa
US Marines move out from a beachhead to assault the Japanese airstrip at Tarawa. The battle for Tarawa cost 1,000 American lives and had a profound effect on public opinion at home.

Attacking Japanese shipping
A B-25 Mitchell bomber attacks a Japanese freighter in Rabaul Harbour, New Britain. US strategy effectively isolated and neutralized the Japanese base there.

of six raids between November 5, 1943, and January 4, 1944. The raids effectively neutralized Rabaul, and thereafter the Americans completed the isolation of the base. In February 1944 they landed on Green Island and in the Admiralties, after which they also moved against central New Guinea. Rabaul itself remained in Japanese hands until September 1945, but the forces left there were helpless.

THE CENTRAL PACIFIC

In any case, by February 1944 the main focus of strategic attention had shifted northward. The raids on Rabaul in November 1943 were part of a series of attacks that paved the way for the main American effort in the Central Pacific. No fewer than six fleet, five light, and eight escort carriers of the Fifth Fleet were concentrated in support of landings on Makin and Tarawa in the Gilbert Islands on November 20. Both islands were secured within three days.

Tarawa came to acquire a certain notoriety in American folklore as a symbol of the supposed costliness of such amphibious landings. Photographs published in the press of corpses floating in the sea reinforced the image of what were dubbed the "bloody beaches of Tarawa." Despite the shocked public reaction in the United States to the cost of the landing, the casualty list—1,009 dead and 2,101 wounded—pales into insignificance when compared with the average of 19,014 dead incurred by the Soviet Union every day of the Great Patriotic War.

thereby bypassed the Japanese garrisons on New Georgia and the island of Kolombangara. The development marked a change in American policy: their goal was no longer the recapture of the Japanese base at Rabaul in New Britain. Instead, they would side-step and isolate what should have been the keystone of Japanese defense. Second, during 1943 the US Navy commissioned into service a tonnage of warships equivalent to the size of the entire Japanese fleet in December 1941. The acquisition of carriers in such numbers as virtually to ensure victory allowed the Americans to launch Operation Galvanic, an offensive in the Gilbert Islands, in November 1943. This was the first operation in a drive across the Central Pacific (see map page 255).

The policy of island-hopping and the American superiority in carrier numbers came together in November 1943, when Rabaul

was reinforced by Japanese carrier air groups and cruiser formations detached from the fleet anchorage at Truk to the north. Warned by signals intelligence, the Americans used carrier task groups to savage both the carrier groups and the cruisers in a series

Aftermath of Tarawa
Dead US Marines lie among the wreckage of vehicles on the beach at Tarawa, November 22, 1943. The Japanese defenders were well dug in and fiercely resisted the US assault.

Attack on Nadzab, September 5, 1943
The first airborne assault of the Pacific War on Nadzab was key to the Allied campaign to seize Lae and central New Guinea. Paratroops from the US 503rd Parachute Infantry descend from C-47 planes, while in the distance another battalion descends against a smokescreen.

"The enemy received all his supplies from the air, while we had to swallow our tears and throw away strategic positions because of supply difficulties."

LIEUTENANT COLONEL YOSHIHARA TSUTOMU,
CHIEF OF STAFF, JAPANESE 18TH ARMY, ON THE FIGHTING AT LAE

AMERICANS GAIN THE UPPER HAND

On New Guinea, meanwhile, the Allies were helping to complete the isolation of Rabaul. With American forces having secured Lae in central New Guinea during September 1943 and the Australians having taken Finschhafen the following month, December saw American forces landing at Cape Gloucester on New Britain, at the opposite end of the island from Rabaul.

In January 1944 the Americans moved against the Marshall Islands in the Western Pacific. When the island of Kwajalein had been taken, an American carrier force—with four fleet and six light carriers, plus six new battleships—launched an offensive throughout the Western Pacific. With contributions from both submarines and surface units, the attack on the Japanese anchorage at Truk in the Carolines on February 17 resulted in the destruction of three light cruisers, three destroyers, and three minor warships,

Bombs over New Guinea
Bombs from aircraft of the Fifth US Air Force fall on Hollandia in New Guinea. Some Japanese units on New Guinea stubbornly refused to surrender, even after defeat.

along with 32 service auxiliaries, merchantmen, and oilers. The shipping sunk—almost 200,000 tons—made this the most costly single day in naval history.

After the collapse of Japanese resistance in the Marshalls, it was clear that the fleet could not sustain itself at Truk. The fleet abandoned the anchorage, and its shipping, and established itself at Singapore. The new base was close to supplies of oil and gave the Japanese carriers the chance to train groups to replace those lost at Rabaul. Placing a safe distance between the fleet and American carrier formations, however, was achieved only at the cost of giving the Americans a free hand in the Western Pacific.

The result was devastating. On March 30, 1944, an American carrier raid on Koror in the Palaus destroyed 11 minor warships and no fewer than 22 service auxiliaries, oilers, and merchantmen, a total

of almost 130,000 tons. Meanwhile, Liberators from the Fifth Air Force struck Hollandia on the north coast of Dutch New Guinea. Repeated raids in the first half of April destroyed the Japanese 6th Air Division, and paved the way for American landings at Hollandia and Aitape on April 22.

WESTERN NEW GUINEA

The ease with which the Japanese air and ground forces were overwhelmed in these exchanges provided encouragement for the Americans to look west. They recast their plans to provide for landings on Wakde Island and in the Arare–Toem area of western New Guinea on May 17 and on Biak 10 days later. At the same time the Japanese, in the middle of enforced command changes, recognized that they could no longer defend their intended centers of resistance. A plan to fall back to new positions was compromised, however, by the loss of the equivalent of a division when US submarines sank transport vessels at sea. The Japanese were forced instead to base their resistance on Sorong and Halmahera. In just 17 days after American forces had landed at Hollandia, the Japanese high command had in effect drawn back its proposed front line a distance of over 1,000 miles (1,600 km).

AMPHIBIOUS LANDINGS

AMPHIBIOUS WARFARE has been used since the time of the Ancient Greeks. The American armed forces developed the technique in the interwar years, learning much from the mistakes made by the British during their disastrous 1915 landings at Gallipoli in World War I. By 1941 the Americans were well rehearsed in getting thousands of soldiers and their equipment from sea to shore, often under intense enemy fire. Such landings were complex, however, and sometimes did go wrong, as they did at Guadacanal, where men were separated from their units and units from their supplies.

The US forces were formidably well equipped. In the course of World War II the Americans produced 23,398 units of the 36-ft (11-m) Landing Craft, Vehicle Personnel (LCVP), the standard assault vessel that could carry 36 combat-equipped soldiers or 3.5 tons of cargo. They also built 11,392 of the 50-ft (15.24-m) Landing Craft, Mechanized (LCM), which was designed to carry tanks and other armored vehicles, and more than 1,000 of the Landing Craft, Infantry (LCI)—158-ft (48.15-m) sea-going amphibious vessels capable of carrying as many as 200 men. Landing craft were also used as fighting vessels, and many were equipped to provide fire support with rockets, machine-guns, mortars, and even large deck guns.

Amphibious landings were always risky, despite intense preparation. At Tarawa, for example, despite the "softening up" of the landing zone with extensive shellfire, the landing craft ran aground on reefs and the Marines were forced to wade hundreds of yards through the surf across razor-sharp coral.

American amphibious operations increased in size and complexity throughout the Pacific war. The final assault, on the Japanese island of Okinawa, in April 1945, involved 318 US combat ships, 1,139 auxiliary vessels, 1,000 amphibious vehicles, and 500,000 men.

Landing Vehicle, Tank (LVT)

The LVT was an amphibious armored vehicle designed to carry troops into combat. Tracked like a tank, it also provided fire support. Some were equipped with flame-throwers.

Crew/cargo compartment could carry a load of 2.5 tons

Six-wheel drive

Tyre pressure could be controlled by the driver from the dashboard

DUKW

This US amphibious vehicle was capable of carrying 25 soldiers and their equipment. At sea it could maintain a speed of 5 knots.

Disembarkation

US troops storm ashore in the Pacific. The skills of amphibious operations became better honed as more were launched. Despite rigorous training, there was no substitute for experience.

Until this stage of the conflict Japanese policy had defined a perimeter that ran from Saipan through Truk to Timor as the line on which they would make their main defensive effort. Now they established a new defensive line stretching from Saipan through the Carolines to the Vogelkop Peninsula in New Guinea. The Japanese high command ordered forces east of the line to resist American advances in order to buy time for the preparation of defenses to the west.

The Japanese Navy now had five fleet and four light carriers and some 450 carrier aircraft being readied for battle. It was hoped that land-based and carrier-borne aircraft would be able to complement one another and compensate for their separate numerical inferiority to any American carrier force that moved into the Western Pacific. The Japanese also hoped that the next American move might take enemy ships in the direction of the Palau Islands, where they could be attacked by land-based aircraft from the Marianas, the Carolines, the Philippines, and western New Guinea. This second hope proved to be self-delusion.

In New Guinea, American forces came ashore as planned at Arare and Wakde on May 17–18 and on Biak on May 27. Despite having abandoned their former defensive line, the Japanese chose to give battle in defense of Biak. The island's garrison continued to offer serious resistance until July 22, and it was not until August 20 that the Americans declared the island secured. But this resistance, during which Japanese defenders had to resort to cannibalism to survive, was isolated and could not be supported. The Japanese, meanwhile, moved about 170 aircraft to airstrips in the western Carolines and on the Vogelkop Peninsula in readiness for operations, and a battle force sailed from the Philippines on June 10. But malaria swept through the aircrews sent to the south and Japanese land-based air power was neutralized without battle.

At the same time as the Japanese battle force arrived in Batjan on June 11, American carriers struck at Guam, Saipan, and Tinian in the Mariana Islands. The Japanese at once recognized that they would have to fight in defense of the Marianas. On June 12 they suspended the defense of Biak and ordered their forces to regroup in readiness for the imminent sortie into the Philippine Sea.

THE BATTLE FOR SAIPAN

American formations came ashore on Saipan on June 15. On the same day 47 B-29 Superfortresses, operating from India via the Chengtu airfield in southern Hunan in China, bombed the steel factory in Yawata on Kyushu. Aside from raids on the Kuriles, this marked the first raid on the Japanese Home Islands since the Doolittle Raid of April 1942. The coincidence of timing was appropriate: once in American possession, the Marianas would become home to the strategic Allied bombing campaign that would begin in November 1944 and that would result in widespread devastation throughout the Japanese Home Islands after March 1945.

The campaigns on the various islands in the Marianas proved very short. Saipan was declared secure on July 9, but in fact the Americans had cleared all but the rugged northern tip of the island within seven days of the landings. The campaign was effectively over after June 30, with the exception of a final *banzai* charge—named for a Japanese war cry—around Makunsha on July 7. The 32,000-strong Japanese garrison died almost to the last man. Over the previous two years the Americans had become familiar with the practice of Japanese defenders fighting to the death. The situation on Saipan, however, was different in one crucial respect. It was the first place visited by the Pacific war that was home to a sizable civilian population. More than 22,000 of these civilians chose to join the service personnel in death rather than allow themselves to be taken prisoner. Whole families perished, with parents killing their children before killing themselves. Most of the suicides took place on two high bluffs: the 1,000-ft (305-m) Suicide Cliff, over which hundreds of people threw themselves onto the jagged rocks below, and the 80-ft (24-m) drop into the ocean near Marpi Point. There the dead and dying lay so thick in the water that they fouled the propellers of destroyers trying to rescue survivors. In spite of this, hundreds of civilians were plucked to safety.

GREAT MARIANAS TURKEY SHOOT

The first days of the campaign on Saipan saw the covering American carrier task group assault various Japanese bases in the southern Bonins and on Guam and Rota. The Japanese had mustered five fleet and four light carriers, in the hope that their carrier-borne and land-based air formations would complement one another and ensure a rough numerical balance with US carrier aircraft. But by destroying more than 150 aircraft on various islands before June 16, the American carriers had broken the effectiveness of Japanese land-based aviation three days before

Casualty on the beach
A US Marine doubles up as a Japanese sniper's bullet strikes its target during the American landings on Saipan in June 1944.

ANTIBIOTICS

THE USE OF ANTIBIOTICS—SUBSTANCES DERIVED from living organisms, usually bacteria or molds, that kill microorganisms or inhibit their growth—dramatically reduced the number of wounded who died in World War II. The most important of these substances was penicillin, discovered in 1929 by Scottish biologist Alexander Fleming. During the early years of the war Britain's laboratories could not cope with the demand for penicillin, so the United States agreed to produce it on behalf of the British. It was a timely decision, since only six months later the United States was dragged into the war by the Japanese attack on Pearl Harbor and needed penicillin for its own wounded service personnel. The first batches of American antibiotics were administered in 1943 to men of the US Eighth Air Force stationed in Britain.

Penicillin was rationed at first, but by 1944–45 plentiful stocks became available. Although it is impossible to say how many lives were saved by antibiotics—improved surgical techniques also played a part—only 4 percent of the wounded died, the lowest figure in military history until that point.

Saving lives
American medics treat casualties in a portable surgical unit in Burma. Penicillin counters bacteria that cause infections such as pneumonia and diphtheria.

A rare drug
An early ampule of penicillin produced at the Squibb Plant in New Brunswick, New Jersey. Because of its rarity, penicillin was restricted to military uses.

Making penicillin, the "wonder drug"
Bottles of liquid media are planted with penicillin seed by means of a spray gun under sterile conditions. There are several hundred different species of mold, but only one was suitable for yielding the powerful substance that combatted bacterial infection.

Physical conditions of many were pitiful. Most of them were skeleton thin, as they had no nourishment for many days. Many were suffering from shock caused by the shelling and bombing, and fright because they did not have the vaguest idea as to what we would do to them. Civilians caught in a war that was not of their making.

ROBERT F. GRAF, MARINE PRIVATE, ON TAKING CIVILIAN JAPANESE PRISONERS ON SAIPAN

the Battle of the Philippine Sea was even joined. The damage caused by the attacks wrecked the Japanese intention to defend the Marianas. Moreover, by choosing to stand off the Marianas and to fight defensively, US admiral Raymond Spruance was able to concentrate a massive superiority of numbers, specifically fighters. This allowed him to give battle in front

of and above the five formations that made up Task Force 58. What made the American tactics possible was radar and radio facilities, which meant that they were able to locate and report the position of enemy forces. The Japanese did not realize the effectiveness of such technology, and had no answer to it.

The Japanese carrier force, having refueled the previous day, found the American carrier force some 200 miles (320 km) west of the Marianas late on June 18. It was too late to launch a strike operation, partly because of the hazards of landing on carriers in the dark. The next day, however, the Japanese had not managed to get their aircraft into the air before they had lost two fleet carriers, both torpedoed by submarines. Those attacks that were mounted fared disastrously. Only the first and third strike missions managed to make proper contact with American groups, and they had little effect. In the course of the day just two American carriers and one battleship incurred only minor damage. Meanwhile American aircraft accounted for some 80 Japanese land-based

aircraft on or over the southern Marianas and about 360 of the 450 carrier aircraft with which the Japanese had opened proceedings. The Americans themselves lost just 18 fighters and 12 other aircraft. So one-sided were the air battles of June 19, 1944, that they came to be dubbed "the Great Marianas Turkey Shoot." The following day saw the Americans sink a third carrier, and the Japanese fleet was reduced to just 35 aircraft. The battle was a defeat from which Japanese carrier aviation never recovered. For the Americans, victory opened the route across the Pacific to the Philippines and Formosa.

THE ALLIES' GREAT OFFENSIVES
1944

THE SECOND HALF OF 1944 WITNESSED DRAMATIC
DEVELOPMENTS IN EVERY THEATER OF WAR. FOLLOWING
THE SEIZURE OF THE MARIANAS, THE AMERICANS LANDED
IN THE PHILIPPINES AND FINALLY CRUSHED THE JAPANESE
FLEET. A MAJOR SOVIET OFFENSIVE ALMOST DESTROYED
THE GERMAN ARMY GROUP CENTER AND REACHED
POLAND'S VISTULA RIVER. IN ITALY THE WESTERN ALLIES
ENTERED ROME AND ADVANCED NORTHWARD. FINALLY
THE LONG-AWAITED SECOND FRONT IN CONTINENTAL
EUROPE WAS OPENED WITH THE ALLIED LANDINGS IN
NORMANDY, FRANCE, ON JUNE 6.

7

US troops landing on Leyte
A long campaign to drive the Japanese out
of the Philippines began with the landings
on Leyte in October 1944. The Japanese
reaction to the landings led to the last
major naval battle in the Pacific, in which
the Japanese fleet was totally crippled.

THE AXIS IN RETREAT

IT WAS CLEAR BY LATE 1943 THAT THERE COULD BE ONLY ONE OUTCOME OF THE WAR AGAINST NAZI GERMANY AND JAPAN. MUCH, HOWEVER, STILL NEEDED TO BE DONE, AND TOUGH CHALLENGES AND HARD FIGHTING LAY AHEAD FOR THE ALLIES. WHILE THE PACIFIC WAS VERY MUCH THE PROVINCE OF THE AMERICANS, THE WAR IN EUROPE REQUIRED EVER MORE CAREFUL COORDINATION BETWEEN THE SOVIET UNION AND ITS WESTERN ALLIES.

B Y THE MIDDLE OF 1944 Japan's situation was growing increasingly parlous with, in particular, the lack of raw materials beginning to make itself very much felt. The passage of rubber, tin, oil, and other vital items from Southeast Asia had all but dried up as a result of a campaign waged by US submarines—a campaign so successful that a lack of targets would result in the withdrawal of some submarines from the Pacific. Massive B-29 bombers, flying from airfields in China, were also beginning to bomb Japan itself. Admiral Chester Nimitz's advance across the Central Pacific had reached the Marianas, which were secured by early August. He had also broken the back of Japanese naval airpower at the Battle of the Philippine Sea in June 1944. General Douglas MacArthur had isolated Rabaul, the main Japanese base in the Southwest Pacific and had almost completed the clearance of New Guinea. He was now planning to liberate the Philippines, beginning with the island of Leyte.

US OPERATIONS IN THE PACIFIC

Nimitz had been ordered to prepare an assault on Formosa (Taiwan). However, during the summer of 1944 it became apparent that the Japanese were reinforcing Formosa. They had also launched an offensive in China that was beginning to threaten the US air bases there. In view of this, the US planners decided that operations would have to be accelerated. They even considered bypassing the Philippines and Formosa and launching a direct assault on the Japanese Home Islands. Both Nimitz and MacArthur objected to this, arguing that it would be impossible without securing the southern and central Philippines first. MacArthur also believed that if the northern and main island in

the Philippines, Luzon, could be seized, a landing on Formosa would be unnecessary. Nimitz disagreed, arguing that an attack on Formosa would remove the need to occupy Luzon. In early October 1944 it was decided that after securing Leyte, MacArthur was to liberate Luzon, while Nimitz prepared to attack Iwo Jima, followed by Okinawa. The projected Formosa operation was left in abeyance.

MacArthur's landing on Leyte on October 20 provoked an immediate Japanese response. The Combined Fleet set sail, its object the destruction of the US Third and Seventh Fleets, and the amphibious shipping in Leyte Gulf. It was to prove a disaster. The Japanese lost 28 warships, including four carriers. The battle also witnessed a further indication of growing Japanese desperation—the extensive use of suicide aircraft to destroy Allied ships. It was a tactic that was to be used increasingly, but it had little effect on the American advance. MacArthur succeeded in securing Leyte before the end of December and prepared to land on Luzon.

The other active theater of war in the Far East was Burma, which was essentially run by the British. After the gloom of 1942, the first Chindit expedition deep behind the Japanese lines in Burma had at least shown that British troops could match their opponents in the jungle. The time had now come to begin

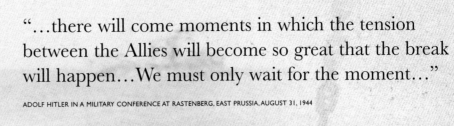

"...there will come moments in which the tension between the Allies will become so great that the break will happen...We must only wait for the moment..."

ADOLF HITLER IN A MILITARY CONFERENCE AT RASTENBERG, EAST PRUSSIA, AUGUST 31, 1944

driving the Japanese out. Lord Louis Mountbatten, the Allied commander, explained his strategy at the conference convened by Churchill and Roosevelt at Cairo in late November 1943. The Chinese premier, Chiang Kai-shek, was also present. Mountbatten envisaged an offensive in Burma's coastal region, the Arakan, a further Chindit operation in central Burma, and an assault by the Chinese into northern Burma. However, Chiang Kai-shek would only agree to the last if there was a major amphibious operation in the Bay of Bengal to capture a port and so improve the supply of equipment to his forces. It was also decided at the conference to maintain the offensive in Italy, even if it meant delaying the planned cross-Channel invasion of Normandy—Operation Overlord—and to give more help to the partisans in the Balkans.

CONFERENCE AT TEHRAN

Churchill and Roosevelt then left for Tehran, in Iran, to meet Stalin. Overlord was foremost on Stalin's mind, and he made it clear that he would accept no postponement to the agreed date of May 1944. While he liked the idea of a simultaneous landing in the south of France, he dismissed the Western Allies' Italian and Balkan strategy. Churchill and Roosevelt therefore confirmed Overlord for May 1944, and, in return, Stalin agreed to mount a simultaneous major offensive on the Eastern Front to prevent the Germans from switching troops to the west. The Western

Allies remained eager for the early capture of Rome. This included mounting an amphibious landing south of the city, which meant that it was impossible to provide sufficient amphibious shipping for a major operation in the Bay of Bengal. This had to be postponed, to the displeasure of the Chinese premier.

Even so, the British began to advance into the Arakan in January 1944. They were aware that the Japanese had been planning an invasion of India, and although they were ready for it, there were four months of bitter fighting before the Japanese finally halted their attacks in July 1944. From this point, the British embarked on an offensive against the Japanese. The Chinese began to advance into northern Burma, while other US-led Chinese forces built a road from India to connect with China.

EASTERN FRONT OFFENSIVES

On the Eastern Front the Soviet Union launched a massive offensive—Operation Bagration—in Byelorussia on June 22. Thrusting into Poland, the Red Army tore the heart out of the German Army Group Center. As Soviet forces closed on Warsaw, the Polish Home Army staged an uprising against the German garrison, but the Red Army now halted its offensive, leaving the Poles to their fate. Farther south, the Red Army advanced into Romania and Bulgaria, forcing them to change sides. It also crossed the border into Hungary, Hitler's last remaining ally in southeast Europe.

PLANNING FOR D-DAY

For the Western Allies the high point of 1944 was undoubtedly D-Day, June 6, when they launched their invasion of Normandy in France. Their attention had been firmly focused on such an invasion from the end of 1943, but it was an operation that had taken almost four years to plan and prepare. Even while Britain had faced invasion in the summer and fall of 1940, Churchill had

The invasion of Normandy
A British-manned six-wheel amphibious vehicle sets out for the shore during the Allied landings on beaches in Normandy in June 1944. While the landings themselves met with limited German opposition, it was to take many weeks for the Allied forces to break out of Normandy.

been looking for ways to strike back at Hitler. On October 5, 1940, he had issued a directive calling for plans to be drawn up for an assault on continental Europe, culminating in an advance to the Ruhr in Germany. At the time Britain had lacked the resources, especially in amphibious capability, to make this possible in the short term.

Late in 1941 the Combined Commanders committee was set up. Consisting of senior naval, army, and air force officers, it became the focus for planning an invasion of continental Europe. It began to gather intelligence on the German defenses in western Europe and to consider where an assault force might be landed. Soviet calls for the opening of a "second front" and US insistence that a cross-Channel invasion should be the

Allied priority concentrated minds still further on the problem. The British, however, were certain that an early invasion was not possible. This was seemingly reinforced by the abortive raid by a largely Canadian force on the French port of Dieppe in August 1942. Few troops managed to get off the beach and casualties were very heavy. But the lessons learned were to prove invaluable.

The Allies now pursued their Mediterranean strategy and the numerous landing operations which took place served to develop the amphibious warfare techniques that were an essential prerequisite for a successful invasion. The decision at the Trident

Conference in Washington, D.C., in May 1943 that a cross-Channel invasion would be mounted in May 1944 accelerated planning. The Combined Commanders committee had concluded that Normandy provided the best option, and an Anglo–US team drew up a detailed plan on this basis.

GERMAN DEFENSES IN THE WEST

On the German side, work had begun in 1940 to build what Hitler was to call the Atlantic Wall—a series of coastal batteries and strongpoints stretching from northern Norway to the Pyrenees. Aside from this, German attention was fixed firmly on the

Hungarian Jews rounded up by SS
In June 1944 the Third Reich was under increasing pressure from all sides, and many of its extermination camps were being liberated by the Red Army. Yet the policy of eradicating the Jews continued, with some 450,000 Hungarian Jews being rounded up between March and July to be sent to their deaths in the camps.

Eastern Front and its forces in western Europe were generally low grade. Indeed, France itself became a sanatorium for divisions decimated in the Soviet Union. Once they had been rebuilt, they returned to the east. Not until the late fall of 1943 was the growing threat of a cross-Channel invasion recognized. Hitler sent Rommel on a tour of the Atlantic Wall and the German forces in France and the Low Countries began to be strengthened.

By the end of 1943 the Allied command team for the invasion of Normandy, Operation Overlord, was in place. Eisenhower, the overall commander, and Montgomery, the groundforce commander, enlarged the existing plan by insisting on an initial assault by five, rather than three, divisions. But much still needed to be done. First, the Allies had to be sure of air supremacy over the landing area. To this end, their air forces set about a systematic degradation of the Luftwaffe in France and the Low Countries. They then switched their attention to the goal of sealing off Normandy —by attacking roads and railroads—in order to prevent the rapid deployment of German reinforcements. They had to be careful, though, to scatter their attacks so as not to draw the attention of the Germans to the assault area.

This itself was part of an elaborate deception plan code-named Bodyguard. One element of this was to pose a threat to Norway, which was partially achieved by stationing a mythical British army in Scotland. Similarly, the equally make-believe US First Army Group was stationed in southeast England to make the Germans believe that the attack would come across the Pas de Calais, the narrowest part of the English Channel. These parts of Bodyguard were remarkably successful in encouraging the Germans to maintain an unnecessarily large garrison in Norway and in believing that the Pas de Calais was the most likely point of attack by the Allies.

Among the lessons learned from Dieppe was that to land at a port was to court disaster, since it was likely to be heavily fortified. Open beaches would have to be used, but this would create resupply problems. Two massive artificial harbors, called

Stalin, Roosevelt, and Churchill at Tehran
During their conference in Tehran, in November 1943, the three Allied leaders confirmed that there would be simultaneous assaults on Germany from east and west in the summer of 1944. Stalin also agreed to declare war on Japan once Germany had been vanquished.

Mulberries, were constructed, to deal with this problem. Positioned off the beaches, they would enable ships to land supplies and reinforcements. Fuel was taken care of through the construction of an underwater pipeline, PLUTO (Pipeline Under The Ocean). Another Dieppe lesson was the need for modified tanks that could get ashore with the leading assault troops and enable them to overcome obstacles on the beaches and beyond. A range of specialized armor was developed, among which were swimming tanks, bridge-layers, and tanks for clearing mines.

D-DAY POSTPONED
Because of the need to bring amphibious shipping back from the Mediterranean, D-Day was postponed until June 5. After the final invasion rehearsals on beaches in Britain, which resembled those in Normandy, the assault troops were deployed to sealed camps close to their embarkation ports. On May 31 the loading of the ships began and messages began to be broadcast to the French Resistance, which had an important role to play in helping to seal off Normandy from the Germans. All now depended on the uncertain weather.

"He told me that if Overlord failed, the United States would have lost a battle, but for the British it would be the end of their military capability."

US PRESIDENTIAL ENVOY AVERELL HARRIMAN
ON A MEETING WITH CHURCHILL, MAY 4, 1944

THE WESTERN FRONT

JUNE 6, 1944–JANUARY 8, 1945

After six weeks of grim fighting in Normandy, the Allies broke out and it seemed that the war might be won before the end of 1944. Supply problems and a rejuvenated German defense, culminating in a major counteroffensive in December, put paid to this hope.

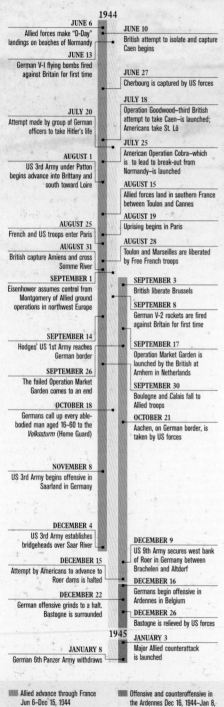

1944

JUNE 6
Allied forces make "D-Day" landings on beaches of Normandy

JUNE 10
British attempt to isolate and capture Caen begins

JUNE 13
German V-I flying bombs fired against Britain for first time

JUNE 27
Cherbourg is captured by US forces

JULY 18
Operation Goodwood–third British attempt to take Caen–is launched; Americans take St. Lô

JULY 20
Attempt made by group of German officers to take Hitler's life

JULY 25
American Operation Cobra–which is to lead to break-out from Normandy–is launched

AUGUST 1
US 3rd Army under Patton begins advance into Brittany and south toward Loire

AUGUST 15
Allied forces land in southern France between Toulon and Cannes

AUGUST 19
Uprising begins in Paris

AUGUST 25
French and US troops enter Paris

AUGUST 28
Toulon and Marseilles are liberated by Free French troops

AUGUST 31
British capture Amiens and cross Somme River

SEPTEMBER 1
Eisenhower assumes control from Montgomery of Allied ground operations in northwest Europe

SEPTEMBER 3
British liberate Brussels

SEPTEMBER 8
German V-2 rockets are fired against Britain for first time

SEPTEMBER 14
Hodges' US 1st Army reaches German border

SEPTEMBER 17
Operation Market Garden is launched by the British at Arnhem in Netherlands

SEPTEMBER 26
The failed Operation Market Garden comes to an end

SEPTEMBER 30
Boulogne and Calais fall to Allied troops

OCTOBER 18
Germans call up every able-bodied man aged 16–60 to the *Volkssturm* (Home Guard)

OCTOBER 21
Aachen, on German border, is taken by US forces

NOVEMBER 8
US 3rd Army begins offensive in Saarland in Germany

DECEMBER 4
US 3rd Army establishes bridgeheads over Saar River

DECEMBER 9
US 9th Army secures west bank of Roer in Germany between Brachelen and Altdorf

DECEMBER 15
Attempt by Americans to advance to Roer dams is halted

DECEMBER 16
Germans begin offensive in Ardennes in Belgium

DECEMBER 22
German offensive grinds to a halt. Bastogne is surrounded

DECEMBER 26
Bastogne is relieved by US forces

1945

JANUARY 3
Major Allied counterattack is launched

JANUARY 8
German 6th Panzer Army withdraws

▓ Allied advance through France
Jun 6–Dec 15, 1944

▓ Allied advance through the Low Countries Sept 3–Dec 15, 1944

▓ Offensive and counteroffensive in the Ardennes Dec 16, 1944–Jan 8, 1945

▓ Other events

ADVANCE INTO NORTHWEST EUROPE

BY THE END OF MAY the Allies were ready to launch Operation Overlord, their long-planned invasion of Normandy. It was intended to begin with landings on five beaches to the east of the Cotentin peninsula on June 5. However, by the 3rd it was clear that a depression was *en route* from the Atlantic, making conditions unfavorable for a landing. When it was predicted that the weather would be slightly better on the 6th, Eisenhower decided to postpone D-Day by 24 hours. He knew that he was taking a gamble and realized only too well that if disaster struck it might be many months before the invasion could be remounted.

Soon after dusk fell on June 5, 1944, two RAF bomber squadrons flew over the Straits of Dover and Boulogne, dropping strips of aluminum foil. This was intended to produce a picture on German radar screens of an invasion fleet heading for the Pas de Calais. Other bombers flew over the base of the Cotentin peninsula dropping dummy parachutes and devices to simulate small-arms fire to the south of where two US airborne divisions were to land.

AIRBORNE LANDINGS

Preceded by pathfinders to mark the drop zones on the ground, the US 82nd and 101st Airborne Divisions began to jump from their aircraft at 1:30 am on June 6. Their task was to secure the area west of Utah beach to the Merderet River and block German reinforcements moving to the beach. High winds, coupled with the fact that many of the pathfinders' indicators on the ground failed to work, resulted in very scattered drops. Once they landed,

Gliders taking part in the D-Day landings
Follow-up waves of the two US airborne divisions were brought in by glider. The operation was, however, fraught with risk, since crashes, collisions, and landings in the wrong place were frequently associated with gliders.

Beach landings at Omaha
Pinned down on the beach by enemy fire, US troops desperately seek cover behind German obstacles. Of the five beaches on which Allied troops landed on June 6, Omaha proved to be by far the most difficult to secure.

their fire onto the coastal batteries. The Germans opened fire first, engaging two destroyers off Utah at 5:05 am. The bombardment groups then set about pulverizing the defenses.

The assault troops now began to scramble down the netting on the sides of their transport vessels and into the flat-bottomed landing craft that pitched in the rough seas alongside. Many men had been seasick during the crossing and few had had much sleep. Patrol boats, equipped with radar and radio, guided in the landing craft, which were supported by other amphibious vessels armed with rocket batteries and guns.

LANDINGS AT UTAH AND OMAHA

Utah beach was the responsibility of General Lawton Collins' US VII Corps. The beach itself—1.5 miles (2.4 km) long—was backed by a sea wall. Behind lay a partially flooded area traversed by causeways, some of which were being secured by the 101st Airborne Division. Just one German battalion defended the beach, with one other in support. It had been intended to launch Sherman DD swimming tanks with the leading US troops 5 miles (8 km) out from the beach, but because of the conditions this was reduced to 1 mile (1.6 km).

D-Day "crickets"
Making a noise like crickets, these devices were used by paratroops to find each other.

the paratroops were disoriented and it took time for parties to gather. Luckily, the Germans, who believed the weather was too poor for the invasion to take place, were initially caught by surprise. This enabled the 101st to secure some of the exits from Utah and for the 82nd to capture Ste. Mère-Eglise, which would prove critical during the next 48 hours, but it was unable to seize crossings over the Merderet (see map page 222).

At the eastern end of the Allied landing area, the British 6th Airborne Division had a similar task. It was to land between the Dives and Orne Rivers, secure bridges over both, and provide a shoulder for the troops landing on Sword beach. The British paratroops experienced the same problems as the Americans over scattered drops. However, five out of six gliders full of infantry landed in precisely the right spot—close by bridges over the Orne River and Caen Canal, which were then captured intact. A coastal battery at Merville, which threatened the eastern flank of Sword beach, was also captured.

While the Allied airborne forces had been in action, aircraft from RAF Bomber Command had been attacking the coastal batteries. Low cloud, however, made accurate bombing difficult. With the coming of daylight, American bombers made similar attacks. Now came the turn of the Allied navies. Their first task was to clear the water of mines, and by 2:00 am minesweepers were hard at work. Each

of the five beaches had a naval bombardment force allocated to it, consisting of larger warships—battleships, monitors, cruisers—11,000 yd (10,000 m) offshore, and destroyers 5,500 yd (5,000 m) from the coast. Bombers laid a smokescreen to help protect the ships, and spotter planes were used to direct

DWIGHT D EISENHOWER

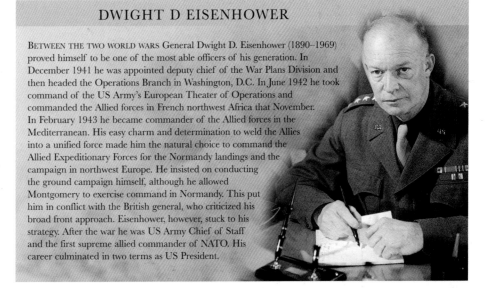

BETWEEN THE TWO WORLD WARS General Dwight D. Eisenhower (1890–1969) proved himself to be one of the most able officers of his generation. In December 1941 he was appointed deputy chief of the War Plans Division and then headed the Operations Branch in Washington, D.C. In June 1942 he took command of the US Army's European Theater of Operations and commanded the Allied forces in French northwest Africa that November. In February 1943 he became commander of the Allied forces in the Mediterranean. His easy charm and determination to weld the Allies into a unified force made him the natural choice to command the Allied Expeditionary Forces for the Normandy landings and the campaign in northwest Europe. He insisted on conducting the ground campaign himself, although he allowed Montgomery to exercise command in Normandy. This put him in conflict with the British general, who criticized his broad front approach. Eisenhower, however, stuck to his strategy. After the war he was US Army Chief of Staff and the first supreme allied commander of NATO. His career culminated in two terms as US President.

NORMANDY
JUN 6, 1944–JUL 24, 1944

- ➤ British and Canadian advance
- ➤ US advance
- ➤ German advance
- ⚐ Allied airborne landing
- ◼ Mulberry harbor

- —— Allied front line Jun 6/7
- —— German front line Jun 12
- —— German front line Jul 24
- ---- German defense line
- ---- Railroad line

D-Day landings June 5/6
On the night of June 5/6, a total of 75 convoys carrying five Allied infantry divisions (3rd and 50th British, 3rd Canadian, and 1st and 4th US) crossed the English Channel to land on five beaches. Only at Omaha did they encounter serious opposition, though the Germans mounted a brief counterattack against the landings on Sword.

❶ Night of Jun 5/6
British 6th Airborne Division lands east of Sword beach

❽ 4:30 pm, Jun 6
German 21st Panzer Division launches counterattack between the Juno and Sword beachheads but is forced to withdraw

❷ Night of Jun 5–6
US 82nd and 101st Airborne Divisions land west of Utah beach

❻ 7:30 am, Jun 6
Men of British 3rd Division land on Sword beach and advance toward Caen

❼ 7:55 am, Jun 6
Men of Canadian 3rd Division land on Juno beach and advance to the west of Caen

❺ 7:25 am, Jun 6
Men of British 50th Division land on Gold beach and advance inland toward Bayeux after some heavy fighting

❹ 7:00 am, Jun 6
Men of US 1st Division land on Omaha beach. They begin to suffer heavy casualties during fight to secure the beach

❸ 6:30 am, Jun 6
Men of US 4th Division land to south of Utah beach. They encounter only light resistance and advance inland to meet up with paratroops

June 6–12
Having established themselves on the five beaches, the next task for the Allied forces was to link up the individual beachheads. This was finally achieved on June 12, when the US troops from Omaha joined with those from Utah. Beyond the beachheads the main British objective was Caen, where the Germans were preparing to counterattack.

❹ Jun 12
Allied troops almost succeed in breaking through center of German line at Caumont

❸ Jun 10
British launch heavy bombardment of Caen at beginning of attempt to capture the town. German forces successfully resist the Allied attack

❶ Jun 9
British and US troops from Gold and Omaha beachheads meet west of Bayeux

❷ Jun 12
US troops from Omaha and Utah beachheads meet east of Carentan

❶ Jun 13
British and Canadian attempt to outflank Caen via Villers-Bocage is halted

❻ Jul 18
St. Lô is taken by US forces

❹ Jul 3
US forces begin to advance toward line between Coutances and St. Lô but meet fierce resistance

❷ Jun 18
US forces reach the coast at Barneville

❸ Jun 20
US forces begin to attack Cherbourg's outer defenses. They capture the port on Jun 27

❻ Jul 18
In Operation Goodwood British and Canadian troops launch attack to east of Caen

❺ Jul 8
Following heavy bombardment, British and Canadian troops advance and take part of Caen west of Orne River but get no farther

June 13–July 24
As British and Canadian forces struggled to capture Caen, tying down the German armor, the Americans captured the port of Cherbourg and made preparations to break out of Normandy.

"Two kinds of people are staying on this beach, the dead and those who are going to die. Now let's get the hell out of here."

US COLONEL GEORGE TAYLOR ON OMAHA BEACH

Wounded US troops
Nearly 3,000 men were killed or wounded during the landings on Omaha beach. Many were forced to huddle against the sea wall, on a narrow strip of shingle, as the tide came in.

The initial bombardment dazed the German defenders and cut their communications to the rear. It was just as well, since the US troops found themselves having to wade through 100 yd (100 m) of water before they reached dry land. They then found that, because of a combination of current and smoke, they had landed 2,000 yd (2,000 m) to the south of Utah. They were ordered inland and northward to secure the correct beach, and they soon made contact with the paratroops. A German gun line on a low but dominant ridge caused some difficulties, but even so, Utah was secure at the end of the day at a cost of just 200 US casualties.

The other American beach—the 6-mile (10-km) long Omaha—would prove to be a very different proposition. At high tide it consisted of a narrow strip of shingle backed by a sea wall, behind which was a 200-yd (200-m) wide plateau with an antitank ditch. To the rear there were cliffs with numerous strongpoints on top. It was the strongest held of all the beaches, with two German regiments deployed. Just 3 miles (5 km) to the west of Omaha there was a battery on Pointe du Hoc, which covered the beach from the flank.

Omaha was the target of the US 1st Infantry Division, which intended to land with two regimental combat teams (RCTs) abreast. Almost all the swimming tanks supporting the RCT on the right were drowned in the heavy swell. Those supporting the RCT on the left only made it to the shore because the skippers of the landing craft carrying them took them right to the beach. Many landing craft were wrecked by underwater obstacles and others were swamped, with the result that most of the supporting artillery never made it to the beach. As for the infantry, many found themselves shoulder-deep in water. Weighed down by their equipment, some drowned, while others fell to the murderous fire from the strongpoints on the cliffs to the rear of the beach. Those who did get ashore often landed in the wrong place and sought shelter at the foot of the sea wall. Many officers trying to gather their men were shot, and few radios worked because they had been impregnated with seawater. Soon, the incoming tide restricted the survivors to a narrow strip of shingle. Meanwhile, 150 Rangers had succeeded in climbing the cliffs that led up to

Arrival of follow-up forces
Following D-Day, it was essential that the Allies reinforce their troops on the Normandy beachhead more rapidly than the Germans.

Pointe du Hoc, only to discover that the guns had
beeen removed. They were then subjected to several
German counterattacks for 48 hours. On the beach
itself, some semblance of order was eventually
established, and groups managed to get off it to
infiltrate the cliffs behind. Even so, by nightfall the
beachhead was still only some 1,000 yd (1,000 yd)
deep and very vulnerable to counterattack.

BRITISH AND CANADIAN LANDINGS

Men of the British 50th (Northumbrian) Division
began to land on Gold beach at 7:25 am, five
minutes before the stipulated time. The defenses

Mulberry harbor
Two artificial harbors were
erected to maintain the
flow of supplies.

within the village of Le
Hamel were the main
problem and it took most
of the day to reduce
them. Nevertheless, by
the end of the day the
division had succeeded
in almost reaching the
town of Bayeux.

Juno beach was the target of the Canadian Third
Division. Offshore reefs restricted the landing places
and the swell slowed the approach to the shore. In
this case, the tanks landed well before the infantry,
who were 25 minutes late. As on other beaches,
while the air and naval bombardments had largely
silenced the coastal batteries, they had not had much
effect on the strongpoints and there were fierce
battles to subdue these. The landing of follow-up
waves of troops caused congestion on the beach,
but by early afternoon the Canadians were moving
inland toward their ultimate D-Day objective, the
airfield in Carpiquet, west of Caen. By dusk they
had reached a point 1.5 miles (2.4 km) short of it
and had linked up with 50th Division on their right.

The final beach, Sword, was to be assaulted by
the British Third Infantry Division, whose ultimate
D-Day objective was the city of Caen. In spite of
heavy German fire, the leading waves of troops
got ashore and by 8:30 am were off the beaches.
A Commando force moved swiftly to relieve the
glider-borne troops holding the bridge over the

Caen Canal. The main
body was held up by
beach congestion, which
delayed the arrival of its
supporting tanks. Matters
were not helped by the
obstinate resistance of a
German strongpoint that
lay on the route to
Caen. Even so, the
troops reached a village
2.5 miles (4 km) north
of the city by 4:00 pm.
Thirty minutes later the Germans launched their
only significant counterattack of D-Day.

GERMAN COUNTERATTACK

There was only one German mobile formation in
Normandy on D-Day. The 21st Panzer Division was
deployed in the Caen area, but was widely scattered.
Rundstedt, the German commander-in-chief, had
a reserve of three other panzer divisions, but
Hitler had insisted that they could not be
deployed without his permission, and not until
the afternoon of D-Day was this forthcoming.
Meanwhile, the 21st Panzer Division,
which had initially been deployed
between the Orne and the Dives, was
ordered to counter the landings on
Sword. The attack, which did not
begin until 4:30 pm, was repulsed,
except for one Panzergrenadier battalion
that managed to advance through the gap between
the Canadian Third and British Third divisions.
It withdrew only through fear of being cut off
by reinforcements for the Sixth Airborne Division.
Meanwhile, the deployment to the beachhead of
the reserve panzer divisions was badly hampered
by Allied airpower, and the leading elements only
began to arrive, too late, on the night of D-Day.

Thus, by the end of D-Day the Allies had landed
150,000 men at a cost of 9,000 casualties, far fewer
than they had feared. The Germans had been
caught by surprise and had failed to prevent any
of the landings from taking place. They were also
still not convinced that there would be no landings
elsewhere, especially in the Pas de Calais.

BEACHHEAD BATTLES

After the success of D-Day, the Allies' first priority
was to link up the individual beachheads. They
finally achieved this on June 12, when Utah was
joined with Omaha. In the British sector the main

Advancing from Sword beach
British forces move inland to join the battle for the capture
of Caen. The city was a D-Day objective, but the Germans
fought grimly to prevent its capture. It took six weeks for
British and Canadian forces to secure Caen.

The destruction of Valognes
The inhabitants of Normandy often paid a heavy price for their liberation. It was not so much the ground fighting which caused destruction and civilian deaths, but the Allied use of carpet bombing from the air.

objective was Caen, but it was here that the Germans were attempting to concentrate their armor for a major counterattack. The 12th SS Panzer Division had joined the 21st Panzer and was able to foil Canadian attempts to capture the city from the west. A British thrust south and then east of Bayeux during June 11–14 proved abortive for the same reason. But while more panzer divisions were arriving, their progress was slowed by destroyed bridges and the constant Allied air threat. At the same time, pressure on the ground meant that they had to concentrate on holding the line rather than mounting a significant attack.

ADVANCE TO CHERBOURG

Once they had secured the beaches the Allies had set about assembling two Mulberry harbors, one in the US sector and the other in the British. The former began to operate on June 16, but three days later it was virtually destroyed by a violent storm. This made it all the more important for the Americans to capture Cherbourg so that it could be used as a resupply port. To this end, they first cut off the Cotentin peninsula by advancing across its base before turning north toward Cherbourg. Hitler had

THE "FUNNIES"

IT HAD BECOME APPARENT after the disastrous raid on Dieppe in August 1942 that tanks should have the capability to overcome beach obstacles and surmount sea walls. There was also the problem of getting the tanks to the beach. Work began on specialized types based on existing tanks, especially the American Sherman and British Churchill.

One of the most important was the Sherman DD (Duplex Drive), which could swim through the sea. It had a collapsible canvas screen and a propellor attached to the main engine to provide propulsion. Once ashore, the gear could be removed and it became a normal tank. Sherman DDs landed with the initial assault troops on all the D-Day beaches, although some did sink, especially off Omaha. On the beaches themselves, a plethora of "funnies," as they became

Browning 0.3-in machine-gun *75-mm gun* *Rotating arm*

Flail of metal chains for clearing mines

SHERMAN V (M4A4) CRAB FLAIL TANK

known, were needed. Tanks with bulldozer blades were used to clear beach obstacles. The carpet-layer Churchill laid trackway on soft sand to enable wheeled vehicles to cross it, while the turretless Churchill Ark was used to ram a sea wall and then become a surface over which other tanks could drive. To deal with antitank ditches, various types of bridging tank were developed. A new method of clearing a lane through a minefield was the Conger explosive hose, which fired from a trailer behind a tank. To deal with strongpoints there was the Churchill Crocodile flamethrower and the Churchill AVRE (Armoured Vehicle Royal Engineers). This had a short-barreled mortar that fired a projectile filled with 26 lb (11.8 kg) of explosive charge.

With the exception of the Sherman DD tank, the Americans usually took little interest in the "funnies," which were very much the province of the British.

Churchill Crocodile flamethrower
The Crocodile tank had a maximum range of 200 yd (185 m). A trailer contained the fuel for the flame-thrower.

INFANTRY WEAPONS ON THE WESTERN FRONT

THE INFANTRY OF BOTH the Allied and the German armies on the Western Front had a wide variety of weapons. They ranged from pistols and grenades, to rifles, submachine-guns, and light and medium machine-guns, as well as mortars and antitank weapons. The rifle, however, remained the basic infantry weapon. On the Allied side, the ammunition for British and American small arms was generally of different calibers and so could not be used in each other's weapons.

3 lb (1.4 kg) projectile

Monopod support

Spring-loaded launch tube

PIAT rocket launcher
The British PIAT ("Projector, Infantry, Anti-Tank") came into service in late 1942. A hollow-charge bomb was launched by means of a powerful spring. It was awkward to handle, but effective up to 90 yd (100 m).

| Length 39 in (99 cm) | Weight 32 lb (14.5 kg) |

Aperture-style rear sights

Hand-operated breechbolt

Detachable 10-round box magazine

Spike-type bayonet

British Lee Enfield no. 4 rifle
The British Army's standard rifle from 1941 to 1959, the Lee Enfield no. 4 was caliber 0.303 in (7.69 mm). It was cheaper to manufacture than its predecessor, the Short Muzzle Lee Enfield (SMLE).

| Length 44⅜ in (113 cm) | Weight 9 lb (4.1 kg) |

Colt .45 automatic pistol
Adopted by the US Army in 1911, the Colt .45 was used in both world wars. It had a 7-round magazine, used large-caliber bullets, and had a reputation for being a "man-stopper."

| Length 8½ in (21.6 cm) | Weight 2½ lb (1.14 kg) |

British M36 or Mills hand grenade
The Mills grenade entered British Army service in 1915 and is still used today. It can be set with a 4- or 7-second delay fuse.

| Length 3¾ in (9.53 cm) | Weight 1¼ lb (0.77 kg) |

"Leaf with aperture"—type foresight

Wooden forward grip

20- or 30- round ammunition magazine

Thin sheet steel canister enclosing powder charge

Removable wooden buttstock

German Steilhandgranate 39
Dating from World War I, the StG 39 contained 7 oz (2.78 gm) of TNT and had a 4.5-second delay.

| Length 16 in (40.6 cm) | Weight 1 lb 6 oz (0.63 kg) |

Threaded safety cap

Thompson M1928A1 "Tommy Gun"
Beloved of American gangsters in the 1920s, the Thompson became the standard US submachine-gun of World War II. It was also much used by British commandos. It could fire 800 rounds of 0.45-in caliber per minute and used a 20- or 30-round box magazine, or a 50- or 100-round drum magazine.

| Length 33¼ in (84.5 cm) | Weight 10 lb 2 oz (4.6 kg) |

Pistole Parabellum 1908
Usually known as the Luger, this pistol had an 8-round magazine and used 9 mm ammunition. It was prized as a souvenir by Allied soldiers.

| Length 8¾ in (22.2 cm) | Weight 1 lb 15 oz (0.85 kg) |

German Karabiner 98K
The last of a long line of bolt-action Mausers, which served the German Army well. It was based on a rifle designed as early as 1898 and became standard issue in 1935. It used 7.92 mm (0.312 in) ammunition and had a 5-round magazine.

| Length 43⅞ in (110.7 cm) | Weight 8½ lb (3.89 kg) |

Bayonet

Bolt

ordered the garrison to defend the port to the last. It fell on June 27, but only after the Germans had destroyed the dock facilities. It would be some weeks before the port was operational. In the British sector there was another attempt to outflank Caen from the west toward the end of June, but again there was no decisive breakthrough.

Much of the Allied lack of progress, aside from the capture of Cherbourg, lay in the nature of the Normandy terrain known as the "*bocage*." It was hilly and often wooded country, with twisting roads bordered by banks topped with hedges, and small enclosed fields. It had a claustrophobic atmosphere, which favored defense, and the Allied troops took time to acclimatize. The Germans had the problem of manpower. In spite of pleas by Rundstedt and Rommel for more men, and even for permission to withdraw from Normandy, Hitler was adamant that the Allies be driven back into the sea. So disgusted was Rundstedt that Hitler replaced him with Hans Guenther von Kluge at the beginning of July.

Searching among the ruins of Caen
Armed with Sten guns, two Allied soldiers search for German snipers in a city that had taken a pounding in successive Allied attacks. The last part to remain in German hands was captured by the Canadians on July 18.

PARIS
ROUEN
LE MANS
LAVA

ATTEMPTS ON ST. LÔ AND CAEN

Montgomery, who was *de facto* still in overall control of the Allied ground operations, was now concerned to tie down the maximum amount of German armor in the east to enable the Americans to get into a position from which they could break out. On July 3 the US First Army began to attack southward toward St. Lô, a key communications center, which it was essential for the Americans to secure if their eventual break-out were to be successful. It was to be a slow and costly business in the face of continuing bitter German resistance. The next day, the Canadians made another attempt to seize Carpiquet airfield, only to be frustrated by the fanatical defense of the 12th SS Panzer Division. Preceded by a massive air attack that destroyed much of Caen, and with naval gunfire and heavy artillery fire in support, British and Canadian troops attacked the city once more on July 8. They managed to break into it and secure the area north of the Odon River, but the Germans held firm on the southern bank.

Although St. Lô was not yet in Allied hands, Montgomery's plan for the break-out was issued on July 10. The Americans were simultaneously to thrust eastward into Brittany to secure its ports and westward toward the line of Alençon–Le Mans.

BOMB PLOT AGAINST HITLER

THERE HAD BEEN A NUMBER of plots against Hitler's life, but the one implemented on July 20, 1944, was the closest to being successful. The plotters were a mixture of middle- and high-ranking army officers and civil servants, many of whom believed that Germany must make peace if it was not to be totally destroyed.

The plot was centered on the Reserve Army, which had its HQ in Berlin, one of whose staff officers, Colonel Claus von Stauffenburg, regularly attended conferences at Hitler's headquarters in Rastenberg in East Prussia. The plan was for him to take a bomb hidden in a briefcase into such a conference and then leave before it exploded. Once Hitler was dead, elements of the Home Army would seize government buildings in Berlin. The same would happen in Paris, whose military governor was involved in the plot.

Stauffenburg duly flew to Rastenberg and attended the conference. Placing the briefcase under the table, he announced that he had to make a

telephone call and left. The bomb detonated and Stauffenburg reported this to HQ Reserve Army. In Paris there were wholesale arrests of SS, Gestapo, and other Nazis, but in Berlin the plot leaders hesitated before ordering the occupation of the key buildings. Government officials in Berlin then learned that Hitler was shaken but had survived. The Berlin plotters were arrested with some, including Stauffenburg, being summarily shot. In Paris the governor was forced to release his captives.

Hitler instituted a massive witch hunt. Hundreds were arrested. After torture, some were subjected to show trials and then hanged with piano wire in Berlin's Plottensee prison. Others, including Rommel and Kluge, who were aware of the plot but not involved, were forced to commit suicide to protect their families.

Bomb damage
Mussolini, who arrived at Hitler's HQ in Rastenberg—the "Wolf's Lair"—later on July 20, is shown the bomb damage.

Eisenhower, however, was beginning to believe that the terrain in the British sector was more suitable for a break-out than that in the US sector.

OPERATION GOODWOOD

As it happened, Montgomery had been planning an attack just to the east of Caen, with the purpose of keeping the German armor tied down, but he let Eisenhower believe that a breakthrough was intended. Rommel sensed what was about to happen and personally briefed his subordinate commanders. On July 17, while returning from a visit to one of these commanders, his car was hit by a marauding fighter-bomber and he was badly injured. Rommel was evacuated back to Germany, and Kluge took over direct command of his Army Group B, as well as continuing to be commander-in-chief west.

Montgomery's assault, Operation Goodwood, opened on July 18. Again, RAF Bomber Command prepared the way. A shortage of approach routes

meant that only one armored division could deploy at a time, but the air bombardment had dazed the defenders and initially there was good progress. The Germans, however, quickly recovered. Antitank guns in villages on the flank of the advance suddenly came to life. Worse, German tanks took up position on a dominant ridge, which marked the first major objective. They brought the British armor to a halt. Attempts to resume the attack on the following day failed and thunderstorms on July 20 brought Goodwood to an end with a loss of 400 tanks. The Canadians had, however, secured the remainder of Caen.

General Omar Bradley, commanding the US First Army, had intended to launch his break-out from St. Lô, which had finally been secured, on July 20. However, he also wanted US bombers to prepare the way, and

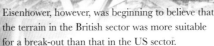

Exhausted German prisoners
Over 50,000 German prisoners had been taken by the end of June. They were put in temporary "cages" prior to being shipped back to Britain.

THE RESISTANCE AND THE SOE

FORCES FRANÇAISES DE L'INTÉRIEUR ARMBAND

THE COUNTRIES OF EUROPE OCCUPIED by Germany and Italy were not totally cowed, as the development of resistance movements testified. For these movements to flourish, their members had to believe that liberation would eventually take place. It was also necessary for the bulk of the population to continue normal life as best it could, since this provided essential cover for Resistance activities. Inevitably, this meant passive collaboration with the occupiers. Furthermore, outside support was vital, and it was to provide this that Churchill established the Special Operations Executive (SOE) in the summer of 1940. This was followed in May 1942 by the founding of the US equivalent to SOE, the Office of Strategic Services (OSS).

The SOE and OSS saw the Resistance as fulfilling two main roles—sabotage and intelligence gathering. The first not only helped to tie down Axis troops, but also hampered the utilization of indigenous industry for the Axis war effort. Intelligence produced by the Resistance was often vital, the progress of heavy water production in Norway for the German atomic bomb program and the development of V-weapons being but two examples. To coordinate the activities of the various groups, the SOE and OSS deployed agents to act as a link and arrange for the necessary weapons, explosives, and other equipment to be delivered to the Resistance.

The Resistance often faced great difficulties. Countries with mountainous terrain provided an easier environment in which to operate than the flatlands of the Low Countries or Denmark, where more effort had to go into establishing places to hide. Another problem was that the groups themselves often held very different political beliefs and it was difficult to get them to work together. In France, for example, there were groups that supported de Gaulle, and others that were communist, with a very different postwar agenda. There was the constant danger of betrayal. Fascist sympathizers often infiltrated the Resistance networks, as did those who were prepared to betray their fellow countrymen for money. The German *Abwehr* was also highly skilled in identifying Resistance members and calling them out. In March 1942 they succeeded in "turning" an SOE radio operator in the Netherlands. For 18 months he continued to transmit to London without the SOE being aware that he was in German hands. As a result, many agents were captured and the Dutch Resistance network was virtually destroyed for a time.

In spite of such difficulties, the Resistance played its part in winning the war for the Allies. On D-Day, for example, the French Resistance succeeded in virtually isolating Brittany from Normandy and thus prevented the movement of German reinforcements. It also helped to delay the movement of German divisions from other parts of France through its attacks on the transportation system.

Sabotaged railroad track
Resistance groups excelled in acts of sabotage that disrupted the movement of supplies.

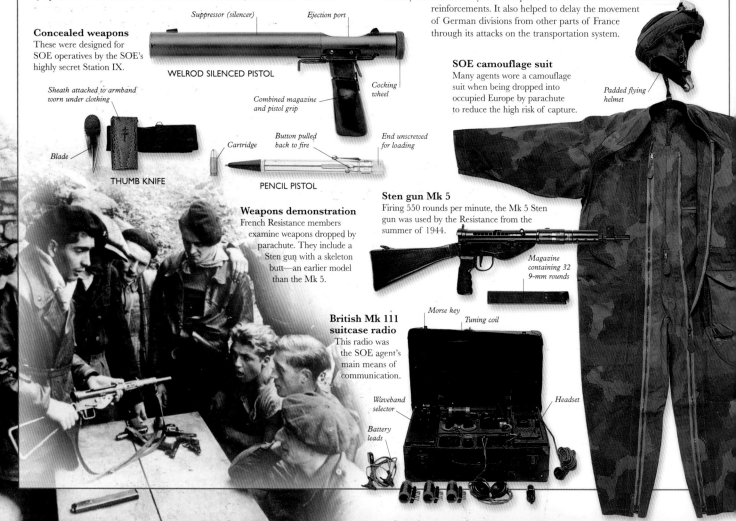

Concealed weapons
These were designed for SOE operatives by the SOE's highly secret Station IX.

Suppressor (silencer)
Ejection port

WELROD SILENCED PISTOL

Cocking wheel

Combined magazine and pistol grip

Sheath attached to armband worn under clothing

Blade

THUMB KNIFE

Cartridge

Button pulled back to fire

End unscrewed for loading

PENCIL PISTOL

SOE camouflage suit
Many agents wore a camouflage suit when being dropped into occupied Europe by parachute to reduce the high risk of capture.

Padded flying helmet

Weapons demonstration
French Resistance members examine weapons dropped by parachute. They include a Sten gun with a skeleton butt—an earlier model than the Mk 5.

Sten gun Mk 5
Firing 550 rounds per minute, the Mk 5 Sten gun was used by the Resistance from the summer of 1944.

Magazine containing 32 9-mm rounds

British Mk 111 suitcase radio
This radio was the SOE agent's main means of communication.

Morse key
Tuning coil
Waveband selector
Battery leads
Headset

the bad weather prevented this. As a result there was an awkward pause, which led to yet further recrimination between Eisenhower and Montgomery over the failure of Goodwood. News of the failed assassination attempt against Hitler did, however, give the Allies some comfort, for it indicated that cracks were appearing in the Nazi regime.

ALLIED BREAK-OUT

Operation Cobra, General Bradley's break-out from St. Lô, was now scheduled for July 24 (see map page 231). The weather was still doubtful and it was decided to recall the bombers after they had taken off. Some did not receive the message and dropped their bombs as planned, inflicting 130 casualties on their own troops. A better weather forecast encouraged Bradley to try again the following day. Inaccurate bombing again inflicted casualties on the attackers, but the attack went ahead and made progress. Further attacks by the Canadians in the Caen area prevented Kluge from switching panzer divisions to counter the threat.

On July 30 the Americans entered Avranches. On the same day the British mounted Operation Bluecoat, with the goal of preventing the German armor from attacking the US flank from the east. Despite a lack of suitable routes, this was largely achieved. The moment to exploit the break-out now arrived. On August 1 Patton's US Third Army came into being and Bradley ordered him to clear Brittany as a priority. He sent two armored divisions to seize Brest and Lorient, but Hitler declared both to be *Festungen* (fortresses) which were to hold out to the bitter end. Brest was to fall in mid-September, but the garrison at Lorient did not surrender until the end of the war. Thus the Allies were denied early use of the Brittany ports.

COUNTERATTACK AT MORTAIN

Some of Patton's forces had begun to advance south and were threatening the German left flank. Kluge wanted to withdraw to the Seine, but Hitler insisted that he mount a counterstroke against Patton's eastern flank. Because of British pressure, Kluge was only able, with great difficulty, to assemble four panzer divisions for the attack, and these attacked in the Mortain area shortly after midnight on August 7. The Americans were initially caught off-balance, and by daylight the Germans had penetrated up to

German POWs near Falaise
On August 20 the remnants from two German armies streamed back toward the Seine, leaving 10,000 dead and 50,000 to be taken prisoner.

6 miles (10 km). With the coming of daylight, the situation changed dramatically as hoards of Allied fighter-bombers took to the skies and engaged the German armor with rockets. The attack was stopped in its tracks and troops on the ground now threatened the flanks of the penetrating forces.

The Canadians now launched an attack south of Caen, Operation Totalize, which was designed to block the withdrawal of the German forces in front of the British Second Army. While it did not reach its final objective of Falaise, the attack further restricted Kluge's options. Worse, the counterattack at Mortain had not inhibited Patton, who had both thrust into Brittany and advanced south to the Loire River. He was now turning east, threatening the main German supply base at Alençon.

Realizing that the German forces in Normandy were being squeezed, Montgomery decided to trap them. The Canadians were to press on to Falaise and then to Argentan, with the British on their left advancing to the Flers-Argentan road. Meanwhile, Patton was to thrust toward the southeast of Argentan. In this way, Montgomery hoped to create a pocket with no decent escape routes to the east. Patton's troops entered Alençon on August 12 and headed for Argentan, to which the Germans hastily redeployed tanks from Mortain. Bradley now ordered Patton to halt at Argentan rather than press on to Falaise as he feared a clash with the Canadians. They had resumed their attacks toward Falaise on

August 14. The 12th SS Panzer Division, held them for a time on the last ridge before Falaise, but by the end of August 17 they had secured almost the whole town. The gap between them and the Americans at Argentan was now a mere 12 miles (19 km).

In spite of Kluge's pleas, Hitler continued to insist on further counterattacks at Mortain as late as August 16. He would not accept that a withdrawal might be necessary, and appointed Model in place of Kluge, who was ordered back to Germany. Fearing arrest on suspicion of being involved in the July bomb plot, Kluge committed suicide *en route*.

TRAPPED IN THE FALAISE POCKET

Immediately grasping how desperate the situation was, on August 17 Model ordered the Seventh and Fifth Panzer Armies to withdraw to the Dives River and take up a new defensive position. However, events were moving too fast for him. The Canadians attacked across the river and by the evening of August 18 had reached Chambois. With the Americans also closing up, there was now a mere 6-mile (10-km) gap through which the German forces were beginning the pour. Just 24 hours later the pocket was finally closed and the Germans still inside it were being hammered from the air. On August 20 desperate attacks by the Germans opened a gap in the mouth of the pocket for a few hours, but by the evening it had been closed again. The battle for Normandy was at an end.

> "The scenes in the Falaise pocket…were horrendous. The various German divisions had taken a terrible pounding in the Normandy battle. Panzer Lehr, for instance, had lost all its tanks and infantry units."
>
> STUART HILLS, BRITISH SHERMAN TANK COMMANDER
> DURING THE ALLIED ADVANCE THROUGH NORMANDY

Searching for Germans
After the Allied landings in southern France, members of the Resistance go into action. The woman has a Schmeisser MP40 submachine-gun.

LANDINGS IN SOUTHERN FRANCE

On August 15, while the Allies were setting about creating the pocket at Falaise, landings took place far to the south on France's Mediterranean coast. The original intention had been for these to be mounted at the same time as those in Normandy, but developments in Italy and the lack of sufficient amphibious shipping had made it necessary to postpone them. Preceded by an airborne drop, General Alexander Patch's US Seventh Army came

Paris liberation celebrations
German snipers were still active even as Parisians celebrated, and several people died in an outbreak of shooting in the Place de la Concorde on August 26.

ashore without the degree of German resistance that the Allies had met on D-Day. The southern half of France contained a mere ten German divisions and the coastal defences were not as strong as in Normandy. Overwhelming Allied air supremacy and powerful naval support also contributed.

Eisenhower's prime objective was to secure Marseilles so that it could be used as a resupply port, a task given to General Jean-Marie de Lattre de Tassigny's *Armée B*, soon to be renamed the French First Army. This consisted of the French Expeditionary Corps, which had fought in Italy, and further troops from North Africa. Hitler had designated both Marseilles and the former French naval base Toulon *Festungen*, but the French ensured that both were secured by August 28. In the meantime, the Americans had begun to advance rapidly northward up the Rhône valley, much assisted by the *Forces Françaises de l'Intérieur* (FFI). This had been formed in February 1944 as an umbrella for all the French Resistance groups, including the *Maquis*, which consisted largely of young men evading compulsory

labor in Germany, who had sought refuge in the forested and mountainous area around the Massif Central. Many would be incorporated into the French First Army. The Allies were helped, too, by the fact that Hitler, appreciating that the situation in northern France was fast disintegrating, allowed the German forces in the south to withdraw.

US ADVANCE TO PARIS

In northern France, Model had hoped to form a new defense line based on the Seine River, but the Allies moved too quickly for him. Patton, frustrated by Bradley's refusal to allow him to advance north of Argentan, had been allowed to continue to advance eastward. Montgomery's intention was that he should strike toward the port of Le Havre so as to create an outer cordon to trap the forces that had escaped from the Falaise pocket. In fact, Patton sent only one corps in this direction, while two others headed for Chartres and Orléans. Once these two

A triumphant General de Gaulle in Paris
On August 26 over 1 million people flocked to the center of Paris to cheer the city's liberation as de Gaulle walked up the Champs Elysées, followed by members of the FFI.

A vibrant crowd surrounds the French tanks draped in flags and covered in bouquets of flowers. On each tank, on each armored car, next to crew members in khaki mechanics' overalls and little caps, there are clusters of girls, women, boys, and fifis (FFI members) wearing armbands. People lining the street applaud, blow kisses, raise clenched fist salutes, call out to the victors their joy at liberation.

BOOKSELLER JEAN GALTIER-BOISSIÈRE DESCRIBING THE SCENE IN PARIS ON AUGUST 25, THE DAY OF LIBERATION

towns had been liberated, Bradley ordered Patton to halt for two days for fear that his advance would become overextended. However, on August 18 he allowed the Third Army to resume its thrust eastward. Late on the following day, Patton's leading elements found an intact footbridge over the Seine west of Paris. They immediately established a bridgehead and then secured another to the east of Paris on August 23. Thus, Model's hopes were crushed and his battered troops were forced to continue their withdrawal eastward.

In Paris itself there had been momentous events. Eisenhower's original intention had been to bypass the city, fearing that to attack it directly would result in unnecessary casualties and collateral damage. Actions within the city caused a change of plan. On August 10, sensing that liberation was close, public sector workers went on strike. The reaction of the Resistance groups in Paris was mixed. Gaullist elements, having been warned that Allied forces would not enter for some time to come, considered it prudent to stand by and wait for events to unfold. The communists, on the other hand, wanted an immediate uprising. Fearing that if this happened the communists would seize the machinery of government, the Gaullists preempted them and on August 19 the insurrection began.

The military governor of Paris, General Dietrich von Choltitz, was known by the Allies to have been involved in the destruction of Rotterdam in May

1940 and the Soviet Black Sea port of Sevastopol in 1942. There was also the knowledge that the Poles in Warsaw were at that very time fighting a desperate battle against their German oppressors.

As it turned out, thanks to the efforts of the Swedish consul-general in Paris, Raoul Nordling, Choltitz agreed to a truce and undertook not to inflict on Paris the terrible punishment that Warsaw was receiving. This was despite a direct order from Hitler that the French capital be defended to the last. The skirmishing continued, however, and on August 22 the FFI commander in Paris called for every street to be barricaded. Finally, on August 23, Eisenhower relented and gave the go-ahead for General Philippe Leclerc's French Second Armored Division and a US infantry division, both part of Patton's Third Army, to dash to the capital. The race was won by Leclerc, who used local knowledge to reach the center via the back streets. Choltitz ordered his troops to withdraw east of the Seine and next day, August 25, surrendered to Leclerc. The next day de Gaulle walked triumphantly up the Champs Elysées.

SPLITS IN THE ALLIED CAMP

Splits now began to appear in the Allied camp. On August 21 Eisenhower had held a meeting at his Advanced HQ in Normandy. He announced that he was taking personal control of the ground forces from September 1 and gave instructions that Bradley's 12th Army Group was to aim for the Franco-German border, while Montgomery's 21st Army Group advanced into Belgium. Montgomery protested, on the grounds that either he or Bradley should continue to conduct the ground campaign and that the Allies should concentrate on a single thrust to the Ruhr, Germany's main industrial region in the west. Eisenhower was adamant that his Broad Front strategy should prevail and that he would take charge. There matters rested.

Advance through France and Belgium

By the time the Allied forces in the south of France linked up with those advancing from Normandy, progress had slowed because of overstretched supply lines. This gave the Germans time to recover and there was to be some hard fighting as the Allies gradually closed on the Rhine.

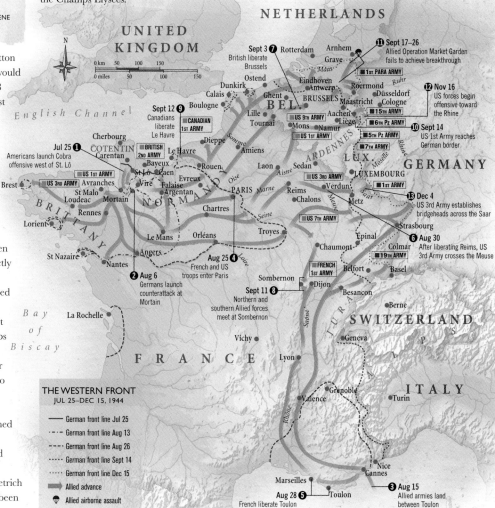

THE WESTERN FRONT
JUL 25–DEC 15, 1944

— German front line Jul 25
–·–· German front line Aug 13
– – – German front line Aug 26
······ German front line Sept 14
·········· German front line Dec 15
➤ Allied advance
Allied airborne assault

OPERATION MARKET GARDEN

The main obstacle barring the Western Allies' way into Germany was the Rhine River. Consequently, Montgomery proposed that airborne troops should seize bridges over the Lower Rhine and other rivers in the southern Netherlands, so allowing ground forces to advance rapidly into Germany. Eisenhower sanctioned Montgomery's plan on September 10 and a week later Operation Market Garden was mounted. The US 101st Airborne Division was to be dropped in the area around Eindhoven, and the US 82nd Airborne Division around Grave, while the British 1st Airborne Division was to seize the bridge over the Lower Rhine in Arnhem. At the same time, a British ground force was to advance north and relieve the airborne divisions in turn.

There were problems from the outset. First, the British paratroops were dropped too far—6 miles (10 km)—from the bridge in Arnhem. There were also two SS panzer divisions reequipping in the area. A US officer was captured with a copy of the operational orders, and the ground force made slow progress, in places being restricted to a single route that was repeatedly attacked. It did eventually link up with the

Paratroops in the Netherlands
Three airborne divisions took part in Operation Market Garden, Montgomery's gamble to break the growing deadlock in the west.

By August 29 the Allies had reached the Seine River, although Patton was already advancing farther east and had reached the Marne. While the Canadians advanced along the Channel coast to secure its ports, the British Second Army launched a lightning thrust, with the US First Army covering its right flank, and succeeded in reaching the Belgian border on September 2. Patton, too, was now across the Marne and heading for the Meuse.

There was a penalty to be paid for these rapid advances. The Allied armies were still being largely supplied from Cherbourg, and the supply lines were becoming dangerously overstretched. The railroads were too badly damaged to be used, and resupply by air was limited by the fact that much of the transport fleet was allocated to the airborne forces. Every available truck had been pressed into service to bring fuel up to the forward supply depots, but the farther the Allies advanced the more fuel was consumed and the less there was for the forward divisions. The Canadians were unable to capture the Channel ports quickly because Hitler had declared them *Festungen*, and the dock facilities of those they did liberate had been largely destroyed.

Montgomery believed that if he could quickly capture Antwerp the problem would be solved. His tanks achieved this on September 4, the day after the Belgian capital, Brussels, had been liberated. So surprised were the German defenders that they had no time to sabotage the docks. Unfortunately, Antwerp as a port was useless unless the Scheldt River, which linked it to the sea, was secured. Montgomery was looking eastward rather than westward and the opportunity was missed. Thus, by the end of the first week of September, Allied fuel tanks were almost dry and the advance ground to a virtual halt.

The slowing of the Allied advance allowed the Germans a vital breathing space in which to regroup. Meanwhile, Montgomery was conceiving an ambitious plan for maintaining the Allied momentum and perhaps ending the war in 1944.

British paratroops in Oosterbeek
Aside from the battle for the bridge in Arnhem, the most intense fighting in Operation Market Garden was in Oosterbeek, a suburb of the town.

US divisions, but Arnhem proved too ambitious an objective. The British paratroops, reinforced by the Polish Parachute Brigade, were subjected to relentless pressure by the two SS divisions and eventually forced to surrender, with only a fifth of their number escaping back to Allied lines. Thus, the chance to end the war in 1944 had been lost.

A STEP-BY-STEP ADVANCE

In the American sector General Courtney Hodges' First Army had begun to penetrate the Siegfried Line, while Patton's Third Army had reached the Moselle and linked up with the US Seventh and First French Armies, now under General Jacob Devers' US Sixth Army Group. Everywhere the Germans were recovering and the Allies were only achieving a step-by-step advance. The Canadian First Army had besieged several Channel ports, all of which, aside from Dunkirk, eventually fell. Montgomery now ordered the Canadians to clear the Scheldt estuary so that Antwerp could be opened. Meanwhile, the British Second Army set about enlarging the salient into the Netherlands that had been created by Market Garden.

In mid-October Eisenhower issued new orders. Montgomery was to continue to clear the Scheldt and, once Antwerp had been opened, advance from

The gun fired 6 rounds per minute and had a maximum range of 9,760 yd (8,930 m)

At 14.6 lb (6.63 kg), the shell was ineffective against solid defenses

The trail was holed to save weight

Airborne howitzer
The US M1A1 75-mm pack howitzer was used by both American and British airborne troops. It weighed 2,160 lb (980 kg) and could be carried in a glider.

V-WEAPONS

V-WEAPONS OR *VERGELTUNGSWAFFEN* (revenge weapons) were one category of Hitler's so-called "miracle" weapons that were designed to turn the tide of war. The three types that entered service were the V-1 flying bomb, the V-2 rocket, and the V-3 long-range, smooth-bore gun, of which only two were actually completed and used.

Development work on the V-1 and V-2 was centered in Peenemünde on Germany's Baltic coast. It was subjected to heavy bombing by the RAF in August 1943, putting back the development program. The V-1 had a preset guidance system and a maximum range of 125 miles (200 km).

V-2 ROCKET

It flew at a top speed of 420 mph (670 kph) and had a 1,875-lb (850-kg) warhead. The Germans launched their V-1 offensive against Britain on June 13, 1944. Initially, it was successful and caused many to evacuate London. The British then installed antiaircraft guns along the south coast and these, combined with fighters, meant that fewer got through. The Allies also overran the launch sites once they broke out of Normandy. A longer-range version was then developed to be launched from the Netherlands, but many continued to be shot down.

By this time the V-2 was in service. This was a very different proposition to the V-1. Flying at speeds as high as 2,500 mph (4,000 kph), it could not be intercepted. It also operated from a mobile launcher, which could withdraw within 30 minutes of firing. The first two were fired on September 8, one hitting Paris and the other London. A steady stream was then launched from the Netherlands, the last on March 27, 1945. The final V-1 against Britain was launched the following day. By this time, Allied air attacks on German oil and transportation targets were starving the V-weapons of fuel. They had in fact come into service too late to affect the course of the war.

V-1 FLYING BOMB

Explosive warhead of 1,875 lb (850 kg)

Pulse jet engine

Damage resulting from a V-2 attack
About 2,000 V-2s were fired at Britain, causing 9,000 casualties. About 16,000 V-1s were fired, some at northern France and the Netherlands, causing 45,000 casualties.

the Maas to the Rhine. Bradley's mission was to advance to the Rhine at Cologne, while Devers in the south closed up to the Rhine via the Belfort gap. The Americans advancing toward Cologne found themselves involved in tough fighting, initially to capture the first German town of any significance, Aachen, and then in the Huertgen Forest. In the south Patton reached the Saar River, while Devers reached the Rhine, although he failed to clear an obstinate German pocket based on Colmar. In the north the Canadians continued to clear both sides of the Scheldt. On November 1 amphibious landings took place on the Walcheren, the island guarding the Scheldt's mouth, and one week later it was secured. The river was then swept of mines and the first supply ships entered the port of Antwerp on November 26, thus easing the supply situation.

While these grim fall battles were being fought, Hitler had been secretly preparing to mount a major counteroffensive. Divisions had been withdrawn from the line and reequipped, all of this unbeknown to the Allies. Hitler planned to attack

US camouflaged Shermans outside Aachen
The tanks carry infantry who are ready to jump off on coming under fire. The fighting for the first significant German town captured by the Allies was very bitter.

GEORGE S PATTON

THE EMBODIMENT OF AGGRESSION, and dubbed by his troops "Old Blood and Guts," General George S. Patton (1885–1945) was one of the few senior American officers to have seen service in tanks in World War I. Following success as commander of the US II Corps in Tunisia in March 1943, he led the US Seventh Army in its invasion of Sicily. A notorious incident in which he struck a US soldier suffering from combat fatigue cost him his position, but he was reemployed as commander of the US Third Army in the build-up to D-Day. In July 1944 he led the Third Army in a race across France from Normandy, but he became embroiled in a battle of attrition on the German frontier before playing a crucial role in the relief of Bastogne during the Battle of the Bulge. Patton crossed the Rhine at Oppenheim on March 22, 1945, ending the war deep in Czechoslovakia. A brilliant exponent of armored warfare, he was one of the few Allied tank commanders who was respected by his German opposite numbers. He was killed in a traffic accident in Germany.

through the Ardennes, his ultimate objective being Antwerp. In this way he hoped to split the British 21st Army Group from the Americans. It was an audacious scheme and, although his generals were not optimistic, he was determined that the offensive should go ahead in mid-December.

BATTLE OF THE BULGE

Hitler's counteroffensive in the west, Operation Watch on the Rhine, was to be spearheaded by two panzer armies, Sepp Dietrich's Sixth, consisting largely of SS divisions, in the north, and Erich von Manteuffel's Fifth in the south. Manteuffel's southern flank would be protected by Erich Brandenburger's Seventh Army. Facing them in the Ardennes were elements of the US First Army. The sector was considered a quiet one and was held by formations recovering from the bitter fighting in the Huertgen Forest and others which had recently arrived from the United States. There were intelligence indicators that the Germans were preparing an attack, but the Allies did not believe that they were capable of mounting a major offensive, especially in the hilly and wooded Ardennes in winter.

On December 16, after a sharp predawn artillery barrage and in thick fog which grounded Allied airpower, the Germans attacked. In the north they found that the narrow winding roads slowed their advance, but one armored battle group did manage to break through the American lines and began to head for bridges over the Meuse. Manteuffel had more

Advancing in the Ardennes
German troops pass an ambushed US convoy in the opening days of their assault. Their initial success made them believe that they could deal the Allies a crippling blow.

favorable terrain and made better progress. The Germans also infiltrated men dressed in US uniforms, who changed signposts around and caused much confusion, including confining Eisenhower in his HQ in Versailles for fear that he might be assassinated. Total confusion reigned in the battle area, with many US units overrun and forced to surrender or caught while on the move. Not until the afternoon did the Allied high command accept

"The present situation is to be regarded as one of opportunity for us and not of disaster."

GENERAL EISENHOWER SPEAKING TO HIS
STAFF ON DECEMBER 19, 1944

that this was a major attack. The fog persisted, but in the north Dietrich's progress remained slow, with enterprising US engineers frustrating the SS battle groups by blocking their advance with blown bridges. Manteuffel, however, continued to thrust eastward and was soon approaching Bastogne, a vital center of communications.

ACTION AROUND BASTOGNE

Eisenhower agreed that Montgomery should take over the northern part of the growing salient and take the US First and Ninth Armies temporarily under command. Montgomery also deployed British troops to guard the bridges over the Meuse River, which the Germans had to seize before advancing to Antwerp. Eisenhower ordered Patton to halt his advance eastward, but Patton had already anticipated this and was swinging his army northward to strike the Germans in their southern flank. Simultaneously, the US 101st Airborne Division was rushed in by truck to reinforce Bastogne, which troops of Manteuffel's Fifth Panzer Army now surrounded.

By December 22 Dietrich's advance had come to a grinding halt and he was ordered to pass divisions to Manteuffel, whose spearheads were continuing to advance toward the Meuse. Two days later they reached it in Dinant, but the Bastogne garrison still

Offensive in the Ardennes

According to Hitler's plan, the German Fifth and Sixth Panzer and Seventh Armies would drive through the Ardennes forests and sweep on to Antwerp. In fact, they did not even succeed in crossing the Meuse and only caused a short interruption in the Allied advance.

BATTLE OF THE BULGE
DEC 16–26, 1944

— US front line Dec 16
···· US front line Dec 20
– – US front line Dec 25
⚑ Area of German parachute drop Dec 16/17
➡ German advance
➡ US counterattacks from Dec 25
–·– Major railroad

Dec 16 ❷ German parachute unit dropped at night to block the roads north of the Ardennes

❶ 5.30 am Dec 16 Germans launch offensive against American front, between Monschau and Echternach

❸ Dec 17 Americans occupy road junction in St. Vith, blocking advance of 6th Panzer Army until 23rd

Dec 25 ❻ Troops of American 1st Army attack near Celles. They overwhelm the Germans on the following day

❹ Dec 20 After rapid advance, 5th Panzer Army reaches outskirts of Bastogne and encircles American troops

Dec 24 ❺ Armored Division in Patton's American 3rd Army begins to advance northward to relieve Bastogne

❼ Dec 26 4th Armored Division reaches Bastogne. Fighting over corridor to Bastogne continues until January 4

held out. The failure to secure the town presented Manteuffel with growing resupply difficulties. Worse, although snow had arrived, the skies had begun to clear and the might of Allied airpower was unleashed on the German forces. On December 26 Patton's forces driving up from the south relieved Bastogne and for the next few days Manteuffel battled desperately to drive them back and take the town. But the momentum had gone and the Germans were increasingly forced on to the defensive.

OPERATION NORTH WIND

On the night December 31/January 1 Hermann Balck's Army Group launched a fresh offensive, Operation North Wind. It was designed to destroy the Allied forces in Alsace, but they were ready. Eisenhower did order Devers' Sixth Army Group to withdraw in order to shorten its line, but the French refused to give up the recently liberated Strasbourg.

In any case, North Wind soon ran out of momentum. In the meantime, on New Year's Day itself, the Luftwaffe launched a major air assault against Allied airfields to destroy as many aircraft as possible. Approximately 900 aircraft took part and they managed to knock out some 300 planes, but lost the same number themselves. More serious was the fact that many of their more experienced pilots were killed, a loss that would be deeply felt during the final air defense of the Third Reich.

Realizing that his offensive had failed, Hitler turned his attention to the east, where the Red Army was about to attack across the Vistula. His attack in the west had temporarily knocked the Allies off balance, but they had recovered quickly and, while the two sides had suffered the same number of casualties, the German loss of 80,000 men and much weaponry was one they could ill afford. The offensive had delayed the Allied advance, but it would not affect the inevitable final outcome.

American wounded soldiers helped ashore
During the Allied landings in Normandy in June 1944, specially converted landing craft were used to carry the wounded back to Britain. A continuous service ensured speedy evacuation from the beaches.

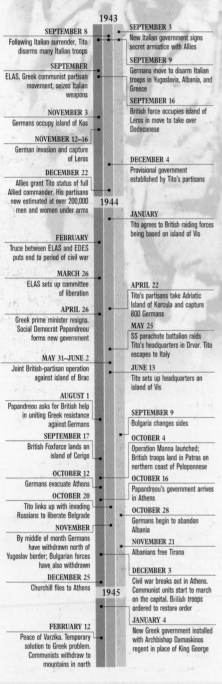

PARTISAN RESISTANCE IN THE BALKANS

SEPTEMBER 1943–FEBRUARY 1945

Under Axis occupation, resistance movements sprang up in Yugoslavia, Greece, and Albania. The most successful campaign was waged by Tito's partisans in Yugoslavia. In all three countries there was bitter rivalry between communist and anti-communist forces and, when the Germans withdrew, these divisions had a lasting effect on postwar Europe.

1943

SEPTEMBER 8
Following Italian surrender, Tito disarms many Italian troops

SEPTEMBER
ELAS, Greek communist partisan movement, seizes Italian weapons

NOVEMBER 3
Germans occupy island of Kos

NOVEMBER 12–16
German invasion and capture of Leros

DECEMBER 22
Allies grant Tito status of full Allied commander. His partisans now estimated at over 200,000 men and women under arms

FEBRUARY
Truce between ELAS and EDES puts end to period of civil war

MARCH 26
ELAS sets up committee of liberation

APRIL 26
Greek prime minister resigns. Social Democrat Papandreou forms new government

MAY 31–JUNE 2
Joint British-partisan operation against island of Brac

AUGUST 1
Papandreou asks for British help in uniting Greek resistance against Germans

SEPTEMBER 17
British Foxforce lands on island of Cerigo

OCTOBER 12
Germans evacuate Athens

OCTOBER 20
Tito links up with invading Russians to liberate Belgrade

NOVEMBER
By middle of month Germans have withdrawn north of Yugoslav border; Bulgarian forces have also withdrawn

DECEMBER 25
Churchill flies to Athens

1945

FEBRUARY 12
Peace of Varzika. Temporary solution to Greek problem. Communists withdraw to mountains in north

SEPTEMBER 3
New Italian government signs secret armistice with Allies

SEPTEMBER 9
Germans move to disarm Italian troops in Yugoslavia, Albania, and Greece

SEPTEMBER 16
British force occupies island of Leros in move to take over Dodecanese

DECEMBER 4
Provisional government established by Tito's partisans

1944

JANUARY
Tito agrees to British raiding forces being based on island of Vis

APRIL 22
Tito's partisans take Adriatic Island of Korcula and capture 800 Germans

MAY 25
SS parachute battalion raids Tito's headquarters in Drvar. Tito escapes to Italy

JUNE 13
Tito sets up headquarters on island of Vis

SEPTEMBER 9
Bulgaria changes sides

OCTOBER 4
Operation Manna launched; British troops land in Patras on northern coast of Peloponnese

OCTOBER 16
Papandreou's government arrives in Athens

OCTOBER 28
Germans begin to abandon Albania

NOVEMBER 21
Albanians free Tirana

DECEMBER 3
Civil war breaks out in Athens. Communist units start to march on the capital. British troops ordered to restore order

JANUARY 4
New Greek government installed with Archbishop Damaskinos regent in place of King George

■ Greece   ■ Yugoslavia   ■ Other events

BALKAN RESISTANCE

AFTER THE AXIS overran the Balkans in April 1941, Yugoslavia was virtually dismembered. Some parts were given to neighboring members of the Tripartite Pact, and others occupied by German or Italian forces. The rump became the puppet state of Croatia. Likewise, the easternmost part of Greece was given to Bulgaria, Macedonia occupied by the Germans, and the remainder of the country by the Italians. The monarchs of both countries established governments-in-exile, that of the Yugoslavs in London and the Greeks in Egypt. Albania remained under Italian occupation.

Resistance movements sprang up in all three countries, but they were initially disparate in nature. Albania saw a split between those who lived in the mountains in the north, who were loyal to King Zog, and the more urban communist-leaning population of the south. The latter eventually became dominant, but looked to Moscow for support and remained deeply suspicious of the Western Allies.

In Greece the main groupings were the Communist National Liberation Front (EAM), with its military arm, the National People's Liberation Army (ELAS), which also absorbed noncommunists. In the summer of 1942 ELAS began to take to the mountains, where it was joined by the noncommunist but also antimonarchist National Republican Greek League (EDES). There were a few small monarchist groups, but of little significance. SOE Middle East, based in Cairo, sent in agents, but its intelligence on the Resistance was virtually nil. Even so, they managed to get ELAS and EDES to combine in the destruction of a bridge carrying the main railroad to the port of Piraeus and an important Axis supply route to North Africa. Thereafter the two groups were mutually suspicious, especially after the British persuaded EDES to declare its support for the monarchy.

In Yugoslavia the situation was even more complicated. The two principal resistance groups were Tito's communists and Colonel Draza

OPERATIONS IN THE DODECANESE

IN THE AFTERMATH of the Italian surrender in September 1943, British Special Forces landed in the Dodecanese, Aegean islands lying close to the Turkish coast, to secure their Italian garrisons before the Germans could react. They succeeded on a number of the islands, but on the largest, Rhodes, there was also a sizeable German force, which preempted the British. Even so, Churchill was sufficiently encouraged that he ordered a brigade to be sent from the Middle East to occupy the other islands. In this way he hoped he could finally persuade Turkey to enter the war, especially since it claimed the Dodecanese, which had been an Italian possession since 1912.

The Americans, who had long been suspicious of British designs on the Balkans, refused to back the operation, stating that the priority was the campaign in Italy. In particular, they would not allow any aircraft under Allied command to be used. In addition, while the British enjoyed naval superiority in the area, the air situation was very different. The Dodecanese were within easy flying range of Luftwaffe units in Greece, while the nearest British aircraft that could be used were based in Libya.

On October 3 the Germans landed on the island of Cos and secured it the following day. They then turned their attention to Leros, which contained the bulk of the British troops. The original intention was to attack on October 9, but that night the Royal Navy intercepted one of the amphibious forces approaching the island and virtually destroyed it. The operation was therefore postponed while the Luftwaffe sank or damaged a number of warships, restricting the remainder to operating by night. Finally, on November 12 the attack went in. The British, helped by the former Italian garrison, repulsed some of the landings, but the use of German paratroops proved decisive. After four days the British were forced to surrender. The remaining British troops on the islands were then evacuated. It was an embarrassing reverse for Churchill, which did little for his standing in US eyes.

Occupied Leros
A small German occupying force remained on Leros until 1945.

Germans come ashore
The amphibious landings on Leros in November 1943 were accompanied by air drops.

The liberation of Yugoslavia
A well-disciplined group of partisans marches through a Yugoslavian village. The young men wear uniforms and carry weapons from many different countries, a good number of them captured from Germans and Italians.

Italian soldier searching suspected partisan
An Italian of the Alpine Corps searches a Yugoslavian for weapons. In September 1943 many of the Italian occupying troops were disarmed by Tito's partisans.

Mihailovic's Chetniks. These drew largely on former members of the Royal Yugoslav Army and Gendarmerie and were Serbian monarchists. Another element was in the puppet state of Croatia, where the right-wing Ustase regime set about removing all who were not pure Croats. In particular, they launched a bloody campaign designed to eradicate the two million Serbs who lived there. They, in turn, rose in revolt and both Tito and Mihailovic sought to improve their positions by lending their support.

CHETNIK STRATEGY

The Germans joined in the persecution of the Serbs and Mihailovic began to accept that the uprisings had been premature and threatened to destroy the Resistance movement. On the other hand, he had scant regard for the communists and became increasingly content to let the Axis occupiers operate against them. Indeed, some of his followers began to give active help to the Italians. The upshot of this was that Tito and his partisans were driven out of Serbia into Bosnia at the end of 1941.

TITO'S PARTISAN MOVEMENT

The British initially supported the Chetniks, even when it began to become apparent that Mihailovic was largely content to await the liberation of Yugoslavia. In the meantime, Tito's partisans were being relentlessly harried by a series of drives by Axis troops against them. Forced marches in the inhospitable mountains, and with little food, were frequent and tested their endurance to the limit. Yet, they maintained their discipline and continued to grow in number, especially after Tito formed the Anti-Fascist Council for the National Liberation of Yugoslavia in November 1942. He was, however, now at war with the Chetniks and during a German offensive against the partisans in early 1943, succeeded in destroying a force of 12,000 of them. The result was that Mihailovic was no longer able to muster significant forces in the field.

The British now began to take note of Tito and in July 1943 Churchill sent a personal representative to establish a system through which the Allies could give Tito active support. The British, however, still maintained contact with Mihailovic, which made Tito suspicious. On the other hand, the Soviets were not in a position to supply him with munitions, while the British and Americans were.

THE SURRENDER OF ITALY

When the Italians surrendered in September, the Germans moved quickly to disarm their garrisons in Greece and Yugoslavia. Tito partly forestalled them, taking the surrender of 10 Italian divisions, adding greatly to his stock of weapons. He was also able to liberate parts of Dalmatia, Croatia, and Slovenia.

In April 1944, the Germans launched their seventh and final offensive against the partisans. Tito was very nearly captured when a German airborne unit was dropped close to his HQ, and he had to be flown to Italy. He then established himself on Vis, which was being used as a base for joint Anglo-partisan raids on German-occupied islands.

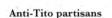

Anti-Tito partisans
Many anticommunist Yugoslavians were armed by the Germans to fight Tito's forces. In spite of this, Tito managed to gain control of large parts of the country.

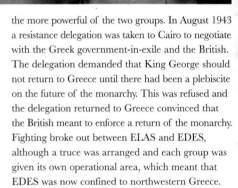

TITO (JOSIP BROZ)

TITO (1892–1980) was born Josip Broz in Croatia. From the early 1920s he was a clandestine revolutionary communist, using a number of pseudonyms, one of which, Tito, he adopted permanently. In the late 1930s he spent time in Moscow, then took over as Secretary of the Yugoslav Communist Party. When Germany invaded in April 1941, the communists stood by, since the USSR was still an ally of the Third Reich. The June 1941 invasion of the Soviet Union changed this, but Tito and his followers were initially more concerned with eradicating rival groups so as to ensure a postwar communist government. When he realized that this could not happen until the Axis occupiers had been driven out, he began to recruit partisans from all sectors. Tito's leadership ensured that he gained the support of the Western Allies to add to that of the Soviet Union. After the liberation of Belgrade in November 1944, he was able to bring the monarchists onto his side and became head of the new federal Yugoslav government in March 1945. Later that year he established a dictatorship, which he maintained until his death. It was marked by his ability to preserve the unity of the state, with its very disparate population, and to steer a neutral line between Moscow and the West.

At about the same time the British finally abandoned their support for Mihailovic. In August 1944 Tito met Churchill in Italy and the following month, with Soviet forces advancing toward Yugoslavia, he flew to Moscow in order to coordinate operations with them.

ALBANIA AND GREECE

The effect of the Italian surrender on Albania was somewhat different. The resistance groups immediately combined and succeeded in capturing much of the Italian equipment in the country and quickly liberated large areas. The Germans reacted by sending troops into the capital Tirana and then went on to place an iron grip on Albania, with harsh reprisals on the population. Enver Hoxha, the communist leader, decided that Germany would lose the war, and split with King Zog's supporters. The latter were now inveigled by the Germans into operating against the communists, thus starting a virtual civil war.

In Greece SOE worked hard to try to create a combined ELAS/EDES resistance movement, even to the extent of establishing a joint HQ, with ELAS members being allowed the majority of the key positions in it. This recognized the fact it was now

the more powerful of the two groups. In August 1943 a resistance delegation was taken to Cairo to negotiate with the Greek government-in-exile and the British. The delegation demanded that King George should not return to Greece until there had been a plebiscite on the future of the monarchy. This was refused and the delegation returned to Greece convinced that the British meant to enforce a return of the monarchy. Fighting broke out between ELAS and EDES, although a truce was arranged and each group was given its own operational area, which meant that EDES was now confined to northwestern Greece.

The fall of Romania to the Soviets at the end of August 1944 and Bulgaria's change of sides a week later dramatically transformed the situation in the Balkans. The Germans immediately began to pull their troops out of the Greek islands in preparation for a withdrawal northward. In October the Soviets thrust into Yugoslavia and, in conjunction with Tito's partisans, liberated Belgrade on the 20th of the month. The Red Army then advanced north into Hungary. Simultaneously, the Germans were withdrawing from Greece.

Ultra had forewarned the British of this. It was also clear to them that ELAS was bent on seizing power as soon as the Germans left. Under pressure from Greek army officers in Egypt, the king formed a new government, which would represent all political parties. Once the German withdrawal

The Soviets reach Belgrade
Following the capture of the city on October 20, 1944, a Soviet soldier with a mine detector makes the streets safe for the passage of vehicles.

Marching into Corinth
Headed by a detachment of ELAS partisans, British troops enter Corinth in October 1944.

"In the midst of our task of… maintaining the rudiments of order… we have become involved in a furious, although not as yet very bloody struggle."

CHURCHILL ON THE SITUATION IN GREECE, IN A TELEGRAM TO ROOSEVELT, DECEMBER 17, 1944

began in earnest, Churchill ordered British troops to be landed in southern Greece. Then, as soon as the Germans evacuated Athens, a parachute brigade was landed at a nearby airfield, while the Royal Navy occupied the port of Piraeus. In the meantime, Churchill obtained Stalin's agreement that he would not interfere in Greece provided he was given a free hand in the rest of the Balkans. On October 16 the reformed Greek government established itself in Athens. The British warned that it must move quickly to disarm the guerrillas, recreate an army, introduce a new currency, and set up the necessary machinery for international aid agencies to feed the population.

The government did its best, but it was not good enough. On December 3 communist demonstrators clashed with police in

Athens and ELAS units began to march on the capital. British reinforcements were quickly sent to Greece, but the fighting spread rapidly through the country. On Christmas Day Churchill arrived in Athens and a peace conference was set up, presided over by the respected Archbishop Damaskinos. Churchill pleaded with the delegates to resolve their differences and to continue helping in the defeat of Germany. He then persuaded King George, who was still in the Middle East, to accept the archbishop as Regent. A new government was formed at the beginning of January and a truce was signed by the warring factions. This was enshrined in the Peace of Varkiza of February 12, 1945. The communists agreed to disband their forces and support the formation of a national army. In fact, ELAS was determined on another bid to seize power once the war had ended and many ELAS members returned to the mountains.

Civil war
Steel-helmeted ELAS troops use a corner building as a shelter as they fire at police headquarters during the fighting in Athens in December 1944.

SOVIET ADVANCE ON THE EASTERN FRONT

JUNE 10–DECEMBER 27, 1944

A number of massive Soviet offensives along the entire Eastern Front began with the launch of Operation Bagration on June 23 in Byelorussia. By the end of July the Red Army had reached the Vistula River and Warsaw. In subsequent months it advanced in the north through the Baltic states, and in the south through the Ukraine into southern Poland, Romania, Bulgaria, Yugoslavia, and Hungary.

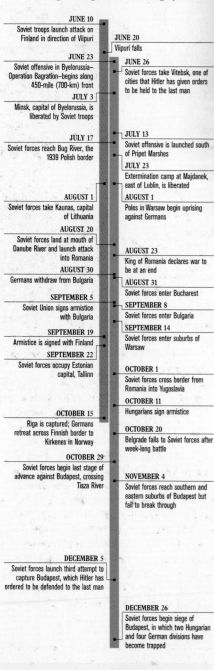

JUNE 10
Soviet troops launch attack on Finland in direction of Viipuri

JUNE 20
Viipuri falls

JUNE 23
Soviet offensive in Byelorussia–Operation Bagration–begins along 450-mile (700-km) front

JUNE 26
Soviet forces take Vitebsk, one of cities that Hitler has given orders to be held to the last man

JULY 3
Minsk, capital of Byelorussia, is liberated by Soviet troops

JULY 13
Soviet offensive is launched south of Pripet Marshes

JULY 17
Soviet forces reach Bug River, the 1939 Polish border

JULY 23
Extermination camp at Majdanek, east of Lublin, is liberated

AUGUST 1
Soviet forces take Kaunas, capital of Lithuania

AUGUST 1
Poles in Warsaw begin uprising against Germans

AUGUST 20
Soviet forces land at mouth of Danube River and launch attack into Romania

AUGUST 23
King of Romania declares war to be at an end

AUGUST 30
Germans withdraw from Bulgaria

AUGUST 31
Soviet forces enter Bucharest

SEPTEMBER 5
Soviet Union signs armistice with Bulgaria

SEPTEMBER 8
Soviet forces enter Bulgaria

SEPTEMBER 19
Armistice is signed with Finland

SEPTEMBER 14
Soviet forces enter suburbs of Warsaw

SEPTEMBER 22
Soviet forces occupy Estonian capital, Tallinn

OCTOBER 1
Soviet forces cross border from Romania into Yugoslavia

OCTOBER 11
Hungarians sign armistice

OCTOBER 15
Riga is captured; Germans retreat across Finnish border to Kirkenes in Norway

OCTOBER 20
Belgrade falls to Soviet forces after week-long battle

OCTOBER 29
Soviet forces begin last stage of advance against Budapest, crossing Tisza River

NOVEMBER 4
Soviet forces reach southern and eastern suburbs of Budapest but fail to break through

DECEMBER 5
Soviet forces launch third attempt to capture Budapest, which Hitler has ordered to be defended to the last man

DECEMBER 26
Soviet forces begin siege of Budapest, in which two Hungarian and four German divisions have become trapped

■ Advance in the Baltic region
Jun 10–Oct 15, 1944

■ Advance through Eastern Europe
Jun 22–Dec 27, 1944

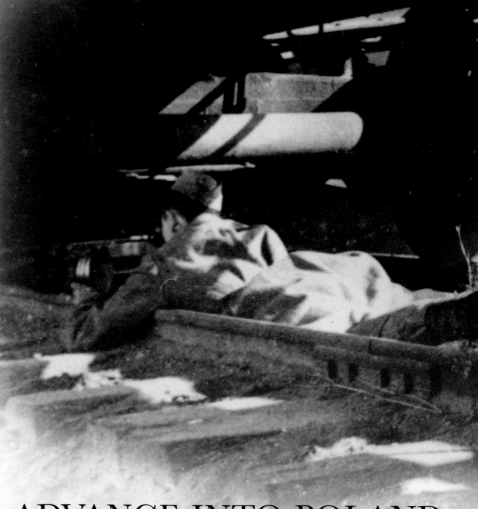

ADVANCE INTO POLAND

THE GERMAN ABANDONMENT of Sevastopol in early May 1944 had resulted in the loss of some 65,000 men. By the end of the month, total German casualties on the Eastern Front stood at approximately 1.25 million dead, over 3 million wounded or sick, and over 500,000 missing.

Casualties had remorselessly eaten away at the Ostheer's morale and fighting efficiency, particularly among the infantry. Since 1943 a growing number of troops had been conscripted from ethnic Germans in eastern Europe, and they now made up nearly one-third of Army Group Center's new intake. Senior commanders doubted both their commitment to the Third Reich and their ability to withstand the shock of their first battlefield encounter with the Red Army. At the same time, the Luftwaffe was becoming alarmed at the transfer of large numbers of day fighters and pilots to the west to defend the Reich against American bombers and at the toll being taken by constant combat.

As the spring rains fell, both sides made plans for their summer campaigns. The Stavka planned a westward drive, of which the largest element—

Operation Bagration—would be launched north and south of the Pripet Marshes, with the goal of expelling the Germans from Byelorussia, trapping and destroying Army Group Center, and then advancing through central Poland, toward Warsaw and Lublin. To the south, another offensive—the Lwow-Sandomiercz operation—was to roll through Ukrainian Galicia into southern Poland.

OPERATION BAGRATION

Operation Bagration envisaged a vast envelopment of Army Group Center along a 450-mile (700-km) front. A northern pincer, spearheaded by the Third Byelorussian Front and supported by the Second Byelorussian Front, was to drive 200 miles (320 km) westward to Minsk, where it was to link with the southern pincer formed by the northern wing of the First Byelorussian Front (see map page 247). Carrying out this encirclement would be 1.7 million troops, over twice the number in Army Group Center. Initially, they would have the support of 2,715 tanks and 1,355 assault guns, approximately six times the number available to the Germans.

Close combat in Lwow
Red Army infantry advance cautiously through the rail yards in Lwow in the Ukraine. The city was abandoned by the Germans and liberated on July 27, 1944, by troops of the First Ukrainian Front.

Bagration was preceded by a closely meshed web of deception measures and, from June 19, by concerted partisan operations against rail communications in occupied Byelorussia. By the summer of 1944 some 270,000 partisans in the region were cooperating closely with deep reconnaissance units of the Red Army and tying down up to 15 percent of Army Group Center's combat strength.

On June 22 a "reconnaissance in force" was launched by the Red Army to probe Army Group Center's defenses. In the early hours of June 23, after a crushing artillery barrage, the blow fell as

the Third Byelorussian Fronts burst on the Third Panzer Army in the area of Vitebsk. Commanded by General G. H. Reinhardt, this was a panzer army in name only, consisting of nine infantry divisions forward and two in reserve. Four of Reinhardt's divisions, comprising LIII Corps, were, on Hitler's insistence, committed to the static defense of Vitebsk. By the evening of the 23rd, Reinhardt was making demands that the commander of Army Group Center, Field Marshal Ernst Busch, allow him to evacuate Vitebsk immediately. Busch relayed this to Hitler, who eventually agreed that three divisions could fight their way out, leaving one behind to hold Vitebsk.

It mattered little, since all four divisions of LIII Corps were lost,

The road to Minsk
A smashed German artillery battery is left in the wake of the drive by the Second Byelorussian Front on Minsk—part of Operation Bagration — in early July 1944.

wiped from the map without a trace. Those who escaped the clutches of the Red Army fell into the hands of Soviet partisans, who had little enthusiasm for taking prisoners. As Army Group Center splintered under the ferocity of Bagration, Reinhardt lost a second corps and was now left with only two of his 11 divisions. To the south, around Bobruisk, the greater part of the Ninth Army was encircled. In the center of the German line the Fourth Army was forced to give ground to the Second Byelorussian Front and was threatened with isolation as the Red Army drove on toward Minsk.

On June 26 Hitler demanded that Orsha and Mogilev, which lay in the path of, respectively, the Third and Second Byelorussian Fronts, should be held to the last man, so condemning another two German divisions to destruction. He then tore himself away from the situation in Normandy to take personal control of plugging the gaping holes that had been torn in Army Group Center's front.

FALL OF MINSK

By June 28 Red Army tanks had already crossed the Berezina River and were racing westward. Busch, completely out of his depth, was replaced by Model, who immediately grasped that the Red Army's

Majdanek discovered
A pile of human remains bears grim testimony to the horrors of the extermination camp in Majdanek, near Lublin in Poland, discovered by Soviet troops on July 23, 1944.

objectives lay far beyond the rear of Army Group Center. Minsk fell on July 3, having been cut off by the Third and First Byelorussian Fronts. The envelopment left large numbers of troops of the German Fourth and Ninth Armies trapped in a giant cauldron east of the city. Between July 5 and 11 the Red Army and partisans began methodically to slice up these pockets while the Soviet armor continued to roll westward, reaching Vilna on July 13 and Bialystok on the 27th.

The scale of German losses in Bagration can only be estimated, but in the course of a month the Red Army had destroyed the equivalent of 25 divisions of the Ostheer—some 350,000 men. This number included 150,000 taken prisoner, of whom at least half would die during transportation to the camps, or from malnutrition and disease after they reached their destinations. The few survivors would not see Germany again until the middle of the next decade. The Red Army lost some 179,000 men.

LWOW–SANDOMIERCZ OPERATION
As the Red Army approached Vilna, preparations were completed for the Lwow-Sandomiercz operation, to be undertaken by Marshal I S Konev's First Ukrainian Front. A mighty force of around 1 million men, 1,600 tanks, 14,000 guns and mortars, and 2,800 combat aircraft was now ready to attack the German Army Group North Ukraine. In early summer the army group's strength on the ground had

nearly matched that fielded by Konev, but it had been much weakened as units had been withdrawn to stem the Soviet floodtide in Byelorussia.

Konev attacked on July 13. After two days of fierce fighting, the center of the German line was breached near Koltov, enabling infantry and two Soviet tank armies to pour through on July 16 and 17. The German XIII Corps and part of the First Panzer Army were encircled and then overwhelmed within a week, while the Red Army tanks advanced westward, bypassing Lwow to the north. By July 30 Konev had crossed the Vistula, having advanced 130 miles (210 km) in 17 days, and gained a lodgment on the western bank in Sandomiercz, later expanded into the Baranow bridgehead.

ADVANCE TO WARSAW
At the end of July, troops of the First Byelorussian Front reached the Vistula and by August 2 they were pushing into the outskirts of Warsaw. The capture of the Polish capital had not played a major role in the Stavka's planning for the summer of 1944. Furthermore, the situation on the ground was complicated by a rising within the city by the Polish Home Army, an armed demonstration of Polish nationalism unwelcome to Stalin. The advance to Warsaw was halted, leaving the German garrison in the city to put down the uprising ruthlessly.

As the major fighting initiated by Bagration came to an end, the Ostheer set about reinforcing the line along the Vistula while the Red Army turned to the task of rebuilding and reequipping its exhausted formations. Offensive operations in Poland were not to resume until January 1945.

OPERATIONS IN THE BALTIC
The Stavka's operational focus now shifted north to the Baltic and south to Romania. In the Baltic the German Army Group North faced four Red Army fronts whose goal was to liberate Estonia, Latvia, and Lithuania. By the end of July the Leningrad Front had captured Narva on the Baltic coast, the Third Baltic Front had driven deep into Latvia and Estonia, and the Second and First Baltic Fronts had thrust toward Riga and Memel, so severing land communications between Army Groups North and Center. On August 16 the Germans launched a counterattack which briefly reestablished a land link between the two army groups and offered Army Group North an opportunity to pull out of the Baltic states with all its heavy equipment.

Confrontation of tanks in Poland
A T-34 noses its way past a damaged German Mk VI Tiger I heavy tank. It usually took about six medium tanks to knock out a massively armored Tiger.

Red Army troops in Poland
Infantrymen race through a blazing street during Operation Bagration. Because Red Army soldiers were not issued with blankets, greatcoats were worn even in the summer.

THE WARSAW UPRISING

FROM 1939 THE POLES had organized an underground resistance movement. Its armed wing was the Polish Home Army, whose members were loyal to the Polish government-in-exile in London. However, in July 1944 the Soviet Union had established its own communist government in waiting in the liberated Polish city of Lublin. On August 1, 1944, with the Red Army only 12 miles (19 km) from Warsaw, 20,000 members of the Polish Home Army, commanded by General Tadeusz Bor Komorowski, rose up against the German garrison. In four days they succeeded in taking control of about three-fifths of Warsaw, but no strategic points.

The First Byelorussian Front did not come to the aid of the Home Army, instead halting to the south and east of Warsaw. Warsaw had never been an objective of Bagration, and if the Red Army entered the city, it would face an army of citizens who were also hostile to the Soviet Union. Stalin prevaricated, even refusing a British and American request to land on Soviet soil to provide the Home Army with arms and medical supplies. When Home Army detachments from outside Warsaw attempted to aid the uprising, they were surrounded and disarmed by Red Army troops.

Freed of pressure from the Red Army, SS troops quashed the uprising with utter ruthlessness. Captured Polish fighters were summarily executed by squads of released convicts, as were doctors and nurses attending the wounded. Civilians were marched in front of tanks as human shields. Gas was used to flush out those who attempted to flee through the sewers.

On September 10 the First Byelorussian Front finally moved on Warsaw, but did not break into the city. On October 2 Komorowski surrendered. In the uprising some 15,000 members of the Home Army and approximately 225,000 civilians had lost their lives. Those who had survived were deported to German camps while the Germans set about the total demolition of what remained of the ancient city.

Injured resistance fighter
Few members of the Polish Home Army managed to escape the terrible vengeance wreaked by the Germans as they suppressed the uprising. Even hospitals, with staff and patients inside, were burned down.

German staff car captured by insurgents
In the early days of the uprising the rebels overwhelmed parts of the German garrison. They failed, however, to capture the railroad stations or the bridges over the Vistula.

Hitler, however, spurned the opportunity. The Red Army went on the offensive again in mid-September. Tallinn, the Estonian capital, was taken on September 22, and Riga fell on October 15. By mid-October the coast around Memel had been secured, but the city itself was to hold out until January 1945. Twenty-six divisions of Army Group North withdrew to the Courland peninsula, where they remained until the end of the war in order to provide the German Navy with continuing access to Baltic waters for the training of U-boat crews.

WAR WITH FINLAND

After the failure of Operation Citadel, Finland had sought to make peace with the Soviet Union, but the negotiations had broken down. In the fall of 1943 Finland had a highly skilled and durable army of 350,00 men who faced just 180,000 Red Army troops of poor quality. In northern Lapland the German 20th

> "…in the final analysis, what can we expect of a front… if one now sees that in the rear the most important posts were occupied by downright destructionists, not defeatists, but destructionists?"

HITLER IN A REVIEW OF THE MILITARY SITUATION ON THE EASTERN FRONT, JULY 31, 1944

Mountain Army was some 180,000 strong, more than a match for the Soviet troops on the Karelian Front. The Finns, however, had no illusions about the likely outcome of the war. While their president, Risto Ryti, pledged to the Germans not to sign a separate peace with the Soviet Union, they were determined to sit out the conflict.

For his part, Stalin was eager to settle with Finland before Bagration. Having reinforced the Red Army's Karelian and Leningrad Fronts, Stalin ordered them to go on the offensive in June 1944 against the vulnerable southeast flank of the Finnish army. The Finns clung on throughout the summer. On August 4 Marshal Carl Gustaf Mannerheim, the hero of the Winter War of 1939–40 and the Finnish commander-in-chief, succeeded Ryti as head of state and repudiated the latter's pledge. Moscow then agreed to resume negotiations with Finland on the condition that Mannerheim broke off relations with

Germany and the 20th Mountain Army left Finnish territory by September 15. The Finns were able to demand this withdrawal following a German attempt on September 15 to seize the Finnish naval base of Suursaari, which was beaten off with heavy German losses. An armistice was signed with the Soviet Union on September 19 as the German withdrawal continued, and by the end of October the 20th Mountain Army was in Norway, bringing an end to Finnish participation in World War II.

BALKAN STALINGRAD

By the end of July 1944 relations between Germany and Romania had badly deteriorated. The Romanian dictator, Marshal Ion Antonescu, insisted on equality

Celebrations in Bulgaria
Bulgarians celebrated their country's signing of an armistice with the Soviet Union on September 5, 1944. Three days later Bulgaria declared war on Germany.

Jewish man mourns in Budapest
Over 60 percent of Hungary's 750,000 Jews were sent to Auschwitz in 1944. Some, however, were still living in Budapest when it came under siege in December.

of command, and the Germans were forced to accept it despite their deep misgivings about the evident inefficiency and corruption of their Romanian allies. In May Antonescu had also opened secret but short-lived negotiations with the Soviet Union. The new German commander of Army Group South Ukraine, General Johannes Friessner, was well aware of the unreliability of his Romanian allies and the possible dangers of shared command. His warnings were ignored by Hitler.

Army Group South Ukraine consisted of two German armies and two Romanian armies, all of which were short of experience, armor, air support, and motor transportation. On August 20 the Soviet Second and Third Ukrainian Fronts fell on Friessner's forces. Within 24 hours the German Sixth Army had been cut off, and—as it became apparent to Friessner that the Romanians were surrendering without a fight—it quickly found itself trapped in a cauldron between the Dniester and the Pruth.

Antonescu was arrested on August 23 and King Carol of Romania then appealed to his troops to lay down their arms. Two days later, Hitler ordered 150 aircraft to bomb the Romanian capital Bucharest, giving the Romanians the pretext to declare war on Germany. Meanwhile, under constant attack from the Red Air Force, the Sixth Army tried to fight its way westward. Another 200,000 German troops were consumed in nine days, a disaster to rank alongside Stalingrad, though the end came more swiftly and in stifling summer heat.

On August 30 the Red Army seized the oilfields in Ploesti, Germany's last major source of crude oil, and on the following day took Bucharest. Romania was rapidly occupied by Soviet troops, together with Bulgaria, which declared war on Germany on September 8. The 500,000-strong Bulgarian Army joined the Red Army as it entered Yugoslavia.

To the north, the Red Army had overextended itself as it pushed into southeast Hungary against more resolute opposition than it had encountered in

Advance from the Baltic to the Balkans

With the opening, on June 23, of Operation Bagration along a 450-mile (700-km) front in Byelorussia, the relentless Soviet advance through eastern Europe got under way. Along the entire Eastern Front, from the Baltic states in the north to Romania, Bulgaria, and Yugoslavia in the south, the Germans were steadily pushed back.

Romania. Its leading forces reached Debrecen, just 70 miles (110 km) from Budapest, on October 8. But then, as panic rose in the Hungarian capital, two German panzer divisions attacked the Soviet spearhead to cut off and destroy three corps. The Second and Third Ukrainian Fronts made further attempts in November and December to advance

to Budapest, but it was not until December 26 that they succeeded in encircling the city. The four German and two Hungarian divisions inside the city were ordered to hold out until relieved. This relief, however, was never to come, and when 30,000 troops attempted to break out on February 11, 1945, fewer than 700 reached the lines to the west.

ASIA AND THE PACIFIC

JUNE–DECEMBER 1944

After victory at the Battle of the Philippine Sea in June 1944, the Americans took the tide of war to the Philippines and thus cut Japan's lines of communication with the Southern Resources Area. With complementary victories in western New Guinea and Burma, by the end of 1944 Japan's defeat was assured.

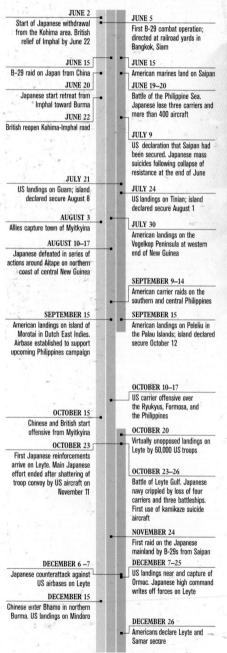

JUNE 2 Start of Japanese withdrawal from the Kohima area. British relief of Imphal by June 22

JUNE 5 First B-29 combat operation; directed at railroad yards in Bangkok, Siam

JUNE 15 B-29 raid on Japan from China

JUNE 15 American marines land on Saipan

JUNE 20 Japanese start retreat from Imphal toward Burma

JUNE 19–20 Battle of the Philippine Sea. Japanese lose three carriers and more than 400 aircraft

JUNE 22 British reopen Kohima-Imphal road

JULY 9 US declaration that Saipan had been secured. Japanese mass suicides following collapse of resistance at the end of June

JULY 21 US landings on Guam; island declared secure August 8

JULY 24 US landings on Tinian; island declared secure August 1

AUGUST 3 Allies capture town of Myitkyina

JULY 30 American landings on the Vogelkop Peninsula at western end of New Guinea

AUGUST 10–17 Japanese defeated in series of actions around Aitape on northern coast of central New Guinea

SEPTEMBER 9–14 American carrier raids on the southern and central Philippines

SEPTEMBER 15 American landings on island of Morotai in Dutch East Indies. Airbase established to support upcoming Philippines campaign

SEPTEMBER 15 American landings on Peleliu in the Palau Islands; island declared secure October 12

OCTOBER 10–17 US carrier offensive over the Ryukyus, Formosa, and the Philippines

OCTOBER 15 Chinese and British start offensive from Myitkyina

OCTOBER 20 Virtually unopposed landings on Leyte by 60,000 US troops

OCTOBER 23 First Japanese reinforcements arrive on Leyte. Main Japanese effort ended after shattering of troop convoy by US aircraft on November 11

OCTOBER 23–26 Battle of Leyte Gulf. Japanese navy crippled by loss of four carriers and three battleships. First use of kamikaze suicide aircraft

NOVEMBER 24 First raid on the Japanese mainland by B-29s from Saipan

DECEMBER 6–7 Japanese counterattack against US airbases on Leyte

DECEMBER 7–25 US landings near and capture of Ormoc. Japanese high command writes off forces on Leyte

DECEMBER 15 Chinese enter Bhamo in northern Burma. US landings on Mindoro

DECEMBER 26 Americans declare Leyte and Samar secure

India and Burma Jun–Dec 1944 | Central Pacific Jun–Sept, 1944 | Invasion of the Philippines Oct 20, 1944 | Other events

JAPAN NEAR THE BRINK

THE JAPANESE CONQUEST of the British possession of Burma between December 1941 and May 1942 cost the victors few casualties and achieved three objectives: the closing of the Burma Road and the main supply route into Kuomintang (Nationalist) China; the possession of a country rich in resources, such as rice; and defense in depth for Southeast Asia. Burma became part of the perimeter on which Japan planned to fight its enemies to exhaustion.

The mountains, valleys, and jungle of the India–Burma border did indeed serve as a line

Aerial resupply of the Chindits
The Chindits—Allied troops commanded by Orde Wingate who fought behind Japanese lines in Burma—depended on efficient aerial resupply missions.

of mutual exhaustion in spring 1942, but events after the monsoon ended in November 1942 changed the attitudes of the Japanese. For the British, the defeat in Burma had to be reversed and, at the insistence of the Americans, the overland route to China had to be reopened. The British began two offensives, one from the Chittagong area on the Indian coast of the Bay of Bengal into the Arakan, and another by a force known as the Chindits, which were infiltrated across the border area. A Japanese division comprehensively and embarrassingly outfought the

The high ground
Sikh machine-gunners look out from Pagoda Hill during the recapture of Mandalay in March 1945, while the battle rages below around Fort Dufferin.

British corps in the Arakan, while the only real achievement registered by the Chindits was measured in column inches in British newspapers rather than on the ground. But the Japanese read the signs correctly: the 1942–43 effort was only a foretaste of what would come as soon as the British recovered their strength in northeast India and the Allies sought to clear Burma in order to reopen overland communications with the Chinese Nationalists. In 1943–44 the situation on the line of mutual exhaustion, which a year earlier had been convenient to both sides, threatened to change, posing new problems for the Japanese. Accordingly the imperial high command undertook the so-called "March on Delhi," a spoiling offensive into northeast India that would secure the border towns of Imphal and Kohima at the end of the dry season. The onset of the monsoon would prevent any Allied counteroffensive to recover the towns.

Chindit insignia
The Chindit badge portrays a Chinthe, the mythical beast that guards Burmese temples. It was from the word Chinthe that the Chindits derived their name.

SETBACKS FOR THE JAPANESE
Before the Japanese offensive began, however, a Sino-American force in northeast India began to advance down the Hukawng valley in the direction of Myitkyina. A Japanese diversionary attack in the Arakan was quickly halted, and while Japanese formations crossed the Chindwin to move against Imphal and Kohima, a second Chindit operation, with units moved by transport aircraft, began in the Japanese rear areas. Again, the Chindits achieved little in real terms. By the time that Myitkyina fell in August 1944, however, disaster had overwhelmed the Japanese at Imphal and Kohima.

The Japanese move through the mountains failed either to encircle British formations or to capture the two towns. The British were therefore able to withdraw in good order to strong new defensive positions, in which they were kept supplied by transport aircraft drawn from as far away as the Mediterranean theater. Although the siege of Kohima was very quickly broken, the Japanese still refused to abandon the offensive. Their supply lines were wholly inadequate, however, and, in effect, the besiegers became the besieged. After Imphal had been relieved on June 22 by Allied forces coming forward from Kohima, the Japanese 15th Army was destroyed piecemeal. The loss of some 50,000 men killed and wounded was to compromise the army's ability to conduct an effective defensive campaign in northern Burma in 1944–45.

The main Allied offensive effort in northern Burma was undertaken by the British. The capture of Ramree Island in December 1944 was the first in a series of operations in the Arakan that ended with the capture of strategic targets. Meanwhile, the main British effort was directed against Meiktila—which was captured on March 4—while the attention of the Japanese was focused on Mandalay. With Chinese forces breaking down resistance on the Myitkyina and Salween sectors, the Japanese hoped to retain Mandalay and retake Meiktila. By the end of March, however, they were pulling back through the lower Salween valley in order to defend Tennasserim and Siam, while the British

Marauders in the Burmese jungle
In 1944 a detachment of "Merrill's Marauders," a US commando force, patrols the Burmese jungle on the lookout for snipers during the advance on Myitkyina.

THE INDIAN NATIONAL ARMY
NOT ALL INDIANS supported the Allies in World War II. The most prominent of those who sided with the Axis powers was Subhas Chandra Bose, who was elected president of the Indian National Congress Party in 1938. Imprisoned by the British, he escaped in 1941 and went first to Germany for talks with Nazi leaders and then to Japanese-held Singapore. With the help of the Japanese, Bose led the 40,000 strong Indian National Army (INA), which advanced across Burma but was defeated in India in 1944. When Japan surrendered in August 1945, Bose fled India and died after a plane crash in Taiwan. Reviled by some, Bose is praised by others for fostering anticolonial sentiment in the subcontinent.

Indian Nationalist
Subhas Chandra Bose was the founding father of the Indian National Army and a fierce advocate of Indian independence from Britain.

Hitler's Indian allies
Before taking over the Japanese-formed INA, Bose created an Indian Legion in the German Army. Some 3,000-strong, it became part of the Waffen-SS in 1944.

advanced down the Irrawaddy and Sittang valleys. The British took Rangoon unopposed on May 3, just ahead of the monsoon. By then the rationale for much of the Allied effort in Burma had been overtaken by events. Although the first convoys to Nationalist China reached Kunming in January 1945, their importance had been reduced by air supply routes. Throughout the next eight months overland communications never accounted for more than a twelfth of the materials supplied to the Chinese. Despite its local significance, the clearing of Burma contributed little to victory over Japan.

THE JAPANESE IN CHINA

In 1937–38 the Japanese overran virtually the whole of China that was worth occupying. Thereafter, aside from some minor operations in the south of the country in 1941, they adopted a primarily defensive stance. Saddled with a crippling manpower and financial commitment, without the military means

Japanese prayer flag
Many Japanese soldiers carried flags inside their combat jackets during World War II. The flags were often decorated with prayers and family names, and were designed to bring good luck on the battlefield.

to defeat the Kuomintang, and unwilling to sponsor a credible alternative to the Chungking regime, the Japanese faced a war that could not be won.

In the north the Japanese devastated considerable areas and neutralized communist resistance in the so-called "Three-All" offensives—"Kill All," "Burn All," and "Loot All." However, between 1938 and 1944 there existed in many areas a "special undeclared peace," despite occasional "rice raids" by the occupying troops. Nationalists, communists, and Japanese effectively observed an unofficial truce, broken by clashes between Chinese factions and local Japanese operations. The Nationalists were unwilling to fight because they felt that Japan's defeat was assured and would come without any major contribution from the Chinese. Their policy was therefore to preserve their strength in readiness for a resumption of the civil war with the communists. The latter naturally reasoned along very much the same lines as the Nationalists.

Chinese infantry
Chinese infantrymen ford a stream in southern Yunnan province on their way to reinforce troops fighting the Japanese on the Salween River front.

After the start of the Pacific war in 1941, however, the United States sought a full Chinese military contribution to Japan's defeat. It undertook to provide supplies for an army of 90 divisions that would undertake major offensive operations. The Americans also planned to use airfields in China from which to bomb the Japanese Home Islands. The first 14th Air Force raid on Formosa, on November 25, 1943—launched from within China—was by common consent the spur for the Japanese high command to consider a general offensive in China. Its aim was to secure the Peking–Hankow, Canton–Hankow, and Hunan–Kwangsi railroad lines and the airfields at Hengyang, Kweilin, Ling Ling, and Liuchow.

The offensive, code-named Ichi-Go, involved some 620,000 troops and began in April 1944 with the conquest of Hunan province. The main effort was made south of the Yangtze, below Ichang, in May. The Japanese secured Liuyang on June 14, Changsa four days later, and Hengyang on August 8. The next phase of operations saw simultaneous offensives from Hengyang toward Kweilin and Liuchow, and from Canton (Guangzhou) toward Wuchow and Nanning. So great was Japanese success that by December they had secured unbroken communications over land from Malaya to Korea. The Japanese occupied Tushan and Tuyün in December 1944 and Sichuan in

Flying Tigers
US pilots in China were known as "Flying Tigers." After July 1942 they were part of the US China Air Task Force. They painted sharks' mouths on their planes to cause alarm among the shark-fearing Japanese.

January 1945, but spring saw the start of a general reduction and withdrawal of the Japanese forces in southern China in readiness for transfer north to Manchoutikuo (Manchuria).

POLITICAL CONSEQUENCES

The Ichi-Go offensive was of dubious military relevance, but it was significant in two other ways. First, the failure of the Kuomintang to offer any kind of coherent or successful resistance to Japanese aggression provoked a full-blown crisis between the regime and the United States. Washington, tiring of Kuomintang ineffectiveness, sought to place its local commander, Joseph Stilwell, in charge of all operations in the region. Without any viable political alternative to the regime led by Chiang Kai-shek, however, the effort miscarried. When the Americans threatened to choke his regime to death, Chiang simply threatened to die. In October 1944 Washington was forced to recall Stilwell and further underwrite the Nationalist regime in Chungking.

Second, and more importantly, the Kuomintang failure to resist the Ichi-Go offensives had a profound effect on the the Chinese public. Hunan province was overrun at the cost of just 869 Japanese dead. The collapse of Kuomintang resistance, or more accurately its failure to materialize at all, enraged local

populations which for years had lived under Nationalist misrule. Angry civilians launched widespread massacres of Kuomintang troops as they tried to desert the people they should have protected. This was Ichi-Go's real significance: it demonstrated clearly the direction in which opinion was moving within China. By this time it was clear that the Kuomintang was too weak to rule, but too strong to be overthrown. The confirmation of its military weakness and incompetence, together

Vinegar Joe
Joseph Stilwell, commander of US and Chinese forces in Burma, takes a break beside the Tani River. Stilwell, whose brusque manner earned him the nickname "Vinegar Joe," led the attack on Myitkyina.

> The temples, cellars, and mysterious chambers covering Mandalay Hill were made of reinforced concrete. No Japanese was alive and visible; but scores of them were alive, invisible, in the subterranean chambers. A gruesome campaign of extermination began, among the temples of one of the most sacred places of the Buddhist faith. Sikh machine-gunners sat all day on the flat roofs, their guns aimed down the hill on either side of the covered stairway. Every now and then a Japanese put out his head and fired a quick upward shot. A Sikh got a bullet through his brain five yards from me.
>
> JOHN MASTERS OF THE GURKHA RIFLES ON THE BRITISH RECAPTURE OF MANDALAY, MARCH 20, 1945

with its long record of corruption and violence toward its opponents, were crucial in the protracted process whereby the political and moral initiatives in China were secured by the communists, who would eventually take power in 1949.

A PLACE TO DIE

Defeat in the carrier battle off the Marianas in June 1944 left Japan in an impossible situation. It was saddled with defensive commitments that reached from the Home Islands to the Indies, but

The assault on Leyte
Rockets from a US Navy landing craft streak toward the beachhead in support of troops assaulting the Philippine island of Leyte in October 1944.

had no carrier force worthy of the name to meet them. The high command also saw that any American move into the Philippines, and thus across Japanese lines of communication with the vital Southern Resources Area, would represent a defeat as comprehensive as an invasion and conquest of the Home Islands. It prepared for a battle that might check or even turn back the American tide. Within the navy, there was a further consideration: as a service it simply could not envisage surviving national defeat.

In seeking a final battle with the enemy it wished to be afforded "a fitting place to die," and "the chance to bloom as flowers of death."

For the Americans in this same period a series of carrier operations revealed a previously unsuspected Japanese weakness in the Philippines. The revelation came at the same time as the possibility of landings on Formosa was set aside in favor of landings in the Philippines, and encouraged an acceleration of the planned schedule of operations. Bypassing the island of Mindanao, troops would land on Leyte in the third week of October. A planned landing in the Palau Islands in the West Pacific, meanwhile, went ahead because it was too late to cancel it.

Defending the invasion fleet
US ships in Leyte Gulf launch antiaircraft fire on a scale that illustrates the overwhelming firepower US forces enjoyed during the Pacific campaign.

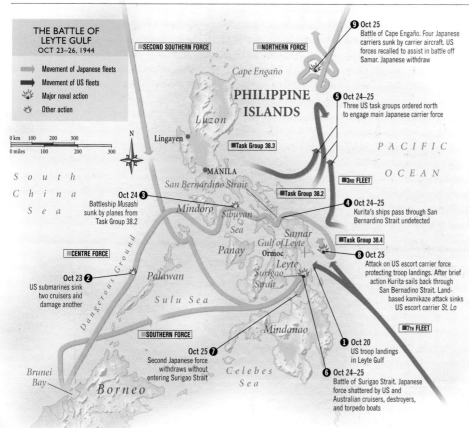

THE BATTLE OF
LEYTE GULF
OCT 23–26, 1944

→ Movement of Japanese fleets
→ Movement of US fleets
✸ Major naval action
✷ Other action

0 km 100 200 300
0 miles 100 200 300

PHILIPPINE ISLANDS

SECOND SOUTHERN FORCE
NORTHERN FORCE

Cape Engaño

Luzon

Lingayen

MANILA

San Bernardino Strait

Mindoro
Sibuyan Sea

Panay

Samar
Gulf of Leyte
Ormoc
Leyte
Surigao Strait

Mindanao

S o u t h   C h i n a   S e a

P A C I F I C   O C E A N

Task Group 38.3
Task Group 38.2
3RD FLEET
Task Group 38.4
7TH FLEET

CENTRE FORCE
SOUTHERN FORCE

Palawan
Sulu Sea
Celebes Sea

Brunei Bay
Borneo
Dangerous Ground

9 Oct 25 Battle of Cape Engaño. Four Japanese carriers sunk by carrier aircraft. US forces recalled to assist in battle off Samar. Japanese withdraw

5 Oct 24–25 Three US task groups ordered north to engage main Japanese carrier force

Oct 24 3 Battleship *Musashi* sunk by planes from Task Group 38.2

4 Oct 24–25 Kurita's ships pass through San Bernardino Strait undetected

Oct 23 2 US submarines sink two cruisers and damage another

8 Oct 25 Attack on US escort carrier force protecting troop landings. After brief action Kurita sails back through San Bernadino Strait. Land-based kamikaze attack sinks US escort carrier *St. Lo*

1 Oct 20 US troop landings in Leyte Gulf

Oct 25 7 Second Japanese force withdraws without entering Surigao Strait

6 Oct 24–25 Battle of Surigao Strait. Japanese force shattered by US and Australian cruisers, destroyers, and torpedo boats

Rallying to the cause
This US propaganda poster was designed to raise morale among Filipino soldiers and recruit more Filipinos for the fight against Japan.

After aircraft from American carriers had bombed airfields and other targets on first Formosa and then the Philippines, the initial landings were made on October 17 on the tiny islands that guarded the approach to Leyte. The main landings on Leyte came three days later, by which time no fewer than four Japanese fleet formations were making their way to the Philippines. The Japanese planned to use their single carrier formation as bait to lure the US carrier force away from the Philippines. They then hoped to use land-based aircraft from the islands to strike against the US carrier formations. The main battle force, without any close air support because of the limited availability of Japanese aircraft and aircrew, was meanwhile to make its way through the San Bernardino Strait. As it turned out, however, this force was divided. One formation was ordered to make its way into Leyte Gulf through the Surigao Strait. It would be joined by another independent force coming from the north.

Leyte Gulf
Although its focus lay in the waters to the east of the Philippine Islands, the naval battle was fought over a vast area of 450,000 sq miles (1,165,500 sq km).

The Japanese lost two heavy cruisers to American submarines even before the main action was joined on October 24. On the first day of the battle US carrier aircraft attacked the main Japanese force moving through the Sibuyan Sea and sank the giant battleship *Musashi*. With the Japanese turning away under repeated attacks, the Americans belatedly discovered the Japanese carrier force to the northeast. The US carrier force—which lost the light carrier *Princeton* to a lone Judy dive-bomber – turned to the north. This left the San Bernardino Strait open. Although the Japanese formation that had been sent to the south lost all but one of its ships in the Battle of the Surigao Strait, the main formation passed

safely through the San Bernardino Strait and emerged off Samar early on October 25. There it engaged the American escort carrier groups in a confused and, on the Japanese side, badly conducted action. The Japanese lost three heavy cruisers in accounting for one escort carrier, two destroyers, and one destroyer escort. The Japanese ships turned away and kamikaze aircraft took up the offensive for the rest of the action, sinking one escort carrier and damaging four more.

Despite the fact that the American force that sailed north succeeded in sinking four aircraft carriers and two destroyers, leaving the San Bernardino Strait unguarded was an undoubted error. The Americans were lucky to escape from the engagement off Samar with only light losses. In the course of the whole battle American ships, aircraft, and submarines accounted for one fleet and three light carriers, three battleships, six heavy and four light cruisers, and 11 destroyers—28 ships of 318,667 tons—plus two submarines and three landing ships.

The full measure of the victory soon became apparent. American carrier aircraft ranged over the Philippines and preyed upon Japanese shipping stripped of any air cover. From October 29 to November 30, the Americans sank 49 warships of

Taking cover
US soldiers are forced to crouch low as the enemy fires rounds overhead on the east coast of Leyte Island, just after the initial landings on October 20, 1944.

"People of the Philippines: I have returned. By the grace of Almighty God our forces stand again on Philippine soil—soil consecrated in the blood of our two peoples.... Rally to me."

GENERAL DOUGLAS MACARTHUR, OCTOBER 20, 1944

JAPANESE SHIPPING LOSSES

THESE GRAPHS SHOW CLEARLY the devastation suffered by Japanese shipping during World War II. As an island nation that was always dependent on imports of food and raw materials, Japan found such losses unendurable. In the second half of 1944 merchant shipping losses were so heavy that in the final year of the war much of the population of Japan came perilously close to starvation. The figures in parentheses in the right-hand table give the number of warships lost in each period.

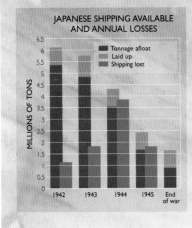

JAPANESE SHIPPING AVAILABLE AND ANNUAL LOSSES

MILLIONS OF TONS

- Tonnage afloat
- Laid up
- Shipping lost

1942 1943 1944 1945 End of war

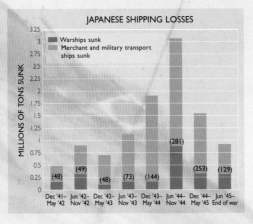

JAPANESE SHIPPING LOSSES

MILLIONS OF TONS SUNK

- Warships sunk
- Merchant and military transport ships sunk

Dec '41–May '42	Jun '42–Nov '42	Dec '42–May '43	Jun '43–Nov '43	Dec '43–May '44	Jun '44–Nov '44	Dec '44–May '45	Jun '45–End of war
(48)	(49)	(48)	(73)	(144)	(281)	(253)	(129)

The basic lack of merchant shipping was compounded by the low priority given to protecting trade—the Imperial Navy was overwhelmingly concerned with battle. When an escort command was belatedly organized in November 1943, it had just 32 escorts of dubious quality. They lacked adequate radio, radar, sonar, and depth charges, while escort aircraft lacked any weapon other than bombs.

The elements of defeat began to come together with the start of the American drive across the Central Pacific. During the first two years of war it was American submarines that carried the burden of the campaign against shipping; by 1944 their effectiveness was increased by the ability to read enemy signals and thus calculate Japanese shipping

US air supremacy
A Japanese destroyer is struck amidships during an aerial attack by a squadron of B-25 Mitchells, the powerful twin-engined bombers that helped to maintain US air supremacy over the Pacific Ocean.

119,655 tons and 48 service auxiliaries, oilers, and merchantmen—a further 212,476 tons—around the Philippines. Such was the finale to a battle fought over some 450,000 sq miles (1,165,500 sq km). The Imperial Navy had found its "fitting place to die." From now on it was reduced to coastguard status.

JAPAN'S SUPPLY CRISIS
The defeat in the Battle of Leyte Gulf left Japanese merchant shipping in crisis. In terms of shipping losses, the three-month period from September to November 1944 was the worst quarter-year of the

war for Japan. In reality, however, the country's position with regard to shipping and trade had been little more than a disaster waiting to happen since the very start of the conflict. Even before hostilities began, Japan lacked both sufficient resources at home to maintain its own population and enough merchant shipping to import what it needed. Once war did break out, there were not enough shipyards and building facilities to build fleet units, escorts, and merchantmen at the same time. Military and trade considerations competed against one another, to the detriment of both. Japan also lacked adequate numbers of high-quality escorts that could protect merchant vessels and the organization to manage shipping requirements.

In 1941 Japan had imported a total of some 48,700,000 tons of food, raw materials, and other goods. Maintaining such a volume of trade required 10 million tons of shipping. On March 31, 1942, however, Japan had under its own flag no more than 6,150,000 tons of shipping, of which over a tenth was laid up. By the end of the war, when Japan possessed just 1,620,000 tons of shipping, more than two-fifths of the total was laid up. By 1944 Japan's imports had fallen to 17,150,000 tons. The following year they fell again, to a disastrous 7,100,000 tons. Some estimates suggest that, had the war continued into 1946, the lack of food imports would have led to perhaps 7 million deaths in Japan as a direct result of malnutrition-related disease.

Rearming the fleet
US sailors supervise the loading of a torpedo into an attack submarine. Each weapon was loaded manually and it could take a number of hours to rearm fully.

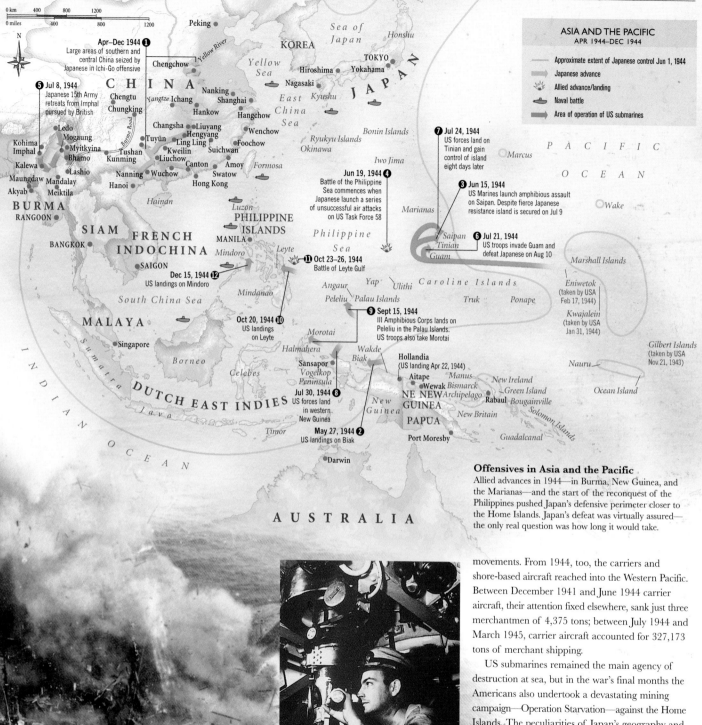

ASIA AND THE PACIFIC
APR 1944–DEC 1944

Approximate extent of Japanese control Jun 1, 1944
Japanese advance
Allied advance/landing
Naval battle
Area of operation of US submarines

Apr–Dec 1944 ❶
Large areas of southern and central China seized by Japanese in Ichi-Go offensive

Jul 8, 1944 ❺
Japanese 15th Army retreats from Imphal pursued by British

Jul 24, 1944 ❼
US forces land on Tinian and gain control of island eight days later

Jun 15, 1944 ❸
US Marines launch amphibious assault on Saipan. Despite fierce Japanese resistance island is secured on Jul 9

Jun 19, 1944 ❹
Battle of the Philippine Sea commences when Japanese launch a series of unsuccessful air attacks on US Task Force 58

Jul 21, 1944 ❻
US troops invade Guam and defeat Japanese on Aug 10

Oct 23–26, 1944 ⓫
Battle of Leyte Gulf

Dec 15, 1944 ⓬
US landings on Mindoro

Oct 20, 1944 ❿
US landings on Leyte

Sept 15, 1944 ❾
III Amphibious Corps lands on Peleliu in the Palau Islands. US troops also take Morotai

Jul 30, 1944 ❽
US forces land in western New Guinea

May 27, 1944 ❷
US landings on Biak

Hollandia
(US landing Apr 22, 1944)

Eniwetok
(taken by USA
Feb 17, 1944)

Kwajalein
(taken by USA
Jan 31, 1944)

Gilbert Islands
(taken by USA
Nov 21, 1943)

Offensives in Asia and the Pacific

Allied advances in 1944—in Burma, New Guinea, and the Marianas—and the start of the reconquest of the Philippines pushed Japan's defensive perimeter closer to the Home Islands. Japan's defeat was virtually assured—the only real question was how long it would take.

Searching for shipping

An officer of the watch peers through the periscope in the control room of a US submarine as it patrols the waters of the Pacific.

movements. From 1944, too, the carriers and shore-based aircraft reached into the Western Pacific. Between December 1941 and June 1944 carrier aircraft, their attention fixed elsewhere, sank just three merchantmen of 4,375 tons; between July 1944 and March 1945, carrier aircraft accounted for 327,173 tons of merchant shipping.

US submarines remained the main agency of destruction at sea, but in the war's final months the Americans also undertook a devastating mining campaign—Operation Starvation—against the Home Islands. The peculiarities of Japan's geography and its inadequate cross-country rail communications meant that ports on the sheltered Sea of Japan were not able to handle any great volume of trade. The ports on the exposed east coast and in the Inland Sea, however, were hopelessly vulnerable to mining. The American effort only exacerbated Japan's shipping crisis. By August 1945 shipping had fallen to only one-quarter of May levels—themselves already low—and Japan's economic collapse was all but complete.

THE FINAL
BATTLES
1945

THE YEAR THAT FINALLY BROUGHT WORLD WAR II TO AN

END BEGAN WITH A MASSIVE RED ARMY OFFENSIVE

THROUGH POLAND INTO GERMANY. THE WESTERN

ALLIES FOUGHT THEIR WAY TO THE RHINE AND THEN

SWEPT ON TO THE ELBE AS SOVIET FORCES PREPARED

TO ATTACK BERLIN. IN ITALY, TOO, ALLIED PRESSURE

BROUGHT ABOUT THE SURRENDER OF THE AXIS FORCES.

JAPAN STILL FOUGHT ON, AND AFTER GRIM BATTLES

TO SECURE THE PACIFIC ISLANDS OF IWO JIMA AND

OKINAWA, THE ALLIES WERE FACED WITH THE

POTENTIALLY COSTLY INVASION OF THE JAPANESE HOME

ISLANDS. THE DEPLOYMENT OF A NEW AND TERRIBLE

WEAPON WAS TO MAKE THIS UNNECESSARY.

Americans crossing the Rhine
US troops huddle down to avoid enemy
fire as they cross the Rhine in March.
The river was the last major obstacle
the Allies had to overcome during their
advance into Germany.

THE DEFEAT OF THE AXIS

IN JANUARY 1945, WITH THE FAILURE OF THE ARDENNES COUNTER-
OFFENSIVE AND THE SOVIET UNION ABOUT TO MOUNT A MAJOR
ASSAULT ACROSS THE VISTULA, TIME WAS RUNNING OUT FOR THE
THIRD REICH. ITS PROBLEMS WERE COMPOUNDED BY THE RENEWED
ALLIED BOMBING OFFENSIVE. JAPAN FACED SIMILAR DIFFICULTIES
AS THE AMERICAN-LED OFFENSIVE CREPT EVER CLOSER TO THE
MAINLAND, WHICH WAS NOW SUBJECTED TO INTENSIVE AIR ATTACK.

THE SOVIET PLAN FOR 1945 called for a continuation of the assaults on East Prussia and Hungary. The main blow, however, would be an offensive across the Vistula River in Poland, its target Berlin. German intelligence became aware of the plan and warned Hitler. Heinz Guderian, the army chief of staff, recommended evacuating Army Group North, now cut off in the Courland peninsula, and thinning out the forces in Norway so as to strengthen the Vistula defenses. But Hitler would have none of it. Apart from the now failing Ardennes offensive, his primary concern was Budapest, which – with its large German garrison – was under siege by the Red Army. An attempt to lift the siege during January 1945 failed, and the city fell in mid-February.

SOVIET ADVANCE FROM THE VISTULA

The main Soviet assault across the Vistula River was launched on January 12 and soon gained momentum, cutting off further German forces in East Prussia and reaching the Oder River at the end of the month. The Soviet troops had been inflamed by propaganda calling on them to exact revenge for the sufferings that their country had endured at the hands of the Germans. Soon, streams of German refugees were heading westward, bringing with them grisly tales of rape, murder, and pillage. This served to heighten the realization that the Third Reich was now facing its Armageddon.

In the west, the Allies soon recovered the ground they had lost during the German counteroffensive in the Ardennes and were now advancing on a wide front toward the Rhine. But wintry weather and often resolute German resistance meant that progress was slow. The Allies' strategic bombing forces were now concentrating on transportation and oil targets, but, to aid the Soviet offensive, they also attacked cities in the eastern part of Germany, notably Dresden, where at least 25,000 people were killed in a single night.

YALTA CONFERENCE

In early February 1945 Stalin, Roosevelt, and Churchill met at Yalta in the Crimea. Roosevelt, now a terminally sick man, was prepared to make concessions to Stalin in return for confirmation that the Soviet Union would enter the war against Japan as soon as the fighting in Europe came to an end. Churchill, worried over Stalin's intentions in eastern Europe, especially Poland, wanted his firm guarantee that its peoples would be allowed to determine their own future. The postconference communiqué, however, contained little of substance, and Churchill was forced to accept that Roosevelt and Stalin had united against him. In truth, Britain's voice no longer counted for much.

After establishing two bridgeheads over the Oder, the Soviets halted their offensive, while they cleared Pomerania and pushed back the remnants of Army Group North in East Prussia toward the Baltic. In the far south, Hitler launched a final offensive to recapture the Hungarian oilfields in the Lake Balaton area. It was soon halted and the Red Army renewed its own offensive in the region, this time aiming at Vienna, which would fall on April 13. The Western Allies eventually reached the Rhine, and were across it before the end of March. The Broad Front versus Narrow Front controversy that had dogged the northwest Europe campaign now resurfaced. With the Soviet Union not yet ready to launch its final assault on Berlin, the British wanted to advance quickly and secure the German capital. Eisenhower, not wishing to provoke clashes with his eastern ally and concerned that the Germans were planning to make a final stand in the Alps, informed Stalin that he would leave Berlin to the Red Army.

Dawn in Berlin on May 2, 1945.
A Soviet soldier waves his country's flag on the roof of the Reichstag building, home of Germany's parliament. This act symbolized not just the end of the 48 hours of fighting required to overcome the defenders of the building, but also the end of the bitter Battle of Berlin.

CROSSING THE RHINE AND ODER

The final act began with the Anglo–US forces breaking out of their Rhine bridgeheads and advancing rapidly eastward. In Italy, after a winter of preparation, the Allied forces broke through the German defenses and were soon advancing toward the Alps. The German forces, realizing they were on the brink of defeat, were able to negotiate their own surrender. Mussolini, however, did not fall into Allied hands alive. He was caught by Italian partisans while fleeing northward and was executed.

Meanwhile, the long-awaited Soviet offensive across the Oder opened on April 16. The previous day, Hitler, now entombed in his underground headquarters near the Reichstag in the center of Berlin and buoyed by the death of Roosevelt on April 12, issued a defiant message to his people. "Berlin stays German," he declared. "Vienna will be German again and Europe will never be Russian." However, within a few days the Red Army was not only across the Oder but had encircled the German capital. On April 25 it had also met up with the Western Allies, who had halted on the Elbe. Now began the break-in battle, as the Soviet forces fought their way toward the center of Berlin. On April 29 they threatened the heart of the Third Reich: the Reichstag and Chancellery. Hitler committed suicide, naming Grand Admiral Karl Dönitz his successor. Forty-eight hours later the last remnants of the German garrison surrendered and the Soviet flag was hoisted over the Reichstag.

GERMANY SURRENDERS

A series of overall German surrenders now took place. The German forces in northern Germany and Denmark surrendered to Montgomery. There followed a capitulation ceremony at Eisenhower's headquarters in Reims and another in Berlin. May 8 was decreed Victory in Europe Day, although hostilities did not formally end until the following day. Even so, fighting continued in Czechoslovakia, Austria, and Croatia until May 14, when the German Army Group E surrendered to Tito's forces in Yugoslavia. Dönitz was allowed to function long enough to ensure that the U-boats at sea had received orders to put into Allied ports to surrender. He was then arrested on May 23. This marked the end of the Third Reich. The Allies were now faced with a range of new problems in Europe, most notably those of governing Austria, Germany, and Italy, the reconstruction of the continent as a whole, and coping with the vast numbers of people who had been displaced by the ravages of war.

"We ask you to cease fire. At 05:00 hours Berlin time we are sending envoys to parley at the Potsdamer Bridge. The recognition sign is a white square with a red light. We await your reply."

RADIO MESSAGE FROM THE GERMAN LVI PANZER CORPS PICKED UP BY THE SOVIET 79TH GUARDS DIVISION, 22:40 HOURS MAY 1, 1945

CLOSING IN ON JAPAN

While the Allies began to grapple with the problems that came in the wake of their victory in Europe, the conflict against Japan continued. In early January 1945 General MacArthur's forces landed on the main Philippine island of Luzon, but it took a month just to liberate the capital, Manila, such was the bitterness of the Japanese resistance. In February 1945, after a lengthy preliminary air bombardment, Admiral Nimitz launched an assault on the island of Iwo Jima. Much of the island was subdued after three weeks of bitter combat, but there were pockets of resistance until late March.

The significance of Iwo Jima was that long-range fighters could reach the Japanese mainland from it. B-29s had been attacking Japan from bases in China since June 1944, but the Japanese offensive had put these under threat. The B-29s had then been transferred to the newly captured Marianas and had begun to bomb Japan from here in November. But the results were disappointing and the loss rate rose, mainly because they lacked escort fighters. In March 1945, both B-29s and P-51 Mustang fighters began to deploy to Iwo Jima. At the same time they launched a new type of offensive based on low-level incendiary attacks by night. The effect on the largely wooden-built Japanese cities was devastating. At the same time, daylight raids were carried out using the P-51s as escorts. The steady destruction of cities combined with the increasingly desperate shortage of raw materials meant that the Japanese war effort was in rapid decline. However, the resolve to continue fighting showed no sign of weakening.

FIRST CRACKS IN THE JAPANESE WILL

The next Allied objective was Okinawa, which represented the last stepping-stone on the route to Japan itself. The initial landings took place on April 1. They were supported by nearly 1,500 ships, including those of the recently arrived British Pacific Fleet. It would take until late June to secure the island in a campaign characterized by fanatical Japanese defense. There were frequent kamikaze attacks, and many civilians committed suicide rather than fall into Americans hands. Yet, for the first time a number of Japanese soldiers did surrender voluntarily—a sign of cracks in the Japanese will.

A further sign came after the Soviet Union renounced its 1941 nonaggression pact with Japan in April 1945. The following month the Japanese Supreme Council discussed peace for the first time and looked to using the Soviet Union as a go-between, believing that Moscow would want a strong postwar Japan to act as a buffer between itself and the US. Yet, on June 6 the Japanese Supreme Council passed a resolution that the country would fight on until the end.

The Allies had begun their planning for the final assault on Japan, which they knew was likely to be costly. However, a new weapon—the atomic bomb—was reaching the end of its development, and by early July the Americans and British had agreed on the possibility of employing it against Japan. On July 17 the Allies met at Potsdam for the last of their great wartime strategic conferences. It soon became apparent that there was an ominous divergence of views between Moscow and the West over Europe. After a recession for the British general election, in which Clement Attlee's Labour Party decisively defeated Winston Churchill's Conservative Party, the Conference turned to Japan.

On July 26 the Allies issued an ultimatum to Japan. It was to surrender unconditionally or face "prompt and utter destruction." Two days later, the Japanese rejected the demand on the grounds that it made no mention of the future of the Emperor and that they were still awaiting a Soviet response to a proposal to send a peace envoy to Moscow. The Americans took the Japanese reply to be an outright rejection and issued orders for two atomic bombs that were on their way to the Marianas to be dropped on Japan. The terrible scenes that ensued were immediately followed by a massive Soviet invasion of Manchuria. Emperor Hirohito now stepped in and on August 15 took the unprecedented step of broadcasting acceptance of the Allied terms on Japanese radio. Japan's formal surrender took place on September 2. It was followed ten days later by the surrender of the Japanese forces in Southeast Asia. World War II had finally come to an end.

Unloading supplies at Iwo Jima
Initially, Japanese resistance to the US landings on the island of Iwo Jima, on February 19, 1945, was light. But the US Marines then came under heavy fire and they suffered many casualties as 30,000 men landed over the course of the day.

Emperor Hirohito inspects Tokyo bomb damage
Tokyo was the first Japanese city to be subjected to an incendiary attack. On the night of March 9/10 a raid by American B-29s caused destruction on a massive scale.

"When the capture of an enemy position is necessary to winning a war, it is not within our province to evaluate the cost in money, time, equipment, or, most of all, human life. We are told what our objective is to be and we prepare to do the job."

GENERAL HOLLAND M. "HOWLIN' MAD" SMITH,
COMMANDING GENERAL OF THE US FLEET MARINE FORCE PACIFIC

ADVANCE INTO GERMANY AND HUNGARY

JANUARY 1–MARCH 31, 1945

On the Eastern Front the year began with a massive Red Army offensive in Poland, which took it from the Vistula to the Oder River. To the north, Soviet forces drove into East Prussia, while to the south they quickly overcame Hitler's last offensive in Hungary. On the Western Front, the Allied forces pushed on to the Rhine and crossed it in mid-March.

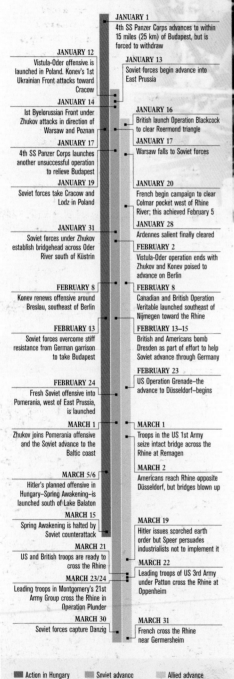

JANUARY 1
4th SS Panzer Corps advances to within 15 miles (25 km) of Budapest, but is forced to withdraw

JANUARY 12
Vistula-Oder offensive is launched in Poland. Konev's 1st Ukrainian Front attacks toward Cracow

JANUARY 13
Soviet forces begin advance into East Prussia

JANUARY 14
1st Byelorussian Front under Zhukov attacks in direction of Warsaw and Poznan

JANUARY 16
British launch Operation Blackcock to clear Roermond triangle

JANUARY 17
4th SS Panzer Corps launches another unsuccessful operation to relieve Budapest

JANUARY 17
Warsaw falls to Soviet forces

JANUARY 19
Soviet forces take Cracow and Lodz in Poland

JANUARY 20
French begin campaign to clear Colmar pocket west of Rhine River; this achieved February 5

JANUARY 28
Ardennes salient finally cleared

JANUARY 31
Soviet forces under Zhukov establish bridgehead across Oder River south of Küstrin

FEBRUARY 2
Vistula-Oder operation ends with Zhukov and Konev poised to advance on Berlin

FEBRUARY 8
Konev renews offensive around Breslau, southeast of Berlin

FEBRUARY 8
Canadian and British Operation Veritable launched southeast of Nijmegen toward the Rhine

FEBRUARY 13
Soviet forces overcome stiff resistance from German garrison to take Budapest

FEBRUARY 13–15
British and Americans bomb Dresden as part of effort to help Soviet advance through Germany

FEBRUARY 24
Fresh Soviet offensive into Pomerania, west of East Prussia, is launched

FEBRUARY 23
US Operation Grenade–the advance to Düsseldorf–begins

MARCH 1
Zhukov joins Pomerania offensive and the Soviet advance to the Baltic coast

MARCH 1
Troops in the US 1st Army seize intact bridge across the Rhine at Remagen

MARCH 2
Americans reach Rhine opposite Düsseldorf, but bridges blown up

MARCH 5/6
Hitler's planned offensive in Hungary–Spring Awakening–is launched south of Lake Balaton

MARCH 15
Spring Awakening is halted by Soviet counterattack

MARCH 19
Hitler issues scorched earth order but Speer persuades industrialists not to implement it

MARCH 21
US and British troops are ready to cross the Rhine

MARCH 22
Leading troops of US 3rd Army under Patton cross the Rhine at Oppenheim

MARCH 23/24
Leading troops in Montgomery's 21st Army Group cross the Rhine in Operation Plunder

MARCH 30
Soviet forces capture Danzig

MARCH 31
French cross the Rhine near Germersheim

■ Action in Hungary
Jan 1–Mar 15, 1945

■ Soviet advance through Poland and Germany Jan 12–Mar 21, 1945

■ Allied advance to the Rhine Jan 16–Mar 21, 1945

THE ROAD TO BERLIN

At THE BEGINNING OF JANUARY 1945 the Allies were fighting to regain the ground they had lost on the Western Front during the German offensive in the Ardennes, while on the Eastern Front preparations were being made for a further massive offensive in central Poland. Here, in the late summer of 1944, the Red Army had established three bridgeheads on the western bank of the Vistula. The southernmost and most substantial bridgehead was at Baranow in the sector controlled by Konev's First Ukrainian Front; the smaller Pulawy and Magnuszew bridgeheads in the sector of the First Byelorussian Front lay some 70 miles 110 km() to the north at the junction of the Vistula and the Pilica, 25 miles (40 km) from Warsaw (see map page 271). These bridgeheads were to provide the springboards for the Red Army's drive to Berlin, which would be spearheaded by the First Byelorusssian Front, placed under the direct command of Zhukov in November 1944.

THE VISTULA–ODER OPERATION

The scale of the preparations for the coming offensive was massive. Along a front of nearly 400 miles (650 km), the Stavka was to launch four major breakthrough operations aimed at Danzig, Konigsberg, Poznan, and Breslau with 30 rifle armies, five tank armies, and four air armies, supported by mobile operational groups and artillery breakthrough

divisions. Packed into Zhukov's Magnuszew bridgehead alone—15 miles (24 km) deep and 8 miles (13 km) wide—were some 400,000 infantry and nearly 2,000 tanks. Zhukov and Konev had under their command approximately 2.25 million men, including one-third of all Red Army infantry formations and 40 percent of all the Soviet armor deployed on the Eastern Front.

These massive concentrations made it all the more important for the Stavka to mislead the Germans as to where the main blows would fall and to blur the enemy's assessment of their size. Complex deception measures included a dummy army of 600 tanks and self-propelled guns, serviced by a network of new roads, on the southern wing of the First Ukrainian Front. This, combined with German intelligence appraisals, helped

***Volkssturm* prisoners**
A form of home guard made up of boys and elderly men, the *Volkssturm* was ill-equipped to face the Red Army. From January 1945 its members were integrated with regular formations whenever possible.

while he was slipping armor, infantry, and artillery across the Vistula by night into the area opposite Kielce, 40 miles (65 km) to the north.

Hitler could not be persuaded that a Soviet offensive was imminent. He was convinced that the Eastern Front would remain quiet while Stalin continued to wrangle with the Western Allies over the status of the puppet Polish government. Stalin was in fact reluctant to go on the offensive in conditions of heavy mud and poor visibility. He was waiting for the rivers and canals to freeze over and the ground to become iron-hard, under a thin covering of snow, which would allow the T-34s to forge across the flat, open plains of western Poland to Silesia with its rich prize of heavy industry.

In the Soviet bridgeheads the final briefings were made on January 11. The ground was now hard, but visibility was poor, eliminating the possibility of close support for the impending attack from Ilyushin IL2 Sturmovich attack aircraft, the "flying artillery" which accounted for about 25 percent of all Soviet combat missions flown on the Eastern Front.

THE ATTACK IS LAUNCHED

Inside the Baranow bridgehead the artillery was ranged wheel-to-wheel in concentrations of up to 500 guns per mile (300 per kilometer) of front.

At 4:35 am on January 12, Konev's artillery attack began, obliterating the German front line, churning the frozen earth and collapsing command posts and bunkers. Half an hour later, Soviet reconnaissance battalions, stiffened by punishment battalions (*strafblats*), stormed the first line of enemy trenches. They then pushed forward to identify the individual strong points between the first and second lines that had survived the initial bombardment. At around 10:00 am the Germans who had survived Konev's first bombardment were subjected to a second pulverizing barrage. For just under two hours it worked its way back and forth across the full depth of the German defenses. The headquarters of the Fourth Panzer Army was destroyed, and the German mobile reserves—deployed close to the main battle line—were broken up.

By midafternoon Konev's Fourth Tank Army had advanced 12 miles (19 km) toward Kielce, crashing through dense forests, crisscrossed with river valleys, which the Germans had thought "untankable." The capture of Kielce secured Konev's right flank, spilling his armor into open country and rolling over the uncoordinated counterattacks launched by General Josef Harpe, the commander of Army Group A. By the evening of January 17, Konev's left flank was encircling

Fighting in Frankfurt an der Oder
The Red Army reached the Oder at the end of January. In the following weeks it fought to secure east German towns as preparations were made for the final assault on Berlin.

the Stavka to persuade OKH that Konev was planning to launch a major assault heading southwest from the left flank of his bridgehead at Baranow. As a result, the German Army Group A, deployed opposite the Soviet bridgeheads, shifted two infantry divisions south to the Tarnow sector to cover Konev's phantom preparations

Bolt · Rear sight · Fore sight · Wooden stock · Air-cooled barrel · Ammunition magazine

Soviet Tokarev 40 7.62-mm rifle
Often issued to Red Army marksmen, the self-loading Tokarev rifle influenced the German MP43 submachine-gun and was the precursor of the postwar Soviet AK 47 range.

Cracow, which was evacuated by its German garrison without a fight on January 19. The way now lay open for Konev's rifle armies to secure the heavy industrial treasure trove in Silesia.

Zhukov's First Byelorussian Front had gone onto the attack against Army Group Center early on the morning of January 14 after a crushing 25-minute artillery bombardment which raked the German lines up to a depth of 5 miles (8 km). By nightfall a bridge had been seized over the lower Pilica, and tanks of the Second Guards Tank Army were pouring over it to swing northwest toward Sochaczew, a rail and road junction 30 miles (50 km) west of Warsaw, whose capture would block the German retreat.

ADVANCE TO THE ODER

By nightfall on the 15th, Konev and Zhukov's forces had torn three gaping holes in the German tactical defense zone. They then joined up to hold a continuous 300-mile (480-km) stretch on the west bank of the Vistula, while tanks and mechanized infantry moved rapidly across open country up to 70 miles (110 km) from their start lines. On Zhukov's right flank, north of Warsaw, the Soviet 47th Army set about clearing the area between the Vistula and the Bug River. Warsaw was liberated on January 17 by the Red Army and Polish troops. They entered a silent city whose prewar population had been reduced to 160,000 famished survivors.

On the 19th, the day Konev took Cracow, units of the Third Guards Tank Army crossed the German frontier east of Breslau. Around 100 miles (160 km) to the northeast, Zhukov's armour was fanning out across western Poland. Simultaneously, Konev was launching a skillfully handled envelopment of the Silesian industrial heartland. By January 27 he was in a position to close off all the Ostheer's escape routes, but mindful of his instructions to seize the region's war industries intact, he left a "golden bridge" for the remnants of Army Group A, now commanded

Soviet attack on Sopot, near Danzig
Troops of the Second Byelorussian Front reached the Gulf of Danzig at the end of March. They attacked the seaside resort of Sopot prior to capturing Danzig on March 30, 1945.

by Field Marshal Ferdinand Schörner, a diehard Nazi. Schörner seized his chance but sensibly delayed telling Hitler that he was withdrawing to make a stand on the Oder until the movement was well under way. Meanwhile, Hitler once again reshuffled his command pack. On January 26 the surrounded Army Group North became Army Group Courland. Army Group Center, also cut off from the Reich, became Army Group North, while Army Group A became Army Group Center. A new formation, Army Group Vistula, under the nominal command of Himmler, was created to cover Danzig and Pomerania.

The Oder was now within the Red Army's sights, but the speed of Zhukov and Konev's advance was outrunning the Soviet supply lines. The situation was further complicated by the fact that the two commanders were vying with each other in a race to reach Berlin. While the Stavka wrestled with this problem, Zhukov's dash to the Oder was delayed by the city of Poznan, located at the junction of six railroads and seven roads, massively fortified and garrisoned by 60,000 determined troops. The city was besieged by six Red Army divisions but held out until February 22. Zhukov pressed on, leaving Poznan in his rear, to reach the Oder and launch a crossing at the beginning of February.

To the south of Küstrin, Chuikov's Eighth Guards Army established a number of bridgeheads on the western bank of the Oder. These were rapidly linked together, although the bulk of the army's artillery and armor remained on the eastern bank. The pontoons needed to bring them over were still deep in the rear of the Red Army. Although the Ostheer was to hold bridgeheads east of the Oder until March 20, Zhukov and Konev had reached the middle Oder along almost its entire length and had gained firm footholds on its western bank. On February 2 the Stavka declared a formal end to the Vistula–Oder operation. The final assault on Berlin would not be made until mid-April.

GERMAN OPERATION SOLSTICE

Zhukov's advance to the Oder had left the flanks of his First Byelorussian Front exposed to a German counterblow, a fact that had not escaped the attention of Heinz Guderian, chief of the army general staff. In Operation *Sonnenwende* (Solstice), Guderian planned to slice off the nose of the huge Soviet salient that had been driven into Germany by Zhukov as far as Küstrin. A pincer attack would be executed in the north by Army Group Vistula and in the south by Army Group Centre, its jaws closing behind the troops of Zhukov in the area of Küstrin. Guderian's plan was undermined by Hitler's refusal to reinforce either of the army groups involved and,

Soviet infantry on a T-70
As Soviet troops advanced across Germany they sometimes rode aboard T-70 light tanks. These were used for reconnaissance duties or direct infantry support.

after making a small dent in Zhukov's right flank, Operation Solstice had petered out by February 19. Guderian was dismissed on March 28.

DRIVE INTO EAST PRUSSIA

On Zhukov's right flank at the beginning of January 1945 was the Second Byelorussian Front under Marshal Konstantin Rokossovsky. Between Rokossovsky and the Baltic were two more fronts, the Third Byelorussian and First Baltic. Rokossovsky's principal task was to protect Zhukov's flank during the Vistula–Oder operation and that of the other two fronts securing the Baltic coast. In this northern sector the going was much tougher for the Red Army, depriving Zhukov of effective flank protection and causing much anxiety in the Stavka. However, by early February German forces had been pinned back into a few pockets of resistance on the Bay of Danzig, and East Prussia had been cut off from the rest of the Reich.

The Red Army drive had sent a tide of refugees pouring both westward and to the Baltic coast, ending 800 years of German resettlement in the east. At the northeastern tip of this vast forced migration, tens of thousands of refugees were trapped in the city of Memel, the port which had been ceded to Germany in March 1939, Hitler's last peaceful conquest. Now it was besieged by troops of the First Baltic Front, into whose hands the refugees were terrified of falling. Red Army troops were all too aware of the barbarity with which the Germans had treated the Soviet people and many were now determined to wreak their revenge. They had acted with great savagery during their advance through East Prussia and Silesia, torturing and killing villagers, and shelling and bombing refugees.

THE BOMBING OF DRESDEN

BY THE FALL OF 1944 the British Bomber Command's target-marking techniques had reached new levels of sophistication, ensuring that the destruction caused by bombing was spread in an unfolding V-shape across the target—the so-called "Death Fan." Such raids were the prelude to Operation Thunderclap, the triple blow delivered to the historic city of Dresden between February 13 and 15, 1945, by the RAF Bomber Command and the US Eighth Air Force. Having largely escaped the attention of Allied bombers, the city lacked an adequate system of civil defense and had been stripped of its antiaircraft guns. In February 1945 it was crammed with at least one million refugees.

Bomb victims
An estimated 60,000 people lost their lives in the Allied bombing raids on Dresden.

Operation Thunderclap had originally envisaged Berlin, 110 miles (70 km) to the north, as the main target, but during the runup to the Yalta Conference the British were eager to help the Red Army in its westward drive by reducing the importance of Dresden as a railhead for reinforcing the Ostheer. On the night of February 13–14, two waves of Lancasters, a total of 773 aircraft, dropped 2,600 tons of high-explosive and incendiary bombs on Dresden with no interference from night-fighters. They caused the worst firestorms of the war, in which jets of flame 50 ft (15 m) high belched across streets and squares, and temperatures rose to 1,800°F (1,000°C). The dead and dying lay where they fell in the melting asphalt of the streets, their clothes burned away, their bodies shriveled like mummies. Hundreds who sought refuge in the tunnels and passageways of the main railroad station were asphyxiated where they sat. Approximately 12 sq miles (31 sq km) of Dresden were devastated in one night. During February 14 and 15 there were daylight raids by a combined total of 516 bombers of the USAAF's Eighth Air Force.

The destruction of Dresden was followed by a propaganda battle waged by both sides. Churchill distanced himself from the operation, and the finger of blame rested on Air Chief Marshal Harris, commander-in-chief of Bomber Command and an unrepentant advocate of area bombing. He was, however, carrying out decisions made by the combined US, Soviet, and British chiefs of staff, fully supported by Roosevelt, Stalin, and Churchill. Thunderclap was the logical climax of the policy of area bombing that the British had been pursuing since 1942.

> "Our pilots report that…a terrific concentration of fires was started in the center of the city."
>
> FROM A BBC NEWS BULLETIN AT 6 PM ON FEBRUARY 14, 1945

Devastation in Dresden
Dresden's fate sparked a fierce debate about the morality of the Allied bombing offensive in Germany that continues to this day.

THE SINKING OF THE *WILHELM GUSTLOFF*

THE ERUPTION OF THE SECOND BYELORUSSIAN FRONT into East Prussia triggered a torrent of German refugees pouring westward in search of safety from the Red Army. By the end of January an estimated 3.5 million German civilians were on the move in the east, all under no illusions about the treatment they could expect from Soviet troops. Over a million headed for Danzig and other Baltic ports in the hope that they would be evacuated. On January 30 the liner *Wilhelm Gustloff* sailed from the Polish port of Gdynia (which Hitler had renamed Gothenburg) with 8,000 refugees crammed on board. With no warships present to escort her, and only 12 lifeboats swinging from her davits, the ship steamed slowly into the Baltic, an easy target for Soviet submarines. At 11:08 pm on the 31st, one of them, S13, fired three torpedoes into her side. The *Wilhelm Gustloff* capsized, immediately drowning 2,000 refugees on the lower promenade deck. Just over an hour later, the liner sank, her siren wailing eerily across the Baltic ice floes. German warships picked up 960 survivors, many of whom later died of exposure. At least 7,000 people perished in the disaster, five times more than the number who went down with the Titanic. A further 23 vessels would be sunk by Soviet submarines before the war's end in May

Some 90 miles (145 km) to the south of Memel, at the base of the Samland peninsula, the fortified Prussian city of Königsberg had also been cut off by the Red Army. Overseen by Marshal Vasilevsky, a plan was now devised to storm the city. Four armies were concentrated in the Königsberg sector, plus an air strike force of 870 fighters, 470 attack aircraft, and 1,124 bombers drawn from the massive Stavka reserve. The storming of Königsberg began on April 2 with a four-day artillery barrage. On the 7th, when the weather lifted, the aircraft flew in to bomb and strafe. By April 8, Königsberg was cut off from the rest of the German forces fighting in the Samland peninsula, and two days later General Lasch, commander of Königsberg's garrison, surrendered. Red Army forces entered the captured city and took their revenge against the Germans amid scenes of almost medieval barbarity.

POMERANIA AND SILESIA

Although it had been a failure, Guderian's Solstice offensive had a disproportionate effect on the Stavka, confirming its fears that Zhukov's right flank was dangerously exposed. He now received the instruction to clear East Pomerania, the result of which was the destruction of Army Group Vistula. Rokossovsky started the ball rolling on February 24, while Zhukov was still reshuffling the forces on his right wing. Zhukov went on the offensive a week later,

Defenders of Königsberg
In East Prussia the resistance of the German defenders was sometimes suicidal. Königsberg, ringed by three defense lines and incorporating 15 forts, was taken after fighting in which some 42,000 of its defenders were killed.

sending three armies on a northward drive to the Baltic, fanning out across East Pomerania and slicing Army Group Vistula into isolated fragments. On March 4 the First Guards Tank Army reached the Baltic at Kolberg, on the boundary between the First and Second Byelorussian Fronts, cutting off the German Second Army to the east and forcing it to fall back on the fortresses of Gdynia, which fell on the 28th, and Danzig, which followed two days later. Hitler immediately declared Kolberg, which was packed with refugees, another "fortress."

By March 16 the German Navy, operating a shuttle service from Swinemünde, had evacuated Kolberg's civilian population. Two days later the last of Kolberg's defenders slipped away. Within 48 hours, Heinrich Himmler had relinquished his command of what was left of Army Group Vistula and had taken refuge in a sanatorium.

SIEGE OF BRESLAU

Some 250 miles (400 km) to the south of Kolberg, on the banks of the Oder, lay the city of Breslau, the capital of Lower Silesia, covered by Army Group Center. Breslau lay directly in the path of a renewed offensive launched by Konev on February 8 with the goal of clearing Silesia west of the Oder. By closing up on the line of the Neisse River in Brandenburg, Konev would bring himself alongside Zhukov in readiness for the assault on Berlin. Breslau was cut off on February 15 by the Soviet Sixth Army and the Fifth Guards Army. The encirclement was completed when the Third Guards Tank Army positioned itself to the west of the city. Trapped inside Breslau were some 35,000 regular German troops, 15,000 *Volkssturm* and 80,000 civilians. By the end of February, Konev's front had reached a 60-mile (90-km) stretch of the Neisse running south from its junction with the Oder, 60 miles (90 km) southeast of Berlin. Breslau, isolated and lacking the defensive features of the fortress cities of Poznan and Königsberg, was vainly waiting for relief by Army Group Center.

For 77 days, the defenders of Breslau occupied the attentions of some 13 Red Army divisions. Inside the improvised fortress, a semblance of normal life, including regular classical concerts, was maintained. Throughout the siege the Aviatik factory turned out half a million cigarettes a day, ensuring that no one went without a smoke. Berlin had already fallen when, on May 6, with about 80 percent of the city in ruins, the commandant

of Breslau surrendered. Of Breslau's garrison of 50,000 troops, 29,000 had become casualties. About half of the city's population of 80,000 had lost their lives in the siege.

HITLER'S LAST OFFENSIVE

At the beginning of January 1945, four German divisions had been trapped in Budapest. A rescue attempt made by IV SS Panzer Corps, called down from Army Group Center, fought its way to within 12 miles (19 km) of the city but was forced to withdraw by the end of the month. The fall of Budapest on February 13 had served only to stoke Hitler's obsession with the Hungarian oilfields at Nagykanisza, 50 miles (80 km) southwest of Lake Balaton, which produced well over half of the oil remaining to Germany. A plan was drawn up, code-named *Frühlingserwachen* (Spring Awakening), in which Army Group South was to trap and destroy the Red Army's Third Ukrainian Front between Lake Balaton and the Danube. The major thrust

88-mm KwK 43 L71 tank gun with 68-mile (109-km) range

12-cylinder Maybach HL 230 P30 engine mounted at rear

Armor 1–4½ in (26–110 mm) thick

7.92-mm machine-gun

Combat tracks 31½ in (800-mm) wide

Panzer Mark VI Tiger II
Introduced in 1944, the "King Tiger" was the heaviest and best-protected tank of the war. Some 485 were produced. Since it had a maximum speed of just 24 mph (38 kph), there was always the danger that it would be stranded in a fast-moving battle. However, it could fight against heavy odds while sustaining minimal damage.

was to be launched by the Sixth SS Panzer Army attacking southeast from the northern end of Lake Balaton to a line on the Danube between Budapest and Baja, around 90 miles (150 km) south of the Hungarian capital. South of Balaton, the Second Panzer Army was to drive east while a supporting attack was to be launched northward from the Yugoslavian border by Army Group E in the direction of Mohacs. Budapest would be retaken, the oilfields retained, and an entire Red Army front struck off Stalin's order of battle.

Preparations for the operation were made in the greatest secrecy and the approach to the start lines was conducted in driving rain and deep mud. The attack went in on March 5. In the vanguard was the Sixth SS Panzer Army, desperate to redeem itself after its recent failure in the Ardennes in Belgium. Among the 600 tanks available to it were a number of Mark VI "King Tiger" heavy battle tanks, armored on a massive scale and each mounting an 88-mm gun.

At the limit of the German advance—a salient driven some 20 miles (30 km) into the Third Ukrainian Front's line—more than 600 tanks and self-propelled guns tried to batter their way through the Soviet line south of Lake Velencze (northeast of Lake Balaton). By March 15 the offensive was all over. Hundreds of tanks were left stranded in the waterlogged Hungarian plains, their fuel tanks empty, to be pounded by Soviet artillery and attack aircraft. The Red Army counteroffensive swept past the gutted hulks of the tanks, smashed through the Hungarian Third Army, covering the Sixth Panzer Army's left flank, and rolled on toward Vienna.

Spoils of war
Some 25,000 civilians died in the siege of Königsberg, which was later incorporated into the Soviet Union and renamed Kaliningrad.

GERMANY IN 1945

GERMANY IN THE EARLY MONTHS OF 1945 was an increasingly grim place. Its already battered towns and cities were receiving further punishment from the Allied strategic air forces by day and by night. Systematic air attacks on oil and transportation targets were making movement ever more difficult. The Luftwaffe was becoming grounded through lack of fuel and was powerless to defend the skies over Germany. Industry, in particular, was suffering. While production actually peaked in 1944, it was now rapidly disintegrating. Earlier bombing had forced much industry to be dispersed to the countryside in the form of satellite factories, but now it was creating enormous difficulties in moving material around the country.

In terms of manpower, Josef Goebbels had declared "total war" in the immediate aftermath of the January 1943 disaster in Stalingrad. All males between 16 and 65 were registered for labor, and members of the Hitler Youth were drafted to help the farmers. Women, too, were gradually conscripted, although never to the same extent as in Britain or the Soviet Union. Some 100,000 of them were called up in September 1944 for duty in air defense. In that same month the *Volkssturm* was created. This was a form of home guard for which all those not yet in uniform and aged 16–60 were liable. Because the vast majority were in reserved occupations in industry, their training was restricted to four hours on Sunday. With the Soviets now close to Berlin, they were to be mobilized for the final defense of the Reich.

Women at war
German women had played an essential part in their country's war effort since the beginning of the war. By 1945 many were being employed in jobs that provided direct support to the armed services. These included the refueling of planes—provided the fuel was available.

Lining up for food
Ration cards became irrelevant as food shortages in urban areas grew because of the disruption of road and rail communications by Allied bombing.

As for the mood of the German people as a whole, it was now one of resignation as the majority were completely caught up in the sheer struggle to survive. With his enemies approaching from both east and west, Hitler tried to inspire the country by drawing parallels with Frederick the Great of Prussia, but with little success. In truth, people were largely cowed through draconian measures that had been instituted after the July 1944 bomb plot. These included tribunals that came down heavily on any suspicion of defeatist talk. They were also well aware of the Allies' demand for unconditional surrender, which appeared to mean that they had little to lose by continuing the fight. Some may have pinned their hopes on the promise of "miracle weapons" that would turn the tide. Others dreamed that the Western Allies would wake up to the real threat to Europe and help turn back the communist hordes that were now engulfing the east of the country. There were, too, the fanatics, notably the SS, who were determined not to surrender. For all these reasons, the war would continue until there was nothing left.

***Volkssturm* conscripts**
Uniforms were often not available for *Volkssturm* conscripts. Most were armed with the Panzerfaust anti-tank rocket projector.

Um Freiheit und Leben
Volkssturm

Destroyed street in Bremen
By early 1945 many of Germany's cities had become virtual shells, but the inhabitants still tried to lead normal lives.

ALLIED ADVANCE TO THE RUHR

During January 1945 the Western Allies regained all the ground they had lost during the recent German offensive. Their main objective now was to get across the Rhine. In the middle of the month, and conscious that the Soviet Union had launched its long-awaited offensive across the Vistula in Poland, Eisenhower issued his orders. In essence, the Ruhr was to be the primary target. To this end, the 21st Army Group under Montgomery was to cross the Rhine to its north, while Bradley's 12th Army Group did so to the south. They would then cut off the Ruhr. In the south, Devers' 6th Army Group would clear the Saarland and reduce an obstinate German pocket around Colmar before advancing to the Rhine. No attempt would be made to liberate the northern Netherlands—a strategy that would result in the Dutch people coming close to starvation.

On the German side, Rundstedt, who had been reappointed Commander-in-Chief West the previous September, wanted to withdraw his forces across the Rhine so as to conserve them for the defense of the Ruhr. Hitler, however, was insistent that Rundstedt hold the West Wall, the German equivalent of the Maginot Line, at all costs. It meant that the Allies would face some very tough fighting.

While the US First and Third Armies continued to regain ground lost in December and the US Seventh and French First Armies set about dealing with the eight German divisions in the Colmar pocket, Montgomery began his approach to the

Action in the Reichswald
Canadian troops played a major part in the grim fighting in the Reichswald, a heavily wooded area close to the Lower Rhine.

Rhine. The first phase was for the German salient in the Roermond area to be eradicated—a task begun by the British Second Army on January 16. Up to this point the ground had been frozen hard, but there was now a sudden thaw which reduced it to mud. This, coupled with resistance by the Germans, meant that it took ten days to clear the Roermond triangle. It was a portent of things to come.

On January 28 the Ardennes salient was finally eliminated and the next task for the US First and Third Armies was to penetrate the West Wall. Their first concern was the dams on the Roer River. If the Germans opened the sluices, much of the surrounding countryside would be flooded and so become a major obstacle. The Americans began their advance on January 31, but they experienced much the same problems as the British had to the north. As a result, they failed to reach the dams in time to prevent the Germans from flooding the whole Roer Valley. A further advance toward the Rhine in the Cologne-Düsseldorf area could not take place until the waters subsided. The one consolation was that the Colmar pocket was finally reduced on February 5, enabling the French and Americans to close up to the Rhine south of Strasbourg. The US Seventh Army then began to clear the Saarland, while the US Third Army began to advance across the Moselle River.

Advance to the Rhine
Men of the US Ninth Army shelter from shellfire during the battle for the German town of Jülich, on the Roer River. They crossed the river on February 23, 1945.

OPERATION VERITABLE

It was now the turn of the Canadians. They were to clear the region that stretched from southeast of Nijmegen to the Lower Rhine between Emmerich and Wesel. Operation Veritable was launched on February 8. Preceded by the fire of over 1,000 guns in the largest artillery bombardment that the 21st Army Group had staged during the campaign, the Canadians quickly broke through the initial German lines. Then, however, they came up against Eugen Meindl's First Parachute Army, which consisted of a significant number of hardened veterans, and the picture changed. The fighting became intense, especially in the wooded area of the Reichswald, where the Germans had constructed five lines of defenses. The situation was not helped by a further thaw, which caused much flooding and restricted the advance to a very narrow front. Even assistance from RAF Bomber Command did not help much, and casualties were heavy.

By February 23 the floods in the Roer Valley had subsided sufficiently for the Americans to resume their advance. General William Simpson's US Ninth Army, which was under Montgomery's command, began to attack toward Düsseldorf. Simpson had the advantage in that German troops had been drawn north to block the Canadians. Once his forces had crossed the Ruhr and advanced farther toward the Rhine, one part turned northeast to link up with the Canadians, while the remainder continued toward Düsseldorf. Simultaneously, the US First Army began to approach the Rhine between Cologne and Coblenz. Meanwhile, Patton's spearheads reached the river at Neuwied on March 7. The US Third and Seventh Armies now set about clearing the remainder of the German forces between the Moselle and the Rhine.

Rundstedt accepted that he could not hold ground west of the Rhine for much longer and embarked on a delaying action designed to buy sufficient time to get the bulk of his forces back over the river. He was, however, particularly concerned that the Allies would capture an intact bridge and consequently organized matters so that there was a phased demolition of all crossings over the Rhine. Thus, when, on March 2, the Ninth Army reached the river at Düsseldorf, the bridges had been blown. It was the same when the US First Army arrived at Cologne two days later, just after the Canadians had finally cleared the Reichswald. Then, on March 7, Rundstedt's worst fear was realized.

CROSSING THE RHINE AT REMAGEN

That afternoon the leading elements of a US First Army task force reached the high ground that overlooked the small town of Remagen. To their surprise, they could see that the Ludendorff railroad bridge spanning the Rhine at this point was still intact. Fighting their way through the town, they reached the bridge, which was defended on the west bank. At this point the Germans attempted to demolish it, but the charges failed to explode. With artillery support, the Americans overcame the defenders and rushed the bridge itself. The Germans now made another attempt to blow it, but this was

Pontoon bridge over the Rhine
By the time they reached the Rhine, virtually all of whose bridges had had been partially or totally destroyed, the Allied engineers were well-practiced in building pontoon bridges.

only partially successful. The attackers charged across the bridge, cutting demolition cables as they did so, and reached the other side. The Western Allies had crossed the Rhine at last.

Rundstedt gave orders that the bridge should be destroyed from the air or by divers. Hitler was furious and immediately sacked the field marshal for the third and final time, summoning Kesselring from Italy to replace him. As for those responsible on the ground for demolishing the bridge, an SS flying tribunal summarily executed five of them. Neither air attack nor divers were able to destroy the bridge, and even V-2 rockets were fired at it, also without success, such was the desperation of the Germans. The Americans quickly reinforced their bridgehead, and soon it contained some four

Fighting in Cologne
US troops reached the heavily bombed city on March 5. They took the Germans by surprise, but the Hohenzollern bridge over the Rhine had already been destroyed.

divisions. However, they feared that if they advanced too far eastward they would lay themselves open to being cut off. In any event, a single thrust from here did not accord with Eisenhower's Broad Front strategy. Hence the US First Army did not exploit this success, although it did cut the Cologne-Frankfurt *autobahn*. The bridge itself collapsed on March 17, but by this time the Americans had constructed two pontoon bridges upstream.

FURTHER ALLIED CROSSINGS

By now the Allies were everywhere closing up to the Rhine and preparing to make other crossings. At this juncture Hitler issued a draconian order. Everything that might be of possible value to the Allies was to be destroyed—communications, industry, and even food supplies. "If the war is lost, the nation will also perish," he declared. Albert Speer, his armaments minister, was horrified, believing that it was the duty of the leadership to ensure that the German people had some means of reconstructing their lives once the war was over. He succeeded in persuading the

YOU ARE NOW CROSSING THE RHINE RIVER THROUGH COURTESY OF 'E' CO. 17 ARMD. ENGR. BN. AND 'C' CO. 202 ENGR. C. BN.

commanders in the west not to carry out the order. The next Allied crossing over the Rhine was in the US Third Army's sector. On the night of March 22/23 Patton's men achieved a "bounce" crossing over the river at Oppenheim, in which they reached the west bank and crossed to the other side without any pause for preparation. They thus caught most of the defenders asleep. The following night the British and Canadians made three crossings. In marked contrast to the hasty action at Oppenheim,

these were deliberate operations, which had been under preparation for the past two weeks. Assault boats, amphibious vehicles, and bridging equipment had been carefully deployed. In addition, a massive weight of artillery had been massed, and RAF Bomber Command had launched two attacks, by day and by night, on the town of Wesel, where the main concentration of German troops in the area was located. Once the assault troops had established themselves on the far bank, the final airborne operation of the war in the west took place. The British 6th and US 17th Airborne divisions dropped by parachute and landed by glider to the east of Wesel in order to provide instant depth to the bridgehead that had been created there. They

actually landed among the German artillery positions, and thus prevented any possibility of a counterattack.

The US Third Army achieved two further crossings on the night of March 24/25 and the Seventh Army was also across the Rhine in two places by the end of the 26th. Finally, the French made a crossing at Germersheim on March 31. It meant that the Allies were now on the east bank of the Rhine on a 200-mile (320-km) front and were still shoulder-to-shoulder, in line with Eisenhower's strategy. During the campaign the Germans had suffered 60,000 casualties, but a further 250,000 had been made prisoner and vast amounts of equipment had been lost. The German forces in the west were crumbling, and the overall picture was very different from that in January, when it appeared that the Soviet offensive across the Vistula would reach Berlin within weeks. Now the Red Army was halted on the Oder and there was every chance that the Western Allies would get to the city first—a prospect that was to trigger the final squabble among them.

German prisoners

As the Allies advanced to the Rhine, many German soldiers were trapped on the west bank and consequently fell into Allied hands.

Closing in on the Third Reich

By the end of March the Red Army was on the Oder River, only 50 miles (80 km) from Berlin, and had virtually overrun Hungary. The Western Allies were about to fan out across Germany. Only in Italy were the Allies yet to resume their assault on the Third Reich.

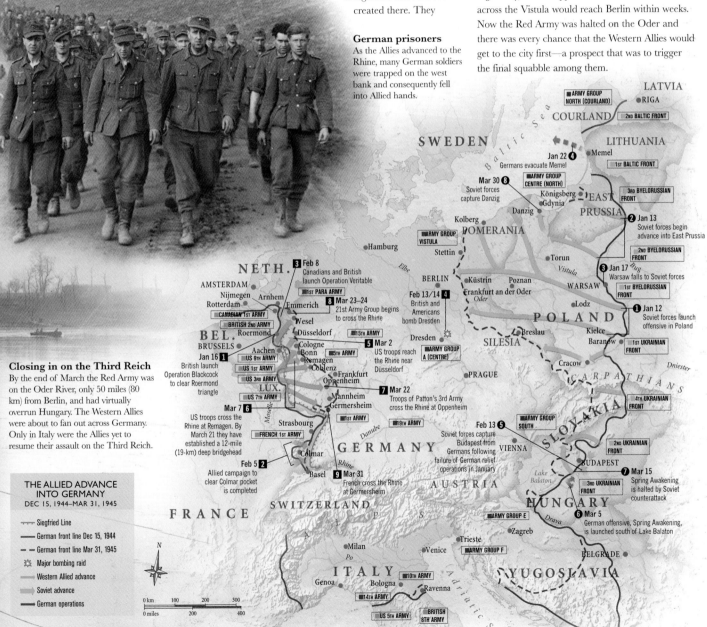

THE ALLIED ADVANCE
INTO GERMANY
DEC 15, 1944–MAR 31, 1945

- ⊤⊤⊤ Siegfried Line
- ▬ German front line Dec 15, 1944
- - - German front line Mar 31, 1945
- ✵ Major bombing raid
- ▬ Western Allied advance
- ▬ Soviet advance
- ▬ German operations

0 km   100   200   300
0 miles   200   400

3 Feb 8 Canadians and British launch Operation Veritable

8 Mar 23–24 21st Army Group begins to cross the Rhine

4 Feb 13/14 British and Americans bomb Dresden

5 Mar 2 US troops reach the Rhine near Düsseldorf

7 Mar 22 Troops of Patton's 3rd Army cross the Rhine at Oppenheim

1 Jan 16 British launch Operation Blackcock to clear Roermond triangle

6 Mar 7 US troops cross the Rhine at Remagen. By March 21 they have established a 12-mile (19-km) deep bridgehead

2 Feb 5 Allied campaign to clear Colmar pocket is completed

9 Mar 31 French cross the Rhine at Germersheim

5 Feb 13 Soviet forces capture Budapest from Germans following failure of German relief operations in January

7 Mar 15 Spring Awakening is halted by Soviet counterattack

6 Mar 5 German offensive, Spring Awakening, is launched south of Lake Balaton

4 Jan 22 Germans evacuate Memel

8 Mar 30 Soviet forces capture Danzig

2 Jan 13 Soviet forces begin advance into East Prussia

3 Jan 17 Warsaw falls to Soviet forces

1 Jan 12 Soviet forces launch offensive in Poland

ARMY GROUP NORTH (COURLAND)
2ND BALTIC FRONT
1ST BALTIC FRONT
3RD BYELORUSSIAN FRONT
ARMY GROUP CENTRE (NORTH)
2ND BYELORUSSIAN FRONT
1ST BYELORUSSIAN FRONT
1ST UKRAINIAN FRONT
4TH UKRAINIAN FRONT
ARMY GROUP VISTULA
ARMY GROUP A (CENTRE)
2ND UKRAINIAN FRONT
3RD UKRAINIAN FRONT
ARMY GROUP SOUTH
ARMY GROUP E
ARMY GROUP F

1ST PARA ARMY
CANADIAN 1ST ARMY
BRITISH 2ND ARMY
15TH ARMY
US 9TH ARMY
US 1ST ARMY
US 3RD ARMY
5TH ARMY
US 7TH ARMY
1ST ARMY
9TH ARMY
FRENCH 1ST ARMY
10TH ARMY
14TH ARMY
US 5TH ARMY
BRITISH 8TH ARMY

THE FINAL PUSH IN EUROPE

APRIL 1–MAY 11, 1945

The last few weeks of the war witnessed dramatic events on every front as Germany was squeezed from the west, east, and south, and split in two by the Western Allies and the Soviet Union. The fall of Berlin to the Red Army at the beginning of May was followed by the signing of four separate surrenders. German troops, however, continued to fight in Czechoslovakia for three days after hostilties ended.

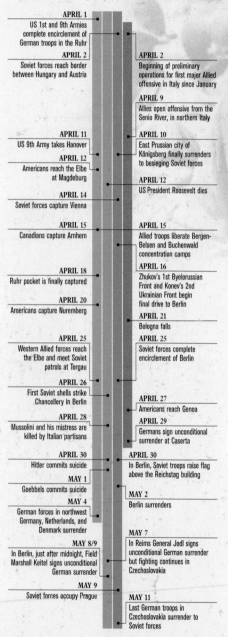

APRIL 1
US 1st and 9th Armies complete encirclement of German troops in the Ruhr

APRIL 2
Soviet forces reach border between Hungary and Austria

APRIL 2
Beginning of preliminary operations for first major Allied offensive in Italy since January

APRIL 9
Allies open offensive from the Senio River, in northern Italy

APRIL 11
US 9th Army takes Hanover

APRIL 10
East Prussian city of Königsberg finally surrenders to besieging Soviet forces

APRIL 12
Americans reach the Elbe at Magdeburg

APRIL 12
US President Roosevelt dies

APRIL 14
Soviet forces capture Vienna

APRIL 15
Canadians capture Arnhem

APRIL 15
Allied troops liberate Bergen-Belsen and Buchenwald concentration camps

APRIL 18
Ruhr pocket is finally captured

APRIL 16
Zhukov's 1st Byelorussian Front and Konev's 2nd Ukrainian Front begin final drive to Berlin

APRIL 20
Americans capture Nuremberg

APRIL 21
Bologna falls

APRIL 25
Western Allied forces reach the Elbe and meet Soviet patrols at Torgau

APRIL 25
Soviet forces complete encirclement of Berlin

APRIL 26
First Soviet shells strike Chancellery in Berlin

APRIL 27
Americans reach Genoa

APRIL 28
Mussolini and his mistress are killed by Italian partisans

APRIL 29
Germans sign unconditional surrender at Caserta

APRIL 30
Hitler commits suicide

APRIL 30
In Berlin, Soviet troops raise flag above the Reichstag building

MAY 1
Goebbels commits suicide

MAY 2
Berlin surrenders

MAY 4
German forces in northwest Germany, Netherlands, and Denmark surrender

MAY 7
In Reims General Jodl signs unconditional German surrender but fighting continues in Czechoslovakia

MAY 8/9
In Berlin, just after midnight, Field Marshall Keitel signs unconditional German surrender

MAY 9
Soviet forces occupy Prague

MAY 11
Last German troops in Czechoslovakia surrender to Soviet forces

■ Allied advance from the west Apr 1–May 7, 1945   ■ Soviet advance from the east Apr 1–May 11, 1945   ■ Allied advance in Italy Apr 2 –29, 1945   ■ Other events

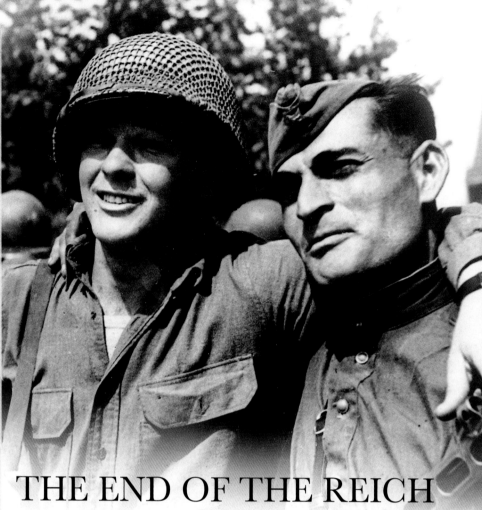

THE END OF THE REICH

ON MARCH 28, 1945 Eisenhower had drafted a message to Stalin to reassure him that he did not intend to make Berlin an objective for his forces. He would leave the German capital to the Soviets, and advance instead to the Erfurt-Leipzig-Dresden line, an area to which he believed the Germans were moving their organs of government. The British were aghast at this. Churchill believed that to wait for the Soviets to capture Berlin would merely prolong the war and enable them to reap the main fruits of victory. Montgomery, too, considered that this was the ideal opportunity for the single-thrust strategy to be used. However, the US chiefs of staff supported Eisenhower, and the British climbed down after he assured them that his decision was not irreversible. Furthermore, Allied intelligence had been warning of the Nazi intention to establish a final bastion in the Alps and he needed to forestall this. Stalin, however, was convinced that Eisenhower was bluffing and took this as a signal to accelerate preparations for the final assault on Berlin.

ADVANCE FROM THE RHINE

Eisenhower's plan for the advance from the Rhine was that Bradley's 12th Army Group was to make the main thrust toward Dresden, taking back the US Ninth Army under command once the Ruhr had been encircled. Montgomery, to his fury, was given the supporting role of covering Bradley's northern flank. Devers' Sixth Army Group was to advance southeastward toward the Bavarian Alps to prevent the establishment of the so-called National Redoubt, where a last-ditch stand might be made.

The various armies were already breaking out of their bridgeheads before the end of March, and the US First and Ninth Armies had the Ruhr encircled

American war correspondent and prisoners
Fred Ramage, one of the many journalists who reported on the advance of the Western Allies, brings in two German air force men on his press jeep.

US and Soviet troops meet at Torgau
On April 25 members of a US reconnaissance patrol crossed the Elbe at Torgau to meet Soviet troops and celebrate the fact that Germany was now divided in two.

on April 1 (see map page 276). Trapped inside was a large part of Army Group B, still commanded by Model. Hitler ordered him to defend the Ruhr to the last and so his troops did not attempt to escape the encirclement. This left a yawning gap in the German defenses. Bradley was quick to take advantage of this and his forces were soon racing to the Elbe. Elements of the Ninth Army entered Hanover on April 11 and reached Magdeburg the following day. Those forces allocated to reducing the Ruhr pocket steadily squeezed it and by April 18 it was no more. Some 325,000 German troops surrendered, but Model chose to commit suicide. To the south, progress was equally rapid. Patton found stiff resistance in Franfurt-am-Main. He left his infantry to deal with this, bypassing the city with his armor, and quickly linked up with the First Army to his north. Kassel was in his army's hands on April 4.

While the French First Army headed for the Swiss border, clearing the Black Forest *en route*, the US Seventh Army advanced quickly to the Main River, reaching Würzburg

> ... orders from the Supreme Command were still couched in the most rigorous terms, enjoining us to "hold" and "fight" under threats of court martial. But I no longer insisted on these orders being carried out. It was a nerve-racking time we experienced—outwardly putting a bold face on the matter ... while we secretly allowed things to go their own way. On my own responsibility I gave orders for lines to be prepared in the rear ready for a retreat.

GENERAL BLUMENTRITT OF THE GERMAN FIRST PARACHUTE ARMY, DESCRIBING THE SITUATION AT THE END OF MARCH

on April 5 and Schweinfurt six days later. German resistance was patchy. Many towns displayed white flags and offered no resistance at all. In others, especially if SS troops were in the vicinity, there was bitter fighting. There was virtually no movement of refugees since there was really nowhere they could go. Civilians stayed in their homes and hoped that the fighting would quickly move on.

The main focus of attention continued to be the Elbe. By mid-April the US First and Ninth Armies had closed up to it. Indeed, Simpson's Ninth Army already had a bridgehead at Magdeburg and he pleaded with Eisenhower to be allowed to go on

to Berlin, just 70 miles (110 km) away. Eisenhower, however, was concerned that US troops were already inside the agreed Soviet postwar zone of occupation. He insisted that there was to be no further advance east of the river or across the Mulde to its south. Instead, Bradley was to turn southeast to the Danube valley and link up with the Red Army so as to isolate the National Redoubt, which did not, in fact, exist. The US Seventh Army captured Nuremberg on April 20 after a fierce battle against SS troops and continued south to the Danube. Meanwhile, Patton led the US Third Army into the Danube valley and into Czechoslovakia, reaching Pilsen before he was halted by Eisenhower.

The burning question was when the Soviet forces would appear. The US First Army on the west bank of the Mulde had sent reconnaissance patrols eastward to a limit of 5 miles (8 km) from the river. On April 25 one of these could not resist going farther and met Soviet troops at Torgau on the Elbe. Germany was now physically split in two.

ADVANCE IN THE NORTH
In the north, Montgomery had also made good progress. The Canadian First Army had the initial task of liberating the northeast Netherlands. In spite of coming across much flooding, it made a rapid

US troops enter Nuremberg
The city—a symbol of National Socialism— was defended fanatically by SS troops. It was finally captured by the Americans on April 20.

THE DISCOVERY OF BERGEN-BELSEN

JUST AS THE SOVIETS had come across extermination camps during their advance through Poland in 1944, so the Western Allies stumbled across similar horrific sites as they overran the western and southern parts of Germany in April 1945. One of these camps was Bergen-Belsen, which lay between Hanover and Hamburg.

On April 12 forward elements of the British 11th Armoured Division on the Aller River received a German officer bearing a flag of truce. He asked that the area around the camp at Belsen be declared neutral, since there had been an outbreak of typhus there and the Germans did not want it to spread. The British agreed and three days later sent a party to inspect the camp. They discovered that there were, in fact, two camps—one for men and the other for women. In both, there were thousands of unburied corpses, as well as mass graves containing another 40,000 bodies. While not an extermination camp, Bergen-Belsen had been crammed with some 60,000 inmates and disease had become rampant. Worse, the administrative system had totally broken down and there was virtually no food for the prisoners, although the British discovered a building crammed with rations for the SS guards.

Some troops were assigned to doing what they could for the 38,000 survivors, many of whom were dying. However, with the advance to Hamburg continuing, the division could not spare any food or medical support and it was to be a few days before this could be provided in sufficient quantities. The local inhabitants, who denied all knowledge of the existence of the camp, were made to help with the burial of the dead so that they could see what had been done in their name. The SS staff of the camp initially had to be protected from inmates determined on revenge. Eventually, they were tried for war crimes and a number, including the commandant, were hanged. The camp of Bergen-Belsen remains to this day a memorial site and a stark reminder of the inhumanity of which people are capable.

Belsen inmates
Around 38,000 people were found alive in the camp on April 15, but as many as 28,000 died in the weeks that followed.

Burying the dead
Guards were made to help with burials in some camps. In others, they were shot by Allied troops.

Corpses in an open pit
In addition to the 40,000 corpses in mass graves, there were 10,000 unburied corpses of inmates who had died from starvation and disease.

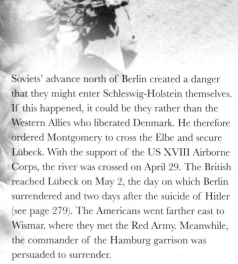

advance and reached Groningen on April 16. The German 25th Army was thus finally cut off, but it showed no sign of surrendering. The plight of the starving Dutch was now of very real concern and so agreement was reached with the 25th Army's commander that the Allies could deliver foodstuffs by air. The strategic bombing forces were given the task—code-named Operation Manna—and dropped supplies from a very low height with no interference from the Germans. Meanwhile, the Canadians began to clear the German North Sea coast.

The British Second Army continued its advance in a northeastward direction, capturing Osnabrück on April 4 and reaching the Weser River the next day. Montgomery's orders were to secure Hamburg and the naval base at Kiel, cut off Schleswig-Holstein, and prepare to liberate Denmark. As the Americans

were finding to the south, some German forces were still prepared to fight and there were some bitter encounters. The fiercest resistance was in Bremen, where the German commander and 6,000 men only surrendered after nine days of fighting. The British were concerned that Hamburg might prove to be an even tougher battle.

Eisenhower was becoming worried about Soviet intentions in the north of Germany. The speed of the

Occupying Bremen
German resistance was fierce on the many river lines in the north of the country. It was particularly obstinate at the port of Bremen, which was finally captured by the British Second Army on April 26.

Soviets' advance north of Berlin created a danger that they might enter Schleswig-Holstein themselves. If this happened, it could be they rather than the Western Allies who liberated Denmark. He therefore ordered Montgomery to cross the Elbe and secure Lübeck. With the support of the US XVIII Airborne Corps, the river was crossed on April 29. The British reached Lübeck on May 2, the day on which Berlin surrendered and two days after the suicide of Hitler (see page 279). The Americans went farther east to Wismar, where they met the Red Army. Meanwhile, the commander of the Hamburg garrison was persuaded to surrender.

By this time many German troops were making their way westward to avoid falling into Soviet hands. This was particularly the case in the British 21st Army Group sector. At the instigation of Grand Admiral

close to the Adriatic coast, and the Reno River. Throughout the winter months there had been an air campaign to throttle German communications and by the spring the Germans' ability to redeploy their troops quickly no longer existed.

After some preliminary operations to tie down the German left flank on Lake Comacchio, the Eighth Army attacked on April 9. The fighting was initially tough, not helped by the numerous waterways, but gradually the defenses crumbled. Delayed by two days because of bad weather, the Americans joined in on the 14th. Argenta fell to the British four days later, and then the Fifth and Eighth Armies jointly seized Bologna. General Heinrich von Vietinghoff, the German commander, realized that his defenses had disintegrated and ordered a withdrawal northward. The Fifth Army then advanced toward Milan, while the Eighth struck northeastward toward Venice.

On April 23 the Germans made further peace overtures and six days later a delegation from Vietinghoff signed a surrender document with the Allies, who included a Soviet representative, at Caserta in southern Italy. It was done without reference to Berlin and came into effect on May 2. By this time the US Fifth Army had reached Milan— already occupied by Italian partisans—and was simultaneously advancing through the Alps toward Austria, eventually meeting up with the US Seventh Army in the Brenner Pass on May 6. At the same time, the British had reached Trieste, where they came face to face with Tito's Yugoslav partisans, who had designs on the port. The arduous campaign in Italy was finally at an end, but Trieste was to create an immediate postwar problem.

Liberation of Milan
Troops of the US Fifth Army enter Milan, already liberated by Italian partisans, on April 29.

Dönitz, who in Hitler's will had been appointed as the Führer's successor and was now in Schleswig-Holstein, a delegation went to Montgomery's tactical HQ on Lüneberg Heath on May 3. They asked him to accept the surrender of Army Group Vistula, which was facing the Second Byelorussian Front, but also requested that he shape his operations so that as many civilians as possible be given the chance to escape falling into Soviet hands. Montgomery replied that Army Group Vistula was a Soviet concern, but that he would accept the surrender of all German forces in northwest Germany, the Netherlands, and Denmark. Dönitz agreed to this, and on the following day the delegation returned and signed the document of surrender. It was a major consolation for the frustration that Montgomery had suffered over the last nine months, but it was not the first German surrender in a major theater.

CAMPAIGN IN ITALY

In Italy the Allies had spent the first three months of 1945 planning their final offensive. The lull had, however, enabled the Germans to send four divisions to assist in the defense of western Germany, not that this had made any difference. The remaining Canadian corps in Italy had also departed, and their place had been taken by a number of Italian partisan brigades. During March 1945 several peace overtures were made to the Allies by the German military governor of northern Italy. He was an SS officer

and his overall boss, Heinrich Himmler, who was also trying to make a deal with the Allies, eventually stepped in and, in the fear of being upstaged, ordered that no more contact be made.

The eventual Allied plan for bringing the war in Italy to an end was to destroy the German forces by trapping them between the US Fifth and British Eighth Armies. The Americans were to attack northward to the west of Bologna, while the British struck through a narrow strip of land, known as the Argenta Gap, that lay between Lake Comacchio,

THE DEATH OF MUSSOLINI

IN THE AFTERMATH OF HIS RESCUE by the Germans in September 1943, Benito Mussolini established himself as head of an Italian Social Republic in Salò in northern Italy, but he had little power. When the German forces began to disintegrate in April 1945, Mussolini declared that he would make a last stand with his German allies in the Alps. Accordingly, on April 25 he left Milan for Lake Como, where he expected to meet a force of 3,000 Blackshirts. On arrival he discovered that the force consisted of just 12 men, and he joined a German convoy heading northward. At 7:00 am the following morning the convoy was stopped at a partisan roadblock. The partisans agreed to let the Germans pass, but not the Italians. Mussolini and his mistress Clara Petacci were then kept prisoner until the afternoon of April 28, when a communist partisan, Walter Audisio arrived to drive them away in his car. After a short way, he ordered them out and shot them. Audisio took the bodies to Milan, where they were strung up by their ankles in a main square. It was a grisly end to Mussolini's dream of creating a new Roman empire.

Fallen Duce
The citizens of Milan threw filth on the corpses of the former dictator and his mistress.

Mussolini and Petacci
The bodies were hung in a square where partisans had been executed.

ADVANCE TO VIENNA

While the Western Allies were crossing the Rhine to advance farther into Germany, on the Eastern Front the Soviet Third Ukrainian Front was overwhelming the German Army Group South in Hungary and Austria. By April 4 it had smashed its way through the Vertes mountains to cut off Vienna on three sides and join hands with the Second Ukrainian Front. A torrent of armor, over which flew fleets of attack aircraft, was followed up by waves of infantry, who poured through every gap that was torn in the Army Group South's lines. There was then a fierce nine-day struggle for Vienna, in which the city's defenders were relentlessly pushed back, and savage hand-to-hand fighting raged in the sewers. By April 14 Vienna had fallen into Red Army hands.

PLANNING THE BERLIN BATTLE

On April 1 Stalin informed his generals that he intended to "take Berlin before the Western Allies did" and launch an offensive into Brandenburg by April 16. Three days earlier he had informed the Western Allies that the coming Red Army offensive would be launched against Dresden and Leipzig, probably in mid-May, and it was not until mid-April that the British and Americans became aware that the offensive was imminent. Stalin calmly reassured them that the principal thrust was to be made on Leipzig. Meanwhile, Hitler had convinced himself that the offensive would be made toward Prague rather than Berlin. Confident that the line on the Oder would hold, and convinced that the Red Army was at breaking point, at the end of the first week in April he transferred three panzergrenadier divisions of Army Group Vistula to the south.

THE ALLIED ADVANCE THROUGH GERMANY
APR 1–MAY 7, 1945

— German front line Apr 1
-- German front line Apr 19
— Western Allied front line May 7
— Soviet front line May 7
→ Western Allied advance
→ Soviet advance
▢ Borders Sept 1939

Apr 16 ❷
Northern Soviet armies restart their advance from the Oder-Neisse Rivers and drive toward Berlin

Apr 1 ❶
Forces in US 1st and 9th armies meet at Lippstadt, so encircling the Ruhr

Apr 10 ❸
US 9th Army takes Hanover

Apr 11 ❹
Americans reach the Elbe at Magdeburg

Apr 20 ❸
Soviet forces begin to shell central Berlin, which surrenders on May 2

Apr 2 ❷
US 3rd Army takes Kassel

Apr 25 ❻
Western and Soviet forces meet at Torgau

Apr 20 ❺
Americans capture Nuremberg

May 9 ❹
Prague is occupied by Soviet forces

Apr 14 ❶
Soviet forces take control of Vienna

Apr 25 ❸
Americans take Parma and Verona

Apr 27 ❹
Americans reach Genoa

Apr 21 ❷
Bologna falls

Apr 9 ❶
Allies open offensive from the Senio River

Advance to the Elbe

The Western Allies advanced from the Rhine on a broad front, with the Americans making the main thrust toward Dresden and the British pushing north. An Allied offensive in Italy made rapid progress, while in the east the Red Army advanced from the Oder and captured Berlin.

The last battle

The Red Army broke into Berlin using assault groups cooperating closely with armor, artillery, and antitank teams. Security detachments mopped up behind.

Meanwhile, Stalin was exploiting to the hilt the simmering rivalry between Zhukov and Konev over who should take Berlin. At a meeting on April 3 it was decided that Zhukov's First Byelorussian Front was to drive to Berlin and seize the city. Konev's First Ukrainian Front was to provide support by attacking the German forces south of Berlin, thus isolating the principal formations of Army Group Center from the units defending the city. However, in the event of stiff enemy resistance on the eastern approaches to Berlin, Konev should also be ready to deliver a blow from south of the city. The Second Byelorussian Front, under Rokossovsky, which had only just completed operations in Gdynia and Danzig, was to join the offensive four days after Zhukov and Konev had gone onto the attack.

A total of 23 Soviet armies set about regrouping on the Oder. On Zhukov's front 7 million shells were brought up by rail and road for 9,000 guns. Meanwhile, 27 engineer battalions kept open damaged bridges on the Oder and built 25 new ones, linking the Küstrin bridgehead with the east bank of the river. No fewer than 120 engineer and 13 bridging battalions on Konev's front worked on bridges over the Oder and Neisse. Four air armies, deploying 7,500 aircraft, were to support the ground forces. On Zhukov's front, the 16th Air Army had assembled 3,200 aircraft, and was augmented by the 800 long-range bombers of the 18th Air Army.

GERMAN PREPARATIONS

Between the Baltic coast and Görlitz, around 100 miles (160 km) southeast of Berlin, there were some 50 German field divisions, five of them armored, supplemented by a patchwork of makeshift battle groups and approximately 100 *Volkssturm* battalions. According to postwar Soviet figures, against them were ranged approximately 190 Red Army divisions, although many of these were very run down, averaging between 2,500 and 5,500 men. For the assault on Berlin, the Red Army was relying on its massive superiority in artillery, aircraft, and armor. On the German side, there was a grim determination to fight on in the east, despite almost universal recognition of impending defeat.

Between November 1943 and March 1944 RAF Bomber Command had tried, and failed, to "wreck Berlin from end to end." By the early spring of 1945, British and American bombers were flying almost at will over the German capital by day and night, forcing Hitler to retreat to his bunker in the Chancellery garden and reducing swathes of the city to rubble. Also in the air over the German capital were Red Air Force reconnaissance aircraft gathering information that was then combined with captured documents and prisoner interrogations to produce detailed assault maps. Zhukov was well aware that a modern city could devour an army committed to a house-to-house battle, as had happened in Stalingrad. He was determined that Berlin would be taken in an all-out power drive, in which specially chosen assault groups would be supported by armor and massed artillery laying down a path of destruction all the way to the center.

The Germans did not give any serious thought to the defense of Berlin until March, when a makeshift "obstacle belt" was thrown up in a ring some 30 miles (50 km) outside the capital. A second ring was improvised around Berlin's rail system, whose cuttings, culverts, and overhead lines provided good cover and a formidable barrier to Soviet armor. The last-ditch defense ring—code-named Citadel and containing eight wedge-shaped command sectors—lay at the heart of the city and contained nearly all the government buildings.

To defend the German capital, its commander General Helmuth Reymann initially had at his disposal some 60,000 *Volkssturm* and a collection of Hitler Youth, engineer, police, and antiaircraft units. The only unit of any operational value was the Berlin Guard Battalion. In Berlin's streets

Escaping destruction
Berlin was ravaged by Allied bombers and Red Army artillery. The battle in the streets produced strange contrasts, with a delirium of fighting in some districts and an eerie calm in others.

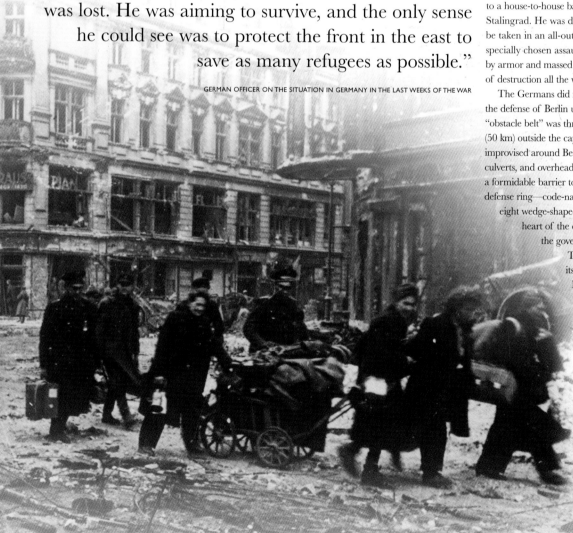

"Even the last soldier was now aware that the war was lost. He was aiming to survive, and the only sense he could see was to protect the front in the east to save as many refugees as possible."

GERMAN OFFICER ON THE SITUATION IN GERMANY IN THE LAST WEEKS OF THE WAR

Firing mortars
Red Army heavy mortars were fired in Berlin to prepare the way for the infantry to leapfrog forward. Each Red Army infantry regiment fielded six 120-mm mortars, which had a range of up to 4 miles (6 km).

the erection of flimsy barricades prompted the sour joke that it would take the Red Army two hours and 15 minutes to break them down—two hours laughing their heads off and 15 minutes smashing them up.

THE RED ARMY'S POWER DRIVE

The terrain facing Zhukov's bridgehead at Küstrin was unsuitable for armored operations—a 10-mile (16-km)-wide valley, heavily mined and crisscrossed with streams, ditches, and canals, and overlooked by the heavily defended Seelow Heights. Zhukov decided to commit his armor to the attack's first phase only when the 200-ft (60-m) Heights had been seized.

The initial thrust was made on April 16, but it met with unexpectedly fierce resistance, and at noon Zhukov sent in his armor—1,300 tanks and self-propelled guns—a full 24 hours before he had thought it would be necessary. The Seelow Heights

were taken after ferocious fighting on the 17th and on the following day the second German defensive line was breached. By April 19 Zhukov had prised open the Oder line on a 45-mile (70-km) front, but was now at least two days behind schedule. On April 20 Berlin's northeast perimeter was breached, and shortly before 2:00 pm the heavy guns of the Third Shock Army opened fire on the city.

To the south, Konev had made rapid progress, clearing the Neisse River by the 17th, and driving a wedge between Army Group Vistula and Army Group Center before swinging north toward Berlin

on the 20th. Hitler, swooping wildly between drug-induced euphoria and deep depression, continued to marshal phantom armies on the map in his bunker. Only on April 22 did he admit the the war was lost.

Berlin was now cut off on three sides. On April 23 Stalin issued the order that decided who was to win the race to Berlin. Konev's troops were placed a crucial 150 yd (140 m) to the west of the Reichstag, the preeminent symbolic objective in the assault on the city. Zhukov had been given the prize. Now the Soviet armies that had encircled Berlin—464,000 men, supported by 12,700 guns, 21,000 rocket launchers, and 1,500 tanks—drove relentlessly forward. Berlin's S-bahn ring was breached on April 26 and by nightfall on the 27th "Fortress Berlin" had been squeezed down to an east–west belt 10 miles (16 km) long and 3 miles (5 km) wide.

On the night of the 26th the first shells struck the Chancellery, sending vibrations through the *Führerbunker* as tons of masonry toppled into the street. Two days later the Red Army had fought its way to within a 1 mile (1.5 km) of the hideout. On April 30 Zhukov's 150th and 171st Rifle Divisions launched their final assault on the Reichstag, which

Arch of defeat
German soldiers march into captivity by the Brandenburg Gate. The Red Army claimed to have taken 134,000 prisoners on May 2, 1945, but this included able-bodied civilians destined for labor camps.

HITLER'S LAST DAYS

ON JANUARY 16, 1945, Hitler descended from the Reich Chancellery into the 13th and last of his headquarters, the *Führerbunker*. With the exception of two excursions, on February 25 and March 16, and occasional brief visits to the Chancellery, the bunker was to remain the center of the shrinking Third Reich until its leader's death. Built in 1944, the *Führerbunker* was contained within a complex of shelters, one of which housed the staff of Martin Bormann, Hitler's secretary, and another a field hospital. Buried 55 ft (17 m) below the Chancellery garden, the main *Führerbunker* was built in two stories. In the bunker's upper level were a kitchen and living quarters, latterly occupied by Josef Goebbels and his family. Below was the *Führerbunker* proper, a series of small rooms that included a telephone exchange, a map room, and Hitler's spartan living quarters.

In the bunker, night merged into day, with the last military conferences often ending at 6:00 am. On April 15 Hitler was joined by his mistress, Eva Braun, who had lived in the Chancellery since mid-March. On April 20, Hitler's 56th birthday, there was a final melancholy reunion of the Nazi paladin in the Chancellery and then the bunker. In the small hours of April 29 Hitler dictated his final testament and married Eva Braun. At about 3:30 pm on the 30th he and Braun committed suicide together, Hitler biting on a cyanide capsule and shooting himself with his Walther 7.65-mm revolver. Their bodies were partially burned in the Chancellery garden, and discovered by an NKVD officer on May 5. Also in the garden were the bodies of Goebbels and his wife Magda, who had poisoned their six children before committing suicide. Bormann, it seems, committed suicide after escaping.

Hitler's grave
Allied troops view the shell crater in the Chancellery garden where the bodies of Hitler and Eva Braun were buried after being burned.

Bunker entrance
The bunker remained intact, even as the Reich Chancellery was being heavily shelled.

Last public appearance
On his 56th birthday, on April 20, 1945, the Führer appeared in public for the last time when he met young defenders of the Third Reich in the garden of the Chancellery.

was defended by over 5,000 SS men, Hitler Youth, and *Volkssturm*. In the early afternoon, as a Red banner was attached to a column at the building's entrance, Hitler prepared to commit suicide.

While fighting continued, the Germans opened negotiations with General Chuikov about a new successor German government and a ceasefire. At 10 am on May 2 General Weidling, Berlin's recently appointed battle commandant, ordered a general surrender. As a chilling drizzle fell on Berlin, its defenders began to lay down their arms. In the battle for the city, the Soviet fronts under Zhukov, Konev, and Rokossovsky had sustained losses of 305,000 men killed, wounded, and missing. They were the heaviest casualties suffered by the Red Army in any battle of the war with the exception of the great encirclements of 1941. In Berlin itself up to 100,000 German soldiers and civilians had lost their lives, while in the fighting since April 16 some 480,000 German officers and men had become prisoners-of-war.

The surrender in Berlin did not end the fighting in the one remaining pocket of German resistance, in Czechoslovakia, where on May 4 the citizens of Prague took to the streets, emboldened by the approach of the US Third Army. However, on May 7 the Americans were ordered to withdraw by US President

Fallen eagle
This massive eagle was captured by the Red Army in the Reich Chancellery.

Truman, who was determined that no American lives were to be risked in so volatile a situation. Murderous confusion had reigned in Prague between May 4 and 8 as Czechs clashed with SS units. In the wee hours of May 9, Soviet tanks reached the outer suburbs of Prague, while its German garrison streamed westward to escape the Red Army. Later that day the Soviet armor rolled into Prague. Just two days before, the Germans had surrendered unconditionally to the Allies. A formal ceremony took place on May 7 in Reims and—as millions of people celebrated in Europe, the US, and elsewhere—on May 8 in Berlin.

Fleeing from the Red Army in Germany
Refugees cross the Elbe River at Tangermünde, to the
west of Berlin, on a bridge blown up by the Germans.
As the Red Army advanced westward in 1945, vast
numbers of German civilians fled in fear for their lives.

ASIA AND THE PACIFIC

JANUARY–SEPTEMBER 1945

The final months of the Pacific war saw frenetic action across the entire region. Landings took place on Iwo Jima and the Philippines, while the British forced the Japanese out of Burma. The infamous fire bombing of Tokyo started in March, and Japanese surrender followed shortly after the dropping of the atom bombs on Hiroshima and Nagasaki.

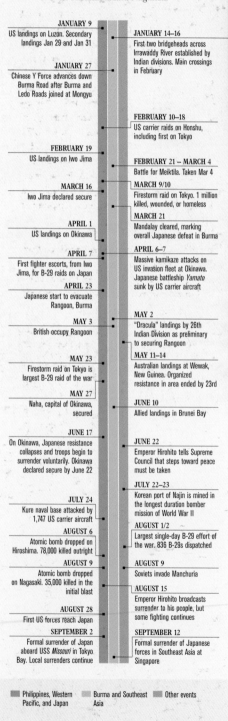

JANUARY 9
US landings on Luzon. Secondary landings Jan 29 and Jan 31

JANUARY 14–16
First two bridgeheads across Irrawaddy River established by Indian divisions. Main crossings in February

JANUARY 27
Chinese Y Force advances down Burma Road after Burma and Ledo Roads joined at Mongyu

FEBRUARY 10–18
US carrier raids on Honshu, including first on Tokyo

FEBRUARY 19
US landings on Iwo Jima

FEBRUARY 21 – MARCH 4
Battle for Meiktila. Taken Mar 4

MARCH 9/10
Firestorm raid on Tokyo. 1 million killed, wounded, or homeless

MARCH 16
Iwo Jima declared secure

MARCH 21
Mandalay cleared, marking overall Japanese defeat in Burma

APRIL 1
US landings on Okinawa

APRIL 6–7
Massive kamikaze attacks on US invasion fleet at Okinawa. Japanese battleship *Yamato* sunk by US carrier aircraft

APRIL 7
First fighter escorts, from Iwo Jima, for B-29 raids on Japan

APRIL 23
Japanese start to evacuate Rangoon, Burma

MAY 2
"Dracula" landings by 26th Indian Division as preliminary to securing Rangoon

MAY 3
British occupy Rangoon

MAY 11–14
Australian landings at Wewak, New Guinea. Organized resistance in area ended by 23rd

MAY 23
Firestorm raid on Tokyo is largest B-29 raid of the war

MAY 27
Naha, capital of Okinawa, secured

JUNE 10
Allied landings in Brunei Bay

JUNE 17
On Okinawa, Japanese resistance collapses and troops begin to surrender voluntarily. Okinawa declared secure by June 22

JUNE 22
Emperor Hirohito tells Supreme Council that steps toward peace must be taken

JULY 22–23
Korean port of Najin is mined in the longest duration bomber mission of World War II

JULY 24
Kure naval base attacked by 1,747 US carrier aircraft

AUGUST 1/2
Largest single-day B-29 effort of the war. 836 B-29s dispatched

AUGUST 6
Atomic bomb dropped on Hiroshima. 78,000 killed outright

AUGUST 9
Soviets invade Manchuria

AUGUST 9
Atomic bomb dropped on Nagasaki. 35,000 killed in the initial blast

AUGUST 15
Emperor Hirohito broadcasts surrender to his people, but some fighting continues

AUGUST 28
First US forces reach Japan

SEPTEMBER 2
Formal surrender of Japan aboard USS *Missouri* in Tokyo Bay. Local surrenders continue

SEPTEMBER 12
Formal surrender of Japanese forces in Southeast Asia at Singapore

■ Philippines, Western Pacific, and Japan   ■ Burma and Southeast Asia   ■ Other events

JAPAN SURRENDERS

THE SETTING OF AMERICAN policy for the war in the Pacific was beset by rivalries between the army and navy. These were compounded by personal differences, specifically between Admiral Ernest King, chief of naval operations, and General MacArthur, commander in the Southwest Pacific theater.

In summer 1944 King wanted the US Navy to advance across the Pacific to Formosa (Taiwan) and on to Okinawa, but MacArthur contended that America should concentrate on the Philippines instead. MacArthur's motives were partly personal—he had made a public pledge to return to the islands after the Japanese invasion in 1942—but he also argued that the Philippines would provide the best base for the next phase of operations and that an attempt to recapture them would be less costly than an attack on Formosa. King's views commanded little support even among his colleagues within the navy, so it was MacArthur's view that prevailed.

RETAKING THE PHILIPPINES

The capture of the Philippines would become the longest and largest US action of the Pacific War thanks to protracted Japanese resistance, first on Leyte and then on Luzon. Seasonal rains, the forced withdrawal of US carriers for replenishment, and the success of kamikaze raids enabled the Japanese to assemble 75,200 troops to defend Leyte. It took until December 1944 to break the defense, by which time the Americans had 200,000 men on the island.

American naval power

US Task Group 38.3 sails to its anchorage at Ulithi, in the Caroline Islands: the light carrier *Langley*, fleet carrier *Ticonderoga*, and three battleships were accompanied by four cruisers and 18 destroyers.

The Japanese Army finally abandoned Leyte on December 19, 1944, although scattered resistance continued into May 1945. Meanwhile US forces had landed on Mindoro on December 15, 1944. They met little resistance there and easily secured useful airfields from which to support landings on Luzon.

The main US assault on Luzon began on January 9, 1945, with landings at Lingayen Gulf, about 100 miles (160 km) northwest of the capital, Manila. Facing 200,000 US troops were 275,000 men of the Japanese 14th Area Army under the command of Lieutenant General Yamashita Tomoyuki. With much of the Japanese Navy lying at the bottom of the Pacific after Leyte Gulf, and only 200 aircraft available, Yamashita had no prospect of supply or reinforcement. He split his forces into three groups and dispersed them to fight delaying actions in key strategic positions, where they dug themselves into cave complexes.

The US Sixth Army's advance to the Philippine capital, Manila, involved two thrusts: XIV Corps under Major General Oscar Griswold proceeded straight to the city across the central plain, taking Clark Field airbase and the town of Calumpit, while I Corps secured the left flank against a Japanese counterattack. Further US forces came ashore at Nasugbu, southwest of Manila, on January 31 and moved north to meet Griswold. Cheering Filipinos welcomed the Sixth Army as it entered the capital on February 4, but the Battle of Manila continued until March 3. Although Yamashita had withdrawn into the mountains, 17,000 naval troops under Rear Admiral Iwabuchi Sanji fought for the city in vicious hand-to-hand fighting. More than 100,000 Filipinos died, along with 1,000 Americans and 16,000

Raising the flag on Iwo Jima

In one of the most evocative images of World War II, US Marines raised the Stars and Stripes on Mount Suribachi. This photograph was not taken in the heat of the battle but specially posed shortly after the island's capture.

Japanese. By March 1945 the city was liberated but lay largely in ruins.

During the battle for Manila the Americans also captured Corregidor, the small rock island located in the entrance to Manila Bay. It was occupied by some 5,000 well-provisioned troops, but after the assault landing on February 15 and a parachute drop the next day, in the words of the official US Navy history, "the defense showed neither spirit nor cohesion." In an action lasting 10 days, the Americans lost some 225 killed and 405 wounded. The Japanese dead numbered over 4,500. Some 500 of these were buried alive, sealed in the caves from which they had been fighting by US bulldozers or demolition charges. Only 20 were taken prisoner.

THE WAR AT SEA

While US land forces were making inroads on Leyte and Luzon, American carrier task groups were operating off the Philippines. In November 1944 the US Navy destroyed 38 Japanese warships and

Manila in ruins

The fighting for the Philippine capital left thousands dead and reduced the old Spanish walled city, Intramuros, to rubble. After Warsaw, Manila was the most heavily damaged of all the Allied capitals during the war.

KAMIKAZE PILOTS

TOWARD THE END OF WORLD WAR II some Japanese pilots undertook suicide missions in which they deliberately flew their aircraft, laden with bombs, into enemy targets such as ships. The pilots had no means of escaping. Both the tactics themselves and the fliers were known as kamikaze, meaning "divine wind." Kamikaze squadrons sank or damaged beyond repair more than 70 American vessels, damaged hundreds of others, and took many lives at Leyte in 1944 and Okinawa in the following year. To some extent kamikaze tactics were adopted through force of circumstance—Japanese aircraft were no match for American aircraft. However, the practice was rooted in the ancient traditions of the Japanese samurai warriors, whose code of honor demanded death before surrender. The name itself is derived from that of a typhoon—the divine wind—which in 1281 destroyed a massive Mongol armada that had been preparing to attack and invade Japan. Kamikaze pilots would go through a ritual ceremony in which they would honor the emperor and drink a cup of sake before taking off on their final mission.

Kamikaze pilots
Kamikaze pilots pose for a last photo before a suicide mission. Around 2,550 kamikaze missions were flown, but their effectiveness lessened as US defenses against the attacks improved.

Kamikaze attack
A Japanese pilot tries to maneuver his Zero fighter into a US warship. In response to kamikaze attacks, the Americans increased their anti-aircraft guns and added fighters to their carrier air groups.

service and merchant ships, while US submarines sank the 64,800-ton carrier *Shinano* and the escort carrier *Shinyo*. During December 1944 and January 1945 Japanese kamikaze attacks sank or damaged 79 US warships, amphibious vessels, and service ships. In early January the US carrier force entered the South China Sea and raided Japanese-held ports in Indochina. On January 12 it destroyed 11 warships and 29 service and merchant ships totaling 115,000 tons. On January 21–22 another two warships and 17 service and merchant ships of 58,000 tons were sunk off Formosa. The relatively small tonnages reflected the lack of any large Japanese ships to sink. However, compelling evidence of American naval power came on February 17, when the carrier force, totaling 119 warships, raided the Japanese Home Islands for the first time since April 1942. Of the

Approaching Okinawa
Sailors on the battleship *West Virginia* keep watch for Japanese aircraft off the coast of Okinawa in late March 1945. On April 1 the ship was hit in a kamikaze attack, which killed four and wounded seven sailors.

ships deployed in this raid, only six—two carriers, two battleships, and two heavy cruisers—had been in service at the time of Pearl Harbor; the others had all been commissioned and built since.

IWO JIMA AND OKINAWA

The capture of two islands south of Japan—Iwo Jima in the Volcano Islands and Okinawa in the Ryukyus—was authorized by the American high command in October 1944 (see map page 290). Once the Americans had decided to launch a strategic air offensive against Japan from the southern Marianas, the small island of Iwo Jima assumed obvious importance as a base from which fighters could escort B-29 bombers on their missions. Similarly, once the decision to retake the Philippines had been made, then Okinawa presented itself as a potential forward base for land, air, and naval formations in the invasion of the Japanese Home Islands.

The campaigns for possession of these two islands are synonymous with the final phase of the Pacific War. Iwo Jima and Okinawa were of critical importance in the final closing of the ring around

Japan. Both also entered the US popular imagination through potent symbolism, such as the famous image of the capture of Mount Suribachi on Iwo Jima.

The campaign on Iwo Jima began on February 19, 1945, that on Okinawa on April 1. The islands were declared secure on March 26 and June 30, respectively. On the 8 sq miles (20 sq km) of Iwo Jima, where the Japanese had deployed about 25,000 troops, some 2,400 further Japanese were killed or captured after the island was declared secure, and resistance continued into June. Just 216 Japanese were taken prisoner. The island cost 6,821 Americans killed and nearly 18,000 wounded, but its value was revealed as early as March 11, when fighters began operations from the first of the airfield complexes that ultimately covered half the island.

The value of Okinawa was somewhat different from that of Iwo Jima. It would also provide airfields to support the campaign against the Home Islands, but its real value lay in the forward anchorage it would provide for the navy and its strategic position astride Japan's lines of communication with Southeast Asia. No tanker reached Japan from the Southern Resources Area after March 1945.

THE STRUGGLE FOR OKINAWA

On Okinawa the Japanese 32nd Army, with some 131,000 troops, ceded the central and northern part of the island in order to concentrate on a defensive campaign on the Shuri Line. The Japanese policy was to force the Americans to fight a protracted campaign within range of aircraft concentrated in the Home Islands. The air campaign was the most important part of the final despairing Japanese attempt to influence events to their advantage by reducing US resources. Suicide aircraft struck at American warships throughout the first four months of the campaign in the Philippines, but the greatest kamikaze effort came in the battle for Okinawa. Its failure demonstrated that there was no effective substitute for conventional air power. In the course of the Philippines campaign as a whole the Japanese armed forces lost an estimated 3,000 aircraft, and in the Okinawa campaign some 7,000 aircraft. In both campaigns, however, the Allies proved able to absorb their losses. Ten American fleet carriers were driven from the battle in the course of 1945, but, with one exception, all were returned to service before the end of the war.

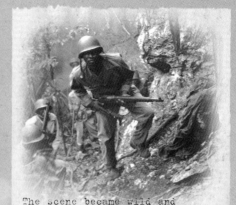

The scene became wild and terrible. More Japs rushed screaming from the caves. They tumbled over the rocks, their clothes and bodies burning fiercely. Soon the flame-throwers paused. There were no shots from the caves. A Jap with his clothes in rags hunched himself out of one hole, his arms upraised. The Marines behind the rocks waved to him to come out. The Jap indicated that there were more who would like to surrender.

ANONYMOUS US MARINE CORPS CORRESPONDENT, IWO JIMA

The Okinawa campaign cost the Allies 48,193 service personnel killed, wounded, and missing. They lost 34 ships of all types sunk and another 25 damaged beyond economic repair; 343 more were damaged to varying degrees. The reality underlying these results was two-fold. First, given their shortages of aircraft, fuel, and personnel, the Japanese could not simultaneously prepare for a conventional air battle and undertake kamikaze offensives. Even the most effective use of suicide missions in the battles for the Philippines and Okinawa could only have one outcome. Second, while the shock created by the employment of suicide forces was very real when they were first employed, it was one that lessened as the attacks themselves became less effective. By the end of the Okinawa campaign the Americans, by adopting new tactics and deployment, had gotten the better of the kamikazes.

In terms of an invasion of the Home Islands, the Americans had moved into a position of strength that ensured victory in the air battle. Sixty fleet, light, and escort carriers saw action off the Ryukyu Islands, and 90,662 missions were flown by US carriers during the Okinawa campaign. Of this total 53,077 missions were flown by the fleet and light fleet carriers between March 14 and June 8, while the rest were flown by escort carriers prior to the end of June. Against such numbers even self-sacrifice was largely ineffective. Tacit acknowledgment of this reality was provided by the fact that 10,755 prisoners were taken on Okinawa, the first occasion on which Japanese soldiers surrendered in any appreciable numbers.

BOMBING RAIDS ON JAPAN

In the American advance across the Pacific the carriers paved the way for landings, and the forces put ashore captured or built airfields from which aircraft were in turn

able to support the fleet against the next objective. The naval, land, and air efforts were mutually supporting, and the capture of the Marianas added another dimension to American strategy. The islands provided the airfields from which a strategic bombing campaign could

Tokyo destroyed by bombing
Little remains standing in this part of Tokyo after waves of incendiary bomb attacks by US aircraft in 1945. More people perished in the Tokyo fire bomb raids than in the atomic bomb attack on Nagasaki.

BOMBARDMENT OF JAPAN
MAR–AUG 1945

- Atomic air raids
- Big Six firebomb raids
- Firebomb raids
- Areas mined by US aircraft
- Allied air attack routes

❶ Mar 9/10, 1945
USAAF launches first major incendiary raid. 279 B-29s attack Tokyo. Firestorm obliterates 16 sq miles (40 sq km) leaving 84,000 dead

❷ Mar 11/12, 1945
Nagoya firebombed by 285 B-29s. City suffers second raid on Mar 18/19

❸ Mar 13/14, 1945
Kobe firebombed by 331 B-29s

❹ Mar 16/17, 1945
Center of Osaka reduced to ashes in firebomb raids

❺ Apr 15/16, 1945
129 B-29s bomb Kawasaki, while 109 others hits Tokyo

❻ May 23, 1945
Tokyo suffers another devastating attack in which 4,500 tons of bombs are dropped on the city. Over 3,000,000 of its citizens now homeless

❼ May 29/30, 1945
Business district of Yokohama (one-third of city) burned out after raid by 454 B-29s

❽ Aug 6, 1945
First atomic bomb dropped on Hiroshima, exploding 2,000 ft (600 m) above ground, devastating the city and killing 78,000 people instantly

❾ Aug 9, 1945
Second atomic bomb explodes over Nagasaki, destroying over 40 percent of the city and killing 35,000 people outright

The final attacks on Japan
In March 1945 the United States began a series of devastating firebomb attacks on major Japanese cities. In August US commanders took the historic decision to drop atomic bombs on Hiroshima and Nagasaki.

from China

from Carrier Task Force 38

from the Marianas

HOKKAIDO
Sapporo
Muroram
Hakodate
Aomori
Hirosaki
Hachinobe
Kamaishi
Sakata
Sendai
Sado
Fukushima
Niigata
Nagaoka
JAPAN
Hitachi
Mito
Utsunomiya
Kumagaya
Maebashi
Isezaki
Kawagushi
TOKYO
Chiba
Kawasaki
Hachioji
Yokohama
Kofu
Hiratsuka
Fujisawa
Numazu
Takaoka
Toyama
HONSHU
Fukui
Shimizu
Izu Islands
Tsuruga
Gifu
Ichinomiya
Nagoya
Shizuoka
Ogaki
Kuwana
Okazaki
Hamamatsu
Yokkaichi
Kyoto
Toyohashi
Tottori
Nishinomiya-Mikage
Matsue
Himeji
Tsu
Osaka
Kobe
Sakai
Uji-Yamada
Akashi
Wakayama
Okayama
Fukuyama
Hiroshima
Takamatsu
Tokushima
Kure
Imabari
Shimonoseki
Matsuyama
SHIKOKU
Yawata
Ube
Kochi
Aki
Kita-Kyushu Moji
Fukuoka
Oita
Uwajima
Saga
Sasebo
Omuta
Kumamoto
Nobeoka
Nagasaki
KYUSHU
Kagoshima

Sea of Japan

Tsushima

East China Sea

PACIFIC OCEAN

Superior payload
A B-29 drops its massive payload over mainland Japan. Its gigantic internal bomb bays could hold 20,000 lb (9,072 kg) of bombs.

Superfortress in flight
With a wingspan of over 140 ft (43 m) and an unladen weight of over 140,000 lb (63,640 kg), the American B-29 Superfortress was the largest bomber to see action during World War II. Its sheer size presented engineering problems previously unencountered in aviation history, but it was a hugely successful aircraft nonetheless.

be staged against the Japanese Home Islands. The bombing campaign began in November 1944, but for its first three months it proved singularly ineffective.

The Americans faced a number of problems. They had insufficient combat aircraft and bombers with which to launch massed attacks. Meanwhile heavy cloud, strong winds at high altitude, and the difficulty of identifying targets reduced the accuracy of their raids. In addition, the B-29 Superfortress still had technical problems. Above all, precision bombing failed to make a significant impact on Japanese industry, much of which was local and small-scale. Consequently, when Major-General Curtis LeMay took over XXI Bomber Command on January 20, 1945, he ordered that its B-29s be stripped of their armor and guns in order to increase their flying range and load capacity in readiness for an area-bombing campaign against Japanese cities. This would be conducted from low altitude at night.

Most Japanese cities were composed of densely packed wooden buildings and had little firefighting capability. They thus became death traps for their citizens during incendiary attacks. On March 9/10, 279 Superfortresses attacked Tokyo and caused greater destruction than the subsequent atom bomb on Hiroshima. Over 2,000 tons of incendiary bombs created a massive firestorm whose glow could be seen 150 miles (240 km) away. The inferno destroyed 16 sq miles (40 square km) of the city, killed or wounded 124,711 people, and left a million homeless. The raid on Tokyo was the first of 18 against Japan's six largest cities in spring 1945.

Both the frequency and the intensity of the raids rose as aircraft were released from commitments in China and Southeast Asia. The raid on Tokyo by 562 Superfortresses on May 23/24 was the largest single B-29 raid of the war, while the greatest number of B-29s committed to a single series of

raids was on August 1/2, when 627 Superfortresses attacked Hachioji, Mito, Nagaoka, and Toyama. By the war's end large areas of 66 major cities had been laid to waste, 13 million civilians were homeless, and a further 8 million had been evacuated. Over 40 percent of Japan's industrial capacity had been destroyed. Such devastation, inflicted in just under seven months, rivaled that inflicted on Germany in the entire last three years of the European war.

With US carrier aircraft flying combat air patrols over Japanese airfields, fighters escorting the bombers, and air groups providing electronic countermeasure operations and night harassing attacks, US air superiority was so great that the Americans were able to announce their targets in advance. The effects on Japanese morale were clear. Rates of absenteeism rose as high as 80 percent in some industrial centers, and touched 40 percent even in

"If you're going to use military force, then you ought to use overwhelming military force…. All war is immoral, and if you let that bother you, you're not a good soldier."

MAJOR-GENERAL CURTIS LEMAY
QUOTED BY ROBERT S. MCNAMARA, *LOS ANGELES TIMES*

Kyoto, which was never bombed. The bombing campaign and the inability of the Imperial armed forces to oppose it were crucial in convincing many ordinary Japanese that the war was lost.

By summer 1945 Japan's situation was hopeless. Its people were on the brink of starvation. Food shortages were so bad that the average adult had lost a minimum of 10 lb (4.5 kg) in weight, and two-thirds of all adults had lost 20 lb (9 kg). Diet deficiency contributed to an increase in tuberculosis, and some estimates suggest that, had the war lasted into 1946, some 7 million Japanese would have died of malnutrition-related disease or starvation. State price controls were ineffective and rationing was haphazard. The average price of black-market goods in July 1945 was 42 times that of official prices; sugar could cost as much as 240 times its official value. Clothing was scarce or unobtainable. It had made up 9 percent of Japanese expenditure in 1936 but accounted for just 1.3 percent in 1944. Taxes, meanwhile, had risen by over a fifth to 61.4 percent of income during the same period.

Industrially, Japan was coming to a standstill. By summer 1945 the country was producing twice as much electricity as it needed. This was because industry was falling idle for want of raw materials. The level of productivity in those industries that were still working was low and falling, as a

Rifle practice
Members of Japan's National Defesce Women's Association perform rifle drill as part of their military training. All Japanese civilians were encouraged to take up arms in readiness for the expected US invasion of their Home Islands.

direct result of conscription policies, which made no provision for reserved occupations. Output per worker in the oil industries fell by half from 1941 to 1945, and the few ships that remained in service had crews some 20 percent greater than in 1941 because of the loss of high-quality personnel.

At sea, summer 1945 was disastrous. One indication of the totality of the defeat now engulfing Japan was the fact that in July 1945 the Allies sank 139 merchantmen, service transports, and auxiliaries—298,223 tons of shipping. Of these, only three merchantmen—just 2,820 tons—were sunk outside home waters. All semblance of strategic mobility had been lost by this stage of proceedings, and, as Japan faced the certainty of

invasion, even its defensive intentions were confounded by reality. The 1945 class of recruits who would be called upon to defend the Home Islands was basically untrained and the 1944 class was little better. Even if the Japanese army could work out where Allied forces would be obliged to land, it faced an impossible dilemma. Formations held back from beaches would be subjected to overwhelming air attack as they tried to move forward. It was highly unlikely that they would be able to get into the battle in an effective way. If they were held in forward positions, however, they would doubtless be subjected to equally overwhelming fire from amphibious and support forces. Even the good-quality Japanese divisions that were available lacked the armor, motor transports, and radios essential to the effective conduct of the defensive battle.

A PREMONITION OF DEFEAT

After the war some Japanese authorities claimed that the most effective course the Allies could have adopted in summer 1945 would have been simply to suspend all offensive operations. This would have made it clear to the Japanese that there was absolutely nothing they could do to redeem the situation. As it was, in what proved to be the last weeks of the war American and British warships bombarded factories and installations on Honshu on five nights during the second half of July and again on August 9. The bombardment of the Hamamatsu aircraft factory on July 29 was the last occasion when a British battleship fired her guns in anger in the conflict.

These final operations of the war are notable for providing a fascinating perspective on the Japanese attack on Pearl Harbor in December 1941. One of the little-known and often overlooked facts of the war was a report received by the Japanese cabinet on August 27, 1941, over three

Mother and child
A Japanese mother bathes her starving child in 1945. The Japanese turned over any available land to growing food, but shortages remained crippling.

JAPANESE PRISONERS OF WAR

ONE OF THE MOST DISTASTEFUL realities of World War II was the manner in which the Imperial Japanese Army treated its prisoners of war. Although by no means all their captives were treated with intolerable cruelty, life as a Japanese prisoner was invariably harsh. Chinese POWs were usually regarded as subhuman and treated barbarically, while Western POWs were treated a little better. Although the Geneva Convention laid down rules for the humane treatment of prisoners, combatants in Japanese custody were routinely beaten, tortured, and killed. They were also used as labor, for which they received a token payment. The construction of the Burma–Siam railroad was a notorious project in which malnourished British and Australian POWs were forced to work under the most extreme conditions. When Allied troops liberated the POW camps they were shocked at the physical and mental state of many of the surviving prisoners, and this galvanized their resolve to continue the fight against the Japanese.

Since the end of the war there has been much speculation about the reasons for Japan's cruelty to its captives. Many Japanese saw themselves as ethnically superior to other races, and believed that surrender was humiliation. One theory is that some of their contempt for their prisoners may have been inspired by the feeling that, if their enemies had been honorable, they would not have allowed themselves to be captured in the first place.

Death railroad
Clearly showing the effects of malnutrition, Australian POWs lay a section of the railroad from Burma to Siam. Its construction cost the lives of around 16,000 Allied POWs.

Canvas straps

Rubber sole for grip

Homemade sandals
When their boots wore away or were stolen by other POWs they made their own sandals from screws, tires, and scraps of canvas.

Hand-carved spoon

Inmate number

Eating equipment
Inmates made their own eating utensils from spare pieces of wood or whatever they could find. They had to purchase their food with the token wages they earned by laboring for the Japanese.

Liberated POWs
American prisoners of war pose in Bilibid Prison, Manila, in April 1945. Their emaciated bodies show the privations they had suffered during three years' Japanese captivity.

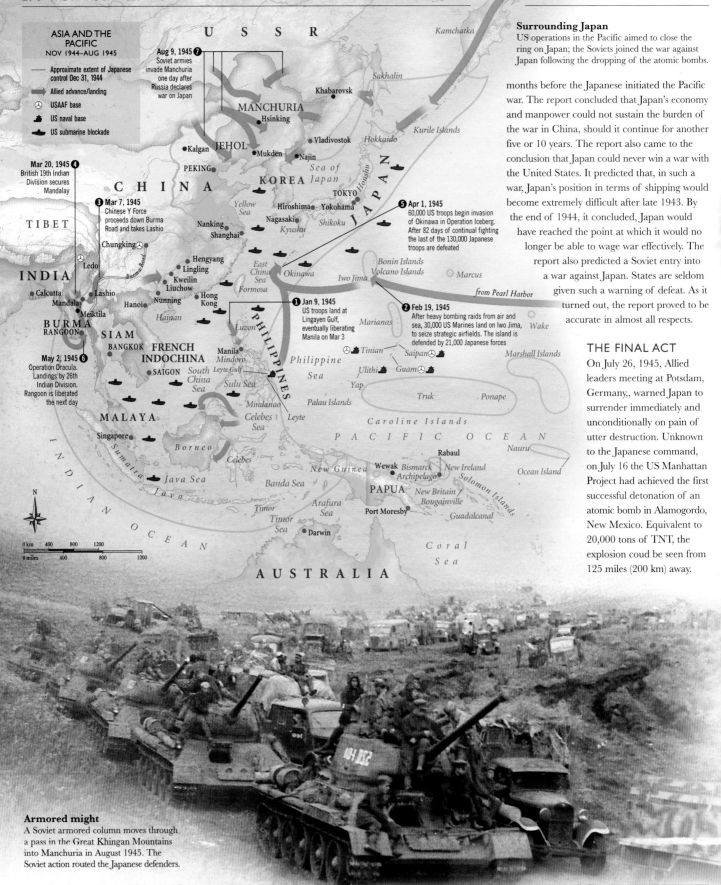

ASIA AND THE PACIFIC
NOV 1944–AUG 1945

⎯⎯ Approximate extent of Japanese control Dec 31, 1944

➤ Allied advance/landing

✈ USAAF base

⚓ US naval base

⚓ US submarine blockade

Aug 9, 1945 ❼
Soviet armies invade Manchuria one day after Russia declares war on Japan

Mar 20, 1945 ❹
British 19th Indian Division secures Mandalay

Mar 7, 1945 ❸
Chinese Y Force proceeds down Burma Road and takes Lashio

Apr 1, 1945 ❺
60,000 US troops begin invasion of Okinawa in Operation Iceberg. After 82 days of continual fighting the last of the 130,000 Japanese troops are defeated

Jan 9, 1945 ❶
US troops land at Lingayen Gulf, eventually liberating Manila on Mar 3

Feb 19, 1945 ❷
After heavy bombing raids from air and sea, 30,000 US Marines land on Iwo Jima, to seize strategic airfields. The island is defended by 21,000 Japanese forces

May 2, 1945 ❻
Operation Dracula. Landings by 26th Indian Division. Rangoon is liberated the next day

from Pearl Harbor

Surrounding Japan
US operations in the Pacific aimed to close the ring on Japan; the Soviets joined the war against Japan following the dropping of the atomic bombs.

months before the Japanese initiated the Pacific war. The report concluded that Japan's economy and manpower could not sustain the burden of the war in China, should it continue for another five or 10 years. The report also came to the conclusion that Japan could never win a war with the United States. It predicted that, in such a war, Japan's position in terms of shipping would become extremely difficult after late 1943. By the end of 1944, it concluded, Japan would have reached the point at which it would no longer be able to wage war effectively. The report also predicted a Soviet entry into a war against Japan. States are seldom given such a warning of defeat. As it turned out, the report proved to be accurate in almost all respects.

THE FINAL ACT
On July 26, 1945, Allied leaders meeting at Potsdam, Germany,, warned Japan to surrender immediately and unconditionally on pain of utter destruction. Unknown to the Japanese command, on July 16 the US Manhattan Project had achieved the first successful detonation of an atomic bomb in Alamogordo, New Mexico. Equivalent to 20,000 tons of TNT, the explosion coud be seen from 125 miles (200 km) away.

Armored might
A Soviet armored column moves through a pass in the Great Khingan Mountains into Manchuria in August 1945. The Soviet action routed the Japanese defenders.

Preparing for the assault
Soviet infantry watch a preliminary bombardment before advancing on a Japanese position in northern China during the invasion of summer 1945.

Bolt   Rear sight   Foresight

Japanese Arisaka Type 99 rifle
This bolt-action rifle was adopted by the Japanese Army in 1939. It fired a 7.7-mm bullet and the magazine held a total of five rounds.

In fact, since the dismissal of Tojo Hideki as prime minister in July 1944, Japanese leaders had been looking for a way to end a war that they knew was lost. In spring 1945 Japan had made contact with the Soviet Union in the hope that it might mediate an acceptable surrender. The Soviet Union, however, had given an undertaking to Britain and the United States at the Tehran Conference in November 1943 that it would enter the war against Japan once the European conflict was over. On April 5, 1945, the Soviet Union announced that it would not renew its 1941 nonaggression treaty with Japan. Although the Soviets did not tell their allies that Japan had made peace overtures, successful codebreaking of Japanese diplomatic signals meant that the American high command was already aware of Japan's search for a possible end to the war.

Privately, Japan's leaders feared that any attempt to surrender would provoke mutiny on the part of an ultranationalist military. The army was not convinced by the reality of defeat but was in any case certain that a final battle would have to be fought in order to uphold the honor of the nation and of the services. The absence of any Allied guarantee to preserve the emperor and the imperial system in the event of a surrender only compounded the difficulties facing the leadership. On July 28 the Japanese high command issued its response to the Potsdam Declaration. It chose to do this in an unfortunately worded statement that seemed to reject Allied demands in a preemptory and dismissive manner.

THE ATOMIC BOMBS

Japan's apparent rejection of the Potsdam demands invited the obvious conclusion on the part of the Allies that it intended to fight on. The American high command naturally sought to bring about Japan's surrender without the daunting prospect of assault landings and a final campaign in the Home Islands. The possession of atomic weapons provided an alternative to invasion, but the decision to use the bombs was underwritten by other considerations.

The prime minister asked me: "Is the Kwantung Army capable of repulsing the Soviet Army?" I replied: "The Kwantung Army is hopeless. Within two weeks Hsinking will be occupied." The premier sighed upon hearing my words and said: "Is the Kwantung Army that weak? Then the game is up."

ACCOUNT BY S. IKEDA, CHIEF OF THE JAPANESE CABINET PLANNING BUREAU, OF A MEETING WITH PRIME MINISTER ADMIRAL SUZUKI KANTARO

The Americans had previously sought a Soviet involvement in the Japanese war, but now that the conflict was clearly in its final stage, that necessity had declined. Instead, there was in Washington an awareness that a demonstration of the possession and use of these new weapons would strengthen the American hand in dealings with the Soviet Union in the aftermath of the war. The Potsdam conference had suggested that relations between the two countries were already becoming difficult.

Accordingly, in the first days of August 1945 the only two atomic bombs that the Americans had so far produced arrived in the Marianas. There they would be loaded aboard specially-modified B-29s. On the morning of Monday, August 6, Colonel Paul W. Tibbetts flew a Superfortress known as *Enola Gay* to drop the first bomb, "Little Boy," on Hiroshima. At 8:15 am three-quarters of the city was destroyed, and more than 78,000 of its citizens were killed instantly in the blast. Many thousands more were condemned to suffer a slow lingering death. Three days later Major Charles W. Sweeney, at the controls of the *Boschcar*, dropped the second atomic bomb, "Fat Man," on Nagasaki. This time two-fifths of the city was destroyed, and more than 35,000 people were killed.

The attack on Nagasaki heralded the Soviet entry into the war. Inside a week the outclassed Japanese forces in Manchuria had been brought to the brink of total defeat. Soviet formations crossed the Greater Khingan Range and the Gobi to reach Hsinking, Mukden, Jehol, and Kalgan, while forces from the

The shock of defeat
Three schoolgirls join other shocked Japanese weeping in front of Emperor Hirohito's palace in Tokyo in August 1945. For many Japanese, defeat in the war was a cause of deep personal shame as well as a national humiliation.

Soviet Union's Maritime Provinces overran northeast Manchuria and were later involved in landings in southern Sakhalin. The Japanese surrender in Manchuria came on August 19 at Khabarovsk. The Soviets then used airborne detachments to secure airfields, towns, and communications centers ahead of their main advance. There was sporadic resistance, but the Soviet occupation of Manchuria and northern Korea was largely unopposed. In the Kuriles, however, there was bitter fighting between August 17 and 23, after which Soviet forces proceeded to occupy the entire chain of islands.

The atom bomb attacks on Hiroshima and Nagasaki and the Soviet entry into the war only served to worsen the divisions that already existed

within the Japanese high command. Fear of occupation by Soviet forces, and the parallel fear of social revolution that might come in the wake of defeat, were major influences in Japan's attempts to search for a way to end the war while the United States still held the power of decision. Within the army, however, there remained a determination to fight a last battle of annihilation that would atone for the military defeat. It took the emperor himself, at a meeting on August 9–10, to indicate that it was time for considerations of his own personal safety and position to be subordinated to national needs. For the sake of Japan, the war had to be ended immediately.

THE SURRENDER

The emperor's decision was considered binding by all the members of the Japanese cabinet and war council. However, when the Japanese attempted to ensure that the Potsdam Declaration did not comprise any demand which prejudiced "the prerogatives of His Majesty as sovereign ruler," the American reply was that "the authority of the Emperor and Japanese government to rule the state shall be subject to that of the supreme commander of the Allied powers." This provoked a second crisis, and Hirohito was obliged to reaffirm his previous

decision. Some junior ranks inside Tokyo, claiming that the emperor had been wrongly advised, attempted a coup, but army discipline, backed by royal princes, who were sent to various commands, ensured compliance with the Imperial decision.

What most ensured an orderly path to national surrender was the emperor's radio broadcast to the people of Japan on August 15. It was the first he had ever made. Using a phrase infamous in Japanese history, he said that it was time "to bear the unbearable," although he did not use the word "surrender." Even after this there were isolated incidents, including an appeal to the people to rise and create a "Government of Resistance," but by the end of August dissent had been stifled.

On August 28 Allied warships entered Sagami Bay; the next day they entered Tokyo Bay. There the instrument of surrender "by command and on behalf of Imperial General Headquarters" was signed on September 2 on the battleship *Missouri*. The actual process of surrender throughout East Asia, the Western Pacific, and Southeast Asia was not complete until spring 1946. It would not be until 1974 that the last surviving Japanese not to have surrendered finally emerged from his hiding place on Lubang in the Philippines. Some Japanese in Malaya deserted after August 1945 and joined the communists. Two survivors did not lay down their arms in southern Thailand until 1991. For some, it seemed, there was no end to World War II.

Hiroshima after the bomb
This panorama of the devastation in Hiroshima was taken in March 1946, more than six months after the city had been subjected to the first atomic bomb attack.

INTO THE NUCLEAR AGE

CODE-NAMED THE MANHATTAN PROJECT, the US and British development of the atomic bomb during World War II was kept secret even from their allies, including the Soviet Union. Based on theoretical work by Enrico Fermi and Albert Enstein, nuclear fission—on which Britain and Germany had been working independently in the 1930s— offered unprecedented levels of destructive capability. The US nuclear fission project began in 1939 and was allocated a budget of $6,000. By 1945, when the first bomb was ready, the government had spent $2 million. The man behind the development of the bombs was J. Robert Oppenheimer, who was based at the Los Alamos Laboratory in New Mexico. Although widely regarded as the father of the atomic bomb, he actually built on foundations laid by scientists at laboratories across America, each working on different aspects of the new technologies and materials needed. The first atomic bomb was tested successfully at Alamogordo air base in New Mexico on July 16, 1945. Three weeks later, the first bomb was dropped on Hiroshima.

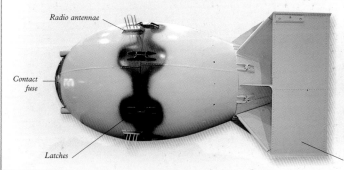

Einstein's letter
The first page of a letter dated August 2, 1939, from Albert Einstein to Franklin D. Roosevelt in which the scientist outlines to the US president his concerns about the implications of nuclear research.

Robert Oppenheimer
The man behind the Manhattan Project, Julius Robert Oppenheimer. A brilliant theoretical physicist, he developed the bombs that were dropped on Japan.

Radio antennae

Contact fuse

Latches

Fat Man
A replica of "Fat Man," the atomic bomb dropped on Nagasaki on August 9, 1945. The bomb was 3 m (9 ft 4 in) long and weighed 545 kg (10,000 lb). Its fission source was plutonium, which gave it an explosive power equivalent to 21,000 tons of TNT.

Fins to stabilize freefall

A NEW WORLD
1945–49

IN THE AFTERMATH OF THE CONFLICT BOTH VICTORS AND VANQUISHED TOOK STOCK OF THE NEW WORLD THAT HAD BEEN CREATED. EUROPE'S AGE-OLD PRIMACY IN INTERNATIONAL AFFAIRS WAS OVER, BROUGHT TO AN END BY THE DESTRUCTION OF WAR, DEBT, AND THE GROWTH OF TWO SUPERPOWERS, THE UNITED STATES AND THE SOVIET UNION. WHILE SHATTERED COUNTRIES IN THE WEST ATTEMPTED TO REBUILD, IN THE EAST THE ECLIPSE OF JAPAN AND EUROPE PAVED THE WAY FOR NEW STRUGGLES AS COLONIES TOOK THE OPPORTUNITY TO FIGHT FOR INDEPENDENCE. IN SOUTHEAST ASIA, INDIA, AND ELSEWHERE, THE END OF WORLD WAR II MARKED ONLY THE BEGINNING OF A NEW ROUND OF BLOODSHED.

9

It's over
New Yorkers gather in Times Square on August 17, 1945, to celebrate the Japanese surrender.

REBUILDING A SHATTERED WORLD

THE IMPACT OF WORLD WAR II WAS FELT IN ALMOST EVERY PART OF THE GLOBE. WHILE VICTORS AND VANQUISHED ALIKE BEGAN TO REBUILD THEIR ECONOMIES, POLITICIANS AND CIVILIANS FACED A CHANGED WORLD IN WHICH FEW CERTAINTIES SURVIVED FROM THE YEARS BEFORE 1939.

BEFORE WORLD WAR II there were many "Great Powers"; by the end of the conflict the United States and the Soviet Union dominated global diplomacy and economics. Europe, the strongest and wealthiest continent at the beginning of the 20th century, was devastated. Many of its nations were on the verge of bankruptcy or communism, while those that had empires were struggling to hold on to their colonies.

ONE WAR IN TWO PHASES

In many ways, World War II was a continuation of World War I. The settlements that had ended the Great War had failed to deal with its causes—mainly nationalism, imperialism, and the balance of power. These matters would not be resolved until the defeat of the Axis powers in 1945.

Just as in World War I, when war broke out in 1939 the European empires called on their colonial subjects for manpower and material aid. In the first war the soldiers and materials had been shipped to Europe; in the second conflagration the war came to them, as European powers fought not only at home but also in their dependencies. What began as French and British resistance to German attempts to dominate Europe became, by the end of 1941, a truly global conflict that involved the United States, North Africa, the Middle East, the Soviet Union, India, China, Japan, and many other parts of Asia.

There were other differences between the two world wars. In the first, the fighting had reached a stalemate by the end of 1914. The Western Front barely moved for four years. Even in the east, where fighting was more fluid, the most significant alteration of the front line came with Lenin's territorial concessions to Germany in 1918 as the price for Russia leaving the war. Mindful of the debilitating effects of another war of attrition, politicians and planners in World War II were determined not to repeat earlier mistakes. Strategists on all sides

prepared for a war of movement: in this they were aided by the development of highly maneuverable weapons, in particular, tanks and aircraft, that lent themselves to offensive warfare in a way that trenches and machine-guns in 1914–18 had not.

CIVILIAN INVOLVEMENT

The use of tanks and aircraft also ensured that many more civilians came under direct attack than in the first war—the air bombardment of entire cities had a particularly harrowing effect. Even though World War I is described as the first total war in the sense that civilians were mobilized to work in domestic industries, noncombatants were rarely directly involved in conflict. In World War II, civilians in many parts of the world faced death and destruction.

For many civilians, tanks and bombs were not the main enemy. For the Jews of Europe, war came in the form of the "Final Solution"—the attempt by the Nazis to exterminate them. World War I had had its own racially motivated atrocities—the massacre of Armenian civilians by Turkish forces being perhaps the most hideous example—but the Holocaust was different in form and substance: it was premeditated and systematic.

SHAPING THE FUTURE

Throughout World War II the leaders of the "Big Three" Allied nations—Roosevelt from the United States, Stalin from the Soviet Union, and Churchill from Great Britain—communicated frequently with one another. They also met to hold discussions about war strategy in Tehran in November 1943 and at Yalta in February 1945. Unlike World War I, in which military officers had largely taken the lead, the overall direction of World War II was always under the command of politicians. Just as civilians defined the shape of the war on the Allied side, so they would define the peace. In July–August 1945, the Big Three met again in Potsdam, just outside Berlin.

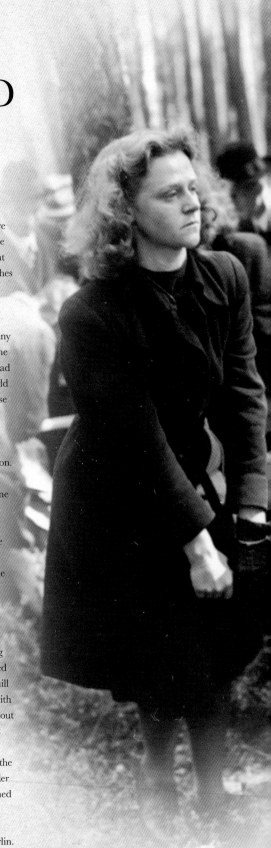

A nation's guilt
Civilians from Nuremberg help rebury victims of the SS, whose bodies had been dumped in a pit. Throughout the country, the Allies forced ordinary Germans to face up to the atrocities committed in the name of the Third Reich.

"If leaders are called to account and condemned, very well, but you cannot punish the German people at the same time. The German people are free of guilt."

NAZI LEADER HERMANN GÖRING IN A CLOSING STATEMENT
TO THE NUREMBERG WAR CRIMES TRIBUNAL, AUGUST 31, 1946

There were new faces around the table: Harry S. Truman, who had become US president on the death of Roosevelt in April, and newly elected British prime minister Clement Attlee. No longer united by their common goal, and facing the task of reconstructing war-torn Europe along with the coming final assault on Japan, the Allied leaders were more tense at this final meeting than they had ever been before.

Potsdam was successful in certain key areas, principally those concerning the temporary control of Germany. The nation was to be divided into four zones and placed under the supervision of an Allied Control Commission consisting of representatives from the Big Three and France, which was included at British insistence as a counterweight to Soviet power. Berlin, the German capital, was also to be divided between the four powers. Furthermore, all territories conquered by the Nazis were to be returned to their former owners. The talks further provided for the conclusion of separate peace treaties with all the defeated combatants, including Austria. The Potsdam Conference also introduced the concept of war crimes so that the Nazi leaders could be tried by an international court. Finally, Stalin, Truman, and Attlee agreed on the creation of a Council of Foreign Ministers. These ministers would meet regularly in an attempt to smooth as much as possible the transition from war to peace.

Despite these manifest successes, a pall hung over the conference. Truman had arrived in Potsdam determined to enforce the Declaration on Liberated Europe, which had been agreed to at Yalta. Under its provisions, all countries conquered by Germany were to be reconstituted and allowed free elections. When it came to the thorny issue of the future of Poland, however, Stalin had already demonstrated that he would take any measures necessary to ensure that the Poles elected a government that was "friendly" to the Soviet Union—in other words, a communist

regime. The British and the Americans feared that if Stalin had his way over Poland, the rest of eastern Europe would also become communist. For their part, Soviet delegates insisted that, since the Soviet Union had been attacked twice by Germany in 25 years, it was only right that they be allowed to establish a western buffer zone.

The Western Allies left Potsdam with grave concerns about Soviet expansionism. Days later the suspicions became mutual as the United States dropped atomic bombs on Hiroshima and Nagasaki to end the war against Japan. The lack of trust between the United States and its allies on the one hand, and the Soviet Union and its communist allies on the other, would soon lead to a new kind of conflict—the Cold War—which was to dominate international politics until the end of the 1980s.

RISINGS IN THE EAST

The total capitulation of Japan was followed by American occupation of the country on August 28, 1945. Commanded by the powerful figure of General Douglas MacArthur, US forces in Japan were given *carte blanche* by Truman. Like Germany, Japan needed almost total political and economic reconstruction; it also needed psychological rehabilitation. In a nation not previously defeated in war, with a strong code of personal and national honor and an emperor who was seen as a god, surrender was regarded as a disgrace.

The United States faced the task of demilitarizing not only Japan's economy and state, but also the attitudes of the people. It reformed the education system to encourage individualism, banned Shinto as the state religion, reduced the prominence of politicians and military leaders, and took control of the press. A new 1947 constitution, drawn up under US influence, created an independent judiciary, guarantees of civil liberty, universal suffrage, and equal land rights. Significantly, Article 9

Empty hope?
Eleanor Roosevelt studies a copy of the Universal Declaration of Human Rights, which was adopted by the United Nations on December 10, 1948. Roosevelt was a prime mover in drafting the document which, for all its bold intent, changed little.

The Nationalists' last stand
Watched by Nationalist troops, a policeman executes a suspected communist in Shanghai moments after killing another, on May 16, 1949. Shortly after, China's civil war ended when the Nationalists fled to Formosa (Taiwan).

"Every segment of the population has united in obedience, to stand behind the great leader Sukarno, to await whatever commands or obligations are put before them. It is our firm conviction that this struggle is a sacred struggle...."

INDONESIAN FREEDOM MOVEMENT REPRESENTATIVE ON GROWING OPPOSITION TO DUTCH COLONIAL RULE, OCTOBER 15, 1945

of the constitution stated Japan's intention of "forever renouncing war." Many Japanese military and political leaders were tried for war crimes; most were imprisoned, but some were sentenced to death. They included former prime minister Tojo Hideki, who was hanged in December 1948.

Throughout the reform process, the Americans took pains to make it seem as if it were the Japanese themselves who were driving the changes and administering justice, even though the majority of the orders actually came from MacArthur and Washington, D.C. Ensuring that the Japanese were able to maintain their dignity did much to expedite the nation's postwar recovery.

DECLINE OF EMPIRE

In other parts of Asia the future looked less certain. In China, civil war, which had been put on hold during the world conflict, immediately erupted again. The United States backed Chiang Kai-shek's Nationalists as the only force that could resist the spread of communism, but they failed to prevent the victory of Mao Zedong's Red Army in 1949. Chiang's Nationalists fled to Formosa (Taiwan), and Mao created the People's Republic of China.

The end of World War II also hastened the decline of European influence in Asia. Britain granted independence to India in 1947, Burma and Ceylon (Sri Lanka) in 1948, and—after a protracted guerrilla war—the Malay states in February 1948. World War II also reduced British influence in Australia and New Zealand. Elsewhere a four-year guerrilla campaign freed Indonesia from rule by the Netherlands in 1949. French influence in Indochina was also weakened, and in the early 1950s Vietnamese nationalism erupted into a war that would eventually also involve the United States, which was now the main force in the region. Just as in Europe, postcolonial Asia would be dragged into the Cold War.

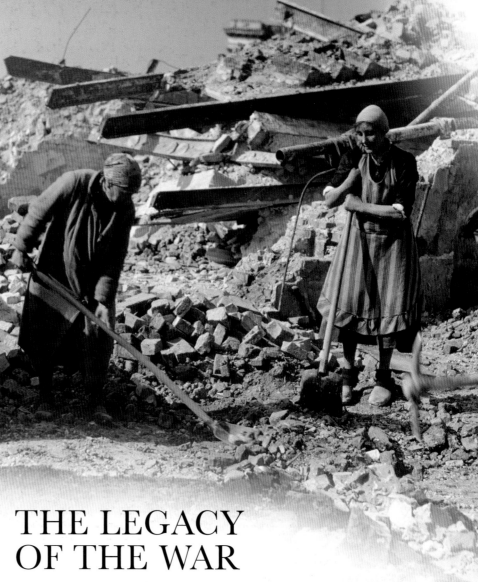

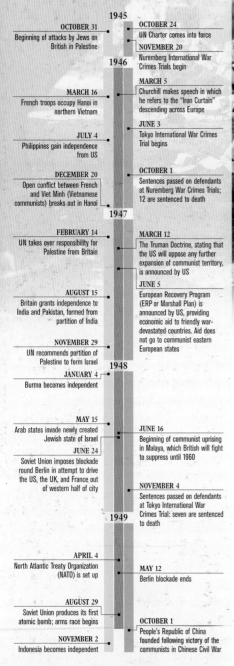

EFFECTS OF THE WAR

SEPTEMBER 1945–DECEMBER 1949

The end of the war saw the emergence of the United States and the Soviet Union as ideologically opposed superpowers. As tensions mounted, the two powers reached a standoff known as the Cold War. Meanwhile, many colonies of European countries began to seek independence from their imperial rulers.

1945

OCTOBER 31
Beginning of attacks by Jews on British in Palestine

OCTOBER 24
UN Charter comes into force

NOVEMBER 20
Nuremberg International War Crimes Trials begin

1946

MARCH 5
Churchill makes speech in which he refers to the "Iron Curtain" descending across Europe

MARCH 16
French troops occupy Hanoi in northern Vietnam

JUNE 3
Tokyo International War Crimes Trial begins

JULY 4
Philippines gain independence from US

DECEMBER 20
Open conflict between French and Viet Minh (Vietnamese communists) breaks out in Hanoi

OCTOBER 1
Sentences passed on defendants at Nuremberg War Crimes Trials; 12 are sentenced to death

1947

FEBRUARY 14
UN takes over responsibility for Palestine from Britain

MARCH 12
The Truman Doctrine, stating that the US will oppose any further expansion of communist territory, is announced by US

AUGUST 15
Britain grants independence to India and Pakistan, formed from partition of India

JUNE 5
European Recovery Program (ERP or Marshall Plan) is announced by US, providing economic aid to friendly war-devastated countries. Aid does not go to communist eastern European states

NOVEMBER 29
UN recommends partition of Palestine to form Israel

1948

JANUARY 4
Burma becomes independent

MAY 15
Arab states invade newly created Jewish state of Israel

JUNE 16
Beginning of communist uprising in Malaya, which British will fight to suppress until 1960

JUNE 24
Soviet Union imposes blockade round Berlin in attempt to drive the US, the UK, and France out of western half of city

NOVEMBER 4
Sentences passed on defendants at Tokyo International War Crimes Trial: seven are sentenced to death

1949

APRIL 4
North Atlantic Treaty Organization (NATO) is set up

MAY 12
Berlin blockade ends

AUGUST 29
Soviet Union produces its first atomic bomb; arms race begins

NOVEMBER 2
Indonesia becomes independent

OCTOBER 1
People's Republic of China founded following victory of the communists in Chinese Civil War

Breakdown of colonial empires Oct 1945–Nov 1949	Developments in the Cold War Mar 1946–Oct 1949	Other events

THE LEGACY OF THE WAR

IN TERMS OF LIVES LOST, World War II was the most costly conflict in history. Estimates of the total number of deaths vary, but there may have been around 55 to 60 million, including 25.5 million Soviet citizens, 13.5 million Chinese, 5.25 million Germans, 2.6 million Japanese, around 290,000 Americans, and 300,000 Britons. Unlike the casualties in World War I, many were civilians, and the loss of manpower had a devastating effect on the recovery of the countries involved. Massive bombardment had reduced many cities to rubble. This was particularly true in Germany, which had suffered intense air attacks by British and US forces, and the Soviet Union, which had lost 70 to 80 percent of its industrial capacity in its bitterly fought campaign to expel the Nazi invaders. Much of the rest of Europe was at a virtual standstill.

The mass destruction of homes, schools, offices, and factories meant that large numbers of people were on the move, looking for new places to live. Some removed themselves voluntarily; others were

Civvy street
Carrying their new civilian clothes in cardboard suitcases, demobilized British troops leave a depot in Olympia in west London. By the end of the conflict, some soldiers had not seen their families for as long as five or six years.

A country in ruins

Three years after the end of hostilities, women in Berlin clear rubble from a destroyed factory. With so many men lost in the war, and German infrastructure in ruins, women were responsible for much of the reconstruction work.

forced to leave. These refugees, officially termed Displaced Persons (DPs), became one of the most distressing features of the immediate postwar era. To care for them, the United Nations (UN)—the world peacekeeping body founded in 1945—set up DP camps throughout Europe. By 1947 there were 700 such camps operated by the United Nations Relief and Rehabilitation Administration (UNRRA). Among the DPs were those who had been brought to German-occupied territory as forced labor, ex-prisoners-of-war, Jews, and other survivors of the concentration camps.

In the immediate aftermath of the war there were as many as seven million DPs. This figure grew alarmingly as a number of newly formed governments began to expel various minority groups. In 1947 the creation by the UN of the International Refugee Organization (IRO) was very much opposed by the Soviet Union, which saw the IRO as a Western attempt to assist the flight of refugees from the communist states of eastern Europe. While it would be many years before the refugee problem was finally resolved, substantial numbers of DPs did find new homes relatively quickly. There were several countries that faced severe labor shortages after the war came to an end, particularly in skilled occupations. Britain was among the nations that actively encouraged immigration, offering the inducement of immediate resettlement to qualified foreign nationals as part of its drive to replace skilled workers who had been killed or incapacitated during the war.

REDRAWING THE MAP OF EUROPE

After the war much of Europe was restructured politically and many of its frontiers were altered. The Red Army had entered Germany from the east, and the countries through which it had passed *en route*—Bulgaria, Czechoslovakia, Hungary, Poland, Romania, and, for a while, Yugoslavia—became Soviet satellites in the postwar world. Britain and the United States had launched their assault on the Axis powers from the south and west, and consequently brought Austria, Greece, and Italy into their sphere of influence. Germany

itself, meanwhile, was divided into four zones by the victors: the east of the country was dominated by the Soviet Union, while the west was shared among the Americans, the British, and the French.

The American, British, and Soviet leaders were united in their determination to de-Nazify Germany, and this policy was carried through with notable success. The main public manifestation of their resolve was a series of war crimes trials held under international law. The most famous of these involved Hitler's top surviving henchmen and were held in 1945–46 in Nuremberg. The location was chosen deliberately by the Allies because it had been the

site of the spectacular Nazi Party rallies of the 1930s and was widely regarded as the symbolic cradle of the National Socialist movement.

While a number of leading Nazis faced the legal consequences of their wartime deeds, Allied civilian administrators in western Germany were mindful of the need to feed, clothe, and find shelter for those worst affected by postwar privations. In the eastern zone, however, Soviet leaders were determined to recover as much industrial capacity as possible. To this end they dismantled many industrial plants and factories in their sector of Germany and shipped the components back to the Soviet Union.

THE NUREMBERG TRIALS

AS EARLY AS 1943 Britain, the United States, and the Soviet Union agreed that, if they won the war, they would put the German leaders on trial. As victory approached and the worst atrocities came to light, the Allies created new international laws enabling them to prosecute Nazis for waging aggressive war and for crimes against humanity.

On November 20, 1945, an International Military Tribunal convened for the trials of 23 leading Nazis, including Hermann Göring, Rudolf Hess, and, in absentia, Martin Bormann. The Tribunal delivered its verdicts on October 1, 1946. It rejected the defense that the accused had had no alternative but to follow Adolf Hitler's orders. Twelve of the defendants were sentenced to death, seven were given various terms of imprisonment, and four were acquitted. Bormann was sentenced to death in his absence, and Hermann Göring committed suicide with a cyanide pill hours before he was due to be executed. On October 16, 1946, ten of the leading figures from the Third Reich were executed by hanging in Nuremberg Prison.

Right-hand man
Hitler's former deputy, Hermann Göring, prepares to give evidence to the court. Göring was the most senior Nazi to stand trial. His request to be shot rather than hanged was refused, and he committed suicide by taking poison.

Nazis in the dock
In the courtroom some of the main Nazi war criminals are guarded by Allied military personnel. Separate trials dealt with Nazis accused of war crimes in specific places.

The Soviet Union turned eastern Germany into a communist society by closing every private bank and confiscating all negotiable gold and silver, foreign currency, and other valuables. As a general rule, Soviet administrators were much more interested in obtaining reparations—direct compensation for the damage caused by the war—than in the well-being of those people who were now under their control.

Acknowledging the victors

A Japanese prisoner bows his head as he passes his American jailer. For many Japanese such humiliations were a devastating blow to national pride.

> "The war situation has developed not necessarily to Japan's advantage. We have resolved to pave the way for a grand peace for all the generations to come by enduring the unendurable and suffering what is unsufferable."

EMPEROR HIROHITO BROADCASTS TO HIS PEOPLE ON THE JAPANESE SURRENDER, AUGUST 15, 1945.

POSTWAR JAPAN

The war against Japan ended with the dropping of atomic bombs on Hiroshima and Nagasaki in early August 1945. On September 2 the government of Japan signed a formal surrender aboard the USS *Missouri*, anchored in Yokohama Bay. World War II was now officially over, and the victorious Allies set about the arduous task of reconstruction in Japan. In comparison with Germany, which it had been agreed to divide into four zones of occupation, Japan was treated as a single political and economic entity under American supervision.

Since the Americans had borne the brunt of the fighting against Japan, they demanded the lion's share of involvement in the peacemaking. American leaders made it clear that, while they welcomed aid from their wartime allies, British and Soviet plans for Japan's future would be subordinate to their own. Truman and his cabinet decided that unconditional Japanese surrender did not necessarily mean the dethronement of Emperor Hirohito. They felt that the Japanese would accept defeat more easily if Hirohito kept his position, albeit with powers that were considerably reduced. One of the conditions imposed by the United States on Japan was that the emperor would no longer be regarded as a deity; Hirohito's public acknowledgment of his own mortality was a central part of the price of peace. General Douglas MacArthur, the Supreme Allied Commander in the Pacific, was placed in charge of Japanese reconstruction, and Truman left him very much to his own devices in the running of the country. In an effort to ensure that militarism would have no place in the future Japan, MacArthur and his advisers decided that those who had led the nation into war would be tried as war criminals, with the important exception of the emperor himself. The postwar Japanese constitution drawn up by the Supreme Allied Commander was intended to rid Japan of the worst excesses of its reliance on tradition while at the same time preserving an emphasis on obedience to authority. Under MacArthur's autocratic leadership, Japan began a transformation from a rigid, hierarchical society into a modern, pluralistic nation. Land reform was introduced, trade unions were established, the role of women in society was vastly expanded, and provision for a parliamentary democracy was written into the new Japanese constitution. These innovations made a significant contribution to Japan's remarkable postwar recovery.

RECOVERY BEGINS

While negotiations continued on a final peace treaty with Japan (it was not finally signed until September 1951), MacArthur concentrated on ensuring that Japan would emerge as an economically vibrant US ally in the Far East. The need to rebuild the Japanese economy became all the more pressing as US–Soviet relations began to deteriorate. US leaders realized that Japan would have to be self-sufficient if it were to serve as a bulwark

Japan's leaders on trial
All 25 defendants in the Tokyo war trials were found guilty. Seven were sentenced to hang; all 16 sentenced to life imprisonment were paroled within 10 years.

The final verdict
Flanked by military police, General Tojo Hideki, Japan's prime minister during the war, listens to the Allied court's sentence of death. He was hanged on December 23, 1948.

against potential communist incursion in the Pacific. MacArthur's efforts to rebuild Japan's economy were aided by the fact that the nation had not been the scene of close combat. Japan had endured heavy bombing from 1944 onward, suffered severe damage to its industrial base, and undergone the physical and psychological trauma of having two atomic bombs dropped on home soil. Yet, in contrast with many Europeans, Japanese civilians had not suffered

the consequences of having huge numbers of troops rampage through their villages and towns. There was also still a semblance of infrastructure in Japan that US planners could harness, along with a central administrative organization that was accustomed to obeying orders. The available workforce was greatly increased as soldiers returned home. When the Cold War flared into military conflict in the Korean War (1950–53), fought between communist China and North Korea on the one hand and South Korea and the United Nations on the other, the huge boost to the Japanese economy from supplying the United States and its allies cemented its recovery.

By the time MacArthur was recalled from Tokyo to focus on the US response to the Korean War, Japan was well on the way to becoming exactly what American leaders had envisioned: a politically stable, economically powerful, Asian ally of the United States. As the Cold War intensified, the leaders of the Western nations appreciated the presence of a democratic, anticommunist bastion in the Far East.

JAPANESE WAR CRIMINALS

Unlike the Nuremberg trials, which were organized by the Allied Control Council, the trials of Japanese war criminals were held under the auspices of one man—MacArthur. In January 1946 he set up in Tokyo an International Military Tribunal for the Far East to bring to justice those responsible for such horrific events as the Rape of Nanking, the Bataan Death March, and the attack on Pearl Harbor. The Tribunal divided the accused into three categories:

WAR LOSSES

ALL THE FIGURES IN the table below are estimates. Historians particularly dispute figures for Chinese and Soviet casualties. Many killings in China took place in rural communities that kept poor or no records during wartime. Soviet dead were often buried in unmarked mass graves; government attempts to establish the number of war dead were based on an unreliable system of interviews with families.

	Troops mobilized	Military dead	Civilian dead
ALLIED POWERS			
Soviet Union	20,000,000	8,700,000	16,900,000
United States	16,400,000	292,000	N/A
France	5,000,000	250,000	170,000
Britain	4,700,000	240,000	65,000
Yugoslavia	3,700,000	300,000	1,400,000
China (Communist)	1,200,000	1,100,000	4,000,000
China (Nationalist)	3,800,000	2,400,000	6,000,000
India	2,400,000	48,000	N/A
Poland	1,000,000	600,000	6,000,000
Belgium	800,000	10,000	90,000
Canada	780,000	40,000	N/A
Australia	680,000	34,000	N/A
Netherlands	500,000	10,000	240,000
Finland	250,000	80,000	10,000

	Troops mobilized	Military dead	Civilian dead
Czechoslovakia	180,000	7,000	310,000
Greece	150,000	17,000	400,000
New Zealand	150,000	12,000	N/A
South Africa	140,000	9,000	N/A
Norway	25,000	5,000	8,000
Denmark	15,000	4,000	3,000
Spain	40,000	12,000	1,000
AXIS POWERS			
Germany	10,800,000	3,250,000	2,000,000
Japan	7,400,000	1,700,000	500,000
Italy	4,500,000	380,000	180,000
Romania	600,000	200,000	460,000
Bulgaria	450,000	10,000	7,000
Hungary	350,000	140,000	610,000

April 1945, President Truman took up the policy of seeking to create the conditions necessary to ensure that the nations of central and eastern Europe would enjoy self-determination.

At the Potsdam Conference (July 17–August 2, 1945), Truman insisted that the Soviet Union establish truly democratic nations in this region. For Stalin, however, the priority was domestic security, not global political freedom. At the end of World War II there were a million Red Army troops in the countries of eastern Europe. This military presence was largely maintained throughout the Cold War: for the next 40 years Poland, Bulgaria, Czechoslovakia, Hungary, and, to a lesser

Before the curtain falls
A US border guard talks to his Soviet counterparts on the German–Czech border on August 1, 1946. The Soviets' advance to Berlin left much of eastern Europe under their control, and the nations of the region remained under communist rule for the next 40 years.

those who had planned and waged an aggressive war, those under whose command atrocities were committed, and those who carried out the atrocities.

For almost three years the tribunal heard evidence of atrocities carried out on a routine basis by Japanese soldiers of all ranks; the testimonies of eyewitnesses to the brutality made for harrowing sessions in court. Finally in November 1948 the Tribunal returned its verdicts. Unlike the outcome in Nuremberg, every one of the accused was found guilty as charged. The major criminals, those found guilty of having prepared and planned Japanese aggression over two decades, were sentenced to death. Among those to suffer this fate was former prime minister Tojo Hideki, who had approved the attack on Pearl Harbor and was widely regarded as the personification of Japanese militarism. The executions of Tojo and his senior cohorts were intended as a message to the world that such acts of inhumanity would not be tolerated in the future.

INTO THE COLD WAR

At the Yalta Conference of February 4–11, 1945, US president Roosevelt and British prime minister Churchill appear to have decided, in private at least, that there was nothing they could do, short of war, to remove the Soviet Red Army from the territories it had occupied in central and eastern Europe during its advance into Germany. Despite this, both leaders signed with Stalin the Declaration on Liberated Europe. This document provided for the restoration of democracy in the countries overrun by Nazi Germany. On the death of Roosevelt in

BERLIN BLOCKADE

ONE OF THE EARLIEST FLASHPOINTS in the Cold War was Berlin, Germany. By the end of World War II the Soviet Red Army had reached the banks of the Elbe River, nearly 60 miles (100 km) west of the capital. Although Berlin was thus within the Soviet sphere of influence, the Allies shared the administration of the old German capital, dividing it into American, British, French, and Soviet zones.

In 1948 the Western powers announced plans to unify their zones of occupation in western Germany. This alarmed the Soviets, who imposed a blockade on road and rail transportation into and out of Berlin. Western leaders saw this as a challenge to their commitment to the independence of western Europe. Berlin became a test case of their desire to check Soviet aggression. They set about supplying West Berlin by air. The Berlin Airlift began in June 1948 and lasted until September 1949, when the Soviets lifted the blockade. With its commitment to remain in Germany now manifest, the next step for the West was clear: the creation of West Germany. In September 1949 the Federal Republic of West Germany was established. The Soviet response was the creation of the German Democratic Republic in East Germany the following month.

Keeping the planes aloft
Giant wheels for transport planes are loaded onto a Dakota freighter during a nightshift at a British airfield in November 1948. During the airlift, Allied planes carried 2.3 million tons of supplies to Berlin.

Airborne lifeline
On July 1, 1948, near the beginning of the Berlin Airlift, a group of Berliners watch from the ruins at the edge of Tempelhof Airfield as a C-47 cargo plane prepares to land with a cargo of food.

extent, Romania would be independent only insofar as they adhered to the Soviet party line. These countries were to form Stalin's buffer zone against the threat of a renewed German invasion. The Allies' failure in Potsdam to agree on a solution to these problems caused a lingering atmosphere of mistrust, fear, and suspicion on both sides. This uneasy situation eventually hardened into a Cold War between East and West. Although it would sometimes erupt into overt but limited confrontation, the Cold War was more often fought with weapons of propaganda, psychology, economics, and subversive undercover operations as the competing ideologies of Western capitalism and Soviet communism vied to win over the people of the world.

THE IRON CURTAIN

In March 1946 Winston Churchill, now out of office, coined a phrase that came to epitomize the Western perception of the Cold War. In a speech in Fulton, Missouri, the former British premier spoke of an "Iron Curtain" that was falling across the middle of Europe, to the east of which lay totalitarian states controlled by Moscow. Churchill's provocative speech was initially viewed by many people as dangerous warmongering—a terrible conflict had just ended, and there was great fear of causing another one. However, as relations between East and West deteriorated, a consensus began to emerge in what became known as "the Free World" that Churchill had been correct in his prognosis.

The deteriorating relations became evident in Greece in 1947. In a secret meeting held in Moscow in October 1944, Stalin and Churchill had agreed that following the war, Greece—which had been occupied by Germany and Italy—should fall within the British sphere of influence. To the surprise of some British officials, Stalin kept to the agreement once the war was over. Thus, when hostilities ended, the British installed a pro-Western monarchist government in Greece.

However, the National Liberation Front (EAM)— a communist group in northern Greece—had a different vision of the country's future. It began a series of military attacks on the government in Athens. The country was soon engulfed in civil war. Britain provided financing and troops in support of the regime in Athens. The civil war ended in early 1945 but flared up again in 1946. Britain then decided that it could no longer afford to maintain its presence in the

The "Iron Curtain"
The position of the "Iron Curtain," dividing Soviet-dominated communist regimes from the rest of Europe, was to change after 1948. Yugoslavia was not a Soviet ally in the Cold War.

THE DIVISION OF POSTWAR EUROPE 1945–49

- Territory under Soviet occupation 1945-55
- Soviet-dominated communist states by 1948
- Members of NATO in 1949
- Iron Curtain in 1948
- ⊗ Cities divided into zones of occupation

Symbol of division
A workman paints a line across Potsdammer Strasse in Berlin to mark the border between the British and Soviet zones of occupation in August 1948. In 1961 the painted line was replaced by a fortified wall across the city that would remain standing until 1989.

country. In response, President Truman took it upon himself in March 1947 to commit the United States to going to the aid of the Greek government in its struggle against the rebels. The Americans supplied military equipment and advice that contributed to the eventual defeat of the rebels in the summer of 1949. In applying to Congress for the necessary funds, Truman asserted that it must now be the policy of the United States to aid free peoples anywhere in the world in their struggle against communism. The Truman Doctrine, as the statement became known, was received badly in Moscow and served as a key catalyst in the intensification of the Cold War.

Another came in 1947, when the US government made public a telegram sent to Washington, D.C., during World War II by George Kennan, the American attaché in Moscow. In it he had warned that the Soviet leadership was intent on expansion and should not be trusted. Kennan had advised that the best way of stopping the Soviet Union was by confining it to the regions in which it already held sway. Within a year of the letter's release, containment of the perceived threat of communism had become the cornerstone of Western foreign policy.

Saving Europe
This poster of the late 1940s was intended to encourage the German people to realize the benefits of the US-funded Marshall Plan for postwar economic regeneration.

CHINESE CIVIL WAR

IN CHINA DURING WORLD WAR II the Kuomintang government of Chiang Kai-shek and the communists led by Mao Zedong maintained an uneasy truce as they united against Japanese invasion. When the war ended, however, they resumed hostilities despite the efforts of the Soviet Union and the United States to broker a deal. Fearing a takeover of China by the communists, President Truman sent George Marshall to persuade the two sides to share power, but the mission failed and fighting was resumed in March 1946.

Chiang's forces had access to US military supplies and enjoyed territorial advantage, while the communists were confined to northern areas of the country and received little aid from the Soviet Union. Nevertheless, the Kuomintang soon lost support among Chinese peasants. Whereas Mao's forces instituted land reform in the areas under their control, the nationalists backed corrupt landowners. Mao's forces became an organized, disciplined movement for revolution, while Chiang's forces lost the will to fight. In January 1949 the civil war ended with the victory of the communists under Mao. Chiang withdrew to Formosa (Taiwan) and set up a dictatorship. In communist China the Soviet Union now had a prospective ally in the Cold War.

Mao's warriors
Victorious troops of the Communist People's Liberation Army assemble in Shanghai on July 9, 1949, after the Nationalists had fled to Taiwan. The soldiers are wearing US combat helmets taken from Nationalist troops.

A landowner's fate
A communist soldier prepares to execute a landowner in the aftermath of Mao's victory. Property ownership was banned in Red China.

Chairman Mao
In Tiananmen Square, Peking (Beijing), on October 1, 1949, Mao Zedong proclaims the foundation of the People's Republic of China.

THE MARSHALL PLAN

Having adopted the policy of containment, the US government began to fear that the rubble of western Europe might provide a fertile breeding ground for communism. In the words of Secretary of State George Marshall, "Europe must have substantial additional help or face economic, social, and political deterioration of a very grave character." As a result, the United States provided 16 countries with enormous financial and material aid to help them rebuild. The European Recovery Program, or Marshall Plan as it became known, was established in June 1947. Under the program, the United States set aside $17 billion to aid the countries of western European—outright grants accounted for seven-eighths of the amount, the rest was in loans. The regeneration of Europe began almost immediately.

As European countries began to recover, Western leaders became concerned that the Soviet Union might strike against them before they could build up their defenses. To forestall such an attack they formed, in April 1949, the North Atlantic Treaty Organization (NATO), a military alliance of western European nations, the United States, and Canada, which guaranteed mutual assistance in the event of Soviet aggression. More pertinently, NATO placed western Europe under the nuclear protection of the United States. The Soviet Union and its allies countered NATO by forming first the Council for Mutual Economic Assistance (COMECON) in 1949, and then in 1955 the Warsaw Pact, a military alliance. Europe was now divided into two armed camps. At the time the NATO alliance was signed, the United States was the world's only atomic power.

Within months, however, the Soviet Union had successfully tested its own nuclear weaponry. The news was greeted by dismay in the West, and set off an arms race with the East.

THE WIDER WORLD

Even before World War II it was clear that the independence movements emerging in Asia would force Western governments to confront the issue of colonial imperialism. Britain, for example, was facing mass nonviolent revolt in India, while France recognized that it would soon have to deal with an increasingly militant nationalist movement in Southeast Asia.

The United States was committed to making the Philippines independent. When war began, Japan invaded many Western colonies in Asia. For a time many local nationalist and independence movements allied themselves to the Japanese cause against the European and American empires in the mistaken belief that Japan planned to establish an Asia of equals. When this did not happen, Asian nationalists found themselves in a dilemma: they did not want to further the cause of Japanese aggression, but neither did they want to bolster the hold of the Western powers on their colonies. In the end, the nationalists came to see the defeat of Japan as their best hope of achieving independence.

After the war, the Philippines gained its promised independence, but with the proviso that the United States retain its military presence there. Elsewhere, the end of empire was less well ordered. Most European countries tried to hold on to their Asian possessions or retake them after Japan's defeat. The exception was Britain, which relinquished control in India. However, there was to be violence, which

Celebrating independence in India
Crowds greet the British governor general of India, Lord Mountbatten, on August 15, 1947. Mountbatten and his wife were in New Delhi to proclaim India's independence.

resulted in at least 1 million deaths in the years following independence. During the war, Churchill had insisted that Britain would never give up India, despite the urgings of Roosevelt and the mass campaign of nonviolent civil disobedience led by Mahatma Gandhi. The British perspective changed, however, with the election of a Labour government in 1945. The new prime minister, Attlee, was determined that India should become independent, and this was achieved in 1947. The transfer of power did not go smoothly. As India approached independence, violence broke out between its Hindu and Muslim communities, and the British decided that the country should be partitioned. A separate Muslim state—Pakistan—was created, but the violence grew worse as millions of Hindu and Muslim refugees sought safety in the two new states. A dispute between the two countries over the border state of Kashmir is still unresolved.

Unlike Britain in India, France made desperate efforts to regain control of its colonies in Indochina. Nationalists in the region had fought long and hard

"Persecution of the revolutionary people only serves to accelerate the people's revolutions on a broader and more intense scale."

MAO ZEDONG, MOSCOW, NOVEMBER 6, 1957

Last flames of empire
Dutch Marines patrol a burning village in Indonesia in 1947 during their ultimately futile campaign to suppress revolutionaries. The insurgents were determined to reinforce independence from the Netherlands, declared in August 1945 by nationalist leader Sukarno.

The people's uncle
A founder of the Vietnamese Communist Party, and later president of Vietnam, Ho Chi Minh led the nationalist struggle against the French from 1945 to 1954.

against the Japanese Army. At the end of the war Vietnamese nationalists, led by Ho Chi Minh, fully expected to be rewarded for their efforts with independence. The French had other ideas. They were adamant that France be allowed to retake its place in Vietnam and the rest of Indochina. Initially, the United States condemned this French reversion to imperialism—after all, the United States had itself been founded after the expulsion of a colonial power in the 18th century. Before long, however, the emerging Cold War forced a rethink. As the United States began to implement the policy of containment of communism, so the Truman administration perceived the need for a stable ally in Southeast Asia, particularly since its main Asian ally, China, was at the time engaged in a civil war between the Nationalist government and communist rebels. The United States supported French efforts to regain control in Vietnam, and nationalist forces now found themselves engaged in another war against imperialists. The direct French involvement in the war against Vietnamese nationalists lasted until 1954; direct American involvement in Vietnam's political conflict began soon after.

The move toward decolonization spread throughout Asia as European powers struggled to recover from the ravages of war. The colonies of the Dutch East Indies were able to re-form themselves as the independent country of Indonesia only after four years of struggle against the Dutch; Burma and Ceylon managed to force the British out, with the latter colony renaming itself Sri Lanka. World War II had played a major

Nowhere to hide
Three generations of a Vietnamese family flee from Hanoi in February 1947, during fighting between Vietnamese revolutionaries and their French rulers.

role in these developments. During the conflict European nations had called on their Asian (and to some extent North African) possessions to help them in their battle against the Axis powers. Most colonies responded positively, but their wartime experience had taught them the techniques and tactics of guerrilla warfare and increased their sense of national identity. By 1945 they not only wanted independence; they now also knew how to use force in pursuit of their objective. World War II made the decolonization of Asia and North Africa inevitable.

THE CONTINUING WAR

As East–West relations deteriorated, both sides began casting about for fresh allies. By the end of the Cold War in 1990, most of the world's nations were regarded as "Eastern" or "Western" on the basis of their political allegiance. The terms had little to do with geography: Cuba, for example, belonged to the "Eastern bloc," while Hong Kong was a "Western" foothold on the edge of Red China.

Having worked so closely together during World War II, Britain and the United States were obvious candidates to head the Western alliance against the Soviet Union. These two democracies did share common interests—largely revolving around the desire to prevent the spread of communism—but nothing about cooperation between them could be taken for

granted. Although Britain was eager to stress its "special relationship" with the United States, American policymakers tended to view Britain as simply a useful ally which was no longer as great a power as it had been at the start of the century, or even at the start of World War II. Nevertheless, the two countries worked well after the war: their similarities generally outweighed their differences, although the United States was clearly the senior partner in the relationship.

The United States supported French resistance to Vietnamese nationalism because it feared that an independent Vietnam would gravitate into the Soviet orbit. The Americans also backed Britain in 1948, when it started to fight communist insurgents in Malaya, because the United States believed that a rebel victory in Malaya would represent a victory for Stalin. In fact, the ideology of the Malayan

rebels was closer to that of China than that of the Soviet Union, but during the Cold War, Western leaders often did not differentiate between forms of communism, even in cases where communist and nationalist ideology were interlinked.

THE FOUNDATION OF ISRAEL
The Cold War also provided the backdrop to the creation of Israel. After World War I (1914–18) the mandate to administer Palestine had been granted by the League of Nations to Britain, which, in the Balfour Declaration of 1917, had committed itself to establishing a homeland for the Jewish people. However, by the end of World War II the issue had not been resolved, and Zionists (Jewish nationalists) waged an increasingly violent terrorist campaign against the British in Palestine. As the details of the Holocaust began to emerge, the Zionist case became even more urgent. When in 1946 Britain refused to allow an influx of 100,000 Jewish refugees from Europe into Palestine, the violence escalated uncontrollably, and Britain handed the matter over to the United Nations in late 1947.

In early 1948 the UN partitioned Palestine into two states—a solution that satisfied neither the Jews nor the Arabs with whom they shared the territory. On May 14 Zionists declared the state of Israel, and both the United States— spurred in part by

sympathy for Jewish wartime suffering—and the Soviet Union recognized it the following day.

The surrounding Arab states of Egypt, Iraq, Transjordan (now Jordan), Syria, and Lebanon went to war with Israel, but the infant state defeated them all and expanded the borders allotted to it by the UN. Almost overnight, more than a million Palestinian Arabs were forced out of Israel and condemned to live as refugees. The resentment felt by the displaced Palestinians festered for years and undermined subsequent attempts at Jewish–Arab negotiation. Both the United States and the Soviet Union sought to increase their influence in the region, with varying degrees of success. Thus the Middle East was drawn into the Cold War.

The pattern was repeated around the world. When colonies sought independence they asked for, or had to accept, intervention from either the United States or the Soviet Union. As far as possible, however, the two superpowers avoided direct confrontation, which might escalate to the use of atomic weapons.

World War I had been dubbed the "war to end all wars." In the aftermath of World War II, few harbored such illusions. Fascism had been beaten, but communism remained. Militarism had been defeated, but at the cost of splitting the world into armed camps. German expansion had been replaced by Soviet expansion. There were also reasons for hope, however, such as the optimistic internationalism that inspired the UN and that organization's key role in settling East–West disputes. Most significantly, perhaps, the democracies of the West had survived one of their moments of gravest crisis. That victory stood democracy in good stead for its ongoing struggle against totalitarianism, and helped encourage its eventual triumph in the Cold War.

> By the end of the 1948 war, hundreds of entire villages had not only been depopulated but obliterated, their houses blown up or bulldozed. To this day the observant traveler of Israeli roads can see traces of their presence: now and then a few crumbled houses are left standing, a neglected mosque or church, collapsing walls along the ghost of a village lane, but in the vast majority of cases all that remains is a scattering of stones and rubble across a forgotten landscape.

PALESTINIAN EYEWITNESS W. KHALDI DESCRIBES THE SCENE AFTER THE 1948 ARAB–ISRAELI WAR

Taking the land
Jewish settlers prepare to defend their new Israeli homes from their previous Arab inhabitants after the creation of Israel on May 14, 1948. The new state managed to survive war with its neighbors.

Ruins of the Reich
Watched by German civilians, Soviet troops ride on a truck through a ruined square in Berlin in July 1945. The two-week long battle for the city had left most of its industrial, commercial, and residential buildings in ruins.

IN MEMORIAM

~

WORLD WAR II BATTLEFIELD MEMORIALS AND
CEMETERIES ARE TO BE FOUND ALL OVER THE
WORLD, EVEN IN SOME OF ITS REMOTEST REGIONS,
GIVING TESTIMONY TO THE SCALE OF THE CONFLICT
AND THE NUMBER OF NATIONS WHO FOUGHT IN IT.
TODAY, MANY OF THESE SITES ARE IMPORTANT
CENTERS FOR REMEMBRANCE AND RESEARCH,
AND CATER FOR THE HUGE POPULAR INTEREST IN
THE CONFLICT. WHEN EXPLORING WAR SITES IT IS
IMPORTANT TO BE GRACIOUS AND RESPECTFUL TO
LOCALS, OBEY THE FUNDAMENTAL COUNTRY CODES,
AND NEVER PICK UP WHAT APPEARS TO BE ORDNANCE
– PEOPLE ARE KILLED EVERY YEAR TAKING
UNEXPLODED ORDNANCE AS SOUVENIRS.

~

Iwo Jima at Sunrise
The US Marine Corps Memorial in Arlington National Cemetery,
Virginia, recreates the moment in which the US flag was raised at the
summit of Mount Suribachi on the Japanese island of Iwo Jima.

NORTH AMERICA

Although there was no actual fighting on US and Canadian soil, the United States nonetheless sacrificed more than 400,000 of its service personnel between 1939 and 1945, and Canada more than 45,000. Throughout the two countries, this sacrifice is commemorated by some internationally respected monuments and museums.

Hall of Remembrance
The Holocaust Memorial Museum houses the Hall of Remembrance. Architect James Freed designed the hexagonal room as a space for private contemplation.

CANADA

CANADIAN WAR MUSEUM

LOCATION: 1 Vimy Place, Ottawa, Ontario K1A 0M8

FEATURES: World War II gallery; vehicles and artifacts; archive and library

VISITOR INFORMATION: Tel: (819) 776-8600 or 1-800-555-5621. Email: info@warmuseum.ca. Website: www.civilization.ca/visit/cwmvisite.aspx

Gallery 3 of this large museum is devoted to Canada's military experience of World War II. It examines Canada's contribution to the land campaign in Europe, and also its roles in the Battle of the Atlantic. Exhibits include a Spitfire, a Sherman tank, personal artifacts, and a black Mercedes-Benz used by Hitler as a parade car. The museum is an important center for historical research, and the George Metcalf Archival Collection and Hartland Molson Library Collection provide comprehensive resources.

UNITED STATES

NATIONAL WWII MEMORIAL

LOCATION: 17th Street, between Constitution and Independence Avenues, at the east end of the National Mall Reflecting Pool, Washington DC

FEATURES: Memorial mall

VISITOR INFORMATION: Open access; Tel: (202) 488-0400; Website (including Email form): www.wwiimemorial.com

Central to Washington DC is the impressive National World War II Memorial, opened in 2004. The peaceful mall and its associated plaques and sculptures remember all US personnel who served and died in the war. It is located between the Washington Monument and the Lincoln Memorial.

A place of reflection
The centerpiece of the National World War II Memorial is a fountain, around which are arranged 56 pillars to represent each US state and the US overseas territories.

UNITED STATES HOLOCAUST MEMORIAL MUSEUM

LOCATION: 100 Raoul Wallenberg Place, SW Washington, DC 20024-2126

FEATURES: Museum, archives, audio-visual displays

VISITOR INFORMATION: Open: 10am–5:30pm every day including weekends, closed only on Yom Kippur and Christmas Day; Tel: (202) 488-0400; Website: www.ushmm.org

A short distance from the National World War II Memorial is the United States Holocaust Memorial Museum. The museum is dedicated to documenting and studying the Holocaust and is the American memorial to the millions of European Jews and others killed by the Nazis. The experience delivered within the museum is undoubtedly traumatic, with exhibitions including photos, piles of shoes collected from gas-chamber victims, and first-hand accounts played on screens, but the educational content is exceptional.

USMC WAR MEMORIAL

LOCATION: Marshal Drive, Arlington VA

FEATURES: USMC War Memorial

VISITOR INFORMATION: Open access; Website: www.nps.gov/archive/gwmp/usmc.htm

The US capital region contains war memorials of international recognition, including the US Marine Corps War Memorial at Arlington, Virginia. This huge sculpture, officially dedicated on 10 November 1954, depicts in 32 ft- (10 m-) high figures Joe Rosenthal's famous photograph of the US Marine flag-raising on the island of Iwo Jima in 1945. It is one of Washington's most powerful landmarks.

NATIONAL WORLD WAR II MUSEUM

LOCATION: 945 Magazine Street, New Orleans, LA 70130

FEATURES: Museum; D-Day exhibits; documentary movie theater

VISITOR INFORMATION: Open: 9am–5pm Tuesday–Sunday; closed Thanksgiving Day, Christmas Eve, Christmas Day, and Mardi Gras Day; Tel: (504) 527-6012; Email: info@ nationalww2museum.org. Website: www. nationalww2museum.org

The National World War II Museum was originally dedicated in 2000 as the National D-Day Museum, until Congress changed its status to become the country's official World War II center. The museum's original purpose is reflected in its extensive exhibitions concerning the Normandy landings and liberation of Europe, but the exhibits cover all theaters and periods of the conflict. The permanent exhibitions include a large area dedicated to the Pacific War, plus material on the US home front. Documentaries are shown daily in the Malcolm S. Forbes Theater.

BATTLESHIP COVE

LOCATION: Battleship Cove, Five Water Street, PO Box 111, Fall River, MA 02722-0111

FEATURES: Collection of public-access warships; World War II and post-War naval museum

VISITOR INFORMATION: Tel: (800) 533-3194 (New England only); (508) 678-1100; Website: www.battleshipcove.org

Battleship Cove has some impressive World War II exhibits at its core. These include the battleship USS *Massachusetts*, the submarine USS *Lionfish*, several torpedo boats and a Japanese attack craft. Most of the vessels are open to access, and the museum also holds major oral archives relating to crew members of the ships. Groups can even spend the night on board some of the vessels, by arrangement, as part of the "Nautical Nights" educational program.

Battleships from World War II and beyond
Among the ships at Battleship Cove is the USS *Joseph P. Kennedy, Jr.* (below left), built in 1945 and named after John F. Kennedy's brother, who was killed in the war.

NATIONAL MUSEUM OF THE PACIFIC WAR

LOCATION: 340 East Main Street, Fredericksburg, Texas 78624

FEATURES: Pacific war artifacts and historical exhibitions; Plaza of Presidents; Memorial Courtyard; Japanese Garden of Peace

VISITOR INFORMATION: Open: every day, except Thanksgiving and Christmas, from 9:00am to 5:00pm; Tel: (830) 997-4379; Website: www.nimitz-museum.org/index.htm

Originally named the Admiral Nimitz Museum, the National Museum of the Pacific War is solely dedicated to education about the Pacific theater. It has much to interest, including a Pacific Combat Zone featuring a hangar deck with PBM Avenger, a PT boat, and an invasion beach mock-up. The George Bush gallery brings the conflict to life through dioramas and collections of personal effects, while the Plaza of Presidents remembers the contributions of ten US presidents who served during the war. Other features include a permanent museum to Admiral Nimitz, a Memorial Courtyard, and the Japanese Garden of Peace.

WESTERN EUROPE
~

The German blitzkrieg and occupations of 1940, followed by the battles of liberation from June 1944, have left a powerful physical legacy across Western Europe. The D-Day beaches of Normandy, France, naturally attract the bulk of visitors, but there is much of interest in other countries and regions.

Spitfire
This Spitfire fighter plane, symbol of British defiance during the war, hangs in the London's Imperial War Museum.

UNITED KINGDOM
~

IMPERIAL WAR MUSEUM

LOCATION: Lambeth Road, London SE1 6HZ

FEATURES: Major World War II exhibition and related archives

VISITOR INFORMATION: Open: daily (except December 24, 25, and 26) 10am–6pm; Tel: +44 (0)20 7416 5000; Email: mail@iwm.org.uk. Website: london.iwm.org.uk

The Museum's permanent World War II exhibition gives the full story of British involvement in the war from 1939 to 1945. The coverage includes "The Blitz Experience," a detailed look at home life during the German bombing campaign, conveyed with authentic street scenes and audiovisual effects. The exhibitions contain thousands of weapons, including a German V-2 rocket, maps, uniforms, and personal artifacts. The museum is also a major depository of photographs, moving images, and official records.

NATIONAL ARMY MUSEUM

LOCATION: Royal Hospital Road, Chelsea, London SW3 4HT

FEATURES: British Army World War II exhibition; related archives

VISITOR INFORMATION: Open: every day 10am–5.30pm, except December 24–26, January 1, Good Friday, early May bank holiday; Tel: +44 (0)20 7881 2455; Email: info@national-army-museum.ac.uk Website: www.national-army-museum.ac.uk

Focusing on the British Army specifically, the National Army Museum (NAM) has a large World War II exhibition, with features including a six-pounder anti-tank gun and a Universal Carrier. NAM is especially useful for seeing how the British Army's equipment and uniform developed throughout the war, and its research library contains regimental histories and service records relating to the conflict. The museum's website features online exhibitions on various themes.

RAF MUSEUM

LOCATION: Grahame Park Way, London, NW9 5LL

FEATURES: World War II aircraft and munitions

VISITOR INFORMATION: Open: daily 10am–6pm, although some exhibits have more limited opening times (see website for details); Tel: +44 (0)20 8205 2266; Email: london@rafmuseum.org. Website: www.rafmuseum.org.uk/london/index.cfm

The air war has a central place in the British memory of World War II. The RAF Museum in Hendon, London, houses a superb collection of more than 100 aircraft, many from the World War II period. The Bomber Hall and Battle of Britain collections are particularly relevant. The museum also features a medals and uniform gallery, a weapons collection, a library and a large archive.

Bletchley Park Estate
The estate of Bletchley Park was bought in 1938 by Admiral Sir Hugh Sinclair, the head of MI6, as a base for his secret Government Code and Cypher School.

BLETCHLEY PARK MUSEUM

LOCATION: The Mansion, Bletchley Park, Sherwood Drive, Bletchley, Milton Keynes, MK3 6EB

FEATURES: Wartime codebreaking computers; Enigma machine; exhibitions of Allied cryptology

VISITOR INFORMATION: Opening times: see website; Tel: +44 (0)1908 640404; Email: see web site; Website: www.bletchleypark.org.uk

As the center of Britain's code-breaking expertise during World War II, Bletchley Park is famous for its achievement in breaking the German Enigma code, although that was only part of the decryption and intelligence work here. The various exhibitions explain the process of code-breaking, and visitors can also see landmarks in intelligence technology such as the Enigma machine and a reconstruction of the Bombe code-analyzing machine. A rebuild of the Colossus computer is underway. There are also numerous personal artifacts and documents explaining life inside this top-secret wartime establishment.

FRANCE
~

D-DAY BEACHES

Location: Normandy coastline between Honfleur and Cherbourg

Features: Defensive positions; battlefield sites; Allied and German cemeteries; museums

Visitor information: The beach areas are mostly open access, although some battle sites are now on private property.

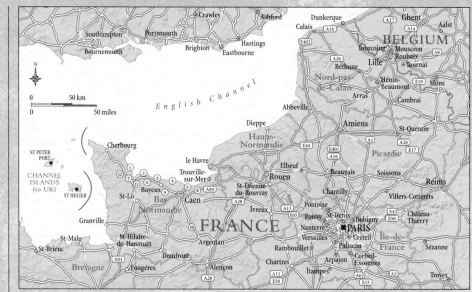

1. Utah beach
2. Omaha beach
3. Gold beach
4. Juno beach
5. Sword beach
6. Colleville-sur-Mer American cemetery
7. Ste. Mère-Église US airborne forces memorial
8. Ranville British cemetery
9. Bayeaux British cemetery
10. Cintheaux Canadian cemetery
11. La Cambe German cemetery
12. Orglades German cemetery

The D-Day beaches, formerly code-named Gold, Juno, Sword, Utah, and Omaha, cover a very extensive stretch of the Normandy coastline. The Omaha Beach site has the remains of concrete casemates and bunkers and the area of the Pointe-du-Hoc assault is definitely worth a visit. Utah Beach also has much to interest, particularly the sites of the Crisbecq and Azeville batteries and an attendant museum (summer season only). Many markers and memorials are to be found in this area, including to the US airborne forces deployed on June 8, 1944, around Ste. Mère-Église. Of the British and Commonwealth beaches, Sword Beach has lost many of its wartime features to development, although traces of some fortified emplacements remain, including an impressive 55 ft- (17 m-) high German fire control post. More is to be found around the areas of the British airborne deployments inland, including Pegasus Bridge and adjacent Café Gondrée (the first house in France to be liberated). The CWCG cemetery at Ranville contains many of the British airborne dead. Gold and Juno beaches feature a number of bunkers and command posts, and at the harbor at Courseulles there is a Canadian tank and a German 50 mm anti-tank gun. At Arromanches are the rusting remains of one of the Mulberry harbors, and the nearby German war cemetery at La Cambes contains more than 20,000 German war dead.

NORMANDY AMERICAN CEMETERY AND MEMORIAL

Location: Overlooking Omaha Beach, east of St Laurent-sur-Mer and northwest of Bayeux in Colleville-sur-Mer

Features: ABMC war cemetery

Visitor information: Open: Daily 9am–5pm except December 25 and January 1; Website: www.abmc.gov/cemeteries/cemeteries/no.php

Established by the US First Army at St Laurent on June 8, 1944, this cemetery contains 9,387 US war dead in a site that covers more than 170 acres (69 hectares). Most were killed during the battle of D-Day and the subsequent fighting in Normandy. A further 1,557 names are inscribed on the Walls of the Missing in a memorial garden, at the center of which stands a 18ft- (6m-) high statue of a young man, entitled *The Spirit of American Youth*. With its view onto Omaha Beach, this cemetery is not the largest in the area, but it is certainly one of the most haunting.

Nazi fortification
This German bunker with anti-tank gun at Longues-sur-Mer was part of the extensive Atlantic Wall, intended to deter an Allied landing.

ORADOUR-SUR-GLANE

Location: Haute-Vienne, Department 87, about 19km (12 miles) west of Limoges on the D9, off the N141 (E603)

Features: Memorial ruins; memorial center

Visitor information: Open: daily 9am–5/6pm, with an extensive period of closure in December and January. Check website for details; Tel: +33 (0)5 55 43 04 30; Website: www.oradour.org

On 10 June 1944, the village of Oradour-sur-Glane in the Haute-Vienne département was destroyed by troops of the 2nd Waffen-SS Panzer Division "Das Reich", who murdered 642 men, women, and children in the process. The ruins of the town have been preserved to this day as a lasting and haunting memorial to the dead, and include artifacts recovered from many of the incinerated buildings. A memorial center includes the full story of the village and its massacre, and holds archive material for those researching the events.

Destroyed village
Cars still stand where they were burned in the village of Oradour-sur-Glane, whose people were murdered by Waffen SS troops who were en route to Normandy.

MUSEUM OF NATIONAL RESISTANCE

Location: Parc Vercors, 88 Avenue Marx Dormoy, 94 500 Champigny-sur-Marne

Features: Museum of Resistance history, thousands of Resistance artifacts

Visitor information: Tel: +33 (0)1 48 81 53 78; Email: see web site; Website: www.musee-resistance.com

The Museum of National Resistance brings to life the activities of the French Resistance between the invasion of 1940 and the liberation in 1944. In total the museum holds more than half a million artifacts and documents relating to the Resistance, from newspapers to weaponry. The museum is arranged chronologically, so the visitor can explore the full evolution of the Resistance war.

CAMBRAI BATTLEFIELDS

Location: Around Cambrai, northern France

Features: Louveral Military Cemetery; Cambrai Memorial to the Missing; numerous other cemeteries and memorials

Visitor information: Cambrai town located on N43 southeast of Arras

The Cambrai area was the scene of bitter fighting, particularly in the last two years of the war. The major site for war burials is the Louveral Military Cemetery. This also features the Memorial to the Missing, which lists the names of more than 7,000 British soldiers with no known grave. Other cemeteries are within easy driving distance.

BELGIUM
~

ARDENNES AREA BATTLEFIELD

Location: Area in and around Bastogne in the Ardennes, eastern Belgium

Features: Battlefield sites, museums, memorials, and cemeteries

Visitor information: The best starting point for exploring the Ardennes is Bastogne itself. For local tourist information, call the Bastogne Tourist Office on +32 (0)61/21 27 11, or visit www.trabel.com/bastogne/bastogne.htm, which has information about the various battle sites

The Ardennes region is a major destination for military history tourists, principally those wanting to explore features relating to the German Ardennes Offensive. The area is replete with armored memorials, including the Sherman tank memorial in the main square at Bastogne, the Panther tank in the village of Celles, a Tiger II at La Gleize, and an M10 Achilles at La Roche. More sombre locations include the Hotton War Cemetery at the village of

The process of finding final resting places for the dead of World War II continues to this day, with bodies still being unearthed from combat zones around the world. US, British, and Commonwealth war dead are either repatriated to their home countries or buried in foreign war cemeteries such as those run by the Commonwealth War Graves Commission (CWGC) or the American Battlefield Monuments Commission (ABMA). The American Graves Registration Service (AGRS), for example, handled US war dead during and after the war, and gave next of kin the option of repatriating the body or burying it in a foreign war cemetery. For defeated nations such as Germany, however, registration became chaotic and random, and countless thousands of soldiers ended up in foreign mass graves, their names etched somewhere on an inventory of the missing.

Hotton, containing nearly 700 Allied war dead (mostly British), and the huge Ardennes American Cemetery and Memorial at Neuville-en-Condroz, with more than 5,000 graves of US soldiers.

FORT EBEN-EMAEL

Location: Rue du Fort 40, BE4690 Eben-Emael, near Maastricht

Features: Fortress complex and related exhibitions

Visitor information: Tel: +32 (0)4 2862 861; Email: info@fortissimus.be; Website: www.fort-eben-emael.be

The fortifications at Eben Emael are impressive examples of ferro-concrete emplacements, and were the target of an audacious and successful German airborne assault in May 1940. Tours of the fortress explore the underground hospitals, kitchens, living quarters, and magazines, and also the defensive arrangements on the surface, taking in surviving evidence of the May 1940 assault.

Lorraine Cross
This 164 ft- (50 m-) high cross was erected in memory of General Charles de Gaulle, leader of the Free French, in his home village of Colombey-les-Deux-Églises.

NETHERLANDS
~

ANNE FRANK MUSEUM

Location: Prinsengracht 267, Amsterdam

Features: Museum of Anne Frank, including her diary and related archives

Visitor information: Open: see website; Tel: +31 (0)20-5567100; Website: www.annefrank.org

This extremely popular museum on the Prinsengracht in Amsterdam was the location in which the young Jewish diarist Anne Frank, her family, and four other Jewish people hid from the Nazis between 1942 and 1944. The Achterhuis ("back house") secret annex in which they lived and were subsequently discovered (Anne died in Bergen-Belsen concentration camp, age 15) is the main focus of the museum, but the collections also bring to life the general experience of Jewish people surviving in wartime Netherlands. Anne's hugely influential diary is on display.

The secret annex
This is Anne's bedroom in the extension at the back of the house on Prinsengracht in Amsterdam. The entrance to the extension was concealed by a bookcase.

LIBERTY PARK

Location: Liberty Park, Museumpark 1, 5825 AM Overloon

Features: National War and Resistance Museum; Marshal Museum

Visitor information: Open: September–June: 10am–5pm, July–August: 10am–6pm; Tel: +31 478-641250; Email: info@libertypark.nl; Website: www.oorlogsmuseum-overloon.nl

The Liberty Park incorporates two major museums over a 14-acre (6-hectare) site – the National War and Resistance Museum, which gives a history of World War II and of the liberation of the Netherlands, and the Marshal Museum, containing 150 wartime vehicles, vessels, and aircraft. Both are well worth a visit, and you can also wander through the main park site, the location of a major tank battle fought in 1944.

ARNHEM-NIJMEGEN AREA BATTLEFIELD

Location: Arnhem-Nijmegen area, the Netherlands

Features: Battlefield sites, museums, memorials, cemeteries

Visitor information: Arnhem town itself is an ideal base for exploring the battlefield sites. For travel, museum, and memorial information, go to www.goarnhem.nl/uk/information.html

The Arnhem-Nijmegen battlefield area is replete with museums, cemeteries, and memorials, and the visitor would do well to obtain a guide book to explore everything the area has to offer. The visitor can walk or drive around many of the key battlegrounds in and around Arnhem and Nijmegen, including Oosterbeck Church, Hartenstein Hotel (now the location of the Airborne Museum), Arnhem Road Bridge, and the bridges across the Waal at Grave and Nijmegen. There are numerous other open access sites where famous engagements took place. The Arnhem Oosterbeck Military Cemetery contains 1,679 British and Commonwealth War dead from operation Market Garden, when Allied forces attempted to capture a number of strategic bridges in German-occupied Holland in 1944.

The Canadian War Cemetery, holding 2,300 Canadian war dead from Operation Veritable in 1945, sits next to the excellent National Liberation Museum at Groesbeek.

DENMARK

MUSEUM OF DANISH RESISTANCE 1940–45

Location: Churchillparken 1, 1263 Copenhagen

Features: Exhibitions on Danish resistance 1941–45; air raid shelter; library, and archives

Visitor information: Open October–April: 10am–3pm, May–September: 10am–5pm, closed December 24, 25, and 31; Tel: +45 3347 3921; Website: www.nationalmuseet.dk/sw23424.asp

The Museum of Danish Resistance forms part of the National Museum in Copenhagen. Opened in 1957, it gives a chronological account of the actions of the Danish resistance from occupation in 1940 through to liberation in 1945. Close to the museum there is also an exhibition in an authentic air raid shelter, an improvised armored car used in the final, violent phase of the resistance against the Danish SS, plus a library and document/photo archives for researchers. The museum also relates the remarkable story of how the Danish resistance rescued all but 500 of the country's 8,000 Jews, by spiriting them by boat into neutral Sweden.

Operation Market Garden
A ceremony held at Arnhem Oosterbeck Military Cemetery to commemorate the 50th anniversary of Operation Market Garden.

NORWAY
~

LOFOTEN WORLD WAR II MEMORIAL MUSEUM

LOCATION: The museum is housed in the old post office building by the coastal-liner dock in Svolvær centrum, Lofoten

FEATURES: Large collections of uniforms and artifacts; wartime documents; library

VISITOR INFORMATION: Open: daily during the summer, and by request the rest of the year; Tel: +47 91 73 03 28; Email: williah@online.no; Website: www.lofotenkrigmus.no/hovengelsk.htm

This museum houses a broad range of exhibits exploring the Norwegian experience of World War II from 1940 to 1945. The collections not only focus on the Norwegian military and the country's resistance movements, but also explore the German forces deployed (including the operations of the local Gestapo), British commando raids on Lofoten itself, and POWs kept in Norway (with a special exhibition on Russian POWs).

NORWAY'S RESISTANCE MUSEUM

LOCATION: Bygning 21, Akershus Festning, 0015 Oslo

FEATURES: Comprehensive exhibition of Norway's experience during World War II

VISITOR INFORMATION: Open: see website; Tel: +47 23 09 31 38; Email: post.nhm@gmail.com; Website: www.mil.no/felles/nhm/start/eng/

This extensive museum was established in 1966, and dedicated to Norway's wartime resistance movement. The exhibition is arranged in a chronological fashion, and each section contains artifacts relating to particular themes, including Operation Weserübung (the German invasion of Norway), the growth of the underground press, the Norwegian Nazi Party, the battle off the Norwegian coast, and resistance operations. The museum is housed in an outbuilding of Akershus Castle, and is next to a memorial on the site where captured Norwegian resistance members were executed by the Germans.

Jewish Museum
The startling design of the museum is the work of American architect Daniel Libeskind. The Garden of Exile can be seen on its left; the old Kollegienhaus is on the right.

GERMANY
~

THE REICHSTAG

LOCATION: Deutscher Bundestag, Platz der Republik 1, D-11011 Berlin

FEATURES: Guided tour of Reichstag building

VISITOR INFORMATION: Tel: +49 30/227-0; Website: www.bundestag.de/htdocs_e/visitors/index.html

The Reichstag building today looks dramatically different from the shattered ruin left at the end of the war. Although the building has been massively redeveloped since then as the seat of the modern German government, including the addition of a glass dome and roof terrace, it is worth a visit on account of its symbolism in the fall of the Third Reich. The guided tours include accounts of the building's wartime experience, and a wall of Russian graffiti left by Soviet troops in 1945.

JEWISH MUSEUM

LOCATION: Lindenstrasse 9–14, 10969 Berlin

FEATURES: Thousands of exhibits, Garden of Exile

VISITOR INFORMATION: Open daily from 10am, see website for closing times; Tel: +49 (0)30 259 93 300; Website: www.juedisches-museum-berlin.de

Germany's most visited museum, which opened in 2001, covers 2,000 years of German-Jewish history. It replaces the original Jewish museum closed by the Nazis in 1938. Exhibits include many artifacts of Jewish life under Nazi rule, from schools and the welfare aid network, and from the Holocaust, including letters, photographs, and documents.

The Reichstag
The building that houses the German parliament was heavily damaged in wartime air raids, and was the central objective in the Battle for Berlin in April–May 1945.

MILITÄRHISTORISCHES MUSEUM DER BUNDESWEHR

LOCATION: Olbrichtplatz 2, D-01099 Dresden (Neustadt)

FEATURES: Large World War II exhibition covering all branches of service

VISITOR INFORMATION: Open Tue–Sun 9am–5pm; Tel: +49 (0)351 8 23 28 03; Email: contact form on website; Website: www.militaerhistorisches-museum.bundeswehr.de

The Federal Army Museum of Military History in Dresden charts the development of all Germany's armed forces from medieval times to the present day, putting the World War II exhibition in context. This section features historical artifacts, vehicles, a German Molch midget submarine, and service uniforms. Altogether it is one of the largest military museums in Europe.

End of the line
This gatehouse was the main entrance into Birkenau, also known as
Auschwitz II, where arriving prisoners faced selection. Most of those
selected to die were killed within about two hours of arrival.

EASTERN EUROPE
~

The wartime experience of Eastern
Europe, including within the territory
of the Soviet Union, was uniquely traumatic.
The political complexities of the region mean
that not every country is forward about its
wartime past, but there is much to interest the
traveler, including the Auschwitz-Birkenau
concentration camp in Poland.

POLAND
~

AUSCHWITZ-BIRKENAU

LOCATION: Near Oswiecim, see Website for
travel details

FEATURES: Auschwitz I and Auschwitz II-Birkenau
death camps; education center

VISITOR INFORMATION: Opening times vary
throughout the year. For these and other conditions
of visits, see the Website: www.auschwitz.org.pl/

Auschwitz-Birkenau was the site of at least
1.1 million deaths between 1940 and 1945,
90 per cent those being the murder of Jews as
part of Hitler's "Final Solution." As the largest
concentration camp in German-occupied Europe,
it was preserved following the war as a testimony
to the Holocaust, and was declared a UNESCO
World Heritage Site in 1979. A visit to the site's
two main camps, Auschwitz I and Auschwitz II-
Birkenau, is a sobering and disturbing experience.
Still in evidence are the appalling prisoner barracks,
the administrative offices, the camp security
apparatus, and the locations of the now-ruined gas
chambers. The *Judenrampe* rail lines show where
the deported Jews arrived and underwent selection
according to whether they would work or die.
Personal artifacts on display include tons of human
hair, eyeglasses, and shoes. The education center,
archives, library, office for information on former
prisoners, collections department and research
department work to further public understanding of
Auschwitz and the Holocaust in general.

REMEMBERING THE HOLOCAUST

The sheer scale and horror of the Holocaust has
resulted in a determined effort by many countries
to preserve the memories of the events as warning
to future generations. Several major concentration
camps remain as living museums, including Auschwitz-
Birkenau, Maidanek, Dachau, Buchenwald, and
Mauthausen, and centers of Holocaust research
include the Yad Vashem Holocaust History Museum
(p.323) in Jerusalem and the United States Holocaust
Memorial Museum (p.311) in Washington DC. In
October 2005, the United Nations declared January
27 to be the international Holocaust Memorial Day, a
day not only for raising awareness about the Holocaust
itself, but also about subsequent and present genocides.
Furthermore, the internet has become a central
depository for education about the Holocaust, such as
remember.org (http://remember.org/), and the Nizkor
Project (http://www.nizkor.org/index.html).

ESTONIA
~

NARVA FRONT BATTLEFIELD

LOCATION: Area extending between Gulf of
Finland and Lake Peipus

FEATURES: Military positions and artifacts; war
memorials and cemeteries

VISITOR INFORMATION: Narva is the best starting
point for exploration. For general Narva tourist
information, see http://tourism.narva.ee/

The battlefields of the Narva front in
Estonia, location of the gigantic clashes
between German and Soviet forces throughout
1944, offer much for the military historian and
artifact hunter, as many of the battlefields remain
undeveloped since the war. Bunkers, gun positions,
vehicles, and anti-tank weapons can still be found
rusting in situ in the landscape, and long trench
lines cut deep scars through forest and woodland.
Regular finds in the area include helmets, military
kit, and personal artifacts of both German and
Soviet origins, although beware of live munitions
and always respect national laws on the collection
of historical material. The swampy and forested
landscape of this region can be especially
treacherous, so exploration of the area is often
best attempted as part of an organized group.
A German cemetery near Narva contains 10,000
war graves, and there are several war memorials
(including one formed by a Soviet T-34 tank) in
the city itself.

FINLAND
~

MILITARY MUSEUM

Location: Maurinkatu 1, 00170 Helsinki

Features: Extensive collection of wartime artifacts

Visitor information: Open: Tue–Thu 11am–5pm, Fri–Sun 11am–4 pm, closed on Mondays; Tel: + 358 (0)9 1812 6387; Email: sotamuseo@mil.fi; Website: www.mpkk.fi/en/museum/

The Military Museum in Helsinki is part of the Finnish National Defense College. Founded in 1929, the museum contains exhibitions and artifacts from Finland's military history, with good displays and information about World War II. The exhibitions include weaponry, equipment, uniforms, medals, flags, and art, plus documentation and photographic archives that give the displays context.

The Winter War
This memorial in Suomussaimi, Finland, commemorates the Finnish dead from the Russo-Finnish war of 1939–40, also known as the Winter War.

SALPA LINE

Location: Stretching from Gulf of Finland to Petsamo, northern Finland

Features: Defensive works, both restored and untouched; museum at Miehikkälä,

Visitor information: See Salpa Center: Tel: +358-5-7490 262; Website: www.salpakeskus.fi

The Salpa Line was an enormous network of defensive fortifications running 746 miles (1,200 km) cost-to-coast from the Gulf of Finland to Petsamo. They were never actually engaged in battle, and for this reason they are well preserved. Hundreds of pillboxes, anti-tank obstacles, infantry dug-outs, and communications posts, plus extensive trench lines still exist. Information boards provide insight into life there between 1941 and 1944. The Salpa Line museum at Miehikkälä is a good starting point for exploration and hikes along the line.

RUSSIA
~

MONUMENT TO THE HEROIC DEFENDERS OF LENINGRAD

Location: Ploschad Pobedy (Victory Square), near the Moskovskaya metro

Features: Memorial area plus underground exhibition

Visitor information: See Website: www.saint-petersburg.com/museums/monument-to-heroic-defenders.asp

This memorial sits in St. Petersburg's Victory Square (Ploschad Pobedy) and is the city's principal act of remembrance to the heroism of the city's population in enduring the 900-day German siege during World War II. A towering column throws its shadow over a ringlike memorial area, on the walls of which are engravings depicting the siege, and torches burn in remembrance of those who died. A memorial hall beneath has an exhibition showing the history of the siege, and English-speaking tour guide staff are often on hand.

MUSEUM OF THE GREAT PATRIOTIC WAR

Location: 121170, Moscow, 3, Victory square

Features: Major World War II collections and historical information; "Victory" monument and statuary; large collections of military vehicles and weaponry; library

Visitor information: Tel: +7 (495) 142-41-85; Website: www.poklonnayagora.ru/

Set in the memorial complex at Poklonnaya Gora, the Museum of the Great Patriotic War is Russia's central state repository for information and exhibits about the war on the Eastern Front. The museum is situated beneath the towering 465 ft- (142 m-) tall "Victory" monument, and containsmore than 110,000 artifacts from the war, ranging from uniforms through to military vehicles. A principal part of the museum is the exposition on the history of the war. Further exhibits display armor and artillery. Larger items, such as a Katyusha rocket launcher (Stalin organ) are arranged in the open-air exhibition.

The Defenders of Leningrad
The monument in Victory Square, St. Petersburg, commemorates the 1.5 million Russians who died during Germany's three-year siege of the city.

MAMAYEV KURGAN

LOCATION: Mamayev Hill, Volgograd

FEATURES: Monumental statuary and reliefs; "Mother Russia" monument; Hall of the Warrior Glory; Military Memorial Cemetery

VISITOR INFORMATION: Use public transportation or taxis to reach the base of Mamayev Kurgan; website: http://mamayevhill.volgadmin.ru/

The Memorial Complex at Volgograd remembers the appalling sacrifices of the Soviet Army and the civilian population during the fighting at Stalingrad in the winter of 1942–43. It is replete with powerful monumental statuary in the socialist realism style, from the somber figure of the Square of Sorrow through to the hand clutching a torch, burning the eternal flame, in the Hall of the Warrior Glory. The defining feature of the complex, however, is the epic "Motherland Calls," a colossal figure of a woman, 170 ft (52 m) high, holding aloft a stainless steel sword 108 ft (33 m) long and weighing 14 tons. She sits atop Mamayev Hill, and creates a dramatic spectacle.

UKRAINE
~
NATIONAL MUSEUM OF THE HISTORY OF THE GREAT PATRIOTIC WAR OF 1941–45

LOCATION: Ivan Mazepa Str. 44, Kiev

FEATURES: Major collections of vehicles, weapons, and artifacts; Memorial Complex park

VISITOR INFORMATION: See Website: www.warmuseum.kiev.ua/

This major museum stands in the shadow of the 203-ft (62 m-) high "Motherland" statue by Serbian sculpor Yevgeny Vuchetich, who also designed the "Motherland Calls" statue at Volgograd. The statue is the centerpiece of the Memorial Complex park that covers 25 acres (10 hectares) and overlooks the Dnieper River. The museum itself houses some 300,000 artifacts, including small arms, aircraft, armored vehicles, artillery pieces, and personal belongings. Outside, the Memorial Complex has further weapons systems and vehicles on display, plus statues in the socialist realism style, depicting facets of the struggle against the German invaders.

KURSK BATTLEFIELD

LOCATION: Prokhorovka, near Kursk

FEATURES: Battlefield site; memorial complex; museum; diorama at Belgorod

VISITOR INFORMATION: Kursk city is the best starting point, and Prokhorovka is generally visited as part of an organized tour

The Prokhorovka area is just one part of the Kursk battlefield, but was the location of the largest tank battle in history in 1943, involving more than 6,000 tanks, and the destruction of the 2nd Waffen-SS Corps. It contains an epic bell-tower victory monument, plus the Prokhorovka tank battle museum, which displays exhibitions relating to the Kursk engagement, including uniforms, weapons, and medals, together with preserved T-34 and German Tiger tanks, Katyushka rocket launchers, and warplanes (Kursk was also the scene of an intense air battle). The battle at Prokhorovka is also represented in creative fashion in the nearby city of Belgorod, in which the Belgorod Diorama depicts a gigantic wall painting of the engagement's various stages. Organized tours of the area follow the "death ride" of the German Fourth Panzer Army and include walks through fields of the Ponyri and Prokhorovka—the northern and southern salients at Kursk—to view the preserved trenches and gun emplacements.

The Great Patriotic War in Kiev
Leading up to the colossal "Motherland" statue is the "Alley of Hero Cities," with sculptures depicting the defense of the Soviet border in 1941, the Nazi terror, partisan struggle, and the 1943 Battle of the Dnieper.

HUNGARY
~
WAR HISTORY MUSEUM

LOCATION: I. Tóth árpád sétány 40, Budapest

FEATURES: World War II permanent exhibition; vehicle displays

VISITOR INFORMATION: Open: 10am–5pm Tue–Sat, 10am–6pm Sun; Website: www.militaria.hu

The War History Museum in Budapest is a major collection of military memorabilia from across Hungary's bloody history. There is a permanent World War II exhibition, which contains displays of Hungarian, German, and Soviet artifacts, and an associated vehicle park with examples of supply vehicles and armor. The museum also has examples of uniforms and flags, and art exhibits.

CZECH REPUBLIC
~
MILITARY HISTORY INSTITUTE

LOCATION: Locations around Prague

FEATURES: Collection of military museums and library facilities

VISITOR INFORMATION: See central MHI Website: www.vhu.cz/en/stranka/vhu-praha/

The Military History Institute (MHI) is run directly by the General Staff of the Armed Forces of the Czech Republic, and is an umbrella organization for several major historical and research institutes located in Prague. These include the Army Museum in Prague-Žižkov, the Aviation Museum at Prague-Kbely, the Military Technical Museum at Lešany (this features over 350 historic military vehicles), and an extensive MHI library for military researchers. All of these museums contain exhibitions relating to World War II. The Army Museum also has exhibits relating to the Sudeten crisis and the run-up to war. Admission is free.

THE BALKANS, ITALY, AND MEDITERRANEAN
~

The battlegrounds of southern Europe and North Africa were as hotly contested as any other theater. Today, the war zones of the Balkans and Italy are generally easily accessible, whereas those in Libya and Egypt may take more planning, and require respect for local religion and customs from the traveller.

ITALY
~
FLORENCE AMERICAN CEMETERY

LOCATION: On the west side of Via Cassia, about 7.5 miles (12 km) south of Florence

FEATURES: US ABMA cemetery; Tablets of the Missing

VISITOR INFORMATION: Open: daily 9am–5pm, except December 25 and January 1; Website: www.abmc.gov/cemeteries/cemeteries/fl.php

The heavy cost of the US campaign in Italy is apparent in this beautifully kept cemetery run by the American Battlefield Monuments Commission (ABMA). There are 4,402 graves arranged on the 70-acre (28-hectare) site, containing mostly soldiers of the US Fifth Army killed in the heavy fighting that followed the capture of Rome in June 1944, and in the Apennines between then and May 1945. Within a memorial area in the grounds are Tablets of the Missing, which list another 1,409 names. There is also a chapel and marble operations maps in one of the memorial's atria.

1. Florence American cemetery
2. Anzio beachhead museum and Commonwealth war cemetery
3. Sicily-Rome American cemetery, Nettuno
4. Cassino memorial & cemeteries
5. Salerno Commonwealth war cemetery
6. Syracuse Commonwealth war cemetery

CASSINO

LOCATION: Southern Lazio, Frosinone province

FEATURES: battlefields; monastery; cemeteries

VISITOR INFORMATION: Website for Monte Cassino: www.officine.it/montecassino

Touring the area around Cassino is physically demanding, but there is much to see. The monastery on Monte Cassino itself, although substantially rebuilt, is worth a visit for its views and for a perspective on the nature of the battle for these heights. The Cassino War Cemetery and Memorial on Mount Cairo contains 4,266 Allied burials, of which more than 1,000 are Poles—on Hill 593 is the main Polish memorial.

Memorial Day
An Italian Carabiniere plays "Silence" during a ceremony at the American cemetery in Florence marking the 60th anniversary of the capture of the city from the German army by US forces.

Commonwealth cemetery
At Suda Bay on the northwest coast of the Greek island of Crete are the graves of more than 1,500 Allied soldiers, most of them from New Zealand or Australia.

MALTA

NATIONAL WAR MUSEUM

LOCATION: Fort St. Elmo, Valletta VLT 02

FEATURES: World War II exhibition, including aircraft and AA artillery

VISITOR INFORMATION: Website: www. heritagemalta.org/warmuseum.html

Set in what was originally a powder magazine, the National War Museum of Malta concentrates primarily on the island's epic battle against the Luftwaffe between 1940 and 1943, and its role in the Mediterranean theater in general. Photographic exhibitions depict the endurance of the islanders under the incessant air raids, and the unhealthy underground shelter living conditions. The main hall contains exhibits that include a Gloster Gladiator biplane, a Bofors anti-tank gun, an Italian E-boat plus, parts of a Spitfire, and a Bf 109 fighter. The island's George Cross is also on display, as is a Book of Remembrance containing the names of those civilians and service personnel who died during the island's defense. An annex is dedicated the role, insignia, and uniforms of the Royal Navy, and the Malta convoys that relieved the island. The air hall includes artifacts relating to German raids.

CRETE

SUDA BAY WAR CEMETERY

LOCATION: Northwestern corner of the Suda Bay, 3.1 miles (5 km) east of Chania

FEATURES: CWGC cemetery.

VISITOR INFORMATION: Website: www.cwgc.org

A total of 2,000 Commonwealth soldiers were killed on Crete during the German invasion of 1941. Originally they were buried by the Germans in four locations around the island (Chania, Iraklion, Rethymnon, and Galata), but after the war the bodies were moved to the present cemetery at Suda Bay. This beautiful cemetery now holds 1,502 war dead, 778 of which are unidentified, owing to the chaotic manner of their original burial.

GERMAN WAR CEMETERY

LOCATION: Near Malame, northwestern Crete

FEATURES: German war cemetery; visitor's center

VISITOR INFORMATION: Provided on location

The German War Cemetery near Malame is testimony to the huge cost of taking the island, and is a somber counterpoint to the CWGC cemetery at Suda Bay. More than 4,400 soldiers are buried here, each grave stone laid flat on the ground with the names of two men inscribed on the surface.

LIBYA

TOBRUK WAR CEMETERY

LOCATION: 7 miles (11 km) inland from Tobruk, on main road to Alexandria

FEATURES: CWGC war cemetery

VISITOR INFORMATION: Open: daily 8am–5pm. Website: www.cwgc.org

Tobruk was a critical supply port fueling the war in North Africa, and changed hands violently or fell under siege several times. The Tobruk War Cemetery is a CWGC-run cemetery and memorial that contains the remains of 2,282 Commonwealth war dead. Foreign travelers are advised to check with the appropriate government office about the requirements for visiting Libya. Other large war cemeteries in Libya are found at Benghazi, Acroma, and Tripoli.

EL ALAMEIN BATTLEFIELD

LOCATION: Around the town of al-Alamein, about 80 miles (130 km) west of Alexandria on the road to Mersa Matruh

FEATURES: Numerous cemeteries and memorials; museums

VISITOR INFORMATION: All sites accessible from al-Alemein village and Marina Tourist Village

The actual desert battlefields of El Alamein are relatively inaccessible because of terrain conditions and travel restrictions on account of the large amount of live munitions that remain. Tell al-Alemein (near the actual town), however, has numerous war memorials and cemeteries, including the Greek Memorial and South African Memorial. A major feature is the CWGC El Alamein War Cemetery, which contains the bodies of 7,240 Commonwealth soldiers, plus memorial panels that remember thousands of other service personnel who died in the North African campaigns. Some 1.8 miles (3 km) west of al-Alemein is a marker that defines the easternmost limits of the Axis advance, and a short distance further west is the German War Memorial at Gebel Alam Abd al-Gawad. This octagonal building serves as the ossuary for 4,280 German soldiers killed in the theater. Some 3 miles (5 km) from here is the Italian Memorial, a large, beautiful complex featuring a chapel, mosque, and a museum. Near al-Alemein itself is the War Museum, which provides a full history of war in the region and displays dedicated to each of the major participants.

Hall of Names
The cupola of the Hall of Names at Yad Vashem in Jerusalem is covered in the photographs and testimonies of victims of the Holocaust.

ISRAEL

YAD VASHEM HOLOCAUST HISTORY MUSEUM

LOCATION: The Holocaust Martyrs' and Heroes' Remembrance Authority, P.O.B. 3477, Jerusalem 91034

FEATURES: Holocaust History Museum; Yad Vashem Archives; Library; Hall of Names; major archive and library resources; exhibitions

VISITOR INFORMATION: Details vary according to department. See Website: www.yadvashem.org/

Yad Vashem is the world's largest institution devoted to Holocaust research. This site, covering 45 acres (18 hectares), features the Holocaust History Museum, the vast archives and library (including the central database for Shoah victims' names), and the powerful Hall of Names. The latter is a place of remembrance that not only contains 600 photographs and pages of testimony covering the ceiling, but also two million short biographies of Holocaust victims in repositories around the Hall. Yad Vashem is an active research establishment, and a visit to the Website is recommended for full details of their exhibitions.

EAST AND SOUTHEAST ASIA

Unfortunately, the turbulent politics of some East and Southeast Asian countries make travel through many of the remote jungle battlefields of World War II inadvisable, and touring with an organized group is strongly recommended. There are some accessible sites, however, that remind of the bitter cost of the Asian conflict.

THAILAND

BURMA RAILWAY SITES

LOCATION: Most accessible sites are around Kanchanaburi, Thailand

FEATURES: Museums; cemeteries; memorials; sections of original railway

VISITOR INFORMATION: Most travelers use Kanchanaburi as a base for exploring the railway sites. For cemetery information, see www.cwgc.org

The 258-mile (415 km) Burma Railway, built by the Japanese between Bangkok, Thailand, and Rangoon, Burma, cost the lives of more than 100,000 forced labor workers, including 16,000 Allied POWs. Travel to key sites is best restricted to those in Thailand. At Kanchanaburi is a CWGC cemetery containing 6,982 Allied POW war dead, with another cemetery just outside the city at Chung Kai with 1,750 burials. Also at Kanchanaburi are two museums relating to the building of the railway, the Thailand Burma Railway Museum, and the JEATH War Museum. Some 3 miles (5 km) from Kanchanaburi is the site of the notorious Kwai River bridge, although little of the original bridge remains, and there is also a museum there. The Hellfire Pass cutting, and its associated museum, is also another key destination for those exploring the history of the railway.

SINGAPORE

KRANJI WAR MEMORIAL

LOCATION: 9 Woodlands Road, Kranji, Singapore

FEATURES: Memorial and cemetery

VISITOR INFORMATION: Open: daily 7am–6pm; For cemetery information see www.cwgc.org

The Kranji War Memorial is found in Kranji, northern Singapore. The site was originally a Japanese military base and, later, a POW camp and a hospital. The memorial itself features 12 columns, on which are inscribed the names of 24,000 Allied soldiers killed in the fighting in Malaya, East Asia, and related Pacific waters (including naval and air force personnel), but whose bodies were never recovered. The war cemetery part of the complex features the graves of 4,458 Allied service personnel, with 850 of the graves containing unidentified soldiers. There is also a grave containing 400 unidentified civilians who died during the Battle of Singapore in 1942.

Bridge over the River Kwai
Although largely rebuilt at the end of World War II, the bridge that now stands over the River Kwai in Thailand still contains the original curved spans built by Allied Prisoners of War in 1943.

CHINA
~

MILITARY MUSEUM OF THE CHINESE PEOPLE'S REVOLUTION

LOCATION: 9 Fuxing Road, Haidian District, Beijing

FEATURES: World War II permanent exhibition

VISITOR INFORMATION: Open: 8:30am–4pm; Tel: +86 10-66817161; Website: www.china.org. cn/english/kuaixun/73574.htm

This extensive museum is devoted to the history of the Chinese revolutionary forces between 1929 and 1949. The entire second floor of the museum, however, focuses specifically on the Chinese struggle against the Japanese in 1937–45. Although the history it tells is highly politicized, it is well worth a visit to see some of the thousands of artifacts on display.

THE PACIFIC
~

The huge geographical extent and the isolated locations of the Pacific conflict make large numbers of the battle sites inaccessible except to the most adventurous travellers. There are, nonetheless, several exceptional battlefields and museums, plus some of the world's finest dive sites.

HAWAII
~

USS *ARIZONA* MEMORIAL

LOCATION: Arizona Memorial Place, Pearl Harbor

FEATURES: Memorial to victims of Japanese attack on Pearl Harbor

VISITOR INFORMATION: Open: 7:30am–5pm, closed on Thanksgiving Day, December 25, and January 1; Website: www.nps.gov/usar/

Dedicated in 1962, the USS *Arizona* Memorial remembers all those who died in the Japanese attack at Pearl Harbor on December 7, 1941. It is located specifically over the partly submerged remains of its namesake, near the mid section of the ship. The memorial features an entry and assembly room, a ceremonial room, and a shrine room that has the names of the *Arizona*'s dead engraved on the marble walls.

Pearl Harbor remembered
A lone trumpeter accompanies the raising of the flag at the USS *Arizona* memorial. The sunken battleship lies directly beneath.

PACIFIC DIVE SITES

Wartime wrecks in the Pacific attract a high number of both professional and recreational divers every year. The Pacific has an unusually large number of accessible wrecks, principally on account of the many sinkings and large numbers of aircraft shot down in shallow littoral waters. The site with the highest concentration of wrecks is Truk Lagoon in Micronesia, which has more than 40 Japanese vessels and several aircraft, most within easy dive range. Further major dive sites are found around the Solomon Islands, Philippine Islands (Coron Bay has 11 Japanese wrecks in its vicinity), and many other minor islands. Remember, however, that many of the wrecks are designated war graves, and there are often strict prohibitions about removing any materials from them.

GUAM
~

WAR IN THE PACIFIC NATIONAL HISTORICAL PARK

Location: Flights to Guam from Honolulu, Hawaii, or Toyko, Japan

Features: Memorials; numerous in situ emplacements and positions; visitor center

Visitor information: Consult the official Website before planning y our visit: www.nps.gov/wapa/

Various locations on Guam make up the National Historical Park, and there is much to see around the island. More than 100 military positions still remain in place, including bunkers, cave defenses, pill boxes, trench systems, and a Japanese communications center. There are also Japanese coastal defense and anti-aircraft guns at various points. At Asan Bay Overlook is the Memorial Wall that lists 16,142 Chamorro and Americans who died in the battles for Guam, while the Liberator's Memorial remembers those who were involved in the 1944 landings to retake the island from the Japanese. A visitor's center provides historical information and displays artifacts from the war.

JAPAN
~

OKINAWA BATTLEFIELD

Location: Sites across Okinawa Prefecture, Japan

Features: War memorials; battlefield sites; bunkers and emplacements; cave complexes; mass grave sites

Visitor information: See official travel information at www.pref.okinawa.jp/tour-e.html

As the location of one of the most intense battles of the entire war, the wartime legacies on Okinawa are numerous and visible. There are several museums dedicated in whole or in part to the 1945 battle, including the Battle of Okinawa Museum (located at Marine Corps Base Camp Kinser), the Himeyuri Monument and Museum, and the Peace Memorial Museum and the Okinawa Prefecture Museum. Many of the battle's most important locations are accessible, including the US landing beach to the north of Naha, Hacksaw Ridge, and the bunker and cave complexes that litter the island. The largest of these, such as the 44th Independent Mixed Brigade Cave, are best suited to guided tours. Some of the sites are particularly dark, such as the Kyan Memorial (Kyan Misaki Enchi), which is located at the point where dozens of civilian committed suicide from the cliffs, and the Konpaku No To mass grave site, holding the remains of some 35,000 dead.

1. US landing beaches
2. Battle of Okinawa Museum, Base Camp Kinser
3. Hacksaw Ridge
4. Sugar Loaf
5. Japanese naval underground headquarters
6. Buckner Memorial
7. Kyan memorial
8. Himeyuri Monument
9. Prefectural Peace Memorial Museum & park
10. 44th Independent Mixed Brigade Cave

HIROSHIMA PEACE MEMORIAL PARK

Location: 1-2 Nakajimama-cho, Naka-ku, Hiroshima City 730-0811

Features: Extensive memorial site devoted to the all aspects of the atomic bomb attack of August 6, 1945

Visitoration: Tel: +81 82-241-4004; Email: hpcf@pcf.city.hiroshima.jp; Website: www.pcf.city.hiroshima.jp/)

The extensive Hiroshima Peace Memorial Park is both absorbing and moving. It explores the horrific effects of the Hiroshima bombing and gives warning of the dangers of nuclear warfare. The Park is replete with monuments, memorials, information centers, exhibitions, and places of reflection, and also features a large three-floor museum. Everywhere are unsettling reminders that on August 6, 1945, the atom bomb exploded directly above this area. The former Industrial Promotion Hall (the A-Bomb Dome) is left standing in its shattered condition, and the Atomic Bomb Memorial Mound contains the ashes of about 70,000 people.

AUSTRALIA
~

AUSTRALIAN WAR MEMORIAL

Location: Treloar Crescent (top of ANZAC Parade), Campbell ACT 2612, Canberra

Features: Memorial; Remembrance Park; museum with extensive World War II exhibitions; Sculpture Garden; Research Center

Visitor information: For opening hours, details of exhibitions and an email contact form, see Website: www.awm.gov.au/visit/index.asp; Tel: (02) 6243 4211

The Australian War Memorial is Australia's national monument to its war dead. Although it was built in the aftermath of World War I, today it serves to remember Australian service personnel killed in all conflicts. The main areas of the Memorial are the Commemorative Area (which includes the Hall of Memory), ANZAC Parade, the Sculpture Garden, the Aircraft Hall (focusing heavily on the war in the Pacific), and the ANZAC Hall (which also contains a Lancaster bomber and a Messerschmitt Bf 109). A large World War II gallery is divided into five zones, together providing a chronological presentation of the conflict. The whole building is set in extensive and well-maintained parkland.

GLOSSARY

ACRONYMS AND ABBREVIATIONS

ASDIC Acronym for the Anglo-French Allied Submarine Detection Investigation Committee, applied to a method of detecting submarines by echo-location. Also referred to as sonar.

DAK Deutsches Afrika Korps

DUKW US 6 x 6 truck fitted with buoyancy tanks. Used to ferry stores from ships lying offshore to beachheads.

Gestapo (*Geheime Staatspolizei*) Secret state police, formed in 1933 by Hermann Göring to replace existing political police. From 1934 it came under the control of Heinrich Himmler, evolving into an independent executive arm of the Nazi Party, with sweeping powers to deal with anyone it considered an enemy of the Third Reich. In 1939 it merged with the criminal police to form the *Sicherheitspolizei* (State Security Police or "Sipo"), commanded by SS General Reinhard Heydrich.

GKO The Soviet State Defense Committee created in June 1941. Oversaw all political, military, and economic aspects of the war.

NKVD (*Narodny Kommissariat Vnutrennikh Del*) People's Commissariat for Domestic Affairs. Soviet secret service, headed by Lavrenti Beria, created in 1934 to control all espionage and counterintelligence activities. Its principal instrument was terror.

OKH (*Oberkommado des Heeres*) The German Army's designated high command for operations on the Eastern Front.

OKW (*Oberkommando der Wehrmacht*) The German armed forces high command which, in theory, was the supreme German joint services high command. It did not have control over the Navy and Luftwaffe high commands, OKM and OKL, whose chiefs reported directly to Hitler.

SAS Acronym for British Special Air Service, formed in Egypt in 1941. It came into its own following D-Day (June 6, 1944), coordinating Resistance activities and carrying out sabotage.

SOE The Special Operation Executive was established in July 1940 to gather intelligence, carry out sabotage, and support Resistance movements in Axis-occupied territories. The American equivalent, established in 1942 was the Office of Strategic Services (OSS).

SS The *Shutzstaffeln*, or Protection Squads, started as Hitler's personal bodyguard and evolved into the most powerful arm of the Nazi administration under Heinrich Himmler. The *Allgemeine* (General) SS staffed the concentration camps and imposed Nazi rule throughout Europe, while the *Waffen* (Armed) SS consisted of military formations dedicated to Hitler.

FORMATIONS AND UNITS

army Two or more corps.

army group Two or more armies.

battalion Usually consisted in the infantry of three to four companies and a heavy weapons company. The total strength was approximately 600–900 men. A tank battalion had three to four companies, with a total of some 50 tanks, while an artillery battalion usually had three batteries.

battery Four to eight artillery guns.

battle group An *ad hoc* German unit formed to meet a particular tactical situation and usually based on an infantry battalion or regiment with tanks and artillery.

brigade Three infantry or tank battalions.

company Usually three to four infantry or tank platoons.

corps A military formation made up of two to three divisions.

division This consisted of two to three infantry/tank regiments or brigades and three to four artillery battalions, a reconnaissance battalion and other supporting arms and army services. Its total strength was 10,000–18,000 men. Divisions were designated infantry ("rifle" in the Soviet Army) or armored ("tank" in the Soviet Army), but mountain and airborne divisions also existed, as well as other types.

platoon In the infantry usually made up of three rifle sections and a HQ section (total 35–40 men). A tank platoon consisted of three to four tanks.

regiment Usually consisted of three battalions, except in British and Commonwealth forces, where it equated to an armored or artillery battalion.

section/squad The smallest subunit in the infantry, consisting of roughly ten men. Squad was the US term.

squadron The equivalent of a tank company in British and Commonwealth forces.

troop The equivalent of a tank platoon in British and Commonwealth forces.

MILITARY ORGANIZATIONS

Kampfgruppe 100 An elite Luftwaffe formation established to exploit the X-Verfahren and Y-Verfahren blind bombing systems, both of which were used against British cities in the Blitz in 1940–41.

Luftwaffe The German air arm.

Ostheer The German Army in the East.

Red Army Front The Soviet high command's term for a distinct operational organization of armed forces. A "front" usually consisted of five to seven armies, with one or two tactical air armies and special armored and infantry formations in support. A "front" could total one million men.

Stavka *Stavka Glavnogo Komandovaniia*, the Red Army's Main Headquarters, formed in June 1941. The Stavka drew up battle plans and through its adjunct, the General Staff, directly organized the preparation and execution of strategic operations.

Wehrmacht The regular armed ground forces of the Third Reich.

WARSHIPS AND LANDING CRAFT

amphibious shipping Vessels designed to support landings from the sea, with the ability to either beach themselves or carry landing craft into which troops transfer when nearing the shore.

battlecruiser A heavily armed ship, built for speed. By 1939 the concept was obsolescent.

destroyer A high-speed, lightly armoured vessel armed with guns, torpedoes, and anti-submarine weapons.

escort carrier A converted merchant ship, it was designed to provide air cover for convoys. It carried 6–35 aircraft.

fleet carrier These large ships provided air protection for the fleet and the means of launching air strikes against opposing fleets. The usual complement of aircraft was 30–95.

heavy cruiser Smaller than a battleship, its main armament was usually 8-in (203-mm) guns. It fulfilled a variety of roles from fleet actions to shore bombardments.

light cruiser More lightly armed than heavy cruisers, normally having 6-in (152-mm) guns, light cruisers were used for reconnaissance and patrolling the sea lanes.

LCT Landing Craft, Tank. An amphibious vehicle designed to carry troops into combat.

LST Landing Ship, Tank. An assault ship designed to beach, and fitted with an opening bow, enabling tanks and other vehicles to drive ashore across a lowered ramp.

pocket battleship Designed by the Germans to circumvent the limit on warship size imposed by the Treaty of Versailles. Officially termed an "armored ship", but reclassified as a cruiser in 1940. Exceptionally fast, with six 11-in (280-mm) guns, its principal role was commerce raiding.

MILITARY TECHNOLOGY

Chain Home British early warning radar system established on south and east coasts of the United Kingdom by the outbreak of war in 1939.

Grand Slam bomb A 22,000-lb (10,000-kg) bomb designed by Barnes Wallis. On March 14, 1945 14 specially modified Lancaster bombers used these bombs to destroy the massive Bielefeld viaduct linking Hamm and Hanover.

Gee A British navigational and blind bombing system which entered service in 1941. First used in raid on Lübeck in March 1942, but thereafter effectively jammed by the Germans.

H2S Downward-looking radar fitted in a blister beneath British bomber aircraft, which gave a clearly defined differentiation between water and land. Radar-equipped German night-fighters were able to home in on H2S emissions, forcing the equipment to be used only in short bursts. The equivalent US system was designated H2X.

Hedgehog An antisubmarine weapon used in conjunction with ASDIC. Hedgehog was a multi-barrel spigot mortar, which threw out a pattern of up to 24 contact-fused bombs.

Knickebein (crooked leg) German blind bombing aid, based on intersecting radio beams, employed in the Blitz. It gave a bomber crew about a 50 percent chance of placing their bombs within 1,100-yd (1-km) diameter circle.

Oboe British radio blind bombing system in use from 1942 and installed in the Mosquito aircraft of Pathfinder squadrons.

Pathfinder Role was to find and mark targets with an increasingly sophisticated range of target markers. The first effective pathfinding unit was the Luftwaffe's Kampfgruppe 100, which used the X-Verfahren and Y-Verfahren to find and mark targets with incendiary bombs and flares for the following main force.

window Codename for lightweight strips of foil dropped from British bombers to form reflectors of German radar signals. The strips were 10 in (26.5 cm). They jammed radar by cluttering its tubes with thousands of false returns. The Germans developed a similar system codenamed "Duppel".

X-Verfahren A German blind bombing system used in the Blitz. A director beam was transmitted from the continent over a target in England. Three other beams, directed from other ground stations, intersected the director beam.

The distance between the two final intersecting beams gave an accurate indication of the aircraft's speed, enabling an onboard computer to calculate the optimum bomb release point.

CODES AND CODEBREAKING

Enigma The commercial name for the encoding machine used in World War II by the German armed forces and civilian organizations such as the railroad system. To the end of the war, the Germans believed that Enigma's encoded messages generated by its system of gears, electric wiring, and drums, were unbreakable.

Magic US codename for decryptions of the Japanese "Purple" cipher and their JN25b naval code. It played a key role in the Battle of Midway in June 1942.

Purple US codename for a Japanese diplomatic cipher system generated on a machine similar to the German Enigma typewriter. The cipher was broken on September 25, 1940, enabling the Americans to read all Japan's diplomatic traffic.

Ultra British codename for intercepts and decrypts of German Enigma coded signal traffic. The name Ultra indicates its security grading and importance. Ultra was arguably the outstanding British scientific-technical achievement of the war.

TERMINOLOGY AND TACTICS

beachhead The initial area captured as a result of an amphibious landing, which provided a base from which subsequent operations inland could be launched.

Big Wing In the Battle of Britain Air Vice-Marshal Trafford Leigh Mallory, commander of 12 Group, advocated that large formations of up to five Fighter Command squadrons be used to fight offensively rather than purely defensively.

bounce crossing Assault across a river, without pausing for preparation on the home bank.

bridgehead Territory seized on the enemy side of a river from which subsequent operations could be launched.

Festung (fortress) From 1944–45, as the Allies advanced in the west and east, Hitler designated cities under threat as "fortresses" to be held to the last man.

Happy Time The period between July and October 1940 in the Battle of the Atlantic when German U-boats sank 217 ships with the loss of only one submarine.

Lebensraum The "living space" in Soviet European Russia which Hitler intended to conquer and seed with German settlements, expelling the Slav population beyond a line drawn from Archangel to Astrakhan (the "A-A" line).

lodgement Bridgehead established in enemy territory by an amphibious landing operation or a river crossing.

open flank A position that is exposed on one side, enabling the enemy to pass round behind it.

rasputitsa The Russian spring and autumn rainy seasons which reduced the countryside to a morass and closed down offensive operations.

screen A lightly armed body of troops deployed in front of the main force to detect the enemy's approach and monitor his progress.

scuttle To sink a ship to prevent it from falling into enemy hands.

INDEX

Note: page numbers in **bold** indicate biographies and features; those in *italics* refer to illustrations. Battles and offensives are indicated by dates in parentheses.

ACKNOWLEDGMENTS

The publisher would like to thank the following for their kind permission to reproduce their photographs:

Firepower, The Royal Artillery Museum, Royal Artillery Historical Trust

Imperial War Museum, Duxford

ABBREVIATIONS KEY:
t=top, b=bottom, r=right, l=left, c=center, a=above, bg=background

akg: akg-images
BPK: Bildarchiv Preußischer Kulturbesitz, Berlin
DK: DK Images
Hulton/Getty Images: Hulton Archive/Getty Images
RHL: Robert Hunt Library
IWM: Imperial War Museum

Endpapers Hulton/Getty Images **1** DK/Andrew L Chernack, Springfields, Pennsylvania (cr), popperfoto.com (b); **2-3** Magnum/Soviet Group; **4-5** National Archives and Records Administration, USA (26-G-4122); **6-7** Corbis; **8-9** Topfoto.co.uk/ Keystone; **10-11** Topfoto.co.uk; **12-13** Corbis/ Bettmann; **13** Hulton/Getty Images (tr); **14** RHL; **15** Mary Evans Picture Library (br), Hulton/ Getty Images (cl), Topfoto.co.uk (bl); **16** Corbis/ Bettmann (bl), (t), Topfoto.co.uk (bc); **17** Corbis/ Bettmann (c), Hulton/Getty Images (tr), RHL (b); **18** Hulton/Getty Images (tl), (b), RHL (cr); **18-19** RHL; **19** Corbis Bettmann (b), RHL/US Library of Congress (cr); **20** Corbis/Bettmann (b); **20-21**Hulton/Getty Images; **21** Corbis/ Bettmann (br), Corbis/Underwood&Underwood (cr), RHL (cl); **22** Corbis/Bettmann (b), (t); **23** Corbis/ Hulton-Deutsch Collection (cl), Hulton/Getty Images (cr), TRH Pictures (tr); **24** RHL (t), TRH Pictures (cl); **25** Corbis/ Bettmann (bl), (br), Hulton/Getty Images (t); **26** Corbis/Bettmann (b), Corbis/Hulton-Deutsch Collection (t); **27** Novosti (London); **28** akg (t), Corbis/Bettmann (b); **29** RHL (c), Peter Newark's Military Pictures (br), popperfoto.com (bl); **30** Corbis/Bettmann (bl), (br), Mary Evans Picture Library (cl), Hulton/ Getty Images (tr); **31** RHL (br), Topfoto.co.uk (t); **32-33** Corbis/ Hulton-Deutsch Collection; **33** Corbis/Bettmann (cr), Peter Newark's Military Pictures (cl); **34-35** Getty Images/Time Life Pictures; **36-37** Corbis; **38-39** IWM (C1748); **40** popperfoto.com (bl); **41** Rex Features Roger-Viollet (cr); **41-42** Hulton/Getty Images; **42-43** Hulton/Getty Images (b); **43** Corbis/ Bettmann (br), Corbis/SYGMA (bl); **44** akg (bl), Corbis (t bg); **44-45** Getty Images /Time Life Pictures/ Hugo Jaeger; **45** Getty Images/Time Life Pictures/Hugo Jaeger (t); **46** DK/MOD Pattern Room, Nottingham (b), Getty Images/ Time Life Pictures (c); **46-47** Hulton/Getty Images; **48** Eden Camp Modern History Theme Museum, Malton (tr), Hulton/Getty Images (b), Rex Features/Roger Viollet (tl); **49** IWM (N65) (b), Peter Newark's Military Pictures (cr), Rex Features/ Roger Viollet (tc); **50** Bundesarchiv, Koblenz (183-LO4481) (tl), Mary Evans Picture Library; **51** akg (cl), Bundesarchiv, Koblenz (183-LO3926) (tr), Getty Images/Time Life Pictures/Carl Mydans/ Stringer (b); **52-53** BPK/Kriegsberichter Ege; **53** Peter Newark's Military Pictures (tr), popperfoto.com (b); **54** Hulton/Getty Images (br); **55** akg (b), Peter Newark's Military Pictures (cr), (t); **56** DK/IWM (c), Hulton/Getty Images (t), IWM (HU2287) (br), Getty Images/Time Life Pictures (bl); **57** Corbis (t), Getty Images/Time Life Pictures (b); **58** BPK; **58-59** Corbis/Hulton-Deutsch Collection; **59** IWM (CH13680) (t); **60** Aviation Picture Library/John Stroud Collection (c), BPK (t); **61** Aviation Picture Library/Austin J Brown (tl); Aviation Picture Library/Austin J Brown (br), Aviation Picture Library/John Stroud Collection (bl), BPK/Ruge (bg), The Art Archive (c), Hulton/Getty Images (tr), (cl); **62-63** IWM (HU36229); **63** Getty Images/Time Life Pictures (t); **64-65** popperfoto.com; **66** Peter Newark's Military Pictures (b); **66-67** IWM (HU44272); **67** Peter Newark's Military Pictures (cl), Rex Features (cr); **68** Hulton/Getty Images (bl), IWM (L103) (t); **68-69** popperfoto.com; **69** Peter Newark's Military Pictures (c), Rex Features/Roger-Viollet (t); **70** BPK/Lauros-Giraudon (t), DK/IWM (br), Hulton/Getty Images (b); **70-71** Corbis/ Bettmann; **72** akg (tl), BPK (cr), DK/IWM (crb), Hulton/Getty Images (tr); **72-73** IWM (IA 37578); **73** BPK (b), Hulton/Getty Images (t); **74-75** Ullstein Bild; **76-77** The Art Archive; **78** Bundesarchiv, Koblenz (101I-164-0349-20) (bl); **78-79** akg; **80** Mary Evans Picture Library (b); **80-81** akg; **81** akg (br), Hulton/Getty Images (tr); **82** akg (br), Corbis (c), DK/IWM (t), Courtesy of The Museum of World War II, Natick, Massachusetts (bl); **83** The Art Archive (tr), (cr), RHL (b); **84** Corbis/Hulton-Deutsch Collection; **85** DK/IWM (cr), Hulton/Getty Images (tr), Rex Features/Roger-Viollet (bg); **86** Corbis/Bettmann (b); **86-87** RHL; **87** akg (tr), The RHL (b); **88-89** akg; **89** Corbis (b), Corbis/Bettmann (t); **90** Corbis/Bettmann (l), RHL (tr); **91** Corbis/ Bettmann (b); **92** akg; **93** RHL (bl); **94** akg; **95** akg (b), RHL (tl); **96-97** Ullstein Bild/Wolff&Tritschler; **98** Corbis (b); **98-99** akg; **99** RHL (b); **100** akg (b), BPK (tl); **101** akg (b); **102** akg (tr), (b), Ullstein Bild (tl); **102-103** Novosti (London); **103** Novosti (London) (t); **104-105** Corbis; **106-107** akg; **108-109** Hulton/Getty Images; **109** Hulton/Getty Images (t); **110** Aviation Picture Library/John Stroud Collection; **111** Corbis/Bettmann (b), Corbis/Oscar White (t); **112** Corbis (tr), Peter Newark's Military Pictures (bl), Courtesy of The Museum of World War II, Natick, Massachusetts (br); **113** Corbis/Hulton-Deutsch Collection (bg); Museum of Flight (c), Hugh Cowin (br), IWM (HU 63027) (t), National Air and Space Museum, Smithsonian Institution (RAC 1074) (bc); **114** Associated Press AP/U.S. Defense (cl), Hulton/ Getty Images (b), Courtesy of the National Security Agency (t); **114-115** Hulton/Getty Images/Archive Photos; **115** Courtesy of The Museum of World War II, Natick, Massachusetts (cr); **116** BPK; **117** Hulton/Getty Images (t), IWM (HU2675) (b); **118** Bovington Tank Museum/Roland Groom (b); **119** Alamy Images (tl), Corbis/Bettmann (b), Hulton-Deutsch Collection (cr); **120** Corbis/ Bettmann (b), Courtesy of The Museum of World War II, Natick, Massachusetts (t); **121** RHL (b), (t), Courtesy of The Museum of World War II, Natick, Massachusetts (c); **122-123** The Art Archive/National Archives; **123** Corbis (t); **124-125** RHL; **125** akg (tr), The Art Archive/ National Archives Washington DC (cr), Peter Newark's Military Pictures (bl); **126** Corbis (t), RHL (b); **127** Corbis (t), RHL (b), Courtesy of The Museum of World War II, Natick, Massachusetts (cl); **128** Corbis (c bg), Corbis/Bettmann (cl), Corbis/Hulton-Deutsch Collection (tr); The Art Archive/National Archives Washington DC (ca); **129** BPK (br), Peter Newark's Military Pictures (bl); **130** Kobal Collection/United Artists (tl), Kobal Collection/Warner Bros (tr), (ca), Getty Images/Time Life Pictures (c), Corbis/John Springer Collection (cl) **130-131** Corbis/Hulton-Deutsch Collection; **131** akg (cr), Mary Evans Picture Library (cl), Kobal Collection/DFG (tr); Kobal Collection/Tobis (crb); **132** Ullstein Bild (t); **133** Novosti (London) (b), (t); **134** Ullstein Bild/ Grimm (b); **134-135** Novosti (London); **135** DK/ IWM (tr), (ca), (cra), Hulton/Getty Images (c), Ullstein Bild (b); **136** Bundesarchiv, Koblenz (Bild101/217/465/32A) (bl); **137** akg (b), Hulton/ Getty Images (t); **138** The Art Archive (b); **138-139** Novosti (London); **139** akg (tr), DK/IWM (c), IWM (NYP38410) (br); **140-141** Ullstein Bild; **142-143** Hulton/Getty Images; **144-145** Corbis; **146** Hulton/Getty Images (tl); **146-147** Getty Images/Time Life Pictures; **148** DK/IWM (bc), Hulton/Getty Images (t); **149** Bundesarchiv, Koblenz (101I-700-0256-38) (t), IWM (FLM1476) (b); **150** Hulton/Getty Images (t), Peter Newark's Military Pictures (b); **150-151** Ullstein Bild/AP; **151** akg (c), Peter Newark's Military Pictures (tr); **152** akg (tl), (cl), Mary Evans Picture Library (cr), Novosti (London) (crb), (b); **153** Hulton/Getty Images (t), IWM (FLM 1474 XF) (b); **154** Ullstein Bild; **155** Hulton/Getty Images (bl), Peter Newark's Military Pictures (cl), Novosti (London) (bg), Getty Images/Time Life Pictures (tr), (c); **156** akg (t); **157** akg (tr), (bl), akg/Michael Teller (t), Hulton/ Getty Images (tl), (br); **158-159** Corbis/Bettmann; **160** RHL (t); **161** The Art Archive/IWM (tr); **162** Alamy Images (t), TRH Pictures (b); **163** RHL (t); **164** akg (b), RHL (t); **165** Bovington Tank Museum (tl), (tr), (c), (cr), Hulton/Getty Images (br), popperfoto.com (bg); **166** RHL; **167** The Art Archive/Musée des 2 Guerres Mondiales Paris/ Dagli Orti, RHL (tl), (br); **168** The Art Archive/ National Archives Washington DC (b); **168-169** Hulton/Getty Images; **169** RHL (b), (tr bg); **170** akg (bl); **170-171** RHL; **171** Hulton/Getty Images (b), RHL (tr); **172-173** akg; **174** RHL; **175** Corbis/ Bettmann (br), Hulton/Getty Images (bl), RHL (t); **176** RHL (b); **177** Corbis/ Bettmann (b), Hulton/ Getty Images (t); **178** akg; **179** RHL (tl), (tr), Getty Images/Time Life Pictures (b); **180-181** Hulton/ Getty Images; **182-183** akg; **184-185** Hulton/ Getty Images; **185** Hulton/ Getty Images (b); **186** Nik Cornish/Stavka (t); **187** Hulton/Getty Images (bl), RHL (tr); **188** Nik Cornish/Stavka (tr), (b); **189** akg (b), Hulton/ Getty Images (t); **190** Bovington Tank Museum (c), DK/IWM (cl), Hulton/Getty Images (br), Ullstein Bild/Scherl-SV-Bilderdienst (bl), Ullstein Bild (bg), Ullstein Bild (t); **191** akg (b), Nik Cornish/Stavka (t); **192** akg (t); **193** akg (b), Corbis (cr), DK/IWM (cl); **194** akg (t), Hulton/ Getty Images (b); **195** RHL (cr), (b); **196-197** RHL (b); **197** RHL (b); **198** Hulton/Getty Images (t), RHL (br), National Archives and Records Administration, USA/US Army ((C-1710) 111-CPF Box 15 and 34) (bl); **199** Corbis/Bettmann (br), The Art Archive/ National Archives Washington DC (bl), RHL (t), popperfoto.com (cb); **200-201** RHL; **202** Hulton/ Getty Images (b), RHL (t); **203** akg (b), Corbis/ Bettmann (t); **204** RHL (c); **204-205** Corbis; **205** Corbis/Jeff Albertson (b), Hulton/Getty Images (tr), Courtesy of Norman Groom (cr), **206** Aviation Picture Library/Austin J Brown (br), aviation-images.com/John Dibbs (cl), DK/Gary Ombler (cra), Hulton/Getty Images (crb), RHL (bg), National Air and Space Museum, Smithsonian Institution (SI 71-338) (bl), National Air and Space Museum US Air Force, courtesy (SI 98-15407) (tl), TRH Pictures (tr); **207** akg (t), Hulton/Getty Images (b); **208** RHL (b); **208-209** Corbis; **209** RHL (b); **210** Corbis/Hulton-Deutsch Collection (b); **210-211** RHL, Bovington Tank Museum/Roland Groom (c), Corbis (t), TRH Pictures (b); **212** Corbis (bl), Corbis/Bettmann (c), (t); **212-213** RHL; **213** RHL/US National Archives (144) (t); **214-215** Corbis/Hulton-Deutsch Collection; **216-217** RHL; **218-219** akg; **219** popperfoto.com (t); **220** popperfoto.com (b); **220-221** Magnum/Robert Capa R; **221** Corbis/ Bettmann (b); **222-223** akg; **223** Hulton/Getty Images (t); **224** Hulton/Getty Images (t), IWM (BS266) (bl); **225** Bovington Tank Museum (cr), Hulton/Getty Images (b), RHL (t); **226** DK/ Courtesy of Firepower, The Royal Artillery Museum, Royal Artillery Historical Trust (cbl), DK/IWM (cr), Courtesy of The Museum of World War II, Natick, Massachusetts (t); **226-227** Hulton/Getty Images (bg); **227** akg (t); Hulton/Getty Images (b); **228** DK/HK Melton (clb), DK/IWM (tl), (cb), (br), DK/MOD Pattern Room, Nottingham (c), Hulton/Getty Images (bl), Rue des Archives (Photo Agency)/Jean Louis Mondange (tr); **229** akg; **230** Hulton/Getty Images (cr), RHL (tl), Getty Images/Time Life Pictures (b); **231** Corbis/Bettmann (tl); **232** The Art Archive (cr), Hulton/Getty Images (t); **233** Hulton/ Getty Images (t), RHL (b), Ullstein Bild/Frentz (tl); **234** Corbis/Bettmann (t); **234-235** TRH Pictures; **236-237** Hulton/Getty Images; **238-239** RHL; **239** RHL (bl), Ullstein Bild (tr), (c); **240** akg (br), RHL (bl); Getty Images/Time Life Pictures (t); **241** Hulton/Getty Images (b), RHL (t); **242-243** RHL; **243** RHL (b); **244** Nik Cornish/ Stavka (tl), (b); **244-245** Hulton/Getty Images (t); **245** Hulton/Getty Images (bl), (br); **246** akg; **247** akg (tl); **248** IWM (KY471207) (b), popperfoto.com (t); **249** RHL (b), Topfoto.co.uk (tr), (cr); **250** RHL (b); **251** Hulton/Getty Images (b), RHL (t); **252** IWM (NYF55918) (b); TRH Pictures (t); **253** RHL (tr), (b); **254** TRH Pictures (b); **254-255** RHL (t bg); **255** RHL/US National Archives (58) (b); **256-257** RHL; **258-259** Magnum/ Soviet Group; **260** Hulton/ Getty Images (b); **260-261** Corbis/Bettmann; **262** akg; **263** Mary Evans Picture Library/Meledin Collection (b); **264-265** akg (b); **265** akg (b), (t); **266** Ullstein Bild (cr); **266-267** akg (t); **267** akg (c), Bovington Tank Museum/Roland Groom (tr); **268** akg (bl), (t), DK/IWM (cl), (cr), Hulton/Getty Images (c), (br); **269** RHL (b), (t); **270** RHL (b), (t); **271** RHL (cl); **272** akg (t); Hulton/Getty Images (b); **273** Corbis/Hulton-Deutsch Collection; **274** akg (c), Corbis/Bettmann (t), RHL (cl); Hulton/Getty Images; **275** Hulton/Getty Images (br), RHL (bc); **276-277** akg (t); **278** akg (t); **278-279** Hulton/Getty Images; **279** DK/IWM (c), RHL (tl), (tc), (bg); **280-281** Hulton/Getty Images; **282** Corbis/Bettmann; **283** RHL (b); US National Archives (156)/Joe Rosenthal, Associated Press (t); **284** RHL (cl), Topfoto.co.uk (t); **284-285** US Naval Institute; **285** Associated Press AP (tr); **286** Corbis (t); **287** Corbis/Bettmann (cr), (t); **288** Corbis/Hulton-Deutsch Collection (b), The Mainichi Newspaper (t); **289** Australian War Memorial (P00406.027) (tr), Corbis/Bettmann (b); **290** Topfoto.co.uk/Novosti (b); **291** Corbis/ Yevgeny Khaldei (cr), Novosti (London) (t); **292** Associated Press AP (t); **292-293** RHL; **293** Corbis (tl), Corbis/Bettmann (tr), DK/ Bradbury Science Museum, Los Alamos (c); **294-295** Corbis; **296-297** RHL; **298** Topfoto.co.uk/ UN (bl); **298-299** Corbis/Bettmann; **300** Corbis/ Bettmann (t), Topfoto.co.uk (b); **301** RHL (b), Topfoto.co.uk (t); **302** Hulton/Getty Images; **303** Corbis/Bettmann (tl), Corbis/Dave Bartruff (b), RHL (tr); **304** Hulton/Getty Images (cr), Getty Images/Time Life Pictures (b), (t); **305** Hulton/ Getty Images (br), Topfoto.co.uk (bl); **306** Corbis/ Bettmann (cr), (t), Hulton/Getty Images (c); **307** Corbis/Bettmann (t), TRH Pictures (b); **308** Hulton/Getty Images (tl), Topfoto.co.uk (b); **309** Hulton/Getty Images (t), TRH Pictures (b); **310-311** Corbis/Bettmann.

Every effort has been made to gain permission from the relevant copyright holders to reproduce the extracts that appear in this book.

p.283: *US Marines on Iwo Jima*, The Dial Press, Inc., 1945, reprinted by Battery Press.
p.179: *The Old Breed*, Infantry Journal Press, 1949, reprinted by Battery Press. Used by permission of Mrs. Cecily McMillan.
p.208: Southern Cross account of the New Guinea Campaigns, translated by Doris Heath. Australia-Japan Research Project at the Australian War Memorial Research Center
p.211: US Marine Corps Reserve, Public Domain.
p.249: *The Road Past Mandalay*, Michael Joseph, 1961, reprinted by Orion Books. Used by permission of the Estate of John Masters.
p.289: Marine Corps Association, Quantico, Virginia, USA.
p.309: *All That Remains: The Palestinian Villages Occupies and Depopulated by Israel in 1948*, Walid Khalidi, Ed., 1992, Institute for Palestine Studies.

DORLING KINDERSLEY WOULD LIKE TO THANK:
Les Smith and the staff at Firepower, the Royal Artillery Museum. Natalie Finnigan and staff at the Imperial War Museum, Duxford. Alex Reay at Advanced Illustration. Neale Chamberlain, DK Picture Library. Helen Peters for the index. Neil Grant for additional contributions. Catherine Day for proofreading.

LOUISIANA STATE UNIVERSITY STUDIES

Social Science Series

Rudolf Heberle, Editor

———

Number Eight

The Pacific Lowlands of Colombia

———

LOUISIANA STATE UNIVERSITY STUDIES

Richard J. Russell, General Editor

The Louisiana State University Studies was established to
publish the results of research by faculty members, staff,
and graduate students of the University. Manuscripts of exceptional merit from sources other than aforementioned are
considered for publication provided they deal with subjects of
particular interest to Louisiana.

The Studies originally appeared as a unified series consisting of forty-two numbers, published between the years
1931 and 1941. In 1951 the Studies was reactivated, and is
now being issued in the following series: Social Sciences,
Humanities, Biological Sciences, and Physical Sciences.
Other series may be established as the need arises.

The Studies in each series will be numbered only serially,
without volume designation. All communications should be addressed to the Louisiana State University Press, Baton Rouge.

The Pacific Lowlands
of Colombia

A Negroid Area of
the American Tropics

by

Robert C. West

LOUISIANA STATE UNIVERSITY PRESS

Baton Rouge

Copyright 1957

By Louisiana State University Press

L. C. Card No. 57-12094

Manufactured in the United States of America

PREFACE

This monograph has two aims. One is to describe a little-known segment of the American humid tropics -- the Pacific lowlands of Colombia and adjacent areas; the other is to describe and interpret the material culture of a predominately Negroid population that has developed in this equatorial area during the past 300 years. Little is known of the role of the Negro and mulatto in the American tropics and of the processes through which the descendents of African slaves in the former Spanish colonies have developed their present cultural status. It is hoped that the data presented in this study may contribute to a better understanding of a Negroid area in the lowland tropics of America.

Since this is a report on the geography of an area, the section on the cultural milieu treats mainly of the material elements that can be visually observed in the field: racial characteristics, settlement patterns, house types, resources and techniques of producing food, clothing, transport, etc. Consideration of non-material elements, such as family and community organization, religion, government, and the like, has been largely excluded.

The study was made under the auspices of the Office of Naval Research, Washington, D. C. Field work was done in Colombia and Ecuador during the summers of 1951 through 1954. Most of the main rivers and much of the coastline of the Pacific lowlands were visited by dugout canoe. A few interfluves and headwater areas were reached by jungle trails. Local officials in the isolated river villages were always helpful in obtaining food, lodging, guides, and transport for my journeys. Without their aid the field work would have been impossible.

During the summer of 1953 Mr. John Cornish, a graduate student in geography, accompanied me in the field. The result of his work is contained in his M. A. thesis, "The Geography of the San Juan Delta," Louisiana State University, 1955. In the summer of 1955 Mr. John Vann, Jr., instructor in the Department of Geography, Louisiana State University, accompanied me to the lowlands, where he made a detailed geomorphological study of the Atrato Delta.

Archival and library work were undertaken in Bogotá and Popayán, Colombia; Quito, Ecuador; and Sevilla, Spain. For aid in consulting documentary material I extend thanks to Dr. Enrique Ortega Ricaurte, director of the Archivo Histórico Nacional de Colombia, Bogotá; Dr. José María Arboleda Llorente, director of the Archivo Central del Cauca, Popayán; Dr. Jorge A. Garcés, director of the

Archivo de la Ciudad, Quito; and Dr. José María de la Peña y Cámara, director of the Archivo General de Indias, Sevilla. I am grateful to Dr. Armand Dugand, director of the Instituto de Ciencias Naturales, Bogotá, for his help in identification of plant specimens.

R. C. W.

Baton Rouge

October, 1956

CONTENTS

MAPS

FIGURES

TABLES

Page

xi

PHOTOGRAPHS

CHAPTER I
THE PACIFIC LOWLANDS
CULTURE AREA

The area of study comprises the Pacific lowlands of western Colombia; the northern part of Esmeraldas province, northwestern Ecuador; and most of the province of Darién southeastern Panama -- a strip 600 miles long and from 50 to 100 miles wide. Excepting Darién, the area lies between the Pacific Ocean and the western versant of the Andean Cordillera Occidental. Within Colombia the lowlands constitute the entire department of Chocó, the northwestern edge of Antioquia, and the western portions of the departments of Valle, Cauca and Nariño (Map 1).

Although Europeans have exploited its mineral and forest wealth for 300 years, the Pacific lowlands are scientifically one of the least-known areas in Latin America. In 1825 Alexander von Humboldt wrote that "The geography of this part of America ... is in a most deplorable state ..."[1] More than a century later the American naturalist Robert Cushman Murphy stated that the coast of this lowland area was one of the world's most "rarely viewed and the least known in every geographical aspect."[2] During the mid-nineteenth century, however, the British Admiralty surveyed portions of the coast; the British charts were used as bases for the construction of maps of this coast recently published by the United States Hydrographic Office.[3] The last half of the nineteenth century saw the scientific exploration of small sections of the northern part of the Chocó by several expeditions sponsored by private individuals and the United States government to study possible trans-oceanic canal routes via the Atrato, Truandó, and Napipí rivers.[4] In the last few years American oil companies have made skeleton surveys based on line traverses along various rivers, and for the first time have produced fairly accurate maps of most of the lowland area.

The Pacific lowlands form but a small part of the American humid tropics, but in terms of both the physical and cultural milieux they are perhaps as representative as any moist equatorial area. Although low in elevation, the land surface varies

1

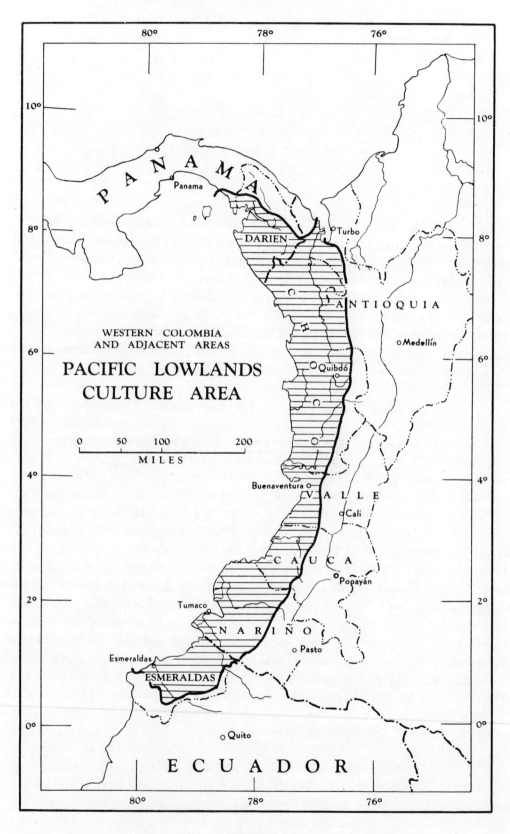

WESTERN COLOMBIA
AND ADJACENT AREAS

PACIFIC LOWLANDS
CULTURE AREA

0   50   100   200
MILES

MAP 1

from swampy plains to rough hill lands. At least two distinct types of shorelines occur along the Pacific margin: in the south, a low deltaic mangrove coast; in the north, a rugged mountainous coast.

If the area has any physical unity, it is to be found in the hot, humid climate and the vegetation cover of dense tropical rain forest. Colombia's Pacific lowlands are the rainiest part of the Americas, with average annual totals from 120 to over 400 inches. The area's position between 1° and 8° north of the equator gives it high year-round temperatures and contributes to an almost continuous relative humidity above 90 per cent. But the most striking physical feature of the area is the rain forest. Seen from the air the canopy formed by the giant trees resembles a sea of green, overlapping umbrellas, broken only by streams and occasional clearings. Hundreds of rivers, often in flood, run through the forest from hill and mountain slope to the sea. They are the pathways for human travel and their banks are the main sites of human habitation. The hot, steamy climate and the tropical rain forest, however, extend beyond the limits of the defined area of study; they continue southward along the lower slopes of the Andes in Ecuador to a point beyond the latitude of Guayaquil; to the north there is no break between the rain forest of Darién and that which follows the Caribbean shore of Panama into Costa Rica and Nicaragua.

The limits of the area of study, therefore, are determined more by cultural than by physical phenomena. Culturally the area is one chiefly because of its predominant Negroid population; because of a common way of life based mainly on subsistence agriculture, fishing, and primitive mining; and because of a similar historical development which differs from that of adjacent areas. Today nearly 80 per cent of the scant population of the lowlands is Negroid, with a large proportion of unmixed African blood. This area, then, may be considered one of the major Negroid areas of Latin America. Descendants of slaves whom the Spaniards introduced from Africa during the seventeenth and eighteenth centuries to work gold placers, the Negroes have pushed the few remaining forest Indians into the headwater areas of small streams. The Negroes have lost practically all of their African cultural heritage; they have adopted primarily Indian and secondarily European (Spanish) ways of life. Like the forest Indians, they are riverine people, living in small farming hamlets or isolated huts along the river banks, practicing Indian subsistence agriculture or placer mining, and travelling and fishing in Indian dugout canoes. The few whites and mestizos of the area are found mainly in the larger trading towns, mining camps, and seaports.

Like most cultural boundaries, the limits of the Pacific lowlands culture area are not static. Since colonial times the area of Negro settlement has been expanding in the lowlands. The last twenty-five years have seen the migration of large numbers of Negroes from the Colombian lowlands into Darién in Panama and into Esmeraldas in Ecuador. These movements are gradually extending the limits of the culture area southward and northward along the Pacific coast. The eastern boundary has been comparatively stagnant since the end of the colonial period. Negroes have had little inclination to move into the cool, foggy uplands of the westward-facing Andean slopes. Many, however, have recently migrated from the Pacific lowlands into the dry, mild Cauca Valley to work on sugar plantations and in such industrial centers as Cali. Recent encroachment of the white Antioqueño peasant farmer down the western slope of the Cordillera Occidental indicates that the eastern boundary may eventually retreat westward.

PART I -- THE PHYSICAL MILIEU

CHAPTER II
SURFACE CONFIGURATION

The surface of the Pacific slope of Colombia and adjacent areas can be classified into three simple landscape types: (1) the flattish plains of Recent alluvium, (2) hill lands of dissected Tertiary sediments, and (3) complex mountain areas composed of Mesozoic rocks (Map 2). The first two categories form the lowlands, the elevations of which rarely exceed 2,000 feet above sea level. In terms of the present study the surface configuration of the lowlands is paramount. The third category forms the highlands with elevations usually above 2,000 feet.

The Lowlands

The dominating geological feature of the Pacific side of northwestern South America is a long structural depression known as the Bolívar Geosyncline.[1] This structure forms the present interior basins and parts of the coastal plains of the lowlands. The main axis of the geosyncline extends for nearly 900 miles from the Gulf of Urabá, northwestern Colombia, southwestward to the Gulf of Guayaquil in southern Ecuador (Map 3). Nygren has shown that a branch or an earlier axis of the same structure continues northwestward into eastern Panama.[2]

The Bolívar Geosyncline formed a sea connection between the Atlantic and Pacific periodically from Eocene to late Pliocene. Today it forms a long series of lowland basins, each with its river systems. These lowland depressions are separated by weak anticlinal structures which lie athwart the geosyncline at right angles to its axis. The northern depression is drained by the northward-flowing Atrato River, which empties into the Gulf of Urabá.[3] To the south the San Juan drainage basin is separated from the upper Atrato by a low divide, 200 feet above the sea, caused by the Istmina anticline. In its lower portion the San Juan River is deflected westward to the Pacific Ocean by another structural high immediately north of Buenaventura. The

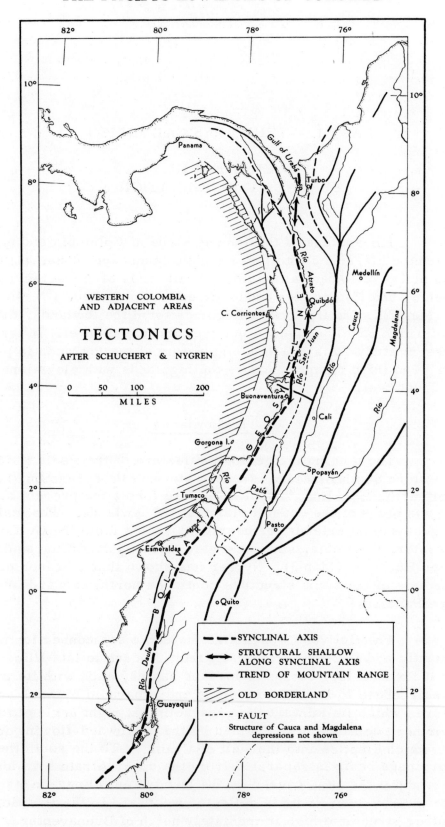

MAP 3

The hills that reflect the latter structure separate the San Juan Basin from the coastal lowlands which extend from Buenaventura southward to the vicinity of Guapi. The axis of the geosyncline corresponds to the present shoreline of these coastal lowlands, the western flank of the structure having been destroyed by submergence and erosion. Gorgona Island, twenty-five miles off-shore represents one of the few remnants of the western borderland along this stretch of the coast. South of Guapi lies the Tumaco high, expressed by low hills lying across the geosyncline; the Patía River has cut its course antecedently through the Tertiary rocks of this weak structure. The axis of the geosyncline continues southward near the coast, forming the lowlands of the Mira, Mataje, and Santiago river drainages. In Ecuador a slight rise in elevation separates the Santiago drainage from that of the Esmeraldas, and farther south another structural high divides the Esmeraldas-Quinindé system from the large basin of the Guayas-Daule river system, which forms the southernmost extent of the geosyncline.

According to Nygren,[4] 20,000 to 35,000 feet of Tertiary sediments comprise the maximum thickness of the Bolívar Geosyncline. Some parts of the depression, such as the Atrato Valley and along the coast south of Buenaventura, are covered by substantial amounts of Recent alluvium, ranging from a few feet to several hundred feet in thickness. Whether subsidence is continuing along the axis of the geosyncline is difficult to ascertain; probably sinking is taking place in the lower Atrato Valley, where large amounts of sediment are continually being deposited. Although a well-defined fault borders the southern half of the geosyncline near the foothills of the Cordillera Occidental, the only strong seismic activity that has occurred in the lowlands in the past 150 years has been centered on the ocean bottom, off the Pacific Coast.[5]

As indicated above, the lowlands formed by the Bolívar Geosyncline are characterized by two distinct physiographic areas: (1) flattish plains of Recent alluvium and (2) hill sections formed by recent stream dissection of Tertiary and Pleistocene sediments. The largest alluvial plains are within the Atrato River Basin and in the deltaic areas along the Pacific Coast from Cabo Corrientes southward to the Santiago River drainage in northwestern Ecuador. Bordering the alluvial plains are wide belts of rough, hilly country, having a local relief between 300 and 800 feet. Examples are the hills along the eastern and western flanks of the Atrato Basin and along the entire course of the San Juan River. The most extensive hill area, however, is that which extends for 200 miles from Buenaventura to Ecuador, forming a belt twenty to forty miles wide between the narrow fringe of coastal alluvium and the Cordillera Occidental.

The Alluvial Plains

Landforms of the alluvial plains are formed chiefly by stream deposition (Plates I and II). Natural levees, levee remnants, and backswamps are the most conspicuous forms in the river basins. Special forms occur along the low coastal fringe where mangrove swamps prevail and where wave and current action is dominant. Discussion of the coastal features is presented in Chapter IV.

The Atrato River Basin, 200 miles long, affords the best examples of alluvial morphology in the Pacific lowlands. From a narrow band of alluvium in its upper section, the flood plain widens to fifty miles in its lower or northern part. The Atrato is a relatively short river, only 175 miles long from its entrance into the basin near Quibdó to its mouths on the Gulf of Urabá. But it is a relatively wide and deep river, and thus must discharge an enormous quantity of water.[6] The anomaly of shortness and large discharge is a reflection of the excessive rainfall and runoff that occur in this part of the Pacific lowlands.

In spite of its large discharge the Atrato has built surprisingly small natural levees (vegas) along its banks. At no place along its course are the levees more than 100 yards wide.[7] They rise from three to four feet above the immediate backswamps to form the highest alluvial land near the river. Below Riosucio the levees become lower and narrower as the delta is approached. During much of the year, however, the river is in flood, and many sections of the levee are capped by water a few inches to three feet deep flowing into the backswamp. During low stages, however, the river banks rise abruptly four to eight feet above the water surface. Occasionally flooding waters cut crevasse channels (caños) through the levees in the upper course of the river; in the lower sections of the river, where flood waters cover the levees almost completely, crevassing is rarely evident. Tributaries of the Atrato have also built up small levees along their middle and lower courses. In many cases the tributary levees are higher and less subject to flood than those of the Atrato. For that reason, and because the levee material is composed of easily worked sand and silt, the tributary banks afford the best farm land within the Atrato Basin.[8]

The most distinctive feature of the Atrato lowland is the extensive swamps that lie back of the narrow levees. In this respect the Atrato is quite similar to the lower Sinú and Magdalena river

PLATE I. ALLUVIAL PLAINS:
LOWER ATRATO RIVER VALLEY

9

(U. S. Army Air Forces photo. Project 2-2016; 2-217L 5; 1943)

Aerial view of the lower Atrato River Valley, looking upstream. In the center is the first bifurcation of the river and the beginning of the Atrato Delta. The natural levees are indicated by bands of dark vegetation along the river banks. The backswamp, often containing <u>ciénagas</u>, is shown by the light tones. The dark tones along the Bahía de Colombia to the left represent mangrove. At the extreme right is the southeastern corner of the Ciénaga de Unguía, and in the center background, the Ciénagas de Tumaradó. In the right background are parts of the highlands that form the boundary between Colombia and Panama. The northern part of the Serranía de Baudó may be seen in the extreme center background.

Natural levee of the middle Atrato at Mercedes, ten miles downstream
from Quibdó; high river stage.

The deltaic plain at the first bifurcation of the lower Naya River,
south of Buenaventura. Fresh-water tidal flats and natural levees
border the channel.

basins of Colombia and the lower Amazon Basin of Brazil. In the
lower half of the Atrato Basin the swamps cover the greater part of
the lowlands and are occupied by numerous shallow lakes, or ciénagas.
Many lakes lie immediately behind the levee, occupying river flank depressions; others of ephemeral nature occur along the inner edge of the
swamp where rapid alluviation by streams rushing down the slope of
the flanking mountains seasonally obliterates old ciénagas and creates
new ones (Map 11). During the drier months of January, February
and March the shallower lakes dry out completely. The extensive
backswamps thus serve as a catchment area for most of the sediment
carried by the tributaries of the lower Atrato. Consequently a relatively
small amount of sediment enters the main stream. For this reason,
probably, the Atrato has failed to build either an extensive levee
system along its course or a large delta at its mouth. As indicated
above, most of the alluviation in the Atrato Basin occurs along the
inner edge of the backswamp, where tributary streams enter the lowlands. There low alluvial cones are built by a maze of anastomosing
channels, called regaderos. In the lower part of the basin many of the
tributaries, such as the Río Sucio, Salaquí, and Truandó, wander
through the swamps in ill-defined channels and enter the Atrato in a
complex system of distributaries, each having its set of low, narrow
natural levees.[9]

In contrast to those of the wide, swampy basin of the Atrato,
the alluvial plains of the San Juan drainage immediately to the south
are restricted in size, and along much of the river's course are absent.
The San Juan is even shorter than the Atrato, being 120 miles long;
but as it drains an area of excessive rainfall, its discharge is great.

Throughout most of its course the San Juan flows through
low hills composed of highly-dissected folded Tertiary sediments.
The river's course is thus largely controlled by structure; high,
steep banks occur where the river impinges against NW-SE trending
folds; pockets of alluvium, varying from several square miles to a
few acres in size, have been deposited along the river between the
confining hills. Extensive levees and backswamps are found mainly
in the extreme lower portion of the river near the delta. Upstream,
sizeable alluvial plains occur in the lower portions of left-bank tributaries, such as the ill-drained flats between the lower Condoto and
Tamaná rivers and those bordering the lower Cajón and Sipí rivers.
Such flats appear to be filled structural basins; their sediments contain the greater part of the alluvial gold and platinum now being
dredged in the upper San Juan area (Plate III).

Lacking an extensive backswamp area to serve as a

PLATE III. RIVER FLOOD PLAIN:
RIO SIPI, CHOCO

(U. S. Army Air Forces photo. Project 2-2016; 2-219L 17; 1943)

Aerial view of the Río Sipí, looking upstream. This river is one of
the larger gold-bearing left tributaries of the San Juan. Cultivated
plots are much in evidence on the flood plain, which is cut by many
meander scars. The rain forest blankets the areas between the rivers.
The tributary, lower left, is the Río Cajón. Portions of the Cordillera
Occidental are seen rising above the clouds in the far background.

catchment basin, the San Juan probably carries much more sediment than the Atrato, as evidenced by the former's larger delta area. Despite strong wave, tidal, and longshore current action along the Pacific Coast, the arcuate delta of the San Juan has an area three times that of the Atrato's bird's-foot delta.

The narrow coastal plain that extends southward from Cabo Corrientes into northwestern Ecuador is another significant area of recent alluviation in the Pacific lowlands. For most of its length this alluvial strip is only five to fifteen miles wide; but in the Patía area north of Tumaco it widens to thirty-five miles. In places, such as near Buenaventura and Tumaco, Tertiary material interrupts the continuity of the alluvium, and outcrops in low cliffs along the ocean front. A great number of streams, large and small, have been responsible for deposition of the coastal alluvium. Among the larger rivers are the Baudó, San Juan, Patía, and Mira, the latter two draining interior basins east of the western Andean range. The smaller rivers, twenty-five to fifty miles long and often less than ten miles apart, originate on the western slope of the low Serranía de Baudó in the north and, in the south, on the western slope of the Cordillera Occidental. Along its entire length the coastal alluvial fringe appears to have been formed by the coalescing of the deltas and lower plains of these rivers. The familiar low natural levees and backswamps are common forms throughout, while mangrove, backed by fresh-water swamp, predominates along the seaward margins. Occupied by the short Tapaje, Sanguianga and Satinga rivers, the wide alluvial plain immediately north of the lower Patía appears anomalous, and may be chiefly the result of former deposition by the larger Patía. The largest delta plain along the coast attributable to a single river is that of the Río Mira, which has deposited a body of alluvium thirty by fifteen miles.

The Hill Lands

Hills comprise by far the greater part of the Pacific lowlands of Colombia and adjacent areas (Plate IV). In Darién, southeastern Panama, the surface of the Chucunaque and upper Tuira basins is mainly hill land; either side of the Atrato Basin is bordered by hills, the wider belt being on the western side between the flood plain and the Serranía de Baudó; except for the small areas of alluvium as noted, a rough, hilly surface characterizes most of the drainage basins of the San Juan and Baudó rivers; south of Buenaventura a belt of low hills, twenty to forty miles wide, lies between the alluvial coastal fringe and the Cordillera Occidental, forming the greater part of the so-called Pacific Coastal Plain of Colombia; in northwestern Ecuador, save for

PLATE IV. HILL ZONE IN COASTAL PLAIN:
RIO YURAMANGUI AREA

(U. S. Army Air Forces photo. Project 2-2016; 2-211L 84; 1943)

Aerial view of the narrow coastal plain between the Cordillera Occidental and the Pacific Ocean south of Buenaventura, showing the belt of hills (dissected Tertiary sediments) back of the coast. The river in the center is the Yurumanguí; that in the right background, the upper Naya.

the alluvial pocket of the lower Santiago river system, hills abut upon the coast.

A product of recent stream dissection of Tertiary and Pleistocene sediments, the hill lands present a variety of landforms distinct from those of the alluvial plains. Although steep slopes prevail in most sections, along streams narrow alluvial Pleistocene terraces, with rolling to flattish surfaces, often occur. Such terraces are usually the sites of habitation and afford the better farm land within the hills. Along the east side of the upper Atrato a large, slightly dissected terrace of highly weathered reddish gravels rises fifty to seventy feet above the narrow flood plain. Traces of this terrace continue for more than twenty-five miles below Quibdo.[10] Less extensive terraces occur along parts of the San Juan, Patía, and Mira rivers. In their upper courses the streams have incised themselves deeply into the Tertiary sediments, in places creating sheer rock cliffs that rise fifty to a hundred feet above the water's edge. Fed by frequent downpours, small falls cascade over the cliffs into the rivers. Rapids and swift currents in the smaller streams make canoe navigation difficult in the hill areas. Slightly folded structures that trend north-south occur in many parts of the Tertiary hills south of Buenaventura.[11] These small structures in many cases appear to control the trellis stream pattern that characterizes the middle and upper sections of the main rivers in this area.

Away from the main rivers a maze of steep, jungle-covered slopes prevails, with local relief between 100 and 200 feet. Often, however, the bottoms of narrow stream valleys between the hills are filled with water-logged sediment and masses of rotting vegetation, forming long stringers of palm-covered swamp. Such alluvial fills result either from damming by log jams or by erosion of the small stream beds to base level.[12] Occasionally swampy spots (bajadas) occur in ill-drained inter-hill depressions. Interfluves are usually narrow, knife-like ridges which afford the best trail sites in the hills. Examples of flat to slightly rolling interfluves occur in the low divide between the headwaters of the Atrato and San Juan rivers. Similar topography is found farther south between the Mira and Caunapí rivers, where a gently sloping plain affords an excellent route for transport lines from the highlands to Tumaco on the coast. The entire Tumaco-lower Patía area appears to be one of recent uplift, evidenced by former sea cliffs now stranded one to two miles inland from the sea and by the steep box canyons incised by the Mira and Patía rivers in their middle courses; hanging tributaries on the Mira further emphasize the recency of uplift. Moreover, numerous flat-topped hills in the lower Patía area and the extensive elevated plain north of the Mira, mentioned above, suggest old erosion surfaces.

The Highlands

The lowlands of the Bolívar Geosyncline are bordered on the east by the high Andean Cordillera Occidental. On the west the geosyncline is flanked by mountains only in its northern part, where the Serranía de Baudó and its Panamanian extension, the Serranía de Sapo, border the Pacific Coast. Both the Baudó and the Andean cordillera have complex geologic structures and rock of mainly Mesozoic age (Map 4).

The Serranía de Baudó

The Serranía is a relatively low mountain range; generally, elevations above sea level range from 2,000 to 4,000 feet; the highest point (Alto de Buey) slightly exceeds 5,000 feet above the sea. Forming a complex en échelon pattern of folds and normal fault blocks, the main part of the serranía is composed chiefly of basic intrusives consisting of gabbros and diorites and sedimentary rocks of marine shales, limestones and sandstones.[13] From Punta Garachiné in Panama to Cabo Corrientes in Colombia the mountains rise abruptly from the sea, forming a steep, rocky coast of superb beauty, in contrast to the low, swampy coast to the south. South of Cabo Corrientes the Mesozoic rocks of the mountains are submerged beneath the sea. Remnants appear as Gorgona Island off the Patía-Sanguianga Delta and as hard-rock hills near the Esmeraldas coast in northwestern Ecuador. The low southern end of the Serranía de Baudó, however, belongs to the hill zone of dissected Tertiary sediments discussed above. These hills border the seacoast immediately west of Buenaventura Bay.

Steep, jungle-covered slopes characterize most of the surface of the serranía. In terms of form and appearance the major difference between the adjacent hills and the mountains is that of local relief, which in the latter area varies between 500 and 1,500 feet. In the lower section of the serranía, swampy creek bottoms alternate with knife ridges between steep slopes, but in the higher sections clear mountain streams flow in rocky channels. Various flat-topped elevations near the coast suggest former erosion surfaces and recency of uplift. Such surfaces are frequently encountered in the vicinity of Cupica and the upper Napipí River (Plate V). On the eastern flank of the serranía the contact of hard metamorphic rock of the mountains with the softer sediments of the hills is marked by a series of swift rapids along many of the eastward-flowing streams. The most celebrated of the rapids are the mile-long "falls" or saltos on the Truandó River.

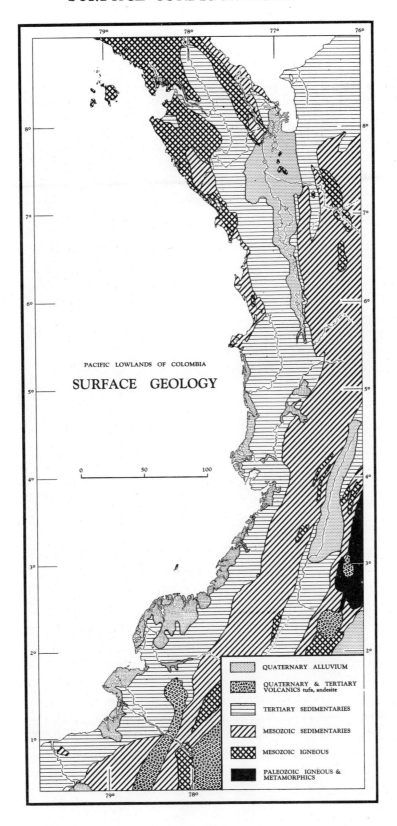

PACIFIC LOWLANDS OF COLOMBIA

SURFACE GEOLOGY

0   50   100

QUATERNARY ALLUVIUM

QUATERNARY & TERTIARY
VOLCANICS tufa, andesite

TERTIARY SEDIMENTARIES

MESOZOIC SEDIMENTARIES

MESOZOIC IGNEOUS

PALEOZOIC IGNEOUS &
METAMORPHICS

MAP 4

PLATE V. SERRANIA DE BAUDO: UPPER VALLE AREA

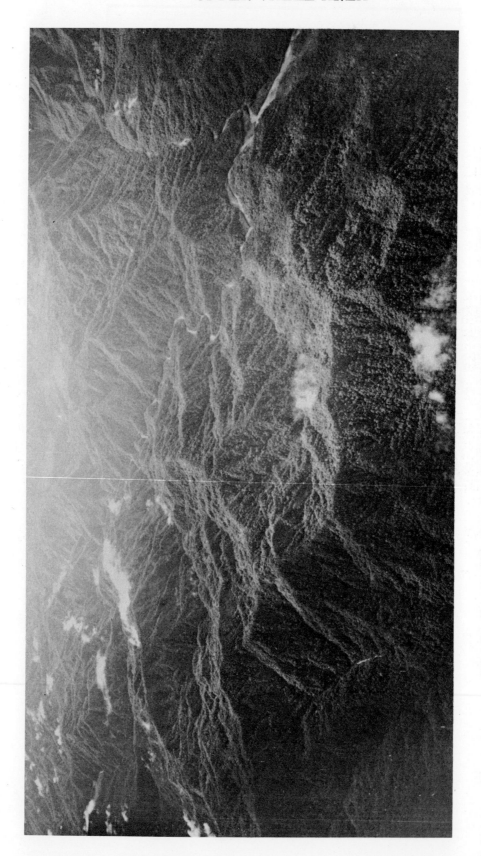

(U. S. Army Air Forces photo. Project 2-2016; 2-225R 23; 1943)

Aerial view of the western slope of the Serranía de Baudó, showing the extremely rough nature of the rain forest-covered area. Steep slopes, knife-like ridges and landslide scars are in evidence. Upland flats probably represent old erosion surfaces. The streams on the right are the headwaters of the Río Valle, southeast of Punta Solano.

The Cordillera Occidental

        The westernmost range of the Andean trident of Colombia, this cordillera rises above the Pacific lowlands to general elevations of 10,000 feet. The range is composed mainly of sedimentaries (shales and sandstones) and metamorphics (slate and quartzite) into which have been intruded numerous large batholiths, whose rocks are largely granodiorite, diorite, and gabbro. Near the Ecuadorian border volcanics such as andesites and tuffs prevail. When exposed by erosion, the batholiths are the main sources of gold and platinum found in the Tertiary gravels of the lowland basins.

        The western versant of the cordillera has undergone extreme dissection. Streams fed by excessive rainfall characteristic of windward slopes have cut deep canyons into the western wall; some of these canyons have been used since pre-Columbian times as corridors of travel from the lowlands eastward across the cordillera to the Cauca Valley. Faulting accompanied by stream dissection has broken the mountain crest into a series of isolated clusters of serrated peaks, some of which rise to 13,000 feet above the sea. Where the igneous rocks of the batholiths have been exposed at the summit of such peaks, tall domes of bare rock, called farallones, stand out like rows of lighthouses. In some cases faulting and dissection have isolated large masses from the range proper, such as Cerro Torrá (12,000 feet) in the upper San Juan drainage and Cerro Jarapeto (9,000 feet) in the middle Atrato drainage.

        In terms of the present study the hydrography and landforms of only the foothill sections of the cordillera are significant. Even there, owing to strong gradients, the stream beds are filled with rapids and falls; during heavy rains even small tributary streams become raging torrents, carrying large boulders into the beds of the main streams (Plate VI). Thus on most rivers in the foothill area, boat travel is possible only a few miles upstream. Along the courses of most of the larger streams there are occasional narrow alluvial terraces, but usually steep, forested slopes and sheer rock walls rise abruptly from the river's edge. During the drier parts of the year (February-March), point bars or playas of gravel and sand are exposed along the banks which can be used for foot travel.

        In both hill and mountain areas within the Pacific slope of Colombia the dense forest cover, with its intricate system of shallow roots, prevents serious erosion by slope wash or gullying by small streams. A more effective degradational agent is mass movement of saturated soil in the form of landslides and slumps on steep slopes.

PLATE VI. UPPER STREAM COURSES:
GUELMAMBI AND NAPI RIVERS.

Boulder-strewn <u>playa</u>, upper Guelmambí River, Barbacoas area.

Rapids and falls (<u>saltos</u>) on the upper Napi River at the mining village
of Belém, near the foothills of the Cordillera Occidental.

As in most areas of the humid tropics, scars of red clay, newly exposed by slides, are abundant in most parts of the high hills and adjacent mountains. Probably much of the load carried by lowland streams comes from the erosion of the loose material of landslides. Rapid growth of vegetation in the slide area, however, quickly heals such scars. The prevailing concavity of slope and the characteristic knife ridges of the area appear to be products of mass soil movement.

CHAPTER III
WEATHER AND CLIMATE

The weather and climate of the Pacific lowlands of Colombia embody most of the characteristics that the midlatitude dweller usually associates with the tropics: high, but not excessive, temperatures; moist, muggy air; and abundant rainfall. Although the temperature even in the interior lowland basins seldom exceeds 30° C. (90° F.), the air is highly most with relative humidity between 80 and 95 per cent. The most striking feature of the weather and climate however, is the excessive precipitation. The Pacific lowland area of Colombia is probably the wettest section of the New World, with annual rainfall between 200 and 400 inches. In most sections heavy rains occur almost daily throughout the year, but there is a slackening of precipitation in some periods, especially in February and March. In the north toward Panama and the Caribbean Sea and in the south near the Ecuadorian border a definite dry season begins to appear, together with a considerable decrease in total rainfall.

Owing to the paucity and unreliability of weather data, even a gross description of the climate of the Pacific lowlands is difficult. Map 5 indicates that of the twenty-five lowland weather stations only one -- Andagoya -- has a record of more than twenty years; the majority of the stations have records of less than ten years. Moreover, most of the stations have been operated sporadically by the Colombian government with inadequate equipment and untrained personnel; published data derived from these stations are usually fragmentary and unreliable. The most dependable weather data come from the records kept at the camps of the American mining companies (e.g. Andagoya, Mongón) and at landing fields (e.g., Tumaco).[1]

Temperature

Air temperatures as recorded by weather stations in the Pacific lowlands are typical of most humid equatorial areas. The monthly means show a remarkably low seasonal range, usually less than one degree Centigrade (1.8° F.) for most stations (Figures 1 and 2). Monthly mean temperatures rarely exceed 28° C. (82° F.);

22

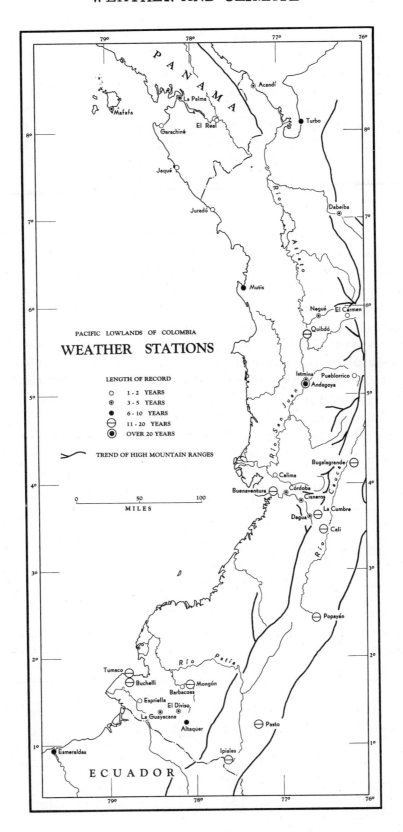

PACIFIC LOWLANDS OF COLOMBIA
WEATHER STATIONS

LENGTH OF RECORD

○ 1 - 2 YEARS
◉ 3 - 5 YEARS
● 6 - 10 YEARS
⊖ 11 - 20 YEARS
◎ OVER 20 YEARS

TREND OF HIGH MOUNTAIN RANGES

0   50   100
MILES

MAP 5

average monthly maxima seldom pass 31.5° C. (88.7° F.); and average minima infrequently go below 22° C. (71° F.). The hottest area of the lowlands corresponds to the Atrato-San Juan depression, where most stations record an annual mean of over 27° C. (80.6° F.). As would be expected, due to oceanic influence less extreme temperatures prevail along the coast. For example, the port of Tumaco has an annual mean of 25.9° C. (78.6° F.), whereas Andagoya in the upper San Juan Basin records 27.3° C. (81° F.). With increase of altitude along the western slopes of the Cordillera Occidental, temperatures naturally decrease.

The figures given above, being averages, are largely fictitious and do not indicate the actual temperature extremes, which are the critical ones for plant growth and human comfort. Such data can be obtained only from the daily weather records. For Andagoya, a typical interior station, maximum daily temperatures over 35° C. (95° F.) are relatively infrequent, occurring on 173 days during a seven-year period (1945-1951), a frequency of only 7 per cent. During the same period temperatures of 38° C. (100.4° F.) or over were recorded on four days only, the highest temperature being 38.5° C. (101° F.). The extreme minimum temperature recorded at Andagoya during the same seven-year period was 16.7° C. (62° F.), which occurred in the early morning hours. Only 94 days in seven years had temperatures lower than 21° C. (70° F.).[2] Table 1 indicates the absolute minima and maxima recorded at various lowland stations, according to data published by the Colombian government.

Table 1

Minimum and Maximum Temperatures from Selected Stations.*

Station	Absolute Maximum	Absolute Minimum
Quibdó (interior)	41° C. (105.8° F.)	15° C. (59° F.)
Tumaco (coastal)	32° C. (89.6° F.)	19.6° C. (63.4° F.)
La Guayacana (interior)	40° C. (104.0° F.)	19.0° C. (66.2° F.)

Cloud cover is instrumental in preventing excessively high temperatures in the lowlands. Except in the drier portions of the year (February-March) the sky is usually completely overcast by three or four o'clock in the afternoon. The first half of the morning is also heavily overcast, the sun breaking through around ten or eleven. During the months of heavy rain the sun may not appear through the cloud cover for periods of several days.

* From Anuario Meteorológico, 1934-1947 (Bogotá).

The well-known phrase "night is the 'winter' of the tropics" is particularly applicable to the Pacific lowlands of Colombia. As in other equatorial areas, the diurnal temperature range far exceeds the seasonal one. At Andagoya daily temperatures reach their maxima between two and three in the afternoon (usually around 32° C. [89.6° F.]), while minimum temperatures come around five o'clock in the morning (commonly 23° C. [73.4° F.]), making a diurnal range of about 9° C. (16.2° F.). In the equatorial areas such temperature variations, seemingly small to a mid-latitude dweller, are acutely sensible to the body. A light blanket is always a welcome comfort to the sleeper during the early morning hours in the Pacific lowlands.

Relative Humidity

One of the first aspects of the lowland climate that strikes the visitor is the depressingly excessive humidity of the air. Dampness prevails even on clear, sunny days. The heavily moist, still air combined with the relatively high midday temperatures, has a depressing effect, particularly on the newcomer. Table 2 gives daily relative humidity figures of a selected month for Andagoya.[3] Percentages are highest in the morning hours, owing to relatively low temperatures; with rising temperatures toward noon the relative humidity decreases and again rises in the late afternoon with increasing cloud cover.

Precipitation

The annual rainfall of the Pacific lowlands of Colombia is not only the highest in the Americas; it probably exceeds that of any other equatorial area in the world.[4] A belt 50 to 100 miles wide and 500 miles long within this lowland zone receives an average annual rainfall exceeding 4,000 mm. (150 inches) (Map 6). A small area with yearly rainfall over 10,000 mm. (400 inches) lies in the upper Atrato Basin, where the station of Quibdó records an average of 10,545.7 mm. (415 inches) annually.[5] This area forms part of a discontinuous belt of high yearly rainfall (over 7,500 mm., or 250 inches) that extends for more than 300 miles along the lower slopes of the Cordillera Occidental. Above 4,000 feet on the western, or windward, slope of the cordillera precipitation decreases. In deep canyons eroded into this slope rain-shadow situations create spots of relative dryness. The deep valley floor in the vicinity of Cisneros (average annual rainfall, 1500 mm., or 60 inches) on the Cali-Buenaventura route represents one of the most pronounced of these dry spots.[6] Others are the upper Garrapatas Valley in the vicinity of El Cairo; the headwaters of the San Juan near Pueblorrico; the headwaters of the Atrato around El Carmen; and the valley of Urrao in the upper Murrí-Penderisco drainage. East of the crest of the cordillera lie the relatively dry basins of the upper Cauca, the upper Patía, and of Pasto -- a world apart from the coastal lowlands.

Table 2

Relative Humidity (dry and wet bulb readings)
Andagoya, Chocó, January, 1953*

Day	7 A M	12 noon	4 PM
1	97%	85%	89
2	92	71	86
3	90	73	87
4	98	91	81
5	91	65	87
6	96	74	77
7	95	87	79
8	95	78	82
9	95	85	80
10	93	86	90
11	98	90	88
12	95	84	86
13	97	87	72
14	97	71	72
15	93	71	80
16	95	79	84
17	84	71	93
18	91	86	84
19	91	66	66
20	95	85	82
21	96	74	81
22	97	67	80
23	90	72	62
24	95	70	74
25	98	92	91
26	98	92	91
27	95	92	93
28	95	75	77
29	93	78	83
30	90	78	79
31	95	89	86
Daily Average	94.2	79.5	82.0

* Data from the Cía. Minera Chocó Pacífico, Andagoya, Chocó. Percentages are highest in the morning hours, owing to relatively low temperatures; with rising temperatures toward noon the relative humidity decreases and again rises in the late afternoon with increasing cloud cover.

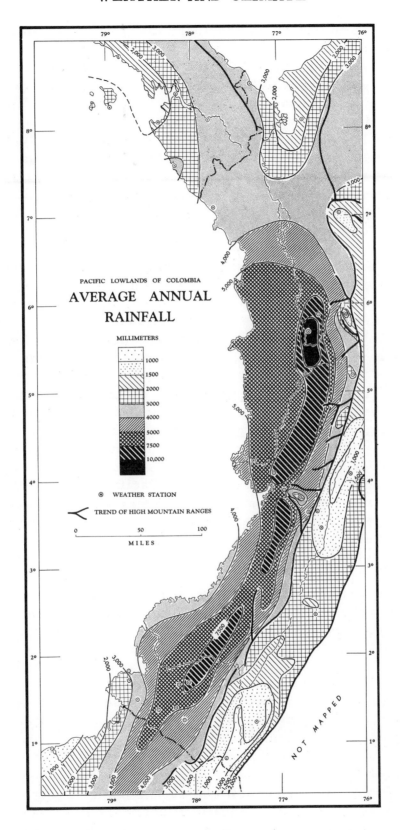

PACIFIC LOWLANDS OF COLOMBIA

AVERAGE ANNUAL
RAINFALL

MILLIMETERS

1000
1500
2000
3000
4000
5000
7500
10,000

⊙ WEATHER STATION

✕ TREND OF HIGH MOUNTAIN RANGES

0   50   100

MILES

MAP 6

The northern and southern margins of the lowlands are characterized by decreasing precipitation. In the north the lower Atrato Valley comes under the influence of the drying Trade Winds from January through April; Turbo, for example, receives yearly only 1,660 mm. (65 inches) of rainfall. Moreover, the Pacific coast of Darién reflects its winter dry season in the decreasing precipitation northward. In the south the coastal area southwest of Tumaco is frequently influenced by cool off-shore waters and diverging air; Esmeraldas in northwestern Ecuador receives only slightly more than 800 mm. (31.5 inches) annually. According to reports of local inhabitants, throughout the coastal area rainfall decreases from the wet belt of the interior toward the seashore. [7]

The averages cited above hide the great variability in amount of rain that actually falls in a given month or year. In terms of actual amounts, rather than percentages, there appear to occur greater rainfall variations in humid equatorial areas than in desert regions. Table 3 presents maximum and minimum rainfall figures for the more reliable stations within the coastal lowlands of Colombia.

The high precipitation of the central portion of the lowlands appears to be associated with the presence of the zone of equatorial convergence, which extends across the Pacific Ocean at 5º N. latitude to Southeast Asia. Being a zone of convergence with moist, unstable air rising over the warm equatorial counter current, the entire zone is one of heavy oceanic rainfall. [8] The Pacific lowlands of Colombia lie at the eastern end of this zone and form its rainiest section; the Caroline Islands, with less annual rainfall (125-180 inches) lie near the western end. The greater precipitation of the Colombian section is due probably to local conditions, among which the most significant is the highly heated land surface (leading to strong convection) combined with orographic rise of air up the lower slopes of the western cordillera. The presence of strong frontal action within the zone of equatorial convergence, suggested by Garbell and others, [9] has not been proved, and has been questioned by Reihl. [10]

Except in the northern and southern extremities of the Pacific lowlands, a definite dry season is absent, no station in the central part of the area recording an average monthly rainfall of less than 130 mm. (5.1 inches). Accordingly, most of the area falls under Koeppen's Af classification. (Aw conditions appear in the north around the Gulf of Urabá and the Gulf of San Miguel in Panamá; in the south the coast of western Esmeraldas is also Aw). Two periods of minimum rainfall, however, usually prevail, although they are hardly discernible in the data of some stations (e.g., Andagoya) (Figures 1 and 2). In the area north of 2º N. latitude the less rainy of the two minimum

Table 3

Variability of Rainfall

Selected Stations Pacific Lowlands of Colombia*

Mongón, Nariño

	Minimum recorded	Maximum recorded
Rainiest month (May)	21 in. (1950)	57 in. (1952)
Driest Month (Nov.)	10 in. (1949)	30 in. (1951)
Annual total	272 in. (1946)	392 in. (1951)

Quibdó, Chocó

Rainiest month (May)	242 mm. (1951)	3,090 mm. (1940)
Driest Month (Feb.)	139 mm. (1932)	658 mm. (1950)
Annual total	5,026 mm. (1951)	15,058 mm. (1939)

Andagoya, Chocó

Rainiest month (May)	370 mm. (1945)	1,013 mm. (1938)
Driest month (Feb.)	242 mm. (1939)	837 mm. (1938)
Annual total	5,350 mm. (1951)	8,341 mm. (1950)

Tumaco, Nariño

Rainiest month (May)	183 mm. (1937)	520 mm. (1940)
Driest month (Nov.)	31 mm. (1937)	509 mm. (1940)
Annual total	2,260 mm. (1946)	3,888 mm. (1940)

*From sources specified in footnote 1, above.

periods, called verano, comes in February and March; the second, called the veranillo, if does come, occurs in July and August.[11] South of 2° N. the two minimum seasons are reversed, indicating the influence of the southern hemisphere climatic regime. Beginning around Tumaco the least rainy period corresponds to the months of September, October and November, while the second minimum period comes in February and March. At Esmeraldas (0° 57' N. latitude) a definite dry season begins in August and ends in the last days of November (Maps 7-10).

The large annual totals as well as the slight seasonal variations in precipitation are reflected in daily frequency of rainfall (Figure 3). Andagoya has an average of 297 rainy days per year;

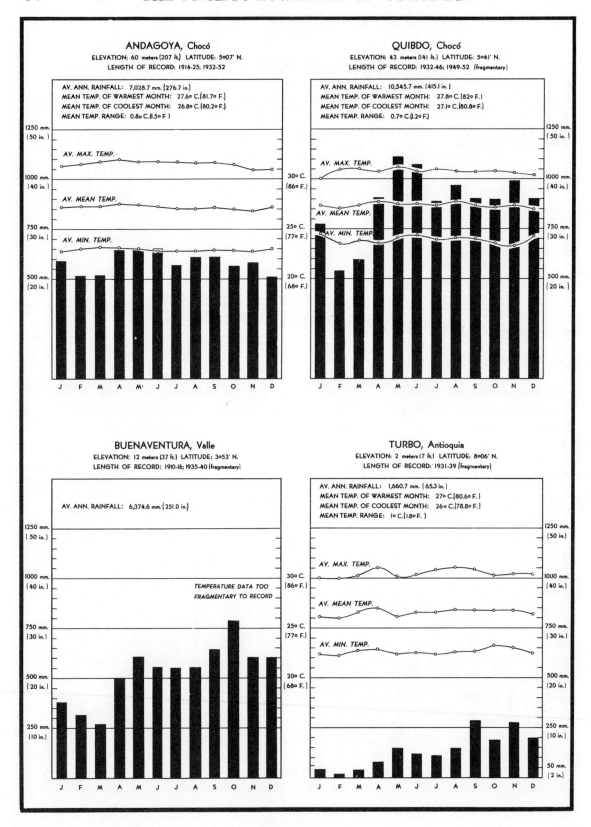

FIGURE 1

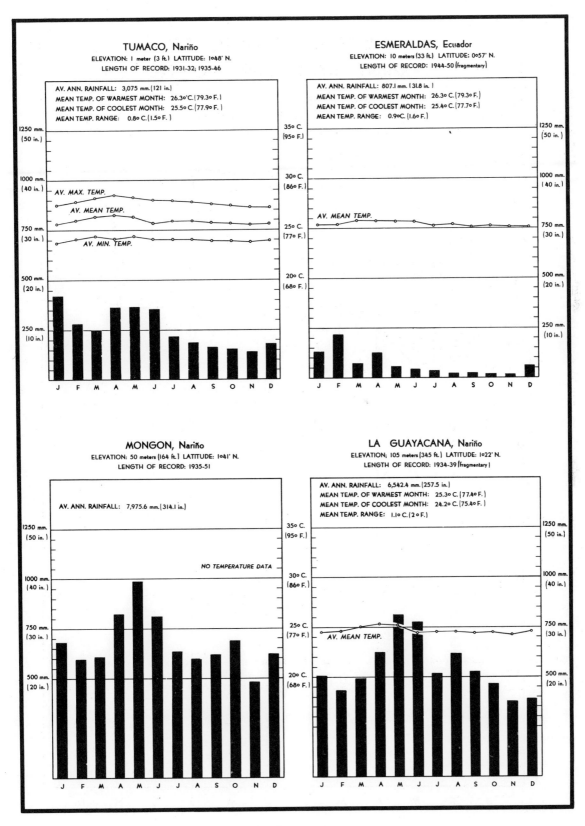

FIGURE 2

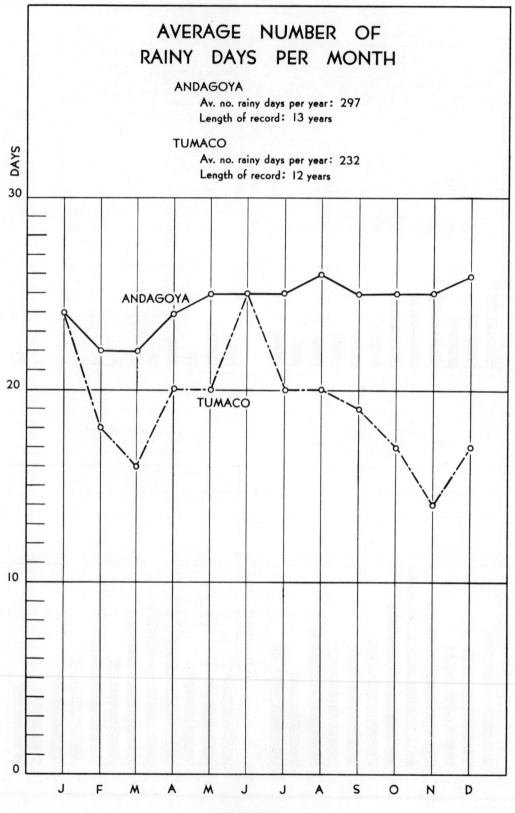

FIGURE 3

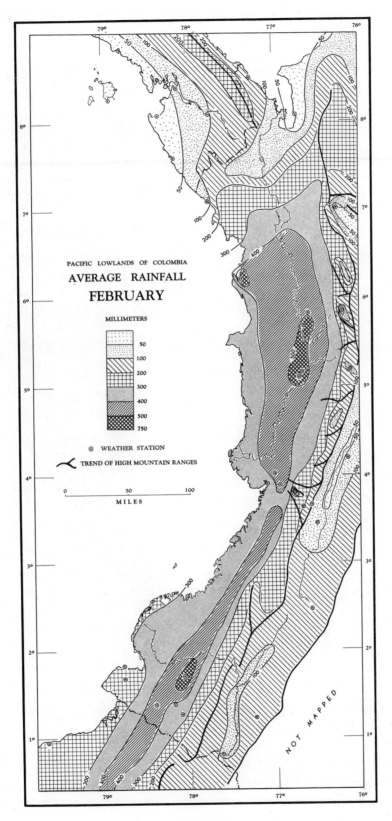

PACIFIC LOWLANDS OF COLOMBIA
AVERAGE RAINFALL
FEBRUARY

MILLIMETERS

50
100
200
300
400
500
750

⊙ WEATHER STATION
TREND OF HIGH MOUNTAIN RANGES

0   50   100
MILES

MAP 7

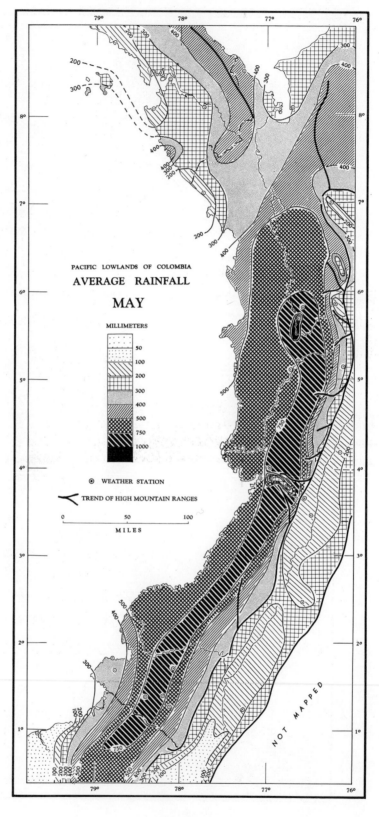

PACIFIC LOWLANDS OF COLOMBIA
AVERAGE RAINFALL
MAY

MILLIMETERS

	50
	100
	200
	300
	400
	500
	750
	1000

⊙ WEATHER STATION

⟨ TREND OF HIGH MOUNTAIN RANGES

0   50   100

MILES

MAP 8

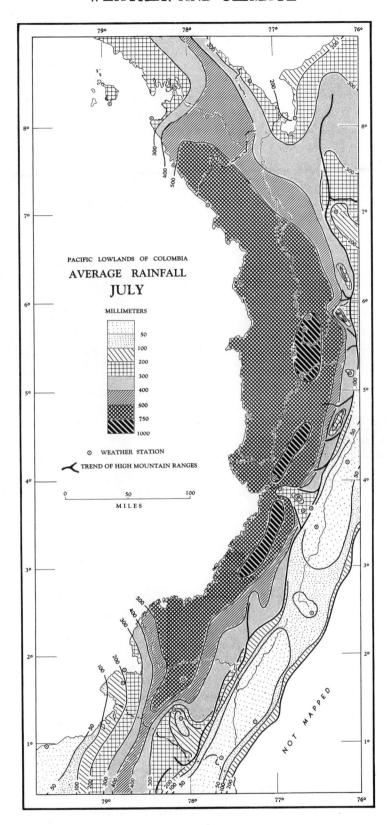

PACIFIC LOWLANDS OF COLOMBIA

AVERAGE RAINFALL
JULY

MILLIMETERS

50
100
200
300
400
500
750
1000

⊙ WEATHER STATION

TREND OF HIGH MOUNTAIN RANGES

0   50   100
MILES

MAP 9

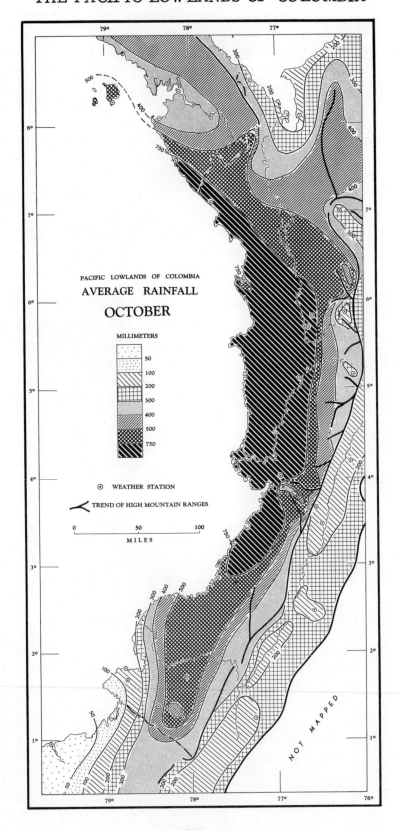

MAP 10

Tumaco has 232. As would be expected, at both stations the months with the least number of rainy days correspond to the drier periods. The popular local statement, "it rains every day in the Chocó", has, of course, no factual basis; however, periods of one week without rain are rare. In Andagoya, within a twenty-one year period, seven consecutive days without rain were recorded three times.[12] According to local inhabitants, longer periods of complete drought occur more frequently along the coast than in the interior of the lowlands. Stories of droughts of thirty days or more in length are common. In February, 1949, the area around Guapi is said to have experienced a rainless period of three weeks. This drought caused a severe shortage of drinking water, as the river near the town was invaded by sea water flowing upstream with the tide against the reduced current; in the surrounding forest, trees and shrubs began to shed their dessicated leaves, and the maize crop was completely ruined.[13]

In terms of rainfall, weather in equatorial areas is characterized more by variety than by the monotony that is often pictured for the tropics. Nevertheless, in the Pacific lowlands of Colombia there is a semblance of a daily rhythm in rainfall and cloud cover. Although some rain may fall at any time during the 24-hour period, most precipitation occurs at night and usually continues into the morning hours. At midday clear or partly-clouded skies usually prevail, and bright sunlight gives a brilliant aspect to the green, forested landscape.

There appears to exist a temporal progression in diurnal periodicity of rainfall from mountain slope westward to the sea. The western slope of the cordillera is almost continually covered with cloud and fog, with heavy downpours in the early afternoon and light rains continuing through the night. On the lower slopes and in the interior lowlands the intense heat of mid-afternoon gives rise to strong convection and the formation of large cumulus clouds; by six or seven in the evening heavy rain, accompanied by lightning and thunder, begins to fall; light rain and occasional heavy showers continue through the night, ending in light drizzles falling from a dull, overcast sky between seven and eight in the morning. Along the coast rains are almost completely nocturnal, often beginning as heavy downpours around midnight or the early morning hours and ending in drizzles about nine o'clock. At that time from the shore one can observe the heavy rains still in progress at sea until the clouds dissipate completely around midday.

Nocturnal precipitation appears to be common in many equatorial areas, both over oceans and land surfaces. At Andagoya in the Chocó approximately 90 per cent of the rainy days are characterized by precipitation at night.[14] Bernard cites the nocturnal maximum as characteristic of several stations in the interior of the Congo Basin.[15] Night rains in the equatorial areas of the Pacific are well known. The rains of the late afternoon are undoubtedly the result of thermally induced convection (heating from below), while the continuance of heavy precipitation throughout the night may be due to cooling aloft through thermal radiation, inducing continuing instability. The night rains and the usually clear, brilliant midday periods are one of the notable aspects of the weather of the Pacific lowlands. Those who have taken the night flight from Lima to Panama will scarcely forget the magnificent lightning display and the rough, turbulent air as the plane passes at 15,000 feet over the west coast of Colombia. Again, standing on a hilltop near Popayán on a clear, cool night, one can witness the continual lightning flashes that permeate the thick cumulus cover lying over the coastal lowlands to the west.

The thunderstorm rainfall of the Pacific lowlands is intense. Although no data on hourly maxima are available for any station in the area, officials at the Andagoya mining camp estimate that rains of two to three inches per hour are not uncommon. Records at Andagoya indicate that maximum rainfall within 24-hour periods range between five and seven inches, with an absolute maximum of 10.37 inches (Feb. 17, 1938). These figures, however, are exceeded in other parts of the world, such as the southeastern United States and southeast Asia, where thunderstorms and hurricanes induce remarkably intense rains.[16]

Aside from thunderstorms few other storm types have been recorded in the Pacific lowlands. The infrequent periods of two to three days with continuous light rains in various parts of the lowlands suggest weak frontal action. Such storms are most common along the rocky coast north of Cabo Corrientes, but may be the result of adiabatic cooling of unstable oceanic air as it rises over the coastal range.

Another remarkable storm type, called locally the choco-sana, occurs frequently at the lower end of the Atrato Basin and in the Gulf of Urabá from June to October. The storm usually comes up between six in the evening and midnight; it is preceded by light northerly winds from the sea; there is a sudden windshift from north to south accompanied by a sharp squall line of dark, rolling scud, which is followed by strong gusts of wind and heavy rain. The storm lasts between one-half to one hour. Winds sometimes approach hurricane force, and it is said that as much as four inches of rain may fall in one storm. The center of origin appears to be in the vicinity of Ríosucio, 100 miles inland from the Gulf of Urabá. There, high heating in the

late afternoon creates an intense local low pressure area, inducing the
inflow of cool air from the gulf. A front is probably formed along the
contact of cool gulf air and the warm interior air over Rfosucio.[17]

Occasionally the traveller in the Pacific lowlands encounters
stories and even apparent evidence of severe tornado-like storms which
may occur any time of the year, but usually during the months of highest precipitation. For example, at Santa Rosa on the upper Rfo Saija
I was shown in the rain forest nearby a long swath of fallen timber
some 200 feet wide, said to have been caused by a borrasco, or severe
storm the year previous (1950). Again, in August, 1954, the village
of Cértegui on a tributary of the upper Atrato was partially destroyed
by a severe wind storm, which, according to witnesses, was a ciclón,
a term often applied to waterspouts.[18] Destructive storms, however,
are extremely rare in the lowlands, for the area is well outside the
hurricane zone. In the interior river basins one is impressed by the
stillness of the air, particularly along streams, which are protected
from even strong breezes by the dense forest. Along the coast, on the
other hand, the sea breeze, prevailingly from the southwest, characterizes daily weather and helps to lower sensible temperatures by evapora-
tion.

CHAPTER IV
VEGETATION

The rainy equatorial climate of northwestern South America gives rise to a dense tropical forest cover -- the outstanding geographical feature of the Pacific lowlands. In general the forest cover may be classified into two large types, based chiefly on plant forms resulting from differing drainage conditions: (1) the true rain forest, which is found mainly on slopes and plains of fair drainage and (2) the swamp forests and other aquatic formations, which develop in areas of poor drainage. The latter type may be subdivided into (a) littoral, or tidal, swamp, characterized by mangrove, backed by brackish-to fresh-water plant formations and (b) the fresh-water swamp and marsh vegetation, which occupies the ill-drained back-water areas on river flood plains.[1] The true rain forest and the swamp forests are floristically, ecologically, and physiognomically distinct. The former is characterized by a great variety of plant species within small areas, the latter by the predominance of a few, or even single, species. The floristic contrast, coupled with differing ecological conditions, gives each major forest type a distinctive appearance.

The Rain Forest

The true rain forest occupies by far the greater part of the Pacific lowlands of Colombia.[2] It also covers the Serranía de Baudó and climbs the western slope of the Cordillera Occidental to elevations of over 5,000 feet above sea level. Southward it extends into Ecuador along the lower slopes of the Andes and to the north it continues into the Province of Darién, southeastern Panama. In the northern and southern extremities near the coast, where a definite dry season occurs, the number of deciduous plants in the forest increase, forming a transition zone between the semi-deciduous forest of coastal Ecuador and southeast coast of Panama and the true rain forest of Colombia.[3]

The appearance of the Colombian-Pacific rain forest is similar to that of most humid equatorial areas of the world.[4] At least two and sometimes three vegetational "stories," or strata, characterize the structure of the virgin stands. Tall evergreen broadleaf trees of numerous species, sixty to one hundred feet high, comprise the upper stratum; occasionally their spreading crowns form a solid canopy, shutting out sunlight from the forest floor; sometimes scattered giant trees rise thirty or more feet above the canopy, giving the forest roof an irregular appearance as seen from the air. The straight columnar trunks of the taller trees are often supported by large buttresses or by a complicated arrangement of serpentine surface roots; rarely do such trees have deep tap roots (Plate VII). [5] Although the large trees are of many unrelated species, a large number belong to the laurel family (Lauraceae), such as the commercially valuable chachajo (Aniba perutilis) and the jigua (Nectandra, spp.); the bombax family (Bombacaceae), such as the giant ceibo (Ceiba pentandra); the mulberry family (Moraceae), which includes many milky-sapped plants, such as the red-barked sande or cow-tree (Brosimum utile), various kinds of tropical figs, or higuerones (Ficus, spp.), and the majugua or damajagua (Poulsenia armata), the source of bark cloth still made and used in the Pacific lowlands. Other important trees of the upper stratum belong to the Bignonaceae, represented by the dark, hard-wooded guayacan (Tabebuia, spp.); the mahogany family (Meliaceae), best characterized by the tropical cedar (cedro, Cedrela odorata); only in northwestern Chocó and in Darién is the true mahogany (Swietenia, spp.) found within the Pacific lowlands.

A second stratum in the forest is formed by a large variety of scattered slender trees and many palms, both growing to a height of twenty to thirty feet. This growth is open and rarely forms a solid canopy. Many of the trees are composed of young plants belonging to species mentioned above, which eventually become part of the top stratum. Other small trees include members of the pepper family (Piperaceae) and the madder family (Rubiaceae), while palms, such as the milpeso (Jessenia polycarpa) and the palma amarga (Welfia regia), occupy much of the second-story element. In parts of the Serranía de Baudó almost solid stands of milpeso palm grow under scattered giant trees; such areas are frequented by droves of wild pigs (peccaries) that feed on the fallen clusters of palm nuts. In other areas, such as the northern Chocó and Darién and the Tumaco and Esmeraldas districts, thick clusters of the valuable tagua, or ivory nut palm (Phytelephas, spp.), occur as understory vegetation especially on natural levees. Such close stands, however, may be the result of protection by man, rather than a wholly natural occurence.

A third stratum of trees sometimes occurs as an intermediate story between the first and second already described. This intermediate stratum is extremely difficult to discern in the forest, and is usually non-existant. Richards states that in most normal

Large **higerón** (Ficus, sp.) with well-developed buttresses and typically covered by lianas and epiphytic growth. Coastal plain, north of San Juan Delta.

Typical undergrowth and second story vegetation, Serranía de Baudó. Palm-like Cyclanthaceae and members of the Piperaceae appear in the foreground.

primary rain forest communities three tree strata exist, though they
are often ill-defined. [6]

In addition to the tree strata, the forest of the Pacific lowlands, like most rain forests the world over, is characterized by a
ground cover made up of low ferns, herbs, woody shrubs, vines, and
tree seedlings. The ferns and shrubs rarely exceed five feet in height.
Like the plants of the second story, these ground elements are scattered and seldom form closed thickets; one can usually walk through
the ground vegetation without difficulty, swinging his machete occasionally to cut away an interfering shrub or vine. The low herbaceous
growth abounds in many wide-leafed aroids (e.g., Calathea, spp.),
palm-like cyclanthaceous plants, gingers, cannas, and many small
plants of the Bignoniaceae. In the low flood plains bordering the lower
Atrato, large areas of low understory growth are composed almost
wholly of thick clusters of a bromelia (Aechmea magdalenae), called
pita, long expounded as a natural source of fiber, but never exploited
commercially. One of the most striking features of the rain forest is
the absence of grasses on the forest floor. Only along low stream
banks open to sunlight and subject to flooding do grasses grow in abundance.

In addition to stratification the appearance of the Colombian
rain forest is distinguished by a luxuriant array of shade-tolerant
climbing vines (lianas) and epiphytic shrubs that grow on the trunks and
branches of the taller trees. Epiphytes range from the pineapple
plants (Bromeliaceae) and orchids (Orchidaceae), both with their
brilliantly and delicately-colored flowers, through the less showy dark-
green aroids to grey-green mosses and lichens. Many of the lianas
are strangler figs (Ficus, spp.), which start as epiphytes; by means
of hanging aerial roots they envelop the entire host tree, eventually
killing it. Other lianas are poisonous, but most of the smaller climb-
ers (bejucos) can be used as rope for tying all manner of things.

Contrary to popular accounts of the equatorial rain forests,
that of the Pacific lowlands usually lacks an abundance of brilliantly
colored flowers. The brightest colors are shown by the epiphytic
plants on the gloomy understory vegetation or by an occasional deciduous flowering tree during its molting period. The general color of
the rain forest is a deep, dull, monotonous green, blurred here and
there by whitish to dark-brown tree trunks which have not yet been
clothed by green epiphytes.

Although the Pacific lowland forest is described as evergreen it contains many scattered deciduous trees, all of which are tall
members of the upper stratum. Such trees undergo a short molting

period of four to six weeks. During that time some flower, then suddenly burst forth with new leaves. Some of the more common deciduous trees in the rain forest include the ceibo, the castilla rubber tree (Castilla elastica), and the tropical cedar (Cedrela, spp.). Such trees usually shed their leaves during the drier part of the year (February to March), but some may molt at any season and at irregular intervals (e.g., the ceibo). The evergreen trees are continually shedding old leaves and putting forth new, although usually a given tree will produce a new set in a short period of time. The amount of leaf fall in the rain forest is consequently enormous; it has been estimated that from forty-five to ninety tons of leaves and other litter fall yearly on every acre of floor in the equatorial forest.[7] The leaf fall acquires great importance when it is considered that the rapidly decaying ground litter forms the chief source of plant nutrients for the forest vegetation.

Disturbed Vegetation

The foregoing description of the equatorial forest refers to climax conditions. Certain factors, natural and human, disturb the forest in various situations and lead to temporary changes in vegetation. Naturally disturbed areas include (1) banks of rivers where erosion and deposition continually operate and (2) tree-falls and landslides, which affect small spots of surrounding forest. Areas disturbed by man are mainly those where original vegetation is partially cleared for cultivation or pasture, or where sections have been logged for timber.

Riparian vegetation in the rain forest is quite distinct from that of well-drained interfluve areas. Low trees and tangles of undergrowth characterize most low river banks subject to erosion and deposition, although occasionally giants like the ceibo and choibá (Tabebuia, sp.) grow on levees near the water's edge. On newly-formed point bars and slip-off slopes a succession of plant types takes place. Various aquatic grasses, one to three feet high, (Panicum, spp., Paspalum, spp.) are pioneers and compose the outer plant fringe, called locally the pajonal or chuscal. This fringe is backed by a zone of higher cane-like grass, usually the widespread caña brava (Gynerium sagittatum), which forms an almost impenetrable thicket along the river bank. The interior of the older alluvial deposits is covered by growths of the slender, wide-leafed tree, yarumo (Cecropia, spp.), a neo-tropical indicator of new or disturbed ground. In time, as the alluvial deposits become higher and better drained, the cecropia thickets may be succeeded by various palms and eventually by a true rain forest. Often these four stages of plant succession form a distinctive step-like vegetative zones of increasing height inland

along low river banks and around alluvial islands within the river
(Plate VIII).

On relatively stable banks, particularly in the upper
courses where rock outcrops along the stream edge, many low water-
loving trees overhang the river like willows. Among these are the
pichindé (unidentified), the chípero (Zygia longifolia) and the fruit-
bearing guamo (Inga, spp.). High, almost vertical river banks of
solid rock are often completely covered by large-leafed herbs, such
as many of the Escitamineae, and large ferns; except for short dry
periods these green river walls are continually dripping with water
from daily rains and from small springs that issue from bedding
planes. Frequently waterfalls tumble over the herb-covered cliffs
into the river.

A characteristic feature of the true rain forest, or of any
forest, is the presence of fallen trees and the gaps made in the vegetation cover by such falls. A falling forest giant, coupled to neighboring trees by a tangle of lianas, may bring down a considerable area of
vegetation, causing a sizeable gap in the forest cover. In such gaps,
where the ground is exposed to direct sunlight, vines, creepers, and
herbs soon develop a chaotic tangle; with the rapid decay of the fallen
vegetation, low trees, especially the familiar cecropia, take over.
Finally these plants are gradually succeeded by true rain forest species,
and the gap is eventually closed. Such gaps caused by tree-falls are
probably significant in the process of rain forest regeneration, especially for the survival of the more light-dependent species that make
up a good part of the upper story of the forest. Tree-falls, however,
often block jungle trails; either detours must be made around the fall
or a way hewn through the rotting mass of vegetation.

Similar disturbed spots are caused by landslides on steep
slopes. In such cases small areas of bare red clay soil are exposed.
Lacking the fertile mulch of rotting vegetation, the slide areas are re-
vegetated much more slowly than the gaps left by tree-falls; but the
process of plant succession is practically identical in both cases.
Minor natural alterations of the rain forest include small, bare spots
in the undergrowth caused by hills of the arriera, or the leaf-cutter
ant, and the wallows made by peccaries.

Man has altered considerably certain sections of the primary rain forest in the Pacific lowlands, principally through periodic
clearings for cultivation. The areas so affected have been chiefly (1)
the natural levees along rivers, where the best agricultural land prevails and (2) the hill and terrace sections inland from the rivers. In

those areas primitive shifting agriculture has been going on for centuries -- first practiced by Indians and, since the eighteenth century, chiefly by Negroes using Indian farming techniques. Probably only in the remote parts of the interfluves and in the lower mountain slopes has the rain forest remained completely free of human interference. Thus a considerable part of the so-called original vegetation of the Pacific lowlands is actually a man-made secondary forest.

The levee vegetation along the rivers is in a continual state of disturbance (Plate VIII). Abandoned fields are almost immediately taken over by creeping vines and many varieties of wide-leafed herbs, such as the banana-like plantanillo (Heliconia, spp.), bijao, or hoja blanca (Calathea, spp.) and Costus, spp. In this state the levee vegetation forms a serious barrier to human movement between the river bank and the interior.[8] If left untilled for several years, this low vegetation is often succeeded by stands of cecropia and other small, softwoods, such as the commercially valuable balsa wood (Ochroma, spp.). The best stands of commercial balsa wood are usually found in the secondary forest along levees of streams.[9] Remnants of cultivated plants, such as the castilla rubber tree and tropical cedar, clumps of bamboo (Guadua angustifolia) various palms, and plantains add to the dense old-field growth along the levees.

Abandoned fields on hill slopes are also rapidly occupied by a secondary forest, which is low in height (twenty to thirty feet) and composed of many light-demanding soft woods, such as Cecropia, Inga, Byrsonima, Ochroma, and Vismia, spp. These plants all bear seeds that are well adapted for transport by wind and animal. The dense herbaceous undergrowth and the tangle of vines, characteristic of young secondary forest plots, disappear after several years; as the vegetation on the disturbed areas increases in age, it becomes difficult to distinguish it from the rain forest. In the Pacific lowlands native grasses never become dominant in secondary vegetation as they do in cleared areas in southeast Asia and parts of equatorial Africa.

Swamp Vegetation

A distinguishing feature of the Pacific lowland landscape is the backswamp vegetation of the middle and lower courses of larger streams. In these wet areas almost solid stands of palms, fifteen to thirty feet high, take the place of the true rain forest. Consequently common local terms used for the backswamp are palmar and guandal (palm thickets), although fangal (quagmire), bajal (low area, and mangual are also used in various sections of the lowlands. Palms which commonly inhabit the backswamp include the fan palm, quitasol

PLATE VIII   47
STREAMSIDE AND DISTURBED VEGETATION

Streamside vegetation, lower Río Mira. Water hyacinth (<u>Eichhornia</u>,
spp.) in foreground, backed by thickets of <u>chuscal</u> (<u>Paspalum</u>, spp.).
Low cecropia trees grow along the edge of the levee forest in background.

Disturbed vegetation along natural levee, upper Guapi River, showing
clumps of chontaduro palm, old plantain groves, and vine-covered
ground.

(Mauritiella pacifica); the frond palms, guángare or jícara (Manicaria saccifera); the nut-yielding táparo (Attalea, spp. and Orbignya Cuatrecasana); and often clumps of the graceful naidí or palmiche (Euterpe Cuatrecasana). In some backswamps, particularly in the lower San Juan drainage, an interesting cycad, called chigua (Zamia chigua) grows singly or in thickets; the starchy, acrid, pinkish seeds of this plant are sought as food by both Indians and Negroes (Plate IX). [10] Associated with the palms are various aquatic shrubs and grasses; a thick tangle of epiphytic vines often covers large areas.

The palmares of the backswamps are difficult of access. During floods, the water is often too shallow to penetrate easily by canoe; entrance to the swamp may be made only through small crevasse channels. During drier periods the soft, much clay and tangles of vines impede the walker. Nevertheless, the palmares furnish a large number of valuable products which are gathered by local inhabitants: fronds for thatching; hard, durable palm trunks for flooring and walls of houses; and many palm fruits rich in starch and oil for food.

Certain sections of many backswamps near the smaller streams are palmless, having instead low shrubs and grass growing on a peat-like surface. Within such areas occur pools and sluggish streams with the clear, highly acid "blackwater" that is so often reported from the humid tropical forests. The brownish or blackish appearance of the water stems from a colloidal suspension of organic or humic material. [11]

The most extensive backswamp in the Pacific lowlands is that of the lower Atrato, where impeded drainage of varied degrees has led to the formation of a corresponding variety of aquatic plant associations (Map 11). A low marsh vegetation, composed of aquatic grasses and herbs, characterizes the edges of numerous shallow lakes, or ciénagas, that lie immediately back of the narrow natural levees of the Atrato. A mass of floating water plants, ranging from the tiny flowering lechuga (Pistia, spp.) to the wide-leafed water lily (Limnanthemum humboldtianum), the abundant water hyacinth (Eichhornia azurea), and the weed-like tabaquillo (Polygonum densiflorum), often cover large areas of the lake surface; sometimes these plants form a solid floating mat, similar to the sudd of African lakes and the flotant of the Louisiana coastal marshes. On the indefinite lake margins a zone of aquatic grasses, such as the common chuscal (Paspalum, spp.) and cattail (Typha angustifolia) mixed with clumps of tall cyperaceous reeds (Cyperus, spp.) form impenetrable thickets. Beyond on higher ground are veritable forests of palms of the species typical of the backswamps. A ring-like zonation of plant associations

PLATE IX. BACKSWAMP VEGETATION   49

The fresh-water swamp along the Quebrada Sequihondita between El Charco and Iscuandé. Clumps of naidi palm (Euterpe, sp.) are mixed with tall nato trees (Mora megistosperma).

The cycad, Zamia chigua, abundant in the backswamps around the lower San Juan area. The fruit can be seen between the fronds at the top of the stem.

(hydroseres) around each lake is thus typical; the plants of each association become progressively taller outward from a given ciénaga (Plate X).

Throughout the marshy section of the backwater areas of the lower Atrato a few species of water-tolerant trees mark the position of old natural levee remnants and the inner sections of small levees that border crevasse channels and esteros leading from the river into the ciénagas. The most common of these trees is the tall and valuable cativo (Prioria copaifera) which is often mixed with a low, spiny palm (chuscará, unidentified) and a variety of tropical figs (higuerón, Ficus, spp.). The same association is found also on the backslope of the present natural levee of the Atrato (Plate X).

The most extensive area of the "cativo" association, however, occurs in a broad belt on the inner side of the backswamp of the Atrato, forming a transition between the palm-marsh and the true rain forest of the adjacent well-drained hills (Map 11). During the periods of heavy rains the cativo forest is completely flooded, but is usually dry during January through March. The seasonally wet conditions appear to limit the vegetation of this belt to almost pure stands of cativo; individual trees with straight, columnar trunks are commonly 80 to 100 feet tall. Although the actual extent of the forest has not yet been determined, large areas are known to exist west of the Atrato in the lower Truandó drainage and east of the river in the Jiguamiandó drainage. Probably these belts follow the inner edge of the backswamp southward to the vicinity of Buchadó and northward to the Gulf of Urabá.

The littoral swamps, including the mangrove forest, are discussed in the following chapter.

PLATE X. CIENAGA VEGETATION: 51
LOWER ATRATO BASIN

Ciénaga de la Isla, lower Atrato Basin. The Cordillera Occidental lies in the far background. Swamp grass (Paspalum, spp.) and tabaquillo (Polygonum densiflorum) in foreground.

A cativo swamp, lower Atrato Basin. The large trunks are cativo; the palm is chuscará.

CHAPTER V
THE PACIFIC LITTORAL

As indicated previously, the Pacific littoral of Colombia and adjacent areas is characterized by two distinct coastal types (1) a high, mountainous coast that extends northward from Cabo Corrientes to Punta Garachiné in southeast Panama and (2) a low alluvial coast, fringed by dense tidal forests and sandy beaches, which stretches southward from Cabo Corrientes for more than 400 miles into Esmeraldas province, northwestern Ecuador (Map 12). These highly contrasted coasts present not only distinct scenery and geomorphic processes, but also offer differing problems for travel and subsistence.

Both coastal types, however, are affected by certain common phenomena, one of which is the large tidal range characteristic of most parts of the eastern side of the northern Pacific Basin. A mean range of eight to ten feet and a spring range of eleven to thirteen feet occur along most of the Colombian coast.[1] Along the low alluvial coast the tide may reach many miles up the courses of the larger rivers.[2] Along the immediate shore, deposition and scour by tidal currents become important factors in shaping various coastal landforms, such as tidal channels, bars and beaches. Longshore currents also are effective depositional and erosional agents along both coasts. The prevailing southwest winds motivate a northward-flowing longshore current, which transports and redeposits quantities of mud and sand immediately off-coast. Moreover minor local and variable currents help to form spits and bars at river mouths and beach ridges along the shore.

The longshore current is significant also in terms of coastwise navigation. Small craft travelling southward often have difficulty in bucking the northward-flowing waters. Coastal inhabitants reckon direction from this current; at any given point along the coast the area to the north is termed costa abajo, or "downcoast", i. e., with the current, while the area to the south is known as costa arriba, or "up coast", i. e., against the current.

The Low Alluvial Coast

The long extent of the tidal swamp south of Cabo Corrientes is not continuous; at three places consolidated Tertiary material reaches the sea to form a steep, rocky coast, which, save on sheer sea cliffs, is covered by rain forest. As shown on Map 12 these interruptions are the 25-mile wide Istmo de Pichidó, between the bays of Buenaventura and Málaga; a short section south of Buenaventura, called Las Tortugas; and a 15-mile stretch of coast on the Ensenada de Tumaco, between the Isla del Gallo and the mouth of the Chaguï River. Excepting these three rocky areas, the entire alluvial coast from Cabo Corrientes to slightly beyond the Santiago River in Esmeraldas is distinguished by four geographic belts arranged in sequence from the sea inland: (1) a belt of shoal water and mud flats immediately off coast; (2) a series of discontinuous sand beaches, interrupted by tidal inlets, estuaries, and wide mud flats; (3) a zone of mangrove forest, usually one-half to three miles wide; (4) a belt of fresh-water tidal swamp, lying immediately back of the brackish-water mangroves. Inland from the tidal swamps on slightly higher ground lies the equatorial rain forest that covers the greater part of the Pacific lowlands (Map 13). Each of the three latter littoral zones -- the discontinuous beach, the mangrove, and the fresh-water swamp -- is distinguished by a given arrangement of certain types of landforms and vegetation associations. Each also presents peculiar problems in terms of human travel and subsistence. This zonation appears to be typical of most mangrove coasts of the world, although the beach zone is frequently absent. It is described for the Malaya Peninsula by Watson and Dobby,[3] for the west coast of Africa by Grew and Pynaert[4] and for the Guina coasts of northern South America by Martyn.[5]

The Shoal Belt

The large quantity of stream-deposited material along the shore has been reworked by longshore currents and waves to form a wide bank of fine silty sand immediately off the mangrove coast. From Buenaventura southward to the Patía Delta a bank of shoal water, three to four miles wide extends seaward from shore. Elsewhere the bank is less extensive, but along its entire length it slopes steeply away to depths of twenty fathoms and more on its seaward side. At low tide the higher portions of the bank, called bajos, are exposed a few inches to three feet above the sea surface. Large waves break on the seaward side of the partially exposed line of bajos, which in places form a discontinuous barrier beach two or more miles from shore. One of the most lasting impressions of the mangrove coast during low tide is the distant roar of the white wall of breakers far off-coast.

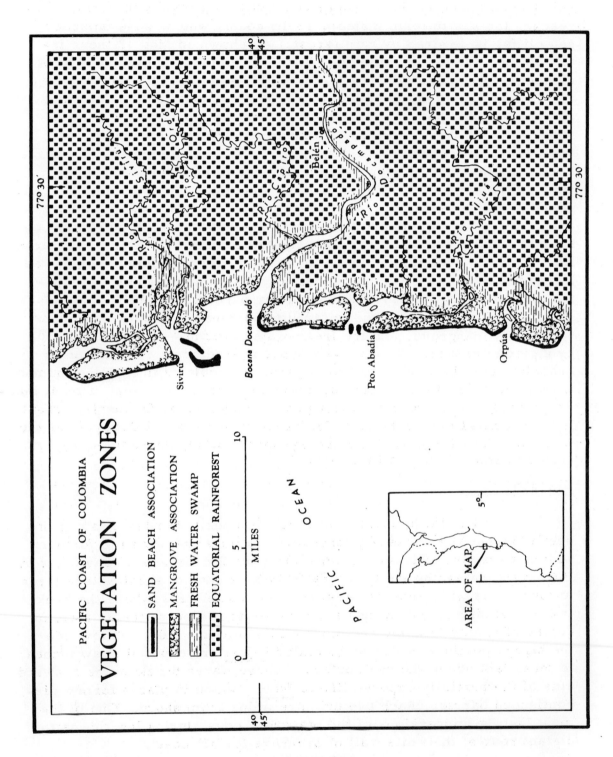

PACIFIC COAST OF COLOMBIA

VEGETATION ZONES

SAND BEACH ASSOCIATION
MANGROVE ASSOCIATION
FRESH WATER SWAMP
EQUATORIAL RAINFOREST

MILES

PACIFIC OCEAN

AREA OF MAP

MAP 13

Often small banks of fine, brownish sand are exposed close into shore; free from breakers, such banks, called cuervales, become temporary roosting places for large numbers of aquatic birds, among the most common of which is a large tern, the cuerval, or "sea crow." At high tide practically all of the bajos and cuervales are submerged, and large waves then reach the shore.

As the higher portions of the banks constantly shift position due to wave and current action, navigation is extremely hazardous immediately offshore even for shallow draft boats and canoes. During high tide the large swells that reach the shore make canoe navigation almost impossible.[6] The shoal belt also makes entrance into the river estuaries dangerous. Shoals, or bars, some of which are exposed at low tide, form at the mouth of every river along the low coast. Craft drawing more than three or four feet must wait off-coast until high tide to attempt the crossing of the bar to enter the river mouth.[7]

Occasionally small sand banks near the shore grow to be low islets. Those composed of fine, silty sand with high clay content are sometimes colonized by low mangrove; those composed of coarser sand are invaded by beach vegetation consisting of creeping vines, reeds and grasses. The shifting of local currents and wave action, however, often destroy such islets a few years after their formation.

Mud flats form another significant feature of the shoal belt. These occur mainly in areas protected from strong wave action, such as bays or large estuaries, and are usually bordered by mangrove on their landward side. At low tide some flats extend seaward for more than one mile, but are completely covered at high tide (Plate XI). The ports of Tumaco and Buenaventura are noted for their extensive mud flats that impede navigation at low tide. Composed of soft mud, the surface of such flats are infirm underfoot; in places a heavy man may sink to his knees in muck. Where wave action is extremely slight the higher mud flats are often colonized by mangrove seedlings and the tidal swamp may thus be extended seaward.

The Beach Zone

Broken by thousands of tidal inlets and estuaries, the low alluvial coast presents an extremely irregular shoreline. However, the outer portions of the shore that are directly exposed to strong wave and current action are fringed by short lengths of straight sand beaches. Approximately 45 per cent of the total shoreline of the alluvial coast is fringed by such beaches; the remainder is bordered by mud flats and mangrove in protected bays and estuaries (Map 12). The beaches are

Extensive mud flats at low tide off Tumaco.   Isla de Guamo in far
distance.

Stranded at low tide in an <u>estero</u> on flats near Orpúa along coast north
of San Juan Delta.

composed of fine, dark, compact sand which comes mainly from stream
load, effectively sorted by wave action; minor amounts of sand probably are derived from erosion of the occasional rocky headlands
enumerated above. The beaches vary greatly in length -- from ten
miles to a few yards, but the majority average five to six miles. Their
foreshore width varies from 100 to 400 yards at low tide and from
zero to twenty-five yards at high tide (Plate XII). As most of the
foreshores are smooth and firm, they could support heavy motor vehicle traffic during the low tide period, which lasts from four to five
hours. Most beaches, however, are crossed by small rivulets, whose
beds are often composed of quicksand. Tidal ponds, called pozos,
form in slight depressions on the seaward side of the beaches . At
low tide such ponds often afford an abundant supply of fish which the
natives catch by spearing.

Back of the areas affected by daily tides lies the beach
ridge which is formed by wave action during infrequent storms and the
highest spring tides. With its steep side facing seaward, the back of
the ridge slopes gradually downward to mud flats bordering a lagoon or
a mangrove swamp (Figure 4). The ridge crests rise from three to
four feet above the average spring tidemark. Their width varies
greatly. Some, which are being prograded, are 300 to 400 yards
wide; often these are composed of a double ridge or even a series of
low ridges with low swales between, as in the case of Orpúa, sixty
miles north of Buenaventura. Most of the beach ridges, however are
narrow (100 to 200 yards wide), and appear to have been undergoing
erosion for the past fifty years.

Up and down the coast old inhabitants, sixty to seventy
years of age, relate that in their youth the beach ridges were much
wider than now, many having been covered with large coconut groves.
Such stories have a grain of truth, for old stumps and root masses of
coconut palms now well within the foreshore of the beach give evidence
of retrogression. Much of the retrogression has been due to gradual
erosion by waves and currents. But probably most of the changes re-
counted by the inhabitants have been sudden, in some cases catastrophic. Such changes have been due to disastrous tsunamis, or giant
waves caused by earthquake shocks, the epicenters of which are located along faults in the sea bottom a few miles off-shore. At least
three tsunamis have been recorded along the coast of northwestern
South America in the last 150 years, all of which affected the Colombian
shoreline. One occurred in 1836 (epicenter off Guapi ?);[8] another in
1868 (epicenter off Cabo Manglares ?);[9] and the last and most disastrous on January 31, 1906 (epicenter off the coast of northwestern
Ecuador, 0°50' S., 81° 32' W.)[10] One of the largest tsunamis ever

PLATE XII
BEACHES AND BEACH VEGETATION

Sandy beach, approximately 500 yards wide at low tide; near Pilizá, north of the Baudó River mouth. The surf can be seen in far distance at right.

Beach vegetation near Orpúa, north of San Juan Delta. The foreshore vegetation consists of trailers (Ipomea pre-caprae), grasses (Cyperus and Uniola), and hibiscus thickets backed by rain forest.

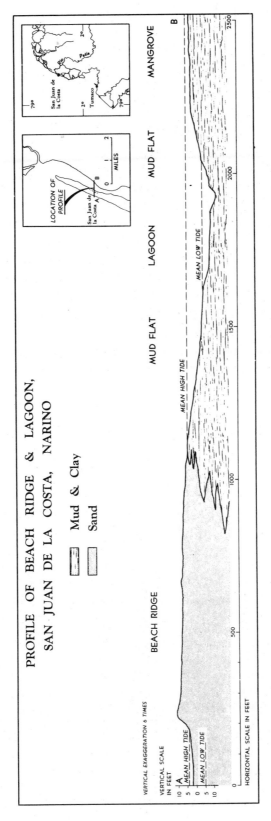

FIGURE 4

recorded,[11] this series of enormous waves destroyed several coastal
villages and coconut plantations and eroded large sections of beaches
and mangrove swamp for a stretch of sixty miles along the coast in the
vicinity of Tumaco. Many low, sandy islands off Cabo Manglares and
Tumaco were destroyed or radically changed in outline.

Despite active erosion, beach formation has been one of
the major factors in the seaward extension of the low alluvial coast.
Remnants of beach ridges separated by mangrove-enclosed lagoons
occur in abundance back of the present beaches. Due probably to
slight sinking and alluviation, the beach ridge zone is invaded by the
mangrove and eventually becomes part of the swamp.

In terms of travel and subsistence the beach zone is of outstanding importance. At low tide the foreshores of the beaches are
used as routes of travel, but only for short distances, as the frequent
tidal estuaries are barriers to foot travel. Moreover, the ends of
beaches adjacent to river estuaries are usually littered with accumula-
tions of driftwood, which impedes travel by foot or by vehicle. On the
other hand, the abundance of fish, the groves of coconut palms, orange
trees, and small patches of maize and manioc cultivated in the sandy
soil of the beach ridges near fishing villages afford sufficient food for
the traveller. Moreover, fresh to slightly brackish water can usually
be found on the beach ridges by digging a few feet below the surface.
Open wells abound near beach settlements.[12]

The beaches of the alluvial coast of the Pacific lowlands
bear a series of vegetational associations that appear to be typical of
tropical sandy shores the world over. Two definite zones can be distinguished: (1) On the upper foreshore there is a belt of low herbaceous
plants, while (2) behind it on the beach ridge occurs a zone of low
bushes and taller trees (Plate XII). The first zone is composed mainly
of halophytes. These plants are tolerant of occasional submergence in
sea water and of the high salt content of sandy beach soils. This zone
is often called the Pre-caprae formation, for the chief member of the
plant assemblage is a low morning-glory runner (Ipomea pre-caprae),
which criss-crosses the upper part of the beach with its trailing vines.
Equally abundant is the climbing and trailing legume, Canavalia rosea;
the composite trailer, Wedelia brasiliensis; and a trailing, milky-
sapped dogbane, Rhabdadenia biflora. High reeds, such as cortadero
(Cyperus, spp.); a tall, reedy grass (Uniola pittieri); and low salt-
tolerant grasses (Stenotaphrum, spp.) make up the inner portion of the
Pre-caprae formation. Located on the higher ground of the beach
ridge, away from salt water and sea spray, the second zone is comprised of dense thickets of the flowering Hibiscus tiliaceus, locally

called majagua. This woody shrub grows to ten or fifteen feet and is
usually mixed with other shrubs, such as Dalbergia, spp. Many of the
older, wider beach ridges contain patches of rain forest, with the giant
tropical fig, higuerón (Ficus, spp.) as a common component. According to Richards,[13] a zonation similar to the one described above is
found on tropical beaches in other parts of the world. The Pre-caprae
zone seems to be pan-tropical. In southeast Asia, a belt of woody
vegetation composed mainly of Barringtonia and in the Caribbean a
zone of Coccoloba shrubs and trees correspond to the hibiscus thickets
of the Pacific lowland beaches.

The Mangrove Zone

Mangrove swamp forests occur in the tidal zone of most
low, alluvial coasts in the humid tropics. The peculiar morphological
adaptation of the plants to a saline environment, as well as the characteristic hydrography and landforms of the swamp, make the mangrove forests one of the most distinctive of tropical areas. Mangrove
forests best develop under the following physical conditions:

1. Tropical temperatures. Well-developed mangrove is
    found usually along coastal areas where the average
    temperature of the coldest month exceeds 20° C.
    (68° F.), and where the seasonal temperature range
    does not exceed 5° C. (9° F.).

2. Fine-grained alluvium. Mangrove best develops along
    deltaic coasts or near river mouths where abundant
    soft mud composed of fine silt and clay, rich in organic
    remains, is available for the growth of seedlings. (In
    the western Pacific basin, however, mangrove occurs
    on coral reefs; but such growth is stunted and can be
    considered abnormal).

3. Shores free from strong wave action. Mangrove cannot
    tolerate destructive wave action, neither for the growth
    of seedlings nor for the maintenance of mature forests.
    Thus mangrove best develops along the shores of pro-
    tected bays and estuaries.

Mangrove is said also to develop best along tropical coasts having
abundant rainfall evenly distributed throughout the year. Such a cor-
respondence does occur usually, but the areas of heavy rainfall are
also those having many sediment-laden streams, which make available
large quantities of loose, wet alluvium at their mouths and along the

edges of bays. Moreover salinity does not seem to be a physical requirement for the growth of mangrove. It has been shown that some members of the mangrove community (especially Rhizophora) will thrive as well, or even better, in fresh-water conditions as in a saline habitat.[14] Thus, it appears that mangrove, being physically adapted to saline conditions, occupies tidal areas where more aggressive fresh-water swamp plants, intolerant of salt, cannot exist. Again, a large tidal range is often cited as a pre-requisite for optimum growth of mangrove.[15] Although the tide per se probably has little importance in determining the existence of mangrove, with a given gradient of shore, the greater the tidal range, the wider the belt of alluvium affected by saline water; consequently, relatively wide belts of mangrove occur on low coasts affected by large tidal ranges, whereas narrow belts are usually characteristic of tropical shores with small tidal ranges.

Along the low Pacific coast of Colombia the three prime requisites for mangrove development listed above are present. Moreover, at high tide salt to brackish water penetrates inland along tidal channels for several miles, flooding a wide area of coastal alluvium. Generally, the mangrove belt is one to four miles wide, but in the Tapaje-Sanguianga Delta north of Tumaco it reaches a maximum width of fifteen miles, while near Cuevitas, south of Cabo Corrientes, mangrove occupies a narrow fringe of mud not more than five to ten feet wide at the base of jungle-covered sea cliffs. Narrow ribbons of mangrove penetrate inland many miles along the banks of streams as far as salt or brackish water occurs at high tide (Map 13).

The mangrove forest of the Pacific coast of Colombia is one of the most luxuriant in the world. One component of the mangrove association -- red mangrove (Rhizophora) -- grows to heights of over 100 feet, some trees having a diameter of over three feet. Only two other mangrove forests in the American tropics are characterized by such luxuriance: (1) the eastern shore of Guayas Bay, southern Ecuador,[16] near the southern limit of mangrove on the Pacific coast of South America and (2) the Ten Thousand Islands area of southwestern Florida,[17] again near the poleward limits of mangrove in the northern hemisphere. Mangrove along other coasts of tropical America are characterized by relatively low, scrubby forests. Elsewhere tall mangrove forests comparable to those of the Colombian Pacific Coast are found on the shores of the Cameroons and eastern Nigeria in the Gulf of Guinea, West Africa;[18] along the coast of Tanganyika, East Africa,[19] and in various parts of southeast Asia, such as the north coast of Sumatra and much of the coast of Borneo,[20] where mangrove forests probably reach their maximum development.

Composition and structure of the mangrove forest. Botanically the mangroves of the Pacific coast of Colombia belong to the Occidental Mangrove District, which encompasses tropical America and the Atlantic coast of Africa. Four major genera form the bulk of the mangrove trees in this district: Rhizophora (red mangrove), Avicennia (black mangrove), Laguncularia (white mangrove), and Conocarpus (sometimes called "button wood").[21] On the Pacific Coast of Colombia Rhizophora brevistyla and, occasionally, Rh. samoensis are the species of red mangrove that form the dominant component of the tall swamp forest. Avicennia nitida, Laguncularia racemosa and Conocarpus erecta are low trees, and in terms of area, are less significant members of the swamp. A fifth mangrove tree, Pelliciera rhizophora, a member of the tea family, is found only on the Pacific coast of tropical America.[22]

Although unrelated botanically, the trees of the mangrove forest exhibit certain common morphological adaptations to their saline environment; these adaptations are reflected in the strange physiognomy of the plants. One of the most spectacular features is the aerial root system. The red mangrove has developed (1) large arched prop (or stilt) roots which raise the trunk high above the ground and (2) long drop roots that grow from the branches into the mud below. When exposed at low tide these gnarled roots, often ten to fifteen feet high, form an almost impenetrable maze of vegetation (Plate XIII). The prop and drop roots rise from a surface of soft, brackish ooze, into which a man would sink to his knees. Black mangrove (Avicennia nitida) is characterized by a system of surface roots, which send up sharp-pointed asparagus-like shoots five to six inches above the ground. The rigidity and sharpness of these pneumatophores, together with the soft, slippery ooze in which they grow, make walking through black mangrove thickets at low tide a difficult procedure (Plate XIV). Another peculiar adaptation of mangrove plants is called vivipary, or the germination of seeds inside the fruit before separation from the mother plant. Once dropped and anchored in the mud, the seedling rapidly produces roots and gives rise to a new plant. Mangroves, therefore, should reproduce and colonize new mud flats quickly, but due to destructive wave and current action, such is often not the case.

Like most tropical swamp vegetation, the mangrove forests are characterized by relatively few species and the formation of solid stands of single species. Moreover, belts of single species tend to develop from the shore inland, due chiefly to decreasing salinity and increasing acidity of water and soil landwards. Belted patterns of mangrove have been reported especially from southeast Asia,[23] East Africa,[24] Florida,[25] and the Caribbean.[26] Such zones have been

PLATE XIII. MANGROVE VEGETATION:
                RHIZOPHORA SWAMP

Typical prop roots of Rhizophora brevistyla in mangrove forest north
of Tumaco. Rhizophora seedlings are almost covered by the rising
tide.

Interior of Rhizophora forest on peaty surface, near Buenaventura.
The fern is Acrostichum aureum. Orchids and bromelias grow as
epiphytes on trunks and prop roots.

PLATE XIV. MANGROVE VEGETATION: 65
AVICENNIA AND PELLICIERA

Young stand of black mangrove (Avicennia nitida) south of Buenaventura.
In the foreground the pneumatophores protrude above the mud like
sharpened pencils.

The iguanero (Pelliciera rhizophora) north of the San Juan Delta. The
trees with their curious buttressing are reminiscent of the bald cypress
of North America.

assumed for most mangrove areas in the humid tropics. Along the
Pacific coast of Colombia, however, definite belts of given species
are difficult to observe in the field, and such arrangements may be
obscured by many local factors, such as variation in salinity from
place to place, exposure to wave and current action, and grain size
and organic content of alluvium. Nevertheless stands of almost pure
giant Rhizophora are usually best developed in a belt of varying width
along the edge of tidal channels where there is an accumulation of soft
clayey mud and complete flooding by the tide twice each 24-hour period.
Inland, belts of Avicennia and dwarf Rhizophora often occur. Proceed-
ing up an estuary, one often encounters stands of Rhizophora in the
lower section, followed by stretches of Avicennia and Laguncularia,
and finally growths of Conocarpus erecta in the drier and less saline
areas. These formations gradually merge with fresh-water swamp
vegetation further upstream. On the other hand, the following arrangement is often observed from the edge of the tidal channels inland:
Laguncularia racemosa, forming a low growth on the channel edge, is
followed by a narrow belt of Avicennia nitida farther inland; finally in
the interior an extensive forest of giant Rhizophora brevistyla is found.
Along the coast immediately back of sand beaches the belted arrangement is even more confused, and in many cases nonexistent. Often
solid stands of Avicennia nitida, fifteen to thirty feet high, occur immediately behind the beach along the edges of lagoons; behind this belt
is Rhizophora forest. In other cases Rhizophora fronts on the lagoons
and even the open coast, if protected from wave action by mud flats
and bars off-shore. The belted arrangement of mangrove by species
is further confused by the odd-looking Pelliciera rhizophora, which
occurs in small communities in exposed positions, such as the seaward
tips of point bars in estuaries or in spots having hard, clay soils
(Plate XIV).

Many low plants are associated with the main mangrove
types mentioned above. A brackish-water fern (Acrostichum aureum),
five to eight feet high, is often seen growing along the tidal channels in
the midst of high Rhizophora, but it is especially common in the inner
mangrove zone near the fresh-water swamp. Wherever the mangrove
forest has been disturbed by man or by windfalls, the Acrostichum
fern is the first intruder, forming spots of low, dense growth in the
swamp. Low, woody shrubs, such as the yellow-flowered Pavonia
rhizophorae, the blue-flowered Conostegia polyandra and Rustia
occidentalis, and the legumes Muellera frutescens and Dalbergia, spp.
are other minor mangrove associates. Growing on the trunks and prop
roots of Rhizophora are epiphytes, mainly orchids and bromeliads
(Tillandsia, spp.) which give a further eerie aspect to the swamp.
Many of the bromeliads contain reservoirs of fresh rain water, which

make ideal breeding places for various species of the Anopheles mosquito within the mangrove swamp.[27]

Associated with the belted arrangement of vegetation in the swamps is the existence of curious rounded patches of low scrubby growth in the center of the high Rhizophora forest inland from the tidal channels. The vegetation in these patches is only four to six feet high, composed of dwarfed Rhizophora with stunted prop roots, mixed with Avicennia nitida, Acrostichum fern, and other brackish-water plants (Plate XV). These areas occupy ground that is slightly higher and drier than the channel banks. They are flooded usually by semi-monthly spring tides only. The soil is peat-like, soggy and quaking underfoot; a heavy man sinks to his ankles in the top muck. Often in the center of these patches one finds hammocks of the naidí palm (Euterpe Cuatrecasana), a plant characteristic of the fresh-water swamp or, in some instances, even clumps of equatorial rain forest. The centers of the patches are the highest, driest, and firmest parts of the mangrove swamp, but they are extremely difficult to reach. The occurrence of these rounded areas of low growth is typical of other mangrove forests; for example, along the coast of Malaya such patches are called "byiaks," and are readily noticed on areial photographs.[28] The formation of these features is probably due to the slow elevation of land through decay of mangrove vegetation. The underlying peat contains remains of large Rhizophora roots and trunks. Such features may be identical with the so-called "ombrogenous moors" found behind mangrove swamps in Sumatra. These moors are characterized by stunted growth developed on highly acid soil underlain by lens-like deposits of peat.[29] Owing, perhaps, to acidity and lack of fine muddy sediment rich in organic matter, tall mangrove forests fail to regenerate themselves in the inner channel areas.

Hydrography, landforms, and soils. The interior of the mangrove swamp is occupied by a complex system of short, meandering tidal channels, known as esteros. Wide in their lower courses, the esteros suddenly narrow to small creeks a short distance upstream. During high tide the channels are brim full, and brackish water overflows into the surrounding swamp forest. At low tide the smaller esteros become dry, while the deeper ones are transformed into shallow creeks, with exposed parts of fallen logs projecting above the water at all angles, making navigation extremely hazardous (Plate XVI). Immediately back of the present beaches and sections of mangrove swamp, lagoons and tidal channels are arranged parallel to the coast and thus connect the lower parts of river estuaries. Such channels form an almost continuous inland waterway along the entire length of the mangrove coast. They also separate sizeable areas of swamp,

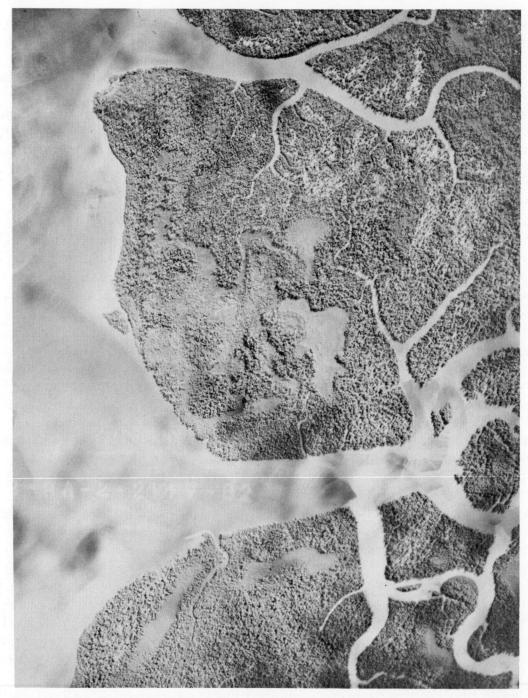

(U. S. Army Air Forces photo. Project 2-2016; 2-211V 82; 1943)

Aerial view of mangrove swamp, Bay of Buenaventura. Estuary of Río Poted6, center. Rhizophora forms the dominant high growth along the stream and tidal channels. The lighter growth along the coast is probably Avicennia. The light patches in the interior represent growth of low shrubs, including dwarf Rhizophora. Hammocks of Euterpe palm can be seen in the light patch near center of photograph.

PLATE XVI. TIDAL CHANNELS WITHIN MANGROVE SWAMP 69

An estero in the mangrove forest at high tide; near Tumaco.

An estero at low tide; between the lower Cajambre and Yurumanguí
rivers.

(called islas) from the mainland. Canoes and small launches use the
quiet waters of the esteros for coastwise travel, rather than risk the
turbulent swells and waves at sea, or "por afuera."[30] Travel "por
adentro" along the inland channels, however, must be closely timed to
correspond with periods of high tide. More than once the writer has
been stranded for several hours in a canoe stuck on the muddy bottom
of an estero at low tide, being pestered to distraction by black flies
and mosquitoes until the water slowly rose with the incoming tide.

Fine, soft mud, deposited and reworked by tidal currents,
accumulates on the edges of the channels between the prop roots of
Rhizophora and the asparagus-like pneumatophores of Avicennia. Low
tide exposes the muddy banks of the channels as well as mud flats,
three to ten feet wide, on the slip-off slopes of meander bends. The
soft mangrove mud is blue-black in color, composed of sediments
with grain size of less than 0.02 mm., and rich in remains of partially
decayed organic matter. The decomposition of organisms in the oxygen-
poor mud, combined with the activity of anerobic bacteria, gives rise
to the quantities of hydrogen sulphide that cause the characteristic
stench of the mangrove swamp.[31] Along the banks of tidal channels,
where sediment is newly deposited, the mud is extremely soft, into
which a heavy man readily sinks to his knees; alighting on the bank
from a canoe at low tide is thus a formidable task, and can be done
best by supporting one's self on the slippery prop roots of Rhizophora.
Inland from the channel banks the mangrove soil becomes firmer; by
reason of the growth of countless capillary rootlets growing from the
props of Rhizophora just below the surface, the soil gradually becomes
hardened, taking on a peaty texture. On such a surface one can walk
rather easily at low tide, sinking up to the ankles in peaty muck. As
one goes farther inland the soil becomes firmer, until the patches of
low growth described above are reached; there, one must cut his way
through the thickets with a machete.[32]

Although fauna in the mangrove swamp is relatively poor
in species, at least two kinds of animals are significant in the development of soil and vegetation. Various crabs,[33] by digging holes in the
mud, help aeriate the soil; these animals thus perform the same function as earthworms in fresh-water soils. Their holes also cause
small depressions in the mud surface, which serve as loci for further
sedimentation by tidal waters. On the other hand, crabs destroy seedlings and thus help to prevent the formation of undergrowth in the mangrove forest. Many mollusks, including oysters and clams, attach
themselves to the prop roots of Rhizophora and their shells become
important sources of calcium carbonate needed by red mangrove in
large amounts for proper growth.[34]

Although black mud and peat comprise most of the soils of the mangrove swamp, small spots of sandy material occur. Within the swamp, back from the seacoast for a distance of one-half to one mile, one frequently encounters along tidal channels small areas of sandy soil which rise slightly above the general level of the swampy muck. These sandy spots are locally called firmes. They are sites of human habitation within the mangrove swamp; fresh water is usually found at a depth of three to four feet below the surface; and coconut palms, patches of maize and other crops are grown (Plate XVII). Some of these firmes appear to be remnants of old beach ridges that have been largely destroyed with the general seaward advance of the coast. Others, farther inland, may be the remnants of natural levees built by former stream channels. The greater number of the firmes along the Colombian coast are found in the extensive mangroves of the Patía-Tapaje-Sanguianga delta system north of Tumaco. There, sizeable villages, such as Mosquera and El Cocal, are located on such sandy "islands." Many of the firmes in this area and farther south toward the Ecuadorean border contain an abundance of highly-weathered potsherds, indicating the presence of pre-Columbian Indian sites within the mangrove. Moreover, today much of the coconut production of the coast of Nariño comes from small groves planted on the firmes.

Relation of mangrove to shore progradation. It is commonly stated that mangrove, and in particular Rhizophora, is an important agent in the seaward advance of low tropical coastlines.[35] It is supposed that Rhizophora is the pioneer colonizer of partially submerged mud banks and shoals, that the growth of young plants fixes the shoal, and that the later development of prop roots is instrumental in entrapping sediments carried by tidal currents, thus aiding in the advance of the shoreline. Consequently, Rhizophora is often termed "land-builder," or "mother of islands." This function of young mangrove has been overemphasized, and cannot be said to occur universally. It is probably true that the prop roots of mature Rhizophora serve to catch some fine particles carried by tidal currents and thus aid in deposition; however, the electrolitic precipitation of suspended materials in river water on contact with salt water is possibly of greater importance as a cause of deposition of fine particles within the mangrove section of the coast.[36] Along the Colombian coast and elsewhere it is observed that land must be entirely emerged during low tide before it is colonized by mangrove, that the first colonizers are often not Rhizophora but black mangrove (Avicennia), and that Rhizophora will not establish or even maintain itself except in quiet saline to brackish water in sheltered bays or along coastlines protected from wave action by offshore bars or shoals.[37] Avicennia is usually the first mangrove plant to invade lagoons immediately back of newly formed beaches; it appears to be

The coconut palms in the background give evidence of a <u>firme</u>, or "island" of sandy soil amidst the mangrove. Another <u>firme</u> is seen at the far left. In the foreground logs are being rafted downstream to a sawmill. Patía-Sanguianga Delta area, north of Tumaco.

more tolerant of highly saline sea water than does Rhizophora; moreover, Avicennia can establish itself in soil having large amounts of coarse quartz sand, whereas Rhizophora demands mud of finely-divided particles of high organic content for full development.[38] In any case the preference of mangrove for fine sediment, be it Rhizophora or Avicennia, tends to localize these plants in those areas that would experience vigorous alluviation regardless of the plant cover; vegetation would seem to play a minor role in progradation of shorelines.

Mud flats along the Colombian coast are not colonized gradually by mangrove; the term "walking out to sea," often applied to the growth of Rhizophora outward from a mother stand probably does not occur except perhaps along the sides of tidal channels. Rather, seaward advance of mangrove on tidal flats seems to occur suddenly with the chance transport of floating masses of seeds by irregular tidal currents to a flat where they are stranded at low tide. If undisturbed by subsequent current and wave action, the seedlings may become established as a colony, all plants of which are of a single age group. As the plants mature, the entire colony maintains an even height. Thus along those parts of the Colombian coast where mangrove fronts directly on the sea, a step-like vegetional profile develops landward each step represents a plant colony of a given age group. Once a colony of Rhizophora is established, only occasionally do young plants develop within it. Moreover, the seaward edge of the colony is usually cut by waves to form a sharp vegetational "bluff," a feature which appears to be typical of mangroves the world over.[39]

Despite the solid appearance of the large prop roots of mature Rhizophora and the matted root system of Avicennia, forests of both are easily driven back by strong wave action. Constant shifting or destruction of mud shoals and offshore bars causes continual change of the locale of wave action along mangrove-bordered bays and estuaries. At such points waves immediately begin to erode the muck and underlying peat which support mature mangrove, eventually killing extensive area of Rhizophora and Avicennia forest.[40] Furthermore, the deposition of sand in stands of Rhizophora soon kills the mature trees. Sediment of nearly pure quartz sand apparently contains insufficient nutrients for the maintenance of that species. A common sight at many points along the Colombian Pacific Coast is the presence of a newly-formed beach along the outer edge of mangrove with bare, grey branches of dead giant Rhizophora silhouetted against the green forest in the background (Plate XVIII).

Like most low, alluvial coasts, the mangrove littoral of Colombia is unstable; the coastline is in continual flux, one section now

Mangrove forest being rapidly destroyed by wave action along the coast north of Tumaco. The peat-like nature of the soil of mature mangrove forests can be seen in foreground.

Mangrove being destroyed by sand deposition, near Puerto España, San Juan Delta.

retreating, another advancing. Despite its instability, in general, the coast appears to be advancing, as evidenced by remnants of beaches (firmes) in the present mangrove belt. Owing to the lack of historical data, determination of the rate of advance is not possible, but it has probably been extremely slow; certainly it is not comparable to the rapid advance of the delta mangrove shorelines of southeast Asia where wave and current action is much less and stream load is much greater.

The Fresh-Water Swamp Zone.

Landward from the mangrove lies a belt of fresh-water swamp, one-half to two miles wide. Incoming tide causes fresh or slightly brackish water to back up in the lower stream courses and to overflow their banks, inundating extensive areas of low-lying land twice each 24-hour period. Like the mangrove, the fresh-water swamp penetrates inland for some distance upstream along the banks of rivers strongly affected by tide.

A plant assemblage of comparatively few species composes the vegetation of the fresh-water swamp. Being aggressive plants, they have crowded out the more salt-tolerant mangrove into the brackish and salt-water areas closer to the sea. As the inward edge of the mangrove becomes higher and less saline, the fresh-water plants invade. The most dominant tree of the swamp is the giant nato (Mora megistosperma). It grows to a height of more than 100 feet and develops huge buttresses at its base. Tolerant of brackish water, the nato often mixes with Rhizophora in the inner edge of the mangrove zone. Associated with nato is the graceful naidí, or palmiche, palm (Euterpe Cuatrescasana) which grows in clumps on the higher, drier spots, such as along the low stream levees or on levee remnants in the interior (Plate XIX). Another typical associate is the manguillo (Tovomita rhizophoroides), a large, prop-rooted tree.[42] Two large trees often form solid stands in the less brackish portions of the swamp: the sajo (Campnosperma panamensis) and cuángare (Virola, spp.). The latter is now being logged in substantial amounts in the vicinity of Tumaco. A small but conspicuous stream-bank tree is a bombax called sapotelongo, or bambudo (Pachira aquatica), which drops its large, round seed pods into the water with a resounding splash. The low stream banks are also covered by many types of grasses. Two of these, pará (Panicum barbinode) and and arrocillo (Oryza latifolia), introduced in the last fifty years, have gone wild. The former is present especially in the swamp areas in the lower Patía, Mira and Mataje rivers, where numerous attempts have been made to establish small pastures farther upstream; elsewhere it may have been transported by streams from headwater areas on the Pacific slope of the Cordillera Occidental, where Antioqueño colonists

Cliffed coast of the Istmo de **Pichidó**, west of Buenaventura Bay. The waves have eroded the Tertiary material, forming stacks, undercut cliffs, and caves.

The southern end of Cabo Marzo along the mountainous coast of the Chocó. The rainy coast is usually shrouded in cloud.

The Rocas de Otávira, off Cabo Marzo. These rocks represent the remnant of an eroded cape.

have established pastures. Arrocillo is probably an accidental introduction with rice cultivation. Today both grasses occur chiefly on
abandoned clearings along the main stream banks in the swamps.

The fresh-water swamp affords greater ease of travel and
better possibilities for food supply than the mangrove. The prop roots
of Rhizophora and the soft, brackish muck are absent. Yet the semi-
diurnal flooding by river overflow makes most of the swamp penetrable
only by canoe during high tide. During the past twenty-five years
Negroes and Indians from up-river have been utilizing the flooded river
banks for growing rice. This development has lessened the problem
of obtaining food within the coastal area, and will be discussed more
fully in the section on agriculture.

Although malaria occurs throughout the Pacific Coast, the
Anopheles mosquito is most prevalent in the fresh-water swamp zone.
Pools of standing fresh water, left by the retreating tide, form excellent breeding places for these insects. At dusk and at dawn swarms of
mosquitoes and other biting insects (mainly black flies and gnats) occur
around every hut and canoe to pester unprotected occupants to distraction. Fewer mosquitoes are encountered along the middle and upper
portion of streams.

The Mountainous Coast

The longest stretch of cliffed, rocky coast of northwestern
South America is that which extends from Cabo Corrientes nearly 250
miles north to Point Garachiné in Panama (Map 12). The shores
around the Gulf of San Miguel are chiefly mountainous; a low alluvial
shore is found only along its eastern end. As indicated previously,
small stretches of cliffed headlands occur south of Cabo Corrientes,
such as that west of Buenaventura and the one north of Tumaco. A few
miles below the Santiago Delta in northwestern Ecuador low headlands
again border the coast.

The neat zonation of landforms and vegetation found in the
low alluvial coast is absent along the mountainous shoreline, where
cliffed headlands alternate with short, sandy beaches. In some cases
beaches, exposed only at low tide, fringe portions of the headlands. In
contrast to the low, monotonous mangrove shoreline, the steep mountainous coast is one of great variety of landscape and rare natural
beauty. [43]

The Offshore Area

Deep water prevails off most of the mountainous coast. The

mud and sand shoals so characteristic of the mangrove coast are lacking, except at the mouths of some of the larger rivers, such as the Río Valle south of Punta Solano and along the shore of the Gulf of Tribugá north of Nuquí. Bars form across the mouths of most of the rivers, making entry difficult into their lower courses. In contrast, thirty to forty fathoms of water occur 500 yards off the headlands formed by Cabo Marzo, Cabo Corrientes, and Punta Utría.[44]

The Headlands

Ridges of hard black gabbro, dark grey andesite, and reddish rhyolite that descend from the main mass of the Serranía de Baudó to the sea have been eroded by waves to form headlands, some with sheer cliffs 200 feet high. Most of the headlands, however, although sloping steeply, are covered with dense rain forest; bare rocks are exposed only in the areas of active wave erosion. At low tide large boulders, having fallen from undercut cliffs are exposed at the base of promontories (Plate XIX). From Punta Ardita southward the headlands are rarely continuous for more than two or three miles, being interrupted by occasional coves with sandy beaches. Small headlands between beaches are called longos locally and at low tide can be rounded on foot. As one must leap from one slippery boulder to the next, to negotiate a longo is at best hazardous; moreover, a particularly high wave dashing on the rocks can easily sweep a person to sea. The larger promontories are by-passed over difficult inland trails. Except for the short trips along the smooth beaches, foot travel along the coast is not easy.

The erosional features usually associated with headlands -- stacks, caves, arches -- are present in profusion. Headland remnants in the form of rocky islets and shoals abound; these features give added beauty to the coast, but present hazards to navigation. The Rocas de Otávira off Cabo Marzo and the cluster of islets off Punta Jurubirá are the best examples of headland remnants along the coast. A curious semi-arid vegetation, composed of aloes and trailing cacti, is characteristic of these islets. Moreover, most are used as rookeries by various sea birds, especially a seasonal black tern. Some islets and rocks have been eroded to form dangerous reefs, partially submerged at high tide, such as the Negritos near the entrance to Buenaventura Bay and the Isla la Viuda near Tumaco. Behind the larger headlands there are bays protected from swell and waves caused by the prevailing southwest winds. For example, Bahía Solano lies in the lee of the point of the same name; Humboldt Bay (Bahía de Coredó) behind Cabo Marzo; and the Bay of Cupica in the lee of Punta Cruces. The most spectacular bay, however, is that of Utría, a drowned graben cleft into the coast north of Cabo Corrientes. Sheltered by a high peninsula and off-shore islands, and ten to twelve fathoms deep, this bay for years has been considered by Colombians as the best natural harbor along the coast of northwestern South America.[45] Unfortunately, the bay is only one mile across and five miles long and stream alluvium has shoaled its eastern or landward shore. Still more unfortunate, it is one of the most isolated points along the Pacific Coast of the Americas.

The Beaches.

Of the 245 miles of mountainous coastline from Cabo Corrientes to Punta Garachiné, approximately 100 miles, or about 40 per cent, is fringed by sand beaches. Those that occupy the heads of coves are no more than a few hundred yards long. Longer beaches extend from one to ten miles along the lower mountain sections, where streams debouching from the coastal hills have formed small alluvial plains (Map 14). The longest beach area of the entire coast is that which stretches for fifteen miles from Coredó northward to Punta Ardita near the Panamanian border. Like most of the long beaches, it is not continuous, but is occasionally interrupted by longos and stream estuaries. The curved pocket beaches that form along the base of the headlands or at the heads of coves are narrow; at low tide most are forty to fifty yards wide, but high tide may cover them completely. The longer beaches that fringe the small alluvial plains are often more than 100 yards wide at low tide; some are compound bay-head bars formed by a series of beach ridges and backed by narrow lagoons. Such features are the sites of many of the more important coastal villages along the mountainous coast, such as Cupica and Juradó in Colombia and Jaqué in Panama (Plate XX).

The vegetation of the larger beaches is similar to that described for the strands along the alluvial coast. On the beach ridges a low mat of salt-tolerant creepers is backed by hibiscus thickets and occasional clumps of rain forest. Along the small lagoons flooded by tide are small areas of mangrove, the prop-rooted Rhizophora brevistyla being the most common component. In many cases the mangrove is backed by a narrow strip of fresh-water swamp forest, with nato (Mora megistosperma) and cativo (Prioria copaifera) as the principal trees. Today most of the original vegetation of the long beaches has been replaced by the coconut palm. The location of beaches along the coast can be readily ascertained from sea by the light green fronds of these palms.

Beach and <u>longo</u> near Juradó, Chocó, at high tide. The town of Juradó
is built on the beach ridge which is backed by a narrow lagoon and a
small area of mangrove.

A short bay-head beach north of Juradó, typical of those encountered
along the rocky coast of the Chocó. The <u>longo,</u> or headland, of Juradó
is in the background.

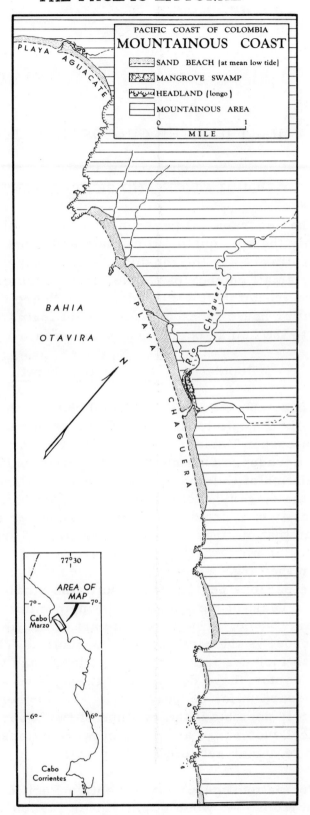

MAP 14

PART II -- THE CULTURAL MILIEU

CHAPTER VI
POPULATION AND SETTLEMENT

The geographical personality of the Pacific lowlands is molded not only the hot equatorial climate and densely forested terrain; even more significant are the inhabitants and their cultural heritage. The relatively small number of people, the characteristic riverine distribution of the inhabitants, the predominant Negroid racial composition, the peculiar house types and settlement forms -- all give an especial stamp to the human occupance of the area.

Population, Density and Growth

Today approximately 335,000 people inhabit the tropical rain forest of the Pacific lowlands.[1] Of these about 300,000 live in Colombia, the rest in Darién, southeastern Panama and in Esmeraldas, northwestern Ecuador. This number comprises only 2.5 per cent of the total population of Colombia, whereas the lowlands make up about 7 per cent of the country's total area. The Colombian lowlands have a population density of approximately ten persons per square mile. This is greater than that of other American rain forest areas, such as the upper Amazon Basin. Densities, however, vary from one person per square mile in the large municipality of Ríosucio, lower Atrato Valley, to thirty-three persons per square mile in the small municipality of Condoto, in the heart of the gold and platinum mining area of the upper San Juan River, Chocó. The southern part of the lowlands near the Ecuadorian border is the more densely occupied. The municipality of Tumaco, which includes fair agricultural land, and that of Barbacoas, an old mining center, have densities of twenty-five and twenty-two persons per square mile, respectively. The northern part of the lowlands is sparsely populated; the swamps of the lower Atrato and large sections of the Baudó range and its northward extension into Darién are almost devoid of human settlement (Map 15).

Population figures for the entire Pacific lowlands of Colombia date from 1843 when slightly over 51,000 persons were enumerated.[2] Figure 5 shows that in the 70-year period, 1843-1912 the population almost tripled, chiefly by natural increase; in the 40-year period, 1912-1951, the population doubled, and is still increasing, despite continual emigration and high death rate. The rate of population increase of the lowlands, however, is not as great as that of Colombia as a whole. Moreover, the percentage of the total Colombian population living in the Pacific lowlands has remained between 3.2 and 2.5 for more than a century.

A longer record of population data is extant for the Chocó, the northern part of the lowlands. Figure 5 shows a slow increase of population in the Chocó during the late colonial and early republican periods (1778-1850). Owing chiefly to the heavy migrations from the mining areas after emancipation of slaves in 1851, the population of the Chocó was stationary for fifty years. Although a sharp increase occurred after the close of the disastrous "Thousand-Day" civil war in 1903, the department in the past forty years has again experienced a decrease in the rate of population growth. The latter fact, coupled with the large increase of people in the lowlands as a whole in the last forty years, indicates that a relatively rapid growth of population has taken place in the southern section, especially around the Tumaco area.[3]

Disease

Among the various factors that underlie the paucity of people in the lowlands are lack of good agricultural land, isolation and lack of adequate transportation, and disease. Of these the latter is outstanding. As in most other humid equatorial areas of northern South America, tropical diseases abound. Rare indeed is the native lowlander who has not contracted one or several of the endemic maladies, which range from various intestinal ills to the dreaded bubas, or yaws. Infant mortality is high -- probably greater than 200 per 1000.[4] Old people are few; according to 1938 census figures, out of every 1000 inhabitants in the Chocó, only 41 are over 59 years of age.[5] Since colonial times the highland people of Colombia have maintained an exaggerated dread of the Pacific lowlands mainly because of its reputation for diseases. But it should be emphasized that these lowlands are no more disease-ridden than other humid equatorial areas of South America and are probably less so than regions of similar climate in West Africa and southeastern Asia.

Malaria is the most widespread and debilitating disease in the lowlands. It is estimated that in the Atrato and San Juan valleys of the Chocó over 50 per cent of the inhabitants are periodically incapacitated by malarial fever; along the Pacific Coast the percentage is between twenty-five and fifty.[6] Most of the nine Colombian species of the

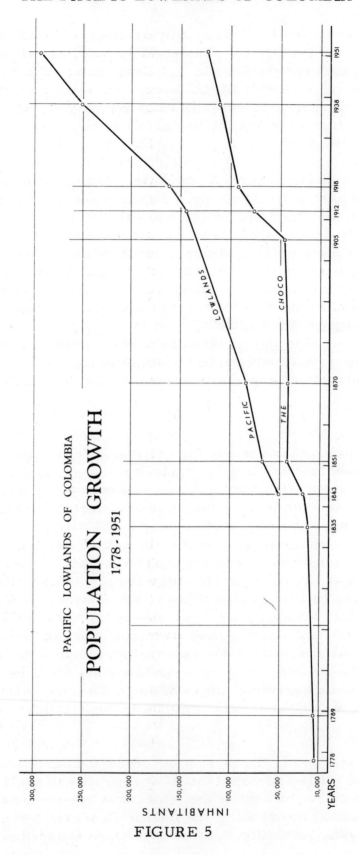

FIGURE 5

Anopheles mosquito -- all vectors of malaria -- are found in the Pacific lowlands. Anopheles albimanus and A. pseudopunctipennis, the larvae of which thrive best in the quiet back-water swamps and marshes, are probably the most common.[7] Anopheles aquasalis probably breeds in the brackish water behind the coastal mangroves.

Dengue and yellow fever, both carried by the Old World mosquito Aedes aegypti and by some native American species,[8] formerly were scourges of the Pacific lowlands; today, although dengue frequently occurs throughout the area, yellow fever is occasionally endemic only in Darién and the northern part of the Chocó.[9]

Several relapsing fevers are common in the lowlands. One is carried by the common bedbug which infests the floors, walls and rafters of practically all huts along the rivers. The parasite injected into the human bloodstream through a bedbug bite is a spirochete (probably Borrelia, spp.) which infects the red corpuscles. Most of the lowland inhabitants have developed an immunity to this malady, but the fever incapacitates an outsider for several weeks, and sometimes can be fatal. Today the disease is quickly cured with penicillin.

Next to malaria, probably the most widespread and crippling sickness in the lowlands is yaws, or frambeais (pián, bubas). Well over 40 per cent of the present inhabitants are infected by this disease which causes ugly skin lesions, running sores particularly on the legs and arms, and in its final stages leprous decay of the flesh and crippling of the limbs.[10] It is usually fatal only to infants. Caused by a syphilis-like spirochete, Treponema pertenue, yaws is usually contracted by direct contact with an infected person; thus small children easily catch the disease from infected mothers. Though yaws is often said to occur more frequently among Negroes than other races, many of the Indians of the Chocó and some whites are infected. The origin of the disease is obscure. It is probably Old World, having been carried from Africa to America by slaves. Today the disease is widespread in the humid tropics, but is especially prevalent in West Africa, southeastern Asia, Oceania, northern South America and the Caribbean. Its area of occurrence appears to be spreading. Presently, the Colombian government, in co-operation with the Interamerican Health Service, is rapidly completing an inoculation campaign against yaws in the Pacific lowlands. Intermuscular injections of penicillin both prevent and cure the disease.[11]

The high rate of infant mortality in the Pacific lowlands is caused mainly by a number of intestinal diseases. Amoebic and bacillary dysentery and hookworm are surprisingly uncommon in the rural areas. Possibly this is because of the torrential rains which daily clean

the ground of human feces. Also significant is the fact that rain collected in barrels and jars is the main source of drinking water. However one parasitic worm, Ascaris lumbricoides, which incubates more
deeply in the soil, is not carried away by rain wash; thus, this worm
has become the principal cause of intestinal ailments in children. [12]
Malaria, yaws and intestinal ascaridiosis thus make up a deathly trilogy
that kills thousands of infants yearly in the Pacific lowlands. Around
urban centers, such as Quibdó and Buenaventura, the accumulation of
rubbish heaps on the outskirts of town attracts large numbers of buz-
zards. As these scavengers often roost or rest on housetops, they
transfer a variety of intestinal parasites, including amoebic forms of
dysentery, which contaminate drinking water collected off roofs.

Pulmonary diseases such as acute bronchitis, pneumonia,
and tuberculosis occur frequently in all parts of the lowlands. Tuberculosis is extremely lethal among the Indians of the Chocó, and, with
measles and smallpox, may well have been one of the principal diseases
that has decimated the Indian population since European contact. The
indigenous population has apparently acquired some immunity against
smallpox and measles, but not against tuberculosis.

One of the major causes of meager population density and
growth in the lowlands today, disease is a detriment that can be controlled. Increasing concern of the national government about the health
problems of the Pacific Coast, as exemplified by the anti-yaws campaign, is an encouraging sign in the modern development of humid tropical areas. With the increased use of insecticides such as DDT and the
introduction of sanitation measures, malaria and the intestinal diseases
may be reduced to a minimum.

The success of health programs in most tropical lowland
areas, however, depends on adequate financial backing, skilled and devoted medical personnel, and a native population receptive to sanitary
innovations. To date, Colombia and other countries in the American
tropics have been dependent upon international health organizations for
financial and technical aid in carrying out campaigns against tropical
diseases. Effective malaria control alone is inordinantly costly, as
evidenced by the expense incurred by European nations in their West
African possessions. Furthermore, the immunity against DDT quickly
reached by some species of Anopheles; the physical difficulties of eradicating breeding places of mosquitoes in a rain-drenched swamp-covered
land such as the Pacific lowlands, and the slowness in educating a
superstitious population in methods of local malaria sanitation are some
of the problems faced by the Colombian officials of the anti-malarial
programs. Although physically possible, effective control of all tropical

diseases in the Pacific lowlands of Colombia appears to be in the distant future.

Riverine Pattern of Settlement

One of the outstanding features of the Pacific lowland population is its riverine distribution, a pattern of settlement that often prevails in rain forest areas (Map 15). River banks have attracted settlement in the lowlands since preconquest times. Along the lower courses of streams natural levees afford the highest land the best soils for cultivation. Similar advantages are found on alluvial terraces along the middle and upper courses of rivers. Even for non-farmers the river banks are attractive by reason of the usual abundant supply of fish, fresh-water crustaceans and mollusks, and a variety of aquatic and amphibious mammals. Moreover, rivers are the highways in this forested land where interfluves, because of their swampy or rugged nature, are hard to traverse. Today, along short stretches of some rivers, such as the lower Rosario near Tumaco, or the Río Condoto in the upper San Juan drainage, population density may be as high as 200 persons per square mile.

Another, though less important settlement pattern is seen in a coastwise arrangement of small fishing and farming hamlets along beach ridges fronting the mangrove swamp or located in sandy coves at the base of rocky shores. Since colonial days various seaport towns have been established in sheltered bays and lagoons along the coast or near river mouths in the lower part of the tidal reach. As indicated earlier, a few small settlements are found on the sandy firmes of the mangrove swamp.

In contrast to the river banks and the sandy seashore, the interfluves are empty areas, or despoblados. Except for occasional small clearings for crops or an isolated gold placer, the dense forests of the interfluves are used mainly as hunting grounds by the local population. Temporary shelters or ranchos may be set up along a miry trail near a cleared plot or beside a placer mine, but permanent settlement is almost invariably found along the streams. Map 15 shows the extensive unoccupied interfluves, even in the areas of dense riverine settlement around Tumaco and near the Ecuadorian border. The vast despoblados of the lower Atrato, the Panama-Colombian border area, the western slopes of the Cordillera Occidental, and the rough Serranía de Baudó are among the most striking features of population distribution in the Pacific versant of Colombia.

The riverine settlement pattern is reflected in social and

political groupings within the lowlands. People living on a given river
consider themselves as a single community, apart from the inhabitants
of an adjacent stream system separated by a despoblado difficult to
traverse. Negroes and mixed bloods speak of "nuestro río," or mention
for example, that "somos del Río Guapi," or "somos Guapiseños," indicating their social attachment to a given river. The relative ease of
travel by water; the common problems involved in the exploitation of
the soil, fish, game, and mineral resource along the river; the inter-
marriage of families on the same stream system -- such factors underlie communal interest along hydrographic lines. Moreover, the minor
civil divisions (corregimientos or inspecciones) of the lowlands often
correspond to river systems, with the largest village on the river as
the administrative center.

Racial Composition

Three races -- Indian, Negro, and White -- and their mixtures comprise the present population of the Pacific lowlands. Negroids,
including mixtures with whites (mulattoes) and Indians (sambos), make
up at least 85 per cent of the total population, while Indians and whites
account for 7 and 8 per cent, respectively. [13]

One of the main themes of the history of settlement in the
Pacific lowlands has been the gradual displacement of the Indian by the
Negro. [14] Several thousand forest Indians, mainly the Chocó linguistic
group, still hold out in their isolated headwater retreats in the Serranía
de Baudó and in various sections of the western versant of the Cordillera
Occidental. With increasing Negroid population, however, the Indian
will probably disappear eventually from the Pacific lowlands. Since
colonial times few Caucasians have resided permanantly in these hot,
forested lands. Those who now make that area their home are confined,
as in colonial days, to the larger towns, where they serve as merchants,
mine owners, and professionals.

The Indians

Long before the Spanish conquest the aboriginal inhabitants
of the Pacific lowlands were living in scattered groups along the river
banks as primitive farmers, fishermen and hunters. At least three
large language groups were represented at Spanish contact: (1) the Cuna,
of Chibchan stock, occupied most of the territory of eastern Panama
between the present Canal Zone and the Gulf of Urabá, including the
province of Darién and the extreme lower Atrato Basin. (2) The Chocó
and the closely related Waunamá (Noanamá), both of probable Cariban
affiliation, were the more numerous. [15] They inhabited most of what is

now known as the Chocó, including the middle and upper Atrato and the
entire San Juan river basins, plus the western flank of the Cordillera
Occidental; apparently they also occupied some territory east of the
Cordillera, particularly in the upper reaches of the Sinú and San Jorge
rivers of Antioquia where remnants are still found today.[16] It is not
certain that the Chocó occupied the Pacific Coast between the present
Panama-Colombia border and the mouth of the San Juan River; other
unrelated Indians, now extinct, may have inhabited parts of the coast
as late as the seventeenth century.[17] Moreover, during the same period
enclaves of non-Chocó people may have existed within the middle Atrato
drainage. For example, a primitive nomadic group known as the
"Suruco" was reported in 1671 to be living on the eastern flank of the
Serranía de Baudó, while further north along the Bojayá River were the
more culturally advanced "Poromea."[18] (3) Groups of several related
Chibchan tribes, including the Cayapa, Coaiquer, Sindagua, Chupa, and
others, inhabited the southern part of the Pacific lowlands and adjacent
mountain slopes from northern Esmeraldas to the Río Timbiquí, south
of Buenaventura.[19] Between the Bay of Buenaventura and the Naya
River lived several unclassified tribes, one of which was the Yurumanguí.

   The Cuna today live mainly outside the Pacific lowlands,
but historically they have been significant in the colonial development
and trade in Darién and the lower Atrato. During the sixteenth century
the Cuna began to migrate from the Gulf of San Miguel and the adjacent
Pacific Coast eastward to the Gulf of Urabá.[20] On the western shore
of the Urabá they supplanted the related Cueva, whom the Spaniards had
practically obliterated after the founding of Santa María la Antigua just
west of the Tarena mouth of the Atrato in 1510. Eventually, the Cuna
spread eastward as far as Jaraguay, near the Sinú River.[21] The warlike nature of these Indians delayed Spanish settlement in central Darién
until the end of the seventeenth century, and their frequent raids discouraged river traffic until the mid-eighteenth century. Still fiercely
independent of white authority, the modern Cuna of Panama are feared
by the neighboring Chocó in Colombia; the Cuna retain a consumate hate
of the Negro.

   Probably during the seventeenth century the Cuna began a
northwestward movement up the Chucanaque River and its northern
tributaries, reached the headwaters of the Bayamo, and by the eighteenth
century had crossed the Serranía del Darién to settle along the Caribbean
coast.[22] By 1800 most of the Cuna had left the lower Atrato. During
the past 150 years a final migration took them to the San Blas Islands
of the Caribbean coast of Panama, where the majority now reside as
fishermen and coconut farmers.

A few Cuna are still in the lower Atrato area (Map 16).
About 200 live on the Río Caimán, near the eastern shore of the Gulf
of Urabá. In 1947 a small number were reported to be on the upper
Arquía, Tigre, and Cutí rivers, immediately west of the Atrato Delta, [23]
and some are still found on the upper tributaries of the Tuira River in
Darién. [24] Although the interior Cuna still retain some of their old
forest culture, such as boat types, isolated river settlement, and shifting agriculture, the bulk of the population on the Caribbean coast is no
longer representative, and should be excluded from a study of the Indian
cultures of the Pacific lowland forests.

The Chocó (who call themselves the Emberá, or "the people")
form the core of primitive forest Indians today in western Colombia
and, since Spanish contact, have set the cultural pattern for Negroes
and mixed bloods throughout most of the Pacific lowlands. Balboa's
short excursion up the Atrato in 1511 probably represents the first
Spanish contact with the Chocó. It was on this expedition that the
Spaniards first learned of the Chocó's bellicose nature and of his
poisoned darts. Drawn by rumors of abundant gold deposits, Spaniards
next penetrated Chocó territory in the 1540's by sending a party from
the newly conquered Cauca Valley down the western slope of the Cordillera Occidental. [25] Despite the failure of this and other forays, due
mainly to the hostility of the Chocó, a mining settlement called San
Francisco de Nóvita was finally established in the last quarter of the
sixteenth century on the Tamaná River in the well-populated country of
the upper San Juan drainage. [26] Farther upstream on the slopes of the
Cordillera Occidental the administrative city of Toro was founded, and
the entire gold-bearing area of the upper Tamaná came to be known as
the "Minas de Toro." [27] Encomiendas of Chancos, Chocó, Ingará, and
Totuma tribes, all of Chocó speech, were apportioned to various
Spaniards, who forced the Indians to work gold placers. [28] The re-
bellious character of the Chocó and their intense dislike of forced work
soon obliged the Spaniards to resort to Negro slave labor. The first
serious Indian uprising took place in 1586, and by the close of the century the Chocó had forced most the Spaniards from the lowlands. [29]
Not until 1636 were mining settlements re-established with Negro slave
labor on the Tamaná. [30] By the mid-seventeenth century the Chocó
Indians of the upper San Juan and Atrato basins were partially pacified,
mainly through missionary activity. [31] Occasional rebellions, such as
that of 1684, however, occurred within the mining area well into the
eighteenth century. [32] Although the Spanish crown prohibited the use
of these Indians for mine labor, tribute for the royal treasure was
levied on heads of families; moreover, Indians near the mining camps
were forced to grow maize, sweet manioc, and plantains to feed the
mines; they were also obliged to construct huts in the camps, to build

and repair aqueducts in the placers, and to make canoes and furnish labor for transport to and from the mines.[33] This relationship between Spaniard and lowland Indian persisted until the end of the colonial period.

During the late seventeenth and eighteenth centuries many Chocó migrated to areas outside their homeland. These movements in some cases were made to avoid payment of tribute and labor. The most significant migration was that into the Pacific side of Darién, which the Cuna had abandoned in the sixteenth and seventeenth centuries. Near the close of the eighteenth century many Chocó were fleeing the mining districts of the upper Atrato to settle on the short rivers along the Pacific Coast and on the longer Balsas and Sambú rivers of Darién.[34] Today western Darién is recognized Chocó territory. Even Chocó typonomy is replacing Cuna place names; though names of several of the larger rivers still carry the Cuna suffix, -ti, those of many of the smaller streams now have the Chocó suffix, -do, both terms meaning river. Movement of Indians from the department of Chocó into Darién still goes on, especially during times of civil stress in Colombia.[35]

During the latter part of the colonial period a few Chocó fled the upper San Juan-Atrato to settle along the Saija, Yuramanguí, Cajambre and Naya rivers south of Buenaventura.[36] Today descendants of these migrants are found mainly on the Saija and its tributaries, but many have moved farther south to the Iscuandé, Tapaje and Sanguianga rivers between Guapi and Tumaco. Superb canoemen, these Indians are even more migratory than those in Chocó department. Some families on the Río Tapaje often go to the lower Saija for a stay of one or two years; those of the Saija think nothing of paddling to Tumaco or Buenaventura (journeys of 150 and 250 miles, respectively) to trade or just to see the country; on important festive occasions most of the Chocó along this coast gather at one of the two Indian "villages" (actually religious centers, each with its Catholic chapel) on the upper Saija (Plate XXI).

To estimate with accuracy the numbers of a primitive, semi-sedentary people is practically impossible. Spaniards who ventured into the Chocó in the sixteenth century reported a "large" population along the river banks. During subsequent centuries the disastrous epidemics of European diseases greatly reduced the number of forest Indians. About the year 1600 missionaries estimated the number of Chocó and Waunamá to be approximately 60,000.[37] In 1768 the number of Indians of the province of Chocó (which included both the Chocó and Waunamá) was thought to be 36,000; twenty-five years

PLATE XXI
FOREST INDIANS OF THE CHOCO

Chocó Indian of the Río Saija in festive dress.

Left: Waunamá Indians of Río San Juan. Men wear the pampanilla, or breachclout; women wear a wrap-around skirt. Right: A group of Chocó-speaking women and children in a multi-family hut, Nazareño, upper Patía del Norte drainage.

later this number had decreased to 15,000.[38] According to 1951 census figures, about 6,800 Indians, including possibly 1,000 Waunamá, lived in the department of Chocó. There are approximately 2,600 Chocó in Darién; 1,000 in Antioquia, including those on the upper Sinú and San Jorge rivers; and possibly 500 in the lowlands south of Buenaventura.[39] The present-day total Chocó population is probably between 8,000 and 9,000 souls.

Today the largest concentration of the Chocó is in the Baudó River drainage, where about 2,000 Indians live on the upper courses of the small tributaries (Map 16). The Catholic mission center of Catrú, established on the Río Dubasa in the 1930's, is probably the only large Chocó village. Other important concentrations of the Chocó include those of the upper Andágueda and its tributaries (1,000 Indians) and the Balsas and Sambú rivers in Darién.[40]

The Waunamá (Noanamá). Of the Chocó languages and dialects extant at the time of Spanish contact, probably the most distinct was Noanamá, or, more correctly, Waunamá. The Indians who spoke this language lived in the middle and lower San Juan drainage and probably as far up the Pacific Coast as the mouth of the Baudó River. A southern group of Waunamá apparently inhabited the area around Buenaventura Bay and the lower courses of the Dagua, Anchicayá and Raposo rivers.[41]

As most of their territory contained few gold placer deposits, the bulk of the Waunamá had less direct contact with the Spaniards than did the Chocó to the north. Spanish accounts of the late sixteenth and early seventeenth centuries describe these people as "indios de guerra," who made bothersome forays against the small port of Buenaventura.[42] Such an unfriendly attitude on the part of the Indians gave the Spanish officials stationed at Buenaventura political license to make occasional raids into the lower San Juan drainage for the purpose of taking numerous Waunamá as slaves. They were then sold to sugar growers in the upper Cauca Valley.[43] In 1631 the Waunamá were finally pacified,[44] and by 1660 they were being assessed payments for the royal tribute.[45] Sometime later those living on the Raposo River were growing food for the mines nearby.[46]

In the early eighteenth century a few Waunamá began to migrate southward settling, like the Chocó, on some of the rivers in the coastal lowland between Buenaventura and Tumaco. The most important Waunamá colony was on the Micay River where Nuestra Señora del Pilar de Zaragoza was established with the help of Catholic missionaries.[47] By the last quarter of the eighteenth century Waunamá were found as far south as Tumaco; many of these had migrated voluntarily from the Raposo, but others were serving as canoemen for Spanish traders.[48]

As mentioned previously, today the Waunamá have been reduced to approximately 1,000 persons who live mainly in the lower San Juan area. The largest concentration is isolated on the Río Siguirisúa, a tributary of the upper Docampadó, which flows into the Pacific. A small number still inhabit certain sections of the lower San Juan, including the delta area, and a few families can be found in isolated parts of the Munguidó, Copomá and Cucurrupí rivers, eastern tributaries of the San Juan. The sole remnant of the southern Waunama is composed of about twenty families who live along the lower Micay River, having been ejected from their old lands around Zaragoza by intruding Negroes.

The "Indios Bravos." The western slope of the Cordillera Occidental and the coastal hill area between Buenaventura and Guapi is almost an ethnological blank in terms of its aboriginal inhabitants. One of the first Spanish entradas into this area was in 1610, when a party led by one Francisco Ramírez de la Serna was ordered to punish various forest tribes called Timbas, Piles, Cacahambres (Cajambres?), and Paripesos, who had been raiding the port of Buenaventura and gold mines nearby. According to the Ramírez report and map, these tribes, of unknown linguistic affiliation, lived on the upper and middle courses of the unidentified rivers "Timbas" and "San Juan," which could correspond to the modern Saija and Micay.[49] The Ramírez party returned to Cali with 130 captives taken from the Timbas area; these were sold as slaves to encomenderos in the upper Cauca Valley. This operation may have touched off a series of slaving parties into the area, for Spanish documents dated 1630 refer to slaves in Cali from the "tierra de Nayabe" (Río Naya area?) and the provinces "de los Piles y los Cacajambres."[50]

In 1743 miners discovered an unknown tribe on the headwaters of the Río Yurumanguí; later, missionaries penetrated into the area to convert these Indians, who were found to speak an unknown and unrelated language. Other tribes, each speaking a distinct tongue, were said to exist at that time on the headwaters of the Micay and Guafuí rivers. A few years later a smallpox epidemic practically wiped out the newly-found Indians.[51] The only trace of these ephemeral people today are legends told by the Negro and mixed-blood inhabitants of the various rivers concerning the "Indios bravos," or wild Indians, who are said to inhabit isolated sections on the slope of the cordillera.

The southern Chibcha groups. At the time of Spanish

contact the Pacific lowlands from the Río Timbiquí southward into
Esmeraldas were inhabitated by a primitive tropical forest people
who represented a large number of Chibchan languages. Pascual
de Andagoya, exploring southward from Buenaventura in 1540, was
probably the first European to report on the dense population and the
large pile houses (barbacoas) of the Indians within the Patía Delta.[52]
It was the abundance and size of these pile dwellings that later gave the
name "Provincia de Barbacoas" to the coastal lowlands between the
Timbiquí and Mira rivers. Spaniards did not again enter the lower
Patía area until the first years of the seventeenth century. On the
upper western slopes of the Andean cordillera they first encountered
the primitive Coaiquer and Mayasquer Indians, whom they called
"indios de la Montaña."[53] Farther downslope in the hilly coastal lowlands along the Patía and Telembí rivers were many nomadic and can-
nibalistic tribes (caribes); the greater number of them spoke the
Sindagua dialect of a Chibchan language that is often called "Barbacoas"
and sometimes "Malla"; minor dialects in the same area and south to
the Mira were Nulpe, Panga, Guelmambí and Cuasminga.[54] As early
as 1601 the Sindagua were raiding Spanish highland farms near Pasto
and stock ranches in the upper Patía Valley.[55] After attempts to pla-
cate the cannibals with gifts of cotton cloth had failed, the Spanish
governor in 1610 finally dispatched a punitive expedition from Pasto into the Sindagua country.[56] On this expedition rich gold placers were
discovered in the Telembí and adjacent rivers, leading to the establishment of the mining center of Santa María del Puerto (present-day
Barbacoas) on the Telembí sometime after 1610. The Sindagua were
not completely subdued until 1635; most of the survivors were apportioned in encomiendas to the Spanish mine owners on the Telembí,[57]
but some Indians taken in combat has been sent as slaves into the highlands around Cali.[58] Later in the seventeenth century the remaining
Sindaguas, mine workers decimated by disease, were replaced by
Negro slaves, and were permitted to commute payment of tribute into
agricultural and transport labor for the mine owners.[59]

North of the Barbacoas area the Chibchan groups extended
to the Timbiquí River, where Spanish miners entering in the 1630's,[60]
found Indians speaking mainly the Chupa and Boya dialects.[61] The
rivers immediately to the south of the Timbiquí, including the Guapi,
Iscuandé, Tapaje and Sanguianga, contained Indians speaking Guapi.[62]
These people were apparently more docile than their Sindagua neighbors, for the Guapi were prized as farm laborers along the coast, especially by the Spanish officials of Santa Bárbara de la Isla del Gallo,
a town that guarded the entrance to the Patía River and the Telembí
gold fields.[63]

From various comments made by miners as to diminution of Indians and the need of more Negro slaves, it is evident that by the end of the eighteenth century disease and shock of conquest had taken their toll of the Indian population in the Barbacoas and Timbiquí mining areas. A few Sindagua remained on the Telembí at mid-century, [64] but by the beginning of the next probably all of the Chibchan groups that once inhabited the area had died off or had been absorbed into the Negro element. Today about 2,000 Coaiquer, a group little molested by the colonial Spaniard, live on the western slope of the Andes between the Mira and Coaiquer rivers; these people are still "indios de la Montaña" and do not fit into the lowland picture. [65] But a vaguely-known people, called "indígenas" by the local Negroids, inhabit the headwaters of the Guelmambí and its tributaries south of Barbacoas and the upper reaches of the Río Rosario to the west. These groups may be of either Coaiquer or Sindagua affiliation. [66]

One important group of primitive forest Indians of Chibcha speech remains -- the Cayapa of Esmeraldas in Ecuador. [67] In the sixteenth century these Indians inhabited the western slopes of the Andean cordillera which overlooks the lowlands of present Esmeraldas. Having moved into the low country in the past 300 years, the remaining 2,000 Cayapa today live mainly on the upper Onzole and Cayapa rivers. Some are found a few miles to the north on the Río Bogotá, a tributary of the Santiago. In recent years, a few Cayapa families have been migrating westward to settle on the upper Río Verde and, west of the Esmeraldas River, on the upper Sucio and Viche rivers. Although in contact with Spanish miners and missionaries since the latter part of the sixteenth century, the Cayapa are still true forest Indians who have changed little through European contact. [68]

Archeology offers little help in reconstructing the history of Indian settlement in the coastal lowlands. The only known area of archeological significance in the entire lowland lies in the Esmeraldas-Tumaco district in the south. [69] There, one finds today large numbers of grave mounds, or tolas, built by an unknown people along river banks and on old beach remnants within the mangrove and fresh-water swamp near the coast. Expertly-molded clay figurines, well-made pottery, and fine metal work in the form of gold, copper, and platinum pins, breastplates, noserings, and small animal and human figurines make up much of the evidence for a people of relatively high culture who once occupied these coastal lowlands. Although this culture centers in the province of Esmeraldas, similar grave mounds and artifacts are found in lesser numbers along the lower and middle Río Mira, around Tumaco, and along many of the rivers to the northwest of Tumaco, such as the Rosario and Chagui. [70] Saville guesses that the Esmeraldas culture may have extended to the Guapi River, [71] but I have found nothing but crude potsherds at small sites along the rivers north of the Chagüí. Nevertheless, native miners along the Timbiquí and Saija rivers, north of Guapi, tell of the frequent discovery of small objects of worked gold in their ground sluices, indicating the probable extension of metallurgy within the lowlands far north of the Esmeraldas culture area.

When the Esmeraldas culture flourished is a matter of conjecture; certainly it had vanished long before the Spanish conquest. A Spanish account of 1600 mentions the extensive sherd-strewn mound area at La Tolita near the mouth of the Santiago River, and relates how the Cayapa and other Indians had for years been washing from the rubble gold ornaments to sell to Spaniards and mulattoes. [72] Until a few years ago this same site was still being exploited for its worked gold. [73] Along the steep Esmeraldas coast west of La Tolita, waves have exposed scores of tolas and have strewn their contents along the beaches, where some people still make a precarious living by panning the sands for small pieces of gold artifacts. [74]

Little archeological research has been done in other parts of the Colombian Pacific lowlands. Reconnaissance points to rich and numerous sites along the Pacific Coast of the Chocó, but finds within the Atrato and San Juan valleys appear less promising. [75]

The Negroid People

The Spanish colonies in the Caribbean and northern South America were among the principal centers of Negro slavery in the New World. Except for the advanced Chibcha culture in the high Colombian Andes, these areas were inhabited by primitive Indian farmers, most of whom quickly collapsed under the heavy death toll caused by the Spaniards' diseases and the psychological shock of conquest. After the first few decades of occupation, when the aboriginal collapse had become apparent, Spaniards turned to Africa for slave laborers to be used particularly in the mines. Since Colombia (or New Granada as it was called in colonial days) was one of the major gold-mining areas of the colonies, large numbers of Negro slaves were introduced, beginning in the last quarter of the sixteenth century and continuing until the end of the colonial period. Every mining center of Colombia was, and still is, marked by predominant Negroid population.

As emphasized in the foregoing section, the Pacific lowlands of Colombia were significant to Spaniards only for the rich gold placers along the upper and middle courses of rivers. The intractableness of some Indians (the Chocó) and the rapid collapse of others (the southern

Chibcha), together with royal prohibition and ecclesiastical disapproval of Indian labor, forced the Spaniards to import Negro slaves into the lowland mines. The descendants of these slaves today form the bulk of the population of the Pacific lowlands from the Gulf of San Miguel in Panama to Esmeraldas in Ecuador (Plate XXII).

During the colonial period at least three mining districts in the lowlands became centers of Negro slave population: (1) the eastern tributaries of the upper San Juan and Atrato drainages -- the heart of the Chocó; (2) the Barbacoas district, which included the Telembí and Magüí rivers and their tributaries; and (3) the upper and middle courses of the numerous rivers that cross the narrow coastal plain between Buenaventura and the Bay of Guapi. From these three core areas Negroes and mixed bloods have spread to all parts of the lowlands.

Although Spanish mining activity in the Chocó began on the upper Tamaná in the 1570's, Indian hostility prevented intensive placering and the importation of many Negroes for more than a century. [76] In 1689 miners from the upper Cauca around Anserma, Cartage and Cali and, especially, Popayán began to bring their quadrillas, or slave gangs, to work gold deposits in the upper San Juan drainage. [77] This area was known as the province of Nóvita, with its administrative center at the old camp of San Gerónimo de Nóvita, (the sixteenth century San Francisco) on the Tamaná. It included the mining centers of Zaragoza de Tadó on the upper San Juan, Santa Getrudis on the Taguato, San Agustín on the Sipí and Santa Bárbara on the Cajón. The upper Atrato mining area was called the province of Citará, and comprised mining camps on the Cértegui, Andágueda, Neguá, Bebará, Murrí and upper Sucio rivers, with the village of Citará, or Quibdó (the modern capital of the Chocó) as the administrative center. [78] Having the richest gold placers, the Province of Nóvita was the center of greatest Negro concentration in the Pacific lowlands. In 1778, for example, this area contained 5,692 Negro slaves and freedmen, while the province of Citará to the north had but 3,316[79] (Map 17). Table 4 shows the trend of Negro population in the Chocó for a 140-year period prior to the emancipation of slaves. The peak slave population was reached in the last quarter of the eighteenth century; with the decline of the African slave trade in the early years of the next century, the number of Negroes in forced servitude began to decrease and finally disappeared with emancipation in 1851. At the same time the number of freedmen, including both Negroes and mixed bloods, gradually increased.

PLATE XXII   99

NEGROES AND MIXED BLOODS OF THE PACIFIC COAST

Negro youths of the Río Naya, south of Buenaventura. The home-made pipe, or <u>cachimba</u>, is common throughout the lowlands.

<u>Left:</u> Mixed Negro-Indian-White women of Coquí, Pacific Coast north of Cabo Corrientes. <u>Right:</u> Sambos, or Negro-Indians of Diaguilla, upper Guelmambí River, Barbacoas.

Table 4
Negro Population in the Chocó, 1704-1843

Year	Slaves	Freedmen	Total
1704[a]	600	?	--
1759[b]	3,915	?	--
1778[c]	5,828	3,160	8,988
1789[d]	5,916	3,342	9,258
1806[e]	4,608	?	--
1843[f]	2,505	[18,000][g]	--

[a] AHNC, Minas del Cauca VI, f. 651[r] (1704)
[b] AHNC, Negros y Esclavos del Cauca IV, f. 358[r] (1759)
[c] "Relación del Chocó ..., 1780," in Historia Documental del Chocó, 205-241.
[d] Silvestre, "Descripción del Reyno ...," 152
[e] AHNC, Visitas del Cauca V, f. 228[v] (1806)
[f] Estadística Jeneral de la Nueva Granada (Bogotá, 1848).
[g] As the 1843 census gives no information on freedmen or mixed bloods, this figure, suggested as an estimate, was derived by assuming that 80 per cent of the total 1843 population was Negroid.

Imporatation of Negroes into the Barbacoas area did not begin on a large scale until the last years of the seventeenth century, after Indian labor had been decimated. In 1684 numerous Negro cuadrillas were working gold in twenty-eight camps strung along the upper Telembí, Magüí, Guelmambí and Tembí rivers.[80] Santa María del Puerto (Barbacoas) was established as the administrative center on the Telembí. Beginning around 1640, Spaniards brought Negro slaves into the mining area between Guapi and Buenaventura. By the mid-eighteenth century every major river of the coastal plain -- the Iscuandé, Guapi, Napi, Timbiquí, Guafuí, Saija, Micay, Naya, Yuramanguí, Cajambre and Raposo -- contained gangs of Negro slaves.[81]

The northern and southern extremities of the Pacific lowlands -- Darién and Esmeraldas -- had relatively few Negroes in colonial days. In Darién a few slaves were brought in to work placers along the Río Balsas after 1665 and to mine the rich gold veins at Santa Cruz de Caná after their discovery in the 1670's.[82] The Negroid population of colonial Esmeraldas consisted chiefly of sambos, offspring of local Indians and escaped slaves shipwrecked along the coast during the sixteenth century.[83] In both areas the present Negro population is

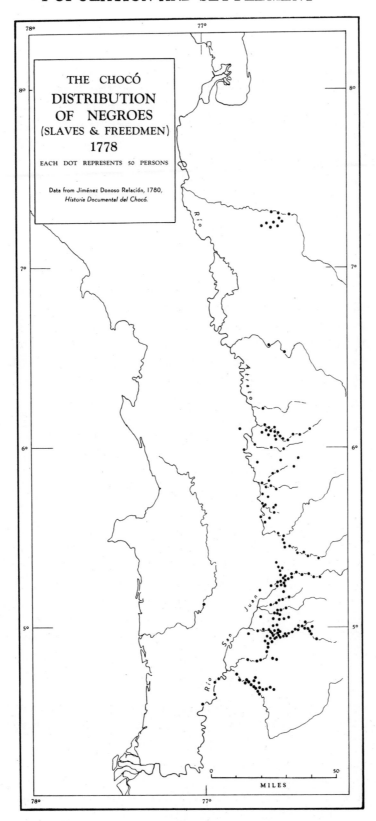

MAP 17

largely the result of migrations from Colombia during the last 100 years.

Provenience of slaves. During the early years of gold exploitation, most of the slaves that entered the mining areas of the Pacific lowlands were seasoned laborers from the Cauca mining camps. Later in the eighteenth century blacks were imported directly from Africa, entering through the port of Cartagena (the official slave mart of New Granada), whence they were taken overland and across the Cordillera to the Chocó or to Barbacoas.[84] Owing to governmental restrictions on transport, few slaves entered via the Atrato River, but some were shipped from Panama to the port of Chirambirá at the mouth of the San Juan, thence upriver to the camps of Nóvita and Citará.[85]

The majority of Negroes imported directly from Africa came chiefly from the Guinea Coast and the Congo; some were probably western Sudanese and Angolese. Customarily, a bozal, or Negro slave recently arrived from Africa, was given the surname corresponding to the name of his tribal language, or sometimes from the name of the African slaving station from which he was purchased; thus, from the name lists in account books of mining camps, a rough, but often erroneous idea can be obtained of the provenience of the slaves. (Slaves born in the New World were usually designated as criollos in the account books.) Several eighteenth-century account books of mines around Nóvita in the Chocó give a total of fifty-six different African names, most of which appear to be tribal or names of slaving stations.[86] Among those the most common surnames are Mina, Biáfara, Carabalí, Cetre, Lucumi, Arará, Congo, and Mandinga. According to Aguirre, Beltrán[87] and Arboleda,[88] who have studied the relationship between slave surnames and provenience, the first six names listed appear to indicate a Guinea Coast origin.[89] Mandinga is a name of a tribe in the western Sudan, (Senegal) and Congo undoubtedly refers to many Bantu-speaking groups in the lower Congo Basin, who made up a large part of the slaves sold into the Spanish colonies.[90] Other African names frequently encountered in account books include Angola, Chambá, Bran and Luango.[91]

Still today on many of the isolated rivers, especially those between Buenaventura and Guapi, many Negro family names are derived from the old tribal ones applied to the slaves during colonial days. For example, on the Yurumanguí, Mina is one of the most common surnames; Congo, Mandinga and Cangá are also numerous. Again, along the middle and upper courses of the Río Guapi one finds the names Biáfara, Cambindo (from the old slave station Cabinda in Angola?), Mina, Cuenú; and on the Río Iscuandé the names Carabalí and Congolino are not uncommon. Generally, however, on emancipation most Negroes took the surname of their former Spanish masters.

The Freedmen. During the colonial period a large number
of free Negroes, known as libres, evolved in most of the mining areas
of western Colombia. The figures in Table 4 (page 100) indicate that
by 1778, 35 per cent of the Negroid population of the Chocó were freedmen. These people were composed of Negroes who had been able to
buy their freedom; the runaways; and many mulattoes, most of whom
had been emancipated by compassionate masters. Most of the libres
continued to placer gold on their own or to work as wage laborers in
Spanish mines; others migrated to other parts of the lowlands to become subsistence farmers and fishermen. After independence a law
of 1821 proclaimed gradual emancipation of slaves in Colombia and
Venezuela,[92] but public disregard of the law and bureaucratic inefficiency made its enforcement impracticable, if not impossible. As previously mentioned, it was not until 1851 that slavery was finally abol-
ished in Colombia.[93] In the more isolated localities of the lowlands
Negroes still call themselves libres; in most areas, however, the term
moreno (dark-complexioned person) is used, rarely negro, which is
deprecatory.

Negro migrations. One of the most significant aspects of
the Negroids has been their expansion from the mining areas to all
parts of the Pacific lowlands in the past 150 years. Small numbers of
freedmen and runaways began to migrate in the latter part of the
eighteenth century. In 1780, for example, a group of runaways, or
cimarrones, fled the Chocó mining camps and settled on several tributaries of the Río Tuira in Darién.[94] By the end of the century several
groups from the upper Atrato and San Juan had established small settlements, such as Cupica and Juradó, along the Pacific Coast and in
the Baudó River Valley.[95] Along the coast some Negroes mixed with
Indians, forming a sambo element which, now diluted with white blood,
is common in many coastal towns.

A marked increase in Negro migrations occurred during
the period of gradual emancipation of slaves from 1821 to 1851.
Bolívar's numerous emancipation proclamations made between 1816
and 1821 touched off a series of Negro rebellions in various parts of
the lowlands. In 1821 a particularly bad uprising took place on the Río
Saija, where, incited by white revolutionists, the slaves burned mining
camps and fled downriver and along the beaches fringing the mangrove.[96]
Moreover, during the wars of independence many Negroes from
Barbacoas and the Chocó joined the revolutionary forces; at the close
of hostilities large numbers of these settled in the Cauca and Magdalena
valleys.[97]

The years following final emancipation saw the largest exodus of Negroes from the mining centers (Map 18). While the majority continued to work as laborers in the camps, a large number of freed slaves migrated downstream to settle the better agricultural lands. In the Chocó Negroes from Tadó, Condoto and Nóvita in the upper San Juan swarmed through the low divides across the Serranía de Baudó and occupied the rich natural levees along the Baudó River; others continued to the coast, where they settled along the better beaches and the short coastal rivers, such as the Orpúa, Ijúa, Docampadó and Virudó. [98] Negroes from around Quibdó and the upper-Atrato mining area settled as farmers in the upper Baudó and in fishing villages, such as Arusí, Nuquí and Nabugá along the rocky coast north of Cabo Corrientes. Many also travelled down the Atrato to settle the banks of the western tributaries, such as the Bojayá, Taguchí and Buey.

During this period (1850-1900) the Chocó and Waunamá Indians began to retreat into the upstream areas of the Serranía de Baudó in the face of Negro penetration into the better agricultural lands of the lower stream courses. It was not that the Negro forcibly ejected the Indian from his home in downstream areas; rather the Indian retreated quite voluntarily in order to be as distant as possible from a race that he held in disrespect.

In the mining area between Buenaventura and Guapi, Negro migrations after emancipation were mainly downstream to the better farming lands within and immediately landward from the fresh-water swamp zone of the coast. As along the Chocó coast, fishing villages and coconut plantations were established along the beaches. For instance, according to local inhabitants, the coastal fishing-farming village of Papayal was founded in 1875 and that of Mayorquín in 1890 by Negroes from the mining section on the Raposo; owing to depletion of placers, Negro miners from San Isidro and Barco on the upper Río Cajambre as late as 1913 moved to the coast to establish the fishing and mangrove bark-collecting camp of Pital, on a tidal channel near the mouth of the river. At the present time practically all upstream dwellers till land in the lower sections of the rivers at least during one period of the year.

From the Barbacoas mining district Negroes moved into the coastal streams north of Tumaco. The fathers or grandfathers of most of the present farmers along the Mira, Rosario, Chaguí, lower Patía and Sanguianga rivers were Barbacoanos. Most of the people of these rivers have relatives still living in mining villages on the Telembí, Guelmambí and Maguí rivers in the Barbacoas district. Many others from Barbacoas moved into the relatively unsettled ares of northern

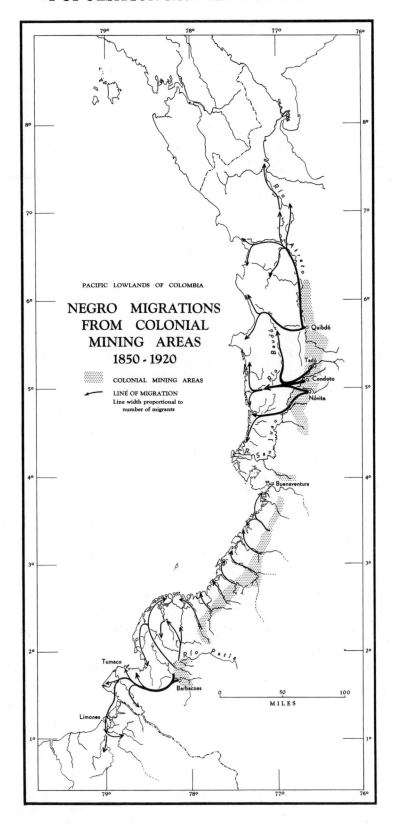

MAP 18

Esmeraldas, a movement that continues today.

The predominant Negroid population of Esmeraldas dates only from the last 100 years. During the mid-nineteenth century, after emancipation, hundreds of Negroes migrated from the haciendas of highland Ecuador into the hot country along the banks of the Santiago River and its tributaries. [99] At the turn of the century an English mining company imported a large number of Jamaican Negroes to work gold placers along the Santiago. Although English is no longer spoken, family names such as Whitley, Brown, Francis, Carr and Wilson are not uncommon along the Santiago today. At the same time many Colombian Negroes from Barbacoas began to enter Esmeraldas to take up farms and to gather rubber and tagua nuts. Today two-thirds of the present population of the canton of Eloy Alfaro, northern Esmeraldas, is said to be made up of Colombian Negroes or their descendants. [100]

The last twenty-five years has seen the migration of particularly the younger Negroes from the river settlements to various rapidly growing urban centers and expanding agricultural sections of western Colombia, northern Ecuador, and eastern Panama. Attracted by high wages and apparent amenities of city life, hundreds of Negroes have flocked into the booming port of Buenaventura to work as stevedores and construction hands. Since 1918 Buenaventura has grown from a village of 3,500 to a city of 35,000 (1951); most of the increase has been due to the influx of Negroes from (1) the coastal rivers between the Patía in the south and the Docampadó in the north and (2) the Río San Juan in the Chocó (Map 19). Many of the river dwellers entering Buenaventura have continued over the western cordillera to the Cauca Valley, where they have settled in the rapidly expanding industrial city of Cali or have sought work in the large sugar cane plantations and refineries nearby. In the south, Barbacoanos and farmers from adjacent rivers persist in their movement into the growing port of Tumaco and into the developing banana lands of Esmeraldas; in the latter area the Colombians are expanding into the coastal river valleys south and west of the port of Esmeraldas. In the north a movement of Negroes from the coastal villages and rivers of the Chocó into the fertile banana lands of Darién and into the high-wage area of the Canal Zone has been underway for many years. Like the Indian migrations, the Negro movement into Darién was accelerated during the recent political disturbances in the Chocó. [101] Other minor Negro migrations have taken place in recent years within the Chocó. Subsistence farmers along many of the Atrato tributaries are slowly giving up their precarious existence to seek a better life in the market towns of Quibdó and Istmina. Some try to find work at the big American mining camp of Andagoya in the upper San Juan, while others have gone to Cartagena on the Caribbean Coast

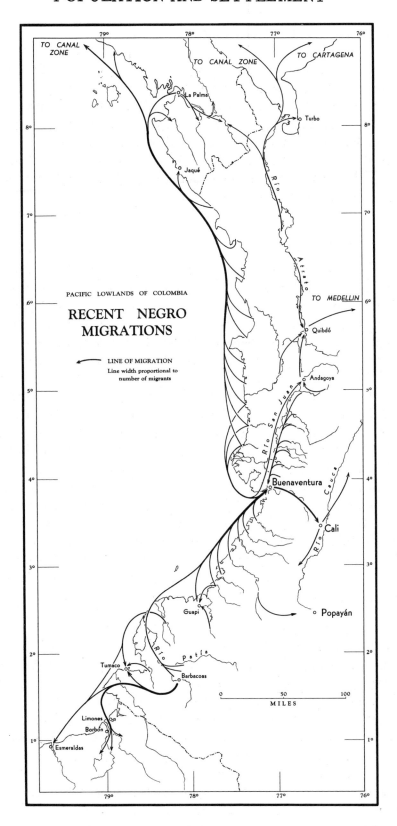

MAP 19

and to industrial Medellín in Antioquia.

Despite the recent emigration of Negroes from the subsistence farming and mining areas of the lowlands, the population of most of the rivers continues to increase or at least to hold its own by natural reproduction. Not all of the young people are moving out, and few of the conservative oldsters would consider leaving their patches of plantains and maize or the hut in which they were born. Nevertheless, owing to the depletion of gold deposits, many mining villages in the upper stream courses are being abandoned.

The White Population

As stated previously, the present white population of the Pacific lowlands of Colombia is estimated to comprise only 8 per cent of the total; a similar proportion is likely for Esmeraldas and Darién. According to the census of 1778, the number of whites in the Chocó made up only 3 per cent of the total;[102] 140 years later, in 1918, the percentage of white population of the same area had increased to 9.5.[103]

During colonial days the white element consisted chiefly of owners and administrators of mines, government officials, the clergy and occasional merchants. Most of these lived in the larger administrative centers, such as Nóvita, Citará (Quibdó), Iscuandé and Barbacoas. The latter town became renowned for its relatively large number of wealthy white families, all of whom were mine owners and merchants. Though greatly depleted in numbers, many descendants of these old families still live in Barbacoas. After the wars of independence and following the final emancipation of the slaves in 1851, most of the white mine owners, their wealth gone and their mining properties no longer economically exploitable, migrated to the highland towns of Pasto, Popayán, Cali, and Medellín.[104]

Probably sometime during the first half of the nineteenth century the beaches north of Tumaco were occupied by a group of Spanish-speaking whites of undetermined origin.[105] Today their descendants, many with some Negro blood, live in fishing and agricultural villages such as San Juan de la Costa, La Vigía, Amarales and Boquerones. Other villages along this coast, possibly formerly white, are now composed of mulattoes. Aside from the urban centers this stretch of coast offers one of the few examples of white rural settlement in the Pacific lowlands. The villages, however, are being slowly invaded by Negroes from the rivers; miscegenation is in progress, and within a few generations the white element will have been strongly diluted by black (Plate XXIII).[106]

PLATE XXIII   109
WHITE INHABITANTS ALONG COAST NORTH OF TUMACO

White farmer-fisherman of Majagual along coast north of Tumaco.

White and mulatto girls of San Juan de la Costa, north of Tumaco.

As in colonial times, the present-day white element in the lowlands is concentrated in the urban centers such as Quibdó, Istmina, Buenaventura, Guapi, El Charco, Barbacoas, Tumaco, Limones and Borbón. While the descendants of some of the old Spanish mining families operate various businesses in the towns, most of the modern merchants are either from the adjacent highlands or from the Near East. In the Chocó, for example, Antiqueños and Syrians own most of the general stores, local transport lines, and forest product-collecting stations. Throughout the Chocó and occasionally in the coastal lowlands south of Buenaventura one encounters the famous itinerant merchants of Antioquia, called paisas.[107] These whites buy and sell all manner of articles up and down the rivers. The paisa is probably as significant as the imported white and mestizo military personnel in the production of mixed bloods in the Chocó.

In the past fifty or sixty years actual Antioqueño settlement has spilled over the crest of the Cordillera Occidental and is now slowly descending into the drier, upper river valleys above the Chocó lowlands (Map 20). Most of the white colonists, however, rarely pass below an elevation of 3,000 feet into the malarial zone. In the upper valleys the Antioqueño is clearing the dense forest, planting grass for his characteristic blanco-orejinegro cattle and coffee for a cash crop. At the present time important colonies have been established in (1) the Dabeiba area in the upper Río Sucio along the newly completed Medellín-Turbo highway; (2) the Urrao district on the upper Río Penderisco; (3) the upper San Juan River valley, where the Antioqueño town of Pueblorrico was established in 1876 on one of the old trails that leads from the Cauca to the Chocó; (4) the upper reaches of the Atrato, where the towns of El Carmen and Guaduas were founded in the 1880's near the present Bolívar-Quibdó road into the equatorial forest; (5) the Ingará and Hábita river valleys, tributaries of the Tamaná, which are being settled by whites from the towns of El Águila and La María on the eastern slope of the cordillera, and from El Cairo and Albán, Antioqueño coffee towns on the western slope (the settlement of Valencia at an elevation of 1500 feet and not far from the old mining Negro town of Las Juntas de Tamaná represents the Antioqueño frontier in this sector); (6) the slopes above the middle Garrapatas River, settled by pioneers from Versailles, on the western slope of the cordillera; (7) the upper Sanguinini, a tributary of the lower Garrapatas, settled from the Antioqueño village of Naranja, near El Porvenir; (8) the upper Aguaclara River, tributary to the Munguidó, the white settlers coming from Trujillo and Ríofrio in the Cauca Valley; (9) the upper Calima River valley, where recently Antioqueños have established experimental farms near Bellavista, at an altitude of approximately 1500 feet; (10) the dry upper Dagua Valley, for centuries the main route of travel between the

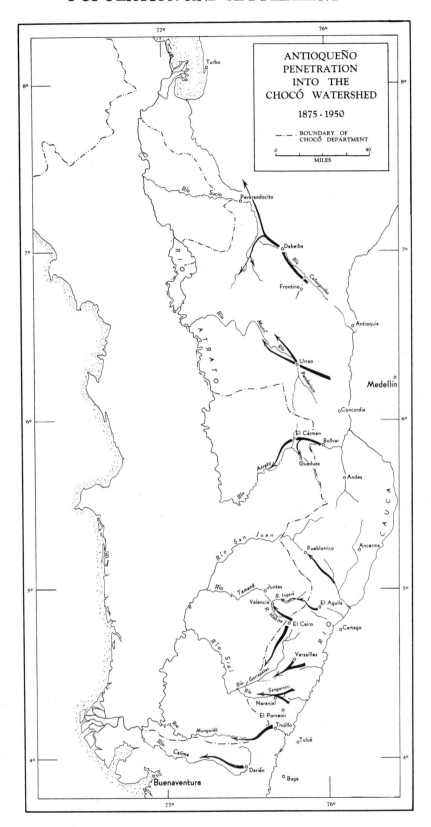

ANTIOQUEÑO
PENETRATION
INTO THE
CHOCÓ WATERSHED

1875 - 1950

BOUNDARY OF
CHOCÓ DEPARTMENT

0   40
MILES

MAP 20

Cauca and the Pacific, occupied by white Antioqueños and Vallecaucanos as far as the village of Cisneros (elevation 2,000 feet).[108]

Colonization Schemes. Various attempts to form agricultural colonies of white highlanders within the Pacific lowlands have been made during the past twenty years. To date none has been successful. In 1935 the Colombian government initiated a colony of mainly Antioqueño farmers on a 10,000 hectare tract near the Bay of Solano 180 miles north of Buenaventura. Colonists received small, partially cleared holdings within the basins of the Jella and Valle rivers. Attempts were made to introduce livestock on planted pastures and to begin plantings of cacao, bananas, coconuts and rice. After eight years of administrative mismanagement the colony was bankrupt, and was turned over to the government of the Chocó intendency.[109] Discouraged, most of the colonists left this isolated spot, and today a few dilapidated buildings housing stragglers at Ciudad Mutis, the administrative center, are all that remain of a once hopeful settlement.

More recently, in 1953, a group of thirty Antioqueños, sponsored by the Colombian Ministry of War and aided by merchants in Cali and Buenaventura, attempted to found an agricultural colony on the Bay of Limones, near Cupica. Owing to lack of organization, the settlement was soon abandoned. In the same year a Dutch company, which had obtained a concession to establish a lumber mill and exploit the surrounding forests on the Bay of Utría, induced the settlement of a few Antioqueño families as farmers on the east side of the bay to furnish food for the mill. In spite of good equipment and organization, the colonists abandoned their plots within a few months after settlement.[110]

Settlement Forms

It is often difficult to distinguish between dispersed and agglomerated rural settlement in a riverine pattern of population distribution like that of the Pacific lowlands. Dwellings constructed near the river bank on a natural levee or on a terrace are often spaced one quarter to one-half of a mile apart, making for truly dispersed settlement. In areas of denser population houses may be only a few hundred feet, or perhaps a few yards apart, forming a "line settlement," possibly one-fourth to one-half of a mile long. Such forms take on aspects of a small village, or caserío; each has a name, often a church or capilla, perhaps a school, and possibly one or two houses where cloth, bottled beverages, and food staples may be purchased. By far the greater part of the "village" names that appear on maps of the lowlands represent settlements of the caserío type (Plate XXIV). Rarely do such

PLATE XXIV. SETTLEMENT FORMS 113

Line settlement, or <u>caserío</u>, of Guachal on natural levee of the lower Río Mira.

<u>Left</u>: Village of San Francisco, on alluvial terrace bordering middle Río Naya. Grid street pattern; plaza, right center. <u>Right</u>: The old mining town and administrative center of Barbacoas on the Río Telembí. The vacant space in center is a burned-out section.

agglomerations exceed 300 people. On the immediate coast, settlement is usually clustered in small fishing hamlets from five to twenty huts often arranged in a single line along the inner part of the beach (Map 21).

In the gold-bearing areas along the middle and upper stream courses are many old villages, former reales de minas, or mining camps, and administrative centers founded in the eighteenth century. Many of these settlements have a double row of dwellings with a street or path between; where the site permits, some are characterized by the familiar colonial Spanish grid street plan with a small plaza. Calle Larga on the Río Napi near Guapi is such a colonial village, where even the late eighteenth century cobbled streets are still intact.

A few of the colonial reales, administrative centers, or ports have grown today into towns of commercial importance, all with the grid street arrangement; Quibdó, Tumaco, and Buenaventura, ranging in size from 5,000 to 35,000 inhabitants, are examples. Comparitively new commercial centers include Guapi (early nineteenth century), Istmina (founded about 1850), El Charco (founded in 1875), and Borbón (founded in 1886).

House Types

Probably the cultural feature of the Pacific lowlands which most quickly attracts the eye of the outsider is the type of house used by the rural Negroid population. This is the square or rectangular pile dwelling with four-shed hipped roof of thatch, a peculiar roof crown, and palm-lath floor and walls. Building materials consist entirely of wood and leaves gathered from the adjacent forest. This type of pile dwelling is one of the diagnostic traits of the Pacific lowland culture area; its distribution extends from western Darién southward to the Santiago River system in Esmeraldas, where it has been introduced by Colombian immigrants. Like most of the present material traits of the lowland Negroid people, their houses appear to be a modified form of an Indian prototype.

Indian Houses.

Descriptions of pre-conquest Indian houses in the Pacific lowlands are extremely fragmentary. Accounts of sixteenth-century Spanish entradas into the Chocó describe the "barbacoa" or tree dwelling used by the Chancos of the Pacific slope of the Cordillera Occidental and the people of the lower San Juan. Apparently such dwellings were no more than roofed platforms constructed on beams lashed to tree

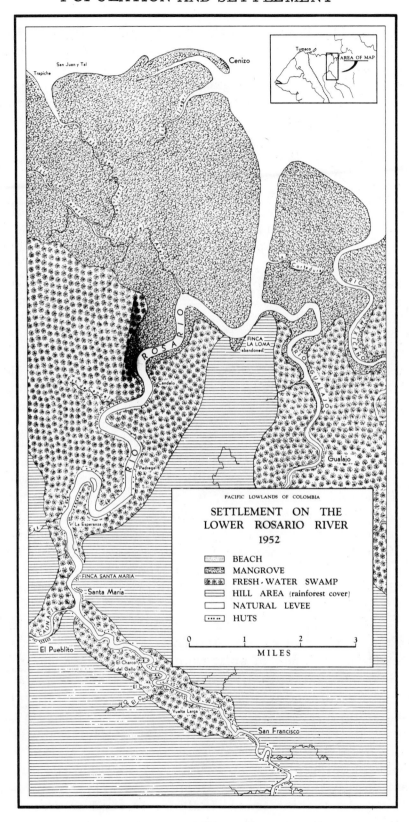

PACIFIC LOWLANDS OF COLOMBIA

SETTLEMENT ON THE
LOWER ROSARIO RIVER
1952

BEACH
MANGROVE
FRESH - WATER SWAMP
HILL AREA (rainforest cover)
NATURAL LEVEE
HUTS

0   1   2   3
M I L E S

MAP 21

trunks and elevated from ten to fifteen feet above the ground as protection from animals and neighboring enemies.[111] Another type of "barbacoa" that the Spaniards found in the lowlands is the true pile dwelling supported high off the ground by several heavy wooden pilings. Most of these were large multi-family houses, roughly round in floorplan and covered by a conical roof.[112]

Today the Indian houses in the lowlands are in many ways similar to the pile dwellings described by the early chroniclers. Called tambos by the Negroes and whites, the Indian houses are generally of two types. The apparently more ancient conical-roofed house with a roughly rectangular or square floorplan is found among the Waunamá in the lower San Juan and upper Docampadó areas,[113] among the Chocó in the upper Río Andágueda and adjacent tributaries,[114] and among the Chocó-speaking Indians in the upper Sinú and San Jorge river drainages of Antioquia.[115] The second type has a rectangular floorplan with a low-angle, four-shed hipped roof, the ridge pole being parallel to the long side of the house. Today the latter type is the more common, being found among most of the Chocó, the Cuna of the Chucunaque in Darién, and the Cayapa in Esmeraldas.[116] According to Nordenskiöld, the true Chocó house is round with a conical roof; the Indians themselves believe that the rectangular plan was introduced by the Spaniards or by the Negroes.[117] Both the "round" and rectangular Indian tambo is today distinguished from the Negro house by the lack of walls, the elevated platform being protected from rain and wind only by the thatched roof. As in pre-conquest times Indians build their pile dwellings on both low, floodable land and high, well-drained sites; the trait of an elevated floor thus cannot be attributed to poor drainage alone; doubtless the element of security from predatory animals and men, important in ancient days, carries over to the present. To reach the raised floor, five to ten feet above the ground, Indians use the notched log, or chicken ladder, as did their ancestors in pre-conquest times (Plate XXV).

Indian houses are usually large (often sixty by fifty feet) and may contain a number of related families or at least an extended family. Floors are made of lathes of split trunks of the tough barrigona palm (probably Socrates durissima); the roof is thatched with the fronds of a variety of palms, among which the corozo (Corozo oleifera) is common. Within the tambo, the hearth or low clay platform built on the floor at one end of the building, is the women's place. Numerous high storage platforms of palm slats, together with baskets and sacks, hang from the rafters. Sleeping platforms are arranged along the edges of the house, each family having its appointed place. (The hammock, important among the Amazonian forest Indians, is used only to sleep infants in the Pacific lowlands.) In the center of the tambo is often found the

PLATE XXV.   INDIAN HOUSE TYPES   117

Multi-family tambo of Chocó Indians, Quebrada de Injuí, upper Río Patía del Norte drainage.   Rectangular floor plan; four-shed roof; chicken-ladder.

Round tambo with conical roof, Waunamá Indians, lower San Juan River.

Spanish-introduced molino, or sugar cane press, in which cane is squeezed to obtain juice for making guarapo, or cane beer. Stinking vats filled with fermenting maize or cane beer vie with dogs and children in cluttering the floor of the tambo.

The Rural Negro House (Plate XXVI - XXVII; Figure 6).

Although the modern Negro house differs from that of the Indian in many respects, it retains the fundamental aboriginal traits of pilings, materials, roofing techniques and interior features, such as the hearth and sleeping platforms. The process by which the Negroes and mixed bloods took over and modified Indian techniques of house construction is fairly clear. During colonial times lowland Indians were forced to construct huts for Negro slaves in the mining camps.[118] In such work Indians must have used their own building techniques, though they may have been instructed to make modifications to suit the Spanish mine administrators. Such modifications may have been the rectangular, four-shed roof structure, which the Chocó may not have known. At any rate, it is fairly certain that Negroes learned the construction of the pile dwelling through the Indian workers at the mining camps.

A contemporary rural house of a Negro or mixed-blood family rests on four (sometimes six) heavy, well-hewn pilings (horcones, puntales) of the extremely hard and durable guayacán (Tabebuia, spp). Often four sets of double pilings are driven, each set consisting of (1) a short piling on which the floor beams (madres) rest and (2) another piling driven snug against the first and sufficiently long to serve as a corner post for walls and a rest for the roof beams. Uprights of guadua (bamboo) or light wood serve as intermediate wall supports. Before the introduction of cheap nails within the past twenty-five years, all beams and uprights were securely lashed, Indian fashion, with lianas, a trait still practiced in isolated areas. The floors, like those of the Indian tambo, are made of split sections of hard palm-wood, usually barrigona or chontaduro (Guilielma, spp.). Walls are also constructed of split-palm trunks or of bamboo, spread out to make thin, lath-like sections two to three feet wide. The roof frame is so constructed that a short ridge pole (burro), supported by uprights (buzos) resting on the center roof beam, is formed in the center. Thus the roof is composed of two large sheds (cuerpos), which slope to the front and back of the house, and two small sheds (culatas), which slope to either side. To support the thatch, small cross-poles (latillos) are lashed to the roof poles (guindaduras). The natives have at their disposal a variety of wild palms for thatching material; the most-used are the fronds of amargo (Welfia regia), corozo (Corozo pleifera) and naidí (Euterpe, spp.). Temporary huts in the forest or near the fields are

PLATE XXVI. NEGRO HOUSE TYPES   119

Negro pile dwelling at beach village of Boca Grande west of Tumaco.
Note four-shed roof; the culata, or smaller shed at right; smoke hole
at apex. The roof crown is held in place by burros. Walls are of
split bamboo. Storage space is below.

Pile dwellings in caserío of Naranjo, Río Guapi

House abuilding at left shows roof construction common in the Chocó.
Note the long Chocoano roof crown and the overlapping burros at top.
Lower San Juan River area.

Detail of piling construction at San Antonio, Río Yurumanguí. Note
double pilings at corner; notched log ladder at left; split-palm wall
construction. The plant near the boy below serves to keep evil spirits
from entering the house.

CHOCOANO HOUSE

CARVED BURROS
LOWER RIO SAN JUAN

FIGURE 6

thatched with the wide leaves of the herbaceous bijao (Calathea, spp.). Spaces are left unthatched at the apex of the culata, just under the ends of the ridge poles, to permit smoke to escape from the hearth inside. However, these vents are often ineffective, and smoke seeps through all parts of the roof. At mealtime a village may appear to be afire as the smoke pours from every roof.

After thatching is completed a curious roof crown, called the caballete, is placed over the ridge pole to keep rain from entering through the opening left at the top. The caballete is ordinarily a long triangular-shaped thatching held down over the roof pole by a series of straddling wooden beams and cross-pieces (burros or caballeteros). Often the straddling beams are elaborately carved and project cross-wise over the roof. In the Chocó the caballete extends far beyond the edge of the ridge pole, giving the Chocoano house its distinctive appearance.

To gain entrance to the pile dwelling, one must often negotiate the slippery notched log, or chicken ladder, a tricky and sometimes dangerous undertaking for the leather-shod visitor. Many Negroes however, have now adopted the European ladder. At night the log or ladder is raised into the house to keep out hungry dogs and wild animals. Doors and window shutters are seen only on the more pretentious rural dwellings.

The house interior is often partitioned into two or more rooms. In front is the largest room, the cuarto, used for sleeping, entertaining guests, storage of grain and equipment, and for dancing during fiestas. Some houses have built-in sleeping platforms; in others the Negroes merely curl up on the floor on mats of bark cloth over which is draped a mosquito netting. Hammocks are rarely used. Behind the cuarto may be the cocina, or kitchen, which contains the hearth (fogón), a mere box of clay set on a raised platform. Three short logs, the burning ends facing into the center of the fogon, Indian fashion, serve as pot-rests. A few home-made chairs and benches and possibly a table complete the house furnishings of a typical rural Negro casa.

The ample space among the pilings beneath the floor is often used to shelter canoes and to store extra lumber and thatching. Sometimes a portion of the space is enclosed to form pens for chickens or hogs, the usual animal domesticates kept by the rural household. Such an arrangement helps to protect the animals from predators, but the stench and noise that penetrate into the living quarters from below may at first be disconcerting to an outsider. The only out-buildings to grace the area around the house may be a crude chicken house (gallinero), consisting of a small thatch-covered box elevated on a post, small sheds to house the sugar cane mill or to protect boats, and, occasionally, a Spanish-type outside bake over placed under a palm-thatch shelter (Plate XXVIII).

The "Spanish" Urban House (Plate XXIX)

The rural house type is found also on the outskirts and in the poorer sections of the mining towns and trade centers. The commercial sections of the towns, however, are distinguished by another building type with elements of Spanish architecture. These structures usually have two stories, plank or split-palm lath walls, and thatched four-shed roofs. Fundamentally the town house is a pile dwelling, with the living quarters on the second floor; below, the empty space among the pilings has been enclosed to form the first floor, used as a store, saloon, or office. Usually a balcony, often highly decorated with wood carving (calado), overhangs the street side of the bottom floor. Entrance to the second floor is gained by means of a European-type stairway. In the old days walls were made exclusively of split trunks of guadua or palm, often whitewashed or plastered on the outside. With the introduction of the power saw in the last thirty years, planks have replaced the lath walls, and palm-wood floors. Moreover, the old thatch roof is rapidly losing out to the more modern and easily applied galvanized sheeting.

Although the use of brick and concrete is increasing in the larger commercial towns, such as Quibdó, Buenaventura and Tumaco, most of the structures are still made of wood and thatch. The latter material is the cheapest, most easily available, and best suited to the tropical habitat and mores of the area. Yet its use in the growing towns has been highly disadvantageous because of fire. There is probably no town of any size in the Pacific lowlands that has not been entirely or partially destroyed by fire, not once, but several times in the past century. One of the most common sights in any town today are charred pilings or remnants of concrete floors in vacant lots where conflagrations have occurred. In 1941 the thriving mining center of Tadó on the upper San Juan was almost completely destroyed by fire; in 1947 nearly half of the port town of Tumaco, including the commercial section and the dock area, was burned; in 1953 the growing commercial village of El Charco was half-destroyed by an accidental fire. Such disasters bring economic ruin among commercial families and cause dislocation of town population.

PLATE XXVIII
DETAILS OF NEGRO HOUSE AND OUTBUILDINGS

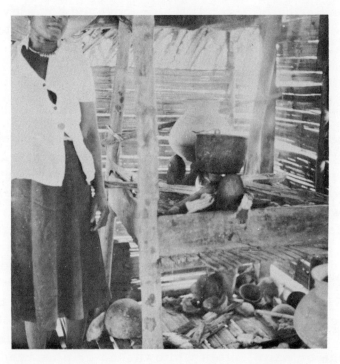

The fogón, or raised hearth in a Negro pile dwelling, Naranjo, Río Guape.

Left: In foreground a hog pen, in background a duck and chicken pen of bamboo, Orpúa. Note notched corners of bamboo stems in chicken house. Right: Covered bake oven, Payón, Río Magüí, Barbacoas area.

PLATE XXIX. "SPANISH" URBAN HOUSES. 125

"Spanish" type wooden building, Calle Larga, Río Napi. Note ornate carving on balcony front.

Main street in market town of López, Río Micay.

CHAPTER VII
ECONOMY

Since the Spanish conquest people have been making fantastic claims concerning the great treasure of natural resources stored in the Pacific lowlands of Colombia and adjacent areas. Yet despite the wealth extracted from gold- and platinum-bearing gravels, poverty has been the keynote of local economy for the last 300 years. Most of the lowland people still eke out a miserable existence through mere subsistence activities. Practically all of the Indians and most of the Negroes and mixed bloods are primitive farmers, fishermen and hunters, gaining just enough food to live by. Within the gold and platinum area, Negroes are small-scale miners as well as farmers and fishermen. But wherever transport and market conditions are favorable most of the inhabitants attempt to raise extra crops and to gather forest products on a small scale to sell for cash. In the larger towns white and colored merchants often do a thriving business, supplying the surrounding rural folk with imported items such as cloth and metal ware. Many local whites and some outsiders have attempted to develop tropical plantation agriculture, but with little success to date. Probably the only ones to gain substantial wealth from the lowlands have been owners and stockholders of mining concerns. Most of these people have been outsiders who were little concerned with the economic improvement of the area aside from their local interests. The reasons for the economic backwardness of the lowlands are many and complex, but some are common to most humid tropical areas. A fundamental drawback is geographic isolation and lack of good transport facilities. Another, contrary to popular belief, is paucity of extensive tracts of good agricultural land. Still another involves the attitudes and cultural heritage of the local inhabitants, who to date have felt little incentive to raise their low living standard.

Subsistence Agriculture

Subsistence farming is by far the most important occupation of the lowland population. Good farm land, however, is scarce, for most of the soils are highly leached and infertile. As in most humid tropical areas there prevails a type of shifting agriculture, which in

126

the Pacific lowlands is based on Indian cultivation techniques. Today the basic food crops represent a mixture of Old and New World plants. Indian maize and the Old World plantain are the main starch foods; the native sweet manioc and other American tubers, the New World peach palm (chontaduro), and Asiatic rice (recently introduced) are secondary.

Soils and cultivation.

At least three types of land, each with its peculiar soils, are utilized today by the lowland farmer: (1) the natural levees and low river terraces subject to occasional flooding; (2) the wet backswamps behind the natural levees and the fresh-water swamps near the coast; and (3) the hill slopes (Plate XXX). The natural levees and the low terraces, whose top soil is periodically enriched by deposition of new alluvium during floods, are the best farm lands. Their silty loam soils are high in organic content, moderately to slightly acid, and well drained.[1] On such soils fields locally called rastrojos are often cultivated for five or six years before they are abandoned;[2] if planted in maize, levee or terrace plots are farmed every other year. The alluvium best suited to primitive farming is usually located not on the low levees that border the large rivers, but along the smaller streams and quebradas, where rich soil is less subject to long periods of inundation. Unfortunately, these fertile strips of alluvium are extremely limited in area and comprise a small percentage of the total land surface of the lowlands. Furthermore, flood waters erode the cut banks of rivers and quebradas, causing large quantities of good soil and crops to topple into the water.

Swamp soils, although high in organic content, are ill-drained and composed of heavy clays low in lime and strongly to moderately acid.[3] But in recent years the swamps have been increasingly utilized for growing rice, tolerant of acid soils. According to local inhabitants, artificially drained backswamps also produce fair crops of bananas and plantains.

A great variety of soils, all relatively infertile, occur in the hill areas, where farmers practice a purely shifting type of agriculture. Almost all of the lowland soils have developed on deeply weathered Pleistocene gravels or semi-consolidated Tertiary clastics. In the Serranía de Baudó they have formed on many kinds of parent material ranging from young volcanic and old crystalline rocks to consolidated limestones and sandstones. The most common hill soils are red and yellow tropical clays. Leached, very strongly acid,[4] and extremely infertile for crop growth, these clays are rarely utilized even

A <u>rastrojo</u> on natural levee, Río Saija. A great variety of plants are cultivated: chontaduro palm (center); breadfruit tree (immediately to right of the chontaduro); coconut palms (extreme right); sugar cane patch (right); plantain patch (left); interspersed are fruit trees of many kinds.

A <u>peña molida</u> on hillside near Noanamá, middle Río San Juan, Chocó. The bush has been newly felled on top half of clearing; bottom half is in plantains. The narrow flood plain along the river is planted in maize and plantains.

by the shifting cultivation. Hardpans of consolidated ferruginous nod-
ules, so characteristic of the lateritic soils in West Africa and Brazil,
seem to be absent in the wet Pacific lowlands of Colombia. In various
hill sections, particularly on elevated flats, top soils having a light-
yellow to grey color and clay-loam texture appear to develop on highly
silicious gravels or on sandstone parent material. These may be a
type of podzol, which seems to be widespread in the humid tropics.[5]
The most desirable hill soil for cultivation occurs on steep to moderate
slopes called peñas molidas. Here a thick humus layer (five to ten
centimeters) gives a black to dark-brown color and friable texture to
the topsoil. The latter is usually underlain by a thick zone of red clay;
occasionally a thin layer of whitish clay (podzolic?) separates the
humus zone from the underlying red material.[6] Although strongly acid
(5.2 to 5.8 pH values), the high humus content affords sufficient plant
nutrients for the growth of one or two good crops of maize and several
of plantains before the soil is exhausted. Thereafter plots on such
soils are abandoned to the forest for seven or eight years; with the
humus layer regenerated through decay of litter, they may be recleared
and replanted.

For most of the humid tropics of the world, native shifting
agriculture is usually described as "slash-burn" cultivation, implying
the use of fire in the clearing of the plots. Throughout most of the
Pacific lowlands, however, the heavy precipitation and lack of a dry
season precludes the effective use of fire. Instead a peculiar system,
which might be called "slash-mulch" cultivation, of probable Indian
origin, has evolved. Seeds are broadcast and rhizomes and cuttings
are planted in an uncleared plot; then the bush is cut; decay of cut vegetable matter is rapid, forming a thick mulch through which the sprouts
from the seeds and cuttings appear within a week or ten days. Weeds
are surprisingly few, and the crops grow rapidly, the decaying mulch
affording sufficient fertilizer even on infertile hillside soils. In the
latter part of the sixteenth century the cultivation of maize by this
system was described for the Indians inhabiting the coastal areas in the
vicinity of Barbacoas and northern Esmeraldas.[7] In 1780 the same
system was noted as an Indian practice in the Chocó,[8] and today its use
extends from the latitude of Ríosucio and the Truandó River in the Chocó
southward to northwestern Ecuador.[9] North of the Truandó and south of
the Río Santiago in Esmeraldas a sufficiently long, dry season occurs to
make burning possible.[10] Except for the excessively wet Cordillera de
Talamanca in Costa Rica, where its practice has been reported,[11] in
the Americas the slash-mulch system appears to be limited to the area
of high rainfall in the Pacific lowlands of Colombia.[12]

Tools needed for such a system of cultivation are few and

simple. In pre-conquest times stone axes and a digging stick must
have sufficed. Today the agricultural tool par excellence used by the
Indian, Negro, and the mixed blood is the steel machete, which is employed to cut the bush, to dig holes for planting rhizomes and cuttings,
to weed, and to harvest plantains, bananas and other fruits. Axes are
employed for felling larger trees and a crude pointed stick may be used
to punch holes in the earth for rice-planting. Plows and hoes are unknown in the lowlands; they have no place in the present cultivation
system.

Negroes appear to have learned Indian agricultural techniques, just as they learned Indian methods of house construction. In
colonial times the Spanish miner in the Pacific lowlands relied upon
forced Indian labor for the feeding of his slave gang. Indians were
either required to furnish certain amounts of maize and plantains from
their own fields or were forced to cultivate fields belonging to the mine
owner.[13] In times of food shortage occasionally fields were cultivated
by slave gangs, probably under the instruction of Indian farmers. Today the Indian is considered to be the best farmer in the lowlands.
Even in his upstream sites he produces a better quality and greater
quantity of crops than his Negro and mixed-blood neighbors.

Main Food Crops

Maize. Before the coming of the Spaniard maize was the
leading food crop throughout the Pacific lowlands. Today in most of
the area plantains vie with maize as the principal item of diet. Along
some rivers, such as the Cajambre and Raposo south of Buenaventura
and in many parts of the Chocó maize foods still are favored.

A single, curious type of maize called maíz criollo or
maíz común predominates. A small short-eared, narrow-grained
corn, usually yellow or white but sometimes black in color, it grows
on short spindly stocks and yields rather meagerly. According to Dr.
Edgar Anderson, Missouri Botanical Gardens, this maize has highly
conservative characters, quite unlike the present-day corns of the adjacent highlands, but more similar to the ancient, primitive pre-Inca
maize found in burials on the Peruvian desert coast.[14] The northern
limit of the lowland maize seems to be Darién; the southern, Esmeraldas;
its eastern boundary coincides with the western slopes of the Cordillera
Occidental, for it is never seen in the highlands.[15] The distribution of
this corn might be taken as another diagnostic trait of the Pacific lowlands culture area.

A white flour corn, called maíz capio, is sometimes

cultivated in the lowlands. It is undoubtedly an introduction from the adjacent highlands where it is grown abundantly, for the lowlanders speak of it as coming from the outside. A large-grained yellow Andean maize is raised on the upper Guelmambí in the Barbacoas area. In southern Esmeraldas many highland corns have become more significant than the lowland type.

Like most of the crops raised in the lowlands, maize is cultivated by means of the slash-mulch method (Plates XXXI - XXXII). Seeds are broadcast (never are they planted) in the tall second-growth vegetation, which is then immediately cut and permitted to rot over the seeds. The sprouting maize takes root in the shallow humus layer on the ground surface and appears through the rotting mulch in a few days' time. The ears are ready for harvesting in four months. Usually two crops of corn are raised in one year, but in different plots. One is planted in July or August, the other in January or February, both periods being those of least rain during the year.

The cutting of the bush (la roza, rozando) during maize-planting time in the plots of the individual farmers is often a community affair -- a kind of minga which Negroes still practice on many rivers below Buenaventura and in parts of the Chocó.[16] A long line of ten or fifteen men and women swing their machetes to the rhythm of communal chants, stopping occasionally to rest and to quaff deep draughts of guarapo, or sugar cane beer. The owner of the plot cut over by the groups is obligated to furnish the guarapo and a meal at the end of the day; he also incurs the obligation to reciprocate when called upon to help his neighbor. Although the minga, or co-operative labor group, is applied to other activities, such as house-roofing and sluice construction in the mines, its use in bush-cutting seems to apply only to maize cultivation. Such labor groups occur still today among many Andean Indian communities, but such a device is foreign to the Chocó and Waunamá tribes. The institution as practiced by the modern Pacific lowland Negroes contains many African elements, such as chanting, which involves a lead singer and chorus, beer drinking during progress of work, and feasting at the end of the day.[17] According to local inhabitants, the minga, one of the few African cultural survivals of the Pacific lowland Negro, is rapidly disappearing as a social institution.

Like his Indian neighbor the Negro farmer gathers his harvest with the help of the immediate family in large baskets of loosely-woven strips of palm leaf. He stores the unhusked ears in baskets that hang from rafters in the house. He has his woman turn back the husks of seed corn and hang them, Indian fashion, in round bundles (ensartos, piñas) from a rafter near the hearth, where smoke will thoroughly dry

Broadcasting maize seed into the growing bush.

The roza, or cutting of bush in area where maize seed has been broadcast. The workers swing their machetes in unison.

PLATE XXXII. MAIZE CULTIVATION 133

A newly cleared corn patch. The cut bush is left to rot over the broadcast seed.

A crop of maize about one month old, cultivated by the slash-mulch method.

the seed and discourage insects and worms. In the Chocó shelled corn
is shipped from the farming sections into the mining areas in calados,
or cylindrical containers lined with tough bijao leaves enclosed in a
loose weave of palm-leaf strips; each calado contains one almud, or
twenty-five pounds of shelled maize.

Both Negroes and Indians have a surprisingly large number
of maize foods, many of which are related to those of the highlands.
Preliminary to the preparation of many corn foods, the kernals are
soaked in water and wet-ground on a crude mealing stone (piedra
moledora) somewhat similar to the Meso-American metate and mano
(Plate XXXIII). To separate the tough, indigestible kernal skins, the
ground maize is strained through a perforated gourd (sisunga). The resulting masa, or maize dough, is the base for the preparation of the
most common corn food in the Pacific lowlands -- the envuelto. This
is a kind of tamale made of an elongated piece of maize dough, finely
ground and slightly fermented, which is tightly wrapped in a bijao leaf
and tied with thongs of palm. To prepare it for eating, the envuelto is
either baked in the coals of the hearth or is pot-boiled. This food is
often preserved for months by smoking over the hearth.[18] True
tamales, possibly introductions, are sometimes made with a meat,
fish, or chile sauce filler.

Various gruels, akin to the Meso-American atole, are made
from the wet-ground maize dough. Casabe, for example, is a thick,
insipid soup of almost pure starch and water. If made from green corn
in the milk stage, slightly fermented, it is called birimbí in the Chocó,
champú in the Tumaco and Esmeraldas areas.[19]

From the masa is made a third class of corn foods, similar to the famous arepa, or maize cake of highland Colombia and
Venezuela. The arepa (also called cachín, tatapú) of the Pacific low
lands is slightly larger than the small, roundish Antioqueno variety; it
is fashioned with the hands and baked in open coals or on iron or clay
plates. When made of fresh corn the cake is called majaja.

A fourth type of maize food is derived from the boiled and
decorticated whole maize kernel, or hominy. The lowland otaya, a
watery, unseasoned mixture of hominy and grits, is identical to the
highland mazamorra of Colombia and Venezuela. Negroes also make
sango, a soup of hominy grits, meat, onions, and chile sauce, which
is similar to the Meso-American pozole. In the Tumaco and Esmeraldas
areas natives prepare mote, a semi-dried hominy common in the
Ecuadorian and Peruvian highlands.

PLATE XXXIII. GRINDING INSTRUMENTS   135

The piedra moledora, or stone used for grinding maize, Balsitas, upper Río Guapi. Similar stones are found throughout the Pacific lowlands.

The pilón, or wooden mortar with pestle, used for hulling rice in the lowlands. Barbacoas, Río Telembí.

Chicha, or maize beer, one of the common aboriginal intoxicants of Andean America, is made by all of the surviving lowland Indians, and has been adopted by many of the Negroes and mixed bloods. Those on the rivers south of Buenaventura make chicha by soaking hard grains in water and adding a bit of raw sugar to hasten fermentation. The Negroes of the Chocó, however, deny the use of chicha, which they deprecate (at least to outsiders) as an Indian drink unworthy of the attention of "gente de razón," accustomed to guarapo and rum.

Finally, maize is utilized as food in the fresh, or milk stage. Throughout the Pacific lowlands, as in most of Andean America, fresh corn (called choclo) is boiled, parched, and made into various dishes, some of which have been described above. According to Barrett, the Cayapa of Esmeraldas utilize only the tender choclo to prepare the few maize foods that they have retained. [20]

Plantains. After more than a century of research and speculation scholars have not yet decided whether the Old World plantain (Musa paradisiaca) was cultivated in the American tropics before the Discovery. [21] With few exceptions early sixteenth-century chroniclers and observers in tropical America fail to mention the plantain as a native food crop. Nevertheless, documentary sources indicate that by the last half of the sixteenth century, Indians and Negro slaves from Mexico to Brazil were growing this plant. If the Spaniards introduced the plantain into America, its spread was extremely rapid. [22]

Most of the sixteenth-century accounts mention maize, sweet manioc, and the peach palm as the main plants cultivated by the Indians in the Chocó and other parts of the Pacific lowlands. [23] According to Fray Pedro Simón, in 1590 Spaniards connected with one of Melchor Velásquez' ill-fated expeditions found Indians cultivating plantains along the banks of a wide river, presumably the Atrato. [24] Evidence of plantain culture among the Pacific lowland Indians is abundant in documents of the mid-seventeenth century. [25] It may be guessed that Spaniards first introduced the crop into the Chocó via the Tamaná River, where the earliest mining camps with Negro slaves were established in the last quarter of the sixteenth century. Other routes of its entry into the lowlands from the east may have been along the Caribbean Coast, where by the 1630's large groves had been established west of Cartagena;[26] via the old Cali-Buenaventura foot trail to the Pacific; and probably by many trails from the upper Cauca, Patía, and Pasto areas. Once introduced, it appears that the plant spread among the lowland Indians faster than Spanish mining settlement. To a people already versed in planting cuttings such as sweet manioc and sweet potatoes, the cultivation of plantain corms should have offered little difficulty.

When or however introduced, today plantains are considered to be the main element of diet among both Negroes and Indians in most parts of the Pacific lowlands.[27] More than twenty varieties are cultivated. The large-fruited "hartón," the "enano" (Musa cavendishi?) with its dwarfed stock and large fruit stems that almost touch the ground, the red-fruited "manzano," and the small-fruited "dominico" are the more commonly planted. Indians and Negroes living in isolated upstream areas seem to have accumulated the largest variety of plantains. In such places one finds the curious "cajeto," the fruit sheath of which is said to contain a "poisonous" ingredient, and the "chimbalo" which yields a fruit bearing large, sterile seeds.[28]

Since the plantain, like the banana, bears no viable seed, it is one of the plant domesticates most dependable upon man for its reproduction. The latter is done by planting the corm, or rootstock, called the colino by the Pacific lowlanders. After the colinos have been planted in holes dug with the machete or pointed digging stick, the bush is cut down, forming a rotting mulch through which the plantain shoots emerge. Nine to eleven months elapse after planting before the stems are ready for harvest. A stalk bears a single stem of fruit, and is therefore cut down after harvest; but new shoots sprout from the rootstock and in turn bear fruit. Thus with good cultivation and fertilization of soil a platanar will yield for years without replanting. However, rapid soil depletion in the tropics forces frequent replanting on new plots.

Plantains are grown both on vegas, or natural levees and alluvial terraces, and in the peñas molidas on slopes. The dwarf "enano" and the "manzana" varieties do best in the alluvial areas, while the "hartón" and "dominico" are usually planted on the infertile slopes. Like most musas, the plantain is tolerant of acid soils; thus plots are being planted in drained portions of the backswamp areas with good results.

The fruit is harvested and usually eaten green. If left on the stalk until ripe, parrots and other pests would soon destroy the fruit; moreover, a green plantain will keep for days in the hut without spoiling. Throughout the lowlands the plantains are counted for consumption and sale by the ración, which consists of sixty-four fingers or individual fruits. The ración is a holdover from the days of slavery when the masters would give each black a week's ration of sixty-four plantains.

In most parts of the lowlands ten to fifteen different plantain foods are prepared by both Indian and Negro. Green fruits are most commonly prepared whole by boiling, baking, or frying. These have a consistency of a half-baked potato and are practically tasteless. Indians often bake ripe plantains in the coals of the hearth, but Negroes and mixed bloods eat them prepared only in special ways. As the ripe fruit contains some sugar, it is somewhat more acceptable to the Western palate than in the green state. Less common are the numerous dishes prepared by grinding or pounding the fruit. Bala is made by pounding boiled green plantain on the stone with the muller to a rubbery paste; salt or dried meat may be added for flavor. Ripe fruits mixed with coconut milk are ground on the stone to prepare chucula, often a fiesta dish. The whole mess is cooked and beaten to a smooth, watery paste. A thiner gruel called colado de plátano is made from sun-dried plantains ground to a powder on the stone, mixed with water, and cooked. Envueltos are prepared by wrapping macerated ripe plantains in bijao leaves and roasting in the coals. Tamales are similarly màde but with the addition of meat or fish as filler. As in most parts of northwestern South America, in the lowlands plantains form an important ingredient in various thick potages, the most widespread of which is sancocho, a mixture of various vegetables and meat. Piscán is a similar Ecuadorian dish made in the Tumaco and Esmeraldas areas. It may be significant that only the Indians have adopted (or retained?) plantain beer, which they call masato.

Bananas. The cultivation of bananas (Musa sapientum) is quite similar to that of plantains. However, since the lowlanders raise bananas only as a cash crop, this plant will be discussed under commercial agriculture.

Today the root crops, all cultivated by vegetative reproduction, are minor in Pacific lowland agriculture. The most important one is sweet manioc, or yuca (Manihot utilissima), but it is cultivated mainly by Indians. The lowlands form part of the large sweet-manioc area of northwestern South America, where the bitter or poisonous variety, so important in the eastern part of the continent, did not penetrate in pre-conquest times. From the early descriptions of Indian agriculture it is apparent that in the lowlands manioc cultivation, although always subordinate to maize, is now much less significant than in colonial times. Usually Negroes plant a few cuttings around their huts or in sandy portions of the rastrojos along stream banks, whereas the Indian cultivates large hillside plots and often intercrops yuca and plantains. Negroes raise yuca in significant quantities only along a few streams in the upper Atrato drainage (e.g., Río Quito, Río Cavŕ, Río Munguidó). When grown in plots sweet manioc, like the plantain, is cultivated by the slash-mulch process. At maturity (six to seven months after planting) the long, slender tubers are dug and prepared by boiling, baking on coals, or frying in grease. Sweet manioc is never grated to form a paste or to make flour for bread.

Batatas, or sweet potatoes (Ipomea batatas) are cultivated
in small amounts chiefly in loose, loamy soil on levee, terrace, or
beach sites. Near the hut Negroes occasionally plant a few vines of
ñame, the Old World yam (Dioscorea alata), possibly introduced into
Colombia from Africa through the slave trade. One of the most interesting of the native tubers is a taro-like aroid, locally called rascadera,
or badú (Xanthosoma sagittifolium). Both Indians and Negroes plant
the tuber around their huts, particularly near the kitchen, where the
soil in enriched with refuse and human urine. The large, tuberous root
is eaten boiled or baked. Another rascadera (probably X. violacea),
the heart-shaped leaves and stalk of which are blemished by violet veins,
grows spontaneously in the house lots on disturbed ground, where it becomes a pesky weed. Said to be "poisonous," the tubers are never
eaten.

Owing to the hot, humid climate, the Old World wheat, of
course, cannot be grown successfully in the lowlands. In colonial times
Spaniards living in the lowland mining centers imported wheat flour
from the adjacent highlands to make bread -- a food which the European
stubbornly retains. The Spaniards also introduced the European outdoor bake oven specifically for wheat bread. Today at least one or two
families in every Negro or mixed-blood community in the lowlands
weekly prepare a batch of panes made from imported wheat flour and
baked in the outdoor oven to sell to the villagers mainly as a delicacy
(Plate XXVIII).

Palms and fruit trees. The rastrojos, or cultivated patches
on levee and terraces near the huts of the farmers, are used not only
for field crops, such as maize, plantains, and tubers; various fruit-
bearing palms and trees are scattered over much of the rastrojo, so
that such plots often resemble unkept gardens choked with a hetero-
geneous mixture of plant life (Plate XXX). Probably the cultivated
plant that is most conspicuous along inhabited river banks of the Pacific
lowlands is the tall, graceful, spiny-trunked peach palm, known locally
as chontaduro (Guilielma Gasipaes), cultivated in clumps around the
house and in the rastrojos[29] (Plate XXXIV). This valuable palm yields
large clusters of red to yellow fruits, whose mealy pulp is rich in
starch, protein, ascorbic acid, carotene, niacin and other essential
dietetic elements. It has a wide but spotty distribution from Nicaragua
south to Bolivia and Brazil; it grows best under rain forest conditions
where elevations do not exceed 4,000 feet; except in the Huallaga Valley
on the eastern Andean slopes of Peru, where it appears to grow wild,
its presence is always associated with human settlement.

In the Pacific lowlands the farmers propagate the chontaduro

PLATE XXXIV
CHONTADURO PALM, GOURD TREE, CACAO

Clumps of chontaduro palm, upper Guelmambí, Barbacoas. Fruit clusters develop just below the fronds.

Left: The gourd tree, or totumo (Crescentia cujete), on lower Sanguianga River. The large gourd fruits can be seen hanging from the limbs. Right: Cacao beans curing in the sun, Cajapí, Río Mira.

either by planting the seed or by transplanting suckers that grow from the base of older palms.[31] Two harvests are gathered each year; the principal one in January and February, a minor one (called the atravesía) in July. During these months, which coincide with the interharvest periods of maize and plantains, the chontadura fruits become the main item of diet throughout the Pacific lowlands. Individual fruits are about the size of large walnuts, and are prepared by boiling in salty water. To preserve chontadura for storage a basket of boiled seeded fruits are either dried and smoked over the hearth or dried in the sun. Indians consume not only the fruits of the palm but also the terminal buds, which are eaten raw or boiled. Both the Chocó and Waunamá groups still make a beer (urnagá) from chontadura fruits, macerated and fermented in water sweetened with raw sugar. Probably the most important palm in the Pacific lowlands, the chontaduro also furnishes building material, such as fronds for thatch and hardwood for floors and walls of huts.

The coconut has become more important as a commercial product than a significant subsistence food in the lowlands. O. F. Cook has propounded the hypothesis that this palm was domesticated by the American Indian probably in the dry, low mountain valleys of northwestern South America, and that before the European conquest is was widely distributed along the Pacific Coast of Central America, the West Indies, and probably along the coast of Brazil.[32] If the coconut was cultivated in the Colombian Pacific Coast before 1500 A.D., it probably was of little importance as a food. Early colonial accounts of the Chocó, for example, fail to mention it. Today coconut culture is limited almost entirely to the sandy beaches along the coast and to the low levees along the tidal sections of streams, where within the past 150 years groves of various sizes have been planted for commercial production. Coconuts appear to thrive best on slightly alkaline soils, such as the salt-impregnated sandy loams on beach ridges and high ground within the tidal zone. Upriver, however, one finds a few coconuts planted in the rastrojos near the huts as far as good alluvial soil prevails. I have seen coconut palms thriving in the old gold-mining towns of Balsitas in the upper Guapi and Belém on the upper Napi, both located at the foot of the Cordillera Occidental south of Buenaventura. Half-way up the Atrato River one finds an occasional coconut palm along the natural levee, but in the upper parts of the Atrato and the San Juan it becomes a rarity.[33] Negroes especially are fond of the refreshing water of the green coconut, or pipa. Ripe coconut meat is widely used in the lowlands as a source of fat for frying and for mixing with maize and plantain foods for flavoring. The coastal folk often pole canoe-loads of coconuts upstream to sell for cash or to barter for plantains.

Among the native American tropical fruit trees planted near the hut or in the rastrojo one may find the papaya (Carica papaya); the milky-sapped caimito or star-apple (Chrysophyllum caimito); guayaba (Psidium, spp.); guamo (Inga, spp.), with its long pods of pithy fruit; aguacate or avocado (Persea, spp.); several fruits of the Annonaceae, including the anón or sweetsop (Anona squamosa), the larger guanábana or soursop (Anona muricata), and the delicate chirimoya (A. cherimola); cacao (Theobroma, spp.); zapote (Matisia cordata); mamey (Mammea americana); and madroño (Rheedia chocoensis). Old World fruits that Negroes and Indians now commonly cultivate along the streams include the common citrus (oranges and lemons) which, like the coconut, grow best in the slightly alkaline and sandy soils of the beach ridges. The Asiatic breadfruit (Artocarpus communis) introduced into Colombia via the West Indies in the 1820's has now spread to all inhabited areas of the Pacific lowlands. Like the chontaduro palm, the wide, deep green, lobate leaves of the breadfruit tree is one of the infallible signs of human habitation along the river banks. Curiously, the Colombian Negroes have never learned to eat the pulp of the fruit, a significant food in various areas of southeastern Asia and Oceania; rather, the Chocoano, for example, prepares only the seeds by boiling or roasting and discards the pulp of the fruit as useless.

Besides the food-bearing plants many other useful cultivated trees and shrubs clutter the rastrojo "gardens": the totumo (Crescentia cujete) producer of gourds used for containers of all sorts, indispensible in the life of the rural folk of tropical America; the native rubber tree, or caucho negro (Castilla elastica), the latex of which is occasionally gathered and sold for a few pesos; the tropical cedar (Cedrela oderata), propagated from seeds and cut for building material; clumpy thickets of guadua manso or native bamboo (Guadua angustifolia) which, propagated by cuttings, also produces valuable building material and whose presence along river banks is another indication of human disturbance; achiote (Bixa orellana), sometimes grown by Negroes, invariably by Indians, for its red dye-yielding seeds used for food coloring and body paint; Indians also cultivate around the hut the jagua (Genipa americana) for black dye and usually a variety of plants producing fish poisons.

Sugar Cane. Since its introduction by the Spaniards in colonial days sugar cane has become an important subsistence crop grown by the lowland farmers in small plots along the rivers. By the eighteenth century, and probably earlier, the Chocó Indians had adopted the plant into their agriculture; the new crop provided an abundant source of sweetening in the form of raw sugar as well as an easily prepared intoxicant in the form of guarapo or fermented cane juice.[34]

To make sugar products both Indians and Negroes adopted various Spanish processes and tools, such as the hand mill (trapiche) and the copper caldron (paila); many Negroes and the Cayapa of Esmeraldas took over distillation, devising crude stills made of clay pots to manufacture brandy (aguardiente).[35] (Plate XXXV). Although cane is grown along almost all of the rivers, Negro and mulatto farmers living in the lower courses of the Tamaná in the Chocó and the Saija, Iscuandé, and Mira in the south, have become renowned for their extensive cane patches and high-quality sugar products; they sell surplus products to miners upstream or to people of other rivers. A popular confection and energy food, the sweet, watery pith of the mature cane stock is chewed and sucked by young and old. To prepare either raw sugar or guarapo, the cane juice is squeezed from the stock by means of the simple hand mill, which consists of two horizontal corrugated rollers of wood. The trapiche with verticle rollers, operated by either men or donkeys harnessed to a long sweep, is more common in the interior highlands, but it has been introduced into the Tumaco and Esmeraldas lowlands. Panela, or raw, brown sugar, the common sweetening in most parts of rural Latin America, is made by boiling cane juice in the copper caldron; syrup is poured into rectangular wooden forms to crystallize, producing the familiar panela bricks that are later wrapped for storage and transport in bijao leaves. Panela has become one of the most important energy foods in the lowlands, and the Negro canoeman or miner is rarely satisfied without a chunk of the sickeningly sweet substance to munch on throughout the day.

The Platform Gardens (Plate XXXVI).

One of the most curious features of Pacific lowland agriculture is the small gardens of annual plants grown on soil-covered platforms elevated five to ten feet above the ground by means of poles. These are the azoteas, or 'soteas, found at the side of every rural house. The saturated nature of the soil and the presence of the destructive arriera, or leaf-cutter ant and rodents preclude successful cultivation of delicate annuals on the ground. The platform garden appears to have been an ancient lowland Indian trait, for in 1593 it is described for the Waunamá, who used it for growing medicinal plants.[36] Two types of raised platforms are used today; the more common is a rectangular frame of palm wood slats; the other is nothing more than a discarded, half-rotted canoe perched on two crotched poles. A mixture of macerated termite nests and clay loam is placed on the platforms as a planting surface for vegetables and medicinal plants, most of which have an Old World origin. The onion, used in flavoring soups and meat dishes, is

Hand-operated sugar mill with horizontal rollers common in most parts of the Pacific lowlands. In photo at right juice is being collected in canoe placed below the rollers. The small container in canoe is made from the totuma gourd.

Sugar mill with vertical rollers, powered by mule or man-operated sweep, near Limones, Esmeraldas, Ecuador. Cane juice is boiling to a syrup in copper caldron (paila) at left.

PLATE XXXVI. ELEVATED PLATFORM GARDENS   145

An azotea, or platform garden, in the village of Tadó, Chocó. Onions and medicinal plants are growing in the soil that has been placed upon the platform.

Rice seedlings ready for transplanting are growing in a crude type of azotea made from a piece of discarded dugout canoe. The metal pot at left contains onions. Mercedes, upper Atrato drainage.

the most important vegetable that the Negroes cultivate on the azotea. Tomatoes and chiles are also planted occasionally. A large number of medicinal plants cover much of the surface of the azotea. Eighteen different plants were counted on one platform in San Bernardo on the upper Río Patía del Norte.[37] Usually isolated from dispensaries of modern drugs, the lowlanders have been obliged to retain the remedies of colonial times.

Animal Husbandry.

If farming in the Pacific lowlands is rudimentary, animal husbandry is even more so. Paucity of forage, prevalence of animal diseases, and lack of interest on the part of the rural folk have not been favorable for the development of animal industries.

Probably the dog and the muscovy duck (Cairina moschata) were the only animal domesticates of the lowland Indians in pre-Spanish times. They likely acquired the Old World chicken, however, soon after the arrival of the Spaniards in Colombia during the mid-sixteenth century. Today muscovy ducks and chickens are the most common animals around Negro and Indian huts, for these fowls are easily raised, serve as scavengers around the house, and afford a readily available source of food for festive occasions. Eggs are rarely eaten, but if the price is suitable, they are eagerly sold to passing merchants or taken to market. The Mexican turkey, called the bimbo, has been introduced on some rivers, and in the northern part of the Chocó the gallinaceous guan, locally called pavo, (Penelope, spp.) is tamed and kept around the house for food.

In the Tumaco, Barbacoas, and Esmeraldas areas a few Negro families keep the "guinea pig" or cavy (Cavia, spp.) around the house as a scavenger and also for food. Probably introduced from the adjacent highlands in colonial times, this little animal is one of many central Andean culture traits that have filtered down into the southern end of the humid Pacific lowlands.

One of the Old World animal domesticates most quickly acquired by the Indian, the pig is found around almost every hut in the lowlands. Of both the old European razorback and the eastern Asiatic breeds, the pigs are allowed to roam the rastrajo near the house during interharvest periods, but are fattened on maize and garbage in pens near or under the huts. Cholera, however, has frequently wiped out the pig population in various areas.[38]

During the colonial period Spaniards brought a few cattle

into the mining areas of the upper Atrato and San Juan rivers to supplement food supply. Grasses were planted in plots carved out of the forest to form small pastures, called llanos.[39] It was found that such pastures were difficult to maintain, as they are today, for the forest continually threatens to re-establish itself in the grass-planted clearings, particularly in areas with no dry season. At present a small number of pastures containing a few rachitic, mixed-bred cattle are found around most of the old mining administrative centers and market towns, such as Quibdó, Istmina, Tadó and Barbacoas. Most of the cattle that are raised today in the lowlands are found around the beach ridge settlements along the coast, where native grasses and low succulent shrubs afford good grazing and the porous sandy soil and cool sea breeze reduce annoyance by insect pests and heat. Moreover, in the northern and southern extremities of the lowlands, where a definite dry season begins to appear, pastures and cattle increase in numbers. Along the Rosario, Chaguí, and Mira rivers and southward into Esmeraldas many grassy plots called pampas have been established on the banks to graze cattle brought in from the highlands.[40] Again, on the well-drained lands in the lower Atrato pastures and cattle do well, as in the vicinity of Sautatá. Even there vampire bats, ticks, and disease are discouraging to the cattlemen.[41] (Plate XXXVII).

Fresh beef and pork are still rarities in the Pacific lowlands. Sometimes on Sundays a cow or a pig is butchered in the larger towns; but lack of refrigeration and the humid heat deem that the meat be consumed the same day that it is dressed, or salt-cured and dried. Still today most of meat consumed in the lowlands is the dried and salted tasajo imported from Antioquia, Caldas, and Pasto, as it was in colonial days. The mining companies in the upper San Juan, however, now buy livestock from the Antioqueño highland pastures. The cattle are driven to the head of navigation, where they are lashed on balsa rafts and floated down to the camps.

Pasture of planted grass carved out of the rain forest on the outskirts
of Istimina, Chocó. Note how shrubs are starting to come back.

A fine pampa, or pasture, at Boca Satinga, confluence of the Sanguianga
and Satinga rivers, north of Tumaco.

Commercial Agriculture

Commercial agriculture has been carried on in the Pacific lowlands in one form or another since the end of the eighteenth century. Large quantities of maize and plantains grown along the western tributaries of the Atrato were sold in the mining areas on the eastern side of the river and in the upper San Juan, as they are today. Later in the nineteenth century, cacao and coconuts were shipped out on a small scale. Only since the 1930's, however, has commercial farming become of much importance in the lowlands; even today its significance in the total economy of the Colombian Pacific Coast is far less than that of subsistence agriculture. Two crops -- rice and bananas -- have been the basis for recent commercial developments in lowland farming.

Rice.

As early as 1858 rice was cultivated in small amounts for local use in the lower Atrato and at a few spots along the Pacific coast of Colombia.[42] During the 1930's, through import restrictions on food staples, extention of credit to small local producers and processors, and improvement of transport, the Colombian government encouraged rice production in all parts of the country, including the Pacific lowlands.[43] Local merchants and owners of small rice hullers in market centers of the Chocó and along the coast were also instrumental in persuading the Negro and mulatto farmers to plant rice as a cash crop. Thus in the last twenty years rice cultivation has spread rapidly into most of the farming areas of the lowlands. Although most of the crop is sold to local dealers, the lowlanders are increasing their own consumption of rice, which they still consider a luxury food.

Today rice production is concentrated mainly along the coast and the lower river courses, particularly in the fresh-water swamp within the tidal zone. There, the low levees along the streams have proved to be ideal for wet rice cultivation due to the natural periodic flooding caused by the rise and fall of the tide. The wet, clay soils of the backswamps are also being increasingly used for rice. Even on the natural levees and low terraces far upstream one now sees small patches of the new grain planted in former maize and plantain plots. In the Chocó the tributaries of the lower Atrato and the coastal lands that fringe the Caribbean immediately west of the Atrato delta lead in rice production. But production is rapidly increasing along the Pacific Coast, especially in such centers as Valle, Nuquí, and Juradó, all low alluvial areas within the rocky coast north of Cabo Corrientes.[44] In almost every town there are now one or several rice hullers operated by gasoline motors to process rice for shipment to the big consumption centers of Buenaventura, Quibdó, and even Cali in the interior.

With rice have come new cultivation practices (Plate XXXVIII). Unlike the normal crops such as maize and plantains, rice is planted in fields well cleared of vegetation. This clearing process demands a large amount of labor. In the backswamps the grains are usually broadcast on the wet soil without further cultivation. In the cleaned plots on natural levees and elevated flats in the hills rice is planted in small holes made with a pointed stick; six to eight grains are dropped in each hole, the latter spaced about one foot apart. The plants thus grow in dense clumps. In five months the grain is ready for harvest.[45] Two plantings per year is the rule; one in March or April, the other in August or September. In isolated areas where rice has been recently introduced harvesting methods are extremely backward. Each head of ripened rice is carefully plucked from the stem with the thumb nail and forefinger without shattering the seed; the heads are tied in neat bundles and taken to the hut where they are dried; threshing is done by placing the heads in a canoe and trampling them with the bare feet. In more progressive areas rice is cut with the machete and threshed immediately in the field by flailing the heads against the side of a small canoe that is dragged about the plot. After winnowing, the grains are sun-dried and sacked, ready for shipment to the huller.

For local consumption rice is hand-hulled in a wooden mortar and pestle (pilón), the instrument used in the highlands to decorticate and pulverize maize. It is not clear whether the mortar and pestle were employed in the lowlands before the beginning of rice cultivation. Today Indians and Negroes never prepare maize in the wooden mortar, but use the mealing stone and muller. After hulling, rice is eaten boiled with an abundance of either imported vegetable shortening or ground coconut meat.

Bananas.

Since the end of World War II commercial banana production has been introduced into various parts of the Pacific lowlands of Colombia and adjacent areas in Ecuador and Panama.[46] As with rice cultivation subsistence farmers began to grow bananas as a cash crop through inducements by commercial dealers, in this case agents of small fruit companies located in the Canal Zone and in Ecuador. In the northern and southern extremities of the lowlands -- Esmeraldas and Darién -- banana cultivation has become the basis of the present local economy. In Darién launches from Panama City arrive weekly at the

PLATE XXXVIII. RICE CULTIVATION 151

Newly cleared rice field on back-slope of low levee, Río Quito, near Quibdó, Chocó.

Left: Plucking heads of rice on mature field, near Juradó, Pacific coast of Chocó. Right: Threshing rice in canoe by trampling with feet, Río Guapi.

town of El Real on the lower Tuira to load stems rafted and canoed down-
river by Negro and Indian farmers. Since 1950 banana-growing on a
small scale has spread southward into the northern Chocó. Along the
Pacific Coast from Jaqué in Panama to the Baudó River south of Cabo
Corrientes the farmers of the coastal rivers furnish several thousand
stems monthly to small Panamanian banana boats. Such craft, each
having capacity of 1000 to 3000 stems, often go up the Baudó thirty-
five miles to buy from local growers.[47] Banana cultivation has also
spread up the tributaries of the lower Atrato, where farmers on the
Bojayá, Murrí, and Opogadó rivers have become the leading producers.[48]
In 1954 it was estimated that 35,000 stems were being exported monthly
from the lower Atrato area in banana launches from Colón.[49] In
Esmeraldas the recent banana developments form but a part of the explosive expansion of tropical agriculture that has made Ecuador the
leading banana exporter of Latin America since World War II. Although
some fruit companies have organized plantations, most of the production comes from the small Negro and Indian farmers along the rivers.
The Ecuadorian banana boom and chances for quick profits have been
the chief reasons for recent Colombian Negro migration into Esmeraldas.
It has also been a factor in the sudden growth of the commercial centers
of Borbón, Limones and other towns in northwestern Esmeraldas.[50]
The boom has recently spread over the Colombian border to the Mira
River area where a small American concern operates a plantation and
buys stems from native farmers for shipment to Panama. Production
and transport are favored in this instance by the narrow-gauge El
Diviso-Tumaco railway and the improved port facilities at Tumaco.

Cultivation techniques and soil and drainage requirements
for bananas are practically identical with those for plantains.
The well-drained natural levees offer the best sites for banana groves,
but some backswamp areas are being drained for cultivation. As yet,
the use of the best lands for bananas in the sparcely populated northern
Chocó has not yet affected food supply. Negroes of the Chocó eat
bananas only as a famine food. Rejected and surplus stems, however,
make excellent hog feed; in many areas along the coast farmers are
using the fruit for that purpose.

Other Commercial Crops.

Formerly other agricultural products such as oranges,
cacao and coconuts, were important commercially in various parts of
the Pacific lowlands. Today, due mainly to the incursion of plant diseases, lack of proper cultivation, and difficulties of transport, these
crops are rapidly disappearing from the lowland economy.

During the last quarter of the nineteenth century the cultivation of citrus fruit, principally sweet oranges, was undertaken in various villages along the Pacific Coast. At the present time at least four coastal localities still cultivate oranges on a commercial scale; Cupica, between Cabo Corrientes and the Panama border; Togoramá, at the northern end of the San Juan Delta; La Vigía and San Juan de la Costa, both in the Patía-Sanguianga delta area north of Tumaco. Each of these villages is on either a recent or an ancient beach ridge, where sandy, alkaline soils give optimum edaphic conditions for citrus culture. Within these villages every family cultivates from five to twenty-five orange trees around the house. Cupica is the largest producer, shipping weekly to Buenaventura between 30,000 and 50,000 fruits during the harvest season (August and September). The harvest of Togoromá is marketed also in Buenaventura, but some oranges are transported as far as the mining districts in the upper San Juan River. The oranges of La Vigía and San Juan de la Costa go to Tumaco, El Charco, and Guapi. Unfortunately, the trees are poorly cared for; grafting and pruning are rarely practiced; as old trees die few new ones are planted. Moreover, black scale and other fungus diseases are rapidly devastating the groves; those of Togoramá were practically wiped out in 1954. Lacking funds for disease control and knowledge of modern citrus culture, the coastal orange growers appear destined to lose completely the few groves that remain.

Although some are consumed locally, most of the cacao beans which the Negro farmers cultivate in their house gardens are sun-cured and sold to passing merchants (Plate XXXIV). About 1900 several plantations of cacao trees were started in the Baudó Valley by large Colombian landowners.[51] Disease and transport difficulties, however, have caused the abandonment of most of the plantings. As mentioned previously, during the last 150 years coconut groves were planted for commercial production along the beaches of the Pacific Coast. Many of these groves have been destroyed by beach erosion. The larger plantations are found on the extensive and more stable beaches of the cliffed coast north of Cabo Corrientes; but, as with cacao, disease has ruined many groves, and costly, uncertain transport does not encourage replanting.

Land Tenure

The majority of the inhabitants of the Pacific lowlands are not only subsistence farmers. They are squatters as well, just as their great-grandfathers were after the abolition of slavery. Today probably not one farmer in a hundred holds legal title to the land he occupies and cultivates, nor does he pay rent. Much of the Pacific lowland of Colombia is national domain (terrenos baldíos nacionales), which may be claimed by any person who (1) cultivates or otherwise uses an area amounting to at least a third of his claim and (2) files the requisite papers with the government and pays certain small fees. [52] Most of the lowland farmers who occupy baldíos have neither the money nor the inclination to file claims, for they have been cultivating such lands for years without interference. Some lands are owned or leased by mining concerns; others are held legally by individuals in the interior who have little interest in their development. Although legally possible, it would be difficult and in most cases undesirable to eject the subsistence farmers from such lands. [53]

Among the squatters various unwritten property rules have evolved, based mainly on Spanish custom. In the long-occupied mining districts levee, terrace, and hill lands near the main settlements are considered to be privately owned by families of the community, each having its unwritten title (título de familia) to certain plots. Such lands can be divided by inheritance, and may be sold to members of the community outside the immediate family. At some distance from the river banks are the communal lands, which may be cultivated, logged, or hunted on by any member of the community. People from other rivers usually must obtain permission from the community authorities to till such land. Some villages have "church lands," contributed to the community by the devout. Any villager has the right to farm church property, but first must obtain permission from the mayordomo, or manager, and agree to pay tithes on all produce obtained from the land. [54]

Most of the fresh-water swamp zone in the lower sections of the rivers south of Buenaventura has been considered baldío, or free land open to cultivation by the farmers of any of the adjacent rivers. In the past thirty or forty years most of the up-river folk have taken up plots of rich levee land in the swamp area, doubling their cultivated holdings. For example, maize is planted in July and August in the old upstream lands; in January and February the family goes downstream to plant the newer plots, near which are built crude huts (ranchos) for temporary living quarters. Many people on the Guapi and Timbiquí rivers have new lands as far away as the lower Sanguianga and Satinga rivers north of Tumaco. As long as such plots are in continual use by a given family they cannot be claimed or cultivated by others. Eventually families will permanently acquire possession of these new plots through the unwritten titulos de familia.

A somewhat similar system of "squatters rights" is found in the Atrato Basin and on the Pacific Coast of the Chocó, where new plots have been made along small quebradas five to ten miles from the principal settlements. In 1954 Negroes from various Atrato villages were opening up new plots and constructing temporary dwellings along the middle course of the Río Napipí. Such land is considered to be baldío, and is available to all comers.

A single family may thus cultivate several widely separated plots along a stream or in the adjacent hills. Rarely are the plantain and maize fields larger than one hectare, or cuadra, on which one almud of shelled maize or 1000 plantain corms can be planted. Usually on the fertile levee and terrace lands the plots vary in size from a quarter to a half an acre.[55]

Fishing

The abundance of full-flowing streams, extensive swamps and lakes, and a long coastline afford a natural base for the valuable fish resource exploited by the Pacific lowlanders. Like most rain forest farmers, the lowland Indian relies as much on fishing as on agriculture for subsistence; fish supply the essential protein needed in an otherwise predominately starch diet. The Indian fishing tradition, including his various techniques, has in part passed on to the present Negroes and mixed bloods. Most of the farmers fish in the streams, but some make occasional trips to the sea to supplement the decreasing fresh-water fish resource; a few of the coastal dwellers are full-time professional salt-water fishermen, but most are part-time farmers as well.

Fresh-water Fishing.

A great variety of fresh-water neotropical fishes inhabit the lowland streams and marshes; only a relatively small number of species, however, are economically important. Catfish (order Nematognathi), generally called bagre, are among the largest river specimens and afford a valuable source of food. Some, like the tabuche of the Atrato, grow to five feet in length and weigh up to 150 pounds.[56] Smaller catfish that inhabit the upper stream courses include the barbudo (Pimelodus, spp.), micuro (Rhamdella, spp.) and capitán (Perugia, spp.). In addition, perch-like mojarra and gualajo are also common in the upper courses of rivers.[57] The most abundant of the fresh-water types are the characins, a small, scaley carp-like fish which comprises more than 50 per cent of the South American species.[58] The sábalo and sabaleta (Bryconinae?), the dorado (Salminus affinus), the dentón (Hopias, spp.), and the bocachico (Prochilodus magdalenae) are the characins most commonly found in the lowland streams. Fortunately, the voracious pirañas, scourge of the Orinoco, Amazon, and

Paraná-Paraguay drainages of South America, do not occur in the streams of the Pacific lowlands.

The two characins, dentón and bocachico, are especially abundant in the Río Atrato, where each year in January and February they leave the ciénagas or fresh-water swamps and migrate upstream with other fishes to spawn, returning in April and May. This phonomenon of swarming by the same fish species is found in each of the four major rivers of northern Colombia -- The Atrato, Sinú, Magdalena, and its main tributary, the Cauca. Numerous shallow lakes (ciénagas) connected with the main channel through small creeks (caños) are found in the lower part of each river basin. At the onset of the dry season in January, when the ciénagas begin to recede, the upstream swarming begins. Called the subienda, this is a time of great activity along the Atrato, for the fish, fat and sluggish, are easily caught with various types of nets and even with the bare hands. The bajanza, or the period during March and April when the fish are returning downstream to the ciénagas is another time of frenzied fishing. The tens of thousands of bocachico, dentón, and other fish that are caught are cleaned, preserved by salting, smoking, and drying, and packed in bundles of one-half to one arroba (twelve and one-half to twenty-five pounds) for storage or for sale. Bundles of dried fish from the Atrato are sold all over the Chocó and are even taken across the cordillera to Antioquia and to Cali. The visitor to Quibdó does not soon forget the stench from the arrobas of dried fish stacked along the river wharf.

In other rivers of the Pacific lowlands where swarming apparently does not take place, the fish resource is rapidly declining. The San Juan and the rivers to the south of Buenaventura are particularly poor in fish, and the farmers are now obliged to buy the dried Atrato product or to fish along the coast for a short period each year.

Fishing tools and techniques employed by the river farmers are of Indian and European origin. The traps are probably Indian. A conspicuous feature along river banks from the Chucunaque River in Darién to the Guayas in Ecuador is the corral, a small rectangular enclosure constructed of long bamboo stems or palm strips driven into mud. A sliding guillotine-like door weighted with a stone is tripped by the waiting fisherman when a sábalo or a mojarra has been attracted inside by bait -- usually an ear of corn (Plate XXXIX). Weirs (trincheras) have a much wider distribution. These are constructed of strips of bamboo or palm across the mouths of small quebradas; during low water scores of fish are often trapped behind the barrier. Such a contraption is useful during the bajanza on the tributaries of the upper Atrato, when fish start their downstream migration. Larger weirs

PLATE XXXIX 157
RIVER FISHING TECHNIQUES AND IMPLEMENTS

Left: A corral along the Río Mira during low water. The sliding trap door is fitted behind the front wall of the corral. Richt: A bamboo weir across mouth of small tributary, lower Río Quito, near Quibdó, Chocó.

Left: A catanga, or shrimp pot, village of Conchera, Esmeraldas. Right: A fishing basket (pando), Rio Guelmambí.

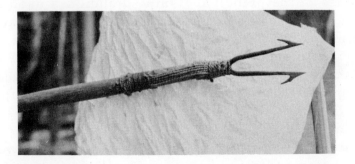

A gig used to catch crab and to hunt guagua, Río Rosario.

(vallados) are constructed on the downstream side of grass-covered slip-off slopes to impound fish during freshets. Women and children often catch small fish in a conical basket (tasa, pando) with which they slowly wade downstream in shallow water. For catching fresh-water shrimp and small catfish a trap (catanga), roughly similar to a New England lobster pot, made of palm slats, is secured with liana thongs along muddy banks and baited with chontadura fruits or maize. A larger pot (tortuguera) is similarly employed to trap turtles.

Most Negroes have adopted the Indian harpón for gigging various river fish and the blue crabs that inhabit the mangrove swamp. In spite of its name the "harpoon" has a nondetachable point consisting of two barbed prongs of iron secured with liana fiber to a long wooden shaft. [59] The fishing arrow is no longer shot with the bow even by the most isolated Chocó Indians.

Nets are today the most valuable tool of the fisherman. Except for possibly some of the dip nets these are of probable European origin. The common dip net (chayo, copón) is nothing more than a piece of heavy netting tied to the ends of a forked stick and used to catch fish from the river bank or to scoop a sábalo captured in the corral. More important is the European throw net (atarraya), a circular piece of netting weighted on the ends by lead pellets. [60] During the fish runs on the Atrato both the copón and the atarraya are the main tools employed to make the prodigious hauls of bocachico and dentón. The long chinchorro, or seine, so important in the coastal fisheries is rarely used in the confined area of a river channel.

The common European pole, line and hook method of fishing is almost never seen in the Pacific lowlands, although occasionally Negro river fishermen employ the trotline with floats attached.

Still significant among Indians and some Negroes in isolated sections are the native piscicides. As in most humid tropical areas, poisoning was one of the principal fishing techniques used in fresh water within the Pacific lowlands before the practice was outlawed by the Colombian government. Most of the poisons employed in Latin America come from various plants generally called barbasco, four of which are found in the Pacific lowlands. [61] The facts that many of the barbascos are cultigens (plants that propagate only with the help of man) and are grown around the house, suggest that the use of piscicides is ancient in tropical America. Quiet water in dammed portions of streams or in lakes is requisite for effective use of poison. Roots, leaves, and stems are crushed in water and the concentrated milky solution dumped into the stream. The poison only stuns or stupifies the fish; it does not kill.

As the stunned fish float to the surface they are scooped into baskets
or they are speared. The government ban on poisoning is obviously a
conservation measure, but like the prohibition of the use of dynamite
in fishing, it often goes unheeded in isolated areas far from centers of
law enforcement.

Salt-water fishing.

          Counterbalancing the decline of the fresh-water fish re-
source, the past 100 years has seen a rudimentary exploitation of the
coastal fisheries. This activity has occurred chiefly along the low mangrove coast between Cabo Corrientes and Esmeraldas. There, large
schools of fish inhabit the shoal waters offshore and the muddy tidal
estuaries, where plankton and river refuse are abundant. Although a
large variety of fish is taken in the coastal waters, two species make
up the greater part of the catch: the lisa, a grey mullet (Mugil cepholus)
and the robalo, a snook (Centroponus, spp.). Both are comparatively
small in size (twelve to eighteen inches long), but they run in schools
of immense numbers in the shoal area and in the brackish tidal estuaries. In addition various crevalles, such as the pámpano (Trachinotrus,
spp.) and the jurel (Carnex, spp.); a croaker, called corbina (Micropo-
gon, spp.); and various salt-water catfish, although more often found
in deeper water, are occasionally caught in the shallows. Deep-water
species which often form part of the fisherman's catch are various
mackerel, including the atún or tuna; the dorado, a yellowtail (Seriola,
spp.), picuda, a barracuda (Sphyraenidae); and sometimes sharks and
swordfish.[62] In spite of their large numbers in the muddy shallows,
few shrimp are taken; but in the mud flats at low tide women and children often dig for clams (almejas, Unio, spp.) and mussels (pianguas,
Mytilus, spp.).

          The coastal fishermen use many old European tools and
techniques that are still seen along most of the coastal areas of Latin
America. To catch the smaller fish in shallow waters two nets are
employed: the common cast net (atarraya) and the seine (chinchorro),
which is like a long tennis net enlarged in the center with lead sinkers
attached to the bottom side, balsa floats to the top side. The cast net
is operated by one person; the manipulation of the chinchorro requires
a crew of five.[63] (Plate XL.) At low tide a crew of chinchorreros
paddle the canoe over a submerged bajo, or shoal; two leap into the
shallow water to arrange the seine, while those remaining in the canoe
pull in the catch. Many fishermen use a process known as the rodeo
in estuaries and channels at low tide to catch lisa. Six to eight men
place a kind of weir (made of wide gill nets fastened to long stakes
driven in the mud) around an area of shallow water some 200 feet in

A crew of chinchorreros near Tumaco.

A barbacoa, or fish-drying platform near hut, Estero de Limones, near Guapi. Unhulled rice is drying in the canoe.

Fishing village of Conchera on shell mound bordering estuary, near Limones, Esmeraldas.

diameter. They gradually make the enclosure smaller by moving the stakes and net inward until the space is small enough to permit easy gathering of fish in baskets. <u>Tajadas</u> are small fences of gill nets which are placed across the mouths of small tributary channels of the estuaries; at low tide the fish caught in the mesh of the net are gathered. Tidal ponds and shallow lagoons on or back of the beach ridges form natural traps for small fish; at low tide sometimes hundreds of <u>lisa</u> are stranded in such ponds and are speared with gigs or poisoned with barbasco.

At sea and also in the deeper parts of the estuaries the Colombian fishermen employ a kind of trotline (<u>belandra</u>) composed of several balsa floats to each of which is attached a line and hook. The larger fish, such as tuna, yellowtail, and sharks are taken either with the <u>balandra</u> or with a harpoon of three detachable barbed points. For their work the fishermen use only small dugout canoes, often equipped with a sprit sail, but expertly handled in the heavy swell that prevails off the Pacific Coast.

Fishing settlements inhabited by Negroes, mixed bloods, and a few whites are found widely scattered on beach ridges along the entire shoal coast of Colombia and northern Esmeraldas. But on the shores of the Bay of Ancón, which straddles the Colombia-Ecuador boundary, and the Ensenada de Tumaco there are nearly twenty-five fishing villages, some with more than fifty huts, making the southern end of the lowland the center of salt-water fishing on the Pacific coast of Colombia. Some of the villages, like Cenizo and Chamorro, are inhabited solely by professional fishermen who sell their catch in Tumaco. Most of the fishers of other villages, however, spend at least half their time tending plots of maize and plantains on the beach ridge and rice in the swamps back of the mangrove.

Another type of fishing settlement prevails along the coast -- the isolated temporary dwellings of the up-river folk who make annual journeys to the sea to fish. Usually the entire family migrates to the beach in January and February in order to obtain fish in time for the fiestas of Holy Week. At the same time they tend their downstream fields in the fresh-water swamps. Both the professional fishermen of the villages and the temporary fisher of the ranchos preserve the catch by drying, smoking, and salting on barbacoas near the huts (Plate XL). Like the Atrateños, the coastal people prepare dried fish for transport and storage by packing them into bundles of various weights.[64]

Hunting

The Animal Resource.

The few remaining forest Indians living in the remote sections of the Pacific lowlands still gain a large part of their subsistence by hunting. To modern Negroes and mixed bloods, however, hunting is of little importance, for after 300 years of European and African occupation the wild life resource has been seriously drained in the areas near the major streams. Although the Chocó is still referred to as a land of venomous snakes, such are rarely encountered except in isolated spots. The only areas where wild game is still adequate for human subsistence are the remoter sections of the Serranía de Baudó and the western slopes of the Cordillera Occidental.

Today the animals most hunted for food by both Indian and Negro are four species of large rodents that live along water courses. All are widespread in the humid tropics of America. The more abundant is the guagua, or spotted cavy (Cuniculus paca virgatus), about the size of a fox terrier.[65] A larger animal is the water pig (lancha), often called the capybara (Hydrochorus capybara), now hunted chiefly in the northern part of the Chocó. The agoutí (locally called guantín or ñeque, Dasyprocta, spp.) is now hard to find in the Pacific lowlands. The flesh of these three animals, although sweet and greasy, is a welcome change from the fetid dried fish that the traveller usually must carry for his boatmen on long river trips. The fourth rodent, the nutria or coypu (Myocastor coypus bonariensis), is hunted for both his meat and hide.

Formerly the most important source of meat among Indians, the hoofed animals of the rain forest have been reduced to small numbers. Two kinds of wild hog, or peccary, were once hunted extensively. The white lipped peccary, or saino (Tayassu pecari spiradens) roamed the forest in small groups; the smaller collered peccary, or tatabro (Peccari tajacu bangsii) fed in large droves of several hundred animals.[66] Both animals have musk glands on the back, and their presence can easily be detected by the peculiar odor as well as their rootings. Today small droves are still common in the Serranía de Baudó, but in the last part of the eighteenth century most of the lower Atrato drainage below Riosucio was noted for its excellent peccary feeding grounds on the palm-covered levees.[67] The tapir, or danta (Tapirella bairdii) is now so rare that it is only a hunter's curiosity. The small brocket deer (Mazama americans reperticia), however, is still plentiful in the Baudó area, where it is hunted mainly by Indians.

Like most animals formerly important for food, the monkeys have been drastically reduced in numbers and the remnants pushed

into the remoter sections of the lowlands. The black spider monkey
(mico, Ateles, spp.), red howler (mono, Alouatta palliata aequatorialis),
and the white-cheeked capuchín (maicero, Cebus capucinus capucinus)
are all eaten by both Indians and Negroes. The tiny marmoset (Mari-
kina, spp.) is often captured for a house pet, but rarely taken for food.
A more abundant tree-dwelling mammal is the small tropical squirrel
(Microsciurus, spp.), a fair source of fresh meat even in the more
densely settled areas of the lowlands.

        In addition to the river rodents the remaining population of
various aquatic and amphibious mammals and reptiles are still hunted
in the swamps and lower stream courses. In colonial times the seacow
or manatee (Trichechus manatus manatus), some weighing from five to
six hundred pounds, abounded in the extensive ciénagas of the lower
Atrato Basin. During the eighteenth century thousands of these animals
were killed annually, their meat dried and fat rendered to ship to the
mining centers upstream.[68] After 250 years of slaughter only a small
number of manatee remain in the lower Atrato. Occasionally a fisherman living near a large ciénaga will harpoon one or two yearly and dry
the meat for his own use or sale. Less useful than the docile seacows
are the offensive crocodiles (Crocodilus acutus) and the smaller cay-
mans (Caiman sclerops) that live along the lower river courses and in
lagoons. In the lower Atrato these reptiles have met the fate of the
manatee, the great swarms of former years having been reduced to a
few stragglers. During the eighteenth and nineteenth centuries the oil
rendered from the crocodiles was used for cooking and illumination in
the mining areas. Today the beasts are hunted mainly for their hides,
and, when discovered in the sand bars along the river, their eggs are
eaten with relish. The common iguana (Iguana iguana), a giant tropical
lizard that grows to three feet in length, still abounds in the fresh-water
and mangrove swamps along the coast. Living in the trees and feeding
on birds, eggs, and tender leaves, this fellow dives into the water with
a resounding splash on the approach of a canoe. His white, tender meat
makes a delicious meal, and he is eagerly sought by Negro canoemen as
they slowly paddle along the tidal channels in the mangrove.

        The cats and other carnivores are hunted for their skins,
which usually bring fair prices in the market towns. Once plentiful,
the jaguar (tigre, Felis onca), puma (leon, F. concolor), and ocelot
(tigrillo, F. pardalis) are now found only in secluded spots, but occasionally the smaller cats will invade a settlement in search of food.
Bears (Tremaretos, spp. ?) have become extremely rare, but spores
of small grey foxes (such as Urocyon, spp.) are seen frequently in the
interfluves.

Minor animals sometimes hunted for food or skin include the armadillo (Dasypus, spp.), sloth (Bradypus, spp.), and ant-eater (oso hormiguero, Tamandua tetradactyla chiriquensis). No special effort is made to hunt snakes for skins, but occasionally a large boa (Constrictor, spp.) is killed and the hide sold to dealers. The highly venomous snakes (mainly the fer-de-lance, Bothrops, spp.) and the bushmaster (Lachesis, spp.) are assiduously avoided. Surprisingly few birds are hunted. Certain galliforms, such as the crested guan (Penelope purpurascens), partridge (Tetrao perdix), and curassow (Crax, spp.), and even the large-billed toucans (Rhamphastus, spp.) are often sought for food in most parts of the lowlands. In the lower Atrato a large tree duck called pato real (Dendrocygna, spp.), well cooked and seasoned, makes a tasty dish, and the large chaverío (Chauna chaveria), a bird of the ciénagas, is sometimes hunted.

Hunting Techniques.

In former days Negroes and mixed bloods used hunting tools and techniques borrowed directly from the forest Indians. These included the blowgun and poisoned darts, spears and harpoons, a variety of traps, and of course the dog. Some of these are still retained, but most have been replaced by the modern gun even among the remaining Indians.

Most of the latter, especially the Waunamá, and a few Negroes living in remote areas still employ the blowgun (cerbatana) with which are shot poisoned darts (pullas) for killing both small and large game.[69] The "gun" is nothing more than a wooden shaft, eight to ten feet long, with a hole through the center. In the Chocó it is constructed of two grooved lengths of hard palmwood fitted together and tightly wrapped with bark fiber. The wooden mouthpiece, through which the hunter puffs to propel the dart, is made separately and attached to the shaft. The darts are splinters of palmwood, eight inches long, sharply pointed, and deeply notched about one inch back from the point, so that the stem will easily break, leaving the poisoned tip embedded in the victim. On the opposite end of the dart is wrapped a small wad of cotton or kapok, which acts as a valve to receive the impact of the air-puff that propels the missle through the bore of the gun. The darts, tipped with poison, are kept in covered bamboo quivers, to which are attached two small round gourds containing cotton for wadding. This weapon complex has a fairly wide distribution in the humid tropics of America. It is found in the Orinoco Basin, the upper Amazon, and the Pacific lowlands of Colombia, Esmeraldas, and Darién.[70] It occurs also among the primitive forest groups of southeastern Asia.

The Chocó and Waunamá Indians make two kinds of poison, with which they coat the tips of the darts. One, called pakuru (Chocó) is prepared by boiling the latex of a tropical mulberry tree (Perebea, spp.); it is probably the only aboriginal cardiac poison used in the New World, the famous curare of the Amazon and Orinoco basins affecting only the motor nerves of the muscles.[71] The other poison, known as kokoi (Chocó), is obtained from secretions scraped from the back side of a tree frog (Dendrobatis tinctorius). Like curare, this poison produces paralysis of the muscles and the central nervous system.[72] Both poisons are deadly to most animals, but both Indians and Negroes claim that various fowl, such as the guan and the common chicken, are immune.

Formerly an important weapon for warfare among the Indians, the bow and arrow is never used for hunting. At the time of Spanish contact in the lowlands probably the blowgun was in the process of replacing the older bow and arrow as a hunting instrument.[73] For killing peccary the Indians used a long lance (aboriginally with fire-hardened point, later with iron point).[74] Negroes and Indians without guns often hunt the water rodents with a barbed spear or gig and a dog. Guaguas are usually hunted at night with the aid of flares or a carbide lamp. Indians employ traps more than the Negroes or mixed bloods. Used by both, however, are the armazón, a pitfall with pointed stakes stuck in the bottom; the llapó, a net fixed along an animal path; various types of deadfalls; and the anjo, a kind of fall trap. The few remaining Negro manatee hunters in the lower Atrato still use the aboriginal harpoon, a shaft four to five feet long having a detachable barbed point fastened with a long rope to a large piece of balsa wood; the latter, fixed to the back end of the shaft, serves as a float to indicate the position of the wounded manatee. Among most of the lowlanders, including the Indians, the gun has become the universal hunting weapon. Some have modern rifles, but the majority must be content with old muzzle-loaders of the last century. Guns are hard to come by, and during the political disturbances of the last few years they have been banned by the government even as a hunting weapon.[75]

Exploitation of Forest Products

Aside from the normal subsistence activities of farming, fishing, and hunting, and the recent development of small-scale commercial agriculture, during the last century the people of the Pacific lowlands have supplemented their livelihood by gathering various tropical forest products for export to foreign markets. Gathering of this sort typifies the early commercial exploitation of most of the world's rain forest areas; but the prosperity of such an activity is usually dependent upon the demand for certain products in the extra-tropical areas. Since this demand frequently changes according to fads, technological developments, and military necessities, gathering industries in the tropics have been extremely unstable; short boom periods are followed by long intervals of depression, and often complete collapse of a given industry. Such as been the case in the Pacific lowlands. Three forest products -- ruber, tagua nuts, and tropical woods -- have been the mainstays of the gathering activities (Map 22). Rubber collecting has seen several boom and depression periods; the tagua nut industry was at its peak during the early years of this century, but now has collapsed; lumbering of tropical woods is the latest phase of forest exploitation, but its life may be shortened by the rapid depletion of forest reserves.

Rubber.

Many latex-bearing trees and vines grow wild in the Pacific lowland forests. Caucho negro (Castilla panamensis), the most valuable, grows on well-drained levee soils and on the lower slopes of hills; almost solid stands occur in the upper Baudó Valley, but these appear to be remnants of abandoned plantations that have become self-renewing. As indicated earlier, castilla is cultivated along the river banks throughout the lowlands, each household having a half-dozen or more trees. Balata or níspero (Mimusops balata), popa (Couma macrocarpa), caucho blanco (Ficus, spp.), and chicle or níspero (Achras sapota) are other wild trees yielding coagulable latex that are commonly exploited for rubber in the Pacific lowlands.

In the early years of the last century Negroes in the Chocó were gathering latex to make rubber candles for illumination. [76] Intensive exploitation of the latex did not begin until the 1850's, after the perfection of Goodyear's vulcanization process had created a large demand for rubber in the United States and Europe. In 1858 the collection of latex from the forest had become the chief occupation of the small number of Negroes and mixed bloods living in the lower Atrato. [77] Collecting methods were extremely destructive, for both castilla and balata trees were felled to gather latex. By the end of the century rubber production had fallen owing to depletion of most of easily accessible stands of trees near the rivers. [78] According to local inhabitants, in 1878 a large area in the Río Mira drainage was planted in castilla and modern tapping methods introduced; later plantings were made on the upper Baudó, middle Patía, and several tributaries of the Atrato. [79] These were abandoned, however, after the start (1913) of the great rubber depression in the American tropics that followed the development of plantation production in southeastern Asia. As in most

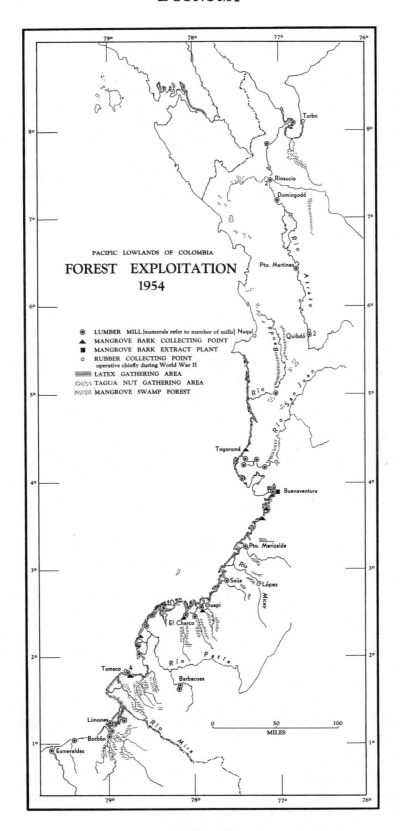

MAP 22

areas of the humid American tropics, rubber collecting was revived in the Pacific lowlands during World War II. The remnants of the abandoned plantings on the upper Baudó, middle Patía and Telembí rivers; the old plantations along the Atrato tributaries; and the wild stands of balata west of the San Juan River were the source of most of the rubber taken out of the Pacific lowlands during the last boom.[80] Today, with the return of the southeast Asian production to the world market and the development of synthetic rubber, latex-gathering in the lowlands has fallen to another low ebb. Farmers and a few professional caucheros occasionally take small amounts of raw rubber to the market centers to sell to dealers -- usually owners of general stores. The castilla tree is usually tapped by making a series of horizontal incisions around the trunk. In each incision there accumulates a band (rueda) of raw rubber. These are ripped off and wrapped in bundles (marquitas) for the market.[81]

Tagua.

The vegetable ivory palm, locally called tagua or cadi, (Phytelephas, spp.; Palandra aequatorialis) has a wide distribution in the wet lowlands from Panama to Bolivia.[82] Within this zone it predominates as a dense, shade-tolerant understory growth along stream levees and low hillsides in three areas: (1) the lower Atrato basin (in particular along the Río León, south of the Gulf of Urabá), (2) the foothills of the northern portion of the Serranía de Baudó in northwestern Chocó and southern Darién, and (3) the coastal lowlands in the vicinity of Tumaco and Esmeraldas.[83] Around the trunk of the palm, just below the bottom fronds, there develops a number of burr clusters, each a foot in diameter, consisting of numerous round carpels. Each carpel contains from four to six brown, egg-shaped nuts, each with a hard, white endosperm -- the vegetable ivory of world commerce. Around 1850 some of the palm nuts were sent to Europe, where they were found to be a good substitute for elephant ivory and an excellent material for making hard, durable buttons.[84] For nearly eighty years the collection of tagua nuts was a profitable business for many Negroes and Indians of the Pacific lowlands, especially for those living in the southern area. The nuts were purchased by dealers and assembled at Esmeraldas and Tumaco for shipment to the United States and Europe. Those gathered along the streams of the Chocó coast were taken to Panama and Buenaventura, while the collections from the Río León and the lower Atrato were sold in Cartagena. But in the 1930's the development of synthetic materials such as plastic for making buttons caused the collapse of the tagua industry of Colombia, Ecuador and Panama. Today Negroes and Cayapa Indians in the Esmeraldas area still gather a few nuts, from which are made the famous Ecuadorian carvings.[85]

The tagua palm is not planted, but it has been protected for so long by cutting out competing vegetation that pure stands now flourish along river banks of Esmeraldas and the Tumaco area.[86] In the Chocó extensive taguales also occur along the streams in the Valle area south of Bahía Solano and in the upper Juradó and Amparadó rivers near the Panamanian border.

Lumbering.

It is well known that the tropical rain forests of the world are ill-suited for large-scale lumbering.[87] Aside from the factors of poor transport and isolation from market center, the inherent drawbacks of heterogeneity of tree species, the predominance of worthless softwoods, and the slow rate of growth of the more valuable hardwoods make commerical logging difficult and unprofitable. In general the Pacific lowland rain forest is poor in logging opportunities, but during the last twenty years a surprising upswing in lumbering activities has occurred in various sections, which has given many peasant farmers a new source of cash income. This development is based mainly on (1) a small-scale, or peasant, logging system and (2) the demand for cheap softwoods in the growing industrial and urban areas of the Colombian highlands and abroad. Although small amounts of certain valuable hardwoods were being shipped from the area by 1900, the present surge in lumbering activity did not begin until the 1930's with the government restrictions on imporation of basic raw materials. Today the forests of the Pacific lowlands and the lower Magdalena Basin supply most of the lumber used in the populous interior.

The large hardwoods scattered through the rain forest have been logged out of the more accessible areas. In the Serranía de Baudó and the Pacific slope of the western Cordillera large specimens of the fine-grained chachajo (Anibo perutilis), chibugá (Cariniana pyriformis), guayacán (Tabebuia, spp.) jigua (Nectandra, spp.) and espavé (Anacardium excelsum) still abound, and occasionally a few logs are floated down-river for sawing. An important source of hardwood lumber are the small protected and cultivated stands of fast-growing tropical cedar (Cedrela, spp.) along the rivers.

The major areas of lumber exploitation in the Pacific lowlands today correspond to the swamp forests, which are characterized by predominance of large softwoods and by single dominant species. The latter characteristic is significant, for logging costs are greatly reduced in exploiting practically solid stands of a single species. In the brackish-to fresh-water swamps immediately landward from the coastal mangrove are large, solid stands of the giant nato (Mora magistosperma), cut for railroad ties; cuángare (Virola, spp.); sajo (Campnosperma panamensis); and tangare (Carapa, spp.); -- all soft-woods used for cheap construction material. Bordering the backswamps of the lower Atrato are the large cativo forests (Prioria copaifera) now being exploited by large-scale logging operations for plywood.

Independent loggers, usually peasant farmers who occasion-ally cut trees for extra cash, float rafts of timbers downriver to large sawmills or prepare lumber themselves in their own small mills near the dwelling along the river. The tiny lumber mill (aserrío), no more than a thatch-covered platform on which is operated a two-man steel cross-cut saw, has become a common feature along the lower course of many rivers. Sawed planks are sold to the river traders who col-lect all kinds of produce in their small sail or motor launches. The greater part of the timber, however, is processed in the large mills located near the mouths of rivers or in the larger market centers. Most have rotary saws powered by Diesel motors. In 1951-1954 over thirty of these mills were operating within the lowlands, including Esmeraldas and Darién (Map 26). Six operate in Buenaventura, the lumber export center of the Colombian Pacific Coast. From there virola logs are shipped directly to Europe, while most of the sawed lumber is taken by rail and truck to Cali and other inland points.[89] (Plate XLI).

Since 1953 two Colombian companies (one is U.S. financed and managed) have been exploiting the cativo forests in the lower Atrato. These companies represent the only large-scale logging operations in the lowlands, although both buy a part of their logs from small cutters. One camp is located on the lower Truandó, the other on the lower León immediately inland from the Bahía de Colombia on the Gulf of Urabá. Cativo logs are shipped by ocean freighter to lumber plants in Barranquilla, Colombia and Pascagoula, Mississippi, where they are processed for veneer and plywood.

Mangrove Bark.

A minor collecting activity is concerned with the stripping of bark from the giant mangle rojo (Rhizophora, spp.), the major com-ponent of the mangrove swamps. Again, the dominance of one species eases exploitation, but that advantage is cancelled by the unpleasant-ness encountered in a mangrove swamp. The value of Rhizophora bark arises from its 50 to 60 per cent tannin content.

Within the last thirty years many up-river folk have estab-lished concheras, or temporary bark-cutters' camps, where, amidst

PLATE XLI. LUMBER EXPLOITATION   171

Logs being rafted down the Atrato to sawmill at Ríosucio. Note paddles, balsa floats, and temporary shelter (<u>rancho</u>).

A small hand sawmill on Río Atrato near Bellavista. The river, at flood stage, overtops the natural levee.

Large lumber mill at Ríosucio, Río Atrato.

the evil stench and swarms of insects, bark is collected and sold to travelling buyers. To strip its bark a tree must be felled; thus considerable destruction of the high mangrove has occurred in many areas along the coast. Most of the bark collected is taken to Buenaventura, where a single plant manufactures tannin extract. [90]

On the outskirts of the larger coastal towns Rhizophora wood is converted into charcoal, the common household fuel in most parts of Latin America. To furnish sufficient wood for the numerous charcoal kilns much of the mangrove swamp around such centers is being depleted of its larger trees.

Other Collecting Activities.

Other minor phases of forest exploitation include the gathering of various medicinal roots and the extraction of oil from seeds of wild palms. Of the medicinal roots the most valuable are those of ipecac, or raicilla (Cephaelis, spp.), a rubiaceous creeper common to the densely shaded ground cover of many rain forest areas in tropical America. Within the Pacific lowlands the forests in the lower Atrato and the northern section of the Serranía de Baudó are particularly productive of ipecac. There the roots, which contain an alkaloid, emitine, are used locally as a painkiller and an emetic but since the last half of the nineteenth century large quantities have been shipped to the United States and to Europe. Also in the northern Serranía de Baudó both Negroes and Indians gather seed clusters of the milpeso palm (Jessenia polycarpa), from which they extract (by soaking in water) a thin oil, used in highland Colombia for lubricating fine machinery.

Mining

The significance of placer mining in the development of the cultural landscape of the Pacific lowlands has been emphasized many times in the foregoing pages. [91] A few points may be summarized as follows:

(1) Rich gold placers alone attracted Spanish interest in the area during colonial times.
(2) The present Negroid population had its origin in the African labor force imported in colonial days to mine gold.
(3) Today a large number of the lowland inhabitants are full or part-time peasant miners, extracting sizeable amounts of precious metals from small placers.

(4) In terms of monetary value gold and platinum, extracted mainly by large-scale dredging operations, are still the most important products of the lowlands.

The Placer Deposits.

The principal mining area of the Pacific lowlands corresponds to a narrow belt of ancient gravels that lies along the western base of the Cordillera Occidental. This belt extends almost continually from the lower Atrato Basin southward into Esmeraldas in Ecuador. [92] The gravels rest on indurated upper Miocene shale and limestone, and appear to have been deposited in late Pliocene and in Pleistocene by streams that had eroded into the gold-bearing batholiths that underlie the cordillera. The gravel richest in gold lies in the beds of old buried stream channels, the pattern of which bears no relation to the modern drainage. Owing to recent uplift, the present streams that drain the western slope of the cordillera have dissected the old alluvial surface, exposing here and there the auriferous layers within the fossil channels. The modern river deposits that form low terraces and point bars derive their gold content from the ancient gravels through which they have cut, rather than from the original lodes.

As indicated previously, since colonial days the chief mining district within the hilly auriferous gravel zone has been the upper Atrato-San Juan area of the Chocó, including the eastern tributaries of those rivers from the Río Bebará southward to the Río Sipí. This area was the first of the Pacific lowlands to be occupied by Spaniards and the first to receive Negro blood. Today this area is still the core of the Chocó, with nearly two-thirds of the department's population and most of its natural wealth.

Other important mining districts within the gravel belt include the area below Buenaventura between the Río Calima and the Río Iscuandé; that of Barbacoas (Río Telembí and its tributaries and the Rio Magüí); and the Santiago River drainage in Esmeraldas. Mining areas of minor significance are those of Darién, based on the lode deposits of Caná and placers of various streams in the mountains that separate Panama and Colombia. Moreover, small scattered placers occur in the southern part of the Serranía de Baudó, such as those of Managrú, west of the upper Atrato and those on the upper Ijuá and Orpúa rivers near the Pacific Coast.

Minute pellets of platinum occur mixed with gold dust in varying amounts in most of the mining districts. The richest deposits are found in the upper San Juan gravels, particularly along the Condoto,

Iró, and Opogadó rivers, where the proportion of platinum to gold is approximately 75 per cent. Minor platiniferous streams are the Jolí (25 per cent), a tributary of the Micay; the Telembí (one percent) in the Barbacoas district; and the Santiago-Cayapa drainage (11 to 17 per cent) in the Esmeraldas. Considered worthless until the last years of the eighteenth century, platinum is now second only to gold as the most valuable product of the Pacific lowlands.

Mining Methods.

Alluvial gold and platinum are extracted in the Pacific lowlands by two types of organizations: (1) the folk, or peasant miners, using primitive colonial techniques, and (2) the large foreign mining companies, using electrified dredges. Despite their primitive methods, the folk miners now produce approximately 25 per cent of the gold and 50 per cent of the platinum mined in the Pacific lowlands.

Folk mining. The peasant miners have probably preserved more of their cultural heritage than any other group in the Pacific lowlands. These people have retained the old placering methods employed by their slave ancestors during the seventeenth and eighteenth centuries. Like so many of the present Colombian folkways, most of the alluvial mining techniques were fundamentally Indian, perfected by the aboriginal gold miners of the Cauca Valley. These Indians taught both Spaniard and Negro slave the art of extracting gold from alluvial deposits. Then as now, the small miners exploited two types of placer deposits, each requiring distinct techniques. There were (1) the recent stream-bed deposits and (2) the old gravel beds on stream terraces or in interfluve areas.

The simplest techniques are employed in stream placering (mazamorreo) -- the extraction of the metal deposited in stream beds, point bars, and low terraces. Usually only women and children carry on such operations during the drier periods of the year (January and February) when water is low and large sand or gravel bars are exposed. Along the edge of the bars Negro women construct small wing dams (burros) of cobbles, which extend from the bank three to four feet into the water. Spaced five to six feet apart, the burros retard the current along the stream banks; in the quiet spaces between the dams the miner scoops up gold-bearing sand which she washes in the batea (a wide, shallow bowl, the counterpart of the tin pan used in the western United States) (Plate XLII). Old women often spend their spare time gouging auriferous sands from small holes along the river's edge without the aid of the wing dam. The taller women wade into the middle of shallow streams to obtain rich sand underneath bottoms of large boulders. In

PLATE XLII   175
NATIVE PLACER MINING TECHNIQUES

A small wing dam, Río Guelmambí. Note batea for washing sand and totumo for holding jagua, or black sand.

Various tools used in placer mining, Río Guelmambí. Large batea in foreground is for hauling tailings; cachos are seen immediately back of the batea; almocafres are the hoe-like instruments with hooked blade.

deeper water the technique of diving is still employed in some of the
isolated headwater areas, such as the Chagüí and Jolí, both tributaries
of the Micay. The diver, or zambullidora, weighted with a heavy
stone tied against the buttocks, sinks to the river bottom to scoop up
gravel; when the batea is filled the diver disengages the stone and
swims to the surface with her load.

The folk miners, however, placer most of their gold and
platinum from the ancient gravels in the interfluves and on high terraces.
Such operations are called minas de oro corrido, as distinguished from
the simpler minas de oro regado, or stream placers described above.
Large co-operative groups consisting of both men and women engage
in this work. Three techniques are employed: ground sluicing, pit
placering, and drifting. Ground sluicing, an old Indian technique, was
the chief method of placering used in Colombia during colonial times;
it is still the most important folk method employed in the Pacific lowlands (Plate XLIII). A sluice channel, or (canelón) is excavated along
the base of a gravel bench to the depth of false bedrock (hardpan, peña),
where the richest pay streaks are usually encountered. With iron bars
(barras) the miners dig into the face of the bench, dumping paydirt into the sluice. Water is then run through the sluice and the finer materials are washed out permitting the heavy gold dust to settle to the bottom of the sluice; large cobbles are thrown from the canelón with pairs
of concave wooden plates (cachos); next, the bottom of the sluice, containing both the settled gold and the highly auriferous clay layer immediately above the false bedrock, is scraped with almocafres, short-
handled dibbles with hooked metal blades; a second washing ensues;
finally the fine residue, rich in gold, is heaped in piles within the
sluice and the precious metal panned out with the bateas. One sluicing
operation from the time of the initial terrace excavation to the final
clean-up requires two weeks of labor by ten or fifteen workers. As
the bench face is excavated in repeated operations, the tailings are
thrown to the opposite side of the sluice until the entire deposit is worked
out. Today the worthless tailings in the upper San Juan, many dating
from colonial days, extend over several square miles of scrub-covered
territory.

The maintenance of an adequate water supply is necessary
for the operation of a ground sluice. Earthen reservoirs (pilas) are
constructed on high ground to impound rain water, which is led to the
mine through canals. The pila system is especially adapted to ground
sluicing in the Pacific lowlands where heavy rains fill the reservoir
nightly and the water is used in the mine during the day. When the
rains fail to come, as they often do for periods of three to five days
during January and February, mining operations necessarily stop.

PLATE XLIII   177
GROUND SLUICING, RIO GUELMAMBI

Ground sluicing in interfluve gravels near Río Guelmambí, Barbacoas district.   Men are excavating terrace face with iron <u>barras</u>; women are washing gold-bearing gravels in ground sluice at left.

<u>Left</u>: Women washing gravels in the ground sluice. <u>Right</u>: The clean-up in the ground sluice; a woman is panning gold with the <u>batea</u>.

Pit placering involves the excavation of a vertical shaft or often a wide pit (hoyo) to reach paydirt in old gravels in interfluves or on stream terraces. Again, a large number of workers is necessary for excavation and draining; both operations are still done by means of the "batea line," a long line of workers passing bateas filled with dirt or water from one to the next. When sufficient capital can be accumulated, pumps powered by one-cylinder engines are used for draining.

Exploitation of alluvial gold in high terraces by means of horizontal drifts (socabones) is a relatively new technique in the Pacific lowlands, having been introduced by a French mining company on the upper Timbiquí River in 1910. From that point the practice has spread to all mining districts of the Pacific coast of Colombia. It is used extensively by folk miners on the upper Saija, Guapi, and Micay rivers. Owing mainly to faulty timbering, however, the socabón has proved to be a dangerous technique when put in inexperienced hands; frequent collapse of the tunnels has killed many.

The product which the folk miners obtain from their placer workings is not pure gold, but a black concentrate called jagua, which consists of a mixture of tiny flakes of heavy magnetic iron oxide, ilmenite, and gold dust. Various methods are used to separate the black sands from the gold. In many areas the Negroes employ an old Indian method, which involves washing the jagua in a solution made from the glutinous sap of various plants, such as the balsa tree, the roots of the rascadera (Xanthosoma, spp.), and species of Piper. By surface tension the iron oxide flakes adhere to the foam of the liquid, leaving pure gold at the bottom of the receptical. Again, magnets purchased at the market centers are often used to separate the black sands from the gold.

Labor organization. Simple stream placering requires no organized labor force; panning for gold along rivers is done mainly by individuals, although a number of women may casually work together for companionship. Moreover, according to Colombian law, all persons are free to pan along streams without having to file a mining claim.

In contrast, the exploitation of the minas de oro corrido in the interfluves and high terraces by means of the more advanced techniques necessitates the use of large work gangs organized and directed by a leader. In addition, to exploit a given area by such methods a mining claim must be filed and fees paid at the land office in the minicipal center. The smaller mines may be worked by a single

family, but to perform a major operation, such as the construction of
a ground sluice or a reservoir, normally the minga, or co-operative
work group of ten or fifteen neighbors is called upon. The mine owner
incurs the usual obligations of reciprocation and ample supply of
guarapo and food for the participants. The institution of the minga is
probably more deeply entrenched among the Negro miners than among
any other group in the Pacific lowlands. The larger mines are commonly worked by a big and formal organization called the compañía,
or company, composed of the mine owner and from five to twenty-five
workers. One half of the gold extracted is divided among the laborers
in accordance with the number of days each works. [93] A person called
the cabo or capitán (a leader, who is often the owner) directs the actual mining operations, keeps records, supplies tools, and organizes
the work gang. Except for the division of the proceeds, the entire
compañía system is highly reminiscent of the organization of the
colonial slave gangs, from which it probably is derived.

Today most of the folk miners devote much of their time
to farming and fishing. Among many mining is merely an occasional
occupation, performed to accumulate sufficient cash to celebrate properly the many religious holidays that occur during the year. One of
the few remaining areas occupied by full-time folk miners is the Río
Condoto in the upper San Juan drainage, noted for its production of
platinum. There, small villages and scattered ranchos are composed
entirely of miners, whose food is shipped in from the agricultural
areas downstream. In the Barbacoas area the Río Guelmambí and
the upper Río Magüí also contain large groups who still devote their
time fully to mining.

The folk miner sells his gold and platinum to licenced
agents in the larger administrative centers, such as Quibdó, Istmina,
and Barbacoas. Precise balance scales, supposedly checked periodically by government officials, are used to weight the precious metal
presented in tiny packages of bijao leaves or of cloth. The price of
gold and platinum paid in the administrative centers is fixed by the
government, but many Colombian agents find it profitable to smuggle
the metal into Panama and Ecuador, where it has a higher purchasing
power.

Large-scale mining operations, financed and managed by
foreign concerns, have centered chiefly in the Chocó mining district.
The first operations began in 1887, when a Boston firm installed hydraulic equipment on the Río Andágueda, a tributary of the upper
Atrato; after a few months of operation, the company failed. Other
unsuccessful attempts to exploit the gravels on the Bebará, Neguá,

and other Atrato tributaries followed.[94] In 1915 the first successful power dredge was installed on the Río Condoto by the Anglo-Colombian Development Company, Ltd., a British concern.[95] A year later this operation was transferred to the present company, the Compañía Minera Chocó-Pacífico, now an American concern, which has built in the upper San Juan area one of the largest gold and platinum dredging operations in Latin America. With its headquarters at Anadagoya Camp at the junction of the San Juan and Condoto rivers, this company now operates five large bucket dredges powered by electricity generated at a hydroelectric plant constructed on the upper Andágueda. The dredges work in stream beds and in "flats," or extensive alluvial pockets in the present interfluve areas (Map 27). The platiniferous deposits on the company's concession along the upper San Juan and Condoto have now been depleted, and operations are slowly moving southward to work the auriferous gravels in the beds and adjacent flats of the Tamaná, Cajón, and probably Sipí rivers. Dredging destroys the once fertile levees and terraces along the streams, but some tailings only twenty years old are now partially covered with alluvium deposited in flood; they support a dense vegetation cover which in places has been cleared for plots of maize and plantains.[96]

The mining districts south of the Chocó have seen many foreign companies attempt to develop mining properties. Few have been successful. As mentioned earlier, in the 1880's, a British concern imported a number of Jamaican Negroes to work gold deposits along the Santiago River in Esmeraldas. In 1910 a French-British company established a large camp at Santa María on the Río Sesé, a tributary of the upper Timbiquí, to work rich auriferous gravels by the drift method; the operations were abandoned in the 1930's.[97] American companies have worked on the Río Llantín, a tributary of the upper Saija (1922-1938), and on the upper Raposo (1935-1938). The most successful operation has been made by the Compañía Minera de Nariño, an affiliate of the Chocó-Pacífico, which in 1937 installed a power dredge on the Telembí. A large, well-equipped camp has been erected at Mongón, approximately ten miles upstream from the town of Barbacoas.

Large-scale mining operations have had little effect on native lowland economy and culture. The companies hire only a few hundred local workers, who enjoy comparatively high wages and the privilege of purchasing various modern clothes and foods at company stores. But the fad of wearing certain American-type clothing, such as overalls, khaki trousers, and galoshes, has not spread much beyond the vicinity of the company camps. Although drift mining was introduced by a foreign mining concern, most of the techniques employed by

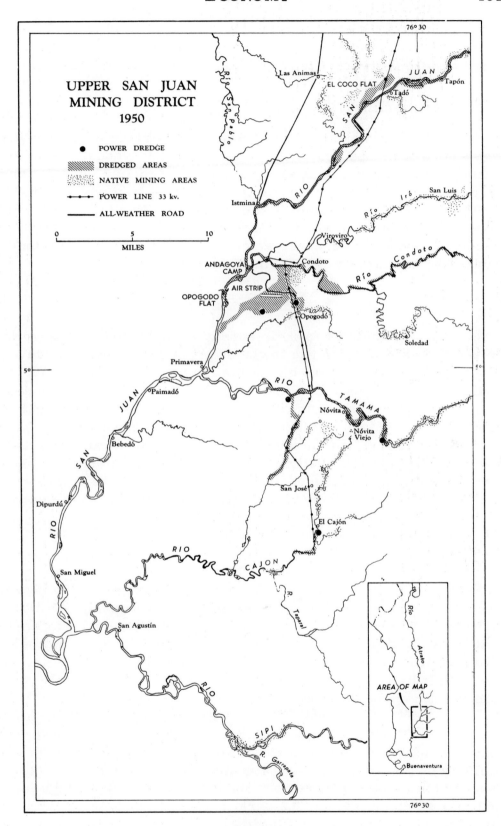

UPPER SAN JUAN
MINING DISTRICT
1950

● POWER DREDGE
DREDGED AREAS
NATIVE MINING AREAS
POWER LINE 33 kv.
ALL-WEATHER ROAD

0   5   10
MILES

MAP 23

large-scale operations cannot be applied to folk mining. Electric power generated at the Andágueda plant for the operation of dredges is supplied also to the nearby towns of Tadó, Condoto, and Istmina.

Petroleum Exploitation.

For more than fifteen years American oil companies have explored and mapped portions of the Pacific lowlands. Despite apparently favorable geological structures for petroleum deposits and surface indications of oil, in the entire lowlands only one well has been drilled -- and that resulted in a dry hole.[98] Further drilling may reveal actual deposits, which, if exploited, will probably induce no more economic and social changes among the Negro and mixed-blood inhabitants than has large-scale mining.

Household Crafts

In contrast to their aboriginal neighbors the Negroes and mixed bloods of the Pacific lowlands practice surprisingly few handicrafts, most of which are direct borrowings from the Indian. The few articles that are made are mainly for home use, rarely for sale. Moreover, the specialization in cottage industries that characterizes so many of the highland villages of Colombia and Ecuador is unknown in the Pacific lowland communities. According to local inhabitants, handicrafts were fairly significant a century ago among Negroes, but as imported household goods became available in the market centers the home manufactures have become less important; eventually they may disappear entirely.

Textiles.

Cloth and dress. The textile crafts are extremely meager. Neither Indian nor Negro have practiced cloth weaving.[99] During colonial days one of the chief imports into the lowland mining districts was cotton cloth, which the miners apportioned among their slaves. Cloth is still today among the main articles imported into the lowlands, for both Indian and Negro rely upon the general store in the market centers for cheap cottons.

For cloth the aboriginals of the lowlands used the inner bark, or bast, of the moraceous damajagua tree (Poulesenia armata). Loin cloths, skirts, and sleeping mats were made of bark cloth.[100] Today both Indians and Negroes make cloth from damagagua bast, but only for sleeping mats. The bark is soaked in water, placed over a smooth log, and pounded with either a grooved wooden mallet or the

large corrugated sea shell of the sangara attached to a short stick
(Plate XLIV). Pieces of cloth sometimes five feet wide and six feet
long are thus prepared. [101]

While Negroes may not have used bark cloth for clothing,
less than 100 years ago the ordinary dress of the rural folk was identical to that of the Chocó and Waunamá Indians. Men wore no more than
the pampanilla, or loin cloth, and the women donned only the paruma,
a piece of cloth wrapped around the waist as a skirt. [102] Under the influence of Catholic missionaries and the spread of modern styles, all
Negroes have today adopted European dress. Whereas the Indians still
cling to the old costume, Negro women wear modern cotton print dresses
and men, trousers and shirts. While at work in the mines or poling
canoes upriver, men and women often revert to the simple Indian dress.

Basketry. All of the Indians of the Pacific lowlands make
fine baskets of strips cut from various types of palm leaves, and from
the inner bark of lianas. Two general weaves are used, both of which
the Negroes and mixed bloods have copied faithfully: (1) a two-element
twill is employed to make closely woven containers, some with tightly
fitted slip-over covers and (2) for large burden baskets a peculiar
loose-lattice weave is used, giving a pleasing hexagonal design (Plate
XLIV). [103] Like the Indians, Negroes also make twilled fire-fans,
but have adopted modern techniques, such as the Singer sewing machine,
to fashion hats of strips cut from palm leaves.

Pottery.

The Indians are today the only potters in the Pacific lowlands.
In isolated sections, such as the upper Saija or the upper Raposo rivers,
old Negroes have told me that their grandmothers made clay pots in
the days of slavery. But now the negro confesses ignorance of such
crafts, and buys the little clay ware he needs -- usually tinajas, or
water jugs -- from the nearest Indian potter. The latter makes rather
crude pottery, using sand for temper and a simple hand technique to
fashion the vessel. Firing is accomplished by simply burning wood
over a batch of newly-made pots and permitting them to cool slowly in
the ashes. As good aluminum ware is now comparatively cheap and
easily available at the market centers, pottery-making is rapidly disappearing from the lowlands.

Woodwork.

Like most forest people, the lowland Negroes and Indians
rely heavily on woodcraft for the manufacture of various household

The man is holding a piece of bark cloth and the <u>sangara</u>, or cloth
beater made of a corrugated sea shell attached to a stick. Río Guapi.

Weaving burden basket, using a loose hexagonal lattice technique.   Río
Guapi.

articles as well as the main vehicle for transport -- the canoe and paddle. (Discussion of the latter items will be found under the section Transport and Trade, to follow.) Among the wooden household articles are containers of various shapes and sizes, including the many kinds of bateas, mixing paddles, stirrers, stools -- all of which appear to have an Indian origin.

In dealing with groups of Negroes who have maintained a simple subsistence economy in an isolated area for generations, one might expect to encounter among them vestiges of West African art, such as the woodcarving similar to that found among the present-day Haitians or the Bush Negroes of the Guianas. There appears to be no trace of the retention of African woodcarving art among the Negroes of the Pacific lowlands. The intricately carved veranda sidings on houses described above are probably of European rather than of African origin. Other woodwork sometimes done by Negroes, such as the low, peculiarly shaped "head-rest" stools or benches are Indian, as are the many kinds of bateas or wooden bowls.[104] Again, the carved burros, or crosspieces which straddle the roof crown of huts on the lower San Juan River appear at first glance to carry an African motif; but the designs are identical with those carved on the handles of old Waunamá pot stirrers.[105]

Musical Instruments.

Among Negroes woodwork is associated with the making of musical instruments. Many of the instruments, together with the type of music, possibly represent examples of the few Africal elements that the Negroes of the Pacific lowlands have retained. Some of the musical devices, however, are of probable Indian or European origin. As in West Africa, percussion instruments prevail. Of these the conuno, or single-head, membrane tubular drum is the most significant, particularly in the area south of Buenaventura. (Figure 7.) Made of a section of a hollowed log two to three feet long and tapered at the bottom, the drum is covered with a piece of dried tatabro skin, secured to the sides with rawhide and liana thongs; the latter are tightened by means of wooden wedges on the sides of the drum. The drummer places the instrument between the knees and beats the skin with the hands. This drum is identical to that of the Pangwe of the southern Cameroons and tribes of Togoland.[106] It has even been adopted by the Chocó and Cayapa Indians.[107] The Guinea Coast single-head drum, the membrane skin of which is fastened and tightened by means of wooden pegs, is unknown in the Pacific lowlands of Colombia, although it is common among the Haitian and Guiana Negroes. Drum types might be taken as one of the clues employed to derive the

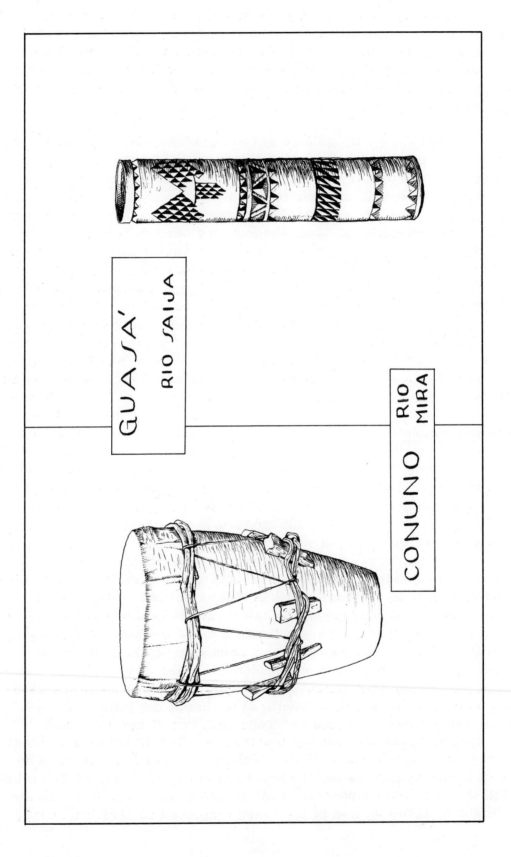

GUASA'
RIO SAIJA

CONUNO
RIO MIRA

FIGURE 7

provenience of African slaves into South America. Another drum which the lowland Negro uses today is the bombo, a large double-head membrane type which is beaten with a cloth-covered stick. Quite distinct from the smaller Indian double-head drum, the bombo is of probably European origin. In the Chocó the requita, or European snare drum is often employed instead of the African conuno.

Other percussion instruments of the lowlands include the marimba, or African xylophone. Like the conuno drum it is used mainly by the Negroes living along the isolated rivers south of Buenaventura. The tubular rattle, or guasá, made of a piece of carved bamboo stem with seeds or pebbles within, may be African in origin. [108] The gourd rattle (calabozo, guacharaco), made from the fruit of the Crescentia, is an instrument which the Negroes have borrowed from their Indian neighbors. The Chocó Negroes have adopted an additional percussion instrument of probable European origin -- the platillos, or iron cymbals. This instrument distinguishes the sound (but not the rhythm) of their music from that of the blacks living south of Buenaventura.

The single non-percussion instrument that prevails throughout the lowlands is the Indian transverse wooden flute (flauta, carrizo). These are manufactured by the Negroes for their own use. String instruments, such as the West African lyre, are not known, although some Negroes who have worked in or visited the adjacent highlands have returned with Spanish guitars. These, however, are never played with the classical lowland ensemble of dance instruments -- the conuno, bombo, guasá and flauta.

Transport and Trade

Except in those few areas where auto "roads," railways and air strips have been constructed, the modes of transport in the Pacific lowlands have changed little since colonial times. Most travel is still by dugout canoe along rivers and estuaries and by foot along jungle trails. Moreover, although changes have occurred in terms of volume and types of products transported, the major lines of trade have undergone few modifications since the eighteenth century. Exchange still predominates between up-river and down-river areas, between the lowlands and the adjacent highlands, and between the humid littoral and the drier coasts to the north (Panama) and the south (Ecuador).

Water Transport (Plates XLV - XLVII).

The dugout canoe is another Indian trait that the Negroes

Left: Canoes and paddles of the Chocó Indians. Río Saija. Right: Agglomeration of canoes belonging to Negro farmers, Puerto Merizalde, Río Naya, on market day.

A painted Cayapa canoe, Río Ónzole, Esmeraldas. Note upward flare of platform ends.

PLATE XLVI. CANOE TYPES 189

A heavily loaded canoe with balsa stabalizers and thatched shelter (rancho). A canoe is so rigged for long coastwise journeys through the esteros. Puerto Merizalde, Río Naya.

A canoe rigged with sprit sail, estuary of Río Tapaje, near El Charco.

Poling up rapids, upper Guelmambí River. In such situations the passenger finds it more comfortable to walk on the river bank, rather than endure the tedious and sometimes dangerous ride in the canoe.

Left: A panga dugout, Ardita, near Panama-Colombia border. Right: An old imbabura dugout, Orpúa, Chocó coast.

A schooner-rigged craft engaged in coastwise commerce, Tumaco.

and mixed bloods of the Pacific lowlands have adopted as an integral part of their material culture. During colonial days Indians were forced to manufacture canoes and serve as canoemen for the Spanish mine owners and government officials in the Chocó, Barbacoas, and other lowland areas.[109] Negro slaves were considered to be of more value as mine workers than as artisans, and the miners emphasized that the blacks had no knowledge of canoe-making and little inclination as canoemen.[110] Negro freedmen, however, through necessity learned to make and operate the canoes from his Indian neighbor. Today the Indian is still considered to be the best canoe-maker, but most Negroes and mixed bloods are as adept at handling the craft as the aboriginees. Rare is the rural Negro child of eight or ten who cannot paddle or pole a small dugout with dexterity and practically every young farmer along the rivers makes an expert boga, or canoeist for long river trips.

The Indians and Negroes of the Pacific lowlands manufacture a canoe which probably has the most pleasing lines of any native dugout craft in the Americas. Both the prow and stern are identical in form, both terminating in a concave, square-ended platform that flares slightly at the edges and overhangs considerably.[111] While gigging fish Indians stand on these platforms, and often the pilot of the canoe sits on the stern platform. The bottom of the canoe is smoothly rounded without a semblance of a keel. This style of dugout occurs from eastern Panama along the Pacific side of the Andes into the Guayas Basin of Ecuador. It is found occasionally in some parts of the upper Amazon.[112] Hewn from a single log of medium weight, cross-grained wood such as chachajo or cedro, the canoes vary in length from six to thirty feet and from eighteen inches to three feet in beam.[113] Roughly shaped with axe and adz in the forest, the half-completed canoe is pulled by a communal work group (minga) to the hut of the maker where the finishing touches are made. Along the gunwales the thickness of the boat varies from three-quarters to two inches; along the bottom, from two to three inches, depending on the length of the craft. The adz is the most useful and probably the only aboriginal tool used in fashioning the canoe. Both Indian and Negro also employ the European plane to give the craft a smooth finish. Today fire is never used to hollow out a log for a boat.[114]

The canoe is paddled downstream, in quiet water, or at sea. It is poled upstream against strong currents. The lowlanders use two types of paddles (canaletes), both with narrow, lanceolate blades and notched hand grips; the long-handled paddle is used by men, who usually stand to propel the boat; a paddle with a short handle and blade is used by women, who invariably sit while paddling.[115] A large canoe requires at least two bogas; the pilot sits or stands aft to steer; the

other boga stands forward to paddle. Both men and women stand to
pole the canoe upstream with the palanca, a long, stout pole often tipped with an iron point. Poling is always done along the side of a stream,
especially on the slip-off slopes where the current is weak and the water
is shallow. Thus there is a constant crossing and recrossing of a
meandering stream to gain the most favorable side for poling. Along
sheer banks the rock wall is pocked with palanca holes made through
years of use.

The river people often go to sea in their flat-bottomed dug-
outs in order to fish or to make coastwise voyages to market centers.
For such trips each canoe is equipped with a simple sprit sail (aboriginal?) of canvas; a perforated strut is placed well forward at the bottom
of the boat to receive the small mast. To increase stability and buoyancy in the swell off-coast, balsa logs are lashed alongside just below
the gunwales.[116] Only the foolhardy, however, would venture por
afuera into rough sea in such craft; instead, for coastwise trips the
longer adentro, or tidal-channel route is taken. The balsa stabilizers
are also employed to increase buoyancy of heavily-loaded canoes in
quiet water.

The coastal fishermen from Panama to Ecuador often make
a dugout with pointed bow and stern, without keel and with little or no
sheer except at the ends which curve slightly upward. Called pangas
or cayuneras, these canoes are highly reminiscent of the Caribbean
cayuco made by the Cuna of Panama and other groups on the north
coast of Colombia and Venezuela. Its presence on the Pacific coast
points to a possible pre-Columbian introduction. Such craft carry the
small sail and the balsa stabilizers described above. Along the rugged
coast north of Cabo Corrientes a curious dugout, called the lancha, is
used as a fishing boat. With pointed bow and square stern and well-developed keel, it carries the sprit sail, and is said to be quite seaworthy.
It has so many European characteristics that an aboriginal origin is
improbable.

Still another coastal craft is the famous imbabura (ibabura),
a large cargo dugout, twenty-five to forty-five feet long, with pointed
bow and square stern, having sides built up with planks above the gun-
wale of the original canoe. It carries one or more sails, and is sometimes sloop-rigged.[117] Although some imbaburas are equipped with
hand-carved wooden rudders, most are steered with a large oar in-
serted through a fulcrum hole in the center of the square stern. A
killick (boya) is used for an anchor. Like the lancha, such craft appear
to be a European adaptation of the native dugout. Keeless and drawing
little water, this boat can carry heavy cargo and still negotiate the

treacherous bars that lie athwart the river mouths. During the last century the imbabura was the principal carrier of cargo between the coastal rivers and the larger Pacific ports, such as Buenaventura, Panama, Tumaco, and Guayaquil. It is still used occasionally, and is frequently seen stored under thatch-covered sheds near the houses along many of the coastal rivers.

Seagoing sailboats such as sloops and schooners still ply the coastal waters off the Pacific, carrying cargo from one port to the next; but such boats have been largely replaced by the motovelero, or Diesel-powered craft of 100 to 200 tons. At high tide most of these boats can clear the bars off the river mouths to enter the estuaries; the smaller ones even go beyond tidal reach. They also ascend the larger rivers, such as the San Juan to Negría, the Atrato to Quibdó. occasionally the Patía to Barbacoas, and the Baudó to Peté. [118]

Land Transport (Plates XLVIII and XLIX).

Despite the difficulties imposed on land travel by the heavy rainfall and dense vegetation, since pre-conquest times foot trails have afforded lines of communication in most parts of the Pacific lowlands. The most important trails are (1) the portages which connect navigable headwaters of tributaries of main streams and (2) the longer roads that join the lowlands with the adjacent highland valleys west of the Cordillera Occidental.

The portages, or istmos, are extremely numerous throughout the lowlands. To travel from one stream system to another, the inhabitants of the middle and upper parts of the rivers naturally use the shorter routes by way of the tributaries and portages, rather than make the round-about trip via the tidal estuaries. Travel across an istmo, however, involves leaving one's canoe at the pie, or head of navigation, crossing the portage on foot, and securing another canoe at the opposite pie to continue the journey down a tributary of the next stream system. A strategic pie may boast of one or more huts in which travelers can obtain shelter overnight. Usually the portages are short, involving a walk of one-half to six hours over treacherous trails.

An important series of portage trails connect the mining centers in the upper stream courses south of Buenaventura. Interstream communication is favored in this instance by the north-south trending tributaries, the courses of which are controlled by the folded structures near the base of the Cordillera Occidental. By crossing ten portages one can travel by canoe more than 100 miles from Santa María on the Río Sesé, a tributary of the Timbiquí, northward to the camp of Leticia

Left: An improved jungle trail, Barbacoas area. Right: The Pie de Suruco, or head of navigation on the Río Suruco and beginning of a trail across portage from the San Juan drainage to the Pie de Pepé, Río Baudó drainage.

Use of the Indian tump line for carrying burden baskets.   Near López, Río Micay.

PLATE XLIX. LAND TRANSPORT   195

One-way all-weather "auto road" between Yuto, upper Río Atrato and Istmina, upper San Juan drainage, Chocó. The bus driver fell asleep at the wheel.

Covered bridge near Condoto, upper San Juan drainage, Chocó.

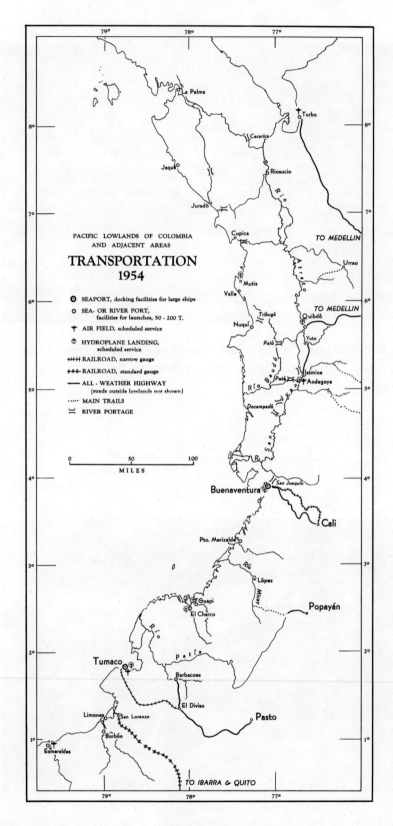

MAP 24

on the upper Raposo, without leaving the foothill section of the lowlands.

Another group of portages facilitate travel between the Pacific Coast across the Serranía de Baudó to the Atrato-San Juan depression. The main route across the southern section of the serranía utilizes the low Istmo de Docampadó to connect the coastal villages with the San Juan River. Northward, the portages of Pepé and Pató link the Baudó River people with the upper San Juan-Atrato mining district. One of the most remarkable of the portages is that of the upper Napipí, an Atrato tributary whose headwaters reach within two miles of the Pacific Ocean. A few hours' walk from the Bay of Limones near Cupica takes one to the pie of Antadó, where in normal times canoes are available for the journey downstream to the Atrato. Before the recent political disturbances in Colombia, the Napipí route was frequently traveled by coastal dwellers going to trade in Quibdó. Immediately northward the Río Truandó route, with two long portages, is another Pacific Coast-Atrato Valley connection. For more than a century both the Napipí and Truandó have been considered as potential trans-oceanic canal routes. [119]

Still another set of portages lies along routes across the mountains and hills that separate the Atrato and Juradó drainages in Colombia from those of the Tuira and Balsas in Panama. The most important of these portages is that of Cacarica, which joins the upper Río Cacarica and the Río Paya, a tributary of the Tuira. Used for centuries as a trailway, this route is now the main line for smuggling between Panama and Colombia, and is a potential site for the most difficult section of the Pan-American highway.

Perhaps the most famous portage of all is the Istmo de San Pablo, which connects the Atrato and San Juan drainage systems. So low is this divide that during periods of exceptionally high water canoemen can drag their boats from one pie to the other, forming an arrastradero. [120] Since the completion of the auto road between the upper San Juan and the Atrato, the San Pablo portage has fallen into disuse. Of almost equal importance is the Istmo de San Joaquín, in former days a significant portage along the main route of travel between Buenaventura and the lower San Juan.

The Mountain Trails. Until the completion of modern roads and railways during the last twenty-five years, the foot and mule trails leading from the head of navigable streams up the western slope of the cordillera to the interior highland valleys, formed the Pacific lowland's best means of contact with the outside. The most heavily travelled trails included (from north to south):

1.   The Urrao-Río Arquí-Bebará route from Antioquia to
     the middle Atrato.

2.   The Chamí-upper San Juan trail from the middle Cauca
     to the Chocó mining centers.

3.   The historic Tamaná route from Cartago to Nóvita.

4.   The old Cali-Buenaventura trail, now occupied by a rail-
     road and highway.

5.   The Mechengue trail from Popayán to the upper Río
     Micay.

6.   The old Barbacoas road from Pasto to the Telembí, now
     covered by a rough auto trail.

7.   The Esmeraldas route from the Ecuadorian highlands
     via the upper Río Mira to the Pacific lowland.

Usually in a state of utter disrepair, the lowland forest
trails are probably among the most treacherous in South America. On
steep slopes the leather-shod traveler slips and slides on the wet, slick
clay. In the flattish swales the trails degenerate into quagmires, into
which the unwary will sink to his knees; to avoid the mire, one must
hop from one surface root to the next, but must eschew the support of
tree trunks to prevent impaling the hand on frequent thorns or receiving
the bites of stinging ants. Portions of some trails have been improved
by laying corduroy, but under the constant dampness and heat the logs
rot quickly, and if not constantly repaired, the improvement rapidly
disintegrates. Near the larger settlements gullies are sometimes span-
ned by narrow plank-floored bridges covered with a thatched or galvanized tin roof. [121] Usually, however, bridges are nothing more than single
logs, notched on the top side to improve footing on the wet, slippery
surface. A slip or misstep will send one plunging into the deep ravine
below.

On the trails in the Pacific lowlands man is the beast of
burden; European pack-animals (horses, mules, oxen) are employed
only in the upper portions of the mountain trails that lead into the interior highlands. The Negroes and mixed bloods have adopted the Indian
method of carrying, which involves the large burden baskets of loose-
lattice weave strapped on the back and supported with the tump line, a
strap around the forehead. During most of the colonial period the
Spaniards used Indian carriers to transport goods along the trails between

the highlands and the Pacific lowlands. The Cali-Buenaventura and
Pasto-Barbacoas trails, for example, were considered too difficult
even for pack mules. [122] Until the close of the last century white travelers were often carried along the lowlands trails in chairs strapped to
the backs of Negro silleros, or chair carriers. [123]

Most of the rail and auto roads have been constructed to
connect the lowlands with the adjacent highlands. Started in 1878, the
narrow-gauge Cali-Buenaventura railway was not completed until 1915. [124]
The gravelled auto road connecting the two cities was not opened until
1938. [125] A one-way all-weather car track, completed in 1944, joins
the Antioqueño towns of Bolívar and El Carmen with Quibdó. Northward,
the lowland section of the Medellín-Turbo highway, long under construction, was finally completed in 1954. In the mid-1930's the port of
Tumaco was joined with Pasto by the completion of a poorly-gravelled
auto road to El Diviso and the construction of a narrow-gauge railway
from that point to the coast. A branch road to Barbacoas was completed
in 1936. At the present time a standard gauge railroad is being constructed between the port village of San Lorenzo (northern Esmeraldas)
and Ibarra (Ecuadorian highlands), with connections to Quito. [126] Steep
slopes and heavy rainfall present extraordinary engineering problems
in the construction of these mountain roads, and today traffic over them
is continually plagued by floods and frequent slides of the saturated,
deeply weathered rock. Service on the strategic Cali-Buenaventura
railway, for example, is often suspended for weeks by enormous landslides that wipe out large sections of track. The Colombian government
goes to great expense to keep the Buenaventura highway open by maintaining road crews with bulldozers at various points along the road.

In the Chocó a few narrow auto paths have been cut through
the forest within the mining areas. For instance, a one-way gravelled
road, ten feet wide, leads from Yuto on the upper Atrato to Istmina on
the San Juan, and the mining company at Andagoya maintains several
all-weather truck roads on its properties for private use (Plate XLIX).

Air Transport

The past fifteen years have seen the construction of several
small landing strips and the use of quiet bays and long reaches of rivers
for land-plane and hydroplane service in various parts of the Pacific
lowlands. Air strips now used by DC-3 planes on scheduled flights are
located at Esmeraldas, Tumaco, Andagoya, and Turbo. Another strip
is under construction at Buenaventura. Small hydroplanes can land on
almost any straight river reach, but in 1954 scheduled hydroplane service was available at Buenaventura, Quibdó, Istmina, Andagoya, and

Ciudad Mutis on the Bay of Solano.

Ports.

        Since the beginning of European exploitation of the Pacific lowlands the development of sea and river ports has been an essential phase of the area's economy. Port towns also have been the centers of white settlement in the lowlands, where merchants, civil and military officials, and clergy still congregate.

        Seaports. During the colonial period a series of small seaports was founded along the Pacific Coast to serve the mines and the interior. Each of these ports was located on or near the mouth of a river that served as an important route of transport. The earliest was Buenaventura, established in the 1540's on the small island of Cascajal at the head of a long bay and near the mouth of the Río Dagua. The latter river formed the lowland section of the old strategic Indian route to the Cauca Valley. A short distance to the north on one of the distributaries in the San Juan Delta the tiny illegal port of Chirambirá was active during the eighteenth century; through it passed cargo for the Chocó gold mines upstream. [127] To serve the Barbacoas mining district in the south, the rocky Isla del Gallo near the mouth of the Patía River was established as the port of Santa Bárbara early in the seventeenth century. [128] During the latter part of the next century Isla del Gallo was eclipsed by the port of Tumaco, established across the bay on a small firme, or sandy island in the midst of mud flats and mangrove swamps, but partially protected by El Morro, a low hill of Tertiary material. [129] Near the mouth of the Iscuande another seaport called Santa Bárbara de Iscuandé was founded in the latter part of the seventeenth century to serve the mines on the upper courses of the surrounding rivers. Later, pirate raids forced its relocation inland on the site of the present town of the same name. [130]

        Today only two of the colonial ports -- Tumaco and Buenaventura -- have survived. Throughout its history Buenaventura has served more as an outlet for the upper Cauca Valley (called El Valle today, La Sabana in colonial times) than as a supply port for the lowland mining districts. By the mid-sixteenth century the Spanish settlements around Cali and Popayán were supplied through the Pacific port, and from it were exported sugar products from the haciendas of La Sabana. [131] In the late 1540's Buenaventura was a hamlet of a few Indians and one or two Spaniards. [132] In 1823 (about 275 years later) it was not much larger, [133] but by 1852 Trautwine describes it as a "mean hole" of a hundred rickety huts. [134] The modern period of the port begins in 1921 with the completion of the first docks sufficiently large to handle ocean freighters on the lee side of Cascajal Island and the dredging of a channel through the shoals in the bay. [135] Subsequent construction has greatly enlarged the dockage space, and today Buenaventura vies with Barranquilla as Colombia's first port (Map 25) (Plate L).

Although its primary function has been to serve the Barbacoas mining district, since the nineteenth century Tumaco has also been an outlet for the adjacent highlands of Pasto and northern Ecuador. With the completion of the railway-highway connection to Pasto in 1934 and the construction of a new dock for ocean freighters on the lee side of nearby El Morro Island in 1953, Tumaco is becoming another significant port on the Pacific coast of Colombia (Map 26). Obviously, the development of modern ports along this coast requires a much larger hinterland than the immediate lowland.

In northwestern Ecuador the small port of Esmeraldas, although important for banana exports, still has no deep-water dock area, and all loading is done by lighter. Farther up the coast the port of Limones can handle only small launches. The completion of the railroad from the highland may transform the sleepy fishing hamlet of San Lorenzo on the Bolívar Estuary into a bustling port. The old port of La Palma at the head of the Gulf of San Miguel in Darién (Panama) is insignificant, and without a productive hinterland will probably remain so. Isolation and lack of large rivers leading into the interior have discouraged the development of significant seaports along the rocky coast north of Cabo Corrientes.

Today there are few river ports of consequence in the Pacific lowlands. Most of those of colonial days on the lower river courses south of Buenaventura have decayed. Formerly the largest river port in the south was Barbacoas, but since the completion of the all-weather road-rail connection with Tumaco and Pasto (1936) river traffic on the Patía and Telembí has practically ceased. The newer towns of Guapi (on the river of the same name), El Charco (on the lower Tapaje), Borbón (on the lower Santiago, Esmeraldas), and Puerto Merizalde (on the lower Naya) are the only southern river ports of any significance.

River navigation and ports have had a checkered history in the Chocó. For eighty-five years (1698-1783) the Atrato River was closed to commerce, due to attacks of the Cuna Indians and to the official attempts to stem smuggling of gold out of the colony. [136] Since that time, the only town along the Atrato that has become a port of any consequence is Quibdó. Beginning around 1850 weekly and bi-weekly

PLATE L
BUENAVENTURA, TOWN AND HARBOR

Left: Main business section of Buenaventura, looking eastward across the coastal plain to the Cordillera Occidental. The gap in the mountains, center, is the route of the Cali-Buenaventura road. Right: The municipal wharf, Buenaventura, used for local trading.

The docks at Buenaventura. A Grace Line vessel appears in foreground.

launch service connected Quibdó with Cartagena; the wood-burning
steamers of those days have not been replaced by motor launches.
Today five 100- to 200-ton vessels make the Quibdó-Caragena run,
each stopping at various river towns and hamlets to take on freight
(mainly lumber and bananas) and passengers.

Local Trade.

Various aspects of trading among the lowlanders have been
mentioned many times in the foregoing pages. Trade ranging from
simple barter to store-credit transactions probably has not changed
appreciably since the abolition of slavery more than a century ago.

On most of the rivers there is active trade between the
upstream and downstream inhabitants. The former bring canoe loads
of maize and plantains to trade for the sugar products, coconuts, and
fish of the down-river folk. At the villages of Cabo Manglares and
Terán at the mouth of the Río Mira primitive barter of such products
still prevails. For example, two to four pounds of dried fish are equivalent to one stem of plantains, depending upon the size of the fruit.

Formal markets are held usually in the river and seaports
on Saturdays and Sundays. On a Sunday, for instance, hundreds of
canoes are seen congregated around the wharf area at Puerto Merizalde,
where people from the Río Naya and the surrounding estero settlements
come to trade and to attend mass at the local church. At such markets
centers trading is done at the general stores and along the wharf which
is lined with canoes loaded with maize, plantains, coconuts, fruit, and
other products of the country.

Along some rivers a series of fairs (ferias) accompany
religious holidays, particularly the fiestas held in honor of the patron
saint of a given village. The association of commercial fairs with important religious festivals closely follows the familiar European pattern introduced by the Spaniards. Such fairs often last for two weeks
in one village. In the Río Saija drainage there is a series of ferias,
one given in each village. That of San Bernardo lasts from August 15
to August 27; this is followed by that at Santa Rosa from August 31 to
September 18; and the series is completed with the fair at Camarones
from September 19 to the 24th. Itinerant priests visit each village to
administer marriage and baptismal rites. Hundreds of Negroes from
the river settlements and traders from the outside jam the streets and
houses, buying and selling and making merry in general.

In general pattern, present trade with the outside differs

little from that of colonial days. The colonial imports of salt from the pans of Santa Elena in southwestern Ecuador and wine from Peru no longer prevail. But the importation of cheese, dried meat, wheat flour, tobacco, cloth of all sorts, and metalware from the adjacent highlands is the same today as in the eighteenth century. The Chocó now receives much of its imports from Cartagena, whence come the launches loaded with beer, vegetable shortening, and other canned products. As in colonial days, smuggling still goes on between Colombia and Panama. Cheap American canned articles and cloth obtained in Panama for gold are encountered in general stores of every coastal village north of Cabo Corrientes.

ABBREVIATIONS

AHNC   Archivo Histórico Nacional de Colombia, Bogotá, Colombia.

ACC   Archivo Central del Cauca, Popayán, Colombia.

AHN   Archivo Histórico Nacional, Quito, Ecuador.

AGI   Archivo General de Indias, Sevilla, Spain.

NAUS   National Archives of the United States, Washington, D. C.

NOTES

CHAPTER I

1
Viaje a las Regiones Equinocciales del Nuevo Continente, hecho
en 1799, 1800, 1801, 1802, 1803 y 1804 por A. de Humboldt y
A. Bonpland. (Edition of Biblioteca Venezolana de Cultura,
Caracas, 1941-42), V, 200.

2
Robert Cushman Murphy, "The Littoral of Pacific Colombia and
Ecuador," Geographical Review, XXIX (1939), 1-33.

3
For example, U. S. Hydrographic Office chart no. 0814, last
published in 1949, shows various key areas along the coast, the
basic data for which are based on British surveys of 1847.

4
The earliest of the 19th century inter-oceanic canal exploratory
reports was made in 1854 by John C. Trautwine, "Rough Notes
of an Exploration for an Inter-oceanic Canal Route by way of the
Rivers Atrato and San Juan, in New Granada, South America,"
Journal of the Franklin Institute, LVII (1854), 145-54; 217-31;
289-99; 361-73; LVIII (1854), 1-11; 73-84; 134-55; 217-26; 289-99.
A few years later Lt. N. Michler, U.S.A., submitted a report
of his surveys on the Atrato and Truandó, northern Chocó.
"[Report of] Lt. N. Michler, corps of topographical engineers,
of his survey for an interoceanic ship canal near the Isthmus of
Darién, via the Atrato and the Truandó rivers, called for by a
resolution of the Senate of June 5, 1860," Senate Executive
Document No. 9, vol. 7, 2nd Session, 36th Congress, 1860-61,
(Washington, 1861). In 1875 another important expedition to the
Chocó was commanded by Lt. Frederick Collins, U.S.N. "Report
of a Survey of the Proposed Route for an Inter-oceanic Ship-Canal
by way of the Atrato, Napipí, and Doguadó Rivers, in the Canton
of Chocó, State of Cauca, United States of Colombia, by the U.S.
Expedition of 1875. Lt. Frederick Collins, U.S.N., Command-
ing," Senate Executive Document No. 75, 45th Congress, 3rd
Session, June, 1875 (Washington, 1879).

CHAPTER II

1 Reliable geological knowledge of the Colombian Pacific versant dates from the early 1930's with the granting of concessions in the area to North American petroleum companies. Unfortunately, these companies have withheld from publication most of the data obtained by their exploration parties; however, some general statements on the surface and structural geology of the area have appeared in various scientific journals. The more important articles include:

1) J. L. Anderson, "Petroleum Geology of Colombia," Bull. American Association of Petroleum Geologists, XXIX (1945), 1065-1142.

2) A. Gansser, "Geological and Petrographical Notes on Gorgona Island in relation to North-western South America," Schweizerische Mineralogische und Petrographische Mitteilungen, XXX (1950), 219-37.

3) Enrique Hubach, "Informe geológico de Urabá," Boletín de Minas y Petroleo, IV (1930), 26-136.

4) W. E. Nygren, "The Bolivar Geosyncline of North Western South America," Bull. American Association of Petroleum Geologists, XXXIV (1950), 1998-2006.

5) Victor Oppenheim, "Geología de la Costa Sur del Pacífico de Colombia," Boletín del Instituto Geofísico de los Andes, I (1949), 1-23.

6) _____, "The Structure of Colombia," Trans. of the American Geophysical Union, XXX (1952), 739-48.

7) A. A. Olssen, "Some Tectonic Interpretations of the Geology of North Western South America," Proc. of the 8th American Scientific Congress, IV (1942), 401-416.

For a general survey of the geology of northern South America Charles Schuchert, Historical Geology of the Antillean-Caribbean Region (New York, 1935) is still the best reference.

2   Nygren, "The Bolivar Geosyncline," loc. cit., 2000. This
     branch has been suggested as a continuation of the present main
     axis of the geosyncline by Carl Troll, "Die geologische Verkettung
     Süd und Mittelamerikas," Mitteilungen der Geographische Gesell-
     schaft in München, XXIII (1930), 53-76; ref., 66-67. The valley
     occupied by the Tuira River and possibly that of the Chucunaque
     in Darién appears to be a topographic expression of the north-
     western branch of the geosyncline. The upper Tuira drainage
     is separated from that of the Atrato by a low divide, 500 feet
     above sea level, which has served as an important route of travel
     between Colombia and Panama. The proposed Pan-American
     highway may pass through this divide.

3   In the vicinity of Sautatá, twenty-five miles upstream from the
     river mouths, the Atrato Valley is crossed by an anticlinal struc-
     ture, which is thought to be a continuation of a western branch
     of the Andean range into Panama, to form the Serranía de Darién
     along the Caribbean Sea. Several hills of Tertiary volcanics and
     clastics extend above the valley alluvium and give topographic
     expression to the cross-basin high. Nygren, "The Bolivar geosyn-
     cline," loc. cit., 2002.

4   Nygren, "The Bolivar geosyncline," loc. cit. 2003. Oppenheim,
     "Geologia de la Costa" loc. cit., 12-13, gives a maximum
     Tertiary thickness of 4,000 to 5,000 meters (13,000 to 16,500
     feet) for the San Juan Basin and for the valleys of the rivers
     Micay and Guapi in the coastal lowlands south of Buenaventura.
     The estimates given by Nygren probably represent thicknesses
     in the Atrato Basin.

5   The seismic disturbances and their effect on the shoreline are
     discussed on page 57.

6   In its upper course at Quibdó, the Atrato River is nearly 250
     yards wide and has a mean depth of ten feet (fifteen to twenty-
     five feet at flood stage). In its lower course at Ríosucio, the
     river is approximately 400 yards wide and the mean depth is 75
     feet. Accurate discharge data for the Atrato do not exist, al-
     though various guesses based on channel profile and current
     velocity have been made. In 1856 Kelley estimated the discharge
     at the Truandó confluence to be about 667,000,000 cubic feet per
     hour (185,260 cu. ft. per sec.). Frederick M. Kelley, "On the
     Junction of the Atlantic and Pacific Oceans, and the Practicability
     of a Ship Canal, without locks, by the Atrato Valley," Institute
     of Civil Engineers, Minutes of Proceedings, XV (1856), 376-417;

ref. 391.

7   At the village of Mercedes, ten miles below Quibdó in the upper Atrato, the width of the levee from the river bank to the beginning of the backswamp measured fifty feet. At Ríosucio, in the lower portion of the river, the levee varies in width from 100 to 300 feet.

8   In colonial times, for example, the plantains and maize consumed in the mines around Quibdó were grown on the levees of the tributaries of the Atrato, as the banks of the main river were considered to be useless for agriculture due to frequent floods. See "Descripción de la Provincia de Zitará y curso de Atrato [1777], " in Antionio B. Cuervo (ed.), Colección de Documentos Inéditos sobre la Geografía e Historia de Colombia (Bogotá, 1891-94), II, 306-344.

9   As seen from the air the land and water features of the Atrato Plain appear to be the products of the gradual filling of a large estuary once occupied by the sea. The narrow levees, the extensive backswamp lakes, and the lack of well-defined meanders within the main river channel indicate a stage of basin filling similar to that of the lower Magdalena River Valley. In contrast, the alluvial morphology of the lower Amazon Basin, with its wide, anastomosing channels, may possibly represent an earlier stage of estuarine alluviation. The features of the lower Mississippi, on the other hand, characterized by well-developed meanders within the main channel, wide levees, and few backswamp lakes, may indicate a much more advanced stage of alluviation.

10   This terrace is particularly conspicuous immediately back of Quibdó, where the Quebrada de Yesca has created a steep escarpment along the terrace face.

11   Oppenheim, "Geología de la Costa, " loc. cit., 9.

12   In the hills between the Baudó River and the upper Atrato, depth of the recent alluvial fills in the narrow interhill valleys measures eighteen or more feet. MS. geological report dated 1946 on file at Richmond Petroleum Co., Bogotá.

13   Oppenheim, "The Structure of Colombia, " loc. cit., 742.

CHAPTER III

1   Most of the weather data recorded by both official and private
stations are published by the Colombian government in its
Anuario Meteorológico, 1934-1947, Departamento de Irrigación,
Ministerio de Economía Nacional, Bogotá. Earlier records
(1930-1933) are found published in the Boletín de Agricultura.
Obvious typographical errors in the published material cited
above decreases the reliability of the data. Other published
data occur in Luis H. Osoria, Estudios Meteorológicos de
Colombia, 1931 a 1935 (Bogotá, n.d.); A. J. Henry, "Rainfall
of Colombia, Monthly Weather Review, L (1922), 189-90; P. C.
Day, "Climatalogical Data for Andagoya, Republic of Colombia,
South America," Monthly Weather Review, LIV (1926), 376-78;
Bruno Franze, "Die Niederschlagsverhältnisse in Südamerika,"
Petermanns Mitteilungen, Ergänzungsheft 193 (1927), 16-17. I
obtained some meteorological data directly from mining companies (e.g., data for Mongón from the Cía. Minera de Nariño
at Mongón Camp; for Neguá from the Neguá Mining Co. records
contained in the files of the Richmond Petroleum Co., Bogotá).
The weather records of Andagoya were consulted in the administration office of the Cía. Minera Chocó-Pacífico, Andagoya
Camp. At Quibdó, where the Colombian government has recently installed new meteorological equipment, reliable data for the
years 1949 through 1952 were obtained from the local agricultural office. The latter data, as well as those for 1953 and 1954
(for Andagoya and Quibdó), are included in recent issues of the
Anuario Meteorológico. (Anuario Meteorológico, 1949; 1950-1951;
1952-1953-1954, Ministerio de Agricultura, Bogotá, 1955.) The
data for 1953 and 1954 were received too late to be used in the
construction of the accompanying climatic graphs and maps.

2   These data were obtained from the daily weather records on file
at the office of the Cía. Minera Chocó-Pacífico, Andagoya.

3   The daily relative humidity averages given in Table 2 for
Andagoya might be compared with similar figures for New
Orleans, noted for its hot, muggy summers. Data for two
Augusts are given below for New Orleans.

	6:30 AM	12M	6:30 PM
Aug. 1938	86%	58%	65%
Aug. 1953	93%	69%	75%

The relative humidity for the morning hours is not far different for Andagoya and New Orleans; Andagoya, however, has a greater relative humidity during the hot midday and early evening periods than does New Orleans.

4   Cherrapungi, on the windward slopes of the Khasi Hills, Assam (Lat. 25° N.), and a station on the windward side of Kauai Island, Hawaiian Group (Lat. 22° N.) still hold the world's records for average annual rainfall, with 424 and 456 inches, respectively. These two stations, however, are outside the equatorial areas. Within the equatorial zone of West Africa the station of Debundscha (4° N.), on the windward side of Mt. Cameroon, records an annual rainfall average of 394 inches for a period of 25 years. See climatic data in K. M. Buchanan and J. C. Pugh, Land and People in Nigeria (London, 1955), 243. This station may thus be the fourth rainiest spot on earth and, in view of its longer and more reliable record, may displace Quibdó as the wettest place in the equatorial areas. In general, however, equatorial stations in Africa, southeast Asia, and Oceania rarely have average annual totals that exceed 200 inches.

5   When the rainfall figures of Quibdó for 1953 and 1954 are considered, the yearly average for that station is reduced to 10,121 mm., or 398.5 inches. Moreover, recent issues of the Anuario Meteorológico, cited in footnote 1, present rainfall data for a new station, Lloró, on the upper Atrato, fifteen miles southeast of Quibdó. A three-year record gives this station an annual average of 13,108 mm., or 516 inches of rain.

6   An even drier spot along the same route is shown at Espinal [?] (772 mm., or 30 inches) by Herbert Wilhelmy, "Die Pazifische Küstenebene Kolombiens," Abhandlungen des Deutschen Geographentages (Essen, 1953), 96-100. Other "dry islands" on the western slope of the cordillera are indicated by R. D. Schmidt, "Die Niederschlagsverteilung im andinen Kolombien," Bonner Geographische Abhandlungen, H. 9 (1952), 99-119.

7   Unfortunately, weather data are not available to substantiate the observations of the local inhabitants. It appears, however, that air over the Pacific lowland coast is more stable than that over the interior; thus it would be reasonable to expect a decrease in precipitation from the interior seaward.

8   H. Riehl, Tropical Meteorology (New York, 1954), 75.

9   M. A. Garbell, Tropical and Equatorial Meteorology (New York,

1947), 125.

10   Reihl, Tropical Meteorology, pp. 236-38.

11   The double minima and maxima distribution of rainfall is especially characteristic of the Andean highlands of Colombia.

12   The Andagoya data come from the period 1930-1951; the Quibdó
data, from 1949-1952. The longer rainless periods for Andagoya
occurred mainly during the month of March; those for Quibdó,
during January, March and July.

13   Such stories were repeated at many places along the coast south
of Buenaventura (e.g., on the lower courses of the Micay,
Cajambre and Naya rivers). At San Juan de la Costa, north of
Tumaco, old inhabitants claimed that in 1908, six months were
completely without rain -- probably a gross exaggeration.

14   From figures given by Schmidt, "Die Niederschlagsverteilung"
loc. cit., 112.

15   Etienne Bernard, Le climat écologique de la cuvette centrale
congolaise (Brussels, 1945), 158.

16   For example, one-hour absolute maxima in the Gulf Coast area
of the United States range between 3.66 inches at New Orleans
to 4.25 inches at Taylor, Texas. Twenty-four-hour maxima,
Gulf Coast area: Taylor, Texas and New Smyrna, Florida, 23
inches each; Alexandria, La., 21 inches. 24-hour maxima,
southeast Asia: Bagui, Philippines, 46 inches; Cherrapunji,
Assam, 41 inches; Funkiko, Formosa, 40.7 inches. Data from
A.H. Jennings, "World's Greatest Observed Point Rainfalls,"
Monthly Weather Review, LXVIII (1950), 4-5; "Maximum Re-
corded United States Point Rainfall," Technical Paper, No. 2
(U.S. Weather Bureau, Washington, 1947); "Maximum 24-hour
Precipitation in the United States," Technical Paper, No. 16
(U.S. Weather Bureau, Washington, 1952).

17   The only published account of the chocosana occurs in the "Sailing Directions for the East Coasts of Central America and Mexico,"
Publication, No. 130 (U.S. Hydrographic Office, Washington,
5th ed., 1952), 81-82. The storm is so remarkable for the
tropics that it deserves detailed study.

18   A newspaper account of the storm appears in El Tiempo (Bogotá),

August 10, 1954.

CHAPTER IV

1   José Cuatrecasas, "Vistazo a la vegetación natural del Bajo
Calima, "Revista de la Academia Colombiana de Ciéncias Exactas,
Físico-Químicas y Naturales, VII (1947), 306-312, suggests a
two-fold division of the tropical rain forest of western Colombia,
based on drainage and salinity: (1) the "Hygrodrymium", or true
tropical rain forest and (2) the "Halodrymium", or tidal and
brackish-water swamp forest along the Pacific littoral. He does
not distinguish between the rain forest and the fresh-water swamp
in the back-water areas along streams.

2   Although numerous scientists have studied the flora of the Pacific
lowlands at various points, the forest is still only partially
known botanically. Among the botanists who have collected
and published on the flora of the Pacific area are José Cuatrecasas,
now of the Chicago Natural History Museum; Richard E. Schultes,
of the U. S. Department of Agriculture; and Dr. Alvaro Fernández
of the Instituto de Ciéncias Naturales, Bogotá. Recently, Dr.
Rafael Romero Casteñeda of the Ministry of Agriculture, Bogotá,
has been doing important taxonomic botony in many parts of the
coastal lowlands of Colombia. Unfortunately, little geobotany or
plant ecology has been accomplished for this area.

3   L. R. Holdrige et al. The Forests of Western and Central
Ecuador (Forest Service, USDA Washington, 1947), 17, use the
terms "wet tropical forest" and "dry tropical forest" as subdivi-
sions of the "semi-deciduous forest" as used in present paper.
The true rain forest they call "evergreen tropical rain forest".
Most of the semi-deciduous forest in the Pacific lowlands can be
equated with the wet tropical forest of Holdridge.

4   Probably the best treatise on tropical rain forest vegetation has
been written by P. W. Richards, The Tropical Rain Forest, an
Ecological Study (Cambridge, 1952). In this book Richards describes the structure and composition of various rain forests in
the tropics, mainly those of Africa, southeast Asia, and British
Guiana.

5   Buttresses and epigeous roots are common for trees of many unrelated species in the rain forest. Various theories that have
been advanced to explain the occurrence of buttressing are discussed by Richards, ibid., 69-74.

6   *Ibid.*, 22 ff.

7   Hans Jenny, Factors of Soil Formation (New York, 1941), 207.

8   For example, the writer and his two guides spent more than one
    hour hacking their way for a distance of about 100 yards through
    an abandoned levee clearing to reach the river's edge from the
    interior.

9   Elbert L. Little, "A Collection of Tree Specimens from Western
    Ecuador," Caribbean Forester, IX (1944), 215-98; ref., 257.

10 The chigua seeds contain an acrid substance which is extracted
    by soaking in water for several days. The seeds are then boiled
    and wet-ground to make a dough, from which a type of tamale,
    wrapped in banana leaves, is made. During inter-crop periods,
    when other foods are scarce, the chigua affords a valuable source
    of nutrition. Thickets of the cycad, like those of the tagua palm,
    may well be the result of protection by man.

11 The association of "blackwater" with peat swamps in the humid
    tropics is discussed by Richards, The Tropical Rain Forest,
    213-215. "Blackwater", however, as Richards points out, oc-
    curs in other ecological situations, such as in highly leached,
    sandy soils in the tropical rain forest. The common statement
    heard in the lower San Juan River that the water of the back-
    swamps is "completamente negra" is probably an exaggeration
    and undoubtedly refers to the special situation described above.
    When the blackwater from such areas is led through drainage
    ditches to the river bank, a brown to orange gelatinous preciptate
    occurs on contact with fresh river water.

CHAPTER V

1   Sailing Directions for South America, III (U.S. Hydrographic
    Office Publ. 174, change No. 1, Washington, 1954), 304-312.
    The following table summarizes tidal range data obtained from
    the publication cited above.

	Mean Range	Spring Range
Tumaco	8.7 feet	10.9 feet
Buenaventura	10.4 feet	12.9 feet
Cuevitas Bay	10.00 feet	12.8 feet
Piñas, Panama	12.0 feet	14.0 feet

Tidal ranges tend to increase northward along the coast from Peru (Chicama: spring range, 2.1 feet), reaching a maximum in the Gulf of Panama (Balboa: spring range, 16.4 feet).

2   For example, along the lower Baudó River tidal effects reach the confluence of the Dubasa River, fifty miles upstream from the Baudó mouth. Again, the tidal reach along the lower San Juan River is at Primavera, 35 miles upstream from the mouth.

3   J. D. Watson, "Mangorve Forests of the Malay Peninsula," Malayan Forest Records, No. 6 (1928), 1-275. E. H. G. Dobby, Southeast Asia (London, 1950), 67.

4   Ferdinand Grewe, "Africanische Mangrovelandschaften. Verbreitung and wirtschaftsgeographische Bedeutung," Wissenschaftliche Veröffentlichungen des Deutschen Museums für Länderkunde zu Leipzig, N.F. 9 (1941), 103-177; L. Pynaert, "La mangrove congolaise," Bull. Agricole de Congo Belge, XXIII (1933), 184-207.

5   E. B. Martyn, "A Note on the Foreshore Vegetation in the Neighborhood of Georgetown, British Guiana," Journal of Ecology, XXII (1934), 292-98.

6   Although the bajos are hazards to navigation, they are excellent feeding grounds for fish; consequently the coastal fishermen know the position of every shoal and bank in the vicinity of their villages.

7   When natives must go to sea in canoes, they invariably wait until the last part of the low tide period, when the water begins rise; for at that time the shoal area between the outer breakers and the shore is least subject to swells and waves.

8   Padre Bernardo Merizalde del Carmen, Estudios de la Costa Colombiana del Pacífico (Bogotá, 1921), 96.

9   August Flemming, "Das Delta des Rio Mira In Colombia," Das Ausland, XLIII (1870), 64.

10   E. Rudolph and S. Szirtes, "Das kolumbianische Erdbeben am 31 Januar 1906," Beiträge zur Geophysik, Zeitschrift für physikalische Erdkunde, XI (1912), 132-99; 207-275.

11   B. Gutenburg and C. F. Richter, Seismicity of the Earth and

Associated Phenomena (Princeton, 1949), 103. The tsunami was registered as far away as the Hawaiian Islands. It is estimated that between 1000 and 1500 persons were drowned in the disaster. The area most badly affected lay between Tumaco and Guapi.

12 Herzberg's theory of the equilibrium between salt and fresh ground water can well be applied to the beaches and beach remnants along the Pacific lowland coast. Even when completely surrounded by salt water, small bodies of pervious material, such as sand, usually contain a layer of fresh ground water overlying the denser salt water. For explanation and illustration of the Herzberg theory see J. S. Brown, "A Study of Coastal Ground Water," Water Supply Paper No. 534 (U. S. Geological Survey, Washington, 1925).

13 Richards, The Tropical Rain Forest, 296-98.

14 Frank E. Egler, "The Dispersal and Establishment of Red Mangrove, Rhizophora, in Florida," The Caribbean Forester, IX (1948), 308.

15 F. W. Foxworthy, "Distribution and Utilization of the Mangrove-swamp of Malaya," Annales du Jardin Botanique de Buitenzorg, suppl. 3, pt. 1 (1910), 319-44.

16 Baron H. von Eggers, "Die Manglares in Ecuador," Botanisches Centralblatt, LII (1892), 49-52.

17 J. H. Davis, "The Ecology and Geologic Role of Mangroves in Florida," Papers from the Tortugas Laboratory of the Carnegie Inst. of Washington, XXXII (1940), 303-412.

18 D. R. Rosevear, "Mangrove Swamps," Farm and Forest, VIII (1947), 23-30, reports red mangrove in Nigeria as high as 151 feet with girth of nearly eight feet.

19 D. K. J. Grant, "Mangrove Woods of Tanganyika Territory, their silviculture and dependent industries, "Tanganyika Notes and Records, No. 5 (1936), 5-16.

20 F. W. Foxworthy and D. M. Matthews, "Mangrove and Nipah Swamps of North Borneo," Department of Forestry, B. N. B., Bull. No. 3 (1917); Foxworthy, "Mangrove-swamp of Malaya," loc. cit. 319-44.

21 In contrast, the Oriental District, which includes the tropical coasts bordering the Indian Ocean (East Africa, Madagascar, India, Malaya and northwestern Australia) and the western Pacific basin (southeast Asia, northern Australia, and the western Pacific Islands) contains fifteen genera and more than twenty species. Rhizophora, Ceriops, Sonneratia, Bruguiera, Acanthus and Avicennia are among the more important genera represented. For a tabulation of species in the Oriental District see Grewe, "Africanische Mangrovelandschaften," loc. cit., 107.

22 José Cuatrecasas, "Mangroves of the Pacific Coast of South America," [Abstract], A Series of Lectures presented before the Department of Botany Seminar, Northwestern University, by the Botanical Staff of the Chicago Natural History Museum, [1952], 8-10.

23 Watson, "Mangrove Forests," loc. cit., 2.

24 B. M. Graham, "Notes on the Mangrove Swamp of Kenya," Journal of East Africa and Uganda Natural History Society, No. 29 (1929), 157-64.

25 Frank E. Egler, "Southeast Saline Everglades Vegetation, Florida, and its management," Vegetatio, III (1950), 213-65.

26 V. J. Chapman, "The Botany of the Jamaica Shoreline," Geographical Journal, XCVI (1940), 312-23; R. A. Howard, "Vegetation of the Bimini Island Group, Bahamas," Ecological Monographs, XX (1950), 317-49.

27 Lyman B. Smith, "Bromeliad Malaria," Annual Report of the Smithsonian Institution, 1952 (Washington, D.C., 1953), 385-98.

28 L. D. Stamp, "The Aerial Survey of the Irrawaddy Delta Forests, Journal of Ecology, XIII (1925), 262-76. Similar features are noted for the mangroves of West Africa by Pynaert, "La Mangrove Congolaise," loc. cit., 189, and be Rosevear "Mangrove Swamps," loc. cit., 23-30. They have also been observed in the mangrove on the north coast of Sumatra by A. Kint, "De Luchfoto en de topografische terreingesteldheid in de Mangrove," De Tropische Natuur, XXIII (1934), 173-89.

29 These moors are described by Richards, The Tropical Rain Forest, 214-16.

30   Probably the first account of the utility of this inland passage
was recorded by Pascual de Andagoya during his explorations
along the Colombian coast in 1540. "From the Santa María
River (south of Buenaventura Bay?) for a distance of fifty leagues
to the Island of Gallo (north of Tumaco) brigs can follow the inland passages from one river to the next without going out to
sea." "Relación de lo ocurrido en el descubrimiento de la mar
del sur... escrita por el Adelantado Pascual de Andagoya," in
Martin Fernández de Navarrete (ed.), Colección de viages y
descubrimientos que hicieron por mar los españoles desde fin
del siglo XV..., III, 387-443; ref. p. 436.

31   The chemistry of mangrove soils has been studied by F.W. Freise,
"Untersuchungen am Schlick der Mangrovküste Brasiliens,"
Chemie der Erde, II (1938), 333-55. The blue-black color of
mangrove mud is probably the result of the reaction between hydrogen sulphide and iron which produces the blackish iron sulphide. Along banks of tidal channels the blue-black mud is often
covered by a thin (1-5 cm.) layer of grey-brown mud, recently
deposited by tidal currents and possibly affected chemically by
oxygen contained in the brackish water.

32   Similar soil types and vegetation sequences are described by
Rosevear, "Mangrove Swamps," loc. cit., 24, for the mangrove
swamps of Nigeria.

33   The tasquero, a small red crab (Pachygrapus cruentatus) is the
more abundant of the crustaceans in the mangrove. The scurry-
ing of these brilliantly colored animals up and down the prop
roots of Rhizophora and across mud flats is one of the common
sights in the mangrove forest. A much larger, edible blue crab
(unidentified) is also found along the muddy banks of the esteros.

34   Freise, "Mangrovküste Brasiliens," loc. cit., 345-46, has
conducted experiments on the rate of decomposition of oyster
and clam shells fixed on mangrove roots along the Brazilian
coast. Rhizophora quickly absorbs the calcium carbonate through
the prop roots.

35   See, for example, statements made by T. W. Vaughn, "The
Geologic Work of Mangrove in Southern Florida," Smithsonian
Institution, Miscellaneous Coll., LII (1910), 461-64; R. Erichson,
"Die Mangrove-Vegetation," Natur, XVI (1925), 190-99; Chapman,
"The Botany of the Jamaican Shoreline," loc. cit., 312-23; Davis,
"The Ecology and geologic role of Mangroves," loc. cit., 394-405;

J. H. Davis, "Mangroves, makers of lands," Nature Magazine, XXXI (1938), 551-53.

36   G. von Freyberg, "Zerstörung and Sedimentation an der Mangrovküste Brasiliens," Leopoldina VI (1930), 69-117, ref. 109-110; Grewe, "Africanische Mangrovelandschaften," loc. cit., 119.

37   This situation has been described for the coast of Brazil between Belem and São Luis by von Freyberg, ibid., 109; for Malaya by Watson, "Mangrove Forests," loc. cit., 1-5; for British Guiana by Martyn, "Foreshore Vegetation," loc. cit., 293. C. G. G. J. van Steenis, "Kustaanwas en mangrove," Natuurwetenschappelijk Tidjschrift voor Nederlandsch Indië, CI (1941), 82-85, states that from data in the literature and from his own observations in Sumatra, natural coastal accretion by mud-silting is the factor responsible for the development of the mangrove, not vice-versa. A similar view was held earlier in 1890 by B. Hagen, "Die Pflanzen- und Thierwelt von Deli auf der Ostküste Sumatra," Tidjschrift van het Kon. Nederlandsch Aardijkskundig Genootschap, 2nd ser, VII 91890), 1-240; ref. 21.

38   Watson, "Mangrove Forests," loc. cit., 56, speaking of mangrove along the coasts of Malaya, suggests that Avicennia, by supplying raw alluvium with organic material through root decay prepares the soil for invasion by more exacting mangrove, such as Rhizophora. Furthermore, the small pneumatophores of Avicennia aid in catching the floating Rhizophora hypocotyls, which quickly take root in the mud. On the other hand, Davis, "The Ecology and Geologic role of Mangroves", loc. cit., 322-31, has shown that in southern Florida Rhizophora pioneers mud flats, while Avicennia, Laguncularia, and Conocarpus form successive bands inland.

39   Egler, "Red Mangrove in Florida," loc. cit., 305.

40   Similar effects of wave erosion on mangrove vegetation have been described for the coast of Brazil by von Freyberg, "Mangrovküste Brasiliens," loc. cit., 109.

41   An account written in 1790 by a Spanish naval officer specifies that Gallo Island, north of Tumaco, was separated from the mainland by a narrow tidal channel, indicating that little change has occurred in that portion of the coast in the last 160 years. Alejandro Malaspina, "Navegación frente a las Costas de Cauca

Panamá, año de 1790, " in Antonio B. Cuervo (ed.), Colección de Documentos Inéditos Sobre la Geografiá y la Historia de Colombia (Bogotá, 1891), II, 129-160; ref. 143.

42 José Cuatrecasas, "Gutíferas nuevas o poco conocidas en Colombia, " Anales del Instituto de Biologiá, XX (1949), 91-112.

43 The mountainous coast is described briefly by Murphy, "The Littoral of Pacific Colombia and Ecuador, " loc. cit., 1-33.

44 U. S. Hydrographic Office Chart No. 0814, 5th ed. (1921, corrected to 1949).

45 Paulo Emilio Escobar, Bahías de Málaga y Buenaventura (Bogotá, 1931), 268-70.

CHAPTER VI

1 The population of the Colombian portion of the lowlands, according to unpublished official 1951 census returns, is 295,666. According to 1950 census figures, 14,600 people inhabit the province of Darién, Panama, giving that area a density of 2.4 persons per square mile. "Quinto Censo Nacional de Poblacíon y Vivienda, 10 de Diciembre de 1950, " Boletín Informative, No. 3 (Direccíon de Estadística y Censo, Contraloría General de la República, Panama, 1952). The 1950 population of the canton of Elroy Alfaro, Esmeraldas province, Ecuador, is 20,470, or 15 persons per square mile. The latter data are from unpublished reports of the official Ecuadorian census, 1950. The grand population total of the Pacific lowland culture area is 335,070, according to the latest census figures.

2 Estadística Jeneral de la Nueva Granada, parte primera (Bogotá, 1848). Nineteenth- and early twentieth-century population statistics for the coastal lowlands are highly questionable. Hardships of travel and frequent migrations of Indians and free negroes made accurate census-taking an almost impossible task.

3 The following sources were used to compile the population curves shown in Figure 5: Data for 1778 were taken from "Relación del Chocó...conforme al reconocimiento del Capitán de Ingenieros don Juan Jiménez Donoso, 15 de noviembre de 1780, " in Enrique Ortega Ricaurte, ed., Historia Documental del Chocó (Bogotá, 1954), 205-41; ref., 212-15; for 1789, Francisco Silvestre, "Descripcíon del Reyno de Santa Fé de Bogotá..., " Anales de

la Instrucción Pública, XIII (1888), 153; for 1835, an article in the newspaper, Constitucional del Chocó, No. 15, Quibdó, 15 February 1836; for 1843, Estadística Jeneral de la Nueva Granada, parte primera (Bogotá, 1848); for 1851 and 1870, Anuario Estadístico de Colombia (Bogotá, 1875); for 1912, Censo General de la República de Colombia, levantado el 5 de Marzo de 1912 (Bogotá, 1912); for 1918, Censo de la Población de la República de Colombia, levantado el 14 de Octubre de 1918... (Bogotá, 1924); for 1905, Censo General de la Población, 5 de Julio de 1938, XVI, Resumen General de País (Bogotá, 1942); for 1938, ibid., XV, Intendencias y Comisarías (Bogotá, 1942); for 1951, unpublished official records, Departamento de Censos Nacionales, Bogotá. Only the cenuses of 1918, 1938 and 1951 are thought to be fairly accurate. That of 1928 is considered so inaccurate that it has not been used in the compilation.

4   The infant mortality rate for the lowlands can be no more than a guess, based on fairly reliable comparative figures for the rest of Colombia. Colombia as a whole has a relatively high infant mortality rate: 136 per 1000. The coffee-producing areas of Antioquia and Caldas and the lowlands of Chocó have the highest rates -- 200 per 1000. Antonio Concha y Vanegas, "Relación entre la geografía y la lucha antimalárica en Colombia," Boletín de la Sociedad Geográfica de Colombia, X (1952), 188-200.

5   Geografía Económica de Colombia, VI, Chocó (Contraloría General de la República, Bogotá, 1943), 160.

6   Concha y Venegas, "Relación entre la geografía y la lucha anti-malárica," loc. cit., 193. In some areas along the Pacific Coast, as in the swamps back of the mangrove belt between the San Juan Delta and the mouth of the Baudó River, the percentage may be well over 50.

7   "Distribution of Malaria Vectors," Atlas of Distribution of Diseases, Plate 3 (American Geographical Society, New York, 1951).

8   Most of the American yellow fever vectors have been found in the Amazon Basin and western Orinoco drainage. Marston Bates, "Observations on the distribution of diurnal mosquitos in a tropical forest," Ecology, XXV (1944), 159-70. The vector Haemagogus spegazzinii falco has been found in Darién and the northern Chocó. "Distribution of Dengue and Yellow Fever," Atlas of Distribution of Diseases, Plate 5 (American Geographical Society, New York, 1952).

9   A yellow fever epidemic occurred on the middle Río Atrato in
     1948-1950; deaths were not reported. Ibid., Plate 5.

10   Concha y Venegas, "Relación entre la geografía y la lucha anti-
     malárica," loc. cit., 191.

11   The Campaña Antipiánica was undertaken by the Servicio Coopera-
     tive Interamericano de Salud Pública (SCISP) in January, 1950.
     Every river and tributary of the Pacific lowlands will have been
     visited and inhabitants inoculated by the workers of this organiza-
     tion probably by the end of 1955. In June, 1954, work on the
     last sector, the Atrato Basin, was begun.

12   Geografía Económica de Colombia, VI, Chocó, 209.

13   The last censuses which break down population figures by race
     were those of 1912 and 1918. The following percentages were
     calculated from the official population data for the Pacific low-
     lands:

	Negro	Mixed	Indian	White	Not Specified
1912	68.0%	17.5%	7.2%	7.0%	--
1918	55.6	21.7	5.4	9.7	4.7

     Judging from field observation the categories "Negro" and "Mixed"
     can probably be classified as Negroid. Thus in 1912, 85.5% of
     the lowland population was Negroid; in 1918, 77.0%. The dis-
     crepancy between the two figures, separated only by four years,
     appears to be due to erroneous census-taking. Jorge Mendoza
     Nieto, Geografía Illustrada del Chocó (Bogotá, 1942), estimates
     the racial composition of the Chocó for 1940 as follows: Negro,
     60%; Mestizo (Negro-White-Indian mixtures), 25%; Indian 7%;
     White, 8%.

14   Robert Cushman Murphy called attention to this phenomenon in
     1939 in his "Racial Succession in the Colombian Chocó,"
     Geographical Review, XXIX (1939), 461-71.

15   See Paul Rivet, "La Lengua Chocó," Revista del Instituto
     Etnológico Nacional, I (1943-1944), 131-96; 297-349.

16   B. LeRoy Gordon, "Human Geography and Ecology in the Sinú
     Country of Colombia" (Ph.D. dissertation, University of

California, 1954).

17   John H. Rowe, "The Idabaez: Unknown Indians of the Chocó Coast," Kroeber Anthropological Society Papers, No. 1 (1950), 34-44. Rowe refers to a heretofore unused seventeenth-century account of Indians called "Idabaez," who inhabited the coastal areas around the Bay of Solano north of Cabo Corrientes. The brief sketch of their culture (1640) suggests that these people were culturally distinct from the Chocó of the Atrato Basin. As Rowe points out, Nordenskiöld, using as evidence their riverine boat types and their lack of native words for marine mammals and fish, suggests that the modern coastal Chocó may have migrated from the Atrato Basin as late as the seventeenth century. Erland Nordenskiöld, "Les Indiens de l'Isthme de Panamá," La Géographie, L (1928), 299-319; ref. 303. Other writers have assumed that the occupants of the Pacific Coast spoke Chocó at the time of earliest European contact (i.e., the forays made by Pizarro and Almagro from 1525 to 1529). For example, Robert Cushman Murphy, "The Earliest Spanish Advances Southward from Panama along the West Coast of South America," Hispanic American Historical Review, XXI (1941), 3-28, argues for coastal occupance by the Chocó on the basis of the reported use of poisoned arrows and the ability of Cueva interpreters to understand the inhabitants. The relationship of Chocó and Cueva speech, however, is not known, and the use of poisoned arrows was apparently widespread in northwestern Colombia at the time of the conquest.

18   Antonio de Guzman, "Descubrimiento y pacificación de la provincia del Chocó..., enero 31 de 1671," Historia Documental del Chocó (ed. Enrique Ortega Ricaurte, Bogotá, 1954), 108-125; ref. pp. 123-24. According to Guzman, the Poromea of the Bojayá made extraordinarily large canoes and were skilled weavers of cotton cloth and hammocks, coveted by the Chocó. The latter periodically raided both the Suruco and Poromea for slaves.

19   J. Alden Mason, "The Languages of South American Indians," Handbook of South American Indians (Bureau of American Ethnology, Bull. 143, Washington, 1950) VI, 157-317; ref. 180.

20   Erland Nordenskiöld, "An Historical and Ethnological Survey of the Cuna Indians," Comparative Ethnological Studies, X (1938), 1-7.

21   Gordon, "Human Geography and Ecology," loc. cit., 208.

22   Henry Wassén, "Contributions to Cuna Ethnology," Etnologiska Studier, XVI (1949), 21.

23   Wassén, Ibid., 29.

24   Cuna are reported to be on the Tesca, Yape, Capití, Pucru and Paya rivers.

25   This expedition, made probably in 1543, was led by Captain Gómez Hernández. It is not known whether he reached the Atrato or the San Juan rivers. A document dated 1553 mentions that the expedition had been made "... ten or twelve years previous..." "Fracaso de la expedición al Chocó del Capitán Día Sánchez de Narváez..., año de 1553," Historia Documental del Chocó, 10.

26   AHNC, Protocolos XXV, ff. 1-24 (1604-1810); AGI, Patronato CCXXXIII, ramo 12 (1630); ibid., ramo 2 (1620-1630).

27   AGI, Patronato CCXXXIII, ramo 12 (1630).

28   Fray Jerónimo Escobar, "Relación sobre el carácter y costumbres de los indios ... de Popayán," in Joaquín F. Pacheco and Francisco de Cárdenas (eds.), Colección de documentos inéditos, relativos al descubrimiento, conquista, y organización (Madrid, 1884), LI, 470.

29   Fray Pedro Simón, Noticias Historiales de las Conquistas de Tierra Firme en las Indias Occidentales (Bogotá, 1892), V, 149. AGI, Patronato CCXXXIII, ramo 2 (1620-1630). The last Spaniards fled the lowlands in 1612 after the Chocó had murdered Captain Melchor Velázquez, military governor of the mining settlements.

30   AHNC, Caciques e Indios LXVII, f. 139^{v} (1637)

31   Missionary work in the Chocó was done chiefly by Franciscans, who first entered the area in 1648. AHNC, Curas y Obispos II, f. 73^{r}, 79^{v} (n.d.); ibid, XXIX, f. 319^{v}.

32   AHNC, Minas de Cauca VI, f. 643^{r} (1684). The 1684 uprising was particularly bad. Most of the Spanish mine owners in the colonial province of Citará (upper Atrato) were killed or forced

to flee to the highlands.

33   Many documents concerning the mining activities in the Chocó that are extant in the Popayán and Bogotá archives describe in detail the labor required of the Chocó Indians in the upper San Juan-Atrato area.

34   AHNC, Caciques e Indios XXIII, f. 1048[r] (1782). The local officials of Quibdó complained bitterly that many of the Chocó reducciones, or resettled Indian villages, on the Atrato, such as Beté and Bebará, were rapidly declining in population because of such migrations.

35   For example, during the political disturbances of 1950-53, many Indians living in the Serranía de Baudó fled to Darién to avoid armed bandits who were scourging the countryside. Some of the migrants returned to their Colombian homes in 1954, but many stayed in Panama.

36   In 1750 there were thirteen heads of families (tributarios) of Chocó origin on the Cajambre and Yurumanguí rivers; there were nine on the Naya River. ACC, sig. 4362 (1750). A document of 1780 indicates that many Chocó families had reached as far south as the Guapi River: "There are now many Indians from the Micay and the Chocó now living on the Saija, Timbiquí, Guapi, and Napi rivers [until now] inhabited only by gangs of Negro slaves and freedmen working in the mines..."; "... every day the settlement of Negro [slaves and freedmen] and Indians from the Chocó is increasing along this coast..." AHNC, Curas y Obispos XXV, ff. 732[r] - 735[r] (1780).

37   Geografía Económica de Colombia, VI, Chocó, 85. Many smallpox epidemics wiped out thousands of lowlands Indians during the colonial period. The early epidemics of 1566 and 1588 are reported to have been the most disastrous.

38   AHNC, Poblición del Cauca II, f. 855[v] (1793).

39   The Chocó population of Darién has been compiled from census data in Boletín Informative No. 3, Quinto Censo Nacional de Población y Vivienda, 10 de Diciembre de 1950 (Contraloría General de la República de Panamá, 1952). The figure for Antioquia was estimated from data presented in the Colombian census for 1918, and is thus hardly more than a guess. The figure for the lowlands south of Buenaventura is an estimate

based on field observation.

40   The numerous local names for Chocó Indians that appear in the
     literature tend to confuse the picture of the present distribution
     of these people. As Gordon points out "Human Geography and
     Ecology" 114, the term Catío as used today usually refers to the
     Indians living in the upper reaches of some of the eastern tribu-
     taries of the Atrato and the upper sections of the Sinú and San
     Jorge rivers; all of these Indians speak Chocó. Citaraes is often
     used for the Chocó Indians of the Andágueda area and Baudoes
     for those of the Río Baudó.

41   A document of 1608 indicates that "... Indians called noanabaes
     [elsewhere in the same document written "noananaes"] live along
     the coast near the port of Buenaventura...." AHNC, Protocolos
     XXV, f. 9^v (1605-1810). In the mid-seventeenth century, Indians
     living on the Río Raposo were known as "indios noanamaes."
     ACC, sig. 440 (1668). Later, these Indians were known as the
     "raposeños," who had great dislike for the Chocó invading from
     the north in the eighteenth century. During the Chocó uprisings
     in the upper San Juan in 1684, Waunamá Indians from the lower
     part of the river and from the Raposo remained loyal to the
     Spaniards and even-aided in putting down the rebellion. AHNC,
     Poblaciones del Cauca II, ff. 9^v , 17^v (1729); ibid., Minas del
     Cauca VI, f. 651^r·

42   AGI Audiencia de Quito XVI, Letter of Francisco de Berrío,
     Cartago, 28 April 1599; relation of Francisco Ramírez de la
     Serna, Cali, 18 April, 1610.

43   AGI, Patronato CCXXXIII, ramo 2 (1620-1630).

44   AGI, Audiencia de Quito XVI, Testimony of Captain Jorge de
     Santa María, Cali, 20 March 1631.

45   ACC, sig. 1184 (1665).

46   ACC, sig. 2307 (1690); ANH, Presidencia de la Real Audiencia,
     Quito, vol. 1724-1725, doc. no. 814 (1724).

47   AHNC, Curas y Obispos XXXV, ff. 727^r - 728^r (1779). In 1779,
     204 Indians were living in the Zaragoza settlement.

48   ACC, sig. 6053 (1778). Those from the Raposo came mainly from
     the village of Guanamía. Still today the mixed bloods around

Tumaco call the Indians from the northern rivers "guanamás," be they Chocó or Waunamá.

49   AGI, Audiencia de Quito XVI, Relación del Capitán Francisco Ramírez, Cali, 8 April 1610. The map, entitled "Mapa de la tierra donde habitan los Piles y Barbacoas en q̃ entró el Capitán Francisco Ramírez" (AGI, map Panamá, no. 30), has been published in J. Jijón y Caamaño, Sebastián de Benalcázar (Quito, 1938), II, 200. As early as the mid-sixteenth century the warlike Timbas tribe, which lived in the upper Pacific slope of the Cordillera Occidental, had been given in encomienda to various Spanish families in Cali. Vexed by the heavy tributes in gold demanded of them, these Indians apparently had rebelled many times previous to the punitive expedition led by Ramírez. Miguel Cabello Balboa, "Verdadera descripción y relación larga de la Provincia y Tierra de las Esmeraldas ...," in Obras (Quito, 1945), I, 7.

50   AGI, Patronato CCXXXIII, ramo 2 (1620-1639).

51   AHNC, Curas y Obispos XLIV (1748). This document was published in part by Paul Rivet, "Un dialecte hoka colombien: le Yurumanguí," Journal de la Société des Américanistes, XXXIV (1942), 1-59, and by Sergio Elías Ortiz, "Los Indios Yurumanguies," Acta Americana, IV (1946), 10-25. On the basis of a word list given in the document, Rivet attempts to relate the Yurumanguí language to the Hokam family of North America. Elías identifies the Yurumanguí Indians as remnants of the Piles and Timbas shown on the Ramírez map.

52   Fernández de Navarrete (ed.), Colección de los Viages, III, 436-37.

53   By 1598 Spanish missionaries from Pasto and Quito had established four reducciones, or villages, among the Coaiquer and Mayasquer along the route of entry into the Barbacoas lowlands to the west. R. P. Fray Joel L. Monroy, "El Convento de la Merced de Quito de 1534 a 1617," Boletín de la Academia de la Historia (Quito), XI (1930), 193-208.

54   The language and dialect names are taken from early seventeenth century documents concerning Indian uprisings and the establishment of encomiendas within the Barbacoas area. AGI, Audiencia de Quito XVI, Juan Bermúdez de Castro to the king, 24 April 1631; ACC, sig. 132 (1659); AGI, Audiencia de Quito XVIII, 15 June 1675.

The last two references concern <u>encomiendas</u> established in 1638. An attempt to identify the Sindagua people linguistically has been made by Henri Lehmann, "Les Indiens Sindagua (Colombie)," <u>Journal de la Société des Américanistes</u>, N.S., XXXVIII (1949), 67-89. On the basis of family-name lists given in seventeenth- and eighteenth-century documents, Lehmann concludes that the Sindagua language (which was sometimes called "Malla" in colonial days) was probably close to that used by the modern Coaiquer; that is, a Chibcha tongue.

55   AGI, Audiencia de Quito XVI, Juan Bermúdez de Castro to the king, 24 April 1631.

56   <u>Ibid.</u> The expedition was led by Captain Moreno de Zúñiga.

57   AGI, Audiencia de Quito XVI, Lorenzo de Villaquirán to the king, 31 May 1635.

58   According to the testimony of one Juan Díaz de Fuenmayor in Buga, December 9, 1630, about 1610 or 1611 a Spanish slave-raiding party (of which he was a member) returned to Cali from the Barbacoas area with more than 100 Sindagua Indians, who were partitioned among the members of the expedition and presumably sold to local farmers and stockmen. AGI, Patronato CCXXXIII, ramo 2 (1620-1630).

59   ANH, Quito, Presidencia de la Real Audiencia, Quito, vol. 1739-1740, doc. no. 1182 (1737). In the vicinity of Santa María del Puerto (Barbacoas) in 1688 there were sixteen <u>encomiendas</u> each with four to forty-three Sindagua Indians (heads of families). ACC, sig. 2134 (1688).

60   At least one mine was in operation on the Timbiquí by 1635, and before 1646 several had been established along the upper and middle courses of the river. AGI, Audiencia de Quito XVI, Lorenzo de Villaquirán to the king, 31 May 1635; ACC, sig. 166 (1646).

61   According to a document dated 1671, Spanish miners on the Timbiquí had seventeen <u>encomiendas</u> of Chupa Indians, fourteen of the Boya dialect, and three made up of Guapi-speaking Indians. ANH, Quito, Presidencia de la Real Audiencia, Quito, vol. 1670-1674, doc. no. 262 (1671).

62   <u>Ibid.</u>, vol. 1729-1730, doc. no. 897 (1730).

63   AGI, Audiencia de Quito XVI, Lorenzo de Villaquirán to the king, 31 May 1635. The port of Santa Bárbara was re-established in 1631, after it had been destroyed by the Sindaguas. AGI, Audiencia de Quito XVI, Relación de Juan Bermúdez, 17 May, 1631.

64   ACC, sig. 4920 (1755); sig. 6056 (1788). In 1788, 328 Sindagua Indians were living on the Telembí and Ispí rivers.

65   For a brief description of the modern Coaiquer see Sergio Elías Ortiz, "The Modern Quillacinga, Pasto, and Coaiquer," Handbook of South American Indians, II, 961-68.

66   To my knowledge no anthropological investigation has been made of these "indigenas." Those that I have seen have been "Europeanized" to some degree, in that they wear modern dress and use many store-bought implements. None admits of an Indian language, and many are obviously sambos (mixed Indian-Negro).

67   The most comprehensive ethnological study of the Cayapa is by S. A. Barrett, "The Cayapa Indians of Ecuador," Indian Notes and Monographs, No. XL (Museum of the American Indian, Heye Foundation, New York, 1925), 2 vols. The modern distribution of the Cayapa is given by Edwin N. Ferdon, Jr., "Studies in Ecuadorian Geography," Monograph of the School of American Research, No. XV (Santa Fé, New Mexico, 1950).

68   Another group of forest Indians, also of Chibchan stock, are the Colorado, or the Tsátchela, who inhabit the western slope of the Andes in Ecuador about 100 miles south of the Cayapa country. However, like the Coaiquer, these Indians are not true lowland river people, and culturally should not be considered in this study. For an ethnographic survey of the Colorado see V. Wolfgang Von Hagen, "The Tsátchela Indians of Western Ecuador," Indian Notes and Monographs, No. LI (Museum of the American Indian, Heye Foundation, New York, 1939).

69   The Esmeraldas culture was first investigated by Marshall H. Saville in 1908 and reported in his "Archeological Researches on the Coast of Ecuador," Verhandlungen des XVI Internationalen Amerikanisten-Kongresses (Vienna, 1908), 331-45. Later contributions to Esmeraldas archeology include Max Uhle, "Las antiguas civilizaciones esmeraldeñas," Anales de la Universidad Central, XXXVIII (1927); Edwin N. Ferdon, Jr., "Reconnaissance in Esmeraldas," Palacio, XLVII (1940), 257-72; XLVII (1941), 7-15; R. d'Harcourt, "Archéologie de la Province d'Esmeraldas

(Equateur). Céramique, Objects en pierre, " Journal de la Société des Américanistes, XXXIV (1942), 61-200; Henry Reichen, "Contribution a l'Etude de la Métallurgie Précolombienne de la Province d'Esmeraldas (Equateur), "Journal de la Société des Americanistes XXXIV (1942), 201-228; Julio Arauz, La Tolita (Quito, 1946).

70   In July of 1951 the writer encountered numerous mounds along the Rosario and Chagüí Rivers, many of which had been undercut by erosion and had slumped into the river. Within such slumps along the river's edge numerous clay artifacts similar to those of the Esmeraldas culture were found. In almost every village along these rivers one or two persons have small collections of such artifacts which they have encountered along the river bank.

71   Saville, "Archeological Researches," loc. cit., 344.

72   "Relación del Pedro de Arévalo sobre la provincia de las Esmeraldas, año de 1600," Documentos para la Historia de la Audiencia de Quito (Madrid, 1949) IV, 15-37, ref., 32.

73   In 1951 gold-washing had practically ceased at La Tolita. In 1940 Ferdon reports that the placer operations there were in the hands of the owner of the hacienda on which the mounds are situated. Ferdon, "Reconnaisance in Esmeraldas," loc. cit., 266.

74   This activity is described by Teodoro Wolf, Viajes Científicos por la Republica del Ecuador (Guayaquil 1879) III, 49-51. Today such activity is carried on chiefly at the small settlements of Lagarto and Lagartillo, between the Río Verde and La Tola.

75   José de Recasens and Victor Oppenheim, "Analisis tipológico de materiales cerámicos y líticos, procedentes del Chocó," Revista del Instituto Etnológico Nacional, I (1943-1944), 351-409.

76   By 1670 practically all of the most important gold placers of the Chocó had been discovered and most were being worked by small gangs of Negro slaves. The Chocó rebellion of 1684, however, forced most of the Spanish miners and their slaves to retire to the highlands until peace was once more established among the Indians in 1688. AHNC, Minas del Cauca V, f. 362^r (1690).

77   Ibid., ff. 359^r, 362^r, 363^r.

78   "Descripción de la Provincia de Zitará..., [1777]," Colección de Docomentos Inéditos..., II, 311.

79   "Relación del Chocó..., 1780," in Historia Documental del Chocó, 213-14.

80   ACC, sig. 1099 (1685). Unfortunately, statistics on numbers of slaves in the Barbacoas area are so fragmentary as to be worthless for comparative purposes.

81   Discovered in 1745, the placers of the Yurumanguí were among the last in the coastal plain to be exploited. AHNC, Minas del Cauca II, ff. 38^V - 39^V (1745). The mines on the Micay and Naya were first worked in 1716. AHNC, Curas y Obispos XLIV, ff. 55^V - 56^V (1716).

82   Vicente Restrepo, Estudio sobre las minas de Oro y Plata de Colombia, 2nd ed. (Bogotá, 1888), 115. The famous Caná mines were abandoned after a Cuna uprising in 1726.

83   "Relación ... de las Esmeraldas, desde 1583 hasta 1585 por Fray Alonzo de Espinoza," Documentos para la Historia de la Audiencia de Quito (Madrid, 1949), IV, 8-13.

84   ACC, sig. 3144 (1730).

85   AHNC, Minas del Cauca II, f. 456^V (1777).

86   AHNC, Negros y Esclavos del Cauca IV, ff. 558^r - 591^V (1759). About two-thirds of the names listed, however, were first names only, or the surname was given as criollo, e.g. Juan Criollo, Mariá Criolla, etc.

87   Gonzalo Aguirre Beltrán, "Tribal origins of slaves in Mexico," Journal of Negro History, XXXI (1946), 269-353.

88   José Rafael Arboleda, S.J., "The Ethnohistory of the Colombian Negroes." (M.S. thesis, Northwestern University, Evanston, 1950); "Nuevas investigaciones afrocolombianas," Revista Javeriana, XXXVII (1952), 197-206.

89   Mina comes from the name of the Gold Coast slave mart of the Portuguese, San Jorge de Mina, where slaves collected from the Ashanti area (between the Bandama and Volta rivers on the Gold and Ivory coasts) were kept for shipment. Biáfara is a Bantu-speaking group living on the Gulf of Biafra, Cameroons. Carabalí comes from the Calabar Coast, east of the Niger Delta. Cetre is a Kru tribe who live on the coast of eastern Liberia and the western

part of the Ivory Coast. Lucumi refers to the Yoruba of the
Nigerian coast. Arará is a tribe from the Guinea Coast west of
the Niger Delta. All the derivations were obtained from Aguirre
Beltrán and Arboleda, cited above.

90 It is quite possible that many more western Sudanese came into
in the mining area, for slave-raiding parties ranged far inland from
the Guinea Coast.

91 Angola probably comes from the Portuguese colony of that name
located on the west coast of Africa. Chamba is the same as
Tjamba, the name of a tribe north of the Ashanti in the Gold
Coast. Bran refers to the Brong Negroes of the Guinea Coast,
conquered by the Ashanti. Luango is possibly from a tribe of
that name in the lower Congo.

92 A result of Simon Bolívar's efforts of many years toward abolition
of slavery, the law provided (1) that after 1821 all children born
to slaves were to be free at the age of eighteen and (2) that a
committee of manumission was to be organized to collect inheritance taxes, which were to be used to pay owners for the freedom
of deserving slaves. See Harold A. Bierck, Jr., "The Struggle
for Abolition in Gran Colombia," Hispanic American Historical
Review, XXXIII (1953), 365-86. In the Chocó the collection of
inheritance taxes for such a purpose proved impossible.

93 Julio César García, "El movimiento antisclavista en Colombia,"
Boletín de Historia y Antigüedades, XLI (1954), 131-43.

94 Restrepo, Estudio sobre las Minas, 117.

95 AHNC, Pueblos del Cauca II, ff. 324^V, 325^r, 328^r (1790). The
Jiménez Donoso census of 1778 reports 79 freedmen (mulattoes
and Negroes) living in the Baudó area. "Relación del Chocó,
1780," Historia Documental del Chocó, 312.

96 AHNC, Secretaría de Guerra y Marina IV, f. 525^V (1821). At
one point along the river the Negroes formed a palenque, or
fortified village, to defy the crown authority.

97 Captain Charles Stuart Cochrane, Travels in Colombia during the
years 1823 and 1824 (London, 1825), II, 419.

98 Most of the old people now living along these rivers and in the adjacent coastal villages were born in the upper San Juan drainage,

chiefly on the Río Tamaná. To them this area is the true Chocó; when speaking of a trip to Istmina or Andagoya, they say, "I am going to the Chocó." Many of the old folk still remember the journey across the Serranía to their new homeland. Most of the villages along the coast north of Buenaventura were settled after 1850 by the grandparents of most of the present-day families.

99   Theodoro Wolf, Viajes científicos, III, 49. Wolf estimates the Negro population of the Santiago drainage to have been between 1500 and 2000 in 1875.

100   Several villages along the Santiago were established by Colombians in the last seventy-five years. For example, the village of Maldonado was founded in 1890 by Colombian Negro immigrants from Barbacoas.

101   Strong commercial and social ties exist between the Chocó coast north of Cabo Corrientes and southeastern Panama. There is probably not a man over eighteen years of age living on the rocky Chocó coast who has not sailed a sloop to Panama to trade or to visit relatives. Around 1900 it was generally accepted that the Colombian province of Panama controlled politically and economically, ipso facto, if not legally, the Pacific Coast southward to the Bay of Utría in the Chocó. News article in El Chocoano, No. 7 (Quibdó, April 1, 1899).

102   "Relación del Chocó..., 1780," Historia Documental del Chocó, 212.

103   Censo de la Poblición, 1918 (Bogota, 1924).

104   Nicomedes Conto, "Notas de la Gobernación sobre Emprestito Forzozo," Unión Chocoana, No. XXII (Quibdó, 26 May, 1855). White families had been leaving the Chocó for the highlands since the 1790's. According to one commentator of that period, "Thus, except for a small number of actual mine owners, the most important people have left the province of Chocó to reside in Santa Fé (Bogotá), Cartago, Popayán, Buga, and Cali; [those who have left] look with horror on returning to such a land... which from any viewpoint offers no advantages whatever...." AHNC, Poblaciones del Cauca II, f. 854^V (1793).

105   Local legend has it that about 1840 one Manuel Moreno, a Spanish immigrant, founded the village of San Juan de la Costa as a center for a coconut plantation along the beach. Other Spaniards entered

later with Negro slaves. The other white settlements along this
coast possibly had the same origin. According to another legend,
told by the people of El Charco, the white inhabitants of La Vigía
are the descendants of shipwrecked crews and passengers. It is
said that until recently the whites would not permit Negroes to
live in some of the coastal villages.

106   A section of the Iscuandé River between the towns of Iscuandé and
Vuelta Larga is inhabited by mulattoes; formerly the town and
most of the lower stretch of the river was largely white. The
river above Vuelta Larga corresponds to the old mining area,
and in colonial days was inhabited by slaves. Today this portion
of the river is completely black. After the liberation of the slaves
most of the white families of the Iscuandé fled to Pasto and
Popayán.

107   Probably a colloquialism for paisano, or countryman.

108   For brief description of Antioqueño settlement in the Chocó, see
Hans Bloch, "La Colonización del Chocó desde el Valle del Cauca,"
"Boletín de la Sociedad Geográfica de Colombia, VII (1948), 40-
42; James J. Parsons, "Antioqueño Colonization in Western
Colombia," Ibero-Americana, No. XXXII (Berkeley, 1949), 86-93.

109   Geografía Económica de Colombia, VI, Chocó, 461-62; Anon.,
"Colonia Agricola de Bahía Solano," Tierras y Aguas, I (1938),
6-9.

110   The writer visited the site of the Limones colony in 1954. Data
on the Utría colony were obtained second hand from informants
in Cupica.

111   Ernesto Restrepo Tirado, "Construcciones Indígenas," Boletín
de Historia y Antigüedades, I (1903), 574-96. Restrepo bases
his study on the printed accounts of the early chroniclers, such
as Cieza de León, Castellanos, Herrera, and Simón. In contrast
to their widespread occurrence in southeast Asia, pile dwellings
in pre-Columbian America had a relatively limited distribution.
Northwestern South America seems to have been the area of
greatest concentration: (1) the Pacific littoral from Darién to
Esmeraldas, (2) many sections of the Venzuelan coast and Lake
Valencia, (3) the Orinoco Delta, and (4) certain areas in upper
Amazonia. Wendell C. Bennett, "Habitations," Handbook of South
American Indians (Washington, 1949), V, 1-20.

112   Such houses are described for the Dabaiba area on the western
      slope of the Cordillera Occidental and for some sections of the
      lower Atrato. The round house with conical roof appears to have
      been dominant among the inhabitants of the Cauca Valley at the
      time of Spanish contact. Restrepo Tirado, "Construcciones
      Indigenas," loc. cit., 582-83. The following brief description
      of Indian houses on the western slope of the cordillera in the
      Chocó is dated 1540: "The areas of Sima, Tatape, and Chocó are
      called the provinces of the Barbacoas, for all the Indian dwellings
      are mounted on high, thick poles ...; they are reached by means
      of ladders, which are raised at night." "Descripción de los
      pueblos de la provincia de Ancerma [1540-1541]," in Pacheco y
      Cárdenas (eds.), Colección de documentos inéditos relativos al
      descubrimiento, conquista y organización... (Madrid, 1864),
      III, 413. In 1540 Andagoya writes that on the rivers between
      Buenaventura and the Isla del Gallo (near Tumaco) the Indian
      houses"... are 300 to 280 pasos (paces?) on the side, and at
      least 100 people live in each one." Martín Fernández de Navarrete
      (ed.), Colección de los Viages, 436.

113   Henry Wassén, "Notes on the Southern Groups of Chocó Indians
      in Colombia," Etnologiska Studier, I (1935), 35-182.

114   "Relación del reverendo Padre Francisco García, "Relación de
      algunas excursiones apostólicas en la Misión del Chocó (Bogotá,
      1924), 8-17.

115   Gordon, "Human Geography and Ecology," 43-45.

116   The San Blas Cuna have discarded the pile dwelling for the caney,
      a gabled long house.

117   Erland Nordenskiold, "Les Indiens de l'Isthmus de Panamá,"
      loc. cit., 299-319; ref. 311.

118   That such work was required of the Indians is evidenced in numer-
      ous documents on Indian labor extant in the colonial archives in
      Bogotá and Popayán.

CHAPTER VII

1   Samples of levee soils on the lower Merendó River, left tributary
      of the Atrato, were taken at several points at various depths.
      These samples were tested for pH values with a La Motte soils
      testing kit.

Depth	Sample 1		Sample 2		Sample 3		Sample 4	
	Texture	pH	Texture	pH	Texture	pH	Texture	pH
25 cm.	sandy loam	5.8	sandy loam	6.0	silty loam	5.8	sandy loam	6.8
50 cm.	silty loam	5.8	silty loam	6.5	silty loam	5.5	silty loam	6.8
1 cm.	clay loam	5.5	clay loam	6.0	clay loam	5.0	clay loam	7.0

These samples are probably representative of most of the levee soils of the Pacific lowlands. Bluish clay material with pH of 5.5 or lower represents the bottom of the levee material, which is highly variable in thickness, depending on the size of the river and levee and the position of the sample locality in relation to the stream mouth. Thickness of the levee material on the Merendó approximately three miles upstream from its confluence with the Atrato varies between four and six feet.

2   In most parts of the Spanish American tropics the term rastrojo (stubble) refers to the rank second-growth vegetation that springs up within a jungle plot after a crop has been harvested. In the Pacific lowlands of Colombia the term has come to mean the actual plots in cultivation along a river bank.

3   Samples taken in the backswamp along the Río Juradó on the northern Chocó coast revealed pH values between 5.2 and 6.0.

4   According to the La Motte color test, various samples of red clay taken at depths of 15 to 30 cm. below the surface in the upper Truandó drainage gave pH values between 4.5 and 4.8.

5   The association of the whitish, podsol-like soil with the weathering of sandstone and silicious gravels corroborates the views of P. W. Richards, The Tropical Rain Forest, 210-14, that tropical lowland podzols are determined largely by parent material. Such soils also appear to develop on sandy terraces above the flood level of adjacent streams. For example, at the farm of Santa María on the Río Rosario, near Tumaco, the following profile was obtained on a terrace cleared for bananas: (1) a humus-clay layer, 10 cm. thick, chocolate brown in color; (2) a whitish sandy clay zone, one meter thick; (3) a thick deposit of sand and sandy loam, which appeared to be the parent material. Podzolic

yellow soils have been noted also on Tertiary alluvial terraces at Córdoba, near Buenaventura. See Hans Jenny, "Great Soil Groups in the Equatorial Regions of Colombia, South America," Soil Science, LXVI (1948), 5-28; ref., 20. On recent developments concerning the question of tropical podzols see E. C. J. Mohr and F. A. Van Baren, Tropical Soils (The Hague, 1954), 398-410.

6   The following profile was obtained in the hills back of the village of Palambí on the Río Chaguí east of Tumaco: (1) a humus zone of black clay loam, 10 cm. thick; (2) a layer of whitish clay, 20 cm. thick; (3) red clay of undetermined thickness.

7   Miguel Cabello Balboa, "Verdadera descripción y relación larga de la Provincia y Tierra de las Esmeraldas," in his Obras (Quito, 1945), I, 16.

8   "Relación del Chocó..., 1780," Historia Documental del Chocó. 200.

9   Victor Manuel Patiño in his interesting article "El Maíz Chococito," América Indígena, XVI (1956), 309-346, describes slash-mulch farming for the cultivation of maiz in the Chocó and gives the present distribution of its use along the wet Pacific coastal areas of northwestern South America.

10   Chocó Indians living along the Truandó burn hillside plots during the dry season in February, but in the fertile spots of alluvium along the rivers they employ the slash-mulch system for raising maize. To native Esmeraldaños along the coast west of La Tola the slash-mulch system is unknown, but it has been re-introduced into the Santiago River area by Colombian immigrants from Barbacoas.

11   Alexander Skutch, "Problems in Milpa Agriculture," Turrialba, I (1950), 4-6. A resident of El General, Costa Rica, Skutch describes the system for raising beans called the picado. The practice is possibly of Indian origin in that area.

12   Some shifting cultivators in parts of southeast Asia employ slash-mulch planting for bananas and coconuts, but not for smaller plants. Recently a mulch system was introduced into the Philippines by agronomists of the U. S. Department of Agriculture for the raising of abacá plants. J. E. Spencer, University of California, personal communication; J. E. Spencer, "The Abacá Plant and its Fiber, Manila Hemp," Economic Botany, VII (1953), 195-213.

13   This system is described for the Barbacoas area in ANH Quito, Presidencia de la Real Audiencia, vol. 1670-1674, doc. no. 262 (1671). For the Chocó it is described in many documents extant in the Bogotá archives, e. g., AHNC, Caciques e Indios XXIII, ff. 955^v - 956^r (1708); Minas del Cauca II, ff. 684^r - 684^v (1720); Curas y Obispos V. f. 40^r (1735).

14   Additional conservative characters noted by Dr. Anderson: grains isodiametrical; ears 14-rowed, tapering gradually to the apex, and slightly enlarged at the basal end; small shanks at base of ear. (Personal communication.) Dr. Anderson kindly examined maize specimens collected from the Timbiquí and Guapi rivers in 1950. The maize types of these rivers appear to be identical to those seen in all other parts of the lowlands. Victor Manuel Patiño, "El Maíz Chococito, " loc. cit., describes the peculiar Chocó corn in detail and also points out some of its primitive characters.

15   An account of around 1540 briefly mentions the maíz menudo as the most significant food of the Indians and living on the western slope of the Cordillera Occidental. "Descripción de los pueblos de la provincia de Ancerma, " Pancheco and Cárdenas (eds.), Colección de documentos inéditos, III, 413.

16   Minga is a Quechua word which originally meant compulsory labor imposed on the common worker by the Inca governors. It retained that meaning under Spanish colonial rule, but since independence it has been applied to the system of co-operative work groups.

17   Hall describes similar elements in the agricultural routine as practiced by the Negro co-operative work groups of Haiti. Similarities to West African customs are pointed out. Robert B. Hall, "The Société Congo of the Ile à Gonave, " American Anthropologist, XXXI (1929), 685-700.

18   A similar maize food is described for the Saija Chocó. Wassén, "Notes on the Southern Chocó" loc. cit., 84; Gordon "Human Geography and Ecology, " loc. cit.

19   The Cayapa of Esmeraldas make an identical dish called tcambose, from which the word champú is derived. Barrett, "The Cayapa Indians of Ecuador, " loc. cit., I, 97.

20   Barrett, ibid., 97.

21   Alexander von Humboldt was among the earliest of the modern
      speculators to favor pre-conquest cultivation of plantains in
      America. Essai Politique sur le Royaumes de la Nouvelle Espagne
      (2nd ed., Paris, 1827), II, 382-97. His views on the subject
      were based principally on legend and the occurrence of Indian
      words for the plantain. More recent proponents of this view are
      Ricardo Latcham, La Agricultura precolombiana en Chile y otros
      paises vecinos (Santiago, 1936) and O. F. Cook, "Food plants in
      Ancient America," Smithsonian Institution, Annual Report, 1903
      (Washington, D. C. 1904), 481-97. Erland Nordenskiöld, "Origin
      of Indian Civilizations of South America," Comparative Ethnologi-
      cal Studies, No. IX (Göteborg, 1931), 25-27; "Deductions sug-
      gested by the Geographical Distribution of Some Post-Columbian
      Words Used by the Indians of South America," Comparative Eth-
      nological Studies, No. V (Göteborg, 1922), 64-76, has to date
      presented the best evidence against pre-Columbian cultivation of
      plantains and bananas in the New World. Recently summaries of
      the culture history of the plantain in America have been published
      by Carl Sauer, "Cultivated plants of South and Central America,"
      Handbook of South American Indians (Washington, D. C., 1950),
      VI, 487-543; ref., 526-27 and by Daniel Mesa Bernal, "El plátano
      su historia y orígen," Agricultura Tropical, VIII (October, 1952),
      23-26; "¿Es el banano indígena de América o es importado?,"
      Agricultura Tropical, VIII (November, 1952), 23-27.

22   Sauer, "Cultivated Plants," loc. cit., 527, emphasizes this point.
      For example, Pedro Cieza de León, who wrote in 1547, mentions
      the presence of large "platanares," or plantain fields, near Cali
      in the Cauca Valley of Colombia. He groups this plant, however,
      with a number of others imported from Europe. La Crónica del
      Perú, Colección Urteaga, Historiadores Clásicos del Perú, VII
      (Lima, 1924), 92.

23   "Descriptión de los pueblos de la provincia de Ancerma," Pacheco
      and Cárdenas (eds.), Colección de documentes III, 413. A report
      of 1593, describing the area around the mouth of the Munguidó
      River, lower San Juan drainage, mentions "... muchas barbacoas
      o casas de Indios, sementeras de maíz, muchas palmas y otros
      árboles frutales." Simón, Noticias historiales, V, 158.

24   Simón, Noticias historiales, V, 152.

25   A report written in 1648 by a Franciscan missionary describing
      the area near the confluence of the Arquía and Atrato rivers
      states, "... [the region] is rich in maize, plantains, peach palms,

and fish, flocks of wild birds and great quantities of wild pigs..."
Fray Gregorio Arcila Robledo, O.F.M., Las Misiones Franciscanas en Colombia (Bogotá, 1950), 18; the same report with
slightly different wording is found in AHNC, Curas y Obispos II,
f. 50ᵛ (1648). In describing the poor life of the Waunamá Indians
on the Río San Juan in 1665:"...[these Indians] have nothing
more to eat than plantains, a little fish, and maize..." ACC,
sig. 1184 (1665). In 1671 the Indians on the Río Timbiquí were
described as having the following "frutas de tierra," or native
foods: plantains, pineapple, papaya, yuca (sweet manioc), maize,
and fish. ANH Quito, Presidencia de la Real Audiencia, vol.
1670-1674, doc. no. 262 (1671).

26   Simón, Noticias Historiales, V, 365, 367.

27   Barrett, "The Cayapa Indians," loc. cit., 73, 96, states that the
Cayapa Indians of Esmeraldas have lost most of their ancient
maize foods, having substituted plantains as their chief item of
subsistence.

28   The large variety of plantains recognized by the local inhabitants
would surely be reduced by scientific classification. Even so,
the number of varieties and the occurrence of oddities, such as
the "chimbalo" and the "cajeto" in isolated spots argues for a
longer period of plantain cultivation than that given by the 300-
odd years of Spanish occupation. W. A. Archer, "Exploration in
the Chocó Intendency of Colombia," Scientific Monthly, XLIV
(1937), 418-34, ref., 432, reports from the Chocó a plantain
called "tahiti," which, like the cajeto reputedly bears a fruit
sheath containing poison that is used for tipping the points of
darts. Wassén, Notes on the Southern Groups of Chocó Indians,"
loc. cit., 107, states that the material taken from the peel is
non-poisonous, and probably is but a substance-forming ingredient
of the dart poison.

29   Other specific terms frequently used for this palm are G. speciosa
and G. utilis. Among the common names are pejibaye (Costa Rica),
macanilla (Venezuela), cachipay (interior Colombia), parijão
(Brazil). R. J. Seibert has emphasized the cultural significance
of the peach palm in his article "The Importance of Palms to
Latin America," Ceiba, I (1950), 65-74. See also Wilson Popenoe
and Otón Jiménez, "The Pejibaye, a Neglected Food Plant of
Tropical America," Journal of Heredity, XII (1921), 154-66.

30   Seibert, "The Importance of Palms," loc. cit., suggests that the

eastern slope of the Andes of Perú and Ecuador might be the center of domestication of the peach palm. He also associates its spread with peoples of Carib linguistic stock. Simón, Noticias Historiales, IV, 169, in describing the hardships experienced by the Gómez Hernández expedition into the Chocó in 1557, states, "... on many days [the Spaniards] found nothing to eat but fruits of a palm called pijibaes, or in other parts I think they call it cachipae...." The Spaniards were probably running across abandoned habitation sites where the chontaduro was growing. Today the presence of clumps of chontaduro is good evidence of a former house site.

31   On many of the rivers south of Buenaventura, chontaduro seeds are planted in a hot bed; the seedlings are transplanted near the house or sometimes in the rastrojo. In some areas of Latin America (Costa Rica) seedless varieties are cultivated.

32   O. F. Cook, "The Origin and Distribution of the Cocoa Palm," Contributions from the U.S. National Herbarium, VII (1901), 257-83; "History of the Coconut Palm in America," Contributions from the U.S. National Herbarium, XIV (1910), 271-93. The Pacific Coast pre-Columbian occurrence of the coconut is based on good first-hand observation before 1526 by Oviedo y Valdés, Historia General y Natural de las Indias (Madrid, 1851), I, 335. The Atlantic Coast occurrence is questionable. Sauer, "Cultivated Plants," loc. cit., 524-25.

33   The oft-mentioned statement that the coconut requires seaside locations for good growth is by no means true. Today in the Cauca Valley there are many coconut groves that produce abundantly.

34   The early accounts of the Pacific lowlands are silent on the cultivation of sugar cane in the Chocó. By the middle of the sixteenth century, Spaniards had established sizeable sugar cane plantations in the Cauca Valley near Cali. Cieza de León, La Crónica General, 92. Possibly cane was introduced into the Pacific lowlands via the Cali-Buenaventura road. In 1780 Captain Jiménez Donoso described Indian agriculture in the Chocó as "... very backward ..., because the only crops cultivated are maize, and sugar cane with a few herbs and roots ...," Relación del Chocó, 1780," Historia Documental del Chocó, 220.

35   Barrett, "The Cayapa Indians," loc. cit., 87-92. Most of the lowlanders, however, consume hard liquor imported from the adjacent highlands.

36 Simon, Noticias Historiales, V, 159. This reference is cited
    also by Wassén, "Notes on the Southern Groups of Chocó Indians,"
    loc. cit., 55-56, who briefly notes the presence of the platform
    gardens among the modern Waunamá. Most travelers who have
    written on the Pacific lowlands have commented on the azoteas.
    See, for example, G. Mollien, Travels in the Republic of
    Colombia in the years 1822 and 1823 (London, 1824), 305; Archer,
    "Exploration in the Chocó," loc. cit., 424.

    Within Latin America the platform gardens occur over
    a large part of the lower Amazon Basin, where they are called
    "hortas." See Antonio Teixeira Guerra, Estudio Geographico do
    Territorio do Amapá (Rio de Janeiro, 1954), 259-61. I have
    heard that they also occur in other parts of Brazil, such as the
    northeastern Sertões, Bahía, and Minas Gerais. It is said that
    in West Africa such gardens are made by the Wolof people living
    along the northern coast of the Cape Verde Peninsula near Dakar,
    and occasionally by the Temne of Sierra Leone. I have seen
    similar devices used in Gold Coast and Nigeria as drying plat-
    forms, but not as elevated gardens. The Brazilian distribution
    within a variety of tropical climates suggests introduction and
    spread by Negroid peoples.

37 Among the European medicinals verbena (Verbena officialis),
    albaca (Ocimum basilicum), malva, or mallow (Malva, spp.)
    yerbabuena or mint (Mentha, sp.), and verdolaga (Portulaca,
    spp.) are the ones most commonly planted in the azotea. American
    plants include various members of the goosefoot family, such as
    paico (Chenopodium ambrodiodes.).

38 In 1948 most of the Pacific Coast of the Chocó was swept by a
    cholera epidemic, killing most of the hogs. In 1943-44 and again
    in 1951 most of the Nariño coast was similarly affected.

39 Cuervo (ed.), "Descripción de la Provincia del Zitará...,"
    Colección de Documentos inéditos, II, 307.

40 For example, on the coast west of Tumaco the Hacienda de
    Matildita grazes 200 cattle and 25 horses on pastures of planted
    grass.

41 For a more optimistic view of cattle raising in the humid tropics
    see Raymond E. Crist, "Cattle Ranching in the Tropical Rain-
    forest," Scientific Monthly, LVI (1943), 521-27.

42   Lt. N. Michler, [Report] of his Survey for an Interoceanic Ship
Canal, Senate Executive Documents, loc. cit., 25, 43, 151. Rice
cultivation in the lower Atrato was probably introduced from
Cartagena. According to local inhabitants, rice was first cultivated in the lower Mira River, near the Ecuadorian border, in
1875; in the lower Patía River area in 1900, and at Nuquí, northern part of the Chocó coast, in 1910.

43   Import restrictions were made during the administration of
Enrique Olaya Herrera (1930-1934), who decreed that no bulky
foodstuff, such as rice, could be imported into Colombia. With
the resulting increase in price of the grain, rice cultivation became profitable in many areas of Colombia.

44   José Angel Córdoba, Bases para el fomento del cultivo del arróz
en El Chocó, Thesis, Facultad Nacional de Agronomía de Medillín,
1952. In 1950 rice production in the lower Atrato area was 6,300
metric tons; in the Pacific Coast and Baudó Valley, 3,900 metric
tons. Statistics are not available for other parts of the Pacific
lowlands. Compared to the large rice production on the mechanized farms in El Valle (the Cauca Valley around Cali), that of the
Pacific lowlands is still insignificant to the national economy of
Colombia.

45   Among the large number introduced, the rice varieties called
"chino" and "fortuno" are those cultivated most widely. The
former is broadcast in the backswamp areas; the latter does best
when planted on the drier rice plots.

46   As early as 1909 a large banana plantation was started by a German concern (Hamburg Columbien Bananen Aktien Gesellschaft)
a short distance inland from Puerto César, a few miles south of
Turbo on the eastern shore of the Gulf of Urabá. With an original concession of 5,000 hectares, 2,000 had been planted to
bananas by the end of 1913; at that time a long concrete loading
pier, a railway ten miles into the interior, and buildings at the
administration center were well under way. Owing to administrative and financial difficulties the company shortly thereafter
abandoned its project, and the entire concession reverted to
forest. NAUS, Consular Post Records, Quibdó, 15 Nov., 1913.

47   During the recent political disturbance (1952-1953) in Colombia,
the coastal banana boats ceased operation, and fruit production
came to a standstill. Since restoration of order in June, 1953,
production has resumed.

48   Bananas are grown extensively on the Domingodó, Tagachí, Sucio, Jiguamiandó, Truandó, and Salaquí tributaries of the Atrato. Prior to the last World War a sizeable banana industry was established on the Caribbean coast of the Chocó around Acandí. In 1938, for example, 220,000 stems from this section were exported to Panama and the United States. Geografía Económica de Colombia, VI, Chocó, 439.

49   Mr. H. A. Hamilton, manager of the Cía. Bananera del Chocó, personal communication.

50   The 1951 banana exports from Esmeraldas were more than 2,500,000 stems, approximately one-fifth of the total exports from Ecuador. In 1953 the national production was 20,000,000 stems, 15,000,000 of which were exported. Figures for banana production in Esmeraldas for the same year are not available, but the percentage of that province's production has been decreasing due to the penetration of sigatoka disease into the Santiago and Esmeraldas river drainages since 1952. Hispanic American Report VI (December, 1953), 27; VII (June, 1954), 30; VII (December, 1954), 30.

51   NAUS, Consular Post Records, Quibdó, 10 Jan., 1914. According to this report, in 1913, 400,000 cacao trees were said to be in production in the lower Baudó Valley. In 1953 most of these trees had been destroyed by the "witches' broom" blight.

52   Peregrino V. Ossa, "Terrenos Baldíos en Colombia," Boletín de la Sociedad Geográfica de Colombia, II (1935), 123-27. A farmer may claim up to 1000 hectares, a stockman up to 2,500 hectares. Legal papers and a topographic plan of the claim must be filed and small fees paid at the nearest national land office.

53   The dredging operations of mining companies, however, have forced farmers to abandon their plots and homes along the banks of various rivers, as in the upper San Juan and along the Telembí near Barbacoas. By law the mining companies are liable to pay occupiers of such land for damage done to crops and buildings.

54   The information on local land tenure among squatters was obtained from various informants in the following communities: Rosario, Río Guapi; Santa Rosa, Río Saija; San Bernardo, Río Patía del Norte; and San Isidro, Río Cajambre. According to the authorities of these localities, the same system was common to most of the rivers south of Buenaventura.

55   The terms cuadra and almud are used in most parts of the low-lands as the major unit of land division. On the Río Sanguianga, however, the Negroes employ the term botija, the name of a local container, which holds four almudes, to describe the unit of land division.

56   Probably Pseudoplatysoma, spp., common also in the Magdalena and lower Cauca rivers. Cecil Miles, Los Peces del Río Magdalena (Bogotá, 1947), 60-62.

57   The mojarras of northwestern South America belong to the Cichlidae family of the order Acanthopteri. The genera Petenia and Aequidens are the more common ones in the rivers of the Pacific lowlands. Miles, ibid., 207-211.

58   The characins belong to the Characidae family of the order Heterognati.

59   Wassén, "Notes on the Southern Groups of Chocó," loc. cit. 91, illustrates a variety of fish spears made by the Chocó-speaking Indians on the Río Saija. Such types can still be seen stored in the huts of these people, but the spear used in fishing at the present time is similar to the type described above.

60   Nordenskiöld believes that the throw (or cast) net is of African origin, and was acquired by some Latin America Indians through Negro contacts. However, he gives no supporting evidence for this belief. Erland Nordenskiöld, "Modifications in Indian Culture through Inventions and Loans," Comparative Ethnographical Studies, VIII (1930), 108-109.

61   Tephrosia toxicaria (barbasco), Clibadium polygynum (catalina), Phyllanthus acuminatus (chirrinchao), Lonchocarpus, spp. (barbasco, commonly cultivated and a source of the insecticide, rotenone). Archer, "Exploration in Chocó," loc. cit. 431; Robert F. Heizer, "Fish Poisons," Handbook of South American Indians, V (1949), 277-81. An interesting description of the use of fish poison on the upper Huallaga River in Peru has been written by Edwin Doran, Jr., "Fish Poisoning on the Río Huallaga, Perú," Texas Journal of Science, V (1953), 204-215.

62   Most of the species of the Pacific coast of Colombia are similar to those of Central America, Mexico, and southern California. Seth E. Meek and Samuel Hildebrand, "The Marine Fishes of Panama," Field Museum of Natural History, Publ. 215,

Zoological Ser., XV (1923). For a general survey of the coastal fisheries of the Pacific lowlands, see Arnold Wilton Janson, "La pesca en la costa del Pacífico," Colombia, I (1944), No. 3 and 4, 99-107.

63 The chinchorro, or seine net, varies in length from 100 to 300 feet and in size of mesh from one-quarter inch to two inches, according to the type of fish sought. The atarraya, or cast net, is either round and ten feet in diameter or oblong with dimentions of fifteen by eight feet. The center cord for hauling in the net is from twenty-five to forty feet long.

64 In the Tumaco and Guapi areas bundles of one-quarter arroba (six pounds), one-half arroba (twelve pounds), one arroba (24 pounds) and four arrobas, or one quintal (96 pounds) are made.

65 Formerly Coelogenys paca. The generic and specific names of the mammals used in this section have been taken from Gerrit D. Miller and Remington Kellogg, List of North American Recent Mammals, U.S. National Museum, Bull. 205 (Washington, D.C., 1955).

66 In pre-Columbian times the peccary appears to have been semi-domesticated by the forest Indians. In the 1540's Andagoya states that in the Barbacoas area" ... most of the [Indian] houses have their pens for wild hogs...." Navarrete, Colección de Viages, III, 437. Writing in the 1620's, Fray Pedro Simón relates that droves of peccaries numbering from 300 to 400 animals roamed the forests of the lower Cauca area. He also states that the Yamací Indians of the same area caught young pigs and fattened them in pens in the houses. Noticias Historiales, V, 77. The same custom was practiced by the Cuna (?) Indians living on the eastern shore of the Gulf of Urabá. Simón, ibid., 172. Still to-day the Chocó tether and fatten in the hut young peccaries that they chance to trap alive during a hunt.

67 "Descripción de la Provincia del Zitará," in Cuervo (ed.), Colección de documentos inéditos, II, 317, et seq.

68 AHNC, Minas del Cauca I, ff. 110^r, 117^r (1751); Protocolos XXV, ff. 82^r - 86^v (1746). Similar exploitation of the manatee occurred in the ciénagas of the lower Sinú, Magdalena, and Cauca rivers. According to Simón, Noticias Historiales, IV, 193, more than 30,000 animals were killed yearly in the backswamps of the lower Atrato.

69   A few old Negroes at San Bernardo on the upper Patía del Norte still keep the blowgun and its related paraphernalia in their huts; occasionally they take the gun into the forest to kill squirrels and monkeys. The younger men scornfully reject such a device, considering beneath their dignity the use of a tool so Indian as the blowgun. Writing in the 1830's, Lafond implies that the instrument was used by both Negro and Indian in the Chocó. Gabriel Lafond, "Excursion dans la rivière de Chinquiquirá, qui a son embouchure dans la baie de Cascajal (San Buenaventura), province du Chocó dans la Colombie," Bull. de la Société de Géographie, Ser. 2, XI (1839), 121-43.

70   Simón, Noticias Historiales, IV, V, gives ample evidence that the blowgun and poisoned darts were used by the Chocó and Waunamá groups at the time of Spanish contact (last half of sixteenth century). Cf. Alfred Métraux, "Weapons," Handbook of South American Indians, V, 248-52; Jens Yde, "The Regional Distribution of South American Blowgun Types," Journal de la Société des Américanistes, N.S., XXXVII (1948), 275-317.

71   Wassén, "Notes on the Southern Chocó," loc. cit., 90-98. The Cayapa also prepare dart poison from a vegetable sap similar to that used by the Waunamá. Barrett, "The Cayapa Indians of Ecuador," loc. cit., I, 114; Wassén, "Notes on the Southern Chocó," loc. cit., 107-108.

72   Wassén, "Notes on the Southern Chocó," loc. cit. 99-101; 105-107. The frog is induced to secrete by singeing him over a fire. Cochrane, writing in the 1820's, gives an interesting description of the methods of obtaining and preparing the frog poison. "The poison is obtained from a small, harmless frog, called rana de veneno, about three inches long, yellow on the back, with very large black eyes. It is only found (as my host informed me) in this place [upper Tamana, the Chocó], and another, called Pelmar. Those who use this poison catch the frogs in the woods, and confine them in a hollow cane, where they take one of the unfortunate reptiles, and pass a pointed stick down his throat, and out at one of his legs. This torture makes the poor frog perspire very much, especially on the back, which becomes covered with white froth: this is the most powerful poison that he yields, and in this they dip or roll the points of their arrows, which will preserve their destructive power for a year. Afterwards, below this white substance, appears a yellow oil, which is carefully scraped off, and retains its deadly influence for four or six months, according to the goodness (as they say) of the frog. By this means,

from one frog sufficient poison is obtained for about fifty arrows. Cochrane, Travels in Colombia, II, 406-407.

73   Métraux, "Weapons," loc. cit., 249.

74   Today the Chocó of the upper Sinú still use the lance for hunting peccary. Gordon, "Human Geography and Ecology," loc. cit., 37.

75   In 1952 the inhabitants of some rivers were complaining that deer were becoming so numerous and bold that they were destroying crops near the settlements.

76   Cochrane, Travels in Colombia, II, 423; Lafond, "Excursion dans la rivière," loc. cit., 128.

77   Lt. N. Michler, "[Report] of his Survey for an Interoceanic Ship Canal," 27, 42, 196-97. At that time eighty tons of rubber were collected annually in the lower Atrato. The product was shipped to New York via Turbo and Cartagena. Later the caucheros antioqueños swarmed over the western slope of the Cordillera Occidental collecting rubber and balata latex. Most of their product was exported via the lower Atrato. Jorge Brisson, Exploración en el Alto Chocó (Bogotá, 1895), 58.

78   According to a U. S. consular report of 1913, 1,500,000 rubber trees (mainly castilla) had been planted in the Chocó, there being plantations of 100,000 trees in the Baudó Valley. These plantations, as well as those on the Río Sucio, were abandoned after World War I. For some years prior to 1913, rubber latex was exceeded only by precious metals as the most valuable export from the Chocó. NAUS, Consular Post Records, Quibdó, 10 Jan., 1914. John C. Treadwell, et al. "Possibilities for Para Rubber Production in Northern Tropical America," Trade Promotion Series No. 40, Department of Commerce (Washington, D.C., 1926), 226-27.

79   As early as 1877 the caucheros had destroyed most of the castilla trees in the Esmeraldas lowlands and were forced to gather latex in the remote mountain areas at increasing costs. Wolf, Viajes científicos, III, 42-43.

80   NAUS, Records of the Rubber Development Corporation. Reports for Western Colombia, 1943-44.

81   The terminology used is from the Río Mira. In the Chocó, diagonal incisions are sometimes made in castilla and the latex collected in receptacles. To coagulate the latex the sap of a vine called batatilla (Rivea campanulata) is introduced. When a large amount of latex has been collected it is made into large balls, called andullos. Most of the rubber now gathered in the Pacific lowlands is consumed in small rubber manufacturing plants in Medellín, Cali, and Bogotá.

82   O. F. Cook, "New Genera and Species of Ivory Palms from Colombia, Ecuador, and Peru," Journal of the Washington Academy of Science, XVII (1927), 218-30.

83   The palm is fairly abundant also in the province of Manabí, western Ecuador. Wolf, Viajes científicos, III, 42. In 1913 export of tagua nuts from the Chocó was as follows: Río León, 8,000 tons; Río Sucio, 3,000 tons; Río Baudó, 1,500 tons; Acandí, 700 tons. NAUS, Consular Post Records, Quibdó, 10 January, 1914.

84   Walter R. Scheiber, "Tagua," Agriculture in the Americas, (1946), 51-53.

85   Small button factories were in operation in Tumaco (one) and Esmeraldas (two) until World War II.

86   According to informants in Tumaco, formerly the Colombian government forbade the cutting of tagua palms in clearing fields for cultivation. It was not ascertained whether such a law is still in force.

87   Pierre Gourou, The Tropical World, 75-77.

88   Until the revision of foreign trade policies by the Olaya Herrera administration (1930-34), Colombia imported most of its cheap construction timber from the west coast of the United States.

89   According to the regional forest inspector, in 1952 the six mills in Buenaventura were producing daily 1,500 board feet of lumber; it was estimated that 20,000 board feet was being produced monthly along the entire Pacific coast of Colombia.

90   During World War II an Italian company established a tannin extract plant on the Atrato Delta, using local mangrove bark for raw material. In 1947 the plant was disassembled.

91 Since the writer has treated various aspects of mining in the
    Pacific lowlands in previous publications, only a summary will
    be presented here. See Robert C. West, "Colonial Placer Mining
    in Colombia," Louisiana State University Studies, Social Science
    Series, No. 2 (Baton Rouge, 1952); "Folk Mining in Colombia,"
    Economic Geography, XXVIII (1952), 323-30.

92 There has been no complete study made of the geology of the
    Pacific lowland placer deposits. Results of investigations of
    small individual districts can be found in E. Bruet, "Sur les
    Formations aurifères du versant pacifique de la Cordillère
    Occidentale de la Colombie au Sud de Buenaventura," Comptes
    Rendus de la Société Géologique de France, XV (1933), 241-42;
    E. Aubert de la Rüe, "Observations géologiques sur les vallées
    du Yurumanguí et du Naya," Revue de géographie physique et de
    géologie dynamique, VI (1933), 191-201; Anon., "Informe cientí-
    fico sobre la región Quibdó-Buenaventura," Minería, V (1937),
    4550-65.

93 The system of equal division of proceeds between the mine owner
    and the workers is used in the Barbacoas mining district. Since
    1945 the compañías in the upper San Juan give two-thirds of the
    gold and platinum mined to the workers, one-third to the mine
    owner. Prior to 1945 the mine owner received all of the gold and
    one-half of the platinum extracted from his holdings.

94 Henry G. Granger and Edward B. Treville, "Mining Districts of
    Colombia," Transactions of the American Institute of Mining
    Engineers, XXVIII (1899), 33-87. In 1893 hydraulicking was
    undertaken in the interfluve gravels between the Bebará and
    Bebaramá rivers by a French-Belgian concern, Mines du Cauca.
    Brisson, Exploración en el Alto Chocó, 310.

95 This concern was an affiliate of the Consolidated Gold Fields of
    South Africa which had acquired title to mining properties in the
    upper San Juan area in 1913. "Informe científico sobre la región
    de Quibdó-Buenaventura," loc. cit., 4558.

96 The British Platinum and Gold Corporation operated a dredge on
    the Río Opogadó between 1922 and 1929. After the dredge found-
    ered in 1929 the company ceased operation.

97 After reorganization in 1915, the company was called "The New
    Timbiquí Gold Mines, Ltd." Sofonías Yacup, Litoral Recóndito
    (Bogotá, 1934), 152.

98   Richmond Petroleum Company began to drill in 1953 on the Río
      Buchadó, a few miles upstream from its confluence with the
      Atrato in the Chocó. Drilling was stopped at approximately 10,300
      feet. The well was abandoned in August, 1954.

99   The Cayapa and Cuna wove some cotton and agave fiber cloth on
      vertical hand looms. Barrett, "The Cayapa Indians," loc. cit.,
      II, 259-74; David B. Stout, "The Cuna," Handbook of South
      American Indians, IV, 257-68. Negro slaves, however, had
      comparatively little contact with these groups.

100   "Relación del Chocó..., 1780," Historia Documental del Chocó,
      221. The Cayapa and Cuna both made bark cloth, but used it
      chiefly for sleeping mats.

101   The manufacture of bark cloth was fairly widespread among the
      American Indians. Although used in some parts of North America,
      the cloth was more significant as a culture trait from southern
      Mexico to Bolivia. Within this area it was used chiefly by the
      forest Indians of the upper Amazon, Orinoco, northwestern South
      America, and the Caribbean coast of Central America. Erland
      Nordenskiöld, "The Ethnography of South America seen from
      Mojos in Bolivia," Comparative Ethnological Studies, III (1924),
      map 30; Alfred Métraux, "Bark Cloth," Handbook of South American
      Indians, V, 67-69; R. B. White, "Notes on the Aboriginal Races
      of the Northwestern Provinces of South America," Journal of the
      Royal Anthropological Institute of Great Britain and Ireland,
      XIII (1884), 240-56; ref., 244. Like so many other Indian traits
      of northwestern South America, bark cloth is also widespread in
      Oceania and southeast Asis.

102   This costume, copied directly from Indian dress, was described
      in 1857 for the lower Atrato by Lt. Michler, "[Report] on his sur-
      vey for an Interoceanic Ship Canal ...," 43; in 1879 for Esmeraldas
      by Wolf, " Viajes científicos, III, 49; and in 1860 for the Buena-
      ventura area by Felipe Pérez, Jeografía física i política del
      estado del Cauca (Bogotá, 1862), 129-30.

103   Both weaves are described and illustrated by Wassén, "Notes on
      the Southern Chocó," loc. cit., 75-83, and Barrett, "The Cayapa
      Indians," loc. cit. 183-251. The lattice weave has a widespread
      but curiously disjunct distribution among the Indians in the rain
      forests of South America: southwestern Amazon, Orinoco,
      Guianas, and Pacific lowlands of Colombia and northwestern
      Ecuador. Nordenskiöld, "The Ethnography of South America

seen from Mojos," loc. cit., map 27. Today burden baskets of a
similar hexagonal lattice weave are made in the lower Amazon
Basin by both whites and Negroids.

104   Wassén, "Notes on the Southern Chocó," loc. cit., 62; Barrett,
       "The Cayapa Indians," loc. cit., 154-59.

105   Wassén, "Notes on the Southern Chocó," loc. cit., 61.

106   Gunter Tessmann, Die Pangwe, völkerkundliche Monographie
       eines west-afrikanischen Negerstammes (Berlin 1913), II, 323-24;
       Karl Izikowitz, "Musical and other sound instruments of the South
       American Indians," Göteborgs Kungl. Vetenskaps-och Vitterhets-
       Samhalles Handlingar, ser. A. Band V (1935), 179-80.

107   Erland Nordenskiöld, "Indianerna på Panamanaset," Ymer, XLVIII
       (1928), 85-110; ref. 105.

108   According to Izikowitz, "Musical and other Instruments," loc.
       cit., 144-47, the tubular rattle used by the Cuna of Panama and
       the Colorado of Ecuador is similar to that of the Pangwe of the
       Cameroons in Africa.

109   Many documents extant in the colonial archives of Colombia give
       evidence of the significant role played by the Indians in river trans-
       port; for example, AHNC, Caciques e Indios X, f. 509^v (1691);
       XXIII, f. 999^r, 1024^r (1708); Minas del Cauca I, f. 121^v (1751).
       In the Chocó the canoe supply was regulated by the Spanish cor-
       regidores, who had legal jurisdiction over Indians within their
       respective territories, Indians usually received a nominal sum
       for each canoe manufactured, but the corregidor made enormous
       profits by reselling the product to the miners. Often the corregi-
       dor kept the canoes and established his own transport system with
       Indian labor, charging the miners exhorbitant freight rates.

110   Probably the miners' opinions on the Negroes' incapabilities were
       highly exaggerated, in order to convince government officials of
       the need to retain Indian labor in such capacities as boatmen and
       suppliers of food to the mines. Negro slaves directly from the
       African west coast surely knew something of canoes, as the river-
       dwelling Africans do today. However, many of the Negroes work-
       ing in the lowland mining camps were criollos (second or third
       generation slaves), and some bozales (recent arrivals), many
       having come from the interior of the Sudan or from Angola, where
       canoemanship is not significant. By the first quarter of the

seventeenth century, Negro slaves had replaced Indians as canoemen on the Río Magdalena. Simón, Noticias Historiales, III,
293.

111   The Cayapa exaggerate the upward flare of the ends of the plat-
forms, which are narrower than those on the canoes made by the
Chocó and Waunamá. Barrett, "The Cayapa Indians," loc. cit.,
I, 141.

112   A dugout of similar appearance is found on the upper Huallaga,
eastern Peru. Doran, "Fish Poisoning," loc. cit., 210.

113   In the Chocó the large dugouts are called champas, from the Chocó
word for canoe, hampa; south of Buenaventura they are called
simply canoa. The smaller canoes go by a variety of names, the
most common of which is potro or potrillo (young horse, or colt).
Along the Río Mira and in Esmeraldas they are often called
chingas.

114   The introduction of iron tools after the Spanish conquest may
have altered both form and construction methods of aboriginal
canoes. Unfortunately, the colonial sources are silent on details
of design and construction of the Indian craft.

115   The blade of the female paddle is so carved as to produce a slight
angle midway between the point and the beginning of the handle.
If held at a certain angle during the stroke, the blade produces a
slight "roaring" sound, which the natives call a ronca. To produce such a noise or roncar while paddling is considered an especially feminine trait among Indian and Negro women. The trait
may also have some erotic significance, or may be simply a
flirtaceous action on the part of the women. Such sounds always
arouse lewd remarks among the men.

116   The balsa log stabilizers are thought to be an incipient form of the
double outrigger introduced from southeast Asia by the Spaniards.
James Hornell, "South American Balanced Canoes," Man, XXVIII
(1928), 129-33.

117   S. K. Lothrop, "Aboriginal Navigation off the west Coast of South
America," Journal of the Royal Anthropological Institute of Great
Britain and Ireland, LXII (1932), 229-56.

118   On the Atrato seagoing craft up to 200 tons reach Quibdó with ease,
and during high water can continue as far as La Vuelta, twenty-five

miles upstream from the capital. Boats of 100 tons ascend the San Juan River to Negría (80 miles from the mouth); those of 50 tons reach Bebedó (95 miles from the mouth); and smaller launches go up as far as Andagoya camp. Hans Tanner, "Verkehrsprobleme Kolombiens," Geographica Helvetica, IV (1929), 137-54; ref., 143. Jorge Mendoza Nieto, Geografía Illustrada del Chocó (Bogotá, 1942), 74-75.

119 There exists a voluminous literature on the possibilities of a trans-oceanic canal via these two routes. The most recent U. S. official survey was published as the Special Report of the Governor of the Panama Canal on the Atrato-Truandó Canal Route, under Public Law 280, 79th Congress, 1st Session (Canal Zone, 1949).

120 According to Humboldt, Viaje a las regiones equinocciales, V, 206, in 1788 a small canal, the Raspadura, was dug to connect the San Juan and Atrato rivers. Further research, however, has disproved this statement. A. Ernst, "Der angeblich Canal des Río Raspadura in Neugranada," Globus, XXIV (1873), 214-15; Admiral Illingsworth, "Remarks on the Isthmus of Cupica," Proceedings of the Royal Geographical Society, I (1856), 866-87.

121 The covered bridge in the Pacific lowlands probably was introduced by the Antioqueños. In Antioquia the covered bridge is common, the roof often being tiled.

122 ACC, sig. 1825 (1633); sig. 8363 (1709).

123 The sillero was a common type of passenger carrier in many parts of Colombia until the beginning of the present century. For a description of the trip along the Cartago-Nóvita trail by sillero see Cochrane, Travels in Colombia, II, 307-411. The silla and sillero may be Indian traits, for in the early sixteenth century they are described by Cieza de León as an ordinary method of travel on the old Cali-Buenaventura trail. La Crónica General del Perú, I, 98.

124 Alfredo Ortega, Ferrocarriles Colombianos, resumen histórico, Biblioteca de Historia Nacional, XXVI, (Bogotá, 1920-1923), I, 462, 498.

125 In 1952 ten kilometers of the auto road out of Buenaventura were paved with concrete slabs. Formerly heavy-truck traffic turned this stretch into a quagmire; two-ton trucks, stuck in a large mudhole, would sometimes sink out of sight.

126 A French firm began construction on this line in 1952. Maps showing the lowland section of this railroad and dated prior to 1952 are in error.

127 ACC, sig. 4828 (1762).

128 Santa Bárbara de la Isla del Gallo was probably founded soon after the settlement of the Barbacoas mining district in 1610. In 1635 the port is mentioned as the outlet for Santa María del Puerto (Barbacoas), and during the last quarter of the seventeenth century it was considered as one of the important ports along the Pacific coast of northwestern South America. AGI, Audiencia de Quito XVI, (76-6-9) (1635); ACC, sig. 723 (1686).

129 A Spanish settlement on Tumaco Island had been established by 1675, and five years later it is mentioned as a military garrison and port. ACC. sig. 1790 (1675); AHNC, Curas y Obispos XXI, f. 710^{r} (1680).

130 ACC, sig. 417 (1688). By 1688 a small shipyard had been established in the port. Apparently, the colonial site was near the present fishing village of Carrizo near the mouth of the Iscuandé. Peréz, Jeografía, 289.

131 Sebastían de Magaña, "Carta de Sebastían de Magaña, visitador de la Real Caja de Popayán, [Dec. 12, 1547]," Colección de Documentos Inéditos relativos al Adelantado Capitán don Sebastían de Benalcázar, 1535-1565. Publicaciones del Archivo Municipal (Quito, 1936), X, 279; Gustave Arboleda, Historia de Cali (Cali, 1928), 198.

132 Cieza de León, La Crónica General, 98.

133 Mollien, Travels in Colombia, 299, describes the port as having a dozen huts inhabited by Negroes and mulattoes, a barrack of eleven soldiers, and the residence of the governor.

134 Trautwine, "Rough Notes . . . ," 299.

135 Escobar, Bahías de Málaga y Buenaventura, v.

136 AHNC, Caciques e Indios XXVI, f. 906^{r} (1788), XXXVIII, f. 725^{v} (1784).

BIBLIOGRAPHY

I Unpublished Documents

Archivo Central del Cauca, Popayán (ACC)

Signatura:	132	1184	4362
	166	1790	4828
	417	1825	4920
	440	2134	6053
	723	2307	6056
	1099	3144	8363

Archivo Histórico Nacional de Colombia (AHNC)

Caciques e Indios, vols. X, XXIII, XXVI, XXXVIII, LXVII
Curas y Obispos, vols. II, V, XXL, XXV, XXIX, XXXV, XLIV
Minas del Cauca, vols. I, II, V, VI
Negros y Esclavos del Cauca, vol. IV
Poblaciones del Cauca, Vol. II
Protocolos, vol. XXV
Secretaría de Guerra y Marina, vol. IV

Archivo Nacional de Historia, Quito (ANH)

Presidencia de la Real Audiencia de Quito

Vols. 1670-1674
1724-1725
1729-1730
1739-1740

Archivo General de Indias, Sevilla (AGI)

Patronato, legajo 233, ramo 2 Sobre la pacificación de indios
Sirambidies, Chocoes, y otros de las montañas de
Toro, 1620-1630.

Patronato, legajo 233, ramo 12 Fray Ambrosio Vallejo, obispo de Popayán al Rey, sobre la población de las Minas de Toro, 9 November, 1630.

Audiencia de Quito, legajo XVI. Francisco de Berrío to the king, Cartago, 28 April, 1599.

Audiencia de Quito, legajo XVI. Relación de los sucesos que tuve yo el capitán Francisco Ramírez de la Serna en la jornada... [que] hice con mi compañía a la pacificación de las provincias de indios Piles, Timbas, y Cacahambres que estan rebelados y alzados ... Cali, 18 April, 1610.

Audiencia de Quito, legajo XVI. Testimonio del Capitán Jorge de Santa María. Cali, 20 March, 1631.

Audiencia de Quito, legajo XVI. Juan Bermúdez de Castro to the king. Popayán, 24 April, 1631.

Audiencia de Quito, legajo XVI. Juan Bermúdez de Castro to the king, Popayán, 17 May, 1631.

Audiencia de Quito, legajo XVI. Lorenzo de Villaquirán to the king. Popayán, 31 May, 1635.

Audiencia de Quito, legajo XVIII. Diego Inclán Valdés to the queen. Quito, 15 June, 1675.

National Archives of the United States, Washington, D. C. (NAUS)

Consular Post Records, Quibdó, 1913-1915.
Records of the Rubber Development Corporation. Reports for Western Colombia, 1943-1944.

Unpublished Theses and Dissertations

Arboleda, José Rafael, S. J. "The Ethnohistory of the Colombian Negroes," Unpublished M.S. thesis, Northwestern University, Evanston, 1950.

Córdoba, José Angel. "Bases para el fomento del cultivo del arroz en El Chocó," Unpublished thesis, Facultad Nacional de Agronomía de Medellín, Medellín, 1952.

Gordon, B. LeRoy. "Human Geography and Ecology in the Sinú Country of Colombia," Unpublished PhD. dissertation, University of California, Berkeley, 1954.

II Printed Materials

Aguirre Beltrán, Gonzalo. "Tribal origins of slaves in Mexico,"
Journal of Negro History, XXXI (1946), 269-353.

Anderson, J. L. "Petroleum Geology of Colombia," Bulletin of the
American Association of Petroleum Geologists, XXIX, (1945),
1065-1142.

Anuario Estadístico de Colombia. Bogotá, 1875.

Anuario Meteorológico, Departmento de Irrigación, Ministerio de
Economía Nacional (Bogotá, 1934-1947).

Anuario Meteorológico, 1949; 1950-1951; 1952-1953-1954, Ministerio
de Agricultura (Bogotá, 1955).

Arauz, Julio. La Tolita. Quito, 1946

Arboleda, José Rafael. "Nuevas investigaciones afrocolombianos,"
Revista Javeriana, XXXVII (1952), 197-206.

Arboleda, Gustavo, Historia de Cali. Cali, 1928.

Archer, W. A. "Exploration in the Chocó Intendency of Colombia,"
Scientific Monthly, XLIV (1937), 418-34.

Arcila Robledo, Fray Gregoria. Las Misiones Franciscanas en
Colombia. Bogotá, 1950.

Atlas of Distribution of Diseases. American Geographical Society
(New York, 1950 -).

Aubert de la Rüe, E. "Observations géologiques sur les vallées du
Yurumanguí et du Naya," Revue de géographie physique et de
géologie dynamique, VI (1933), 191-201.

Barrett, S.A. "The Cayapa Indians of Ecuador," Indian Notes and
Monographs, No. XL. Museum of the American Indian, Heye
Foundation, 2 vols. (New York, 1925).

Bates, Marston. "Observations on the distribution of diurnal mosquitos in a tropical forest," Ecology, XXV (1944), 159-70.

Bennett, W.C. "Habitations," Handbook of South American Indians,

Bureau of American Ethnology, Bull. 143 (Washington, D.C., 1949), V, 1-20.

Bernard, Étienne, Le climat écologique de la cuvette centrale congolaise. Brussels, 1945.

Bierck, Harold A., Jr. "The Struggle for Abolition in Gran Colombia," Hispanic American Historical Review, XXXIII (1953), 365-86.

Block, Hans. "La Colonización del Chocó desde el Valle del Cauca," Boletín de la Sociedad Geográfica de Colombia, VII (1948), 40-42.

Brisson, Jorge. Exploración en el Alto Chocó. Bogotá, 1895.

Brown, J. S. "A Study of Coastal Ground Water," Water Supply Paper, No. 534. U. S. Geological Survey (Washington, D.C., 1925)

Bruet, E. "Sur les Formations aurifères du versant pacifique de la Cordillère Occidentale de la Colombie au Sud de Buenaventura," Comptes Rendus de la Société Géologique de France, XV (1933), 241-42.

Buchanan, K. M. and Pugh, J. C. Land and People in Nigeria. London, 1955.

Cabello Balboa, Miguel. Obras. Quito, 1945.

Censo General de la República de Colombia, Levantado el 5 de Marzo de 1912. Bogotá, 1912.

Censo de la Población de la Republica de Colombia, levantado el 14 de Octubre de 1918. Bogotá, 1924.

Chapman, V. J. "The Botany of the Jamaica Shoreline," Geographical Journal, XCVI (1940), 312-23.

Cieza de León, Pedro de. La Crónica General del Perú. Colección Urteaga, VII (Lima, 1924).

Cochrane, Capt. Charles Stuart. Travels in Colombia during the years 1823 and 1824. 2 vols., London, 1825.

Colección de Documentos Inéditos relativos al Adelantado Capitán Don Sebastián de Benalcázar, 1535-65. Publicaciones del Archivo

Municipal, X (Quito, 1936).

Collins, Lt. Frederick, U.S.N. "Report of a Survey of the Proposed Route for an Inter-oceanic Ship Canal by way of the Atrato, Napipí, and Doguadó Rivers, in the Canton of Chocó, State of Cauca, United States of Colombia, by the U. S. Expedition of 1875. Lt. Frederick Collins, U.S.N., Commanding," Senate Executive Document No. 75, 45th Congress, 3rd. Session, June, 1875 (Washington, D.C., 1879).

"Colonia Agrícola de Bahía Solano," Tierras y Aguas, I (1938), 6-9.

Concha y Vanegas, Antonio. "Relación entre la geografía y la lucha antimalárica en Colombia," Boletín de la Sociedad Geográfica de Colombia, X (1952), 188-200.

Conto, Nicomedes. "Notas de la Gobernación sobre Empréstito Forzozo," Unión Chocoana, No. XXII (Quibdó, 26 May, 1855).

Cook, O. F. "The Origin and Distribution of the Cocoa Palm," Contributions from the U.S. National Herbarium, VII (1901). 257-83.

_____. "Food Plants in Ancient America," Annual Report, 1903, Smithsonian Institution (Washington, D.C., 1904), 481-97.

_____, "History of the Coconut Palm in America," Contributions from the U.S. National Herbarium, XIV (1910), 271-93.

_____. "New Genera and Species of Ivory Palm from Colombia, Ecuador, and Peru," Journal of the Washington Academy of Science, XVII (1927), 218-30.

Crist, Raymond E. "Cattle Ranching in the Tropical Rainforest," Scientific Monthly, LVI (1943), 521-27.

Cuatrecasas, José. "Vistazo a la vegetación natural del Bajo Calima," Revista de la Academia Colombiana de Ciéncias Exactas, Físico-Químicas y Naturales, VII (1947), 306-312.

_____. "Gutíferas nuevas o poco conocidas en Colombia," Anales del Instituto de Biología, XX (1949), 91-112.

_____. "Mangroves of the Pacific Coast of South America," [Abstract], A Series of Lectures presented before the Department of Botany Seminar, Northwestern University, by the Botanical Staff of the Chicago Natural History Museum (Evanston, 1952), 8-10.

Cuervo, Antonio B. (ed.). Colección de Documentos Inéditos sobre la Geografía e Historia de Colombia. 4 vols. Bogotá, 1891-1894.

Davis, J.H. "Mangroves, makers of lands," Nature Magazine, XXXI (1938), 551-53.

_____. "The Ecology and Geologic Role of Mangroves in Florida," Papers from the Tortugas Laboratory of the Carnegie Institution of Washington, XXXII (1940), 303-412.

Day, P.C. "Climatalogical Data for Andagoya, Republic of Colombia, South America," Monthly Weather Review, LIV (1926), 376-78.

D'Harcourt, Raoul. "Archéologie de la Province d'Esmeraldas (Equateur). Céramique, Objets en pierre," Journal de la Société des Américanistes, XXXIV (1942), 61-200.

Dobby, E.H.G. Southeast Asia. London, 1950.

Doran, Edwin Jr. "Fish Poisoning on the Río Huallaga, Peru," Texas Journal of Science, V (1953), 204-215.

Eggers, Baron H. von. "Die Manglares in Ecuador," Botanisches Centralblatt, LII (1892), 48-52.

Egler, Frank E. "The Dispersal and Establishment of Red Mangrove, Rhizophora, in Florida," The Caribbean Forester, IX (1948), 299-320.

_____. "Southeast Saline Everglades Vegetation, Florida, and its management," Vegetatio, III (1950).

Elías Ortiz, Sergio, "Los Indios Yurumanguíes," Acta Americana IV (1946), 10-25.

_____. "The Modern Quillacinga, Pasto, and Coaiquer," Handbook of South American Indians, Bureau of American Ethnology, Bull. 143 (Washington, 1946), II, 961-68.

Erichson, R. "Die Mangrove-Vegetation," Natur, XVI (1925), 190-99.

Ernst, A. "Der angeblich Canal des Río Raspadura in Neugranada," Globus, XXIV (1873), 214-15.

Escobar, Paulo Emilio. Bahías de Málaga y Buenaventura. Bogotá, 1921.

Estadística Jeneral de la Nueva Granada..., parte primera. Bogotá, 1848.

Ferdon, Edwin N., Jr. "Reconnaissance in Esmeraldas," Palacio, XLVII (1940), 257-72; XLVII (1941), 7-15.

_____. "Studies in Ecuadorian Geography," Monograph of the School of American Research, No. XV (Santa Fe, New Mexico, 1950).

Flemming, August. "Das Delta des Río Mira in Colombia," Das Ausland, XLIII (1870), 64.

Foxworthy, F.W. "Distribution and Utilization of the Mangrove-swamp of Malaya," Annales du Jardin Botanique de Buitenzorg, suppl. 3, pt. 1 (1910), 319-44.

Foxworthy, F. W. and Matthews, D. M. "Mangrove and Nipah Swamps of North Borneo," Department of Forestry, B.N.B., Bulletin No. III (1917).

Franze, Bruno, "Die Niederschlagsverhaltnisse in Südamerida," Petermanns Mitteilungen, Ergänzungsheft 193 (1927).

Freise, F.W. "Untersuchungen am Schlick der Mangrovküste Brasiliens," Chemie der Erde, II (1938), 333-55.

Freyberg, G. von. "Zerstörung and Sedimentation an der Mangrovküste Brasiliens," Leopoldina, VI (1930), 69-117.

Gansser, A. "Geological and Petrographical Notes on Gorgona Island in relation to Northwestern South America," Schweizerische Mineralogische und Petrographische Mitteilungen, XXX (1950), 219-37.

Garbell, M.A. Tropical and Equatorial Meteorology. New York, 1947.

García, Julio César. "El movimiento antisclavista en Colombia,"

Boletín de Historia y Antigüedades, XLI (1954), 131-43.

Geografía Económica de Colombia, VI, Chocó. Contraloría General de la República (Bogotá, 1943).

Gourou, Pierre. The Tropical World (trans. R.D. Laborde). London, 1953.

Graham, B.M. "Notes on the Mangrove Swamp of Kenya," Journal of East Africa and Uganda Natural History Society, No. 29 (1929), 157-64.

Granger, Henry G. and Treville, Edward B. "Mining Districts of Colombia," Transactions of the American Institute of Mining Engineers, XXVIII (1899), 33-87.

Grant, D.K.J. "Mangrove Woods of Tanganyika Territory, their silviculture and dependent industries," Tanganyika Notes and Records, No. 5 (1936), 5-16.

Grewe, Ferdinand. "Africanische Mangrovelandschaften. Verbreitung and wirtschaftsgeographische Bedeutung," Wissenschaftliche Veröffentlichungen des Deutschen Museums für Länderkunde zu Leipzig, N.F. 9 (1941), 103-177.

Guerra, Antonio Teixeira. Estudio Geográphico do Territorio do Amapá. Rio de Janeiro, 1954.

Gutenburg, B. and Richter, C.F. Seismiscity of the Earth and Associated Phenomena. Princeton, 1949.

Hagen, B. "Die Pflanzen- und Thierwelt von Deli auf der Ostküste Sumatra," Tidjschrift van het Koninklijk Nederlandsch Aardijkskundig Genootschap, 2d. ser., VII (1890), 1-240.

Hall, Robert B. "The Société Congo of the Ile à Gonave," American Anthropologist, XXXI (1929), 685-700.

Heizer, Robert. "Fish Poisons," Handbook of South American Indians, Bureau of American Ethnology, Bull. 143 (Washington, D.C., 1949), V. 277-81.

Henry, A.J. "Rainfall of Colombia," Monthly Weather Review, L (1922), 189-90.

Holdrige, L.R. et al. The Forests of Western and Central Ecuador. Forest Service, U.S. Department of Agriculture (Washington, D.C., 1947).

Hornell, James. "South American Balanced Canoes," Man, XXVIII (1928), 129-33.

Howard, R.A. "Vegetation of the Bimini Island Group, Bahamas," Ecological Monographs, XX (1950), 317-49.

Hubach, Enrique. "Informe geológico de Urabá," Boletín de Minas y Petroleo, IV (1930), 26-136.

Humboldt, Alexander von. Essai politique sur le royaume de la Nouvelle-Espagne. 5 vols. 2d. ed. Paris, 1824.

_____. Viaje a las Regiones Equinocciales del Nuevo Continente, hecho en 1799, 1800, 1801, 1802, 1803 y 1804 por A. de Humboldt y A. Bonpland. 5 vols. Biblioteca Venezolana de Cultura (Caracas, 1941-1942).

Illingsworth, Admiral. "Remarks on the Isthmus of Cupica," Proceedings of the Royal Geographical Society, I (1856), 866-87.

"Informe científico sobre la región Quibdó-Buenaventura," Minería, V (1937), 4550-65.

Izikowitz, Karl. "Musical and other sound Instruments of the South American Indians," Göteborgs Kungl. Vetenskaps- och Vitterhets-Samhalles Handlingar. ser. A. Band V (Göteborg, 1935).

Jansen, Arnold Wilton. "La pesca en la costa del Pacífico," Colombia, I (1944), nos. 3 and 4, 99-107.

Jennings, A.H. "World's Greatest Observed Point Rainfalls," Monthly Weather Review, LXXVIII (1950), 4-5.

_____. "Maximum 24-hour Precipitation in the United States," Technical Paper No. 16. U.S. Weather Bureau (Washington, D.C., 1952).

Jenny, Hans. Factors of Soil Formation. New York, 1941.

_____. "Great Soil Groups in the Equatorial Regions of Colombia, South America," Soil Science, LXVI (1948), 5-28.

Jijón y Caamaño, Jacinto. Sebastián de Benalcázar. 2 vols. Quito, 1938.

Kelley, Frederick M. "On the Junction of the Atlantic and Pacific Oceans, and the Practicability of a Ship Canal, without locks, by the Atrato Valley," Institute of Civil Engineers, Minutes of Proceedings, XV (1856), 376-417.

Kint, A. "De Luchtfoto en de topografische terreingesteldheid in de Mangrove," Tropische Natuur, XXIII (1934), 173-89.

Lafond, Gabriel. "Excursion dans la rivière de Chinquiquirá, qui a son embouchure dans la baie de Cascajal (San Buenaventura), province du Chocó dans la Colombie," Bulletin de la Société de Géographie, Ser. 2, XI (1839), 121-43.

Latcham, Ricardo. La Agricultura precolombiana en Chile y otros paises vecinos. Santiago, 1936.

Lehmann, Henri. "Les Indiens Sindagua (Colombie)," Journal de la Société des Américanistes, N.S., XXXVIII (1949), 67-89.

Little, Elbert L. "A Collection of Tree Specimens from Western Ecuador," Caribbean Forester, IX (1944), 215-89.

Lothrop, S. K. "Aboriginal Navigation off the West Coast of South America," Journal of the Royal Anthropological Institute of Great Britain and Ireland, LXII (1932), 299-56.

Martyn, E. B. "A Note on the Foreshore Vegetation in the Neighborhood of Georgetown, British Guiana," Journal of Ecology, XXII (1934), 292-98.

Mason, J. Alden. "The Languages of South American Indians," Handbook of South American Indians, Bureau of American Ethnology, Bull. 143 (Washington, D.C., 1950), VI, 157-317.

Meek, Seth E. and Hildebrand, Samuel. "The Marine Fishes of Panama," Field Museum of Natural History, Publication No. 215, Zoological Series, XV (Chicago, 1923).

Mendoza Nieto, Jorge. Geografía Illustrada del Chocó, Bogotá, 1942.

Mesa Bernal, Daniel. "El Plátano, su historia y orígen," Agricultura Tropical, VIII (October, 1952), 23-26.

_____. " Es el banano indígena de América o es importado?"
Agricultura Tropical, VIII (November, 1952), 23-27.

Merizalde del Carmen, Padre Bernardo. Estudios de la Costa
Colombiana del Pacífico. Bogotá, 1921.

Métraux, Alfred. "Bark Cloth," Handbook of South American Indians.
Bureau of American Ethnology, Bull. 143. (Washington, D.C.,
1949), V, 67-68.

_____. "Weapons," Handbook of South American Indians,
Bureau of American Ethnology, Bull. 143. (Washington, D.C.)
V, 248-52.

Michler, Lt. N., U.S.A. "[Report of] Lt. N. Michler, corps of topo-
graphical engineers, of his survey for an inter-oceanic ship
canal near the Isthmus of Darién, via the Atrato and Truandó
Rivers, called for by a resolution of the Senate of June 5, 1860,"
Senate Executive Documents, No. 9, vol. 7, 2d. Session, 36th
Congress, 1860-1861 (Washington, D.C., 1861)

Miles, Cecil. Los Peces del Río Magdalena. Bogotá, 1947.

Miller, Gerrit D. and Kellogg, Remington. "List of North American
Recent Mammals," U. S. National Museum, Bulletin 205
(Washington, D.C., 1955).

Mohr, E. C. J. and Van Baren, F.A. Tropical Soils. The Hague,
1954.

Mollien, G. Travels in the Republic of Colombia in the Years 1822
and 1823. London, 1824.

Monroy, Fray Joel L. "El Convento de la Merced de Quito de 1534 a
1617," Boletín de la Academia de Historia, [Quito] XI [1930]),
193-208.

Murphy, Robert Cushman. "The Littoral of Pacific Colombia and
Ecuador," Geographical Review, XXIX (1939), 1-33.

_____. "Racial Succession in the Colombian Chocó,"
Geographical Review, XXIX (1939), 461-71.

_____. "The earliest Spanish Advances Southward from
Panama along the West Coast of South America," Hispanic

American Historical Review, XXI (1941), 3-28.

Navarrete, Martín Fernández de (ed.). Colección de viages y descubrimientos que hicieron por mar los españoles desde fin del siglo XV .... 5 vols. Buenos Aires, 1945-1946.

Nordenskiöld, Erland. "Deductions Suggested by the Geographical Distribution of some Post-Columbian Words used by the Indians of South America," _Comparative Ethnological Studies_, No. V (Göteborg, 1922).

_____. "The Ethnography of South America seen from Mojos in Bolivia," _Comparative Ethnlogical Studies_, No. III (Göteborg, 1924).

_____. "Les Indiens de l'Isthmus de Panamá," _La Géographie_, L (1928), 299-319.

_____. "Indianerna pa Panamanaset," _Ymer_, XLVIII(1928), 85-110.

_____. "Modifications in Indian Culture through Inventions and Loans," _Comparative Ethnological Studies_, No. VIII (Göteborg, 1930).

_____. "Origin of Indian Civilizations of South America," _Comparative Ethnological Studies_, No. IX (Göteborg, 1931).

_____. "An Historical and Ethnological Survey of the Cuna Indians." _Comparative Ethnological Studies_, No. X (Göteborg, 1938).

Nygren, W. E. "The Bolivar Geosyncline of North Western South America," _Bulletin of the American Association of Petroleum Geologists_, XXXIV (1950), 1998-2006.

Olssen, A. A. "Some Tectonic Interpretations of the Geology of North Western South America," _Proceedings of the Eighth American Scientific Congress_, IV (1942), 401-416.

Oppenheim, Victor. "Geología de la Costa Sur del Pacífico de Colombia," _Boletín del Instituto Geofísico de los Andes_, I (1949), 1-23.

_____. "The Structure of Colombia," _Transactions of the_

American Geophysical Union, XXX (1952), 739-48.

Ortega, Alfredo. Ferrocarriles Colombianos, resumen histórico, Biblioteca de Historia Nacional, XXVI. 2 vols.(Bogotá, 1920-1923).

Ortega Ricaurte, Enrique (ed.). Historia Documental del Chocó. Publicaciones del Departamento de Biblioteca y Archivos Nacionales, XXIV. (Bogotá, 1954).

Osorio, Luis H. Estudios Meteorológicos de Colombia, 1931 a 1935. Bogotá, [n. d.].

Ossa V., Peregrino, "Terrenos Baldíos en Colombia," Boletín de la Sociedad Geográfica de Colombia, II (1935), 123-127.

Oviedo y Valdés, Gonzalo Fernández de. Historia General y Natural de las Indias, Islas y Tierra-Firme del Mar Océano. 4 vols. Madrid, 1851.

Pacheco, Joaquín F. and Cárdenas, Francisco de (eds.). Coleción de documentos inéditos, relativos al descrubrimiento, conquista, y organización de las antiguas posesiones españoles de América y Oceanía, sacadas de los archivos del de Indias, 42 vols. Madrid, 1864-1884.

Parsons, James J. "Antioqueño Colonization in Western Colombia," Ibero-Americana, No. XXXII (Berkeley and Los Angeles, 1949).

Patiño, Victor Manuel. "El Maíz Chococito, noticia sobre su cultivo en América Ecuatorial," América Indígena, XVI (1956), 309-46.

Pérez, Felipe. Jeografía física i política del estado del Cauca. Bogotá, 1862.

Popenoe, Wilson, and Jiménez, Otón. "The Pejibaye, a Neglected Food Plant of Tropical America," Journal of Heredity, XII (1921), 154-66.

Pynaert, L. "La mangrove congolaise," Bulletin Agricole de Congo Belge, XXIII (1933), 184-207.

"Quinto Censo Nacional de Población y Vivienda, 10 de Diciembre de 1950," Boletín Informativo, No. 3. Dirección de Estadística y

Censo, Contraloria de la Republica. Panama, 1952.

Recasens, José de, and Oppenheim, Victor. "Análisis tipológico de materiales cerámicos y líticos, procedentes del Chocó, " Revista del Instituto Etnológico Nacional, I (1943-1944), 351-409.

Reichen, Henry. "Contribution à l'Etude de la métallurgie précolombienne de la Province d'Esmeraldas (Equateur), " Journal de la Société des Américanistes, XXXIV (1942), 210-228.

"Relación del reverendo Padre Francisco García, " Relación de algunas excursiones apostólicas en la Misión del Chocó. Bogotá, 1924.

Restrepo, Vincente. Estudio sobre las minas de Oro y Plata de Colombia. 2nd ed. Bogotá, 1888.

Restrepo Tirado, Ernesto. "Construcciones Indígenas, " Boletín de Historia y Antigüedades, I (1903), 574-96.

Richards, P. W. The Tropical Rain Forest, an Ecological Study. Cambridge, 1952.

Riehl, H. Tropical Meteorology. New York, 1954.

Rivet, Paul. "Un dialecte hoka colombien: le Yurumanguí, " Journal de la Société des Américanistes, XXXIV (1942), 1-59.

_____. "La Lengua Chocó, " Revista del Instituto Etnológico Nacional, I (1943-1944), 13-96; 297-349.

Rosevear, D. R. "Mangrove Swamps, " Farm and Forest, VIII (1947), 23-30.

Rowe, John H. "The Idabaez: Unknown Indians of the Chocó Coast, " Kroeber Anthropological Society Papers, No. 1 (1950), 34-44.

Rudolph, E. and Szirtes, S. "Das kolombianische Erdbeben am 31 Januar 1906, " Beitrage zur Geophysik, Zeitschrift fur physikalische Edrkunde, XI (1912), 132-99; 207-275.

Rumazo, José (ed.). Documentos para la Historia de la Audiencia de Quito. 8 vols. Madrid, 1948-1950.

"Sailing Directions for the East Coasts of Central America and Mexico, " Publication No. 130, 5th ed. U.S. Hydrographic Office, Washington, D.C., 1952.

Sauer, Carl. "Cultivated Plants of South and Central America, "

Handbook of South American Indians. Bureau of American Eth-
    nology, Bull. 143 (Washington, D.C., 1950), VI, 487-543.

Saville, H. "Archeological Researches on the Coast of Ecuador,"
    Verhandlungen des XVI Internationalen Amerikanisten-Kongress
    (Vienna, 1903), 331-45.

Scheiber, Walter R. "Tagua," Agriculture in the Americas, (1946),
    51-53.

Schmidt, R.D. "Die Niederschlagsverteilung in andinen Kolombien,"
    Bonner Geographische Abhandlungen, Heft 9 (1952), 99-119.

Schuchert, Charles. Historical Geology of the Antillean-Caribbean
    Region. New York, 1935.

Seibert, R.J. "The Importance of Palms to Latin America," Ceiba,
    I (1950), 65-74.

Silvestre, Francisco. "Descripción del Reyno de Santa Fé de Bogotá
    escrita en 1789 ...," Anales de la Instrucción Pública, XIII
    (1888), [scattered pagination].

Shands, A.L. and Ammerman, D. "Maximum Recorded United States
    Point Rainfall," Technical Paper, No. 2. U.S. Weather Bureau
    (Washington, D.C., 1947).

Simón, Fray Pedro. Noticias Historiales de las Conquistas de Tierra
    Firme en las Indias Occidentales. 5 vols. Bogotá, 1882-92.

Skutch, Alexander. "Problems in Milpa Agriculture," Turrialba, I
    (1950), 4-6.

Smith, Lyman B. "Bromeliad Malaria," Annual Report, 1952,
    Smithsonian Institution (Washington, D.C., 1953), 385-98.

Special Report of the Governor of the Panama Canal on the Atrato-
    Truandó Canal Route, under Public Law 280, 78th Congress,
    1st Session, Canal Zone, 1949.

Spencer, J.E. "The Abacá Plant and its Fiber, Manila Hemp,"
    Economic Botany, VII (1953), 195-213.

Stamp, L.D. "The Aerial Survey of the Irrawaddy Delta Forests,"
    Journal of Ecology, XIII (1925), 262-76.

Steenis, C. G. G. J. van. "Kustaanwas en mangrove," Natuurweten-schappelijk Tidjschrift voor Nederlandsch Indië, CI (1941), 82-85.

Stout, David B. "The Cuna," Handbook of South American Indians, Bureau of American Ethnology, Bull. 143 (Washington, D. C., 1948) IV, 257-68.

Tanner, Hans. "Verkehrsproblems Kolombiens," Geographica Helvetica, IV (1949), 137-54.

Tessmann, Gunter. Die Pangwe, völkerkundliche Monographie eines west-afrikanischen Negerstammes. 2 vols. Berlin, 1913.

Trautwine, John C. "Rough Notes of an Exploration for an Inter-oceanic Canal Route by way of the Rivers Atrato and San Juan, in New Granada, South America," Journal of the Franklin Institute, LVII (1854), 145-54; 217-31; 289-99; 361-73; LVIII (1854), 1-11; 73-84; 145-55; 217-26; 289-99.

Treadwell, John C., et al. "Possibilities for Para Rubber Production in Northern Tropical America," Trade Promotion Series, No. 40, Department of Commerce (Washington, D. C., 1926).

Troll, Carl. "Die geologische Verkettung Süd- und Mittelamerikas," Mitteilungen der Geographische Gesellschaft in München, XXIII (1930), 53-76.

Uhle, Max. "Las antiguas civilizaciones esmeraldeñas," Anales de la Universidad Central, XXXVIII (1927).

Vaughn, T. W. "The geologic work of mangrove in Southern Florida," Miscellaneous Collection, Smithsonian Institution (Washington, D. C., 1910), LII, 461-64.

Velasco, Juan de. Historia del Reino de Quito, 3 vols. Quito, 1946.

Von Hagen, V. Wolfgang. "The Tsátchela Indians of Western Ecuador," Indian Notes and Monographs, No. LI. Museum of the American Indian, Heye Foundation. New York, 1939.

Wassén, Henry. "Notes on the Southern Groups of Chocó Indians in Colombia," Etnologiska Studier, I (1935), 35-182.

_____. "Contributions to Cuna Ethnology," Etnologiska

Studier, XVI (1949), 1-139.

Watson, J.D. "Mangrove Forests of the Malay Peninsula," Malayan Forest Records, No. 6 (1928), 1-275.

West, Robert C. "Colonial Placer Mining in Colombia," Louisiana State University Studies, Social Science Series, No. 2 (Baton Rouge, 1952).

_____. "Folk Mining in Colombia," Economic Geography, XXVIII (1952), 323-30.

White, R.B. "Notes on the Aboriginal Races of the North Western Provinces of South America," Journal of the Royal Anthropological Institute of Great Britain and Ireland, XIII, (1884), 240-56.

Wilhelmy, Herbert. "Die Pazifische Küstenebene Kolumbiens," Abhandlungen des Deutschen Geographentages (Essen, 1953), 96-100.

Wolf, Theodor. Viajes científicos por la República de Ecuador. 3 vols. Guayaquil, 1879.

Yacup, Sofonías. Litoral Recóndito. Bogotá, 1934.

Yde, Jens. "The Regional Distribution of South American Blowgun Types," Journal de la Société des Américanistes, XXXVII (1948), 275-317.